Microsoft 365 Unlocked

Learn to utilize the latest Microsoft 365 productivity tools efficiently

Nuno Mota

Adina Waffenschmidt

bpb

www.bpbonline.com

First Edition 2026

Copyright © BPB Publications, India

ISBN: 978-93-65893-052

To View Complete
BPB Publications Catalogue
Scan the QR Code:

Dedicated to

My beautiful and amazing family, close and afar.
Without you, I would not be where I am today.

– Nuno Mota

All my family members, whose support and encouragement have been a guiding light throughout this journey. Thank you for standing by my side every step of the way.

– Adina Waffenschmidt

About the Authors

- **Nuno Mota** is a seasoned technology expert and author with deep expertise in Microsoft 365 architecture and enterprise collaboration solutions, with over a decade of experience in designing, implementing, and managing scalable, secure, and user-centric enterprise-scale messaging and collaboration solutions.

  A CISSP-certified professional and EMBA graduate, Nuno combines deep technical expertise with strategic vision and insight.

  This book reflects Nuno's dedication to bridging the gap between technology and business, offering readers a comprehensive and insightful guide to navigating the evolving landscape of Microsoft 365.

- **Adina Waffenschmidt** is a technology expert with over a decade of experience in the Microsoft 365 ecosystem, having held diverse roles across multiple industries. Her career has encompassed responsibilities ranging from technical support to design and implementation, allowing her to build a holistic perspective on the evolving challenges and opportunities within the digital workplace.

  Specialized in architecture, governance, and security, Adina is focused on driving secure, scalable, and efficient Microsoft 365 environments and is always seeking innovative ways to harness the latest advancements to empower users and streamline business processes.

About the Reviewers

❖ **Ed** has been specializing in SharePoint since version 2007. He was a Microsoft MVP in SharePoint for 12 years, and a Microsoft Certified Trainer for over 15. He is also a published author. Over the last 10 years, he has been consulting almost exclusively in Microsoft 365 / Office 365, specializing in SharePoint, search, workflows, compliance, document management, records management and knowledge management.

❖ **Suvidha Shashikumar** is a solutions architect at Microsoft, specializing in low-code platforms, enterprise AI, and business applications. She develops and implements solutions using Microsoft Power Platform, Dynamics 365, and Copilot, helping organizations modernize systems, automate processes, and meet key business objectives.

With experience across a wide range of industries, Suvidha focuses on simplifying the implementation, maintenance, and scalability of complex systems. Her work often involves bridging the gap between technical and business teams, ensuring that solutions are not only technically sound but also aligned with broader strategic goals.

She is particularly interested in how AI and low-code tools are reshaping enterprise technology, and brings a practical, systems-level perspective to her work.

Outside of her role at Microsoft, Suvidha regularly blogs about technology, product thinking, and enterprise architecture. She also runs Speedread, an Instagram channel that offers short, visual book summaries - designed for readers who want to learn quickly and consistently.

❖ **Vaishali Pillai** is a customer service and support specialist with a focus on the Microsoft 365 ecosystem, specializing in Exchange Online. She works closely with end users and administrators to troubleshoot, optimize, and enhance the performance of email and collaboration tools within the Office 365 environment. Her work centers around delivering smooth, efficient user experiences while continuously streamlining backend support operations.

She is especially interested in modern workplace technologies and spends her spare time deepening her knowledge of Microsoft 365, with a strong focus on cloud productivity and user adoption. She is passionate about learning and often explores new tools, features, and updates across the Microsoft 365 platform.

Outside of work, she is an avid reader of thrillers and personal development books. She enjoys reviewing and recommending titles, combining her love for storytelling with her curiosity for growth and self-improvement.

Acknowledgements

Writing this book has been an incredible journey, and I am deeply grateful to everyone who supported us along the way.

First and foremost, I would like to thank my family and friends for their unwavering encouragement, patience, and support throughout this process.

To our publisher, thank you for your trust, guidance, and commitment to excellence. Your support made this project not only possible but also truly rewarding.

I am also indebted to my colleagues, past and present, whose insights, collaboration, and shared passion for Microsoft 365 inspired much of the content in these pages. Your expertise and friendship have been invaluable.

To my co-author, Adina, thank you for your dedication, clarity of thought, and deep knowledge. It has been a privilege to work alongside you, and I am grateful to share this new adventure of bringing this book to life together.

Finally, to you, the reader, thank you for choosing this book. Your curiosity and dedication to learning inspired its creation, and we hope it proves to be a valuable companion on your Microsoft 365 journey.

– Nuno Mota

I would like to express my heartfelt gratitude to my family and friends for their unwavering support and encouragement throughout the writing of this book.

I am sincerely grateful to BPB Publications, and to the reviewers, experts, and editors whose dedication and expertise helped make this book possible.

I also wish to acknowledge the invaluable contributions of my colleagues and co-workers with whom I have had the privilege of collaborating over the years. Their insights, advice, and feedback have shaped my work and broadened my perspective.

A very special thanks to my co-author, Nuno, for his outstanding collaboration and steadfast support throughout this project. Your partnership has been truly invaluable.

Finally, to you, our readers, thank you. Every page of this book was written with you in mind, with the hope that it will inspire you to explore new possibilities and achieve greater success in your journey with Microsoft 365.

– Adina Waffenschmidt

Preface

Technology moves fast, and having the right tools to work and connect with others is more important than ever. Microsoft 365 brings together everything you need to be productive - like Teams, SharePoint, OneDrive, Power BI, and more, into one easy-to-use platform that helps business users, IT professionals, and teams get more done with less hassle, while remaining secure.

Most people know the basics of Microsoft 365 with tools such as Outlook, Word, or Excel, but very few know how much more it can do. There is a whole world inside Microsoft 365, whether it is chatting with your team on Teams, building smart and powerful automations with Power Automate, or creating videos with Clipchamp, there is so much to explore.

Whether you are an IT expert, a manager, a business analyst, or just a curious user about getting the most out of your subscription, this book is your roadmap to discovering the hidden treasures of Microsoft 365. This book provides practical insights, real-world use cases, and guidance on how to unlock the value of these applications in your daily work.

Let us begin the journey beyond the familiar and unlock the full potential of Microsoft 365.

Chapter 1: Understanding Microsoft 365 - It introduces Microsoft 365, detailing its significance for modern businesses and how it differs from Office 365. It outlines the book's scope and the intended audience, and provides an overview of Microsoft 365 plans and licenses. This foundational chapter sets clear expectations and objectives for readers about this book.

Chapter 2: Microsoft Teams - It delves into Microsoft Teams. It explores the various functionalities of Teams, including chats, calls, and video conferencing capabilities. The chapter also covers the use of channels and the integration with SharePoint for seamless collaboration. By the end of this chapter, readers will gain a comprehensive understanding of how to effectively use Microsoft Teams to improve teamwork and collaboration.

Chapter 3: Viva Engage - It explores how Viva Engage can be leveraged to create a vibrant and connected workplace. The chapter delves into the Viva Engage key features, including storylines, communities, creating posts, and engaging with content. By the end of this chapter, readers will have a broad understanding of the features and benefits of Viva Engage within the Microsoft 365 ecosystem.

Chapter 4: Microsoft Loop - It explores how Microsoft Loop can be utilized to create dynamic and interactive content that can be easily shared and edited in real-time. Key features include Loop workspaces, Loop pages, and Loop components, and how they integrate with other Microsoft 365 applications. The readers will descover the benefits of incorporating Microsoft Loop into their worklflow and how this tool improves productivity and collaboration.

Chapter 5: Whiteboard - It delves into the versatile Whiteboard, a dynamic tool for collaboration and creativity in a digital workspace. It explores the fundamental aspects of creating and managing whiteboards, allowing users to brainstorm and visualize ideas seamlessly. Readers will learn how to collaborate effectively with other users, leveraging real-time updates and interactive features to enhance team productivity. Additionally, the chapter covers the integration of Whiteboard with Microsoft Teams, providing a comprehensive guide to utilizing this powerful combination for meetings and remote work scenarios. By the end of this chapter, users will be equipped with the knowledge to harness the full potential of Whiteboard in their professional and creative work.

Chapter 6: Microsoft Copilot - It explores Microsoft's AI-powered Copilot, a revolutionary tool designed to enhance user productivity within the Microsoft 365 ecosystem. It begins with an introduction to the core functionalities of Microsoft 365 Copilot, highlighting how it assists users generating content, providing intelligent suggestions, and more. Readers will gain insights into how to maximize the capabilities of Copilot to streamline their workflows, improve efficiency, and foster innovation in their daily tasks. By the end of this chapter, users will have a comprehensive understanding of how to leverage Copilot to transform their work experience.

Chapter 7: SharePoint - It guides readers through the various functionalities of SharePoint Online, including site creation, site types, document libraries, and lists. The chapter also covers essential aspects of permissions and sharing, ensuring that users can securely manage access to their sites. Additionally, it provides guidance on creating and editing site pages to meet specific needs. The search functionality section will help users understand how to efficiently locate content within SharePoint. By the end of this chapter, readers will be equipped with the skills to build a more organized, secure, and collaborative workspace using SharePoint Online.

Chapter 8: OneDrive - It covers the essential features of OneDrive, including working with and sharing content, managing access, collaborating in real-time on documents, and file synchronization. By the end of this chapter, readers will understand the differences between OneDrive for work or school, OneDrive for home, and the OneDrive sync app, as well as the OneDrive's functionalities and benefits.

Chapter 9: OneNote - It describes how OneNote can be utilized to organize and manage notes efficiently. Key features include creating notebooks, sections, and pages, as well as using tags and the search functionality to find important information quickly. By the end of this chapter, readers will have a comprehensive understanding of how to leverage OneNote to enhance their productivity.

Chapter 10: Microsoft Stream - It covers essential Microsoft Stream topics such as managing video content, video settings, and sharing options. The chapter also explores how Stream integrates with other Microsoft 365 apps, enhancing collaboration and productivity. By the end of this chapter, readers will be able to effectively manage their video content using Microsoft Stream.

Chapter 11: Clipchamp - It introduces Clipchamp, a user-friendly video editing app that simplifies the video creation process for personal, educational, or professional projects. This chapter covers essential features of Clipchamp, including clip editing, auto composition, and using the stock media library. Readers will also explore advanced features like text to speech or autocaptions which enhance video accessibility. By the end of this chapter, readers will be well-equipped to create polished and engaging videos with Clipchamp.

Chapter 12: Sway - Explores Sway, an app designed for creating visually appealing digital content. From stunning reports to engaging presentations, Sway offers a user-friendly platform for crafting professional newsletters and captivating stories. This chapter will guide readers through the various features of Sway, demonstrating how to leverage its intuitive design tools and integration capabilities to produce dynamic, interactive content. Readers will learn how to harness the power of Sway to elevate their digital storytelling and communication.

Chapter 13: Power BI - It covers the core components of Power BI, including Power BI Desktop, Power BI Service, and Power BI Mobile. The chapter illustrates the essential Power BI features and the typical workflow for transforming data into meaningful reports by using an example scenario where we build a sample report step-by-step, from connecting to the sources to get the data, to publishing and sharing the report. By understanding these features, readers will be able to build reports, make data-driven decisions, and enhance their business intelligence capabilities.

Chapter 14: Power Automate - It covers Power Automate, Microsoft's powerful tool for automating workflows and processes. It guides readers through the essentials of creating automated workflows that can save time, reduce errors, and enhance productivity. Readers will learn how to connect various services and applications using connectors and utilize ready-made templates to quickly set up flows. By the end of this chapter, readers will be equipped with the knowledge to streamline their tasks and integrate separate systems efficiently, making the most out of Power Automate's features to achieve seamless automation in their work environment.

Chapter 15: Power Apps - It delves into the fundamentals and core functionalities of Power Apps, a tool that allows users to build low-code custom applications tailored to their business needs. This chapter covers topics such as Power Platform environments, application types, and Power Apps Studio overview, and it is structured to equip readers with the essential knowledge and skills to begin unlocking the full potential of Power Apps. The chapter also guides users through building a simple canvas app, publishing, and sharing it.

Chapter 16: Power Pages - It delves into the essential aspects of leveraging Power Pages to build robust and user-friendly sites. Readers will explore how to create web pages from scratch, design them to meet specific needs, and manage their content and functionality effectively. Furthermore, this chapter will guide readers through the go-live process, ensuring their site is ready for public access. By the end of this chapter, readers will have a solid foundation in using Power Pages to enhance their digital presence.

Chapter 17: Forms - It covers the essential features of Microsoft Forms, including creating and customizing forms and quizzes, sharing them with respondents, and analyzing the collected data. By the end of this chapter, readers will understand the fundamental aspects of Microsoft Forms and will be equiped with the knowledge to start creating and configuring quizzes and forms.

Chapter 18: Personal Insights - It explores Personal Insights within Microsoft 365. Readers will learn how to use Viva Insights in Teams, on the web, as well as in Outlook, and how it can help enhancing their productivity and well-being. This chapter offers practical tips for using this tool to create an effective work-life balance.

Chapter 19: Microsoft Planner - It covers Microsoft Planner, an essential tool for organizing tasks and managing projects within Microsoft 365. Readers will gain a comprehensive understanding of how to effectively use Planner to streamline their workflow, create and assign tasks, and collaborate with team members. This chapter highlights how to set up and utilize tasks and buckets, access insightful reports and dashboards, and customize views and charts to track progress and productivity. By mastering these features, readers will enhance their ability to manage projects efficiently and meet deadlines with ease.

Chapter 20: Microsoft Bookings - It covers the essential features of Microsoft Bookings, including setting up meeting types, and creating and managing shared booking pages. By the end of this chapter, readers will understand the key features of Microsoft Bookings and the differences between personal and shared booking pages.

Chapter 21: Microsoft To Do - It explores the To Do application, a tool for organizing tasks and improving productivity. Readers will learn how to create and manage tasks and lists, ensuring efficient task management. The chapter also covers integration with Planner. By the end of this chapter, readers will be proficient at using To Do for both personal and group tasks.

Chapter 22: Security and Privacy - It explores the security and privacy features within the Microsoft 365 suite for securing and managing an account from an end-user perspective. The chapter covers important aspects such as password change and reset, MFA, device management and sign-in activity. By the end of this chapter, readers will be equiped with the knowledge to safeguard their account effectively.

Coloured Images

Please follow the link to download the
Coloured Images of the book:

https://rebrand.ly/274712

We have code bundles from our rich catalogue of books and videos available at https://github.com/ bpbpublications. Check them out!

Errata

We take immense pride in our work at BPB Publications and follow best practices to ensure the accuracy of our content to provide with an indulging reading experience to our subscribers. Our readers are our mirrors, and we use their inputs to reflect and improve upon human errors, if any, that may have occurred during the publishing processes involved. To let us maintain the quality and help us reach out to any readers who might be having difficulties due to any unforeseen errors, please write to us at :

errata@bpbonline.com

Your support, suggestions and feedbacks are highly appreciated by the BPB Publications' Family.

At www.bpbonline.com, you can also read a collection of free technical articles, sign up for a range of free newsletters, and receive exclusive discounts and offers on BPB books and eBooks. You can check our social media handles below:

Instagram

Facebook

Linkedin

YouTube

Get in touch with us at: business@bpbonline.com for more details.

Piracy

If you come across any illegal copies of our works in any form on the internet, we would be grateful if you would provide us with the location address or website name. Please contact us at business@bpbonline.com with a link to the material.

If you are interested in becoming an author

If there is a topic that you have expertise in, and you are interested in either writing or contributing to a book, please visit www.bpbonline.com. We have worked with thousands of developers and tech professionals, just like you, to help them share their insights with the global tech community. You can make a general application, apply for a specific hot topic that we are recruiting an author for, or submit your own idea.

Reviews

Please leave a review. Once you have read and used this book, why not leave a review on the site that you purchased it from? Potential readers can then see and use your unbiased opinion to make purchase decisions. We at BPB can understand what you think about our products, and our authors can see your feedback on their book. Thank you!

For more information about BPB, please visit www.bpbonline.com.

Join our Discord space

Join our Discord workspace for latest updates, offers, tech happenings around the world, new releases, and sessions with the authors:

https://discord.bpbonline.com

Table of Contents

CHAPTER 1

Understanding Microsoft 365

Introduction

This chapter will guide you to the powerful Microsoft 365 suite of collaboration, communication, data management, productivity, and analytical tools. We will explore everything you need to know about these Microsoft 365 tools, showing you how to use them to boost productivity, enhance team collaboration, and streamline business practices.

In this chapter, we will kick things off by introducing Microsoft 365, highlighting why it is such a big deal for all types of businesses today. We will also break down the differences between Microsoft 365 and Office 365, so you know exactly what each one offers and how they differ from each other. Additionally, we will explain what you can expect from this book and who will benefit the most from it, as well as give you an overview of the various plans and licenses you can choose from.

By the end of this book, you will have a thorough understanding of how to make the most of each application, allowing you to streamline your work and achieve your goals with greater efficiency.

Let us unlock the full potential of Microsoft 365 and transform our work and collaboration.

Structure

This chapter covers the following topics:

- Exploring Microsoft 365
- Reasons to choose Microsoft 365
- Office 365 vs. Microsoft 365
- Scope of this book
- Target audience
- Microsoft 365 plans and licenses

Objectives

By the end of this chapter, you will have a foundational understanding of Microsoft 365, the differences between Microsoft 365 and Office 365, and its multiple plans and licenses.

The scope of this book will provide you with an understanding of its coverage and methodology. Additionally, you will gain insights into the target audience for whom this book is intended.

Exploring Microsoft 365

Microsoft 365 is a subscription-based service that offers access to a suite of Microsoft Office applications, alongside other productivity services, over the internet (cloud services). The main applications available in Office 365 include the familiar Word, Excel, PowerPoint, and Outlook, in addition to many other cloud-based services such as Exchange Online for email or SharePoint Online for collaboration and storage. But Microsoft 365 encompasses much more. It includes a variety of other tools that can assist users and organizations in enhancing their productivity, collaboration, and other functions. It offers a suite of applications and services designed to meet various and different business needs. It provides seamless communication tools such as Microsoft Teams, which facilitates virtual meetings, chats, and collaborations, while OneDrive ensures that all your documents and files are safely stored and easily accessible from any device, anywhere.

Additionally, Microsoft 365 allows users to streamline their workflows. For example, Power Automate enables the automation of repetitive tasks, saving valuable time and reducing human error. Power BI offers advanced data analytics that helps organizations make informed decisions by visualizing data trends and insights. The suite also caters to project management needs with tools like Planner and Project. These applications aid in organizing tasks, setting deadlines, tracking progress, and ensuring that projects are completed efficiently and on time.

Note: **Microsoft 365 includes many other great tools for the readers to explore.**

Reasons to choose Microsoft 365

Microsoft 365 has been a game-changer for businesses since its early days when it was called Microsoft **Business Productivity Online Standard Suite** (**BPOS**). In today's digital world, working from home and collaborating online from anywhere has become the norm, and Microsoft 365 offers a complete package that excels at that, with an unparalleled level of integration and interoperability. The suite's applications are designed to work seamlessly together, allowing users to transition smoothly between tasks and tools. For instance, data from SharePoint can be easily integrated into Teams, while emails from Outlook can be linked to tasks in Planner. This level of cohesion is unmatched by other productivity suites like Google Workspace or Apple iWork, which, while competent, often fall short in terms of deep integration and enterprise-level features.

Moreover, Microsoft 365's security features are robust and comprehensive. For example, two-factor authentication to prevent unauthorized access to files, threat detection, and anti-malware features to identify and address security threats in real-time, and more are crucial for any organization, but they also assure users their files remain confidential and secure, promoting comfort and platform adoption.

Another significant advantage is business continuity. The cloud-based nature of Microsoft 365 ensures that all files, emails, and data are accessible even in the event of physical device failures, which is crucial for maintaining operations during unforeseen circumstances.

Automatic upgrades in Microsoft 365 ensure that users always have the latest features without the hassle of manual updates and eliminate conflicts caused by using different software generations.

Furthermore, the suite's accessibility from anywhere with an internet connection is a must for mobile and remote workforces. Microsoft 365 enables employees to access their work from any device, fostering flexibility and productivity.

Microsoft 365 also includes a myriad of powerful tools designed to enhance productivity. Industry-standard applications such as Word, Excel, and PowerPoint are complemented by innovative tools like Teams for communication, OneDrive for storage, Power Automate for workflow automation, Power BI for business intelligence, and Planner and Project for project management. This extensive array of tools covers nearly every aspect of productivity and collaboration, providing a comprehensive solution that other suites, with their more limited toolsets, struggle to match.

Lastly, Microsoft 365 is backed by Microsoft's extensive support and training resources, ensuring that users can maximize their use of the suite's features. This level of support is often more extensive than what is available from competitors, making Microsoft 365 a more attractive option for organizations seeking a reliable and well-supported productivity suite.

In summary, the comprehensive integration, robust security, business continuity, automatic upgrades, accessibility, powerful tools, and extensive support make Microsoft 365 an exceptional choice for organizations and users. Its advantages over other productivity suites make it a leader in the market and an asset for any organization looking to enhance productivity and collaboration.

Office 365 vs. Microsoft 365

Understanding the difference between Office 365 and Microsoft 365 can be confusing. In a nutshell, and from an end-user perspective, Office 365 is now Microsoft 365. Now, let us explore this difference a bit further.

Consistency in product names is essential, as having products with similar names can quickly become confusing. Microsoft is a prime example of this.

The confusion started when Microsoft introduced *Microsoft 365* in 2017 as a collection of existing products under one license, specifically aimed at businesses. The name was similar to the pre-existing *Office 365*, which led to further confusion as many people had already been accidentally referring to Office 365 as Microsoft 365. This similarity in names contributed to the misunderstanding between the two products.

The situation was further complicated because Microsoft 365 included Office 365. To clarify the differences between these offerings, let us examine them more closely as follows:

- **Office 365**: It is a comprehensive cloud-based suite of applications and services designed to enhance business productivity. It includes familiar applications such as Word, Excel, PowerPoint, and Microsoft Outlook. Depending on the selected plan, subscriptions may also include additional applications and services such as Teams, SharePoint, OneDrive, Planner, and much more, offering robust productivity, collaboration, and security features. The service operates on a monthly, per-user subscription basis, and various plans are available to cater to different requirements. These plans can be combined within an organization, providing flexibility to modify them as needed.

- **Microsoft 365**: It comprises a suite of services, including Office 365, Windows 10/11 Enterprise, and **Enterprise Mobility + Security (EMS)**. Like Office 365, it offers various plans based on different requirements, and its services can also be purchased as separate licenses.

Up to this point, the difference was somewhat clear. However, things started to get confusing when, in April 2020, Microsoft rebranded Office 365 as Microsoft 365 to reflect its strategy of offering a unified productivity platform. Now, the distinction is less clear, especially because certain licensing plans are still called *Office 365*, as we will see later in this chapter.

As it stands, from a user perspective, Office 365 is now called Microsoft 365, and that is the term to use when referring to it. Unfortunately, from an administrator's perspective, there may still be the need to refer to either Office 365 or Microsoft 365 to distinguish between different licensing plans that Microsoft still offers.

> **Note:** Licensing details and application availability are subject to change and you are advised to refer to the official Microsoft documentation for the most current information.

Scope of this book

Given the extensive array of tools and features available in Microsoft 365, this book aims to provide a detailed and practical guide to using the suite to its fullest potential. While Microsoft 365 includes well-known applications such as Word, Excel, Outlook, and PowerPoint, which are universal in office environments, this book will not cover these applications.

The reason is that these are already widely covered in books, tutorials, and guides that comprehensively explore the functionalities and uses of these well-established tools. Most users are already familiar with the basics and even some advanced features of these applications, which makes it redundant to cover this ground extensively in this book. Instead, our goal is to shine a light on the lesser-known and less frequently used applications within the suite that provide significant benefits and are often underutilized.

By uncovering and focusing on these tools, we aim to unlock the full potential of Microsoft 365 for our readers, helping them discover new ways to enhance productivity, collaboration, and efficiency in their work. These tools offer advanced functionalities that can transform how organizations operate and how individuals manage their tasks and projects.

This book will provide a comprehensive guide on using and maximizing the benefits of Microsoft 365 from a user perspective. Rather than delving into setup and configuration, the focus will be on practical usage, offering insights into how to effectively utilize the suite's tools and features.

We will explore productivity and collaboration tools that go beyond the basics, including:

- **Teams**: A powerful communication and collaboration tool that can also be used as a gateway to other tools.
- **Viva Engage**: It enhances employee engagement through personalized experiences.
- **Loop**: a flexible canvas for real-time collaboration.
- **Whiteboard**: A digital canvas for brainstorming and teamwork.
- **Microsoft 365 Copilot**: An AI-powered assistant to enhance productivity.
- **SharePoint**: A platform for creating websites, managing content, and fostering collaboration.
- **OneDrive**: Cloud storage for secure file access and sharing.
- **OneNote**: A digital notebook for organizing notes and ideas.
- **Stream**: A video service for creating, sharing, and managing videos.
- **Clipchamp**: Simplified video creation and editing.
- **Sway**: A tool for creating interactive reports and presentations.
- **Power BI**: Business intelligence and data analysis.
- **Power Automate:** Workflow automation to streamline processes.
- **Power Apps**: Custom app development with minimal coding.
- **Power Pages**: A platform for building and managing web pages.
- **Forms**: A tool for creating surveys and quizzes.
- **Personal Insights**: Analytics to improve productivity and well-being.
- **Planner**: Project management and task organization.
- **Bookings**: A scheduling tool for managing appointments.
- **To Do**: A task management app to keep track of daily activities.

Target audience

This book aims to help users make the most of Microsoft 365 by exploring the powerful yet often overlooked tools and features within the suite. By mastering these tools, users will be able to maximize their efficiency and productivity, making the most of each application to streamline their work. Additionally, the book will showcase tips and tricks for enhancing team collaboration, enabling users to work together more seamlessly and effectively. It will also delve into advanced features and functionalities that can further enhance productivity and collaboration, offering detailed insights into the capabilities of Microsoft 365.

Our focus will be on the practical application of these tools to improve your productivity and workflow. Our aim is to empower end-users by focusing on the functionalities and features that directly impact your day-to-day activities and productivity.

As we journey through the capabilities of Microsoft 365, you will discover tips and tricks that can make a significant difference in how you utilize these tools. From enhancing team collaboration to leveraging advanced features, we will provide you with the knowledge and skills to work smarter and more efficiently within the Microsoft 365 ecosystem.

Microsoft 365 plans and licenses

Microsoft 365 offers a variety of plans and licenses tailored to different business needs and sizes. Understanding these options is essential for selecting the right plan, be that for personal use or for a large organization. This involves assessing your needs or those of an organization and understanding the features and benefits of each plan. By selecting the appropriate plan, you can ensure that your team has access to the tools and resources they need to excel and drive your business forward.

In today's dynamic business environment, choosing the right productivity tools is essential for achieving optimal performance and efficiency. In this section, we will provide an overview of the main licensing plans available for Microsoft 365. Our focus will be on the user services offered by these plans rather than on administrative services or features. We aim to help you understand how each plan can enhance your productivity and align with your specific needs, whether you are an individual user, a small business, or part of a large enterprise. By delving into the user-centric aspects of Microsoft 365's plans, we will equip you with the knowledge to make informed decisions that will benefit your work and collaboration efforts.

Microsoft 365 offers a variety of plans tailored to different business sizes and needs. These plans can be broadly categorized into three segments, *Home, Business, and Enterprise.*

In addition to these, Microsoft also offers specialized plans for education and nonprofits that readers can explore.

Home plans

Microsoft 365 Home plans are designed for personal and family use, providing access to essential productivity tools and services.

There are currently two plans available as follows:

- **Microsoft 365 Family**: It allows up to six users to access premium Office apps, 1 TB of OneDrive cloud storage per person, and additional features such as advanced security and family safety tools.

- **Microsoft 365 Personal**: It is intended for a single user and offers the same premium Office apps and 1 TB of OneDrive storage, along with personalized features.

Refer to the following table:

	Microsoft 365 Family	Microsoft 365 Personal
Number of users	1 to 6 people	1 person
Number of accounts	1 to 6	1
Cloud Storage	Up to 6 TB (1 TB per person)	1 TB
Multiple devices and platforms	✓	✓
Word, Excel, PowerPoint	✓	✓

	Microsoft 365 Family	Microsoft 365 Personal
Outlook	✓	✓
Ongoing technical support	✓	✓
Defender	✓	✓
Clipchamp	✓	✓
Teams	✓	✓
OneNote	✓	✓
Access (PC only)	✓	✓
Forms	✓	✓

Table 1.1: Microsoft 365 Family vs. Microsoft 365 Personal Plans

Business plans

Business plans cater to small and medium-sized businesses, offering robust tools to enhance productivity and collaboration. Microsoft now provides the same plans with and without Microsoft Teams.

In this section, we will just mention those with Teams since they are identical otherwise, as follows:

- **Business Basic**: This plan is ideal for small businesses looking for essential services. It includes web and mobile versions of Office applications, email hosting, and 1 TB of cloud storage per user. Users can collaborate using Microsoft Teams and take advantage of shared calendars and business-class email.

- **Business Standard**: A step up from the Basic plan that offers desktop versions of Office applications in addition to web and mobile versions. It also includes advanced email hosting, higher security features, and additional cloud services to enhance productivity and business management.

- **Business Premium:** It is designed for businesses requiring a more advanced IT infrastructure, this plan includes everything in Business Standard plus robust security features such as advanced threat protection and device management capabilities. Users benefit from comprehensive security measures and additional administrative tools to ensure data protection and compliance

Refer to the following table:

	Business Basic	Business Standard	Business Premium
	Identity, access, and user management for up to 300 employees Custom business email (you@yourbusiness.com) Web and mobile versions of Word, Excel, PowerPoint, and Outlook Chat, call, and video conference with Microsoft Teams 1 TB of cloud storage per employee 10+ additional apps for your business needs (Microsoft Bookings, Planner, Forms, and others) Automatic spam and malware filtering Anytime phone and web support Microsoft 365 Copilot, available as an add-on	Everything in Business Basic, plus: Desktop versions of Word, Excel, PowerPoint, and Outlook Webinars with attendee registration and reporting Collaborative workspaces to co-create using Loop Video editing and design tools with Clipchamp Microsoft 365 Copilot, available as an add-on	Everything in Business Standard, plus: Advanced identity and access management Enhanced cyberthreat protection against viruses and phishing attacks Enterprise-grade device and endpoint protection Discover, classify, and protect sensitive information Microsoft 365 Copilot, available as an add-on

	Business Basic	Business Standard	Business Premium
Word, Excel, PowerPoint	✓ (web only)	✓	✓
OneNote		✓	✓
Outlook	✓ (web only)	✓	✓
Teams	✓	✓	✓
SharePoint	✓	✓	✓
OneDrive	✓	✓	✓
Forms	✓	✓	✓
Bookings	✓	✓	✓
Planner	✓	✓	✓
Clipchamp		✓	✓
Loop		✓	✓
To Do		✓	✓
Exchange	✓	✓	✓
Entra ID			✓
Intune			✓
Defender			✓
Purview			✓

Table 1.2: Microsoft 365 Business Plans

Enterprise plans

Enterprise plans are suited for larger organizations, offering advanced capabilities to support complex needs, and include additional features such as advanced security, compliance tools, and analytics.

As previously discussed, Microsoft still offers Office 365 license plans. Unlike the Business plans, Enterprise plans now do not include Teams, with this now being offered as a complementary add-on.

Office 365 plans

Office 365 Enterprise plans are divided in three categories:

- **Office 365 E1**: This plan includes web-based Office apps, 1 TB of OneDrive storage, and essential enterprise services such as Exchange and SharePoint.

- **Office 365 E3**: Building on the E1 plan, the E3 plan adds desktop versions of Office apps, advanced security features, and additional compliance tools.

- **Office 365 E5**: The most comprehensive plan adds advanced security and compliance capabilities, as well as business analytics with Power BI.

Refer to the following table:

	Office 365 E1	Office 365 E3	Office 365 E5
	Microsoft 365 on the web with create and edit rights for online versions of core Microsoft 365 apps Email, file storage, and file sharing 1 TB of OneDrive cloud storage Anytime phone and web support Microsoft 365 Copilot, available as an add-on	Everything in Office 365 E1, plus: Install Microsoft 365 apps on up to five PCs or Macs, five tablets, and five mobile devices per user Message encryption Rights management Data loss prevention for email and files Microsoft 365 Copilot, available as an add-on	Everything in Office 365 E3, plus: Advanced security and compliance capabilities Scalable business analytics with Power BI Microsoft 365 Copilot, available as an add-on
Word, Excel, PowerPoint	✓ (web only)	✓	✓
OneNote	✓	✓	✓
Outlook	✓	✓	✓
Teams			
SharePoint	✓	✓	✓
OneDrive	✓	✓	✓
Forms	✓	✓	✓
Bookings	✓	✓	✓
Planner	✓	✓	✓
Clipchamp			
Loop			
Exchange	✓	✓	✓
Access		✓	✓
Publisher		✓	✓
Viva Engage	✓	✓	✓
Viva Insights	✓	✓	✓
Stream	✓	✓	✓
Sway	✓	✓	✓
Power Apps	✓	✓	✓
Power Automate	✓	✓	✓
To Do	✓	✓	✓
Power BI Pro			✓

Table 1.3: Office 365 Enterprise plans

Microsoft 365 plans

Unlike Office 365 Enterprise plans, Microsoft has two distinct categories for Microsoft 365 Enterprise plans as follows:

- **Microsoft 365 E3**: It is an extensive option that provides users with full access to desktop, web, and mobile Office applications. This plan includes security features such as data loss prevention and encryption.

- **Microsoft 365 E5**: This plan is currently the *top* license a company can purchase. It encompasses all the features of the E3 plan and adds advanced security capabilities such as advanced threat protection and Cloud App Security. It also provides advanced compliance tools and detailed analytics.

The details are explained in the following table:

	Microsoft 365 E3	Microsoft 365 E5
	Microsoft 365 apps for desktop and mobile* Windows for Enterprise 1 TB of cloud storage Core security and identity management capabilities Microsoft 365 Copilot, available as an add-on	Everything in Microsoft 365 E3, plus: Advanced security and compliance capabilities Scalable business analytics with Power BI Microsoft 365 Copilot, available as an add-on
Word, Excel, PowerPoint	✓	✓
OneNote	✓	✓
Outlook	✓	✓
Teams	✓	✓
SharePoint	✓	✓
OneDrive	✓	✓
Forms	✓	✓
Bookings	✓	✓
Planner	✓	✓
Clipchamp	✓	✓
Loop	✓	✓
Exchange	✓	✓
Access	✓	✓
Publisher	✓	✓
Viva Engage	✓	✓
Viva Insights	✓	✓
Stream	✓	✓
Sway	✓	✓
Power Apps	✓	✓
Power Automate	✓	✓
To Do	✓	✓
Power BI Pro		✓
Visio	✓	✓
Windows for Enterprise	✓	✓

Table 1.4: Microsoft 365 Enterprise plans

Conclusion

By the end of this chapter, we will have gained a foundational understanding of Microsoft 365 and its significance in today's digital world. We discussed the key differences between Microsoft 365 and Office 365, understanding the unique benefits of each, and discussed why this book is all about Microsoft 365. We have also explained what this book covers and what it does not, the primary audience of this book, and finally, the various licensing plans that Microsoft provides.

As you proceed through the subsequent chapters, you will gain a deeper insight into each aspect of Microsoft 365, equipping you with the knowledge to optimize your use of this versatile suite of tools.

By the end of this book, you will be well-versed in the capabilities of Microsoft 365, ready to leverage these powerful tools to transform your work and achieve your goals. This journey will empower you to navigate the digital world with confidence and efficiency.

In the next chapter, we will explore Microsoft Teams and how you can make the most out of it in your meetings, chats, and when collaborating with others.

Join our Discord space

Join our Discord workspace for latest updates, offers, tech happenings around the world, new releases, and sessions with the authors:

https://discord.bpbonline.com

CHAPTER 2
Microsoft Teams

Introduction

In this chapter, we will cover Microsoft Teams, a powerful collaboration platform that combines chat, audio and video calls, meetings, file storage, and application integration. It is designed to facilitate communication and collaboration within teams, making it easier for users to work together regardless of their physical location.

Structure

The chapter covers the following topics:

- Introduction to Microsoft Teams
- Accessing Teams
- Navigating the Teams client
- Teams and channels
- Chat and conversations
- File sharing
- Meetings and calls
- Integrations and apps
- Best practices

Objectives

This chapter aims to provide the readers with insights into Microsoft Teams, emphasizing its role in enhancing teamwork and productivity. Readers will discover how to utilize Teams' core features such as chat, calls, meetings, file storage, and application integration. The chapter will focus on demonstrating the advantages of using Teams for communication and collaboration within organizational teams, ensuring users can effectively leverage these tools to improve their workflow and connectivity.

Introduction to Microsoft Teams

Teams is a versatile and comprehensive platform designed to enhance collaboration and communication within teams. Launched in 2017, it has rapidly become the go-to tool for organizations seeking to enhance productivity and streamline workflows. By integrating various features such as chat, video meetings, file storage, and application integration, Teams ensures that users can work together seamlessly, regardless of their geographical location. This platform empowers team members to communicate effectively, share resources, and collaborate on projects, thereby streamlining workflows and boosting productivity. Through its intuitive interface and robust functionality, Teams has become an indispensable tool for organizations aiming to foster a cohesive and dynamic work environment.

Microsoft Teams offers a diverse array of use cases that can significantly enhance productivity and streamline operations within any organization:

- **Everyday collaboration**: Teams excels in day-to-day collaboration, providing a hub for messaging, meetings, and file sharing. Whether working remotely or in-office, users can communicate effortlessly, share updates, and stay connected with team members. The platform's integration with other Microsoft 365 tools ensures that all necessary resources are readily available.

- **Project management**: Teams is a valuable tool for project management, offering easy access to apps like Planner, and integration with project management apps like *Trello* and *Asana*. Channels can be dedicated to specific projects, ensuring all relevant information is stored in one place. Project managers can create tasks, assign them to team members, set deadlines, and track progress, all within Teams.

- **Remote work**: With the rise of remote work, Teams has become indispensable. Video conferencing, virtual collaboration, and cloud-based file storage enable remote teams to work effectively without the need for physical presence. Teams ensures that remote workers remain connected, productive, and engaged through features like team-wide announcements, virtual meeting rooms, and collaborative document editing.

- **Virtual Events**: Teams supports virtual events, including meetings, webinars and town halls. Its robust video conferencing capabilities, combined with features like live captions, meeting recording, and attendance tracking, make it ideal for hosting online events. Organizers can schedule events, manage registrations, and create engaging presentations using Teams' extensive toolkit.

  The following points explain the main differences between these:

  - **Meetings:**
    - **Capacity**: Up to 1,000 interactive participants. Any extra participants, up to 10,000 more, join in a view-only mode, allowing them to watch the meeting without interacting.
    - **Interactivity**: Full participation—chat, audio/video, screen sharing.
    - **Registration**: No.
    - **Use case**: Team collaboration, daily standups, internal check-ins.
  - **Webinars:**
    - **Capacity**: Up to 1,000.
    - **Interactivity**: Moderated Q&A, structured chat.
    - **Registration**: Built-in registration with customizable forms.
    - **Use case**: External briefings, product demos, training sessions.
  - **Town halls:**
    - **Capacity**: Up to 10,000 attendees, but with a Teams Premium license, organizers can create town halls with up to 50,000 attendees.
    - **Interactivity**: Limited; Q&A only, speaker roles are pre-assigned.

- **Registration**: Advanced options with analytics.
- **Use case**: Company-wide announcements, exec updates, live broadcasts.

Microsoft 365 Copilot and Copilot Chat are reshaping the Microsoft Teams experience, turning it into a powerful, AI-assisted collaboration space. Instead of manually searching through chats or notes, users can now rely on Copilot to summarize meetings, highlight key points, and generate action items, saving time and reducing mental overhead. Microsoft 365 Copilot is covered in detail in *Chapter 6, Microsoft Copilot*.

Teams' components

Microsoft Teams is built on a robust architecture that integrates various Microsoft 365 services to provide a seamless collaboration experience.

Here are the key components:

- **Microsoft Entra ID**: Teams uses identities stored in Microsoft Entra ID (formerly Azure Active Directory) for authentication and authorization.
- **Microsoft Graph**: Microsoft Graph connects Teams with other Microsoft 365 services, enabling functionalities like calendar integration, file sharing, and more. It provides a unified API endpoint for accessing data across Microsoft 365.
- **Microsoft 365 groups**: When you create a team, a corresponding Microsoft 365 group is created. This group manages team membership and permissions, ensuring that only authorized users can access the team's resources.
- **SharePoint**: Each team gets a SharePoint site for storing files and documents. This site provides robust document management capabilities, including version control, metadata, and sharing options.
- **OneDrive**: OneDrive is used for storing individual files and documents. When you share files in a chat or channel, they are stored in OneDrive, making them easily accessible and shareable.
- **Exchange Online**: Teams integrates with Exchange Online to provide calendar functionalities, allowing users to schedule meetings, view availability, and manage appointments directly within Teams. Additionally, chat messages are also stored in Exchange Online for eDiscovery purposes.
- **Power Automate**: Teams integrates with Power Automate to allow users to create workflows that automate repetitive tasks. This can include notifications, approvals, and data collection.
- **Power Apps**: Users can embed custom apps built with Power Apps directly into Teams, enhancing functionality and providing tailored solutions.
- **Power BI**: Teams supports embedding Power BI reports and dashboards, enabling data-driven decision-making within the platform.
- **Loop components**: Loop components allow users to collaborate directly within chat messages. These components can include tables, task lists, and paragraphs, and are saved automatically to OneDrive.
- **Planner**: Teams integrates with Planner to provide task management capabilities, allowing users to create, assign, and track tasks within Teams channels.
- **Stream**: Microsoft Stream is used for managing and sharing video content within Teams. This includes meeting recordings, training videos, and other multimedia content.

Licensing

Teams is available as a free version with limited features, suitable for personal use. This includes group calling for up to 60 minutes and 100 participants, unlimited chat with friends and family, and 5 GB of cloud storage. For additional features, Teams is included in the following home plans: Microsoft 365 Personal and Microsoft 365 Family.

In terms of businesses, Teams is available as a standalone *Microsoft Teams Essentials* package, or as part of Microsoft 365 Business Basic, Standard, and Premium plans.

For enterprises, Teams is no longer included in any Office 365 or Microsoft 365 plans. It is now separate and available as a *Microsoft Teams Enterprise* add-on. There is also an additional license for *Teams Premium* that offers a range of advanced features that enhance the standard Teams experience.

Here are some of its key features that aim to make meetings more personalized, intelligent, and secure:

- **AI-powered meetings**: Intelligent meeting recaps automatically generate notes, recommended tasks, and personalized highlights (Teams Premium license required).

- **Customization**: Personalized touches like branded meetings, organizational backgrounds, and more.

- **Advanced security**: Enhanced meeting protections such as watermarks, sensitivity labels, and end-to-end encryption.

- **Virtual appointments**: Streamlined appointment management with reports and analytics.

- **Immersive experiences**: Host immersive events like town halls and onboarding sessions with Microsoft Mesh.

Accessing Teams

Microsoft Teams offers a versatile range of options to ensure users can stay connected across devices and environments. Whether you want a feature-rich experience on your desktop, seamless access via your web browser, or the convenience of mobile connectivity, Teams adapts to meet diverse needs.

Desktop client

The Microsoft Teams desktop client is available for both Windows and Mac operating systems. To access Teams on your desktop, download the application from the official Microsoft website or through your Microsoft 365 subscription portal. Once installed, open the application and log in using your Microsoft account credentials. The desktop client provides a comprehensive experience, offering all the features of Teams, including chat, calls, meetings, and file sharing, in a powerful, standalone application. It is particularly useful for users who need to multitask and manage multiple Teams windows simultaneously.

The following figure shows the Teams desktop client on a Windows PC:

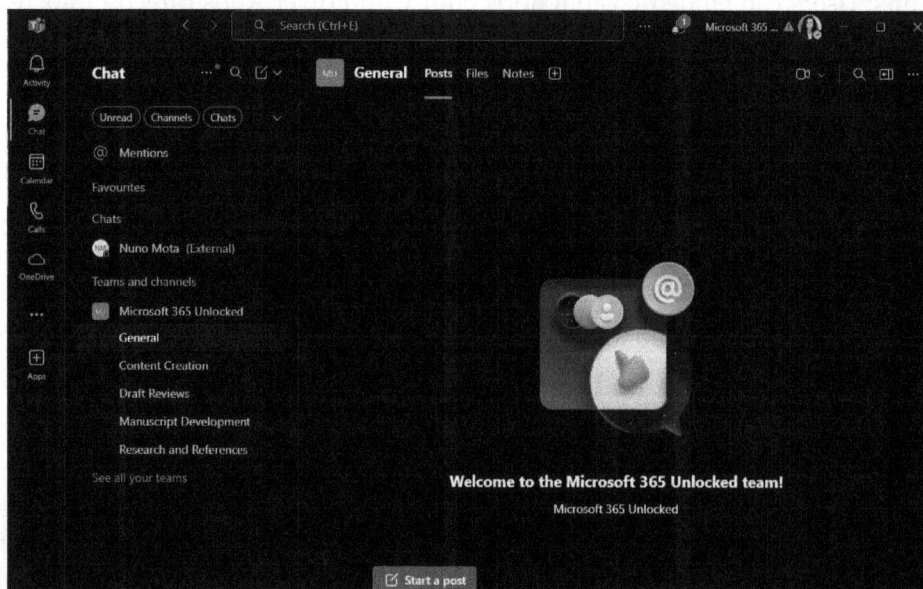

Figure 2.1: Teams desktop client

Web client

The Microsoft Teams web client allows users to access the platform directly from a web browser, without the need for any installations. Simply navigate to the Teams website at **https://teams.microsoft.com** and log in with your Microsoft account. The web client supports most modern browsers, including Chrome, Firefox, Edge, and Safari. This option is ideal for quick access or for users who may not have the ability to install applications on their devices. The web client offers nearly all the functionalities of the desktop client, making it a versatile alternative for working on the go or from different devices.

The following figure shows Teams running on the Edge browser on a Windows PC:

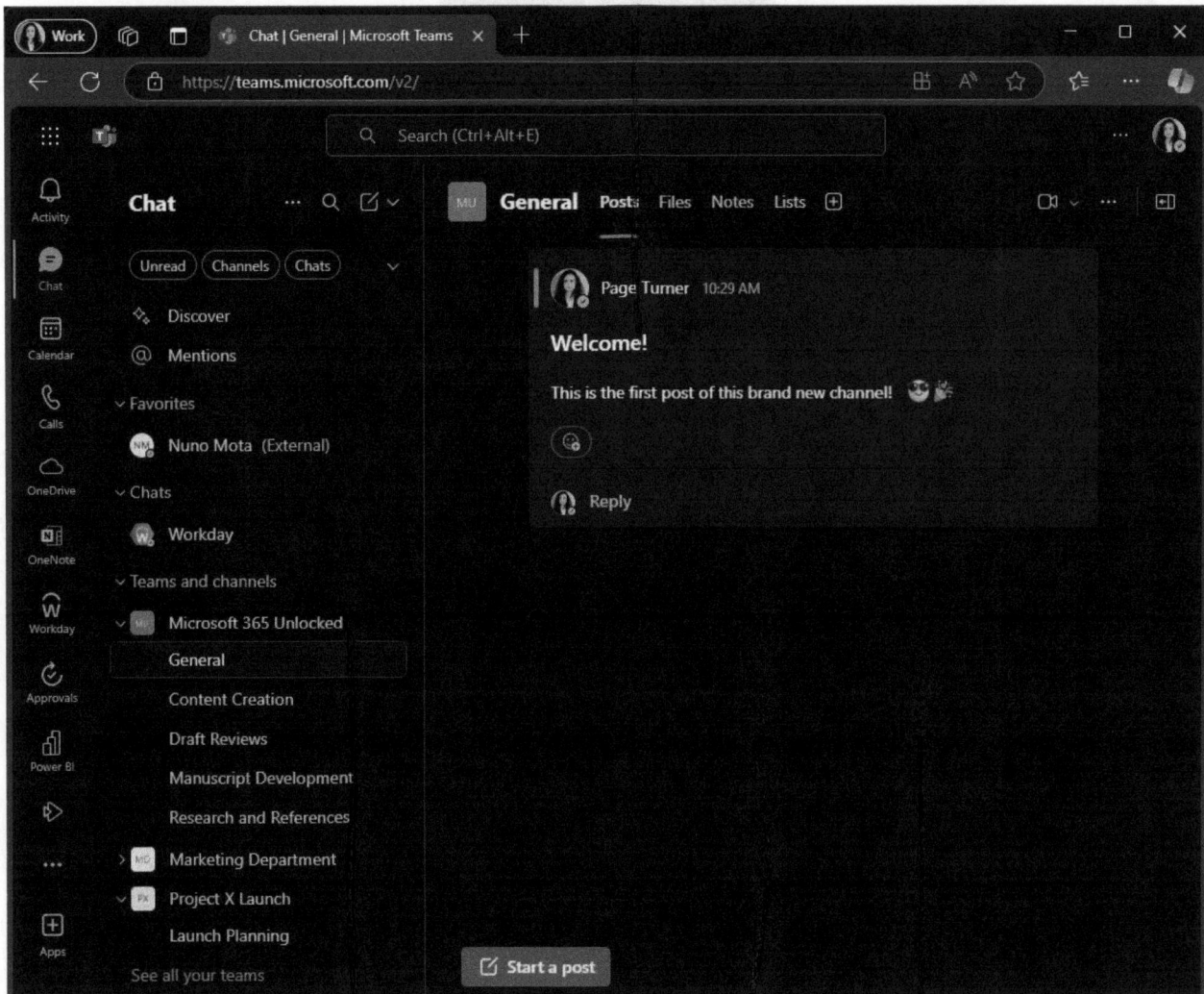

Figure 2.2: *Teams web client*

Mobile client

For those who need to stay connected while on the move, the Microsoft Teams mobile client is available for both iOS and Android devices. Download the app from the Apple App Store or Google Play Store, then log in with your Microsoft account. The mobile client is designed to provide a streamlined experience, with access to chats, calls, meetings, and file sharing, optimized for smaller screens. Notifications and the ability to join meetings directly from your mobile device ensure that you remain up-to-date and engaged, regardless of your location.

The following figure shows the Teams iOS mobile client:

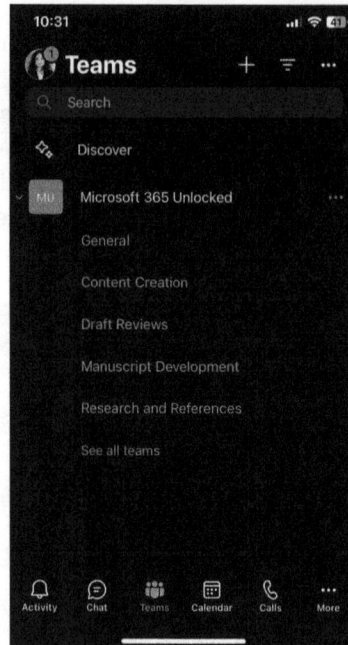

Figure 2.3: *Teams mobile client on iOS*

Navigating the Teams client

Upon logging into the Microsoft Teams client, users are greeted by a clean and intuitive interface designed to simplify collaboration and communication. The main window is divided into several key sections, each serving a specific purpose:

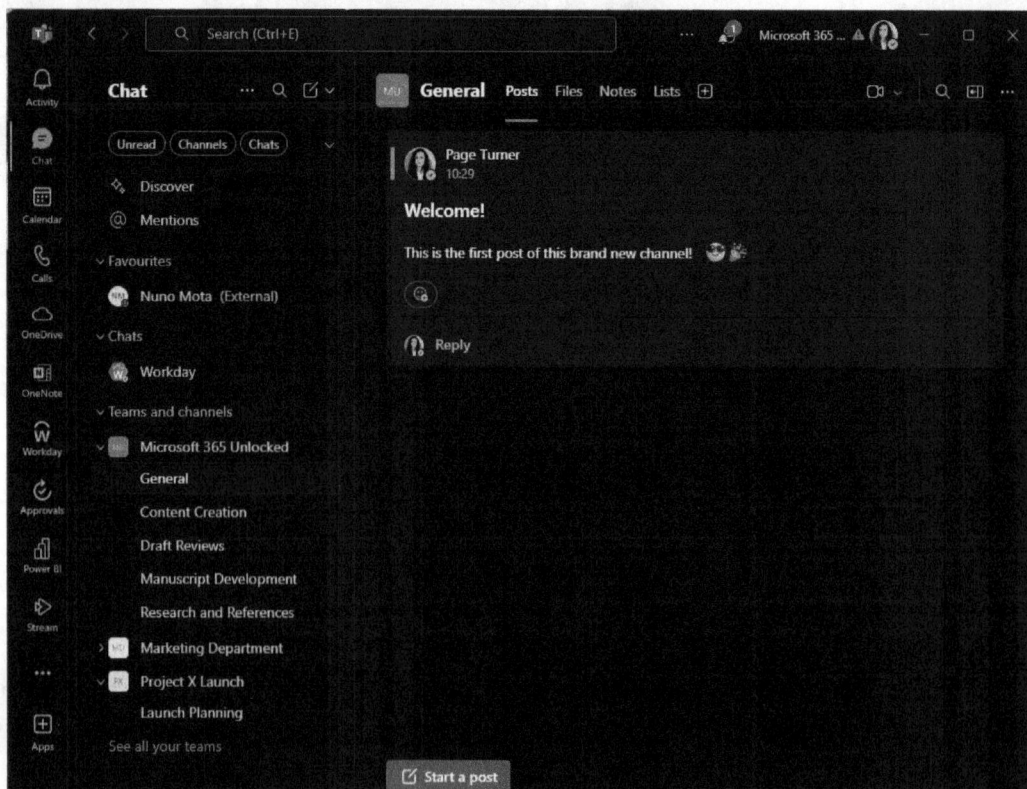

Figure 2.4: *Navigating the Teams client*

The explanation of each section is as follows:

- **Navigation Pane**: On the left side of the main window, the navigation pane provides quick access to the core features of Teams. Here, you can find icons for **Activity**, **Chat**, **Calendar**, **Calls**, and other icons for apps that you or your administrator might have installed. Each icon opens a corresponding view, allowing users to seamlessly switch between different tasks.

- **Activity Feed**: The **Activity Feed** (typically the first icon at the top left side of the client) aggregates notifications and updates from all teams and channels, ensuring users stay informed about new messages, mentions, reactions, and other activities. This centralized feed helps users manage their workload and prioritize tasks.

- **Chat**: The **Chat** section displays recent conversations, including one-on-one messages and group chats. Users can initiate new chats, search for existing ones, and view message history. The chat interface supports rich text formatting, file attachments, and multimedia content, making communication more engaging. Following a recent update to Teams, this view now also lists the teams a user is a member of, along with their respective channels. This hierarchical structure allows users to navigate to specific channels, view ongoing conversations, and access shared files and resources. Users can also create new teams and channels from this view. This new combined view can be changed by going to *Settings | Chats and channels | Viewing chats, teams, and channels* and selecting *Separate* instead of *Combined*.

- **Calendar**: The **Calendar** integrates with Outlook and displays scheduled meetings and events. Users can create, join, and manage meetings directly from this view, ensuring they stay on top of their commitments.

- **Calls**: The **Calls** section provides access to the calling features of Teams, including a contact list, call history, and voicemail. Users can make voice and video calls, either one-on-one or in groups, and manage their call settings.

- **Main content area**: The central part of the main window is the main content area, where the details of the selected view are displayed. For example, when viewing a channel, users will see the channel's conversations, files, and tabs. When in a meeting, this area shows the video feed, participant list, and meeting controls.

- **Command bar**: At the top of the main window, the command bar allows users to search for messages, files, and people across Teams. It also provides quick access to commands and shortcuts, helping users perform actions efficiently.

- **User profile and settings**: On the upper right corner of the main window, users can access their profile, change their status, and adjust settings. This menu includes options for managing account details, notifications, and device preferences, ensuring a personalized experience.

Teams and channels

Microsoft Teams is a powerful collaboration tool that revolves around the concepts of *teams* and *channels*. These two components are integral to how users organize and streamline communication and collaboration within the platform. The following is an explanation of what they are, how they differ, what they are used for, and how to use them effectively.

Teams

Teams in Microsoft Teams are overarching groups created to organize people, projects, or departments. They act as a digital workspace where members can collaborate on specific goals or topics. An organization might create separate Teams for different departments (e.g., marketing, IT, or HR) or for specific projects (e.g., product launch or annual conference). For example:

- A team for the marketing department might include all marketing employees, with channels for campaign management, content creation, and analytics.

- A team for a product launch project might include cross-departmental members working together on the launch strategy.

Membership in a team can be open to everyone in the organization or restricted to a specific group of individuals, depending on the purpose and sensitivity of the content.

The following figure illustrates an example of two teams with several channels each:

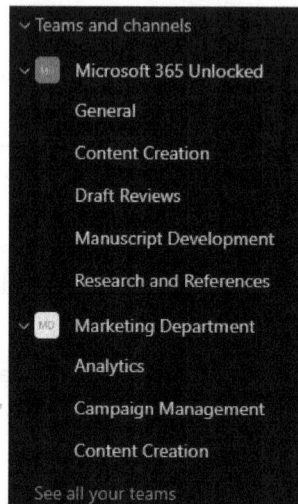

Figure 2.5: Example of two teams and several channels in Teams

To create a new team, follow these steps:

1. Click the **Chat** icon in the navigation pane. If you are using the separate view we discussed earlier, select the **Teams** button.

2. Select the New items icon above your list of chats and channels, and click on **New team,** as shown:

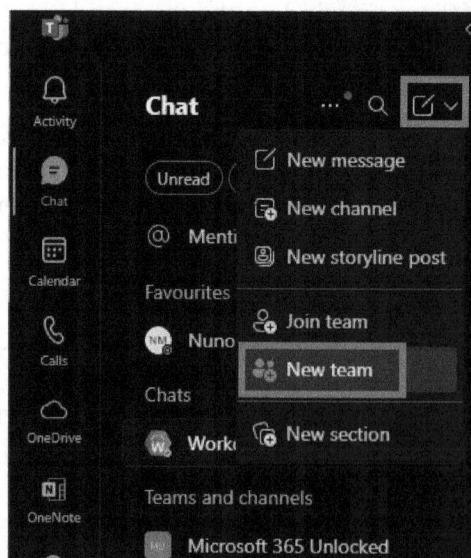

Figure 2.6: Creating a new team

3. Name your team and consider adding a detailed description that highlights its purpose, objectives, and the type of collaboration it will foster. This description can serve as a guide for members to understand the team's focus and goals, such as in the following example:

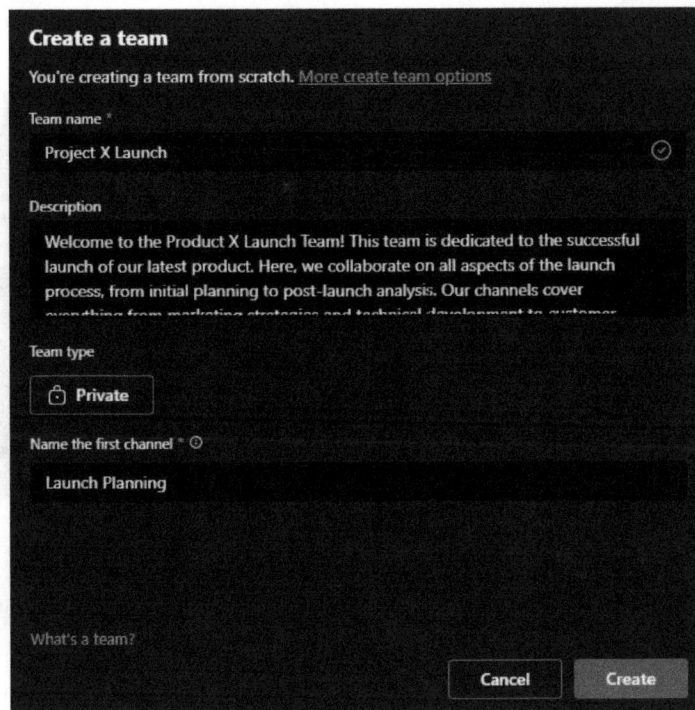

Figure 2.7: Details when creating a new team

4. Next, name your first channel. Each team begins with at least one channel, which serves as a foundational space for organizing discussions and activities. While the initial channel is automatically created for you, it requires a name to establish its identity within the team. As you progress, you have the flexibility to create additional, tailored channels to accommodate specific projects, tasks, or topics, fostering more streamlined and effective collaboration. Up until early 2025, the first channel used to always be called *General*, but users could rename it.

5. Next, setting the privacy level of your team is crucial. Choose between **Public**, which allows anyone in your organization to join, or **Private**, which restricts access to invited members only. This step ensures your team aligns with its intended audience and confidentiality requirements. A team's privacy can be changed at any time after it has been created.

6. When you are done, click on **Create**.

Keep in mind that creating a team results in:

*   A new Microsoft 365 group.
*   A SharePoint site and document library for files.
*   An Exchange Online shared mailbox and calendar.
*   A OneNote notebook.
*   Integration with other Microsoft 365 apps like Planner and Power BI.

If the team is created from an existing group by clicking on the **More create team options** button shown in *Figure 2.7*, its membership, site, mailbox, and notebook are surfaced in Teams.

Team member roles

As the creator of the team, you hold the role of **team owner**, granting you the authority to manage its structure and membership. Once your team is created, you can begin inviting individuals to join. To do this, navigate to the team name, click on **... More options**, and then select **Add member**. Begin by entering a username, distribution list, security group, or Microsoft 365 group. You can also invite external individuals as guests by entering their email addresses (if allowed by your administrator). Once you have added all desired members, click **Add**:

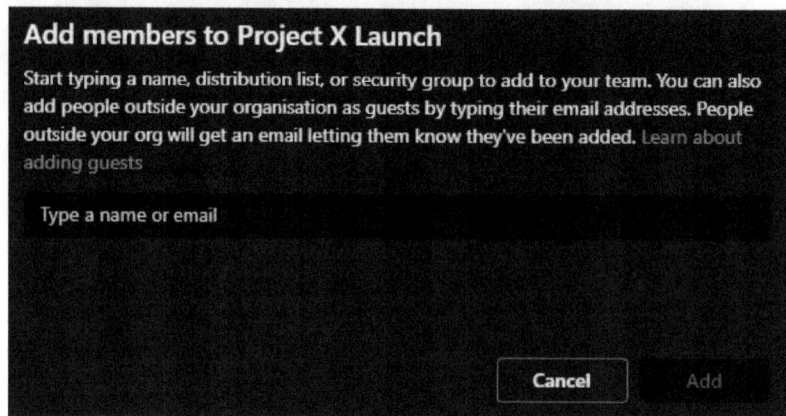

Figure 2.8: Adding members to a team

To assign someone as a team owner, use the dropdown menu next to *Member* and select the appropriate option. Multiple owners can be designated for a single team.

Carefully consider the purpose and needs of your team when selecting members, ensuring that their skills and expertise align with the objectives of the group. Additionally, as the team owner, you can customize settings, monitor activity, and foster an environment of collaboration that supports the team's goals.

Within each team, users can assume different roles that define their level of access, authority, and responsibilities. Understanding these roles is essential for ensuring effective collaboration and maintaining the structure of teams. We will explore the various roles within a Microsoft Teams team in detail.

The team owner is the individual who creates the team and holds the highest level of authority within it. This role is critical for the team's structure and management.

Team owners have the following responsibilities and capabilities:

- **Creating the team**: The owner initiates the creation of the team, naming it, setting its privacy level, and defining its purpose and description.

- **Managing membership**: Owners can invite individuals to join the team, remove members, and assign roles within the team. They are responsible for ensuring that the team includes members whose skills align with the team's objectives.

- **Customizing settings**: Owners can configure settings to control how the team operates, including permissions for posting messages, adding apps, and managing tabs.

- **Monitoring activity**: Owners can view analytics and activity logs to track the team's engagement and identify areas for improvement.

- **Creating and managing channels**: Owners can create standard or private channels, ensuring they align with the team's projects and discussions. They can also manage channel settings and permissions.

Team owners often act as moderators, fostering an environment of collaboration and guiding the team toward achieving its goals.

To assign someone as an owner or view the owners of an existing team, follow these steps:

1. Next to the team name, select **... More options**, and then click on **Manage team**.

2. Select the dropdown next to **Members and guests** to see all team members. The **Role** column on the right indicates if someone is a team member or owner. To designate someone as an owner, select the dropdown and choose **Owner** as shown in the following figure:

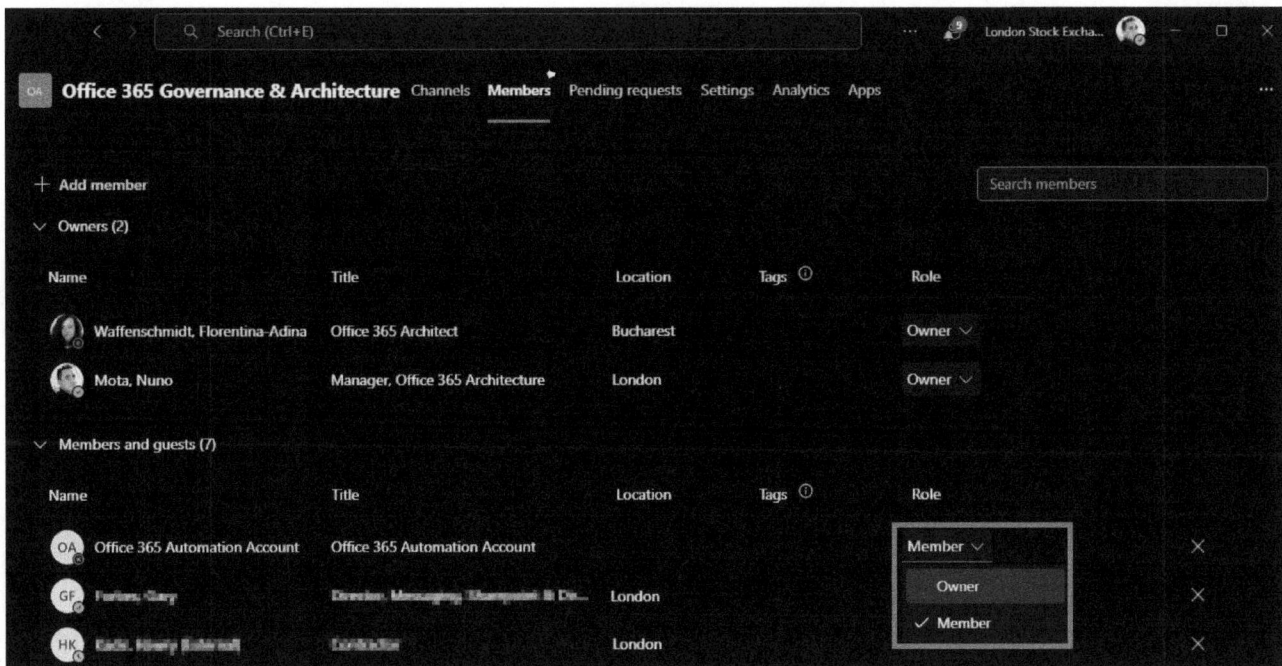

Figure 2.9: Promoting a team member to owner

Team members are users who have been invited to join the team by its owner. They play an active role in collaboration but have fewer privileges than the owner. Their capabilities include:

- **Participating in channels**: Members can contribute to conversations, share files, and collaborate on tasks within the team's channels.

- **Accessing shared resources**: Members have access to resources such as files, shared OneNote notebooks, and other tabs added by the owner.

- **Using apps**: Members can utilize apps integrated into the team, such as Microsoft Planner or third-party tools, for task management and collaboration.

- **Creating content**: In some cases, members may be allowed to create new channels, post messages, or add tabs, depending on the permissions set by the team owner.

Team members form the backbone of collaboration, contributing their expertise and insights to drive the team's objectives.

To remove someone from your team:

1. Next to the team name, select **... More options**, and then **Manage team**.
2. Select **Members** and find the person under **Members and guests** (you can search by name).
3. Select the X icon next to their name to remove them.

To remove a team owner, change their role to member first, then remove them.

Guests are external users who are invited to join a team. They may include contractors, clients, or collaborators from outside the organization. Although their role is limited compared to team members, guests can:

- **Participate in channels**: Guests can access specific channels and contribute to conversations and activities, as long as permissions are provided by the owner.

- **Access files**: Guests can view and interact with files shared within channels.

- **Collaborate on tasks**: Depending on permissions, guests can use apps integrated into the team to complete tasks or contribute to projects.

The inclusion of guests allows teams to collaborate effectively with external stakeholders while maintaining control over sensitive information.

In addition to the team-wide roles, Microsoft Teams allows for channel-specific, moderators. Channel moderators are responsible for managing activities within a specific channel. Their duties include:

- **Controlling conversations**: Moderators can manage who can post messages in the channel, ensuring discussions remain relevant and organized.

- **Setting permissions**: Moderators can adjust channel settings to control access and interaction levels for team members and guests.

This role is particularly useful for channels focused on specialized projects or confidential topics.

Deleting, archiving, and restoring teams

Microsoft Teams provides functionalities to manage the lifecycle of a team, including deletion, archiving, and restoration. These tools are designed to enhance administrative control while preserving essential data and ensuring proper organization.

The **deletion** of a team removes it entirely from Microsoft Teams, including all associated channels, files, and conversations. During the first 30 days following the deletion, the team can still be recovered by its owner(s) by restoring its corresponding Microsoft 365 group. However, after that period has passed, the deletion is irreversible unless a backup or restoration mechanism is in place. Team owners and administrators are the only ones with permissions to delete teams. Deletion is useful for removing inactive or outdated teams that no longer serve a purpose.

To delete a team:

1. Navigate to the team in Microsoft Teams.
2. Click on the three-dot menu next to the team name.
3. Select the **Delete team** option and confirm the action.

The following figure shows the deletion option for a team:

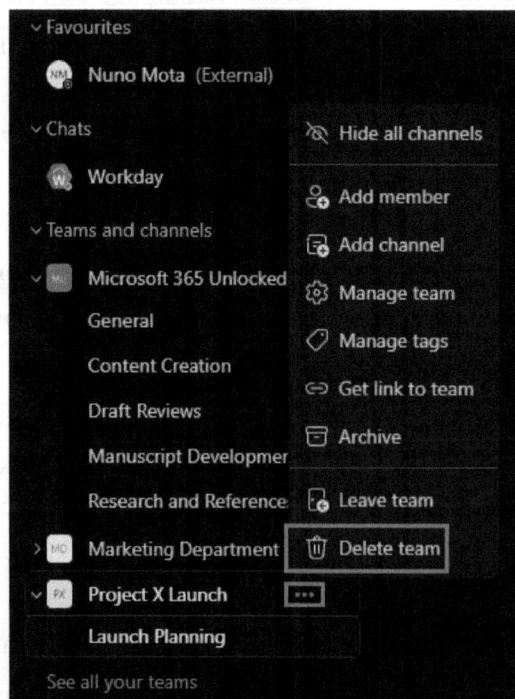

Figure 2.10: *Deleting a team*

Please keep in mind the following when deleting a team:

- Deleting a team removes the team mailbox and calendar from Exchange
- The corresponding SharePoint site and all its files will also be deleted
- And any OneNote notebook, Planner plan, Power BI workspace, or Stream Group affiliated with the team will also be deleted.

To see all the teams you own, from the *combined chat and channels* or the *separate teams* view, select **More list options ...** followed by **Your teams and channels** button, and then select **Teams you own,** as shown:

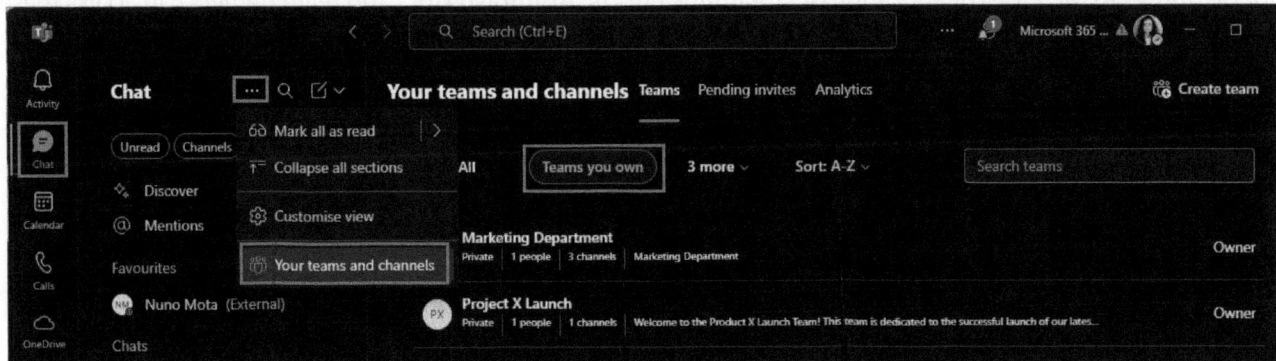

Figure 2.11: Teams you own

Archiving serves as a middle ground between active usage and deletion. When a team is archived, it is placed in a read-only state, allowing members and owners to access its contents without modifying them. This is particularly beneficial for preserving information from completed projects or dormant collaborations while keeping the workspace organized. Files and other resources remain intact, and the team can be unarchived if necessary.

To archive a team, follow these steps:

1. Navigate to the team in Microsoft Teams.
2. Click on the three-dot menu next to the team name.
3. Select the **Archive** option, ensuring that the team is no longer active, but its data remains accessible.

Archiving can help declutter the interface while maintaining a record for future reference or auditing purposes.

Restoration applies to either archived teams or teams that need to be recovered from deletion. It reactivates the team, allowing members to resume their work and interactions. This capability is critical for instances where archived data needs to be revisited, or a mistakenly deleted team must be recovered. To restore an **archived** team:

1. From the *combined chat and channels* view, select **See all your teams**.
2. Find the team you want to restore.
3. Select **... More options**, and finally click on **Restore**.

If the team was deleted, team owners can restore it by restoring its corresponding group in **Outlook on the web** by:

1. Navigating to the **deleted groups** page at **https://outlook.office.com/people/group/deleted**
2. Expand the **Deleted** section and find the team you want to restore.
3. Select the team and click on **Restore**.

Note: **If the group is not listed, you will need to contact your administrator.**

Team analytics

Team analytics in Microsoft Teams provides valuable insights into how teams and channels are being utilized, facilitating better management and optimization of collaboration efforts. These analytics are available at two levels: individual teams and specific channels.

For an individual team, analytics offer data on various key performance indicators. This includes active users, number of posts, replies, and reactions, as well as data on shared files and the team's overall activity level. Such insights help team leaders understand engagement levels, identify inactive members, and pinpoint opportunities to increase collaboration or streamline efforts. Administrators and team owners can access these metrics by navigating to the Teams Admin Center or directly within the Microsoft Teams app by going to **Manage team** and then **Analytics**:

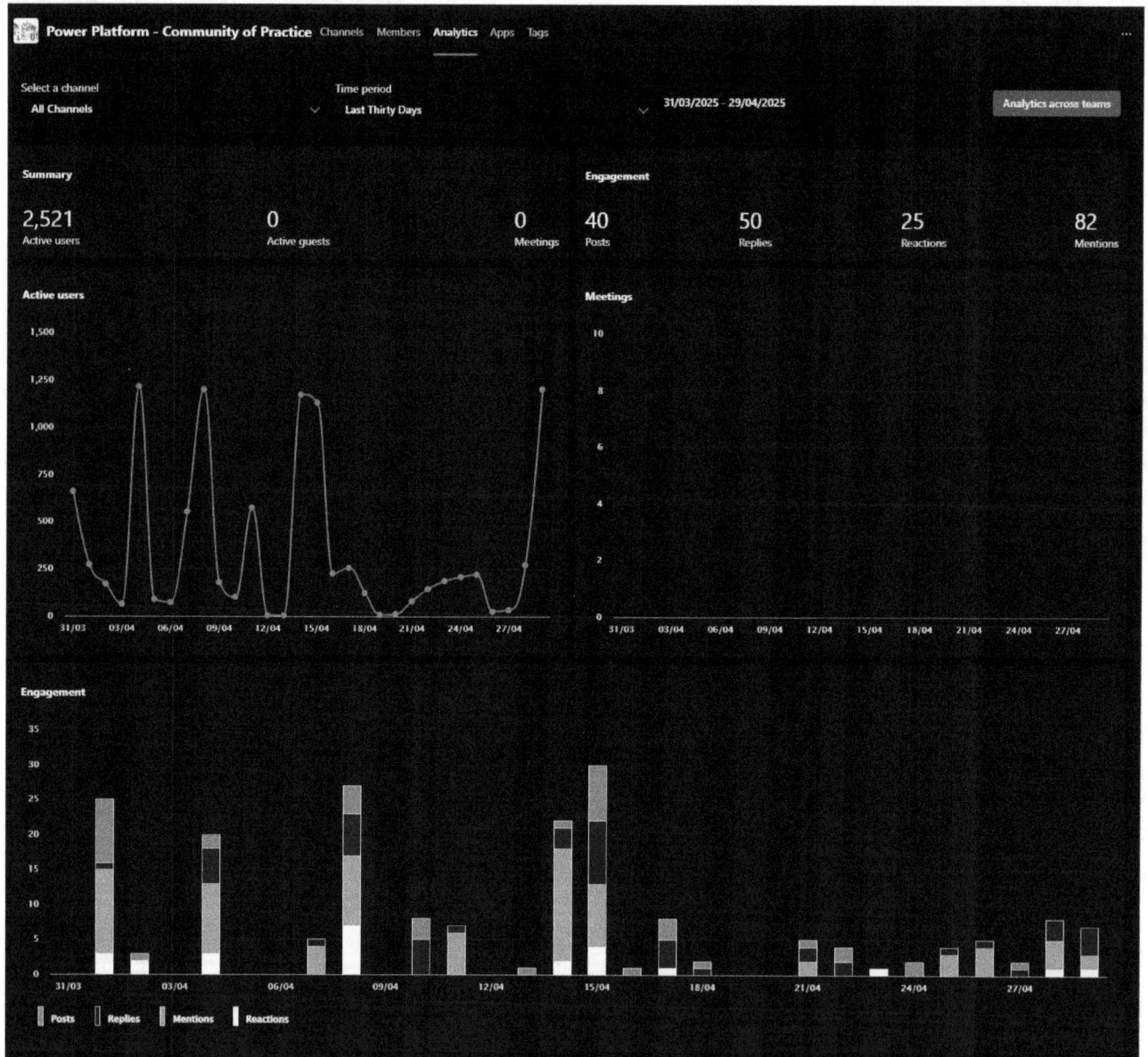

Figure 2.12: Individual team analytics

When focusing on a specific channel, channel-level analytics delve deeper into usage patterns within that specific channel, showing the same metrics as the ones shown above. This information is particularly useful for determining which channels are fostering meaningful collaboration and which may require adjustments, such as redefining their purpose or encouraging more participation.

To access an overview of usage data for all teams you are a member of or an owner of within a single view, follow these steps:

1. From the combined chat and channels or the separate teams view, select **More list options ...**

2. Select **Your teams and channels**.

3. Select **Analytics**, then choose a date range to display the usage data for all the teams of which you are a member or an owner.

The following figure is a screenshot of analytics across all of the teams a user owns:

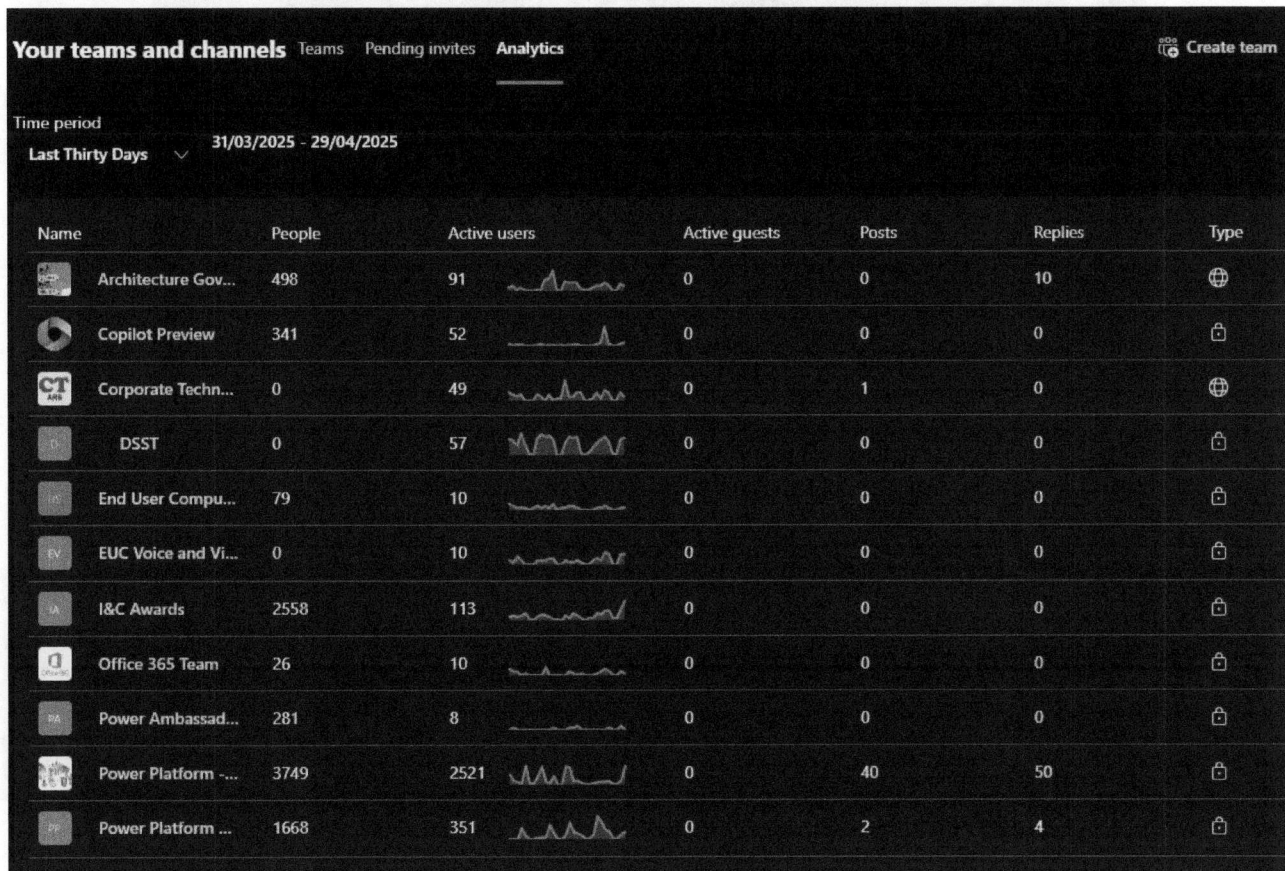

Name	People	Active users		Active guests	Posts	Replies	Type
Architecture Gov...	498	91		0	0	10	🌐
Copilot Preview	341	52		0	0	0	🔒
Corporate Techn...	0	49		0	1	0	🌐
DSST	0	57		0	0	0	🔒
End User Compu...	79	10		0	0	0	🔒
EUC Voice and Vi...	0	10		0	0	0	🔒
I&C Awards	2558	113		0	0	0	🔒
Office 365 Team	26	10		0	0	0	🔒
Power Ambassad...	281	8		0	0	0	🔒
Power Platform -...	3749	2521		0	40	50	🔒
Power Platform ...	1668	351		0	2	4	🔒

Figure 2.13: *Analytics across all your teams*

Team settings

Microsoft Teams provides team owners with a variety of settings to effectively manage their teams and enhance collaboration. These settings not only allow customization of team functionality but also offer tools for ensuring security, productivity, and inclusiveness. The following is a detailed overview of the key settings available to team owners, also shown in the following figure:

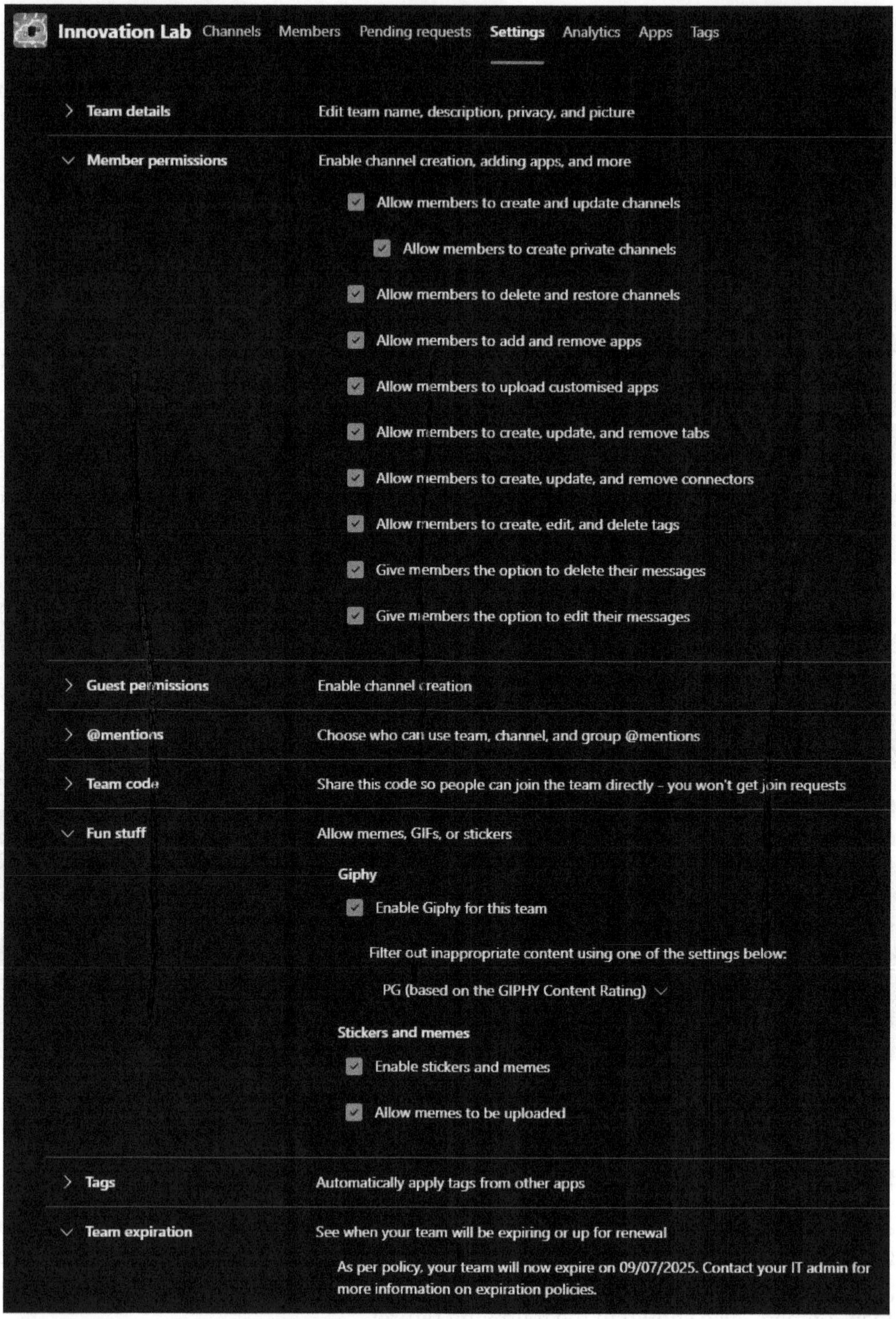

Figure 2.14: Teams settings

The details are as follows:

- **Team details**: This section allows the team owner to view and edit basic information about the team, such as the team name, description, and privacy settings.

- **Member permissions**: Team owners can configure permissions for members to control the extent of their participation within the team. Amongst others, these options include:

  o Allowing members to create, update, and delete channels.

- o Permitting members to add or remove apps and tabs.

- o Controlling whether members can upload custom memes and stickers.

- **Guest permissions**: For teams that involve external collaborators, guest permissions enable team owners to manage what guests can do within the team, such as allowing guests to add or remove channels, deciding whether guests can delete or edit messages, or enabling or restricting file sharing for guests.

- **@Mentions**: This setting allows team owners to control the use of @mentions within the team. Owners can decide:

  - o Whether members can use @team to notify everyone in the team.

  - o Whether @channel can be used to target all members of a specific channel.

- **Team code**: A team owner can generate a unique code for the team, simplifying the process of joining the team. Users can use this code to join without requiring invitations, making it particularly useful for large or frequently changing teams.

- **Fun stuff**: This section allows team owners to enable or disable features like memes, stickers, GIFs, and reactions. These elements can help foster team engagement and creativity but can be restricted if necessary to maintain professionalism.

- **Tags**: Tags in Microsoft Teams enable owners to organize members into specific categories for streamlined communication. For example, tags like *Design Team* or *Project Leaders* allow owners to @ *mention* a particular group instead of notifying the entire team.

- **Team expiration**: Team owners can set an expiration date for the team, which ensures that inactive teams are automatically archived or deleted after a specified duration. This feature helps maintain organizational tidiness and avoid cluttered team lists.

Each of these settings empowers team owners with tools to optimize team management, encourage collaboration, and safeguard the integrity of their workspace. By leveraging these features, owners can create a productive and secure environment tailored to their team's unique requirements.

Channels

Each team comprises channels, which further break down conversations and activities into manageable, focused discussions. Channels are subdivisions within a team, designed for organizing conversations, files, and activities around specific topics, projects, or tasks. Each team must have at least one channel, but typically, additional channels are created to focus on narrower topics or areas of interest. For example:

- The marketing department might have a *Social Media* channel where discussions focus specifically on social campaigns.

- A product launch team might have an *Event Planning* channel for planning the launch event and a *Budget* channel for financial discussions.

Channels can be of three types:

- **Standard channels**: These are accessible to all members of the team and are ideal for general collaboration and discussions. A team can have up to 1,000 channels throughout its lifespan. This limit encompasses both active channels and those that have been created and subsequently deleted.

- **Private channels**: These are limited to a subset of team members and are useful for confidential projects or discussions that should not be visible to the entire team. You can create up to 30 private channels throughout the team's lifespan.

- **Shared channels**: These facilitate collaboration by allowing individuals outside the team to be added to the channel. Access to the shared channel is restricted to users who are designated as owners or members. This feature is particularly useful for collaboration among individuals from various teams, such as engineering, sales, and support, who are working on different facets of the same project or product. Thus, it provides a unified space for cross-functional cooperation.

    Note: **Shared channels support cross-tenant collaboration if B2B Direct Connect is enabled by your administrator.**

Understanding the differences between teams and channels is crucial for effectively using Microsoft Teams:

Aspect	Teams	Channels
Purpose	Serves as the overarching group or workspace for a department, project, or organization.	Organizes discussions, files, and activities within a specific team into focused topics or tasks.
Scope	Broad, encompassing a wide range of members and objectives.	Specific, focusing on a particular topic, project, or interest within the Team.
Access	Controlled at the team level. All members have access to the team's standard channels.	Access can be set for all team members (standard channels) or restricted to a subset (private channels).
Use case	Organization-level, project-level, or team-level collaboration.	Task-focused or topic-specific discussions and file sharing.

Table 2.1: Teams vs. channels

To create a channel, follow these steps:

1. Navigate to the desired team.
2. Click the ellipsis (**...**) next to the team name and select **Add channel**.
3. Enter a name and description for the channel.
4. Choose the channel type—*Standard*, *Private*, or *Shared*—depending on the intended audience and level of access required
5. Click **Create** to create the channel.

Each channel contains its own set of tabs, including **Posts** (for conversations), **Files** (for shared documents), **Notes** (which surfaces the OneNote associated with the team), and other customizable tabs like Microsoft Planner, SharePoint sites, workflows, and many more. To add a new tab to your channel, simply navigate to the channel and click the + icon on the right:

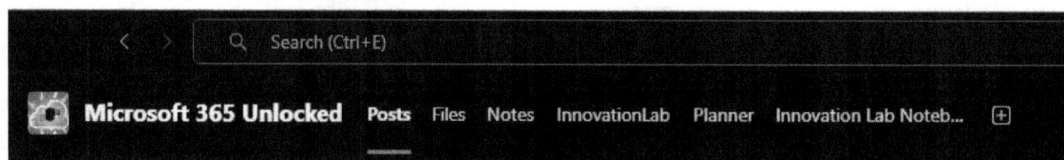

Figure 2.15: Tabs in a channel

Deleting, archiving, and restoring channels

Just like with a team, team owners have the ability to archive channels within a team when they are no longer active yet need to be retained for future reference or potential reactivation. Archived channels will be marked as read-only, preserving the conversations and files while allowing for search functionality within the channel. Retention or deletion policies applied to the channel prior to archiving will continue to be enforced, and the channel may be renewed if necessary.

To archive a channel, first locate the channel you wish to archive in your list of teams and channels. Then, click on **More options ...** next to the channel's name and select **Archive channel**:

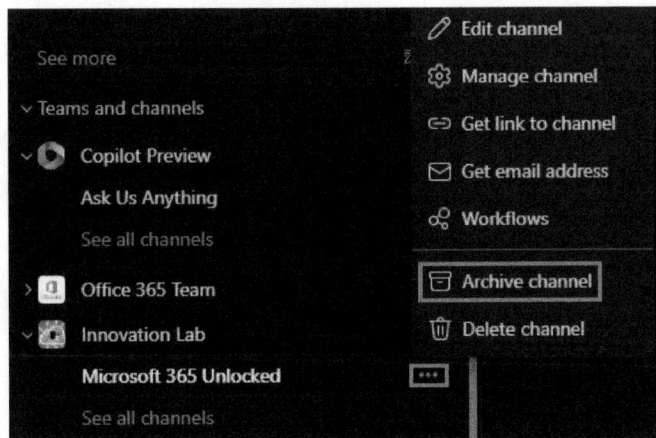

Figure 2.16: Archiving a channel

A new window will open with an option to **Make the SharePoint site read-only for team members** that you can select. This will prevent members from editing the content in the SharePoint folder associated with the channel, but team owners will still be able to edit this content.

After the channel has been archived, it will have an archived icon next to it, and the team's name will be in *italic*:

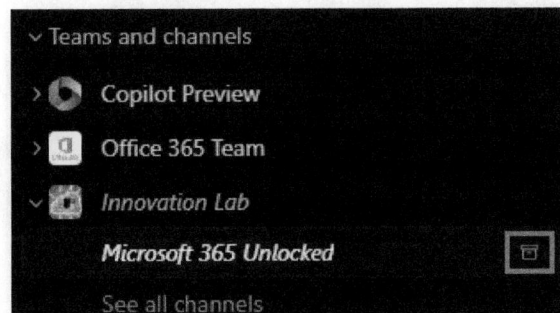

Figure 2.17: Archived channel

Members will no longer be able to initiate new conversations, respond to posts within the channel, modify channel settings, or add tabs/install applications. However, as the owner of a team or channel, you retain the ability to manage membership, update roles, and delete, renew, or restore archived channels.

You can also find the channel by going to **Manage team**, then **Channels**, and finally selecting **Archived** to show only channels that have been archived.

To restore an archived channel, simply navigate to the channel you want to restore, as explained above, select **More options,** and then **Restore channel**.

Channel settings

Channels also offer a set of settings designed to empower team owners with control and customization over their channels. These settings ensure that channels align with the needs of the team and encourage effective collaboration, as follows:

- **Channel details**: This section allows channel owners to rename the channel, update its description, and recommend the channel, which highlights the channel as essential or preferred for new team members, encouraging active participation and visibility within critical areas of the team workspace.

- **Moderation**: Moderation provides team owners with the ability to control interactions within a channel. Owners can designate specific team members as moderators, granting them permissions to manage conversations. Moderators can initiate discussions, respond to posts, and delete inappropriate content, ensuring a productive and respectful environment within the channel. This feature is particularly valuable in channels dealing with sensitive information or high-traffic discussions.

- **Connectors**: Connectors enable team owners to integrate external services and applications directly into a channel. These integrations bring updates and notifications from platforms such as Trello, GitHub, or Twitter into the channel, keeping team members informed and aligned without requiring them to leave Microsoft Teams.

The following figure shows some of the options available for channels, including options around moderation:

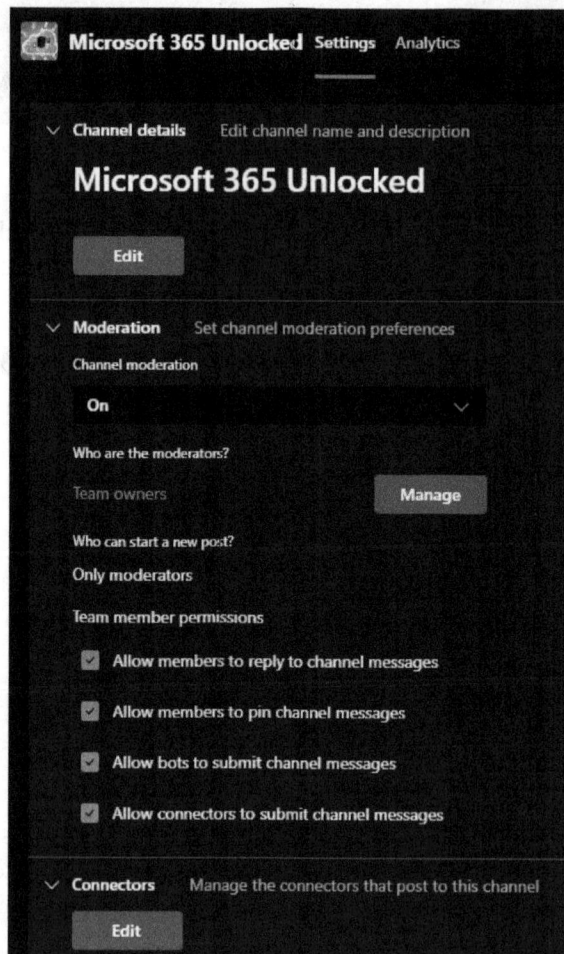

Figure 2.18: Channel settings

Additionally, users can configure individual notification settings for a specific channel. These settings are individual to each user and allow them to tailor their notifications based on their engagement and priorities within the channel. To manage notification settings for Teams channels, follow these steps:

1. Click the ellipsis (**...**) next to a channel name.

2. Select **Channel notifications**.

3. Customize notifications to your preference:

    a. Receive a notification for each new post in the channel.

    b. Receive a notification each time the channel is @mentioned.

    c. Choose to receive no notifications at all.

Chat and conversations

Microsoft Teams provides a comprehensive and dynamic chat experience, enabling users to communicate efficiently, whether in one-on-one conversations, group chats, or within specific channels. Users can share files, emojis, GIFs, and links, making communication more dynamic and engaging. The chat function supports rich text formatting, allowing users to highlight important information, create bulleted lists, and more. These features foster collaboration and engagement, ensuring seamless communication across teams and projects.

One-to-one chats

One-to-one chats in Microsoft Teams are ideal for private conversations between two individuals. These chats are perfect for direct communication, quick decision-making, or confidential discussions. Users can exchange text messages in real time while also sharing files, links, and media such as emojis, GIFs, and stickers, adding a personal touch to their interactions. The chat interface supports rich text formatting, allowing users to emphasize key points with bold or italic text, create bullet points, and even add hyperlinks.

The text composing options in Microsoft Teams chat are designed to enhance the user experience and make communication dynamic and engaging. These include the following:

- **Formatting options**: Teams chat supports rich text formatting, allowing users to structure and highlight their messages effectively. Users can apply bold, italic, and underline styles, create bulleted or numbered lists, and incorporate hyperlinks to emphasize key points or organize information clearly. This flexibility ensures that messages are both professional and visually appealing.

- **Emojis**: Users can insert emojis directly into their messages to express emotions, reactions, or ideas in a fun and relatable manner. Emojis are a universal way to make communication more engaging and approachable.

- **Loop components**: Teams integrates Loop components, enabling real-time collaboration within chat messages. These components allow users to create and edit content such as lists, tables, or ideas collaboratively without the need to switch to another application. All participants can contribute simultaneously, ensuring seamless teamwork and centralized updates. Loop and Loop components will be covered in *Chapter 4, Infrastructure as Code*.

- **Actions and apps**: This option allows users to attach files, schedule the message to be sent at a later time, send the message as important or urgent, record and send an audio clip, or add apps to the chat (just like in a channel).

Together, these options foster creativity, efficiency, and collaboration, ensuring that communication within Teams chat is tailored to the diverse needs of modern workplaces. The following figures shows some of these options:

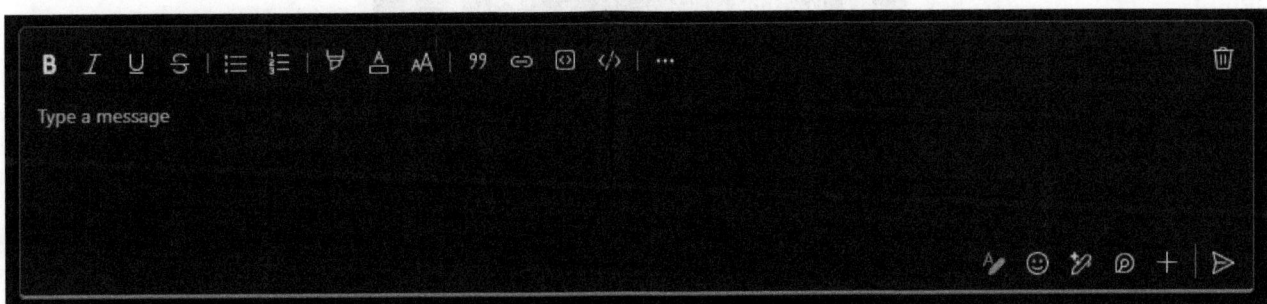

Figure 2.19: Chat message composing options

In the following figure, we have the *Actions and apps* panel:

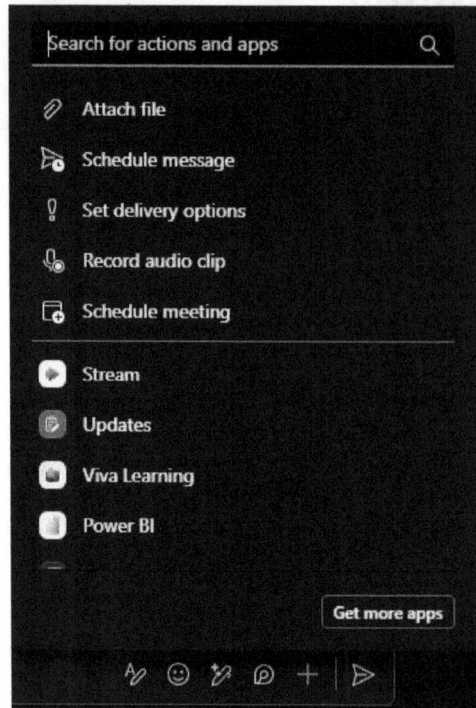

Figure 2.20: *Actions and apps in a one-to-one chat*

When engaging in a Teams chat that includes external users, certain composing functionalities are restricted to ensure compliance with organizational policies and data security standards. For instance, the ability to share files is disabled, preventing sensitive or proprietary information from being inadvertently shared. Features that typically enhance collaboration, such as Loop components and app integrations, may also be unavailable in external chats, limiting users to basic text messaging and media sharing options. These constraints aim to balance functionality with the need for secure and controlled communication across organizational boundaries. The following figure shows a much-reduced *Actions and apps* pane during an external chat:

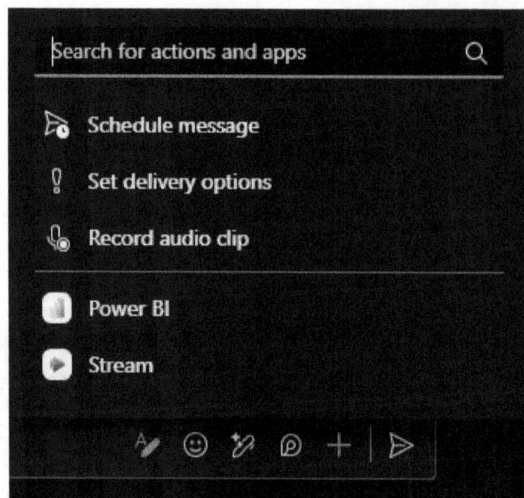

Figure 2.21: *Actions and apps in a chat with an external user*

Users can escalate a one-on-one chat to an audio or video call directly, ensuring that communication is smooth and uninterrupted, by clicking the telephone icon at the top of the chat. In the same place, the **...** icon gives users a few more options for the chat:

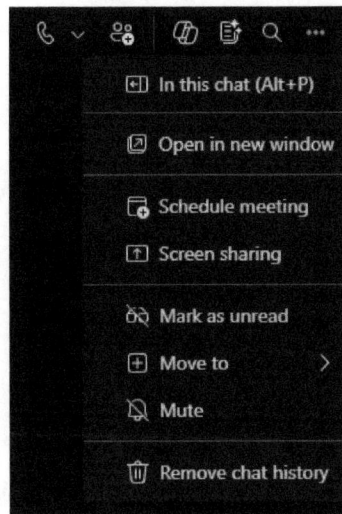

Figure 2.22: More chat options

Teams enables users to pin important group chats, ensuring these conversations remain easily accessible. A pinned message appears at the top of the chat, making it easy for users to go back to that message with the click of a button, as follows:

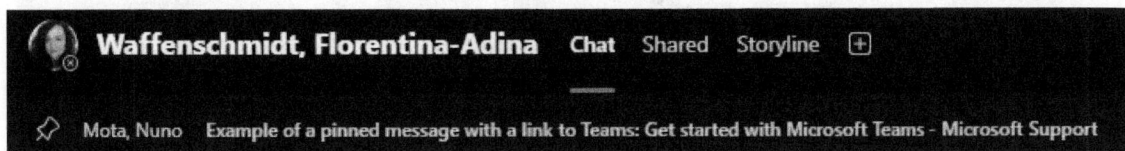

Figure 2.23: Pinned chat message

Messages can also be replied to directly, providing clarity and structure to the discussion, as well as a notification to the original user.

To enhance communication in all types of chats, Microsoft Teams integrates advanced features such as search functionality, read receipts, and the ability to edit or delete messages. These features ensure that every communication is clear, relevant, and easily retrievable.

Group chats

Group chats offer a dynamic space for collaboration among multiple participants. These chats are particularly useful for brainstorming sessions, project discussions, or team updates.

In essence, group chats in Microsoft Teams are identical to one-on-one chats in every way, sharing the same features and functionalities such as file sharing, multimedia options, and direct message replies. The sole distinction lies in the number of participants involved, with group chats accommodating multiple users to facilitate collective discussions and collaboration.

Chats in channels

Channel chats are a unique feature of Microsoft Teams, designed for topic or project-specific discussions. Unlike one-on-one or group chats, these conversations take place within dedicated channels, where all members of the channel can participate. Channel chats help centralize communication, ensuring that all team members have access to relevant discussions and updates. Messages in channels are visible to all members, fostering transparency and inclusivity. Users can reply to specific messages within a thread, keeping conversations organized and focused on particular topics. Additionally, channel chats support tagging with @mentions, allowing users to notify specific individuals, groups, or the entire channel of important updates.

Within channels, users can utilize two message formats to share information effectively, namely *posts* and *announcements*, each serving distinct purposes:

Posts

Posts are the standard message type channels. They are designed for day-to-day conversations, sharing updates, and discussing topics within a channel. Posts are versatile and can include text, images, file attachments, and links. They allow channel members to reply directly within a thread, keeping discussions focused on specific topics.

Key features of posts include:

- Ideal for general communication.
- Supports text, files, multimedia, and links.
- Replies are organized in threads, fostering structured discussions.
- Accessible to all channel members.

Posts work well for quick exchanges, brainstorming ideas, or raising questions that require input from multiple team members.

The following figure shows the composing window of a new post:

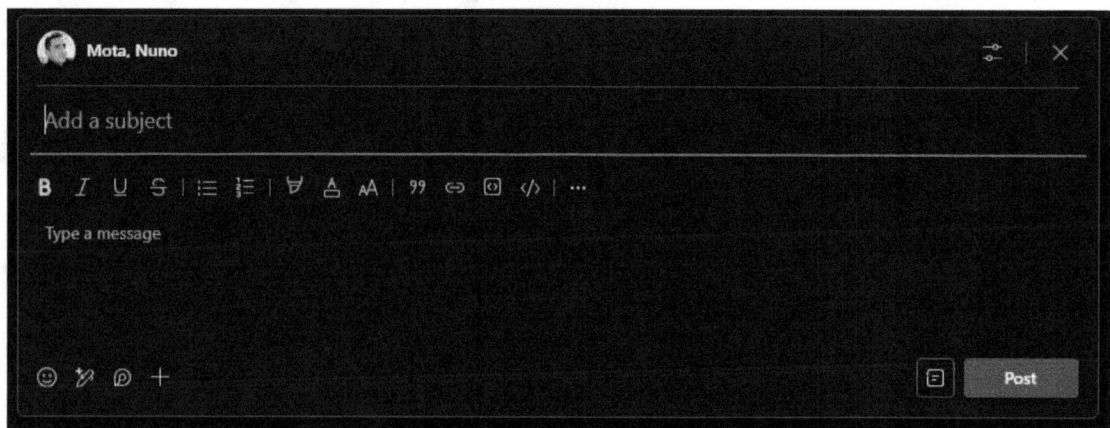

Figure 2.24: Starting a new post

The following is an example of an ongoing channel conversation:

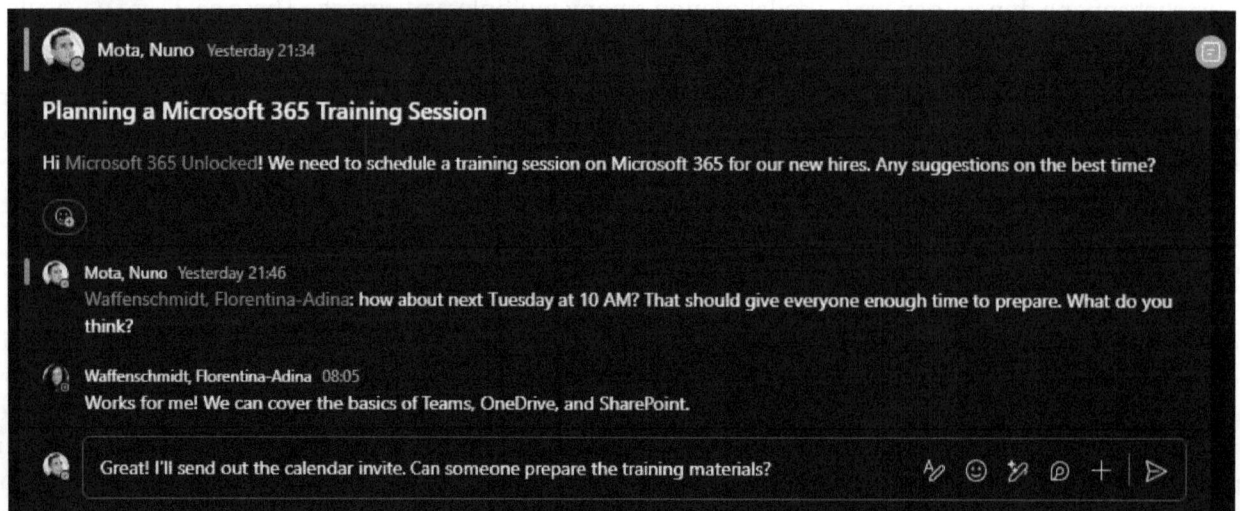

Figure 2.25: Example of a channel conversation

Announcements

Announcements are a specialized type of post designed to grab attention and highlight important updates or information. They are typically used for sharing significant news, deadlines, or changes within the channel. Announcements stand out visually, often featuring larger headers, colorful backgrounds, and options for visual customization, making them more noticeable than regular posts.

The key features of announcements include:

- Emphasizes urgent or noteworthy information.
- Includes visual customization options, such as banners and headers.
- Can be pinned to ensure visibility over time.
- Supports text, files, and multimedia attachments.

Announcements are especially useful for communicating updates that require immediate attention or long-term visibility, such as project milestones, policy changes, or event reminders. In the following figure, we see an example of an announcement being composed:

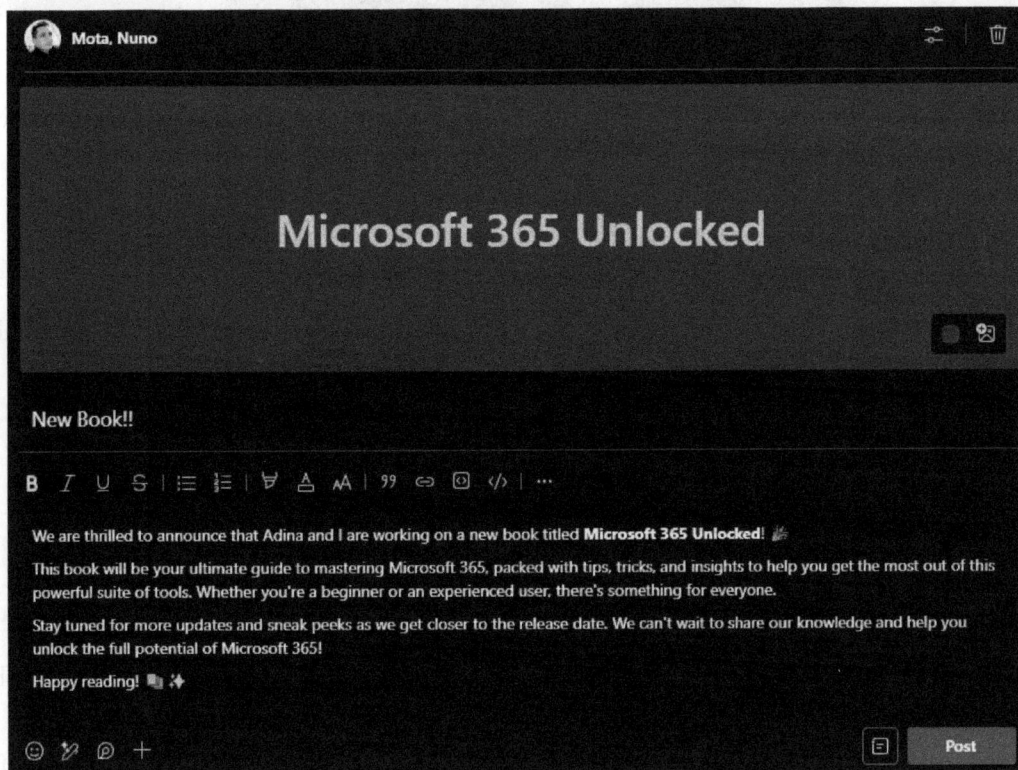

Figure 2.26: Composing an announcement

File sharing

File sharing in Microsoft Teams is a robust feature designed to enhance collaboration and streamline workflows within teams and organizations. It allows users to share files directly within team chats, channels, or meeting chats, making it easy to disseminate information and collaborate on documents. Files are shared as attachments or links and can be accessed by participants with appropriate permissions. These files are integrated seamlessly with Microsoft 365 tools, enabling users to edit and collaborate in real-time.

File sharing in Teams goes beyond this by enabling collaborative workflows. Users can co-author documents in real-time, make comments, track changes, and have discussions directly within the Teams interface. This fosters smooth teamwork and ensures that everyone stays on the same page.

Process of sharing files

Here is how users can share files in Teams:

1. Within **channels**, users can upload files when composing a new post or to the channel's **Files** tab. These files become accessible to all members of the channel, fostering collective collaboration, as can be seen in the figure:

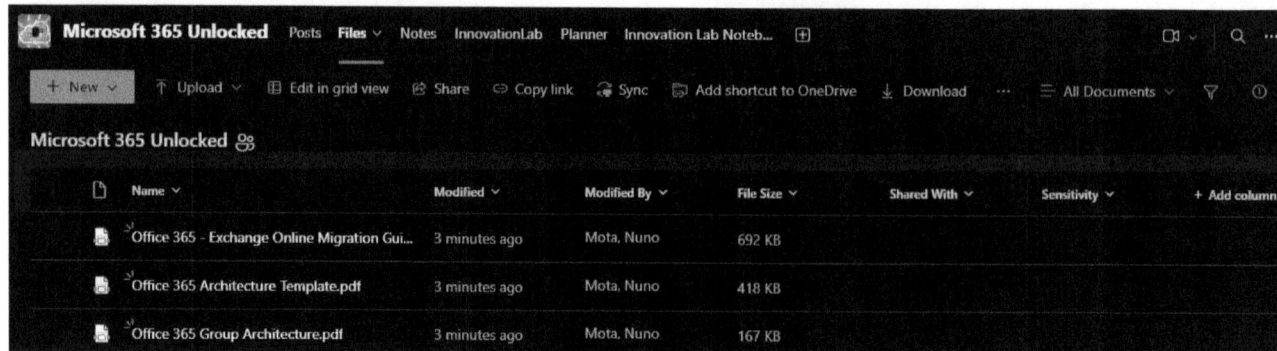

Figure 2.27: Files tab in a channel

2. In **chats**, files can be sent directly through private or group chats by clicking the paperclip icon or dragging and dropping files. Chats are ideal for sharing files with specific individuals or smaller groups.

3. During **meetings**, files can be shared by uploading them into the chat or sharing them via screen-sharing for live collaboration.

4. Via **OneDrive** links, which allow users to share links to documents stored in their personal OneDrive accounts.

File storage

Files shared in Teams are stored securely in SharePoint Online or OneDrive for Business, depending on the context:

- **Channel files**: Files uploaded to team channels are stored in the corresponding SharePoint site associated with the team.

- **Chat files**: Files shared via private, or group chats are stored in the sender's OneDrive for Business in a folder named **Microsoft Teams Chat Files** and shared with recipients.

This centralized cloud storage ensures that files are accessible across devices, protected by Microsoft's security measures, and version-controlled for easy tracking of changes.

Managing access and revoking permissions

Users have full control over who can access shared files and how they can interact with them. Users can adjust permissions through the following actions:

- **Setting permissions**: When sharing a file, users can specify whether recipients can view, edit, or download the document.

- **Revoking access**: To revoke access to shared files, users can modify sharing settings in SharePoint or OneDrive, removing specific individuals or groups from the access list.

- **Restricting links**: If a file is shared via a link, users can disable the link or restrict access to specific recipients, ensuring tighter control over sensitive information.

Version control and recovery

Files stored in SharePoint or OneDrive benefit from version history, allowing users to revert to earlier versions if needed. Additionally, files deleted from Teams can be restored from the SharePoint or OneDrive's *recycle bin*, ensuring that no important document is lost.

Meetings and calls

Microsoft Teams facilitates seamless communication and collaboration within organizations. Its functionalities extend well beyond chat and file sharing by offering robust support for virtual meetings and calling. These features are designed to streamline interactions, making it easier than ever for teams to connect, whether for quick discussions, formal presentations, or collaborative projects.

Voice and video calls

Microsoft Teams supports voice and video calls, making it easy for users to connect whether they are engaging in one-on-one conversations or group discussions. The platform provides a seamless experience across devices, ensuring that users can initiate or join calls from smartphones, tablets, or desktop computers, making it versatile for both remote and in-office scenarios.

Some of its core features include:

- **High-quality audio and video**: Teams can deliver clear audio and HD video, ensuring professional-grade communication. This is especially beneficial for organizations hosting virtual meetings or conferences, offering participants a smooth and immersive experience, even across different time zones.

- **Screen sharing**: Enhance collaboration by sharing your screen during calls or meetings. This feature is invaluable for delivering presentations, conducting training sessions, or troubleshooting issues in real-time, fostering productivity and clarity.

- **Live reactions**: Express yourself during calls with emojis or reactions. This feature makes conversations more interactive and allows participants to communicate non-verbally, which is helpful in scenarios where speaking might disrupt the flow of a meeting.

- **Call queues and auto attendants**: These features empower organizations to handle incoming calls effectively. Call queues ensure that no calls are missed, while auto attendants guide callers to the right department or individual, saving time and improving customer satisfaction.

- **Call history and voicemail**: Teams keeps a record of past calls and stores voicemails securely. This functionality ensures that users can revisit important conversations or retrieve missed messages, making communication management effortless.

Some of these features are built-in into Teams, which others are part of Microsoft Teams Phone, a cloud-based telephony solution that brings traditional calling features into the Microsoft Teams environment. It allows users to make and receive calls to and from landlines and mobile phones over the **Public Switched Telephone Network (PSTN)**, all within the Teams app.

Making calls

The steps to make a call are as follows:

1. Open the Microsoft Teams app and navigate to the **Calls** tab, which provides access to your recent call history, contacts, and dial pad.

2. Select a contact from your list or use the dial pad to enter a phone number. For group calls, click **Add Participants** to include multiple people.

3. Click on the call icon to initiate a voice call. During the call, you can switch between voice and video modes as needed.

The following figure shows the controls and options available in the **Calls** tab:

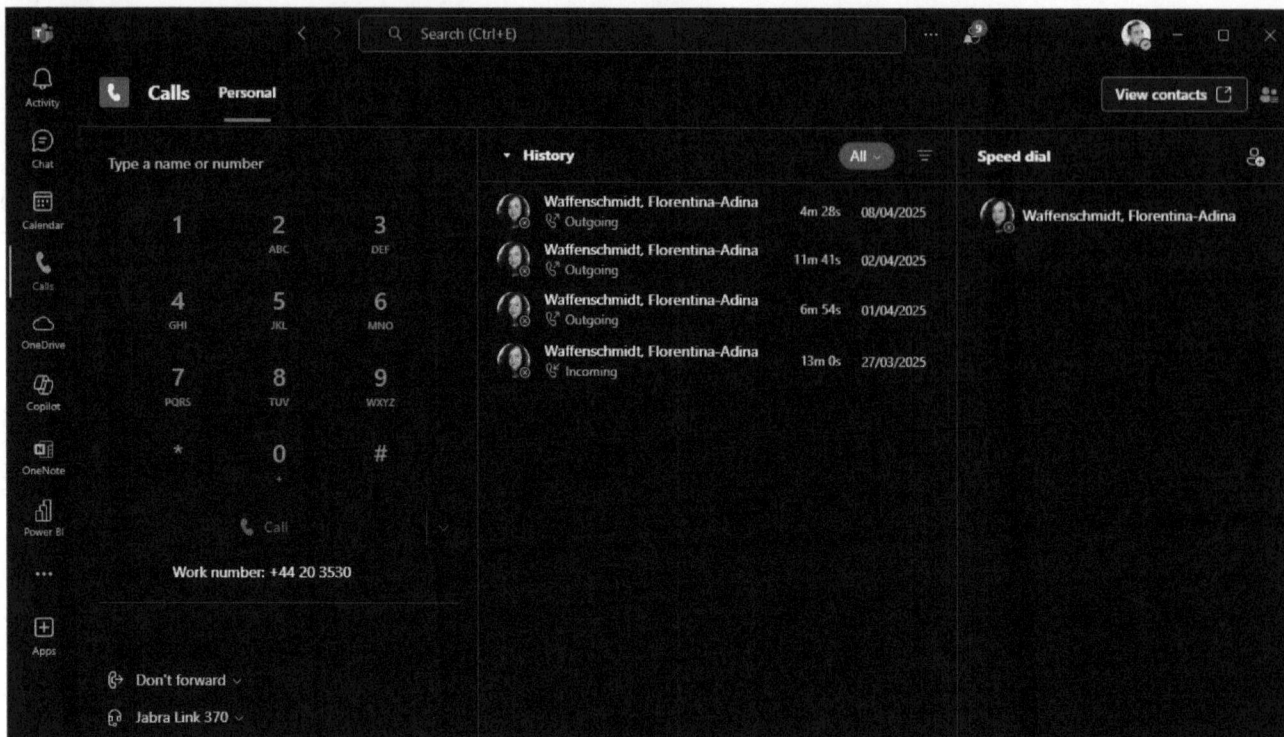

Figure 2.28: Call controls

Call forwarding, delegation, and other options

Navigate to **Settings** by clicking the **...** button next to your profile picture in Teams. The settings menu allows you to personalize your calling experience.

Under **Calls**, you can configure call forwarding by entering a number or assigning a delegate. Forwarding ensures that important calls are not missed, even when you are unavailable.

Delegates can answer calls on your behalf, making this feature ideal for executives and busy professionals who require assistance with managing communications.

In the following figure, you can see these options and a few more:

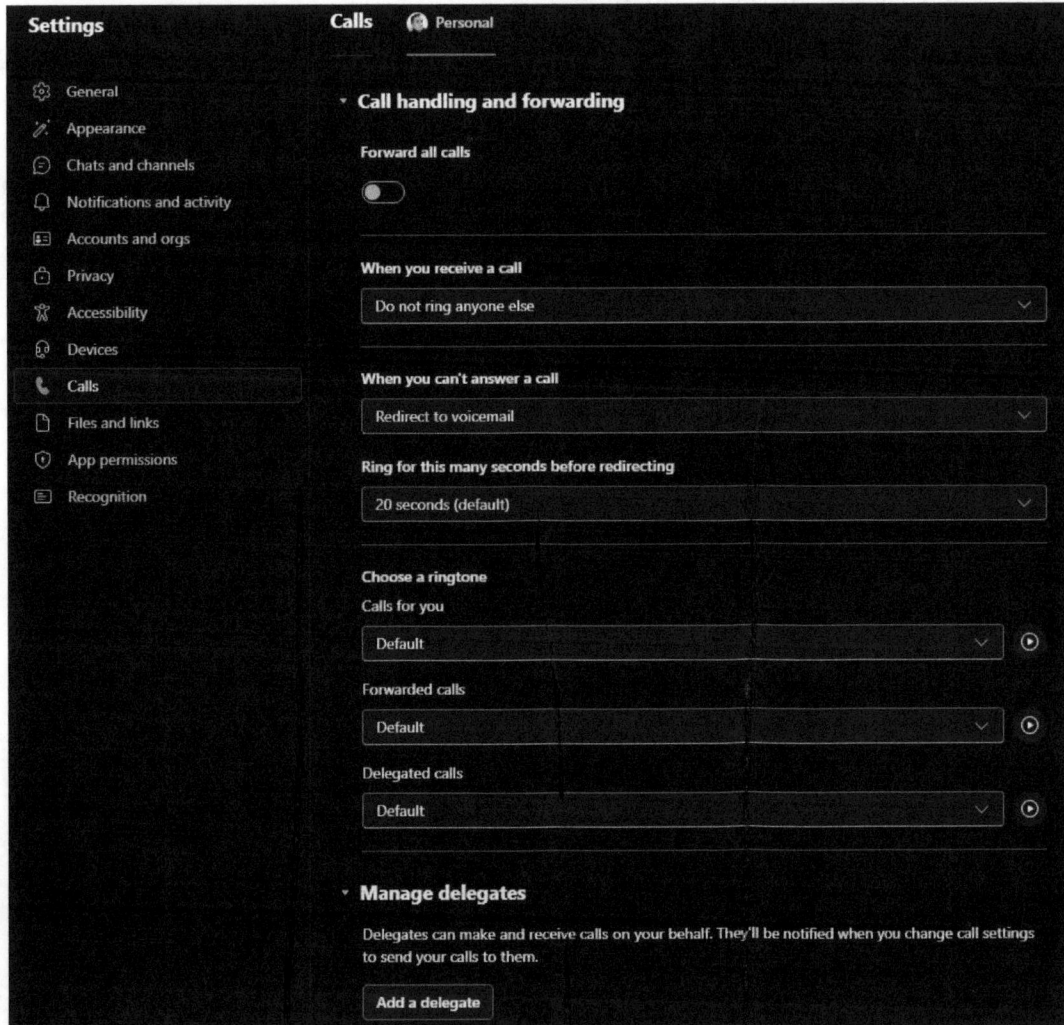

Figure 2.29: Call settings

Setting up meetings

Scheduling and hosting meetings is a breeze with Teams. Users can set up one-time or recurring meetings, invite participants, and share meeting agendas. During meetings, participants can share their screens, collaborate on documents in real-time, and use the chat function to ask questions or share information. Teams' meeting capabilities also include breakout rooms, allowing larger meetings to be divided into smaller, focused discussion groups.

Effective meeting setup is crucial to fostering productive collaboration. By properly organizing a meeting, users can ensure that participants are well-informed, have the necessary resources, and can engage meaningfully.

Using the Teams calendar

Teams offers an integrated calendar feature that allows users to schedule meetings directly within the app. Follow these steps:

1. Open the Microsoft Teams app and navigate to the **Calendar** tab on the left-hand menu.

2. Click the **New event** button located at the top-right corner of the calendar view.

3. Fill in the meeting details, including the title, date, time, and duration.

4. Add participants by typing their names or email addresses. Teams allows you to invite both internal colleagues and external guests.

5. To optimize meeting planning, the **Scheduling Assistant** helps identify available time slots for all participants, ensuring meetings are scheduled conveniently and avoiding conflicts.

6. Toggle the **Teams meeting** button to make it a Teams meeting.

7. Include a description of the meeting in the description box to provide context for the meeting.

8. Click on **Add an agenda** to add some structure for the meeting.

9. Select **Save** to finalize and send the invitations. The meeting will appear in your calendar, and participants will receive a notification with the details.

The following figure shows the meeting creation assistant in Teams:

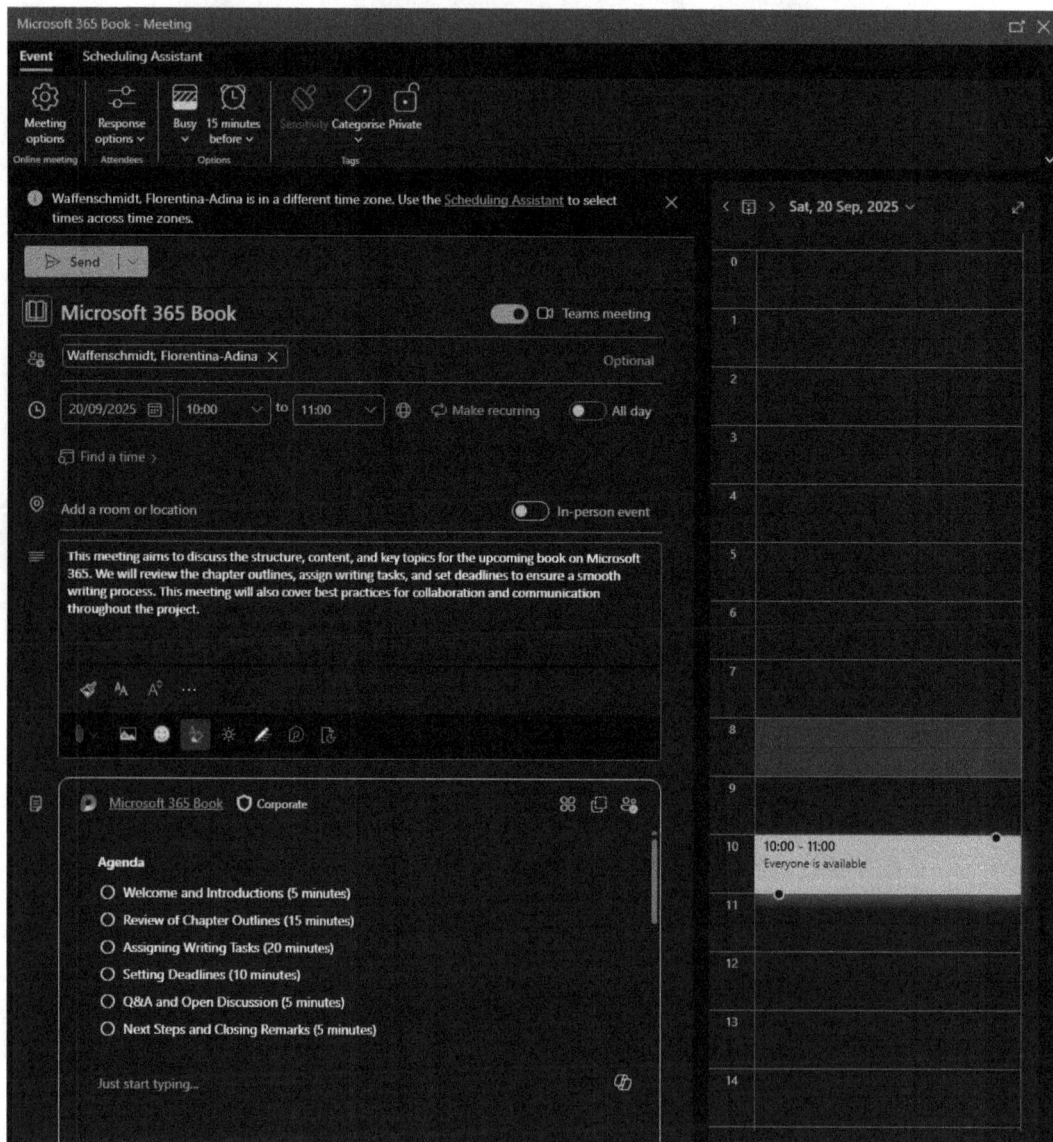

Figure 2.30: Creating a new Teams meeting

The **Meeting options** button provides several customizable meeting options to enhance the experience and manage participation effectively. Some of these include:

• **Who can bypass the lobby**: Organizers can decide whether all participants, only internal colleagues, or specific individuals can enter the meeting directly without waiting in the virtual lobby.

- **Roles**: Participants can be assigned roles such as presenter or attendee, which define their permissions during the meeting, including screen sharing and muting others.

- **Participation settings**: Organizers can manage attendee actions, such as allowing or blocking chat, reactions, or screen sharing, to maintain meeting focus.

- **Recording and transcription**: Meetings can be recorded for future reference, and transcription options allow a text version of spoken content to be generated, making information accessible post-meeting.

Using Outlook

For users who prefer to work within Microsoft Outlook, Teams integrates seamlessly with the Outlook Calendar. To schedule a meeting via Outlook, follow these steps:

1. Open Microsoft Outlook and navigate to the **Calendar** tab.
2. Click the **Teams Meeting** button on the toolbar.
3. Enter the meeting details, such as the title, date, time, and participants.
4. Add any supporting materials or links in the description box.
5. Click **Send** to distribute the invitations. The meeting will be synced with both Outlook and Teams calendars.

In-meeting features

Microsoft Teams has become an indispensable tool for virtual collaboration, offering a suite of features designed to streamline online meetings. At the heart of its functionality are in-meeting features that enhance communication, simplify content sharing, and promote engagement among participants. In the following figure, we can see a typical example of the Teams client during a meeting:

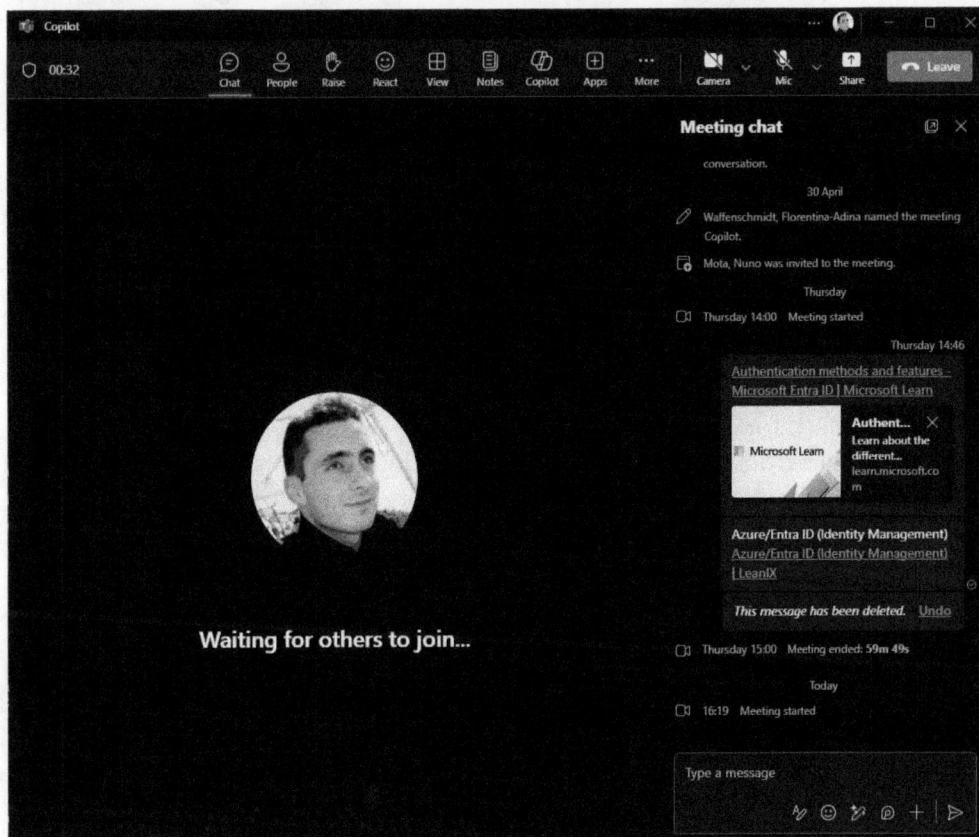

Figure 2.31: Teams client during a meeting

During a meeting, attendees have several features available to them. Let us have a look at some of these.

Screen sharing

Screen sharing is an essential tool for presenting information clearly during meetings. Whether you are sharing slides, documents, or live demonstrations, this feature allows participants to follow along visually. You can choose to share your entire desktop, a specific window, or even just a browser tab. To enhance engagement, ensure that your content is organized and easy to read.

Similar to screen sharing, **PowerPoint Live** sharing allows presenters to upload and display PowerPoint presentations directly within the meeting interface. This has several advantages over the traditional screen sharing:

- Cleaner and more professional experience, as notifications and desktop clutter are hidden.
- Optimized for presenting static or pre-designed content such as slideshows.
- Enhances audience engagement by allowing independent slide navigation for participants.
- *Presenter View* allows presenters to access notes, view upcoming slides, and navigate non-linearly without participants seeing these actions.
- Independent navigation, if allowed by the presenter, allows participants to navigate slides independently, without affecting the presenter's flow.

The only two downsides are that it is limited to PowerPoint files and less effective for dynamic or interactive demonstrations.

Chat functionality

The chat panel provides a dynamic space for real-time communication during meetings. Participants can ask questions, share links, and exchange files without interrupting the speaker. This feature is particularly useful for collecting feedback or highlighting important points.

Reactions and raise hand

Reactions, such as thumbs up, applause, or emojis, allow participants to express themselves non-verbally. These quick responses can help gauge participant sentiment without derailing the discussion. The raise hand feature is ideal for requesting attention or signaling a desire to contribute during a structured conversation. Encourage participants to use these tools to foster a collaborative and respectful environment.

Breakout rooms

Breakout rooms are perfect for dividing participants into smaller groups for focused discussions or brainstorming sessions. These rooms can be customized with unique settings to suit specific agendas, whether for workshops or team-building activities. As the meeting organizer, you can easily monitor and manage breakout rooms, bringing groups back together when necessary. Use this feature to boost productivity and encourage active participation.

Whiteboard

The Whiteboard tool is a collaborative canvas that allows participants to draw, write, and brainstorm ideas visually. It is particularly valuable for planning, problem-solving, and creative sessions. Utilize features such as sticky notes, pens, and shapes to organize thoughts and make the discussion more interactive. The Whiteboard saves these inputs for future reference, ensuring that ideas are not lost. Whiteboard is discussed later in this book in *Chapter 5, Whiteboard*.

Live captions and transcriptions

Live captions and transcriptions enhance accessibility and inclusivity for participants, especially those who are hard of hearing or speak different languages. Captions display text in real-time during the meeting, while transcriptions provide a comprehensive record that can be reviewed afterward. These features ensure that no participant misses crucial information and can also serve as a meeting summary tool for follow-up purposes.

Recording and post-meeting actions

Recording and follow-up actions are critical for ensuring that meetings remain impactful and that their outcomes are effectively realized. By capturing every detail and assigning responsibilities afterward, you can maximize the productivity of your meetings.

Recording meetings

Recording meetings is a powerful tool for capturing content for review and reference. Microsoft Teams makes it simple to record sessions, ensuring that no participant misses important moments. Once the recording is complete, it can be stored securely and accessed by team members at their convenience.

When recording, it is essential to obtain consent from all participants. This ensures compliance with privacy regulations and promotes transparency. Additionally, consider informing participants about how the recording will be used, whether for documentation, training, or follow-up purposes.

Once a meeting recording is complete, it is securely stored in the organizer's OneDrive or SharePoint, ensuring ease of access and data protection. The platform automatically grants meeting participants viewing rights, allowing them to access the recording seamlessly without additional permissions. This streamlined storage system fosters transparency and facilitates post-meeting collaboration, enabling participants to revisit discussions and clarify details at their convenience.

Meeting notes

Taking accurate and concise meeting notes is crucial for effective meeting management. These notes should highlight key points, decisions made, and action items assigned. They serve as a quick reference for those who attended and as an update for those who could not.

Tools like Microsoft OneNote or Teams' built-in note-taking feature can streamline the process. By integrating notes with other software, such as Microsoft Planner or SharePoint, teams can ensure that the information is accessible and actionable. Encourage participants to collaborate on notes in real-time to capture different perspectives and minimize omissions.

Follow-up actions

The end of a meeting marks the beginning of follow-up tasks and actual implementation. Clearly defined follow-up actions ensure accountability and momentum. After each meeting, distribute a summary that includes assigned tasks, deadlines, and next steps.

Leveraging tools like Microsoft Planner enables teams to track progress seamlessly. Set reminders or schedule brief check-ins to ensure that tasks are on track. A well-structured follow-up process not only increases productivity but also reinforces the sense of purpose from the meeting.

Integrations and apps

Microsoft Teams serves as a hub for seamless integration with a wide range of applications, both within the Microsoft 365 ecosystem and beyond. This integration allows users to connect their favorite tools directly into Teams, creating a centralized workspace where collaboration thrives. By bringing together apps like OneDrive, OneNote, Workday, Trello, Asana, and hundreds of other applications, Teams eliminates the need to switch between multiple platforms, saving time and reducing inefficiencies.

The benefits of this integration are vast. Teams' users can streamline workflows, ensuring that all necessary tools are accessible within the same interface. For instance, project management tasks can be managed using Planner, Asana, or Trello without leaving the Teams environment, while GitHub can provide developers with quick access to repositories for collaborative coding projects. This centralization reduces distractions, enhances focus, and fosters a smoother flow of information.

Using integrated apps within Teams is intuitive and highly customizable. Users can add their most-used apps as tabs in specific channels, tailoring their workspace to fit the unique needs of their team or project. Users can also pin their most-used applications directly to the main Teams window for even quicker access. By doing so, essential tools always remain within reach, reducing the need to navigate through multiple menus or tabs. This customization feature empowers users to tailor their workspace to match their workflow, ensuring maximum efficiency. For instance, an HR manager might pin Workday to manage employee schedules, while a developer might prioritize GitHub for streamlined coding collaboration. This flexibility enhances the user experience, making Teams not only a hub for collaboration but also a personalized command center.

Moreover, the ability to integrate third-party apps and services within Teams fosters adaptability. Whether your team relies on customer relationship management tools like Salesforce or creative platforms like *Adobe Creative Cloud*, the flexibility of Teams ensures that your workspace grows and evolves with your needs. It empowers users to work smarter by giving them access to all the essential tools in one unified location.

Best practices

Microsoft Teams has become an indispensable platform for collaboration and productivity, offering a wide range of features to streamline team interactions. To fully harness its potential, it is essential to follow best practices that ensure efficient organization, clear communication, and effective use of integrated tools. By adopting these guidelines, teams can create a well-structured and dynamic workspace that supports seamless collaboration and drives success.

Here are some Teams best practices that users should try to follow:

- **Organize teams and channels effectively**: Structure your Teams environment in a way that mirrors your organizational hierarchy or project structure. Create specific channels for distinct topics or projects to keep discussions focused. Avoid overloading a single Team with too many unrelated topics, which can dilute conversations and make information difficult to find. Naming conventions should be clear and consistent across Teams and channels, enabling users to navigate easily.

- **Use @mentions thoughtfully**: The @mention feature is a powerful tool for drawing attention to specific team members or for alerting an entire team or channel about critical updates. Use @mentions sparingly and only when necessary to avoid overwhelming colleagues with notifications. For urgent matters, direct mentions of specific individuals are more effective than broad announcements.

- **Customize notifications**: Adjust notification settings to suit your workflow and priorities. Customize which alerts appear for Teams, channels, and mentions so that you stay informed about the most relevant updates without being distracted by less critical notifications. This ensures a balance between staying connected and maintaining focus on your work.

- **Leverage integrated tools**: Take advantage of Microsoft Teams' seamless integration with apps like Planner, OneNote, or third-party tools like *Trello* and *GitHub*. Use these integrations to centralize your workflow, manage tasks, and collaborate without needing to switch between platforms. Adding these tools as tabs in relevant channels ensures easy access and encourages team-wide adoption.

- **Enhance meetings with preparation and features**: Make meetings more productive by preparing an agenda and sharing it with attendees beforehand. Use features like breakout rooms, screen sharing, and meeting notes to facilitate collaboration during virtual sessions. Additionally, record meetings for later reference, especially when team members cannot attend, ensuring that everyone stays aligned.

- **Maintain good communication etiquette**: Use clear language and keep messages concise to avoid misunderstandings. Refrain from using excessive emojis or GIFs in professional channels unless they are appropriate for the context. Furthermore, use threaded replies to respond to specific messages within a channel, ensuring that conversations remain organized and easy to follow.

- **Use status updates effectively**: Set your status to indicate availability. Whether you are online, busy, or focusing on specific tasks, your status helps others know when to reach out or when to wait for a response. Utilize the *Do Not Disturb* mode during meetings or deep work periods to minimize interruptions.

- **Keep files organized**: When sharing files within Teams, ensure they are uploaded to the appropriate channel or folder. Use clear file names and organize them logically to make it easy for team members to locate documents. Regularly clean up outdated files to avoid clutter.

- **Periodically review and archive/delete teams**: To maintain a streamlined environment, review inactive Teams regularly. Archive those that are no longer in use but contain valuable information and delete those that are no longer needed. This practice helps declutter your Teams interface while preserving historical data, when archiving, for future reference.

Conclusion

Microsoft Teams is a powerful collaboration and communication tool that enhances productivity, fosters seamless collaboration, and supports remote work. By understanding its core functionalities and advanced use cases, users can optimize their use of Teams and create a more efficient and connected working environment. Embracing best practices and providing adequate training and support will ensure that teams can leverage the full potential of Microsoft Teams.

In the next chapter, we will look at Viva Engage, a platform designed to foster community, connection, and knowledge-sharing within organizations.

Join our Discord space

Join our Discord workspace for latest updates, offers, tech happenings around the world, new releases, and sessions with the authors:

https://discord.bpbonline.com

CHAPTER 3
Viva Engage

Introduction

In this chapter, we will explore Viva Engage, a powerful social platform within Microsoft 365 that helps people across an organization connect, share, and build communities. Whether you are part of a frontline team, a distributed project group, or a leadership circle, Viva Engage provides a space for more open and authentic communication. It is designed to enhance employee engagement, enable knowledge sharing, and bring visibility to voices across all levels of the organization.

Structure

This chapter covers the following topics:
- Getting started with Viva Engage
- Storylines
- Communities
- Creating posts and engaging with content

Objectives

By the end of this chapter, readers will have acquired a broad understanding of Viva Engage and its integration within the Microsoft 365 ecosystem. They will gain a comprehensive grasp of storylines, along with practical knowledge for creating and managing communities. Furthermore, readers will learn how to create posts, understand various post types, and engage in conversations.

Getting started with Viva Engage

Formerly known as Yammer, Viva Engage is part of the Microsoft Viva suite and is integrated with Microsoft 365 services. It is designed to facilitate open communication, promote knowledge sharing, and support employee connection at scale. Unlike Teams Chat, which is focused on real-time, direct, and small-group messaging, Viva Engage emphasizes broad, organization-wide conversations and community building, making it ideal for fostering open dialogue and sharing knowledge across larger groups.

Viva Engage serves a variety of purposes within organizations, supporting communication, collaboration, and engagement across teams and individuals. Some common use cases include:

- **Company-wide announcements**: Leadership can broadcast important updates, celebrate achievements, or share organizational news to keep everyone informed.

- **Knowledge sharing**: Employees can post tips, best practices, or lessons learned from completed projects to build a collective knowledge base that benefits the entire organization.

- **Community building**: Teams or interest groups can create specialized spaces to discuss topics relevant to their roles, hobbies, or shared goals, fostering a sense of community and belonging.

- **Celebrating successes**: Employees can highlight major accomplishments, recognize colleagues, and mark milestones, creating a culture of appreciation and motivation.

- **Employee feedback and pulse checks**: Leaders can gather insights or opinions from staff through polls and open discussions, enabling continuous improvement and responsiveness.

- **Personal and professional storytelling**: Individuals can share their career journeys, project highlights, and everyday experiences, encouraging engagement and visibility across the organization.

Before using Viva Engage, it is important to understand what the licensing requirements are and how to access the service.

Licensing

Viva Engage is available to users with Microsoft 365 and Office 365 Enterprise licenses. This includes Microsoft 365 F1, F3, E3, and E5, as well as Office 365 E1, E3, and E5 plans. The base Viva Engage experience does not require a separate Viva Engage license.

To access enhanced capabilities in Viva Engage, users need a Microsoft Viva Suite or Viva Employee Communications and Communities plan license. These premium features include:

- **Advanced analytics** offer in-depth insight into how employees interact within Viva Engage communities. This information helps organizations measure the effectiveness of their communication strategies, identify active contributors, and discover opportunities to foster greater collaboration and inclusion.

- **Campaigns** represent a way to promote organizational initiatives, to align employees with organizational goals, culture shifts, or major events. Through campaigns, users can create and promote thematic conversations, encourage the sharing of stories and achievements, and track participation.

- **Answers in Viva** connects employees with the knowledge and expertise present across the organization. Users can post questions and connect to subject-matter experts. This feature supports faster problem-solving, knowledge sharing, and learning at scale.

- **Leadership corner** is a dedicated space within Viva Engage where employees can get to know and stay connected with their organizational leaders. Here the users can see the updates shared by the leaders they follow and can engage with the content posted by their leaders. This environment helps build trust, transparency, and a sense of connection between leadership and the broader workforce, fostering a culture of open dialogue and inclusive communication.

Accessing Viva Engage

You can access Viva Engage through the browser by navigating to **https://engage.cloud.microsoft** and sign in with your Microsoft 365 credentials.

The following figure illustrates the user interface of Viva Engage when accessed through a web browser:

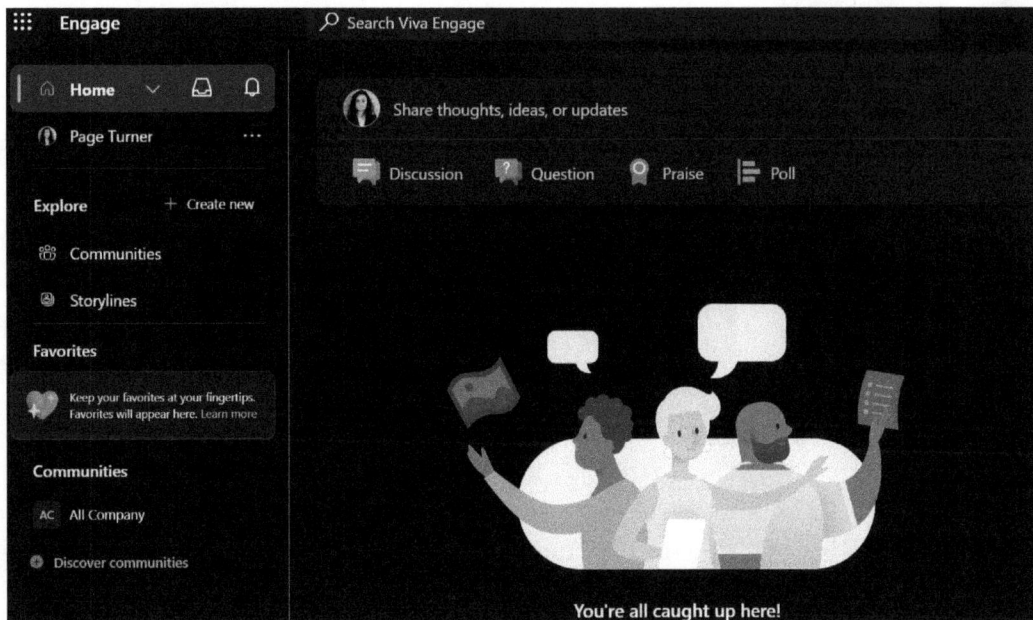

Figure 3.1: *Viva Engage on the web*

Additionally, you can install the Viva Engage app for Teams by following these steps:

1. Access **Teams** either through the web or your desktop client.
2. In the left-hand menu of Teams, click on **Apps**.
3. Search for the **Viva Engage** app, select it, and then click **Add**.

Note: **If Viva Engage is not visible in the Apps section, you might need to reach out to your Teams administrator for assistance.**

After you added the app, you can also pin it to ensure it remains constantly visible.

By adding the Viva Engage app to Teams, you can access it directly within Teams without needing to switch apps.

For users who prefer mobile access, the Viva Engage mobile app is available on iOS and Android. It supports full functionality, including posting, reacting, viewing storylines, and receiving notifications, making it especially valuable for frontline or on-the-go workers.

Storylines

Storylines in Viva Engage are a powerful feature designed to help individuals share their personal and professional journeys within the organization. This feature allows users to create and share posts that highlight their experiences, achievements, and insights, fostering a sense of connection and community.

Every Viva Engage internal user has their own storyline, providing a unique space to share their updates and experiences. Think of your Viva Engage storyline as your personal blog or social media timeline within the organization, where you can share updates, photos, and thoughts with your professional network.

Here are some benefits of using storylines:

- **Personal narratives**: Share milestones, challenges, and successes to inspire and motivate colleagues.
- **Professional achievements**: Showcase major projects, awards, and career milestones to recognize and celebrate hard work.
- **Knowledge sharing**: Share insights, tips, and best practices to contribute to the organization's collective knowledge.

- **Enhancing visibility**: Increase visibility and recognition within the organization by sharing your stories.

To access *Storylines*, go to Viva Engage and click **Storylines** on the left side pane of the screen:

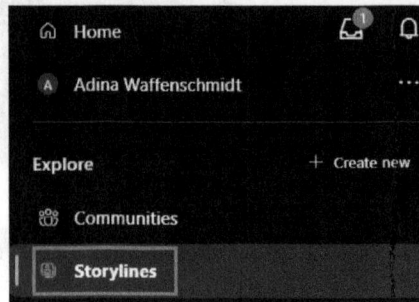

Figure 3.2: Access storylines

Note: If the Storylines tab is not visible in Viva Engage, it is possible that the storyline feature has been disabled by your administrator.

The **Storylines** page aggregates content from people you follow and trending topics, ensuring you stay informed and engaged.

This page provides two feeds to keep you updated:

- **Feed** defaults to sorting posts by relevance, showing content from people followed and trending posts from your organization. The filter can be set to **All** to view all storyline conversations across your organization.

  The following figure displays an example of the **Feed** view:

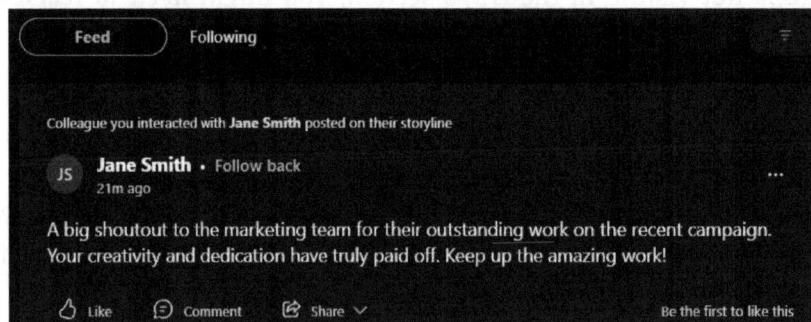

Figure 3.3: Feed view on Storylines landing page

- **Following** displays posts only from people you follow. By default, this is sorted by **newest content**, meaning the most recent storyline content will appear first. It can also be sorted by **recent activity**, which displays storyline content with new comments and reactions first.

  The following figure displays an example of the **Following** view:

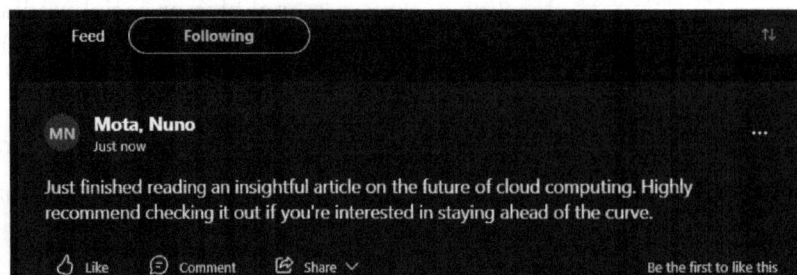

Figure 3.4: Following view on Storylines landing page

Access your storyline page

From the *Storylines* page, you can easily navigate to your personal storyline by clicking on the **Storyline** button under your display name at the top right of the page, as shown in the following figure:

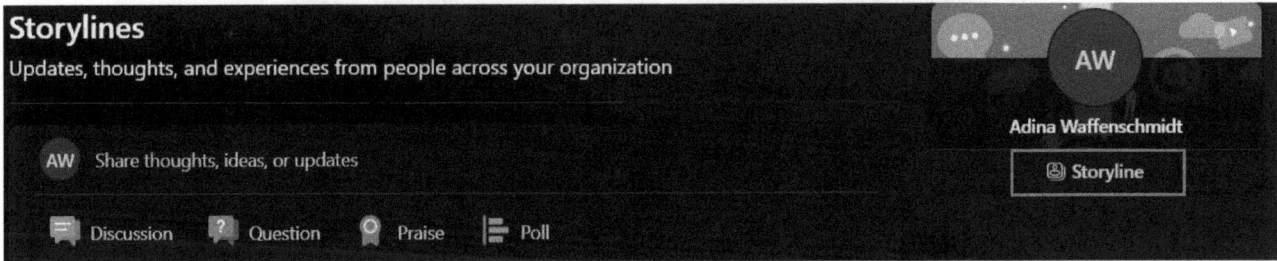

Figure 3.5: Navigate to your personal storyline

On your storyline page, you can view the posts you have created, your followers, and the people you follow. Additionally, you can view your activity on others' posts, including comments and reactions, under the **All activity** tab. The **My bookmarks** tab allows you to access your saved bookmarks.

Visitors to your storyline page can view all your posts and activity. However, your bookmarks remain private and are accessible only to you.

The following figure illustrates an example of a personal storyline page:

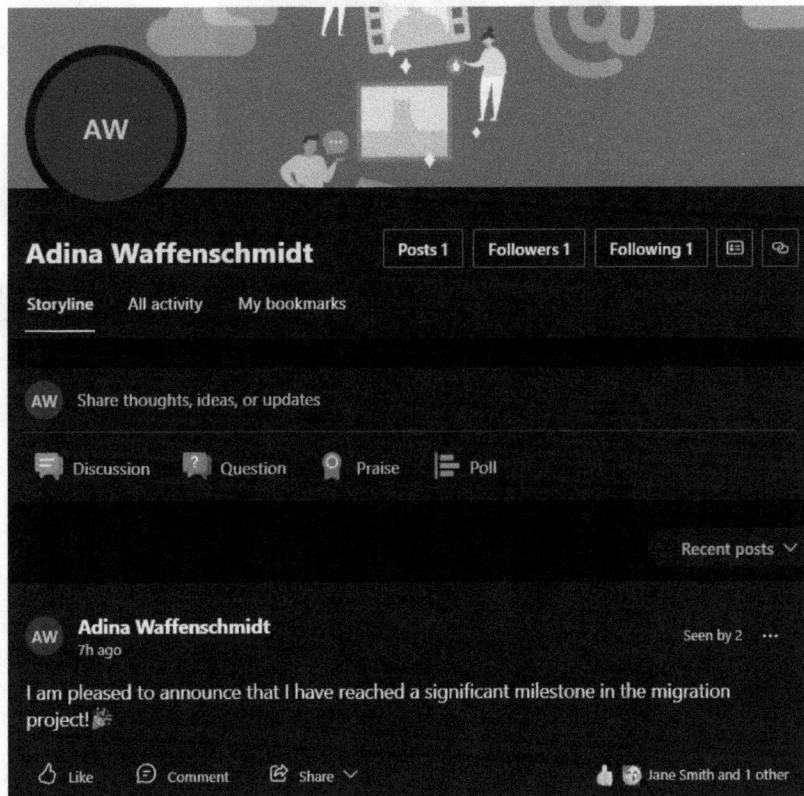

Figure 3.6: Personal storyline page

Visit storyline pages of other users

To access the storylines of other users within your organization, simply enter the user's name in the search box located at the top of the Viva Engage screen and select the desired user from the results. On the user's storyline page, you can view their posts and activities, as well as see a list of their followers. If you wish to receive notifications each time the user publishes new content, you may follow their storyline by clicking on the **Follow** button, as shown in the figure as follows:

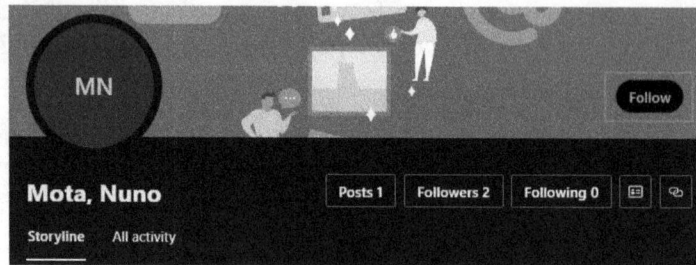

Figure 3.7: Follow a user's storyline

Post on storyline

You can post on your storyline from different areas within Viva Engage, including your storyline page, the *Storylines* landing page, and the *Home* feed. When a post is created from either your personal storyline page or the *Storylines* landing page in Viva Engage, **My storyline** location will be automatically selected. This selection is fixed and cannot be modified, as illustrated in the following figure:

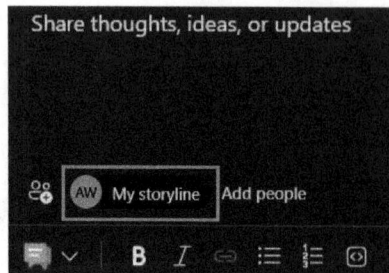

Figure 3.8: Create post from personal storyline or Storylines landing page

You can also post from the *Home* feed or by selecting + **Create new** button on the left side pane and then select **Post**. This allows you to post to your storyline or to a community, as shown in the following figure:

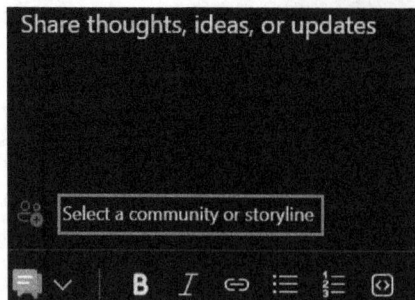

Figure 3.9: Create post from Home feed

To post on your storyline, ensure that *My storyline* is selected within the community picker.

All Viva Engage users in the organization can view your storyline posts when they visit your page. Additionally, your followers will receive a notification each time you publish a new post on your storyline if they did not opt out of notifications.

Communities

Communities in Viva Engage are the heart of collaboration and connection within an organization. They provide a space where employees can come together around shared interests, projects, or goals, fostering a sense of belonging and teamwork. Whether you are part of a project team, a department, or a special interest group, communities offer a platform to share ideas, ask questions, and support each other.

To discover and join existing communities, go to Viva Engage and click **Communities** on the left side pane of the screen:

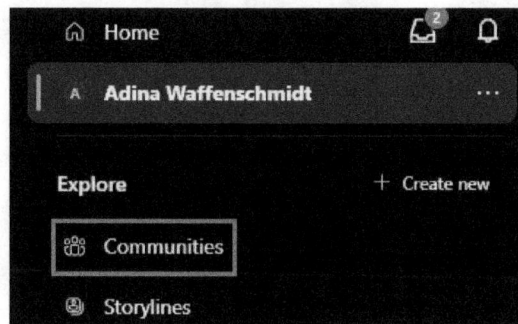

Figure 3.10: Access Communities page

On the **Communities** page, you can see the communities you are a member of, under the **My communities** section:

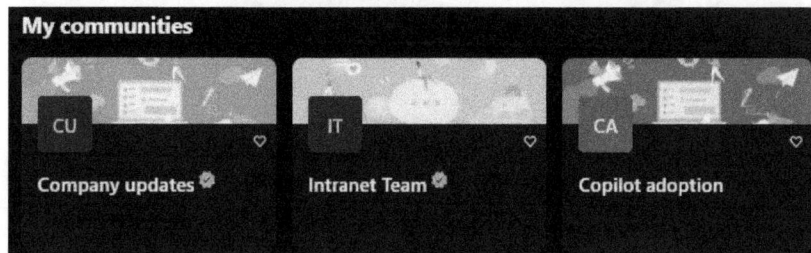

Figure 3.11: My communities

The *Discover communities* section on the **Communities** page displays the official communities within the organization, along with additional recommended communities that you can join.

An official community is established, supported, or acknowledged by an organization to represent its voice. Official communities can be recognized by the *verified* icon, as seen in the following figure:

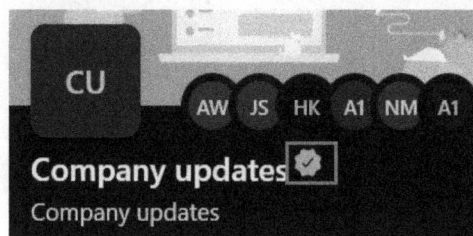

Figure 3.12: Official community

Note: A community can be marked as official in Viva Engage only by an administrator.

By using the search box in Viva Engage, you can search for and find communities within your organization, which you can join directly (for public communities) or request to join (for private communities). Private and public communities are explained in the next section.

Create a new community

To create a new community, follow these steps:

1. Navigate to Viva Engage and on the left side pane, click on + **Create new** and then select **Community**:

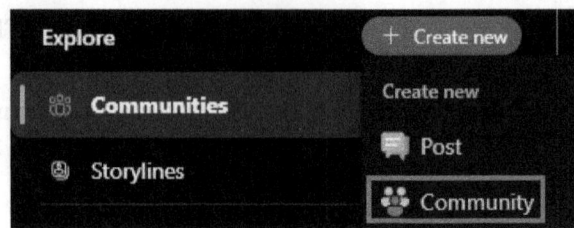

Figure 3.13: Create a new community

2. Provide a name for the community, a description (optional), and add community members (optional):

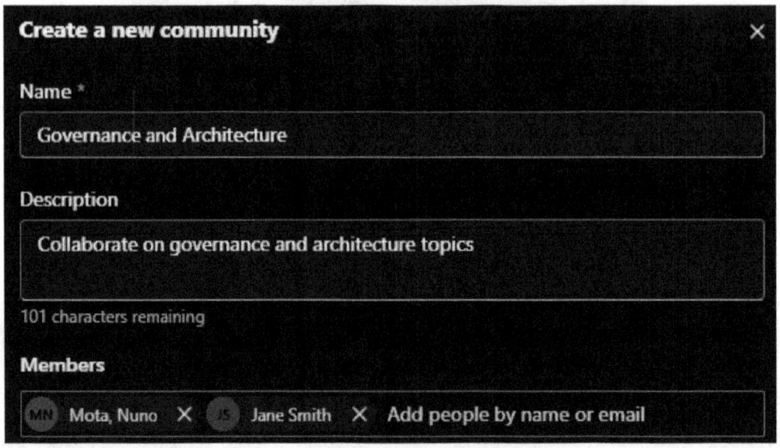

Figure 3.14: Provide community name, description, and add members

You can also add community members after the community has been created.

3. Under the **Edit settings** section, you can configure the following:

   a. **Community privacy settings**: The default is public, allowing everyone within the organization to view and join the community. Alternatively, you can set it to private, restricting access so only members you approve can view and participate:

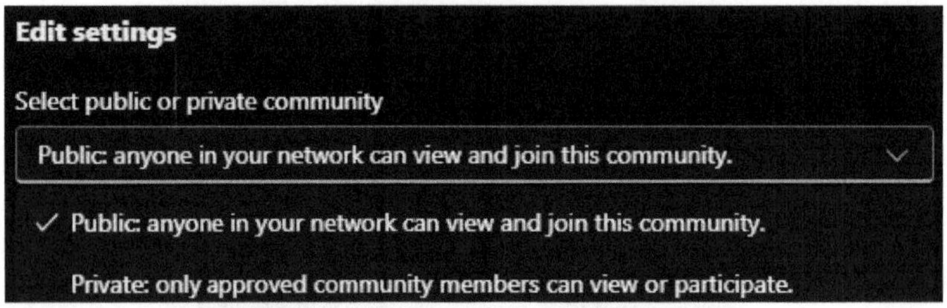

   Figure 3.15: Select community privacy settings

   b. **Default publisher**: The default publisher is the initial post type that appears when you start creating a new post in the community. This is set by default to **Discussion**, but you can also set it to **Question**:

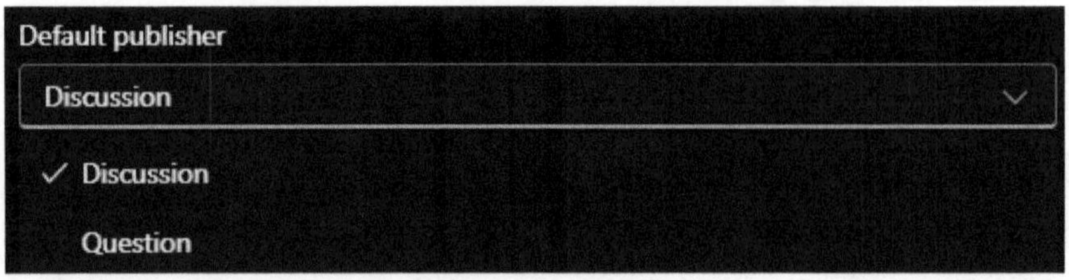

   Figure 3.16: Select default publisher

c. **Allowing users to move conversations to the community**: This feature is enabled by default. To turn it off, use the provided toggle switch:

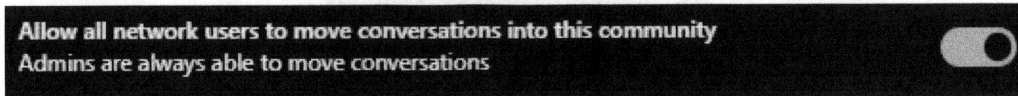

Figure 3.17: Allow all users to move conversations into the community

4. Once you are happy with the details provided and the settings, click **Create** to create the community.

When setting up a new community, a Microsoft 365 group and a linked SharePoint site are created to enable collaboration and file storage. If the community is public, both the Microsoft 365 group and the SharePoint site will be publicly accessible. On the other hand, if the community is private, the Microsoft 365 group and SharePoint site will remain private.

Manage a community

By default, the community creator becomes the community administrator. A community administrator can manage different aspects of the community, such as making other members community admins, removing members, approving requests to join a community (for private communities), managing conversations, changing the community privacy settings, deleting a community, and more.

Next, we will discuss important aspects of community management and how to accomplish them.

Manage members

Community admins can add, remove members, or make other members community admins.

To manage the membership of the community, follow these steps:

1. Navigate to the community you own and on the **Members** tile, click on the + button:

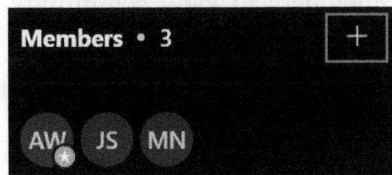

Figure 3.18: Manage membership

2. To add new members, search for the users you want to add by typing their name in the search box.

3. To manage existing members, click on the ellipsis (**...**) next to the member's name and choose the appropriate option from: Make admin (to grant admin rights to an existing member), Remove from community (to remove the member from the community). For members who are already admins, you will see the Revoke admin option instead of Make admin.

Assign community experts

As a community administrator, you can select specific members from your community and assign them as community experts. Community experts act as subject matter experts for the respective community, and they can mark an answer as the best answer on a question post, and they can pin and unpin a post.

To assign community experts, follow these steps:

1. Navigate to the community you own and on the **Members** tile, click on **Assign** under **Community experts**:

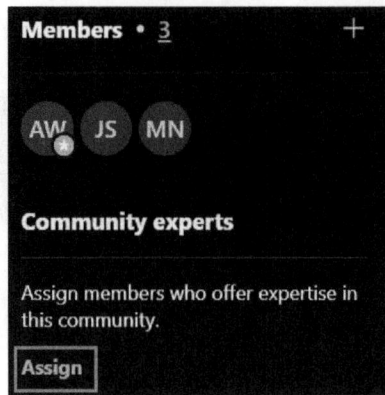

Figure 3.19: Assign community experts

2. Click on **Mark as expert** next to the name of the member you want to assign as a community expert.

Community settings

To access the community settings page, follow these steps:

1. Navigate to the community you own and click on the ellipsis (**…**) in the community header.
2. Select **Settings**.

On the community settings page, you can:

*   Change the community's name and description.
*   Change community privacy from Public to Private, or vice versa.
*   Set the posting permissions to Open (allowing all community members to start a conversation) or to Restricted (restricting the option to start a conversation to admins).
*   Enable or disable community members to view community resource links, such as links to the SharePoint library, SharePoint site, OneNote, and Planner.
*   Enable or disable the Files tab, which provides access to content via SharePoint.
*   Change the default publisher.
*   Assign community experts.
*   Delete the community.

Post to communities

To post to a specific community, you can create the post from the Home feed or by selecting the **+ Create new** button on the left side pane and then selecting **Post.** If you use these options to create the post, you need to ensure that you choose the appropriate community in the community picker, as shown in the following figure:

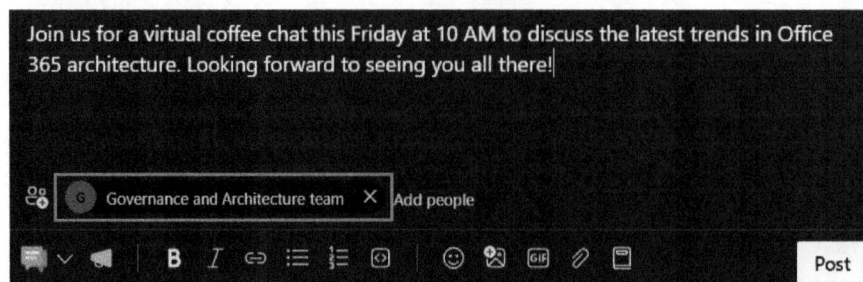

Figure 3.20: Post to a community from the Home feed

Additionally, you can simply navigate to the respective community and create the post from the community landing page:

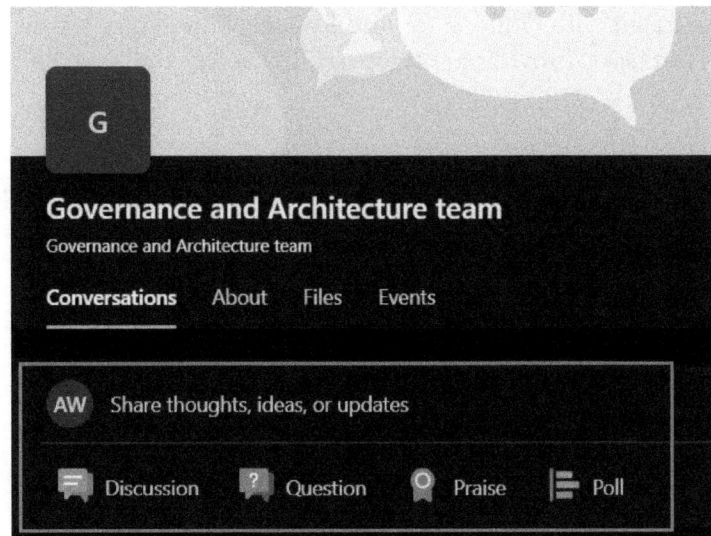

Figure 3.21: Post to a community from the community landing page

Community analytics

Community activity analytics offer insights into the overall activity levels within your communities. You can track metrics such as the number of active members, posts, and interactions over time. This data helps community managers understand participation trends, identify active contributors, and recognize areas that may need additional support or engagement efforts. All licensed users can access public community analytics. Private community analytics are accessible only to community members.

To access the analytics of a community, navigate to the respective community and click on the **Analytics** icon, as shown in the following figure:

Figure 3.22: Access community analytics

Some of the statistics that users can get from the Community analytics page are:

- Member activity, including percentage of members engaged, percentage of members who have viewed community content, percentage of admins engaged, and admin response rate.
- Total posts and percentage of posts by post type in the community.
- Views on posts, messages posted, and reactions on messages.
- Number of unique users who viewed the community content.
- Knowledge sharing, based on the breakdown of question-and-answer impact.
- Top conversations.

Creating posts and engaging with content

In Viva Engage, creating posts and engaging with content are fundamental activities that drive collaboration and communication within the organization. Whether you are sharing updates, asking questions, or celebrating achievements, your posts contribute to a vibrant and dynamic community. Engaging with content through reactions, comments, and shares helps build connections and fosters a sense of belonging among colleagues.

Viva Engage content is integrated with Outlook for notifications, SharePoint for file storage, and Planner for organizing community-driven tasks, providing interoperability across the Microsoft 365 suite.

Creating posts

Creating posts in Viva Engage is very intuitive. You can choose from various post types, such as discussions, questions, praise, and polls, to suit your communication needs. Each post type serves a unique purpose, enabling you to tailor your message and interact effectively with your audience.

Viva Engage supports inclusive communication practices such as alternative text for images and support for screen readers, ensuring everyone can engage meaningfully.

Choosing the right post type

When you start creating content in Viva Engage, you have several post types to choose from:

- **Discussion**: This post type is ideal for brief posts and discussions. This is the default post type and works well for quick updates.

- **Question**: Use this post type to ask questions and obtain responses from subject matter experts.

- **Praise**: A great way to acknowledge and commend coworkers for their achievements.

- **Poll**: Useful for requesting feedback from users. Poll participation is private, ensuring confidentiality.

- **Article**: Ideal for crafting in-depth content, such as blogs and newsletters. Articles support headings, separators, images (both inline and cover), and quote blocks.

The following figure illustrates the post types you can select when creating a post in Viva Engage:

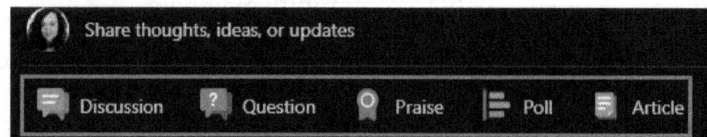

Figure 3.23: Post types

Note: **Articles represent a premium feature, available only with Employee Communications and Communities or Microsoft Viva Suite licenses.**

Community administrators can choose to make their post an announcement before sharing it within a community. When a post is marked as an announcement, it triggers notifications to all community members via Teams, Viva Engage inbox, and mobile push. If the announcement remains unread for 2 hours, an email notification is also sent. Additionally, the post creator can select the **Immediate email delivery** option to send an email notification right away, even to users who have opted out of email notifications:

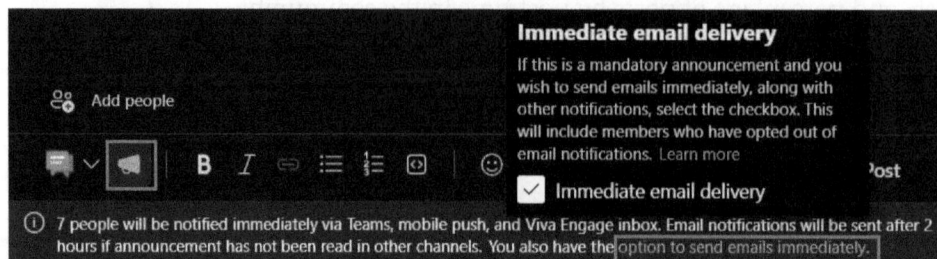

Figure 3.24: Announcements

Storyline announcements are reserved for leaders and their delegates, and it is also a premium feature.

Mention people and add content to your post

When creating a post, you can include or @mention colleagues who may be interested in the content or who might assist with answering a question. You can also add images, files, GIFs, or emojis to enrich your post:

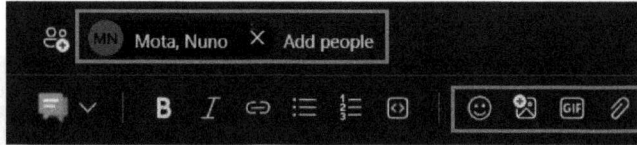

Figure 3.25: Add people and content

When using the Viva Engage mobile app, you have the option to record a short video, add annotations, and then share it through your post:

Figure 3.26: Record a video option

The content you upload through a post is stored in the underlying SharePoint site for community posts. For storyline posts, the uploaded content is stored in the user's OneDrive.

Creating posts using Copilot

With the help of Microsoft 365 Copilot, you can elevate your posts by crafting messages that are both engaging and informative. Copilot offers intelligent suggestions for wording, structure, and tone, ensuring your content resonates with your audience, whether you are sharing important news, asking a question, or simply looking for inspiration. Microsoft 365 Copilot can help you brainstorm ideas, refine your drafts, and polish your final message, providing a valuable resource for anyone aiming to communicate more effectively.

Note: **Microsoft 365 Copilot in Viva Engage is available to users with Microsoft 365 Copilot license assigned.**

Drafts and scheduling

If you begin writing a post and find that you need extra time or more information to complete it, you can save it as a draft. This allows you to edit and publish the post later when you are ready. Viva Engage also enables users to schedule posts up to 15 days in advance of publication.

To save as a draft or to schedule a post, click on the down arrow next to the **Post** button, and from the drop-down menu, select **Save as draft** or **Schedule post**:

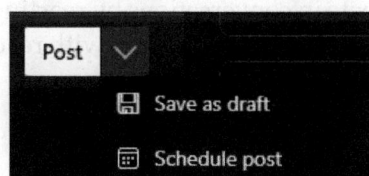

Figure 3.27: Save as draft or schedule post

If you choose to schedule a post, you will then be prompted to select the date and time for when the post should go live.

To access your drafts and scheduled posts, navigate to any page in Viva Engage where the publisher window is available. Then, click on the **Drafts** button located on the publisher window, as shown in the following figure:

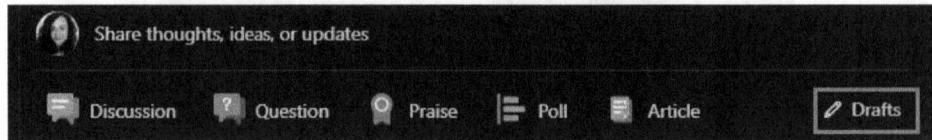

Figure 3.28: Access drafts and scheduled posts

On the **Drafts and scheduled posts** page, you can edit drafts, reschedule posts, or post them immediately:

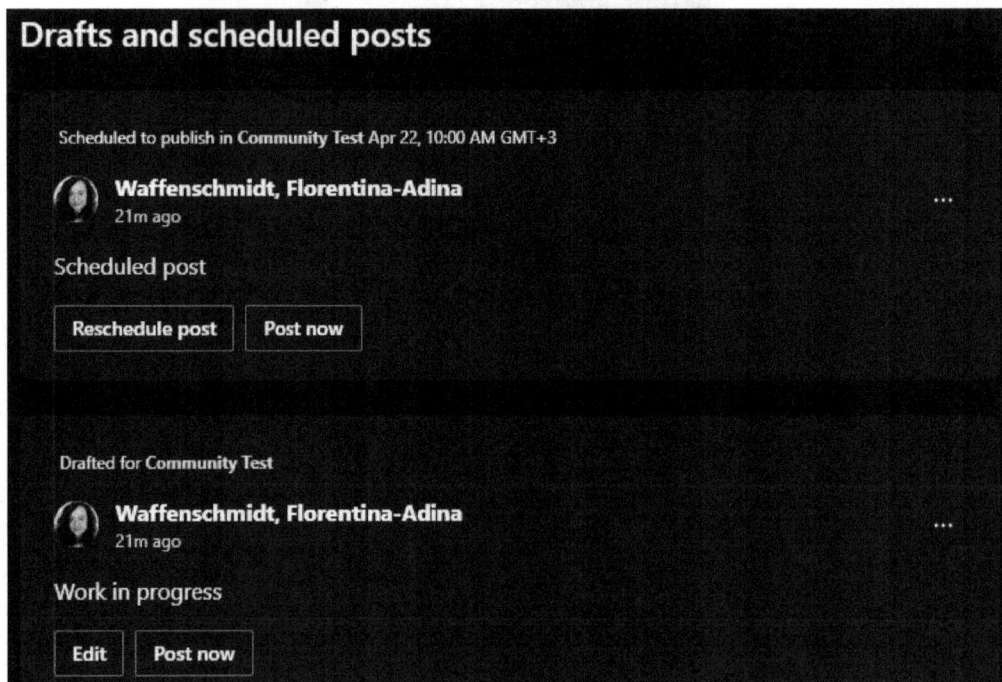

Figure 3.29: Drafts and scheduled posts page

Note: **Drafts and scheduled posts are available as premium features and require either a Microsoft Viva Suite or an Employee Communication and Communities license.**

Engaging with content

Engaging with content is equally important as starting conversations and creating posts. By actively participating in conversations, you not only share your insights but also support and recognize the contributions of others. This engagement enhances the overall experience within Viva Engage, making it a powerful tool for fostering collaboration, knowledge sharing, and employee engagement.

In Viva Engage, you can actively participate in conversations by reacting to a post, commenting, or sharing the conversation. The following figure shows an example of posts with reactions and comments from other users:

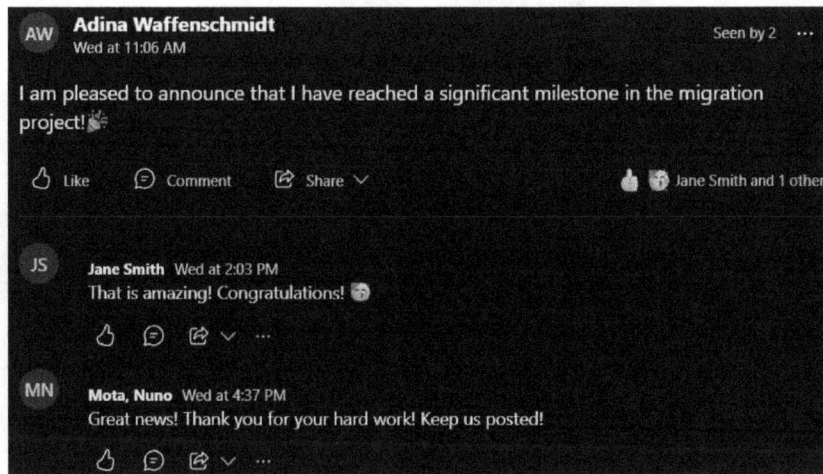

Figure 3.30: Reactions and comments on a post

You can view, react to, and comment on posts directly from connected apps like *Outlook* and *Teams* when you receive a notification with a post.

The following figure shows the interaction with a post from an email in Outlook:

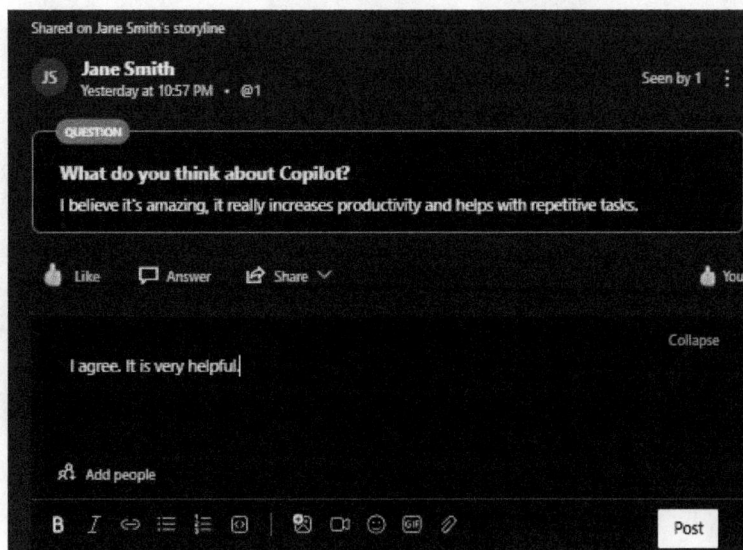

Figure 3.31: Interactions with a post from an email in Outlook

Conversation analytics

To monitor the post activity, Viva Engage provides analytics for all conversations posted on storylines or communities. To access conversation analytics, click on the ellipses (…) located on the top right side of the conversation, and then select **View analytics**:

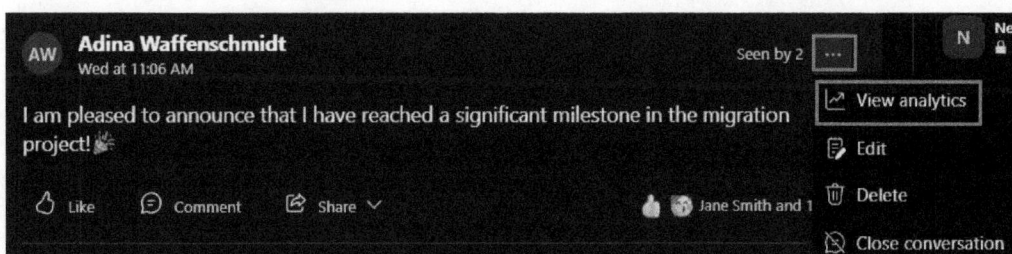

Figure 3.32: Access conversation analytics

Conversation analytics provide valuable insights, such as engagements on the post, conversation trends, reactions, and top comments, as seen in the following figure:

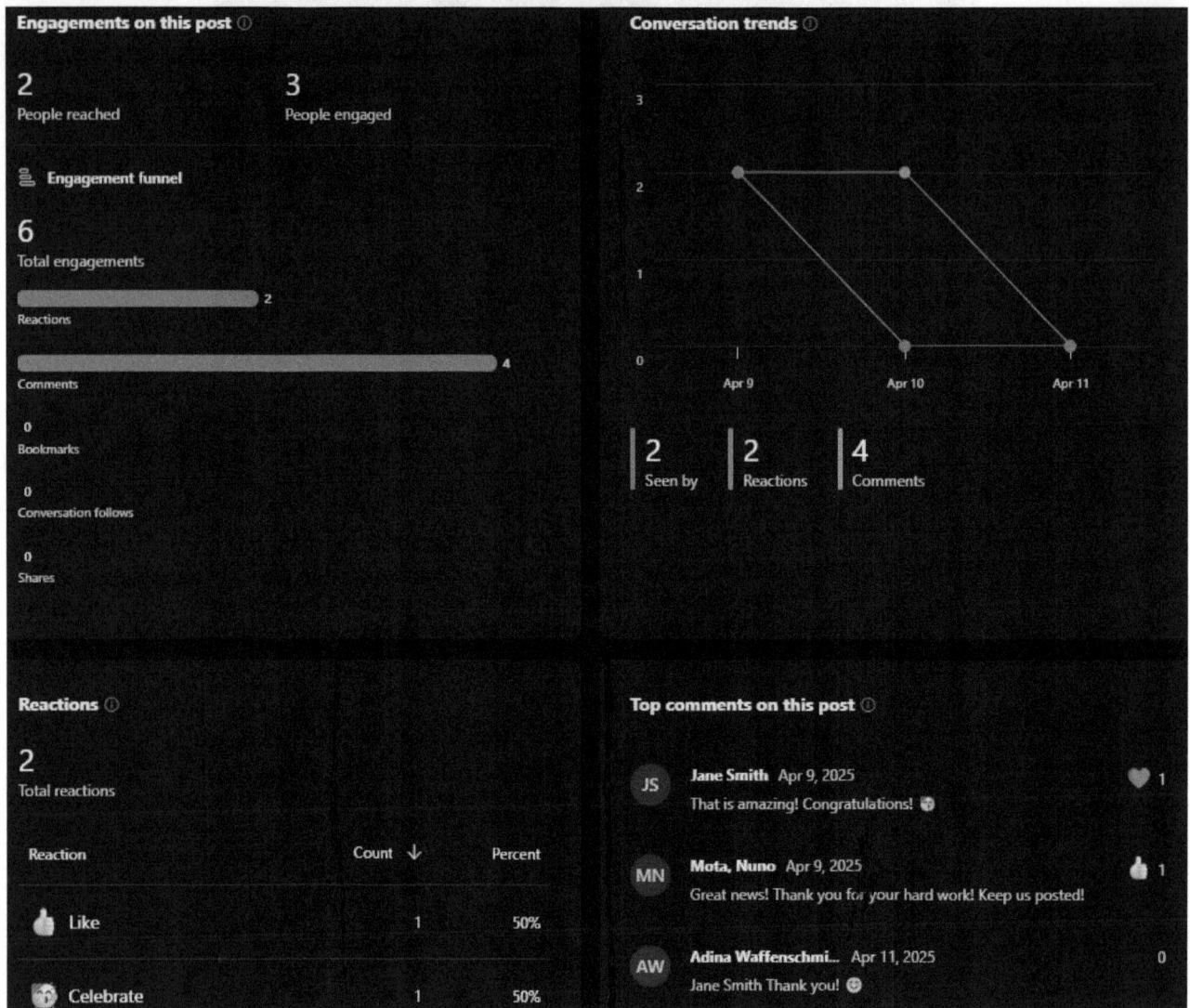

Figure 3.33: View conversation analytics

Conclusion

In this chapter, we explored the various features and benefits of Viva Engage within the Microsoft 365 ecosystem. From getting started with the platform to understanding the importance of storylines and communities, we have covered essential aspects that enhance communication, collaboration, and engagement within an organization. By leveraging the tools and insights provided by Viva Engage, employees can foster a more connected and supportive work environment, ultimately driving productivity and innovation.

In the next chapter, we will explore Microsoft Loop, a collaborative workspace app that allows teams to create, share, and collaborate on dynamic content in real-time.

CHAPTER 4

Microsoft Loop

Introduction

Collaboration and productivity are essential in modern work environments, and having the right tools is key for effective teamwork and successful project development. Imagine a platform that seamlessly integrates various aspects of your work, allowing teams to collaborate in real-time, share ideas effortlessly, and stay organized.

Enter Microsoft Loop, a tool designed to transform the way we work together. Loop brings together components from across Microsoft 365, enabling fluid collaboration and dynamic content creation.

Structure

This chapter covers the following topics:

- Microsoft Loop overview
- Getting started with Loop
- Loop workspaces
- Loop pages
- Loop components

Objectives

By the end of this chapter, you will have a comprehensive understanding of the core features of Microsoft Loop, including workspaces, pages, and components. You will learn how to get started with Microsoft Loop and explore the initial steps required to set up and begin using it effectively within your team or organization.

Additionally, you will discover the benefits of incorporating Microsoft Loop into your workflow, such as enhanced collaboration, streamlined project management, and improved productivity. You will understand how Loop workspaces help to organize project-related content and facilitate team collaboration, and how to use Loop pages to capture, structure, and share ideas in a dynamic and interactive manner.

Finally, you will discover how to integrate Loop components into supported Microsoft 365 applications for seamless collaboration and real-time updates.

Microsoft Loop overview

Microsoft Loop is an innovative platform designed to enhance teamwork and collaboration by bringing together content from different tools, reducing the need to switch between apps to keep track of your work and project tasks. It offers a versatile and dynamic workspace where components can move freely and remain synchronized across different applications. This enables teams to collaborate, brainstorm, and create content together more effectively, ensuring that everyone stays on the same page and contributes in real-time.

The three core elements of Microsoft Loop are:

- **Loop workspaces**: These are collaborative areas you can create in Microsoft Loop to be able to group and organize everything related to your project. They help centralize all relevant information, making it easier for teams to stay aligned and work efficiently.

- **Loop pages**: These are adaptable canvases designed to accommodate content creation according to your needs. They allow teams to share ideas and keep track of project progress and are ideal for brainstorming, planning, and documenting work.

- **Loop components**: These are portable elements (lists, tables, boards, notes, etc.) that can be shared and updated across different Microsoft apps. They enable teams to collaborate seamlessly, as any changes made to a component are reflected everywhere the component is used.

These three elements are designed to work together to create a cohesive and efficient collaboration experience, enabling teams to work seamlessly towards their goals.

Getting started with Loop

In this section we will explore how to begin using Microsoft Loop, considering both licensing requirements and access methods.

Licensing

From a licensing perspective, users with a **work or school account (Microsoft Entra account)** need one of the following **Microsoft 365** subscriptions to be able to access all Microsoft Loop features: **Business Standard, Business Premium, E3, E5, A3, or A5.**

Loop components can be used by anyone with a work or school account and access to supported Microsoft apps such as Teams, Outlook, Whiteboard, OneNote, SharePoint, OneDrive, and Loop.

Table 4.1 shows which Loop features are available based on the license assigned for users with a Microsoft work or school account:

Feature	Available to	Notes
Access to Loop components	Anyone with access to Teams, Outlook, Whiteboard, SharePoint, OneDrive, and other supported apps	
Viewing Loop pages, components and workspaces	Everyone with a work or school account	
Creating new Loop workspaces and adding/removing members	Users with work accounts and one of the following Microsoft 365 plans: Microsoft 365 Business Standard, Microsoft 365 Business Premium, Microsoft 365 E3, Microsoft 365 E5, Microsoft 365 A3, Microsoft 365 A5, Microsoft 365 Copilot	Office 365 E3, E5, A3, or A5 plans do not qualify for these additional capabilities; Microsoft 365 Extra Features plan is required

Table 4.1: Loop licensing

The Loop app is available to anyone with a personal Microsoft account. However, Loop components are not yet supported in Teams, Outlook, or other apps when used with a personal Microsoft account.

Accessing Microsoft Loop

You can access the Microsoft Loop app by navigating to **https://loop.cloud.microsoft**.

Once on the initial page, click the **Get Started** button and sign in with your Microsoft 365 credentials to begin using Loop. After signing in, the Loop homepage opens, as illustrated in *Figure 4.1*, allowing you to start exploring its powerful collaboration and productivity features:

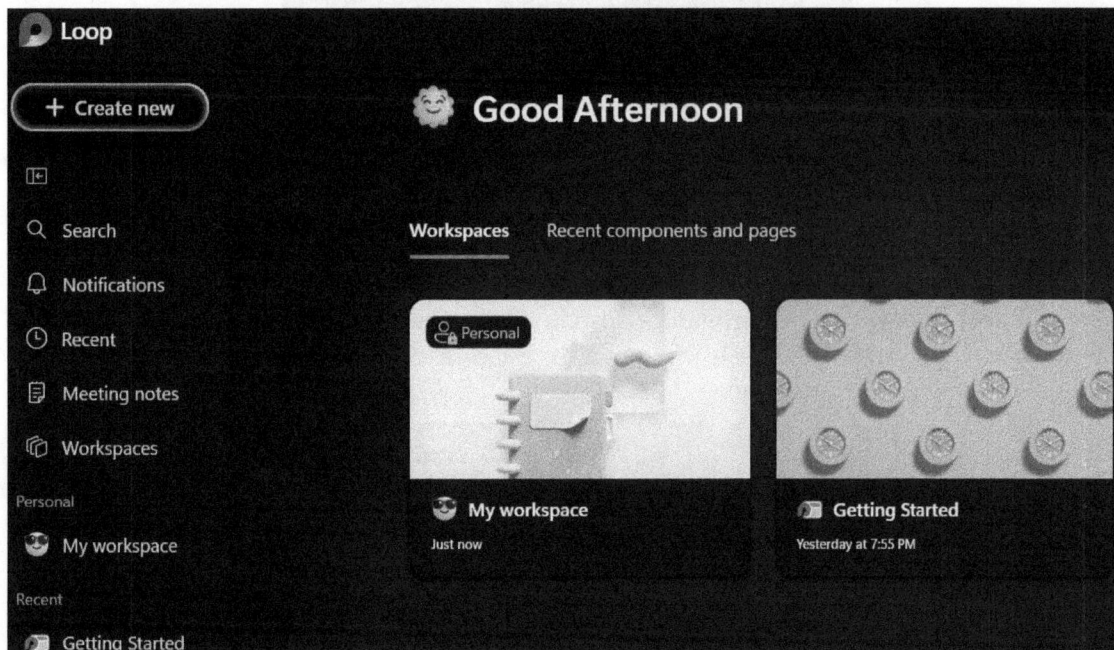

Figure 4.1: *Loop homepage*

Loop workspaces

Loop workspaces are containers designed to organize work items. A dedicated workspace can be created for each project, grouping related tasks and documents. Alternatively, workspaces can be set up to facilitate collaboration with different groups of people on various topics.

Creating a new workspace

To create a new workspace, click the **Create New** button on the left side pane of the Loop homepage, then select **New workspace**.

You will be prompted to provide the workspace details, such as name, sensitivity label (if sensitivity labels have been configured in your organization by an administrator), and the members you wish to invite as part of this workspace. Members can be added after the workspace creation as well.

You can also select an icon for the workspace and update the cover by choosing an image that represents your work or project. *Figure 4.2* shows the **Create a new workspace** dialog box in Microsoft Loop:

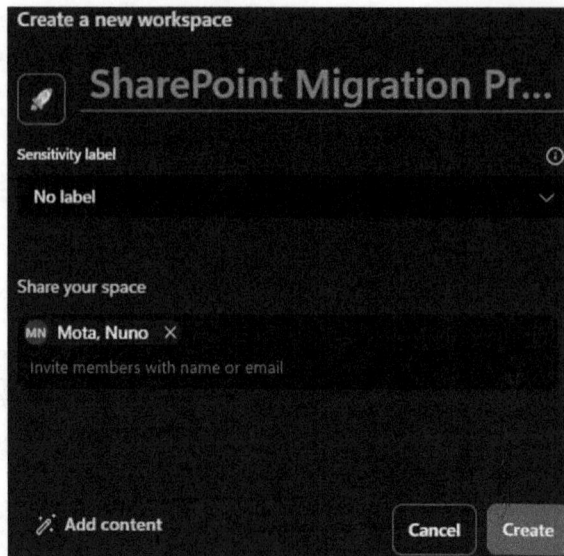

Figure 4.2: Create a new workspace

By clicking on **Add content**, you can provide a description and add files to your workspace. Based on the workspace name and description, suggested files you have access to, from SharePoint, OneDrive or Loop, will appear and will be available for selection:

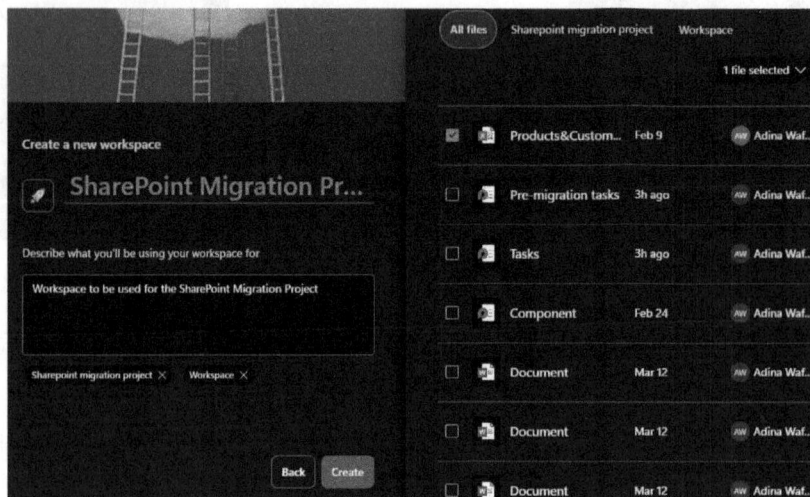

Figure 4.3: Add files to your workspace

Selected files will be added as links to your workspace, to be able to easily access related project files directly from Loop.

Once you click **Create**, your workspace will be set up and ready to use:

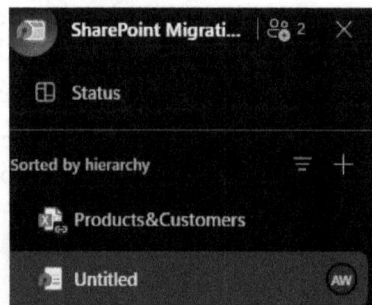

Figure 4.4: Workspace sidebar

As seen in *Figure 4.4*, the file selected in our example appears under the new workspace, together with a blank **Untitled** page that gets created by default with the workspace.

Creating and organizing content

Within a workspace, you can add and organize links, pages, and files. From the + (*Create New*) icon, you can easily add a new page, link, or upload a file:

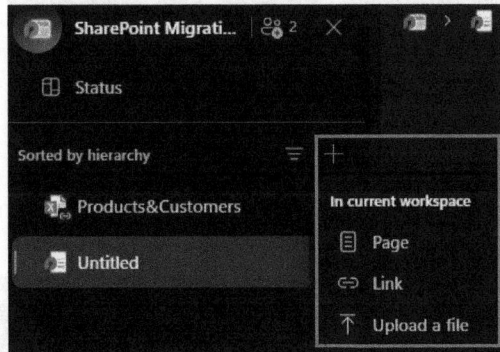

Figure 4.5: Add new items to a workspace

When you add a new page to your workspace, it will first appear as **Untitled** with the default Loop icon, as shown in *Figure 4.5*. To customize the page, simply select it and you can rename it to reflect its content, change the icon for better identification, or add a page cover. These options are available at the top of the page. You can click **Add icon** to select a new icon or **Add cover** to choose a page cover image.

You can also rearrange the workspace items by moving them up or down, and you can create a structure with multiple pages and subpages based on your requirements.

In our example, we created a workspace called *SharePoint Migration Project* to organize all necessary information related to the migration and facilitate collaboration among team members. To manage the project phases more effectively, we created three main pages within the workspace: *Project Overview*, *Migration Plan*, and *Post Migration*. Under each of these pages, we added relevant files and created subpages to further divide tasks and activities. For all the Loop pages created in this workspace, we added relevant icons, as shown in *Figure 4.6*:

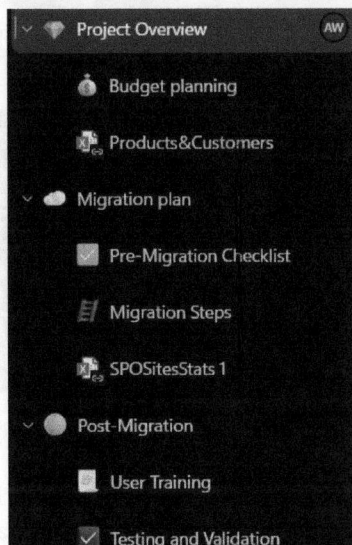

Figure 4.6: Item structure in a workspace

Establishing a clear structure for your content in Loop helps your team work efficiently and stay organized, ensuring that everyone can easily find and collaborate on the necessary information.

Adding members to workspace

Collaboration is key in Microsoft Loop. In most cases, you will want to add team members, co-workers, or project stakeholders to collaborate smoothly and work together effectively.

To add members to a workspace, navigate to the respective workspace and click on the **Invite and manage members** icon, next to the workspace name on the sidebar:

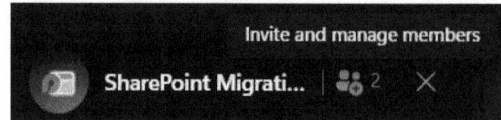

Figure 4.7: Invite and manage members icon

From here, you can easily add new members by typing their names or email addresses and then clicking **Invite**:

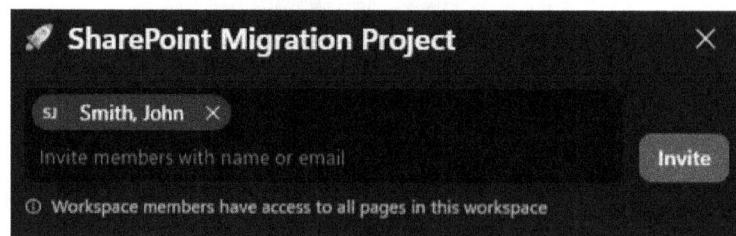

Figure 4.8: Invite members

Additionally, from the **Invite and manage members** dialog box, you can also:

- View the pending access requests (if any) and approve or decline them:

Figure 4.9: Pending access requests

- View the list with current workspace members and change their roles from owner to editor or vice versa, or remove members' access if needed:

Figure 4.10: Change role or remove access

The workspace creator becomes automatically the owner of the workspace. When adding additional users to the workspace, by default they are added as editors, but a workspace owner can promote an editor to the owner role.

Workspace editors can edit content, create and delete pages, and add new members to the workspace. In addition to these permissions, an owner can also change the role of other workspace members, manage pending access requests, remove members, change or apply workspace sensitivity label and delete the workspace.

My workspace

My workspace in Microsoft Loop is a dedicated area designed for individual use. It serves as a private space where you can organize your thoughts, plan your tasks, and manage your projects without any external interference. This workspace is ideal for brainstorming, drafting ideas, and keeping track of personal to-dos.

One of the key features of the personal workspace is its exclusivity. Unlike other workspaces in Microsoft Loop, the personal workspace cannot be shared with anyone. This ensures that content within this space remains confidential and accessible only to you. It provides a secure environment where you can freely explore and develop your ideas without the concern of others viewing or modifying your work. However, if needed, you can share individual pages from your personal workspace. This allows you to collaborate on specific items while maintaining privacy at the workspace level.

Loop pages

Loop pages are designed to bring together people, content, and tasks across various tools. They act as a central hub where teams can create, share, and collaborate on content in real-time. Whether you are brainstorming ideas, tracking project progress, or documenting meeting notes, Loop pages provide a versatile platform to keep everything in one place.

One of the most powerful features of Loop pages is the use of flexible content blocks. These blocks are designed to give users the freedom to organize and present information in a way that best suits their needs. Content blocks can be anything from text, tables, and lists to images and videos. This versatility allows you to create rich and diverse content within a single Loop page. For example, you can have a block of text explaining a concept, followed by a table summarizing data, and then an image illustrating the idea.

Customize Loop pages

Once you add a new page to a workspace, you can start from scratch from a blank page and customize it progressively, adding the desired content blocks suitable for your project, or you can select a template from the **Template Gallery**. To streamline the creation process, Loop pages offer customizable templates that include pre-defined content blocks. These templates can be tailored to fit specific project needs, saving time and ensuring consistency across different pages. *Figure 4.11* illustrates some of the available templates in the *Template Gallery*:

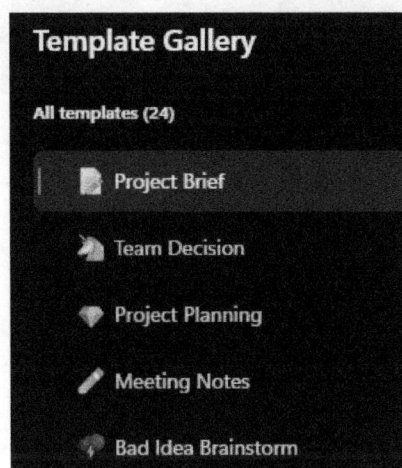

Figure 4.11: Template Gallery

Inserting a content block into a Loop page is easy. Simply type the **/** key and then select the desired block that best suits how you want to create and display the content:

General

- New subpage
- Table
- Checklist
- Bulleted list
- Numbered list
- Date
- Callout
- Code
- Mermaid
- Math equation
- Table of contents

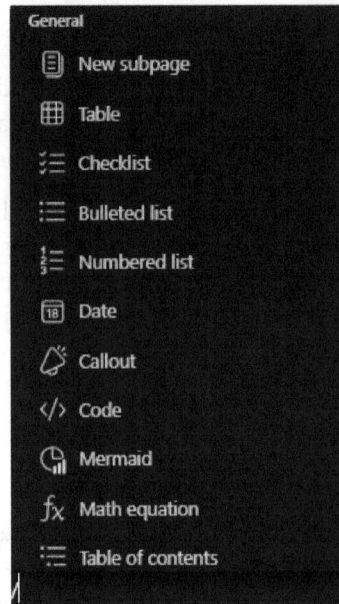

Figure 4.12: Insert a content block

For example, within the *SharePoint Migration Project* workspace, we have added a new page called **Brainstorming Hub: Migration Strategies** and inserted a voting table to help decide the migration strategy to be applied:

Brainstorming Hub: Migration Strategies

Voting table

	Idea	Pros	Cons	Votes
1	Content-only migration	• Easier and faster to migrate • Lower costs • Focus on data	• Limited functionality • Manual reconfiguration of settings, permissions and structure	+0
2	Content & structure migration	• Preserved functionality • Comprehensive transfer	• Complex to migrate • Higher costs • Potential downtime	+0

Figure 4.13: Loop page with voting table

This makes it easier for team members to review the available options and vote, enabling them to make an informed decision. You can effortlessly change column types as your needs evolve. For instance, switching from a voting column to a text column can be done simply by hovering over the column header and selecting the desired option from the dropdown menu.

To keep track of tasks, organize them in buckets, and assign the right task to the right team member, you can use a *task list* as a content block in your Loop page. Task lists can be inserted to the page by typing the **/** key as you would do to insert any other content block and then select *Task list* from the *Templates* section. Task lists are particularly useful as they integrate with both **Planner** and **To Do** applications, allowing team members to track and update their tasks regardless of whether they prefer to work in Planner, Loop, or To Do. From the **Task apps** dropdown menu in your task list, you can easily navigate to Planner or To Do apps, as shown in *Figure 4.14*:

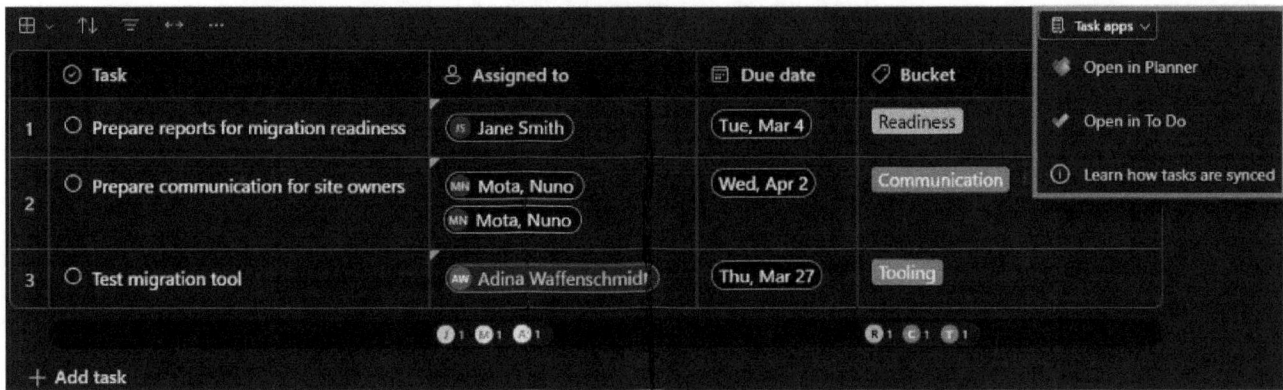

Figure 4.14: Task list

Additionally, an existing plan from Microsoft Planner can be added to a Loop page, ensuring that all tasks and assignments are seamlessly integrated and accessible in one place. This integration helps team members stay organized and up to date with their responsibilities, regardless of whether they prefer working directly in Planner or within the Loop page.

There are a variety of content blocks that can be added to Loop pages, allowing you to organize content in the most suitable way for your work or project. Loop pages provide a flexible and integrated solution that enhances productivity and fosters collaboration.

Sharing Loop pages

There are times when you may want to share just a specific Loop page with others without granting them access to the entire workspace content.

To share a Loop page, navigate to the respective page, click on the **Share** button from the top right corner of the screen in the Loop app, and select **Page link**:

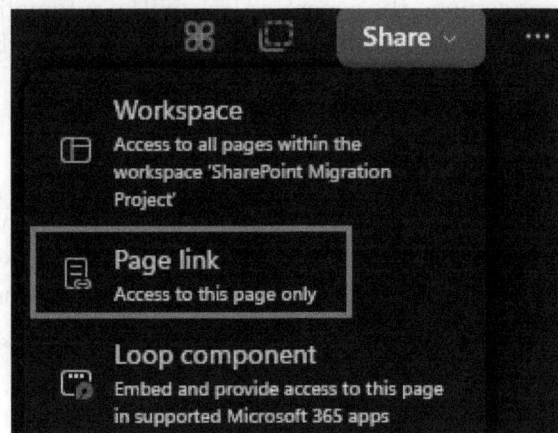

Figure 4.15: Share Loop page

By default, this will generate a link for people with existing access to the page, but you can choose to grant access to everyone in the organization or to specific people, by changing the sharing option under the link **Settings**:

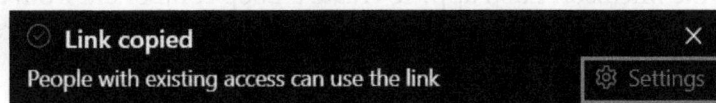

Figure 4.16: Page link settings

From here, you can choose to grant view or edit access to the page, as well as set an access expiration date:

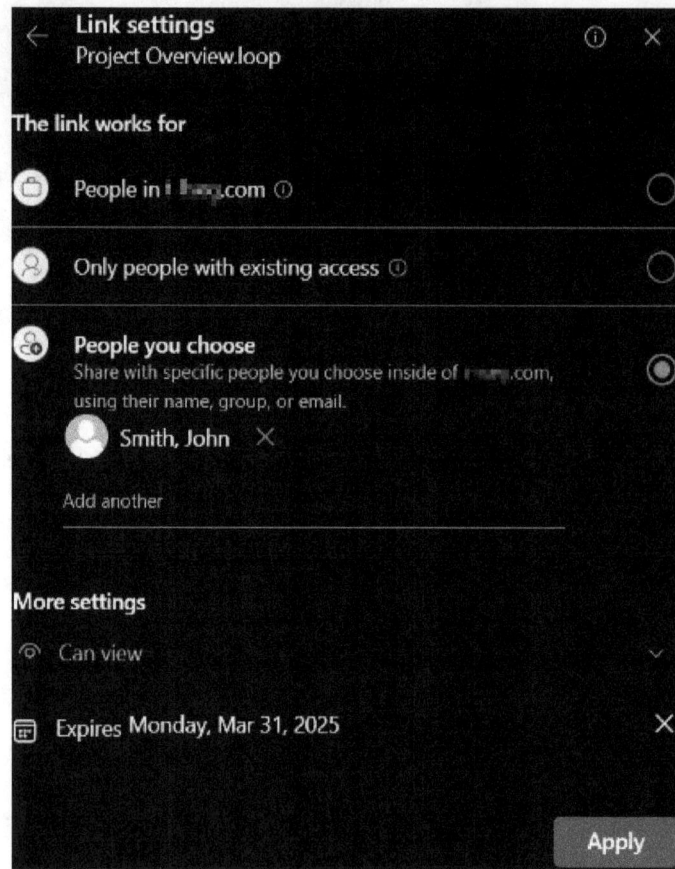

Figure 4.17: Grant access to a Loop page

After applying the preferred sharing settings, the generated link will be automatically copied to your clipboard. You may then distribute it via chat, channel, or email to those users who have been granted access.

Loop components

Loop components are modular pieces of content that can be created, shared, and edited in real-time across different Microsoft 365 applications, such as Teams, Outlook, OneNote, and Whiteboard. They are designed to break down barriers between apps, allowing users to collaborate without switching contexts. Whether it is a table, a list, or a task, Loop components ensure that everyone has access to the latest information, no matter where they are working.

Create and share Loop components

A content block created in a Loop page can easily become a Loop component, which you can then share via supported apps to increase collaboration.

For example, the voting table we created previously can be converted into a Loop component and then shared via a Teams chat or channel or sent via email to the team members for them to be able to vote without the necessity of navigating to the Microsoft Loop app. To create a Loop component from a content block, click on the grid icon next to the content block and select the **Create Loop component** option:

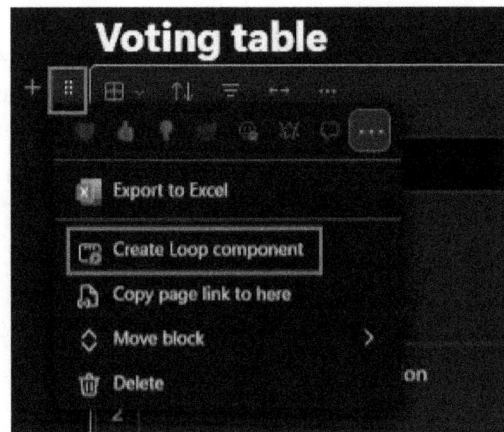

Figure 4.18: Create Loop component

Once created, you can choose to copy the Loop component by clicking on the **Copy component** icon from the top right side of the component, and a link will be generated by default for people with existing access:

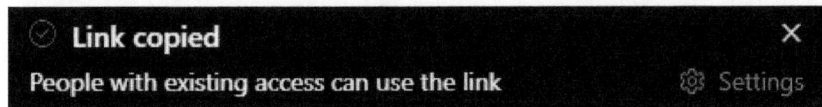

Figure 4.19: Copy Loop component

Alternatively, from **Settings**, you can opt to configure the link to work for all users in the organization or for specific people you choose.

After copying the component, a post can be created on a dedicated Teams channel designed for project collaboration, accessible to all project members. This allows members to vote or suggest additional options directly within Teams:

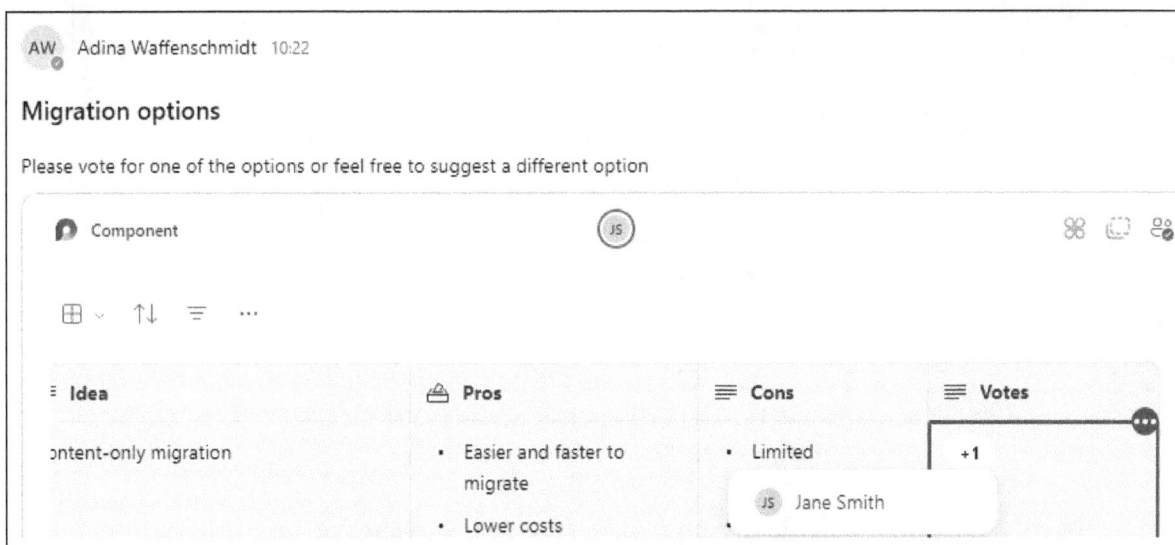

Figure 4.20: Loop component copied in Teams channel

All team members with access to the Loop component can view real-time voting results and modifications made to the Loop component, and they can also make changes themselves. This functionality can be further extended by incorporating the Loop component into an Outlook email, Whiteboard, or OneNote. Regardless of the application where the component is added and updated, it will remain live and accessible to all authorized users.

Create Loop components from supported apps

Loop components can also be created directly from supported apps, such as Teams, Outlook, OneNote, etc. The same benefits apply no matter where you created the Loop component. You can then add it to other Microsoft-supported apps to increase productivity and collaboration.

For example, we created a **Progress tracker** component in a one-to-one Teams chat by clicking on the **Loop components** icon on the chat **Message** bar, as shown in *Figure 4.21*:

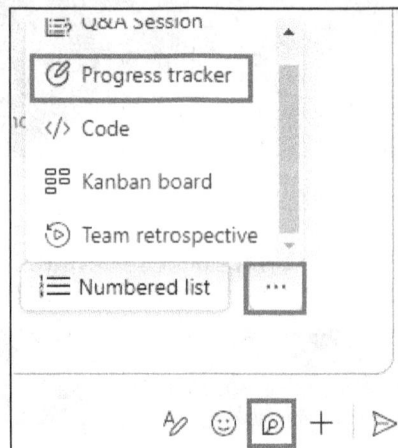

Figure 4.21: *Loop component created in Teams chat*

This helps keep track of different work areas owned by different members directly in Teams:

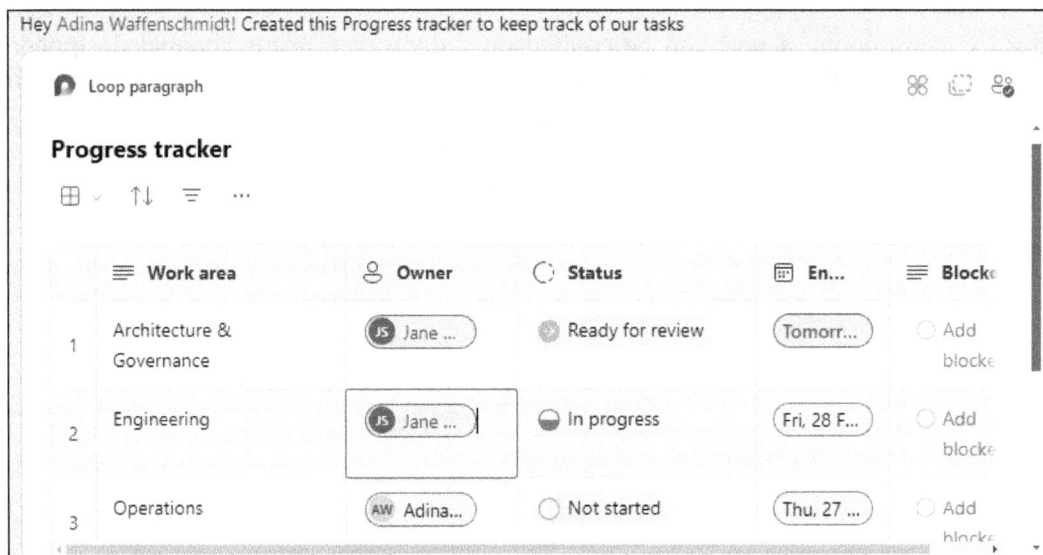

Figure 4.22: *Progress tracker in Teams chat*

All team members with access to the Loop component can view in real-time the modifications made to the component and actively participate by making their own changes and updates, ensuring that everyone is working with the most current information. Regardless of the application where the component is added and updated, it remains live and accessible to all authorized users.

Loop components generated in Teams chats and Outlook are .loop files that are stored in the creator's OneDrive. Loop components created in Teams channels are stored in the underlying SharePoint site connected with the respective team in Teams. Having these files in OneDrive or SharePoint allows users to create, find, and manage Loop components just like any other Office document. Users can also access versioning settings and restore previous versions if required.

Create a Loop component from a Loop page

In addition to converting a content block into a Loop component or creating a Loop component in a supported app, we can also convert existing Loop pages into Loop components. This helps to have live pages with multiple content blocks that can be updated seamlessly from different Microsoft 365 applications in real-time.

To convert a Loop page into a Loop component, select the desired page and click on the **Share** button from the top right corner of the screen in the Loop app and select **Loop component**:

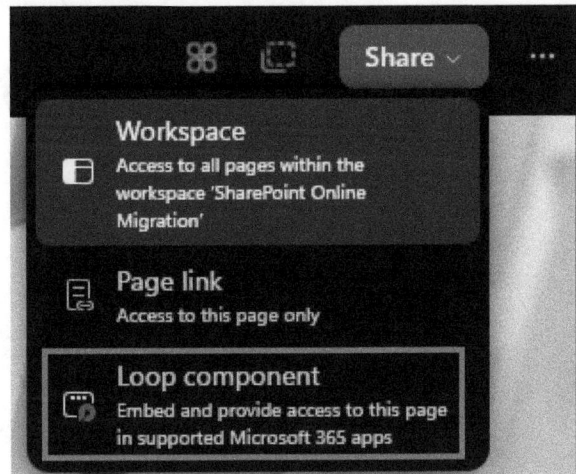

Figure 4.23: Convert Loop page into Loop component

From this **Share** menu, you can also share the entire workspace (add new members to the workspace) or share the page only.

Conclusion

By the end of this chapter, we got a comprehensive overview of Microsoft Loop and its core features, including workspaces, pages, and components. We have learned how to get started with Microsoft Loop, including the initial steps required to set up and begin using it effectively within your team or organization.

We explored the benefits of incorporating Microsoft Loop into your workflow. We also understood how Loop workspaces help to organize project-related content and facilitate team collaboration.

Furthermore, we delved into the use of Loop pages to capture, structure, and share ideas in a dynamic and interactive manner. We also discovered how to integrate Loop components with supported Microsoft 365 apps for seamless collaboration and real-time updates.

Overall, Microsoft Loop offers a versatile and dynamic platform that brings together content from different tools, enabling teams to collaborate more effectively and stay organized. By leveraging the features of Microsoft Loop, teams can work toward their goals more efficiently and achieve better outcomes.

In the next chapter, we will explore Whiteboard, a tool that enables teams to collaborate creatively in real time.

Join our Discord space

Join our Discord workspace for latest updates, offers, tech happenings around the world, new releases, and sessions with the authors:

https://discord.bpbonline.com

CHAPTER 5
Whiteboard

Introduction

In this chapter, we look into Microsoft Whiteboard. We will explore what Whiteboard is, how to use it, how it integrates into various collaborative settings, and the several ways it can enhance productivity. Through this chapter, you will gain insight into the features that make Whiteboard an asset for teams and learn how to maximize its potential for your projects.

Structure

This chapter covers the following topics:

- Understanding Whiteboard
- Getting started with Whiteboard
- Using Whiteboard in Microsoft Teams
- Loop components in Whiteboard

Objectives

By the end of this chapter, you will understand the core functionalities and benefits of Microsoft Whiteboard, gain practical knowledge on how to utilize Whiteboard effectively, and learn how to integrate Whiteboard into collaborative environments, such as Teams. We will also explore the use of Loop components within Whiteboard for enhanced team dynamics.

After reading the chapter, you will have a comprehensive understanding of how Whiteboard can transform collaborative efforts and elevate productivity in your projects.

Understanding Whiteboard

Microsoft Whiteboard is an innovative digital canvas that facilitates the collaboration of people, content, and ideas. It enables team members to work together in real time and express and share their thoughts on an expansive canvas designed for pen, touch, and keyboard inputs.

Whiteboard provides various features aimed at improving collaboration, creativity, and productivity for users, such as:

- **Real-time collaboration**: Whiteboard allows multiple users to work on the same canvas simultaneously, making it suitable for brainstorming sessions, planning, and collaborative projects, regardless of whether the team is in the same location or dispersed worldwide.

- **Flexibility and accessibility**: With support for pen input, touch, and keyboard, users can interact with the canvas in their preferred way. This ensures effective contribution from everyone, regardless of their device or input method.

- **Infinite canvas**: The infinite canvas feature allows users to expand their ideas without constraints. New content can be continuously added, and existing elements can be reorganized without space limitations.

- **Integration with Microsoft 365**: Whiteboard integrates with other Microsoft 365 tools, enabling users to incorporate content from applications like OneNote, Outlook, and Teams, promoting a cohesive workflow.

- **Creativity tools:** With various drawing tools, sticky notes, and templates, Whiteboard facilitates the creation of diagrams, the annotation of documents, and the visual organization of thoughts.

- **Accessibility features**: Whiteboard includes features to ensure participation and contribution from all users, including those with disabilities, supporting inclusive use by diverse teams.

All these features make Whiteboard a great tool to help run effective meetings, brainstorming, sprint planning, problem-solving, and much more.

Getting started with Whiteboard

Whiteboard is available on the following platforms:

- Web browsers by navigating to **https://whiteboard.office.com/**
- In Microsoft Teams meetings, chats, and channels
- Windows
- iOS
- Android
- Surface Hub devices

Once you have downloaded Whiteboard to your device or accessed the web version in your browser, please sign in using your Microsoft account. Upon launching it, you will begin with the board selection screen, as shown:

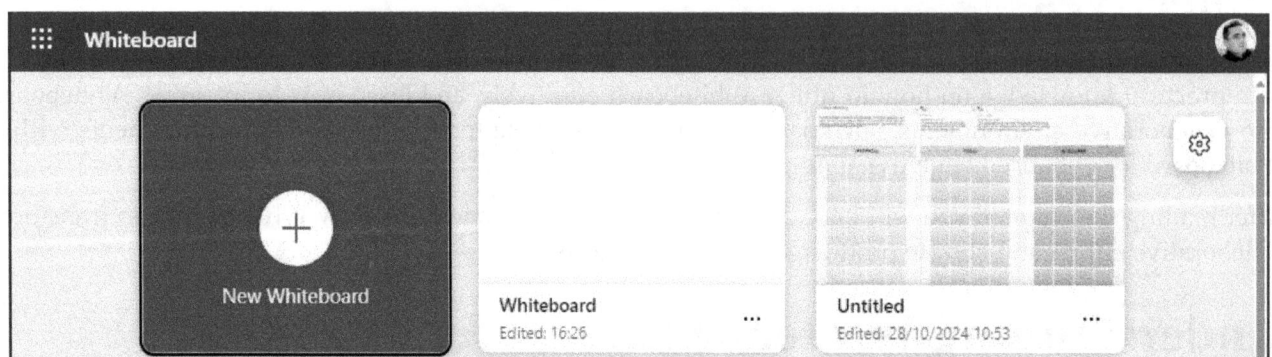

Figure 5.1: *Whiteboard board selection screen*

This section contains all the whiteboards that you have previously created or accessed. To create a new board, select the **New Whiteboard** tile. You are taken to a freshly created whiteboard that is ready for your ideas, as follows:

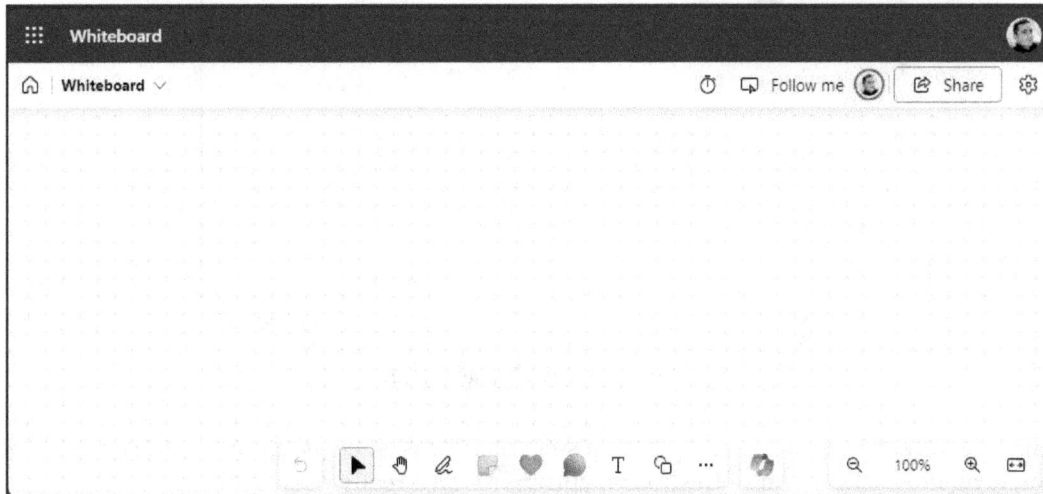

Figure 5.2: Blank whiteboard

Starting with the top left corner, the whiteboard will be named **Whiteboard** by default. You can simply click on this name and rename the board to what you want.

In the top right corner, the first button is the **timer**, which helps keep focus and stay on-task by setting a time limit for all participants:

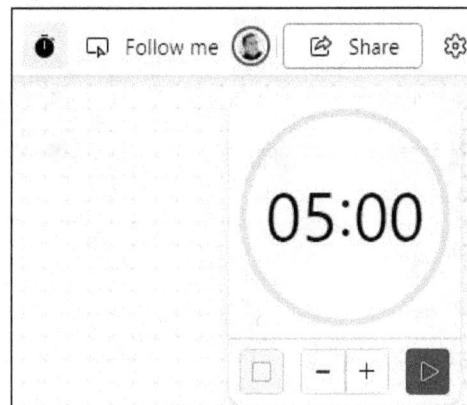

Figure 5.3: Whiteboard timer

With the **Follow me** button, participants will follow your point of view as you navigate the canvas to discuss and make edits. This feature is useful for presenting material created on Whiteboard and guiding participants through activities and sessions. Participants can pause or resume following to contribute independently and rejoin your view at any time. With collaboration cursors on, you will see participants' cursors, but only yours will be visible to them.

The **Share** button allows you to generate a link for collaboration on your current board with others, just like when sharing a file or folder in SharePoint:

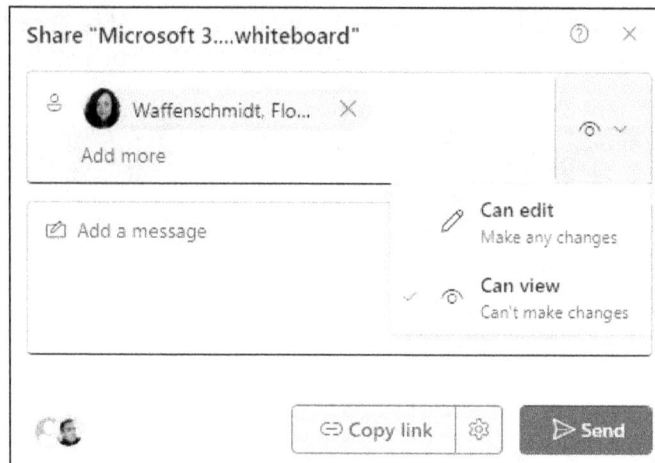

Figure 5.4: *Sharing a whiteboard*

In the **Settings** menu (*Figure 5.5*), you can perform several actions, such as exporting the board as an image or ZIP file, formatting the background of the board, and more. Two really useful settings are:

- **Collaborative cursors** allow you to see other users' contributions in real time. They display other people on the board and show what they are working on, with each user represented by a different color and a name bubble.

- **Enhanced inked shapes** convert hand-drawn shapes into precise shapes.

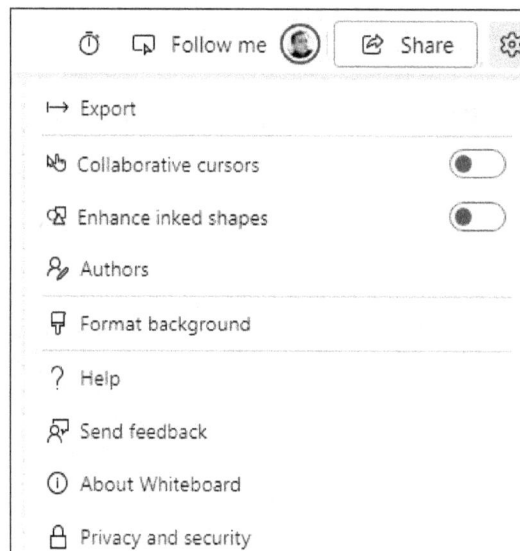

Figure 5.5: *Whiteboard settings menu*

At the bottom, we have the menu with all the inking and content creation tools. Starting with **Templates**, these can jumpstart creativity and enhance sessions for brainstorming, agile rituals, group projects, problem-solving, and more. To access these, click on the ellipsis (**...**) icon and then **Templates**, as follows:

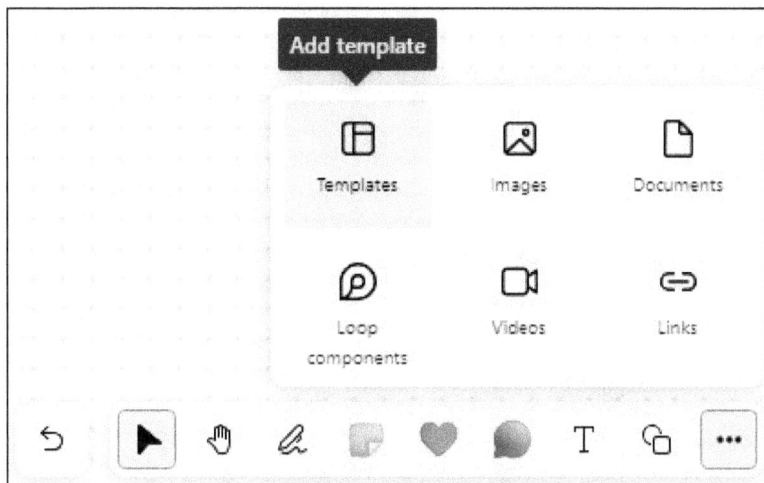

Figure 5.6: Adding a template

As you can see, there is a wide variety of templates to choose from, all aimed at a specific objective:

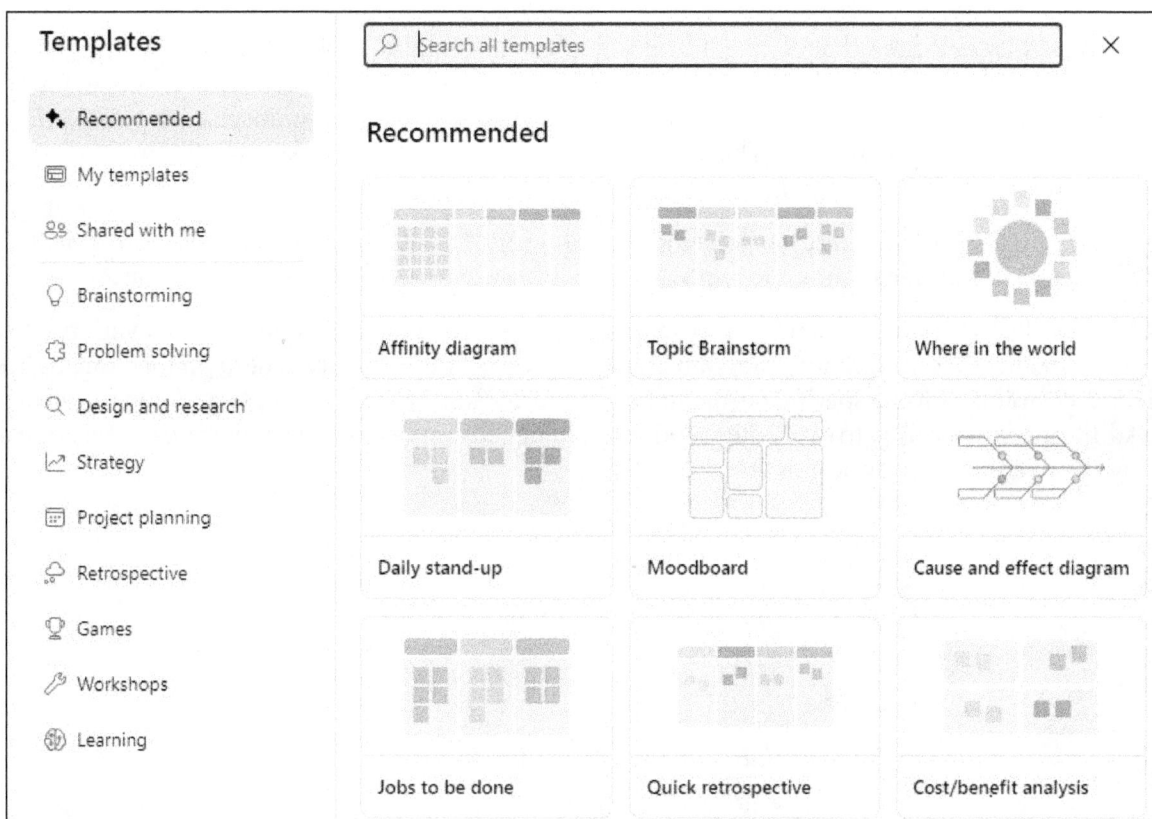

Figure 5.7: Available templates

Digital **ink** plays a crucial role in Whiteboard, whether it is used to convey your own ideas or to provide comments and annotations on the ideas of others. Whiteboard enables everyone to utilize the unique visual expression capabilities that digital ink offers.

The whiteboard features dozens of pens and highlighter color options and a variety of thicknesses to aid in visualizing content and bringing ideas to life. In addition to colors, it also includes other useful features like **ink arrows**, which ensure perfect arrows every time by adding an arrowhead to your ink stroke, simplifying inking, and keeping annotations and diagrams clean. The following figure shows a few of these:

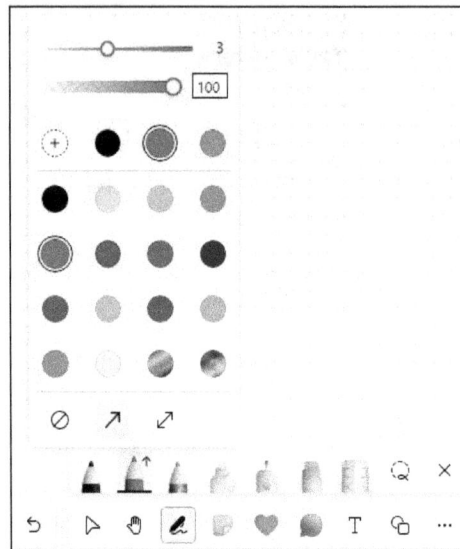

Figure 5.8: Ink arrows

Drawing **straight lines** can be challenging, but if you press the *Shift* key while drawing, a straight line will be created between the starting point of your stroke and your cursor. You can continue to move your cursor, finger, or pen to adjust the length and angle of your line. The line will automatically snap to 0, 45, and 90 degrees and to the nearest stroke end. This feature also works for arrow strokes, facilitating the creation of straight ink arrows.

To delete ink from the canvas, select the **Eraser** tool or press *Alt + X*. As the eraser moves more quickly on the board, it increases in size, facilitating the removal of multiple or large objects from the canvas.

Shapes in Whiteboard are instrumental in structuring and organizing information. With a variety of shapes available, you can create flowcharts, diagrams, and mind maps effortlessly. These shapes can be resized, rotated, and customized to fit specific needs, making it easier to illustrate concepts and communicate ideas clearly. Additionally, the ability to easily align and snap shapes ensures a polished and professional appearance, enhancing the overall visual appeal of the board:

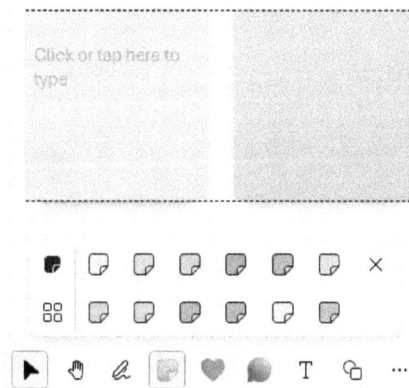

Figure 5.9: Aligning objects with each other

To add substantial text, such as detailed information to explain an image on your whiteboard, use **sticky notes**. Click on the notes icon shown in *Figure 5.9* and select a color from the available options. A sticky note will appear as a square card on your whiteboard where you can type text. You can also modify the text style (bold, italic, underline) and change the background color of the note. To add additional information to your whiteboard, you can also use a **note grid**, a collection of sticky notes arranged in a grid layout, also depicted in *Figure 5.9,* with four small squares. Each sticky note within a note grid can be edited and manipulated like a standard sticky note, including text formatting and background color changes.

Reactions allow you to engage with others and vote on ideas and items on shared boards. Reactions, such as thumbs up, hearts, or other emoticons, are a simple and effective way to show your opinion without posting lengthy comments. They enable quick feedback and help gauge the group's sentiment on various topics.

The following figure shows an example of a whiteboard with several reactions from different users:

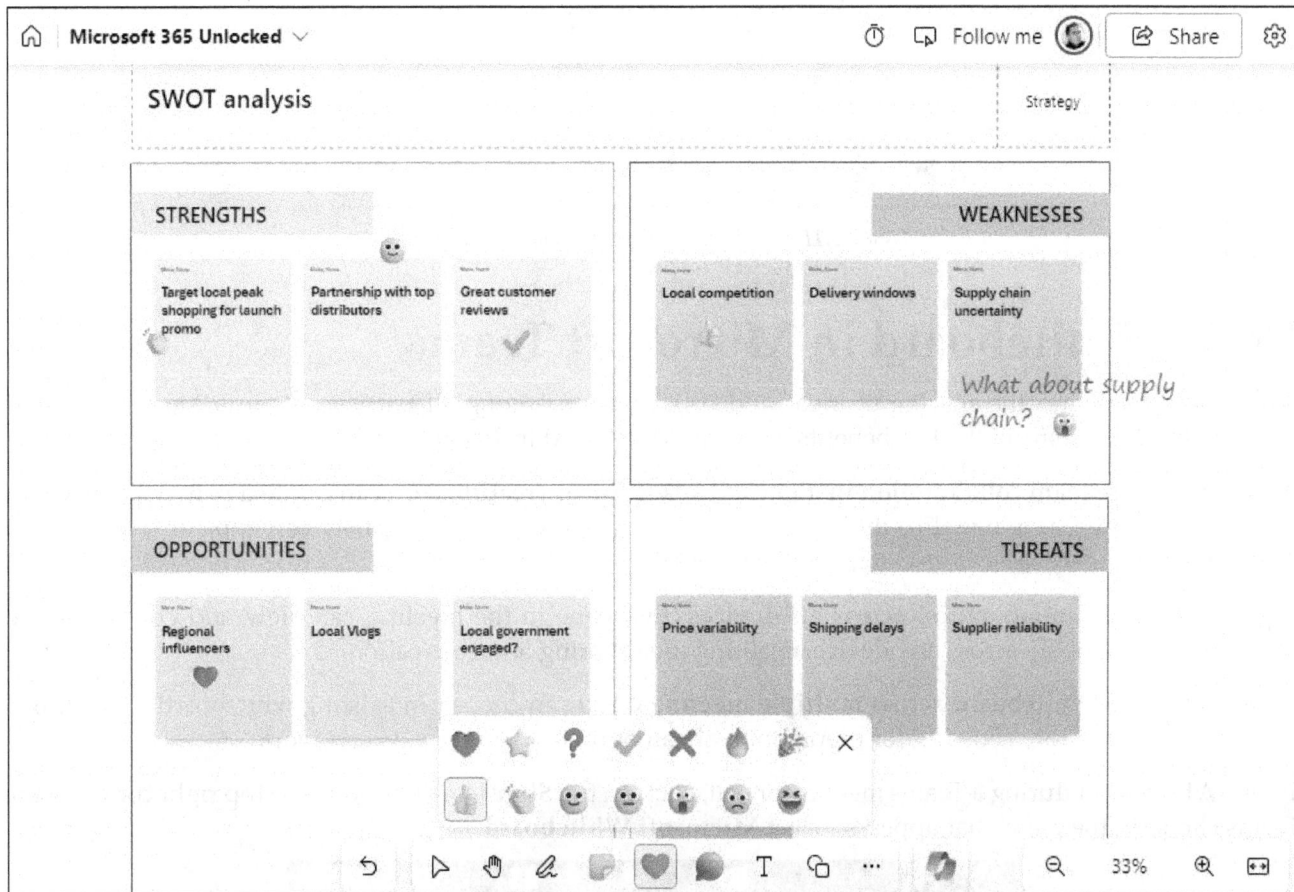

Figure 5.10: *Reactions*

Comments can be added to a note or other elements on a whiteboard. To add a comment, right-click on the note or element and select *New comment* from the toolbar that appears near or over the note or element. Alternatively, you can click the speech balloon icon (next to the heart) or click *Alt + C*. A small panel will open where you can type in a brief comment.

Comments are displayed as a speech balloon containing either the author's initials or a small headshot. By clicking on the balloon, a card will open, revealing the comment. You can enter a response directly on this card. You can also relocate a comment balloon by clicking, holding, and dragging it to a different area on the whiteboard.

Whiteboard allows you to add various multimedia and informational elements, such as images, PDF pages, PowerPoint slides, links to files or web pages, and embedded videos from YouTube or other sources. It also supports embedding Microsoft Loop components, as we will explore later in this chapter.

To add images, links, and videos, click on the **More options** button (...) and select the type you want to add. For documents, you can add individual pages or the entire document.

All these elements can be moved and resized as needed. It is recommended to include media and information-rich elements only when they add clear value and to keep their number minimal for simplicity. A whiteboard should primarily convey ideas through basic drawings, shapes, and text, ensuring ease of understanding.

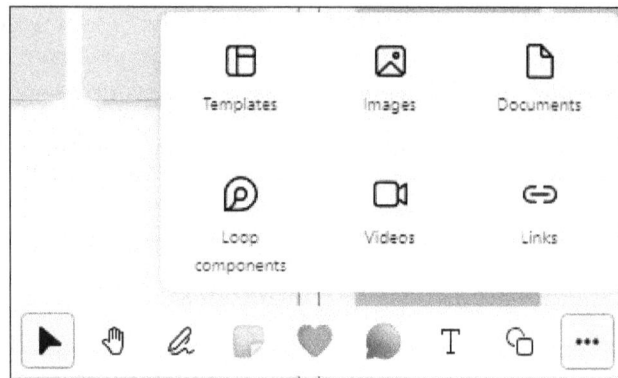

Figure 5.11: Adding media and informational elements

Using Whiteboard in Microsoft Teams

Whiteboard facilitates the sharing of ideas and collaboration among all participants in a Microsoft Teams meeting. Here are some of the key benefits of using Whiteboard in Teams:

- **Facilitate team collaboration in a unified space for co-creation**: You can create a new whiteboard or open an existing one directly in a Teams meeting without switching between apps or sharing your screen.

- **Real-time collaboration across all devices**: Everyone in the meeting can view and edit the board simultaneously across any device, enabling idea sharing and co-creation.

- **Re-use a Whiteboard across multiple meetings**: You can choose an existing whiteboard to share in a Teams meeting, allowing for preparation ahead of time or iterative project work.

To use Whiteboard during a Teams meeting or call, click on the *Share* icon located at the top right corner of the Teams client. In the panel that appears, select **Microsoft Whiteboard**:

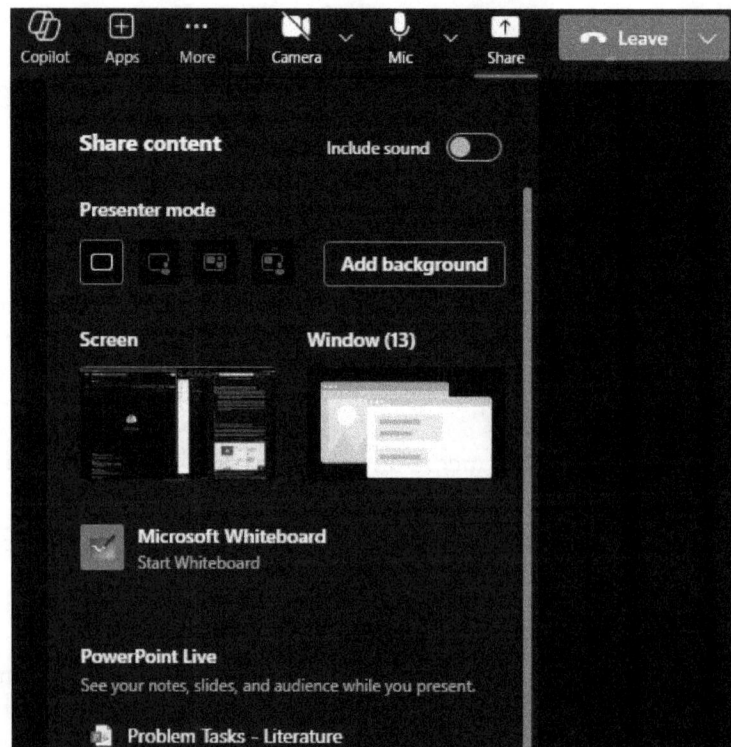

Figure 5.12: Sharing a Whiteboard in a Teams meeting

A new Whiteboard is created and shared automatically with everyone on the call as you can see in the following figure:

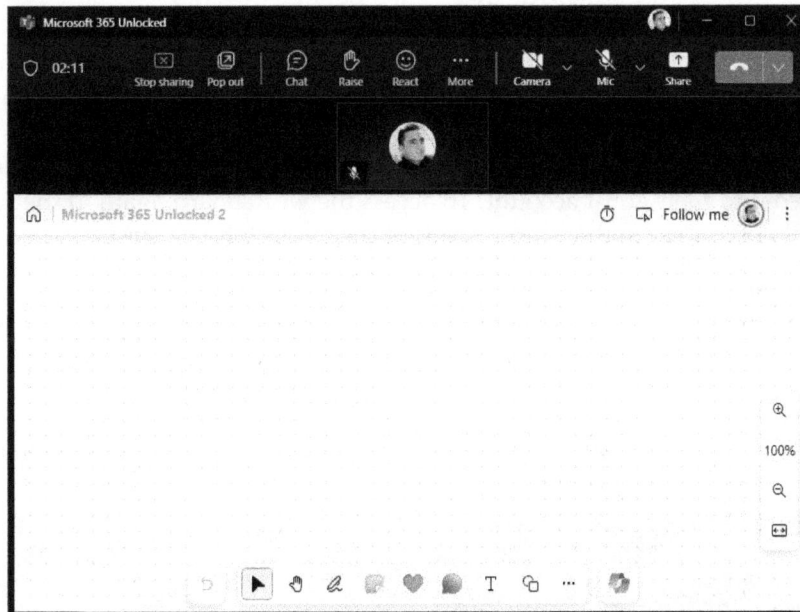

Figure 5.13: Sharing a Whiteboard during a Teams meeting

If you would like to share an existing whiteboard instead, click on the **Home** icon in the top left corner and all your previous whiteboards will be displayed ready for sharing. This means you can prepare your board ahead of time and then present it during the meeting.

Once you have selected a whiteboard to share, you will see the Whiteboard app interface with the same tools in the Teams meeting window. Meeting attendees can then ink and type collaboratively, just like they would directly on the Whiteboard.

Collaboration does not have to end after the meeting has finished! After the Teams meeting has ended, the whiteboard can be accessed by all participants from the Teams meeting chat in a tab labeled **Whiteboard**. The whiteboard will also be available in the **Board Gallery** in the Whiteboard app, allowing meeting attendees to continue collaborating on it even after the meeting has ended.

The following figure shows a whiteboard being accessed within Teams after a meeting has ended:

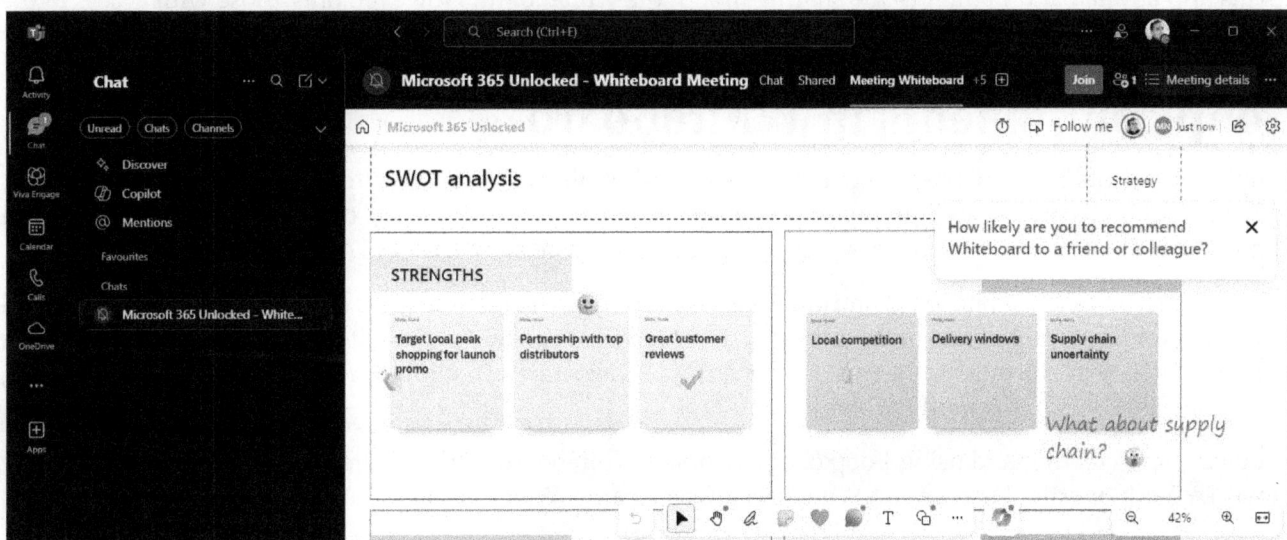

Figure 5.14: Whiteboard after a Teams meeting has ended

Whiteboard allows collaboration with **external participants** during a Teams meeting, provided your administrator has enabled the required settings, but this is only possible *during* a Teams meeting. External attendees will not have access to the whiteboard once the meeting concludes.

Similarly, if your organization allows it, you can also share a whiteboard with an external user just like you would share it with an internal user. External users can only access shared content through *Share with specific people* links. Company-wide share links are not compatible with external users, so you must specify the external user in the share dialog to generate a unique share link. When an external user accesses the whiteboard via the link, they will be signed into their guest account. To access the whiteboard again in the future, they must use the share link, as it will not appear in the board picker of their standard account.

At the time of writing this book, whiteboards shared during a Teams meeting that is being **recorded** do not appear in the recording. If a whiteboard session needs to be recorded, the only workarounds are to either share your screen and bring up the whiteboard or open the whiteboard with the browser and then share the browser window.

To add a whiteboard in a **Teams channel or chat**, click the + button (*Add a tab*) at the top of the screen. On the panel that opens, select or search for **Whiteboard**:

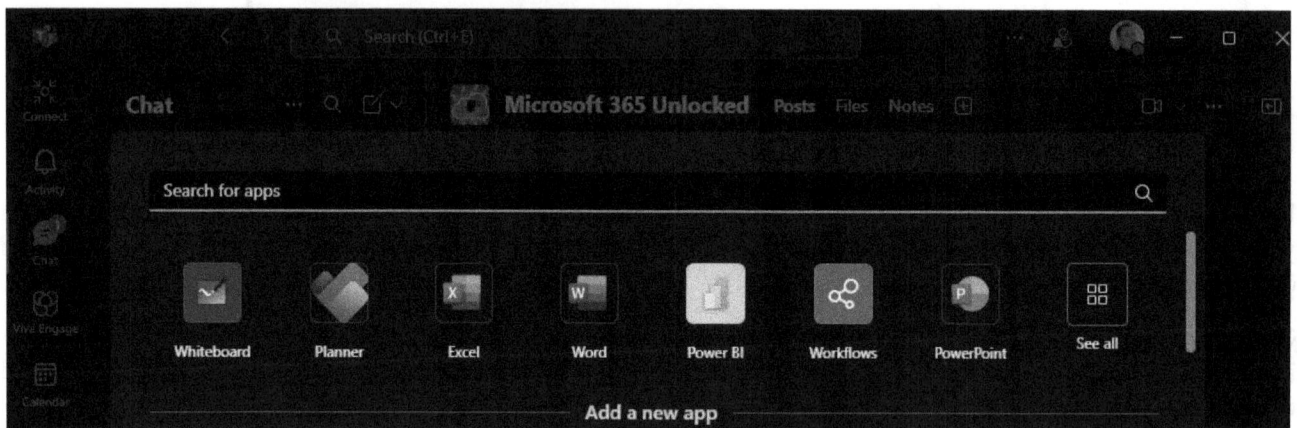

Figure 5.15: Adding Whiteboard to a Teams channel

A Whiteboard panel will appear. Give the new whiteboard a name, select *Save* at the lower right corner, and the new whiteboard will be added to the channel or chat as a tab. Unfortunately, at this stage, it is not possible to add a pre-existing whiteboard to a Teams channel or chat. The only workaround is to add the *Website* Teams app as a tab and point it to the sharing link of the whiteboard. However, only those with access to the whiteboard will be able to access it, and it will open in a new window, not within Teams.

Loop components in Whiteboard

Loop components in Whiteboard are a great feature that allows seamless integration across the Microsoft 365 suite. This deep dive will give you a comprehensive understanding of the capabilities and potential applications of Loop components, ensuring you can make the most of this powerful tool.

Loop components in Whiteboard facilitate continuous team collaboration by allowing members to add information to lists, tables, and more during brainstorming sessions. Any updates made to Loop components within Whiteboard will automatically synchronize across all shared locations like *Teams* and *Outlook*, ensuring everyone has access to the most current information.

Let us explore creating and using Loop components in Whiteboard. This feature is available for users signed in with a work or school account on Whiteboard web, Teams, Windows, and Surface devices.

Limitations exist based on the device and user type, such as:

- On iOS and Android devices, users can view and edit Loop components in Whiteboard but cannot create or copy/paste them. This functionality will be available in a future update.

- On Surface Hubs and Microsoft Teams Room devices, users cannot view, edit, create, or copy/paste Loop components in Whiteboard. This functionality will be available in a future update.

- External and anonymous users collaborating on whiteboards in Teams meetings cannot view, edit, create, or copy/paste Loop components. This functionality will be available in a future update.

To create new Loop components in a whiteboard, follow these steps:

1. First, open the whiteboard where you wish to create a new Loop component.

2. Next, select the **...** option from the bottom menu.

3. Then, choose the **Loop components** option.

4. Select from a **Task list**, **Table**, **Voting table**, **Progress tracker**, or **Checklist** to insert on the canvas as follows:

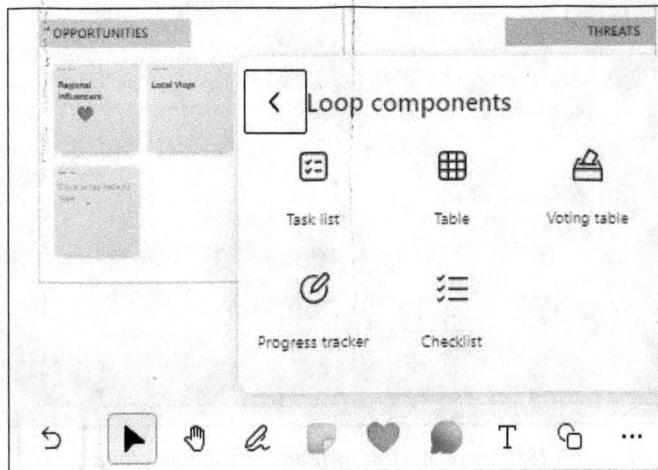

Figure 5.16: Adding a Loop component into a board

The following figure is an example of a **Progress tracker** loop component in a whiteboard:

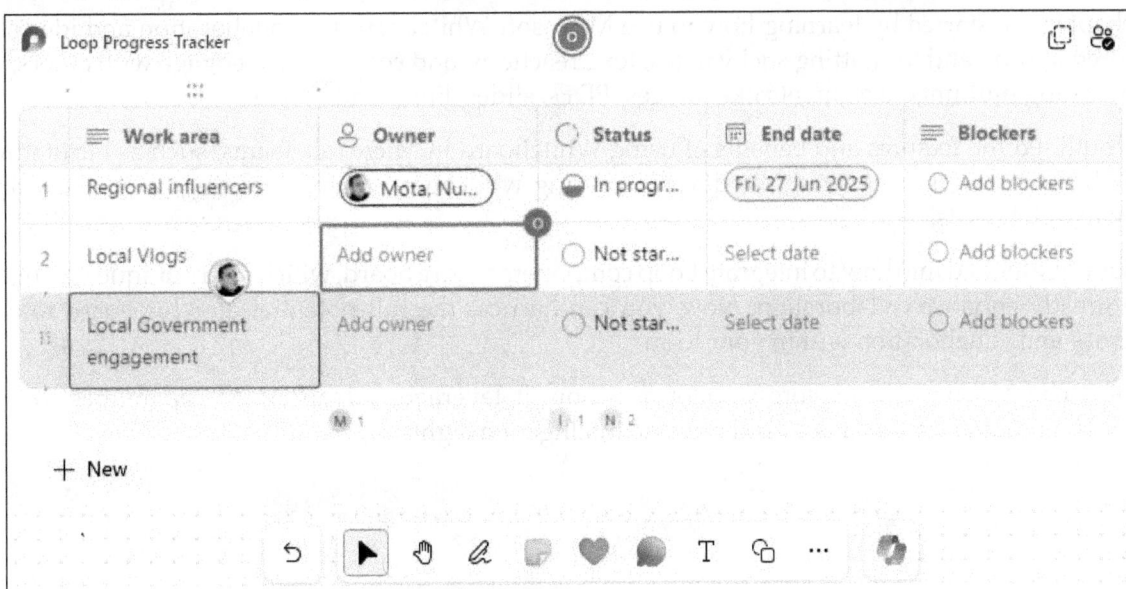

Figure 5.17: Progress tracker Loop component in a board

With the new Loop component on the board, all participants can contribute to it. Updates will be visible in real-time, and everyone will have the ability to edit all content.

To live copy a Loop component from a board and paste it into other Microsoft 365 applications:

1. Select the **Copy link** located in the upper right corner of the component.

2. Open the application, such as Teams chat or Outlook email, and paste the component.

3. The Loop component will look the same, and all users can collaboratively work on it on both platforms, as follows:

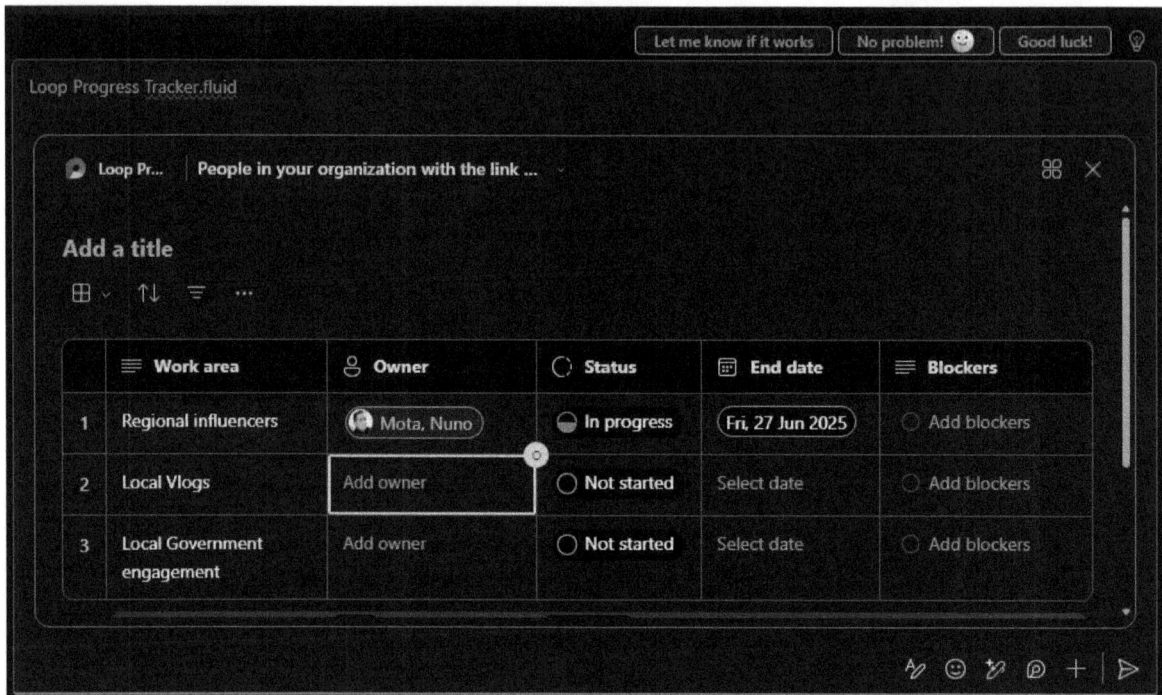

Figure 5.18: Loop component in Teams copied from Whiteboard

Conclusion

In this chapter, we started by learning how to use Microsoft Whiteboard for collaboration and idea sharing. We explored adding and formatting sticky notes, text, reactions, and comments to engage with others, as well as incorporating multimedia elements like images, PDFs, slides, links, and videos.

We then outlined the features and benefits of using Whiteboard in Microsoft Teams, such as facilitating real-time collaboration even across multiple devices, reusing whiteboards across meetings, and preparing and presenting whiteboards.

To conclude, we looked into how to integrate Loop components into a board, which offers unique functionalities that can greatly enhance collaboration. Now, you can harness the full potential of Whiteboard to enhance productivity and collaboration within your team.

In the next chapter, we will explore Copilot and how it leverages advanced AI capabilities to enhance productivity, automate routine tasks, and provide intelligent insights.

CHAPTER 6
Microsoft Copilot

Introduction

This chapter explores the revolutionary integration of **artificial intelligence** (**AI**) within the Microsoft ecosystem through Microsoft Copilot. This revolutionary tool harnesses the power of **large language models** (**LLMs**) to transform how we interact with and utilize several Microsoft 365 applications. From enhancing creativity in Word to boosting analytics in Excel, Copilot redefines productivity and collaboration. By the end of this chapter, readers will have gained a comprehensive understanding of how Copilot can enhance their workflows and drive efficiency in their professional and personal lives.

Structure

This chapter covers the following topics:

- Versions of Microsoft Copilot
- Prompting
- Copilot in Outlook
- Copilot in Teams and Business Chat
- Copilot in Word
- Copilot in PowerPoint
- Copilot in Excel

Objectives

This chapter aims to provide readers with a thorough understanding of the capabilities and applications of Copilot. By the end of this chapter, readers will have a clear understanding of what Copilot is, how it functions, insights into the practical applications and benefits of using Copilot, and knowledge of how to enhance productivity and skills with Copilot's assistance.

This chapter sets the stage for a deeper exploration of Copilot, providing readers with the foundational knowledge and practical insights needed to effectively integrate this innovative tool into their professional and personal workflows.

Versions of Microsoft Copilot

Microsoft Copilot is an AI-driven tool designed to assist users and administrators across various platforms and applications. It leverages advanced AI capabilities to enhance productivity, automate routine tasks, and provide intelligent insights. By integrating Copilot into multiple Microsoft products, from Microsoft 365 to the Power Platform, users can benefit from an AI-enhanced experience tailored to their specific needs.

As expected from Microsoft, there are a variety of Copilots across its ecosystem. Understanding what each one does and how to access them can quickly become confusing. Although this book will focus on Microsoft 365 Copilot, this section will briefly explain what each Copilot is intended for.

Microsoft Copilot

The free version of Copilot provides essential AI-driven assistance without additional cost. It offers basic functionalities to aid users with everyday tasks. Users can access features such as automated text generation and basic data analysis, enhancing productivity and simplifying routine work. While it does not include the advanced capabilities found in the Pro or enterprise versions, it serves as a starting point for individuals and small businesses looking to integrate AI into their daily operations.

Users access it by navigating to **https://copilot.microsoft.com** or **https://m365.cloud.microsoft/chat** and use it by asking Copilot questions through a *prompt* (explained in detail in the next section).

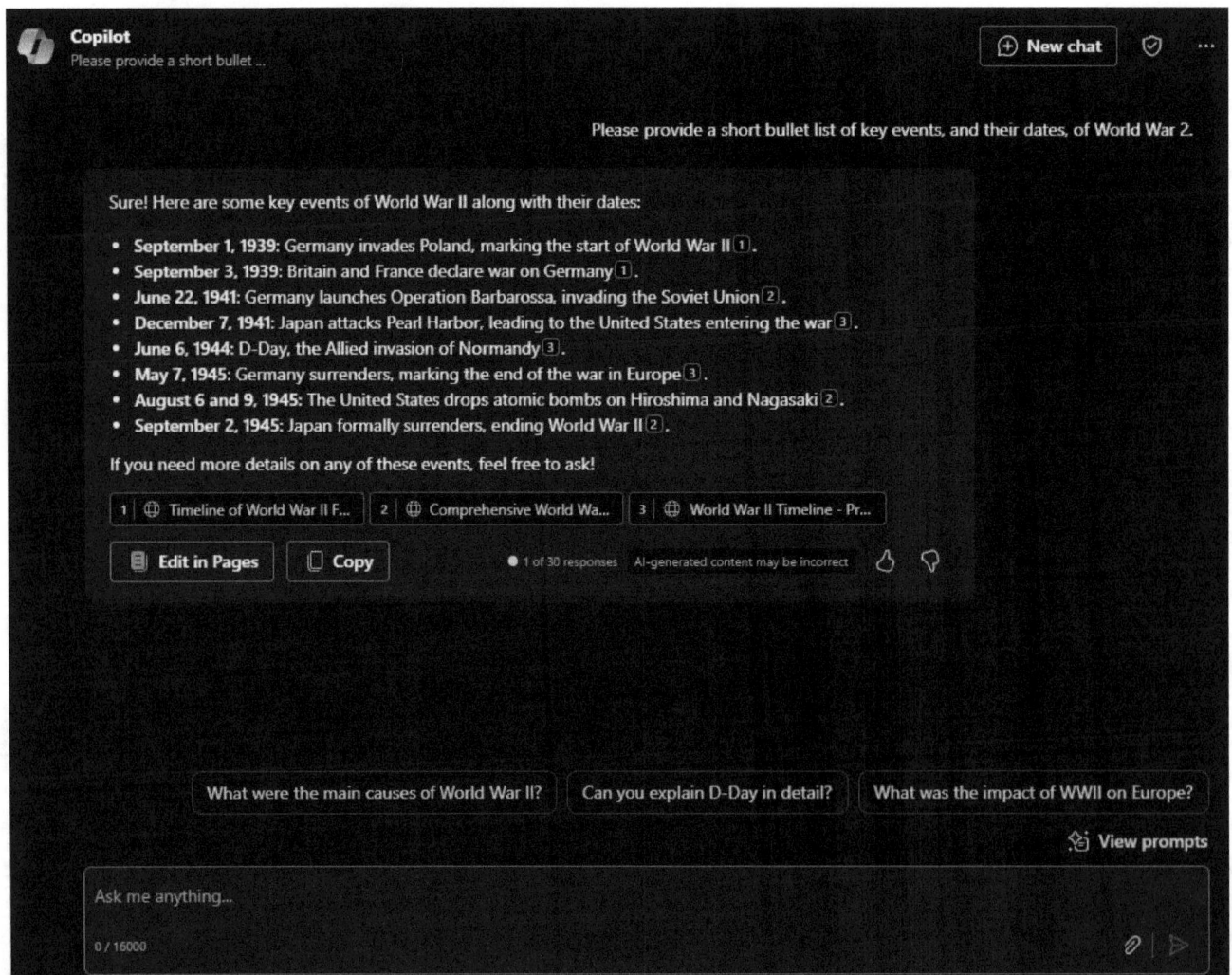

Figure 6.1: Copilot (free)

By default, any activities or uploads made to this Copilot contribute to training its ChatGPT model and are essentially public. The generated results are based on information found on the internet, and it is advised not to use this version in a professional environment.

However, if you go to the same address and log in with your Microsoft 365 username and password, you can access the same functionality as Copilot at no additional cost if you have a Microsoft 365 license. More importantly, your data will not be used to train the model, and all information will remain within your Microsoft 365 tenant. This is part of what Microsoft calls **enterprise data protection** (**EDP**): controls and commitments that apply to customer data for users of Microsoft Copilot and Microsoft 365 Copilot. This means that the security, privacy, and compliance measures available for Microsoft 365 Copilot also apply to Microsoft Copilot (free) prompts and responses. This can be verified by a green shield icon with a tick in the upper right corner, as shown in *Figure 6.1*.

It is important to highlight that this version does not have the capability to directly interact with SharePoint, Outlook, or Teams applications, nor does it display the Copilot icon within Office applications. This is one of the main differences between this version and Copilot Pro or Microsoft 365 Copilot.

Copilot Pro

This paid version of Copilot integrates with the Office suite and allows you to use Copilot directly within these applications. Users with a Copilot Pro subscription can access it via Copilot on the web (at **https://copilot.microsoft.com** or **https://m365.cloud.microsoft/chat**) and through the Copilot app on iOS, Android, and Windows. It can also be used in the web versions of Word, PowerPoint, Outlook, and Excel without a separate Microsoft 365 subscription. Those with a Microsoft 365 Personal or Family subscription can use Copilot in the more fully featured Office desktop apps, as follows:

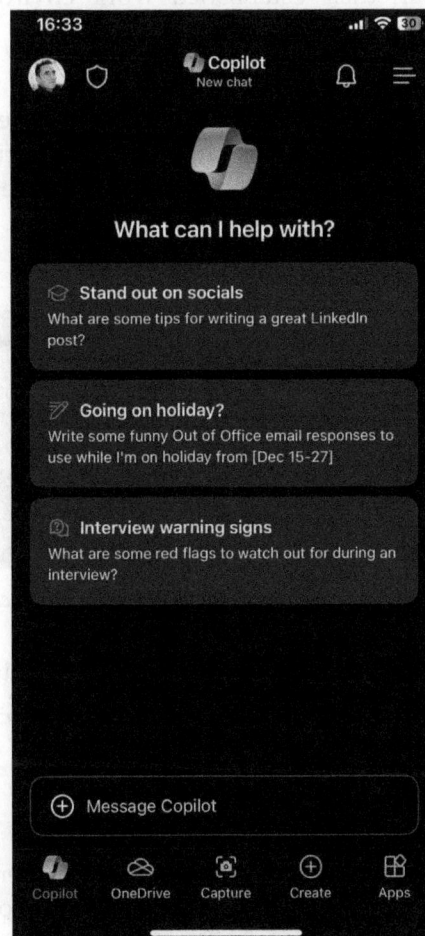

Figure 6.2: Copilot on iOS

Microsoft 365 Copilot

While all Copilots use advanced large language models, this particular Copilot unlocks business value by serving as a bridge connecting those LLMs to internal business data in Microsoft 365 applications. This capability allows Microsoft 365 Copilot to surpass the functionalities of other LLM-powered chatbots and Copilots by accessing data from Microsoft 365 Apps as well as internal resources such as articles, reports, emails, presentations, chat messages, and more.

Microsoft 365 Copilot was designed to integrate seamlessly with widely used Microsoft 365 applications such as Word, Excel, PowerPoint, Outlook, and Teams. Its primary purpose is to enhance user productivity and creativity by utilizing advanced AI capabilities. Among its many features, and similar to Copilot Pro, Microsoft 365 Copilot can generate text, create summaries, and analyze data, making it an invaluable tool for users engaged in a variety of business tasks. For instance:

- In Word, it can help draft documents by suggesting paragraphs, rephrasing sentences, or even generating entire sections based on the user's brief.

- In Excel, it can provide data analysis and insights, automate the creation of complex formulas, and assist in the visualization of data through charts and graphs.

- In PowerPoint, Microsoft 365 Copilot aids in designing presentations by recommending slide layouts, suggesting visual elements, and even generating speaker notes based on the presentation content.

- In Outlook, it can streamline email management by drafting responses or summarizing lengthy email threads.

The incorporation of artificial intelligence into Microsoft 365 applications enables users to leverage intelligent insights and recommendations within their established work environment. This integration enhances workflow efficiency and minimizes the necessity to transition between various tools, thereby promoting a more productive and streamlined work experience.

While both Microsoft 365 Copilot and Copilot Pro leverage AI to enhance productivity, they cater to different user needs and complexities. Microsoft 365 Copilot is targeted at enterprises that leverage Microsoft 365 as it is designed to work with user's data hosted in Microsoft 365 services like *Exchange* or *SharePoint* for example.

With this version, a Copilot icon will appear in the application menu bar, assisting with tasks specific to those applications, as shown in the following figure:

Figure 6.3: Microsoft 365 Copilot in Word desktop client

With this Copilot, Microsoft has introduced *Business Chat*, a feature that integrates LLM, Microsoft 365 applications, and user data to perform tasks like summarizing meetings, email messages, chats, and much more. Business Chat will be covered later in this chapter.

GitHub Copilot

This Copilot is designed for developers as it functions as an AI-powered code completion tool. It assists in writing code more quickly by suggesting entire lines or blocks of code in real-time. Integrated directly into popular code editors such as Visual Studio Code, it supports a variety of programming languages and frameworks, improving the coding process and minimizing the time spent on repetitive code.

Dynamics 365 Copilot

This iteration of Copilot is tailored specifically for business applications, particularly within the Dynamics 365 suite. It facilitates the automation of **customer relationship management (CRM)** and **enterprise resource planning (ERP)** tasks, including data entry, customer service interactions, and financial analysis. By offering intelligent insights and recommendations, Dynamics 365 Copilot empowers businesses to make well-informed decisions and enhance operational efficiency.

Copilot for Sales

Copilot for Sales, or Sales Copilot as it is also known, is designed specifically for sales professionals, integrating sales data and insights seamlessly into their workflow. This tool brings new capabilities to Outlook, Teams, and Dynamics 365 Sales, helping sellers streamline tasks, enhance customer focus, and facilitate deal closures. Operating within Microsoft 365, it connects directly to Dynamics and Salesforce CRMs, providing real-time data and updates to assist sales teams in making informed decisions and improving efficiency.

Power Platform Copilot

This version facilitates the creation of applications, the automation of workflows, and the analysis of data for individuals utilizing Microsoft's Power Platform without requiring extensive coding expertise. It enables users to develop solutions swiftly and efficiently, thereby enhancing the development process and promoting innovation.

Security Copilot

Security Copilot is dedicated to cybersecurity by supporting security professionals in threat identification and mitigation. By utilizing advanced artificial intelligence, it scrutinizes security data, detects anomalies, and provides actionable recommendations to enhance an organization's security posture. Integrated with Microsoft's suite of security tools and platforms, Security Copilot facilitates streamlined incident response, efficient vulnerability management, and adherence to industry compliance standards. By automating routine security tasks and delivering intelligent insights, it empowers teams to protect their digital environments.

Prompting

A *prompt* refers to the request you make for assistance from Copilot, and the information provided by Copilot is the *response*. Copilot does not retain any previous prompts or responses once the application is closed. Each time the application is reopened, it starts from scratch without any prior context. You can see an example of a prompt and the subsequent response from Copilot in the following figure:

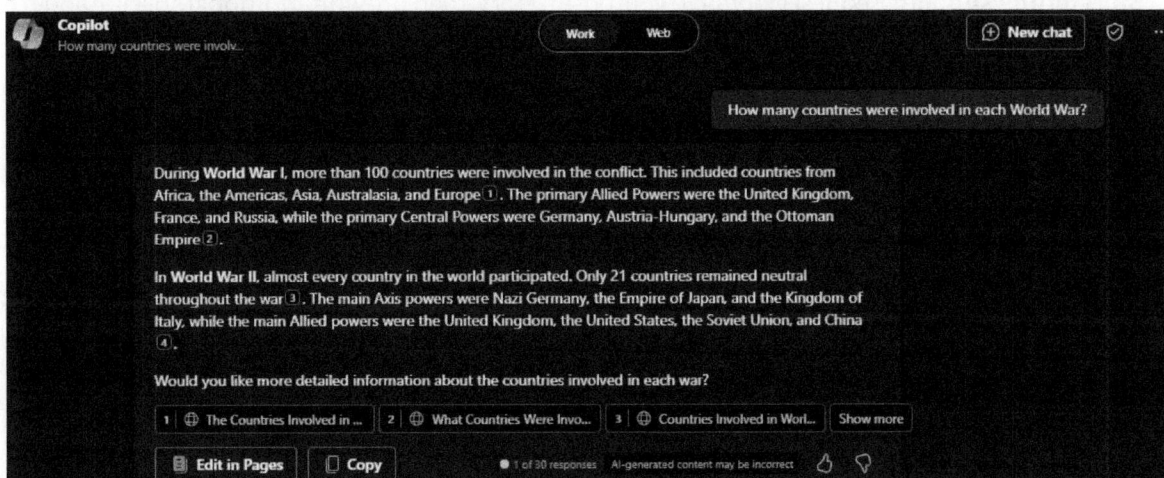

Figure 6.4: Copilot prompt and response

Copilot operates by utilizing the content within your prompt and the file you are currently working on, if that is the case, as well as content from another file or source you might reference. For instance, this could involve asking Copilot to assist in rewriting a paragraph in a Word document or generating a to-do list based on a set of notes from a meeting.

Copilot prompts are directives or inquiries used to communicate with Copilot regarding your requirements. Prompts can encompass four components, the goal, context, expectations, and source. The details are as follows:

- **Goal**: What do you want from Copilot? Example, *I want a list of 3-5 bullet points to prepare me...*
- **Context**: Why do you need it, and who is involved? Example, *... for an upcoming meeting with [client x], focusing on their current state and what they are looking to achieve.*
- **Expectations**: How should Copilot respond to best fulfill your request? Example, *Respond with a tone that is friendly but authoritative...*
- **Source**: What information or samples do you want Copilot to use? Example, *"... and focus on email and Teams chats with [people] over the last two weeks".*

A prompt can be brief or detailed, but it must have a clear objective. To be more precise, you can include additional elements. Often, it is necessary to provide more than just an objective to achieve the desired outcome. The following is an example prompt in Copilot chat that includes both a goal and a source:

> *Provide a summary of all emails received from Adina over the past two weeks.*

Here is an example with a goal, context, and expectations:

> *Prepare an outline of a training manual on time management. The target audience is professionals working in a hybrid environment who frequently attend virtual meetings and need to meet deadlines. The tone of the document should be neutral and informative.*

It is probable that you will follow up on the results with an additional prompt, so anticipate a series of back-and-forth to achieve the desired outcomes. You can also keep the conversation going by following up on your prompts to achieve a more useful and tailored response from Copilot. For example:

- **Generating content ideas**: Begin with general requests and then provide specific details about the content.
- **Obtaining insights**: Request a summary of a specific document, followed by posing pertinent questions to acquire more comprehensive insights.
- **Facilitating productive meetings**: Request a meeting summary and then inquire further for additional relevant information you should be aware of.
- **Language translation**: Request Copilot to translate a sentence into one of the supported languages, then ask for additional context or a specific regional dialect if needed.
- **Storytelling support**: Request Copilot to compose a story, then provide additional specific and relevant details to guide it further.
- **Addressing technical issues**: When presenting a technical issue, clearly define the problem and progressively narrow it down. Alternatively, request step-by-step guidance to resolve the issue.

Things to keep in mind

No matter how great and advanced Copilot is, there are several important considerations to bear in mind:

- **Review and verify responses generated by Copilot**: Copilot is built on sophisticated large language models that predict and generate text based on patterns observed in vast datasets. Due to the extensive and varied nature of LLMs, Copilot may occasionally generate inaccurate content. As such, you should always evaluate Copilot's responses and corroborate with reliable sources when necessary.
- **Repeatedly using the same prompt can generate different responses**: Due to the underlying neural networks and their inherent randomness, Copilot can generate different responses to the same prompt upon repeated use. This variability is a fundamental characteristic of LLMs. You should be mindful

of this, and you might want to refine your prompt or run multiple iterations to obtain the most appropriate response.

- **Use Copilot in a manner that is respectful, ethical, and lawful**: Avoid using Copilot for purposes that could cause harm to yourself or others.

- **Understand Copilot's limitations**: Copilot's functionality is confined to the current conversation context. This means that for optimal results, you need to provide ample and relevant details within each session. Comprehensive and well-structured prompts are essential for achieving a good result. You should recognize this constraint and write your prompts accordingly.

Helpful tips

Writing effective prompts is essential for achieving optimal results with Copilot. Similar to utilizing strategies to communicate proficiently with other people, there are guidelines that can enhance the quality of outcomes when formulating prompts for Copilot.

All about the details

Provide as much detail as possible. When stating your goal (the specific task for Copilot), include relevant context, clarify how Copilot should respond to meet your request, and mention information sources Copilot should refer to (such as a file or email messages). Try using the following two prompts with Copilot in Word and compare the responses. Determine which prompt resulted in a more detailed and concise blog post draft:

- **Prompt 1**: `Compose a blog post on sustainable practices in agriculture.`

- **Prompt 2**: `Develop a comprehensive 1500-word blog post for a general audience interested in sustainability. The focus should be on the significance and benefits of sustainable agricultural practices such as organic farming and agroforestry. Include real-world examples, innovative technologies, and insights from reputable sources. Conclude with an analysis of the importance of these practices and a call to action for collective efforts to embrace them.`

Structure your prompts

You can structure your prompts for optimal results. The sequence of your instructions can affect the response you receive. Instructions given later in a prompt may be given more emphasis than those provided earlier. Test different sequences to understand their impact. If you want Copilot to use specific files or sources, provide that information at the end. Try the following two prompts using Copilot in Word and compare the responses.

Note the following differences between them:

- **Prompt 1 (instruction-context-example)**: `Write a blog post highlighting the benefits of meditation. This age-old practice helps reduce stress. For example, mindfulness meditation improves mental health.`

- **Prompt 2 (context-example-instruction)**: `Meditation has been practiced for centuries and is renowned for its stress-reducing properties. Mindfulness meditation, in particular, has demonstrated significant positive effects on mental health. Considering this, please compose a blog post detailing the benefits of meditation.`

Positiveness

Provide positive instructions. Copilot is designed to execute tasks, so giving precise directives on what *to do* rather than what *not to do* yields better results. Consider using *if-then* instructions for clarity.

Review and regenerate

The initial result may not always be the final or optimal response. If you are not satisfied with the results provided by Copilot, review your prompt and try again. Consider the following three iterations to observe how the responses can improve with each attempt.

- **Prompt 1:** `Tell me about recent developments in renewable energy technologies.`

- **Prompt 2:** `Write a technical article about recent advancements in renewable energy technologies with a focus on solar and wind energy aimed at engineers and environmental scientists.`

- **Prompt 3:** `Compose a technical article for engineers and environmental scientists that explores advancements and innovations in renewable energy technologies, particularly focusing on solar and wind energy. Discuss the scientific principles underlying these technologies, their efficiency improvements, and real-world applications. Refer to recent research papers, patents, and industry reports for accurate and current information.`

Always double-check

We already mentioned this, but it is crucial to review and verify the responses provided by Copilot. Copilot uses large language models, which are trained to predict subsequent words and phrases. However, LLMs may sometimes generate content that is biased, offensive, harmful, or incorrect. Therefore, it is important to always review and validate its responses for accuracy and appropriateness.

Language

Polite language can improve Copilot's responses. It is also important to pay attention to punctuation, grammar, and capitalization. Finally, using quotation marks helps Copilot understand what to write, modify, or replace for you.

Copilot Prompt Gallery

The *Copilot Prompt Gallery*, previously known as *Copilot Lab*, allows you to create, save, and share Microsoft 365 Copilot prompts with colleagues. You can save frequently used prompts within Business Chat, making your work more efficient, as follows:

Figure 6.5: Saving a Copilot prompt

Once saved, you can share with coworkers the prompts you use to prepare for customer meetings or generate ideas for product launches. Leaders in an organization can demonstrate how they utilize Copilot by sharing prompts that help save time or address various tasks.

Prompts can be easily found and reused under the **Saved** tab by clicking **View prompts** in the prompt box of Business Chat, Word, Excel, and PowerPoint.

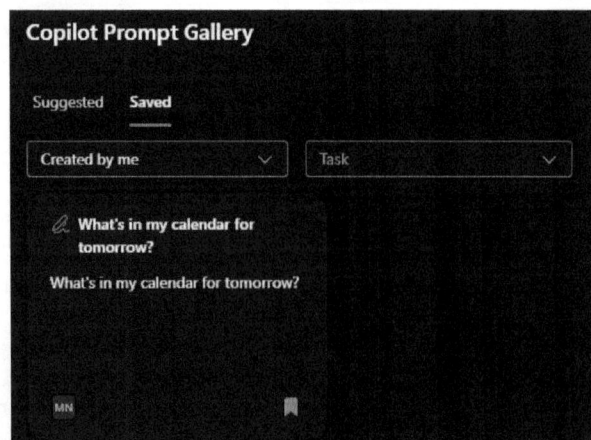

Figure 6.6: Copilot Prompt Gallery

Copilot in Outlook

With Copilot in Outlook, users can easily catch up, prepare, and follow-up on emails and tasks. This integration of Copilot in Outlook offers numerous advantages that can greatly enhance productivity, improve the clarity and professionalism of communications, and save time on routine tasks. The following are some compelling reasons for adopting Copilot in Outlook.

Summarizing emails

You can use Copilot to convert lengthy email threads into brief summaries. This feature is especially useful when dealing with extensive threads that have accumulated over time, allowing users to quickly grasp the main points and key decisions without reading through each message individually. By generating a concise summary, Copilot saves time and ensures that important information is not missed. This can be particularly beneficial for anyone needing to stay up to date with ongoing communications.

To summarize an email, select the email conversation that you want to summarize and click on **Summarize** at the top of the email thread as shown:

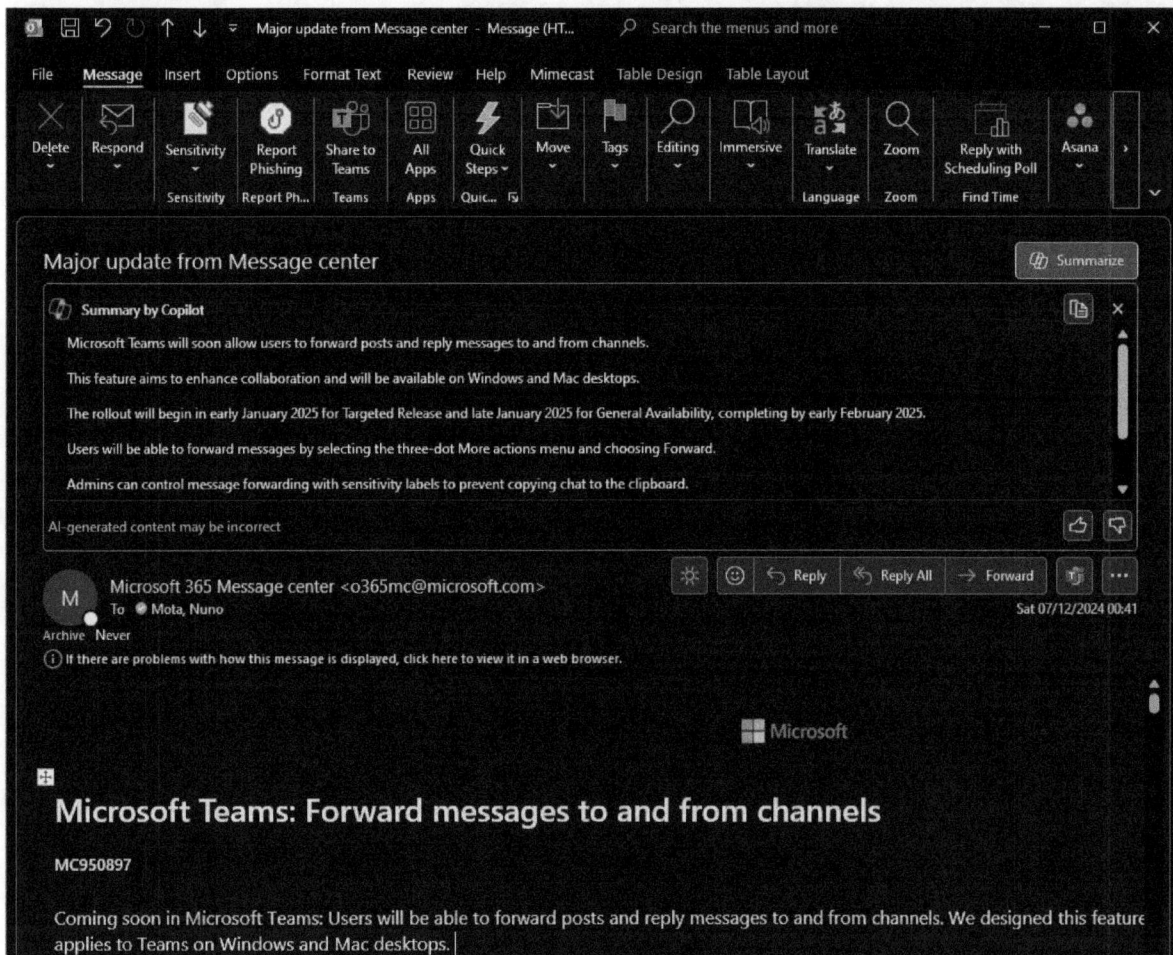

Figure 6.7: Summarizing an email thread with Copilot in Outlook for Windows

Copilot will scan the email thread, looking for key points, and will then create a summary for you, which will appear at the top of the email. The summary might include numbered citations that, when selected, take you to the corresponding email in the thread.

On your Outlook for iOS or Android, you can achieve the same by selecting the email you want to summarize and then clicking on the Copilot icon in the toolbar.

Drafting emails

Writing emails with Copilot is both intuitive and timesaving. By using a good prompt, Copilot can assist users in composing well-crafted emails effortlessly. This feature not only enhances productivity but can also ensure that emails are clear and professional.

A great benefit of using Copilot to draft emails is the ability to tailor responses to specific scenarios, such as a project launch, a formal complaint, etc. Users can simply input their desired prompt, and Copilot will generate a draft that can be reviewed and edited as needed. This automation reduces the time spent on routine email tasks, allowing users to focus on more strategic work, as shown:

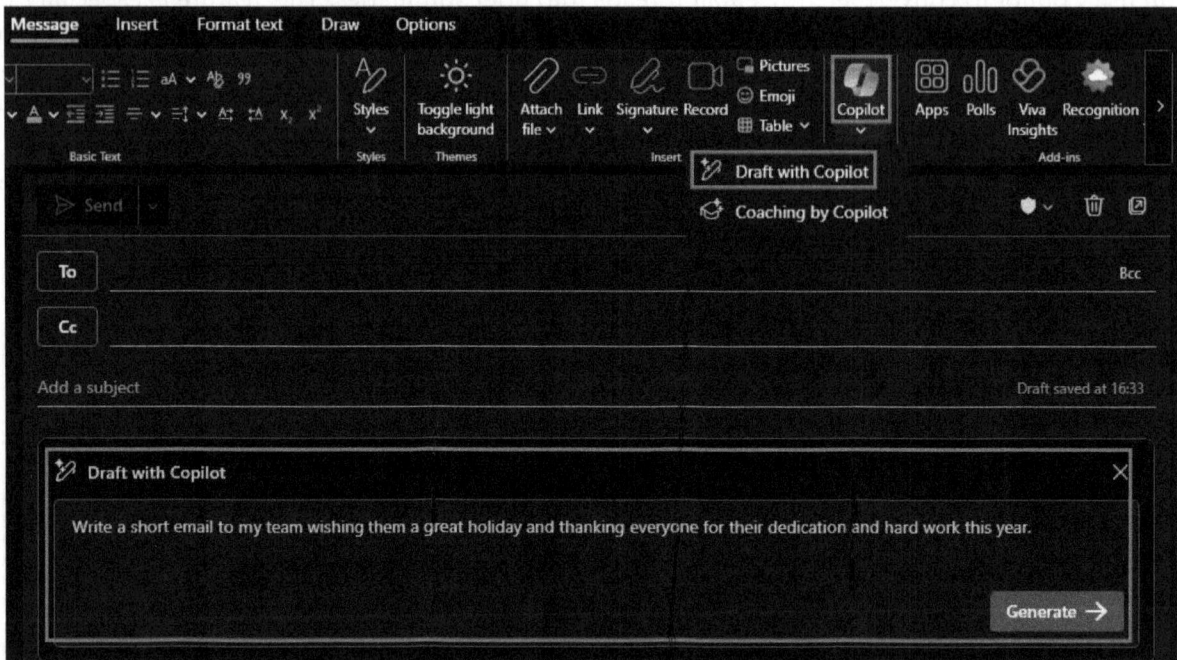

Figure 6.8: Composing a new email using Copilot in Outlook on the web

Once your prompt has been generated, you can select the options icon to modify your desired length and tone, as you can see in the following figure. Alternatively, you can ask Copilot to make whatever changes you want through a follow-up prompt, as follows:

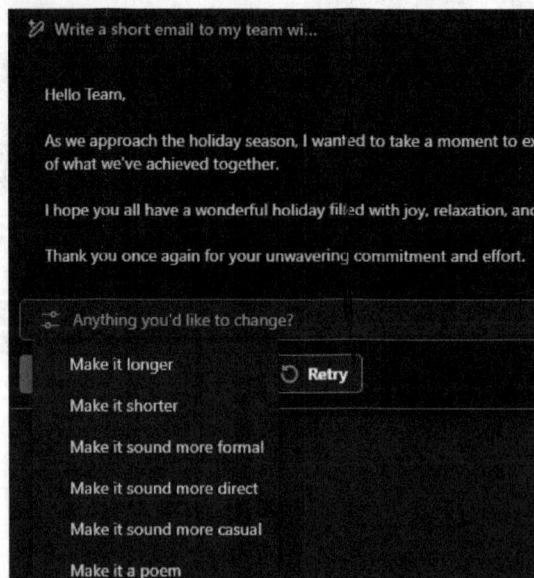

Figure 6.9: Making changes to an existing draft

Email coaching

Email coaching with Copilot in Outlook enhances users' email skills by providing suggestions for tone, clarity, and impact. It offers instant feedback on drafts, highlighting areas needing refinement, like complex sentences or unclear language. Users can follow these tips to make their messages concise and compelling.

Copilot also advises on email etiquette, from greetings and closings to polite language and information structure. This guidance benefits both new and experienced professionals aiming to improve their writing.

By automating drafting and editing, Copilot boosts productivity and ensures consistent communication. With its support, users can confidently send professional and precise emails, improving their effectiveness in digital correspondence.

The following figure shows an example of Copilot providing feedback on an email, coaching the user with suggested improvements:

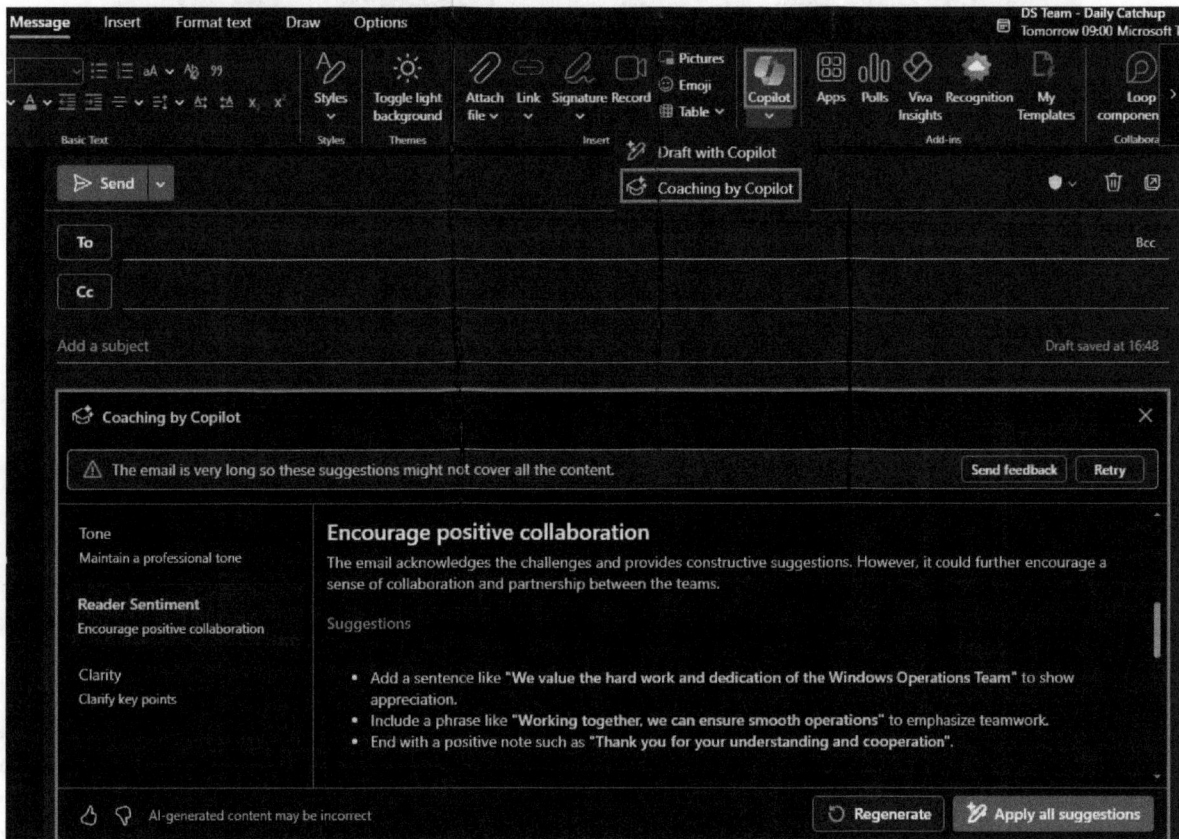

Figure 6.10: Email coaching with Copilot in Outlook

Schedule with Copilot

This feature in Outlook is a powerful tool designed to simplify and optimize the process of scheduling meetings and appointments. It leverages advanced AI capabilities to assist users in finding the best times for meetings by automatically analyzing the calendars of all participants and proposing meeting times that avoid conflicts, as shown:

Figure 6.11: Schedule with Copilot icon in Outlook on the web

Nothing new so far, but Copilot reviews all related emails in the thread and creates a comprehensive agenda with a summary of the conversation to date. This includes the main topics and any initial decisions, ensuring everyone is informed and prepared to participate:

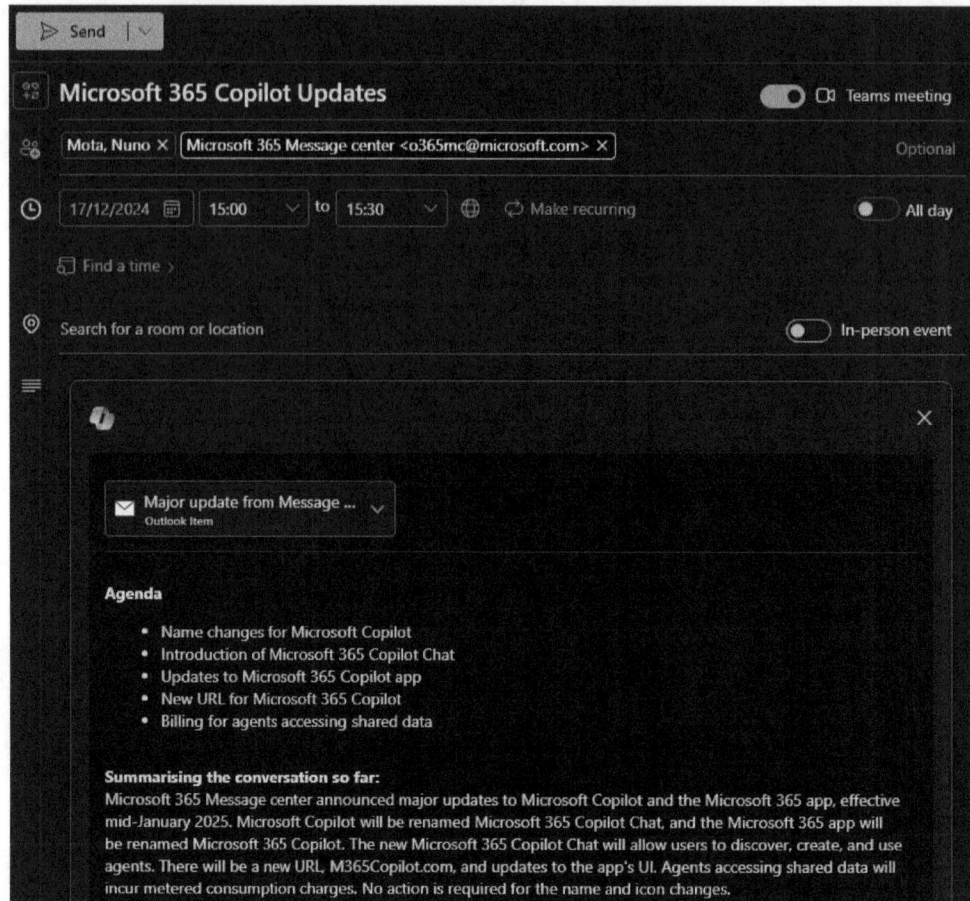

Figure 6.12: Schedule with Copilot agenda and summary

Copilot in Teams and Business Chat

Copilot in Teams and Business Chat transforms the way teams collaborate and communicate and can greatly improve users' productivity. In Teams, Copilot assists users by providing real-time suggestions and responses during chat interactions, catching up on missed meetings, planning a team-building activity, generating ideas for projects, drafting messages, summarizing previous discussions, providing information based on the context of the conversation, and more.

Copilot offers intelligent, contextual support that adapts to your specific needs. By integrating seamlessly into your daily workflow, Copilot ensures that you stay informed, engaged, and efficient in all your professional interactions.

Business Chat

Copilot helps integrate data from your documents, presentations, email, calendar, notes, and contacts in Teams. With this integration, Business Chat can easily provide summaries of projects, meetings, email messages, chats, and more. It can be used to find due dates, recent project updates, or recent communications from colleagues or managers efficiently.

To start using Business Chat, navigate to **https://www.microsoft365.com/chat**. Alternatively, within your Teams client, go to **Chat** on the left side of Teams and select **Copilot** from the top of your chat list:

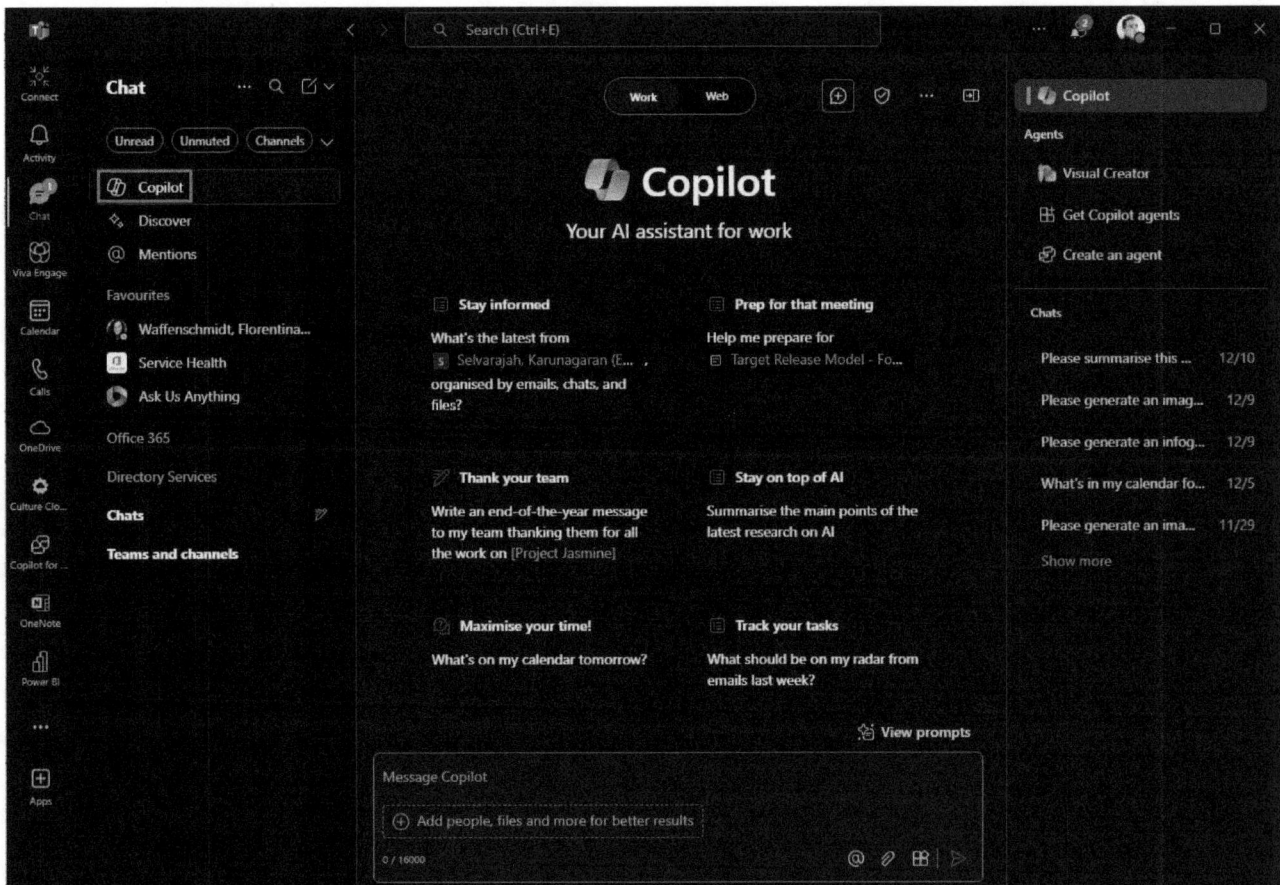

Figure 6.13: Schedule with Copilot agenda and summary

At the very top, you can choose **Work** or **Web** mode. Selecting **Work** enables Copilot to utilize your Microsoft 365 data, including files, emails, and Teams meetings and chats, in conjunction with the LLM. This mode might also incorporate live web content, depending on whether that setting is activated. Choosing **Web** mode ensures that Copilot is grounded solely in the LLM public data it was trained on and current web data, excluding any of your Microsoft 365 data. Both modes provide enterprise-level security, privacy, and compliance.

On the right side of the window, you have your prompt history, and at the bottom, the Copilot chat where you can type your prompt. Here are a few examples of prompts:

- `Summarize my recent messages from /Adina`
- `Summarize my last meeting`
- `Catch up on unread chats`
- `Summarize the documents, email, and chat messages about the Microsoft escalation that happened yesterday`

Once you send the prompt, Copilot will generate a response for you to review. You can obviously use your own prompt and be more specific. Let us say you want to make sure you have not missed any key details from Mark, the project manager you have been working with.

You could use a prompt like this one: `Provide a summary of messages from /Mark over the last two weeks. Highlight any important details, such as deliverables, due dates, and action items for me.`

Or, to summarize updates of a specific project, you could try something like this: `Provide a summary of the recent developments on Project X that would be important for an executive overseeing the product launch, based on collaborations from the past five business days.`

You can also ask broader questions, such as `What is the company policy on remote work?` If the data is available on the company's Intranet or in a public SharePoint Online site, Copilot should be able to find it and provide you with an answer.

It is important to note that Copilot can only access data that the user already has access to. This means that if the response to a prompt is in a file or location that the user does not have permission to access, Copilot will never present that data to the user since they do not have the necessary access rights. This ensures that data privacy and security are always maintained, and users can trust that they will only see information they are authorized to view.

Business Chat can also be used to create content. For example, to translate a complex topic into an easy-to-follow script, you could use a prompt like this: `I need to explain Topic A to a CEO, covering its definition, functionality, and value proposition. Create a script for this purpose, and include one analogy to help a non-technical person understand it.`

Or, if you want to create a presentation for leadership based on a Word file, use a prompt like this: `Help convert /Document1.docx into a 10-minute presentation for a non-technical audience. Include an agenda and for each item, include a duration, objective, and the key talking points. Assume the intended audience is C-suite to whom we will be introducing our product.`

Copilot in chats

Copilot in Teams chat and channels allows you to review the main points, action items, and decisions of conversations efficiently without needing to scroll through lengthy threads. Simply go to a chat in Teams and open Copilot using the icon in the upper-right corner of the chat:

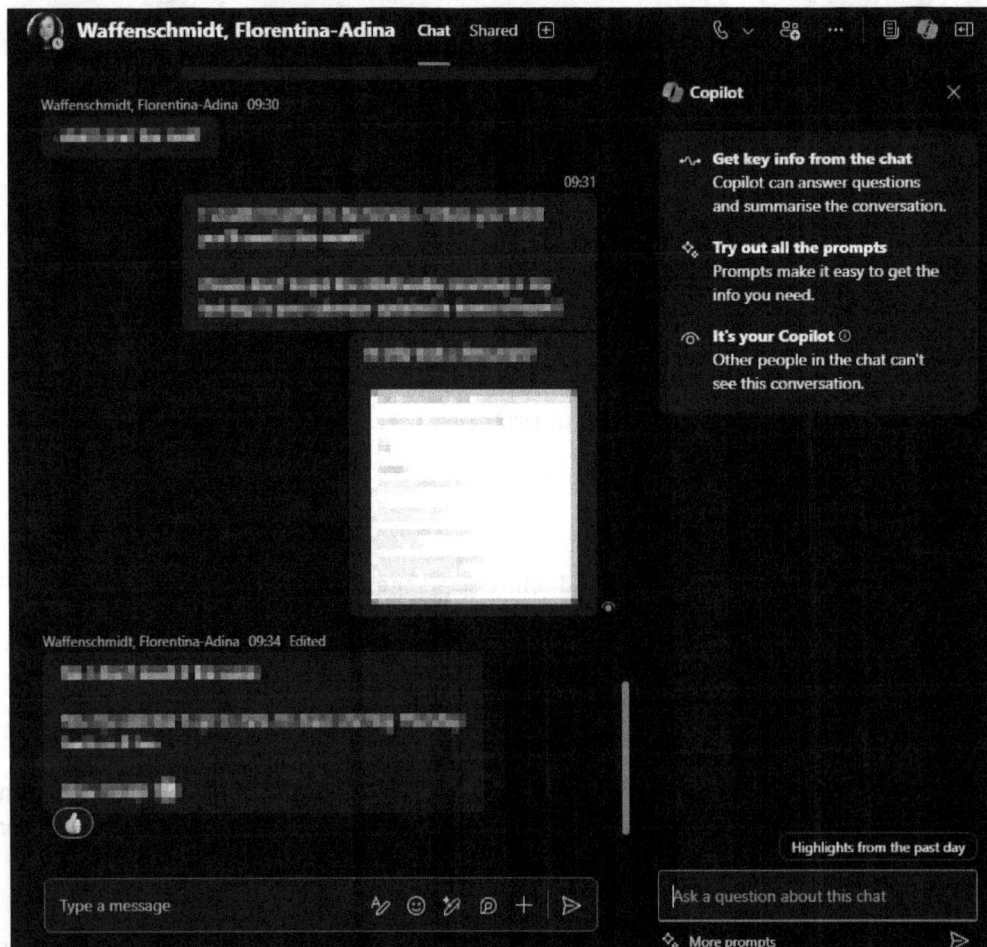

Figure 6.14: Copilot in a one-to-one chat

To the right of your chat box, you will find an option labeled **More prompts**, where you can select from various predefined prompts:

- `Highlights from the past day`
- `Highlights from the past 7 days`
- `Highlights from the past 30 days`
- `What decisions were made?`
- `What are the open items?`

Alternatively, ask Copilot what you would like it to do for you, such as `Summarize what I have missed` or `What were the key takeaways from last month?` and press **Send**. Copilot will reference information from the opened message thread, with a default 30-day history, unless you specify otherwise.

> **Note:** **Copilot does not summarize images, Loop components, or files shared in the chat thread.**

Copilot also enables users to draft responses or messages based on the content and context of the ongoing conversation and suggest edits or provide insights, all within the chat interface, as shown:

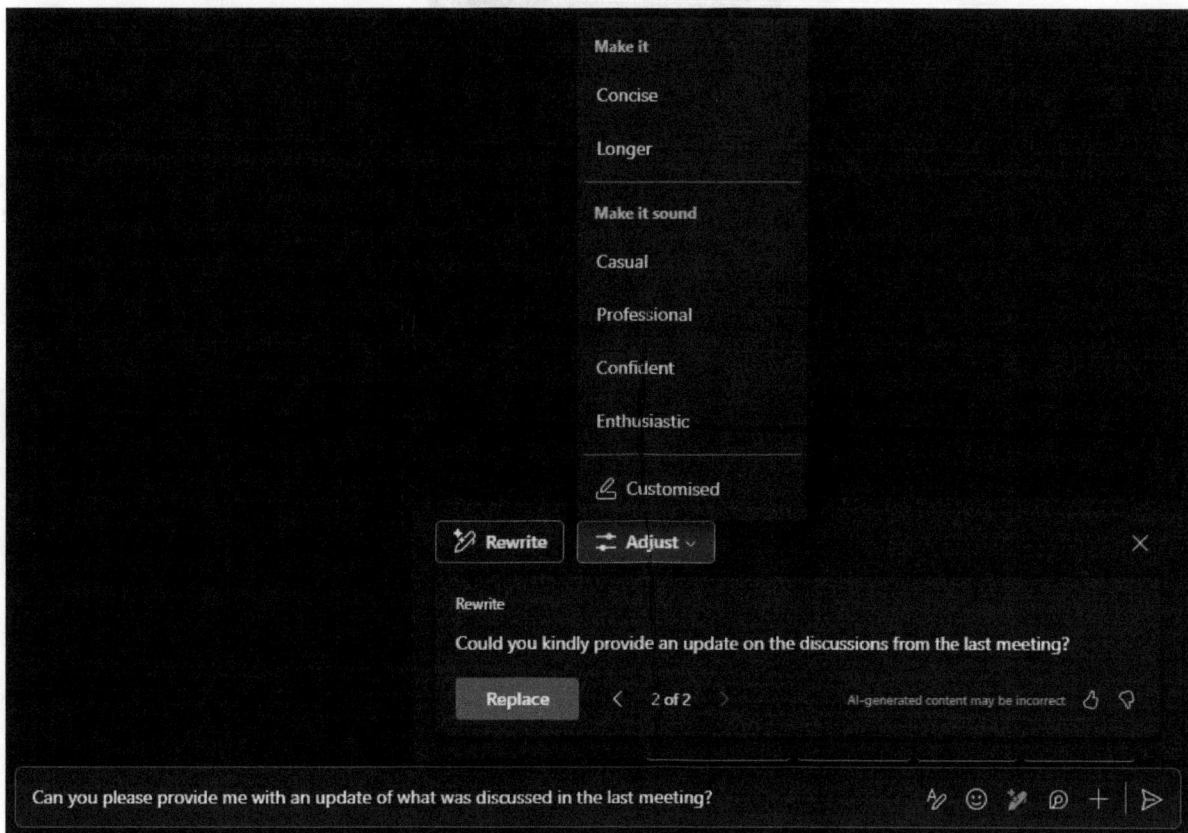

Figure 6.15: Drafting a chat message with Copilot

With **Rewrite**, Copilot can rewrite your message up to 10 times, always with a slight difference. To navigate between previous versions, use the left and right arrows located just below the text. You can modify just a specific part of your message by selecting that section and choosing **Rewrite** or **Adjust**. With **Adjust**, you can change the length and style of your message.

Once you are happy with the new message, click **Replace**. If you highlight part of your message, only that part will be updated.

Also in Teams chats, **AI notes** offer a current, shared summary of vital information, organized by topic as the conversation progresses. These notes capture key decisions, action items, and unresolved questions. They are automatically added to new chats, but it is possible you will have to enable it in existing chats. To do this, navigate to the one-to-one or group chat you would like to enable it for, select the **AI notes** icon in the top right corner of the chat, and click on **Turn on,** as shown:

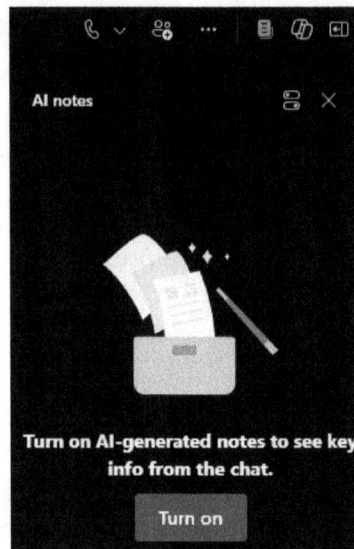

Figure 6.16: Enabling AI notes

As discussions continue, the AI-generated notes are automatically updated to reflect the most recent status of the chat in a concise and easily readable format. The following is an example of AI notes being updated in real-time during a meeting:

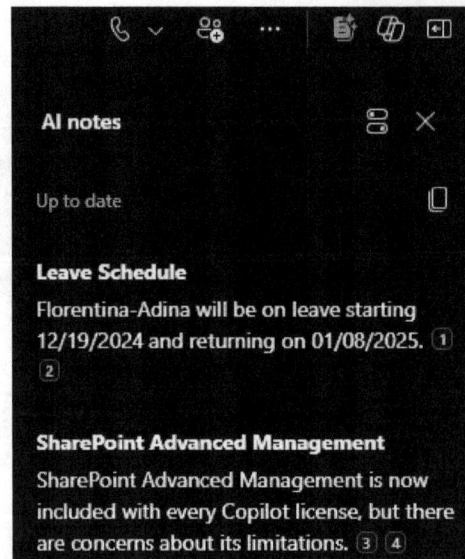

Figure 6.17: Example of an AI note in a one-to-one chat

As shown in *Figure 6.17*, each note summary has a reference to the original message(s) that the summary was generated from.

Note: **AI notes are not available in external chats or meeting chats.**

Copilot in meetings

To use Copilot in a Teams meeting, the meeting must be transcribed. If recording or transcribing confidential meetings in Teams is not preferred, Copilot can still be used when it is set to *Only during the meeting* in the Meeting options:

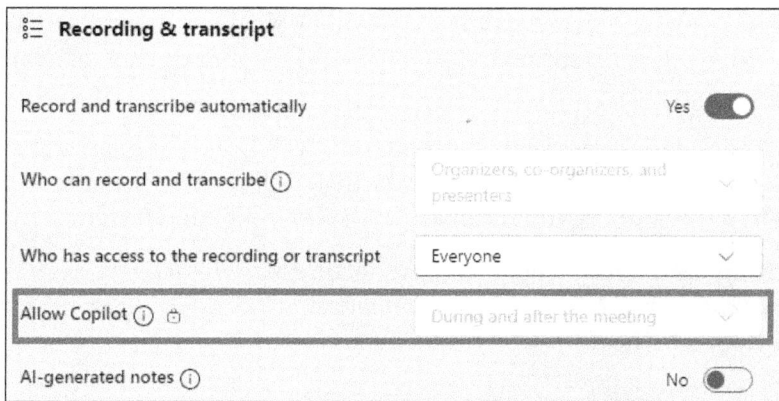

Figure 6.18: Copilot in meetings setting

Please note that if this option is selected, Copilot will not be available in the meeting's **Recap** tab after the meeting has finished. As the name suggests, Copilot will only be available during the meeting and not afterward.

During Teams meetings, Copilot can summarize discussion points, note who said what, highlight alignments or disagreements, suggest action items, and answer questions in real time. If your meeting is transcribed, Copilot references the transcript in its responses. Otherwise, it will use the meeting chat conversation instead. Copilot offers various prompts, some of which are listed as follows, but you can use your own prompts as always:

- `Recap the meeting`
- `List action items`
- `Suggest follow-up questions`
- `What questions are unresolved?`
- `List different perspectives by topic`
- `List the main ideas we discussed`
- `Generate meeting notes`
- `Highlights from the meeting chat`

Copilot will provide a prompt 10 minutes before the scheduled conclusion of a meeting to assist participants in wrapping up. By selecting **Open Copilot**, you can view a summary of key discussion points and identify subsequent steps, including tasks assigned to specific individuals. Additionally, Copilot can be queried to determine if there are any unresolved issues or open topics from the agenda, as well as any other relevant questions that may facilitate the conclusion of the meeting.

After the meeting ends, Copilot provides summaries of discussion points and generates notes reflecting the current status of the chat. These summaries include references to the original messages for clarity and context. Copilot also outlines follow-up questions and unresolved issues to ensure that all important details are noted.

You can also access Copilot after a meeting has ended from the **Recap** tab in the meeting chat. Note that previous chats with Copilot in recurring meetings will be lost if a later meeting is transcribed.

Copilot in Word

Copilot in Word revolutionizes the writing experience by providing ideas and overcoming writer's block. Copilot adapts to your writing style and preferences over time, offering personalized recommendations that align with your unique writing style. Here are some of Copilot's key capabilities in Word:

- **Drafting documents**: Copilot can generate drafts, offer inspiration, and improve content, ensuring professional documents. It can rewrite paragraphs, create outlines, or brainstorm concepts, providing valuable AI-driven assistance.

- **Overcoming writer's block**: When experiencing writer's block, Copilot can offer ideas and suggestions to assist you in progressing. By supplying prompts and inspiration, it aids in maintaining continuous creativity and productivity.

- **Personalized recommendations**: With continued use of Copilot, it adapts to your writing style and preferences, providing customized suggestions that reflect your writing style. This personalized service ensures that the support you receive is both pertinent and efficient.

- **Interactive drafting tool**: Copilot lets you draft documents interactively. Start a new document using the *What do you want Copilot to draft?* box or enhance an existing document by selecting the Copilot icon next to the cursor. In the *Draft with Copilot* box, type prompts to get content generated that can be refined further.

- **Contextual enhancements**: for optimal results, Copilot enables users to provide supplementary context. The more comprehensive the information provided, the more detailed and specific the generated drafts will be. You can also utilize existing documents as sources by clicking on the paper clip icon and selecting the pertinent document.

Drafting documents

Copilot can generate an initial draft, provide inspiration, and enhance existing content. It can help make sure your documents are polished and professional, making it easier to communicate effectively. Copilot can also generate ideas and suggestions to help overcome writer's block. Whether you need to rewrite a paragraph, create an outline, or brainstorm new concepts, Copilot's AI-powered capabilities provide valuable inspiration and support.

On a new document, you can use the **What do you want Copilot to draft?** box at the top of the document to get started. Here is an example in Word for the web:

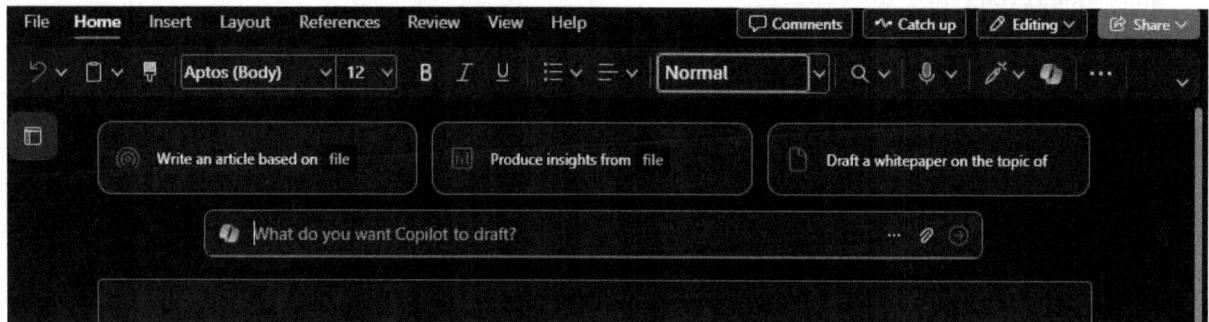

Figure 6.19: Drafting with Copilot in Word for the web on a new empty document

If you have already started working on the document, you select the Copilot icon next to the cursor on an empty line, or press *ALT + I*, to open the **Draft with Copilot** box:

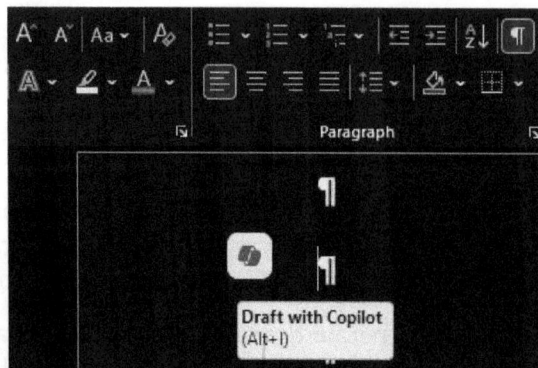

Figure 6.20: Drafting with Copilot in Word for the web on an existing document

In the *Draft with Copilot* box, type or paste your prompt, for example, *write an article on the significance of establishing a work-life balance* and press **Generate**. Copilot will then draft the new content for you. After Copilot has generated the content, you can choose to **Keep it** to retain the content, **Regenerate** to create a new response, **Discard** to remove the content, or refine the draft by entering specific details into the compose box, such as *make it more concise* or *make it sound more professional*.

For improved results, provide Copilot with additional context. The more information you give, the more detailed and specific Copilot's draft will be. For example, you can tell Copilot to use an existing document as a source by clicking on the paper clip icon and then selecting the document from the list that appears or by typing / followed by the name of the document.

In the **Draft with Copilot** dialog, you can also select **Inspire me** to have Copilot generate additional text based on the existing content in your document.

Editing existing content

A useful way to use Copilot in Word is to assist in improving your writing. Simply select the paragraph you want to edit and select the Copilot icon in the left margin of your document. From the Copilot menu, click on **Auto Rewrite**, as shown:

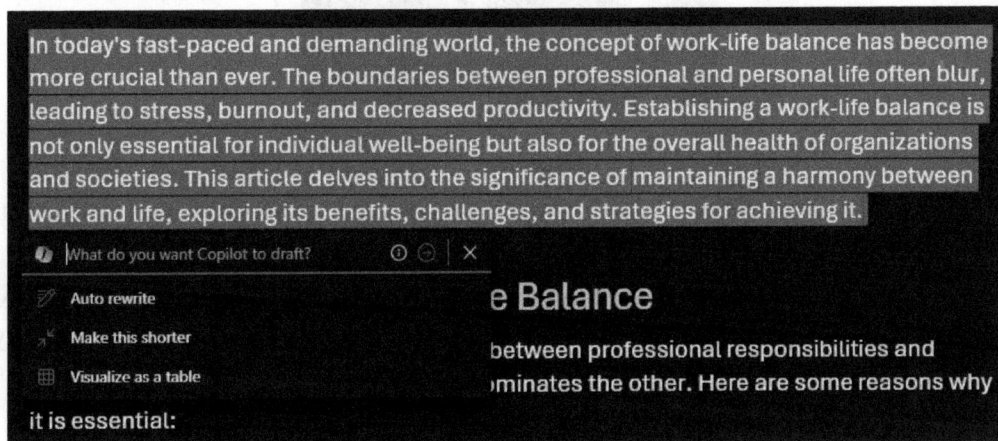

Figure 6.21: Auto rewrite with Copilot in Word for the web

Copilot will show you three revised options to choose from. Select **Replace** to use the chosen revised text, **Insert below** to insert the revised text below the current text, **Regenerate** to regenerate Copilot's suggestions, or type the changes you would like Copilot to make. Instead of rewriting content, you can also visualize it as a table, which can be useful in certain scenarios.

Image generation

Copilot can also help you generate banners or images for your documents and presentations. Provide a description in your prompt, and Copilot will create images based on your specifications. For example, instruct Copilot to `Generate an image of a futuristic office with lots of natural light and many gadgets`. The more specific your prompt is, the more accurately the image will align with your requirements.

The following is an example of images generated by Copilot using a simple prompt:

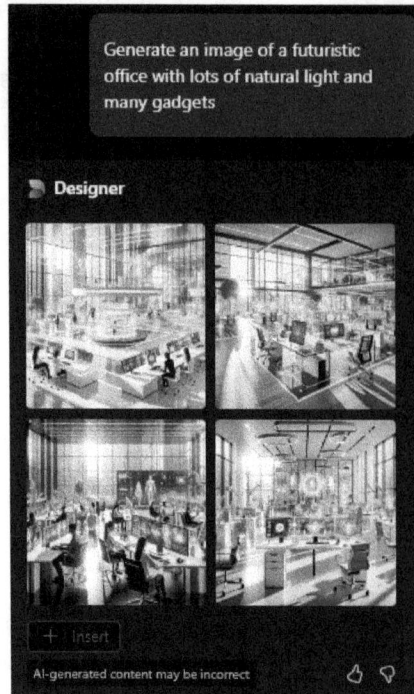

Figure 6.22: *Generating images with Copilot*

Copilot leverages *Designer's Image Creator*, which utilizes an advanced DALL-E 3 model, to generate AI-crafted images in Business Chat, PowerPoint, and Word.

Creating an image is very different from searching for stock images. The **Designer's Image Creator** is most effective when detailed descriptions are provided, including adjectives, locations, or artistic styles such as *digital art* or *photorealistic*. To generate a brand image, it is important to include the term *brand* in your prompt.

Here is an example of how to create an extended, more detailed prompt:

- **Original prompt**: `Create an image of a cat`
- **Descriptive prompt**: `Create a close-up photo of a cat in a busy urban area at sunset`

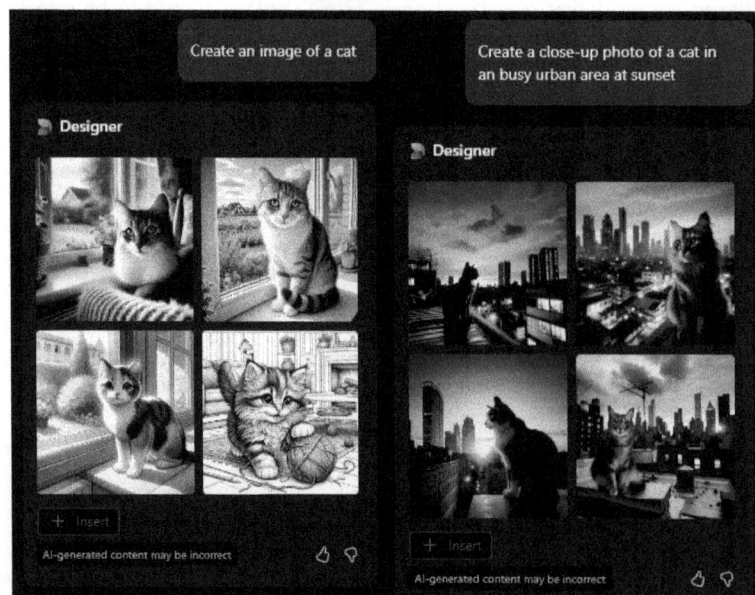

Figure 6.23: *A basic vs. a descriptive prompt in Copilot*

Chat with Copilot

Copilot in Word can both create content and answer questions about the document you are reading. For example, you can ask Copilot to *summarize this document* in the chat pane to receive a summarized version in bullet points or *is there a call to action?* to have Copilot check if the document has a clear call to action. After Copilot responds to a prompt, it also provides references with citations from the document where the information was sourced.

You can also ask an open-ended question if you would like to enhance your document with additional content or context or simply get answers from the document.

For instance:

- `How can I revise this document to make it more professional?`
- `Are there any quotes in this document about work-life balance?`

Another very useful feature is having Copilot summarize a document, especially a lengthy one. This allows users to quickly grasp the key points and essential information without having to read through the entire document.

Upon opening a document, you may view a summary that allows you to scan and identify the topics covered within the document. The summary will be presented in a collapsed or partially open section at the top of the document, as shown:

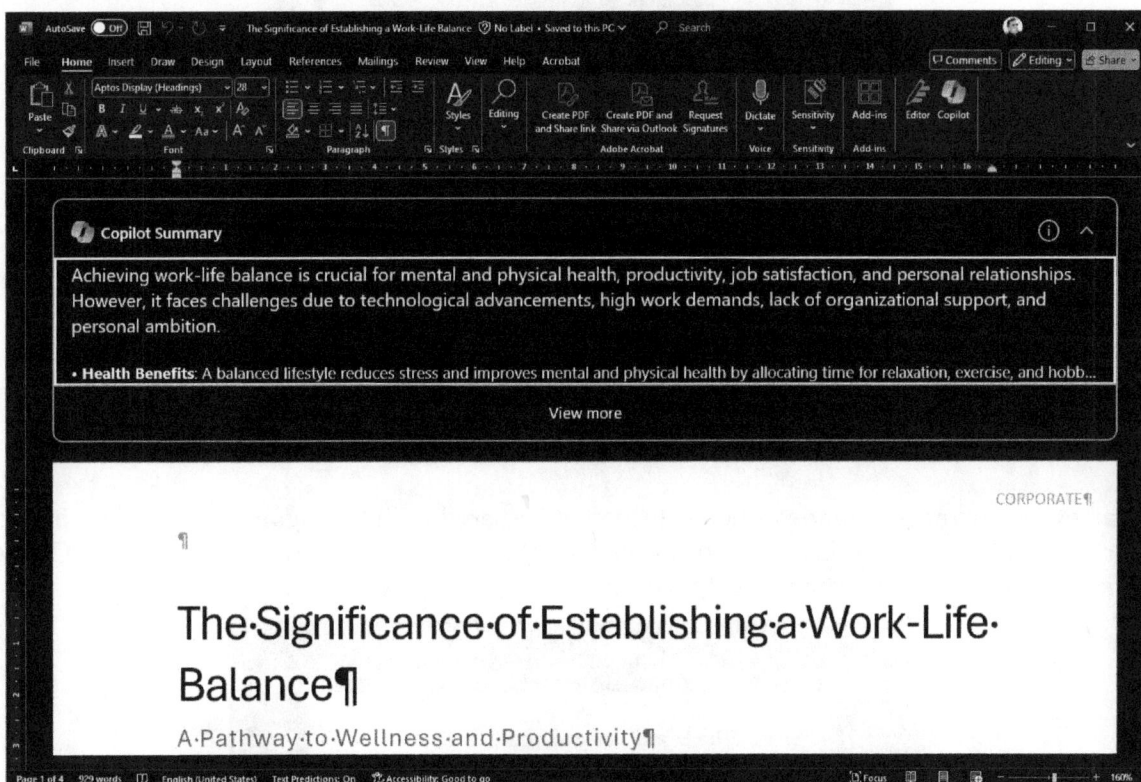

Figure 6.24: Automatic summary with Copilot

To view the complete summary, select the **expand summary** down arrow. To customize the summary or ask follow-up questions about the documents, select the **Open in chat** option at the bottom of the summary and enter your prompt.

If a summary is not automatically generated, select Copilot from the ribbon to open the Copilot pane and either select the suggested **Summarize this doc** option or type **summarize this document** in Copilot's compose box. You can also ask Copilot to **explain this document in three sentences**, as shown:

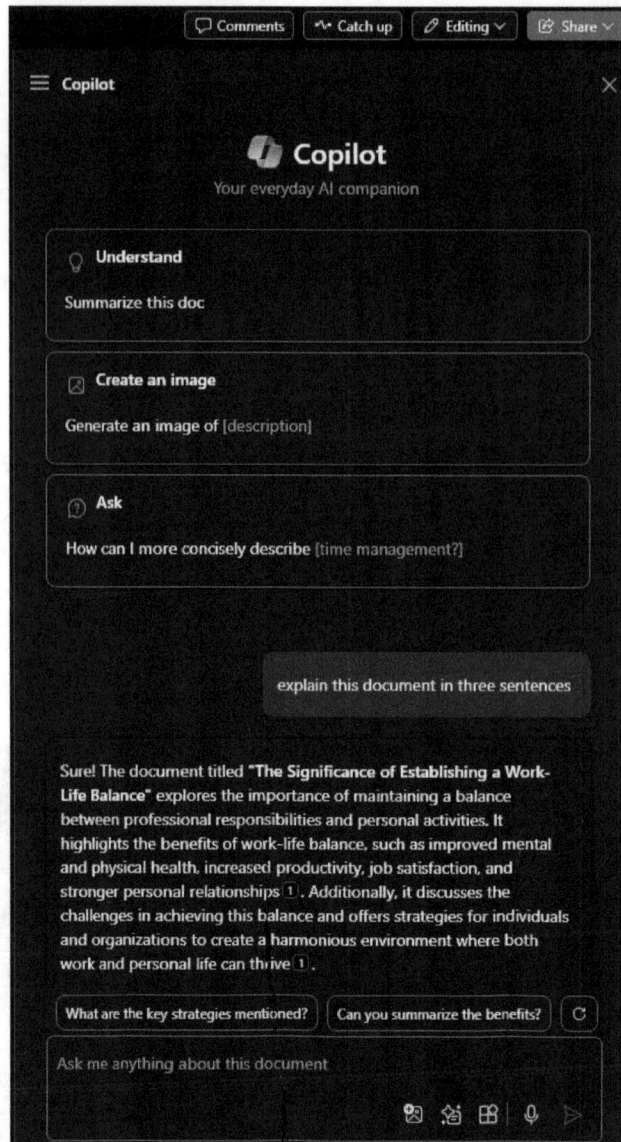

Figure 6.25: *Asking Copilot to summarize a document*

Copilot can even generate summaries when a document is shared with colleagues: click on the **Share** button and then click **Share** again in the list. Click the Copilot logo icon within the *Add a message* box, and Copilot will generate a summary of the document to help with the sharing, as shown:

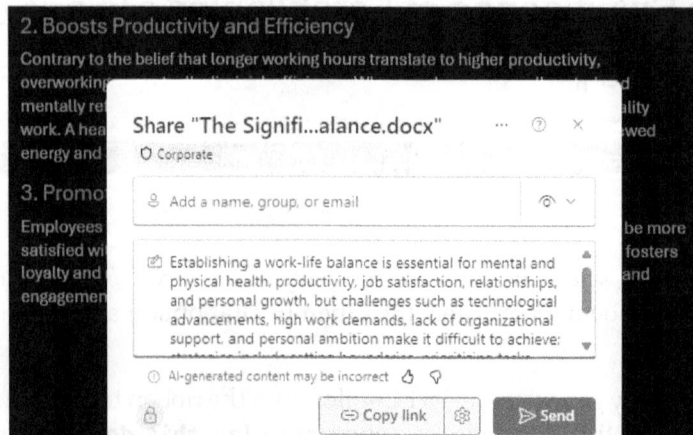

Figure 6.26: *Summarizing a document with Copilot when sharing it*

Copilot in PowerPoint

Copilot in PowerPoint is designed to enhance your presentation creation experience by offering intelligent assistance and suggestions. Whether you need help drafting a new presentation or refining an existing one, Copilot offers a variety of tools to streamline the process.

Creating presentations

When creating a new presentation in PowerPoint, Copilot will automatically present you with the option to **Create a presentation about** or **Create a presentation from file**, as shown:

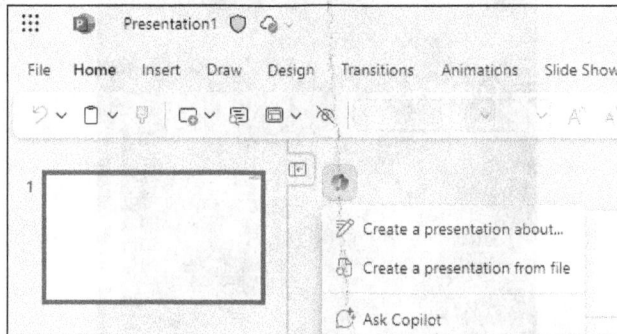

Figure 6.27: Creating a new presentation using Copilot in PowerPoint

If you choose the first option, provide a description of the presentation you would like Copilot to help draft, and Copilot will generate relevant topics and content to assist you with getting started. This feature, called **Narrative Builder**, uses your prompt and file (if one was provided) to turn your work into a compelling narrative, allowing you to guide the story and create a draft with the right flow and information. Next, review and amend the topics generated by Copilot as needed. To refine your prompt and generate a new set of topics, just select the pencil button. To add a topic, select the + button and provide a detailed description of your topic. Once you are satisfied with your topics, select **Generate slides,** and Copilot will prepare a draft presentation for you to review, as follows:

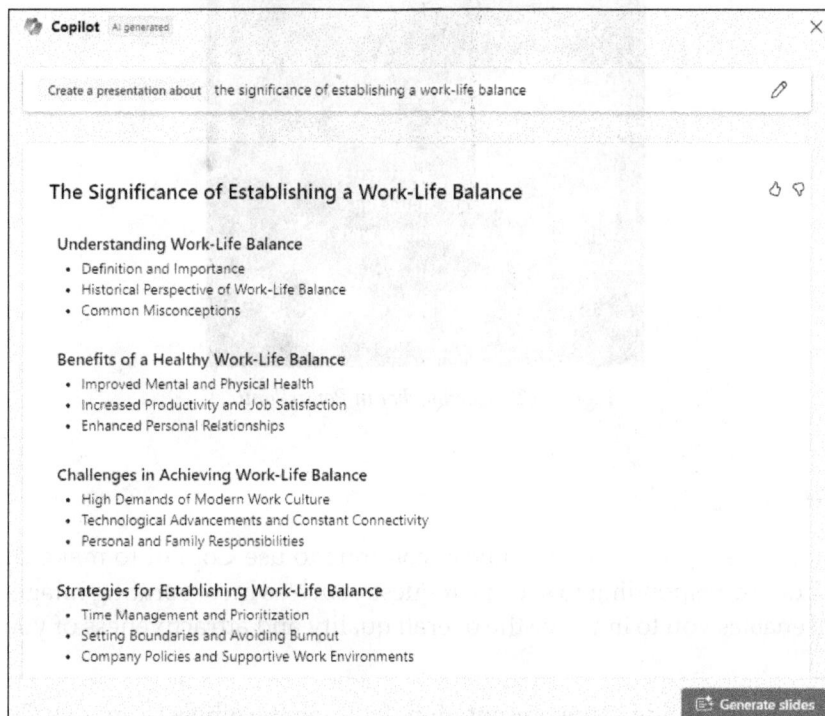

Figure 6.28: Presentation draft using Copilot in PowerPoint

With the **Create a presentation from file** option, you can upload a file for Copilot to reference, ensuring that the generated content aligns with your expectations. This option also makes it possible to create a presentation based on an existing theme or corporate template.

You can also use Copilot chat to create a presentation from scratch or from an existing file by selecting the relevant option and completing the prompt with what you would like Copilot to help you draft:

Figure 6.29: Copilot chat in PowerPoint

Editing presentations

Once Copilot generates a draft presentation, you can continue to use Copilot to make changes to it. Copilot can help refine your slides by responding to specific requests, such as incorporating images or adjusting visual elements. This feature enables you to improve the overall quality and attractiveness of your presentation with minimal effort.

Suppose you want to add a final slide to the presentation thanking the whole team. Ask Copilot in PowerPoint to **add a final slide to thank the entire team for their help with the presentation**:

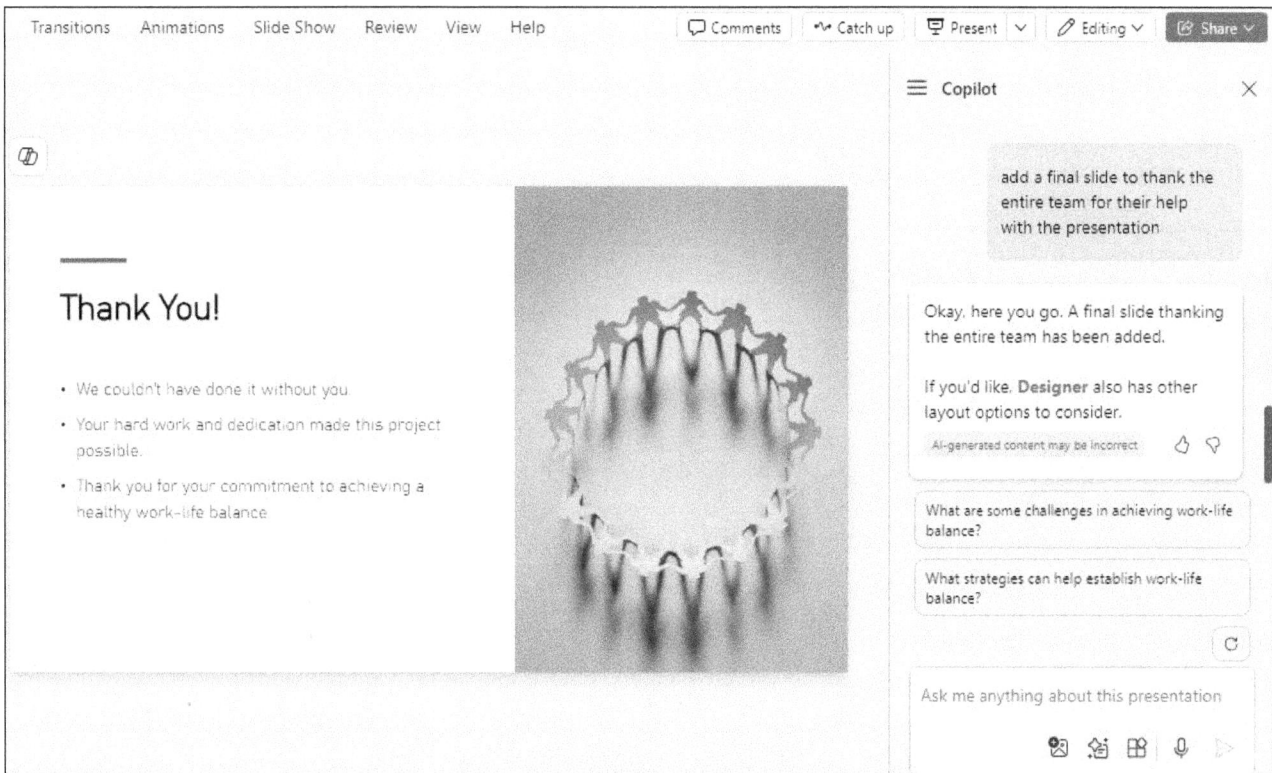

Figure 6.30: *Editing a presentation using Copilot in PowerPoint*

Copilot can also assist in selecting stock images for your presentation by instructing Copilot to *add an image that symbolizes work-life balance,* and it will search through the stock images to find and insert an appropriate image from the collection. Similar to what we have seen with Word in the previous section, you can ask Copilot to *create an image,* and it will use DALL-E 3 to generate an AI-created image that can be incorporated into your presentation.

When creating a presentation, you might be uncertain about how to structure your slides into sections. Copilot can assist by organizing the slides into sections and adding section heading slides. To achieve this, just ask Copilot to *organize this presentation.* If you find that Copilot's changes are not to your preference, you may click the *Undo* button on the ribbon to revert your presentation to its prior state.

To change the style of an existing presentation, open the Copilot pane and request Copilot to *try a new design.* This will alter the theme of your entire presentation, and you can repeat this process multiple times until you find a suitable design.

Summarizing presentations

If you need to get an overview of a presentation, Copilot can provide a summarized bullet-point overview. This feature allows you to understand the key elements of the presentation. Simply ask Copilot to `summarize this presentation`, and Copilot will summarize it for you and even include references to show where it pulled information from in the presentation:

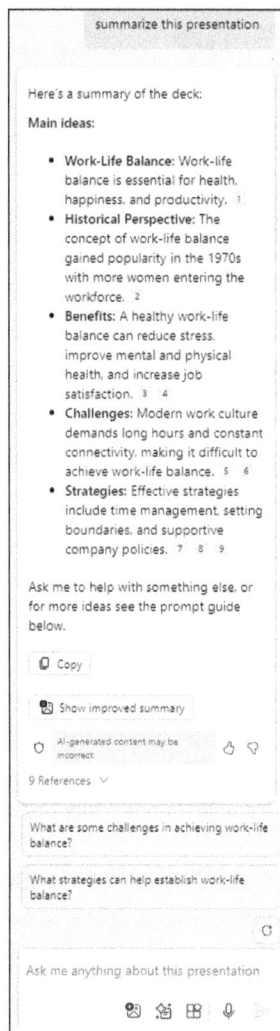

Figure 6.31: Summarizing a presentation using Copilot in PowerPoint

You can even ask Copilot to **show me the key slides** to have Copilot determine which slides might be significant for review.

Copilot in Excel

Copilot in Excel is a powerful tool designed to enhance your productivity and efficiency when working with spreadsheets. Copilot can assist with data by suggesting formula columns, displaying insights in charts and PivotTables, and highlighting notable data, ensuring that your work is both accurate and insightful.

To use Copilot in Excel, there are a few requirements that you need to meet:

1. First, ensure that your workbook is stored on OneDrive or SharePoint Online.

2. Secondly, it is crucial that your data is formatted correctly. This will help Copilot understand and interact with your data more effectively, enabling it to provide accurate assistance with your tasks. This is done by having the data in either an Excel table or as a supported range.

Visualizing and understanding data

Visualization is an area where Copilot excels. Whether you need to create charts, graphs, or pivot tables, Copilot can generate informative representations of your data. You can specify the type of visualization you need, and Copilot will take care of the rest, ensuring that your data is presented in an effective way.

After formatting your data, go to the ribbon, select Copilot to open the chat pane, and type your prompt. For example, `Create a bar graph showing the sales growth between 2023 and 2024`:

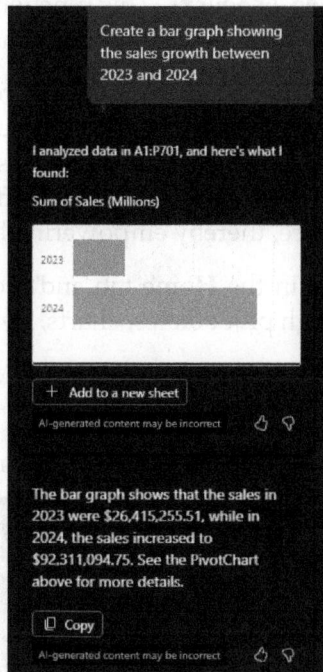

Figure 6.32: Creating charts using Copilot in Excel

If you are happy with the graph, you can click on **Add to new sheet,** and Copilot will add the graph to your Excel document, together with the corresponding pivot table, if applicable.

Copilot enables you to efficiently highlight, sort, and filter tables, drawing attention to critical information. Simply provide Copilot with instructions on how you would prefer to adjust the table for an improved view of specific data sections. For example, let us ask Copilot to `bold the top 10 values and highlight the highest value in the Sales column`:

Figure 6.33: Highlighting data using Copilot in Excel

Sorting and filtering data can be accomplished by providing Copilot with specific criteria. For instance, you can instruct Copilot to **sort the table by Gross Sales from largest to smallest**, or to **filter the table to display only the highest performing products**. This functionality enables users to concentrate on the most relevant information at a glance, thereby enhancing the efficiency and precision of data analysis.

Copilot is capable of providing insights derived from your data or responding to specific inquiries you may have regarding your data. By leveraging sophisticated algorithms and data processing techniques, Copilot can quickly sift through extensive datasets to extract meaningful patterns and trends. Whether you are looking to understand sales performance, customer behavior, or operational efficiency, Copilot's insights will help you translate raw data into actionable intelligence, thereby empowering better decision-making.

Click on the **Copilot** button on the ribbon in the **Home** tab and then select **Understand**. Copilot will then process your data to display insights through pivot tables, charts, trends, summaries, or even anomalies.

Alternatively, describe your query regarding your data using clear and precise language in the Copilot prompt box. Copilot will then try to extract the information you are after.

The following are the two examples of Copilot extracting information based on our data:

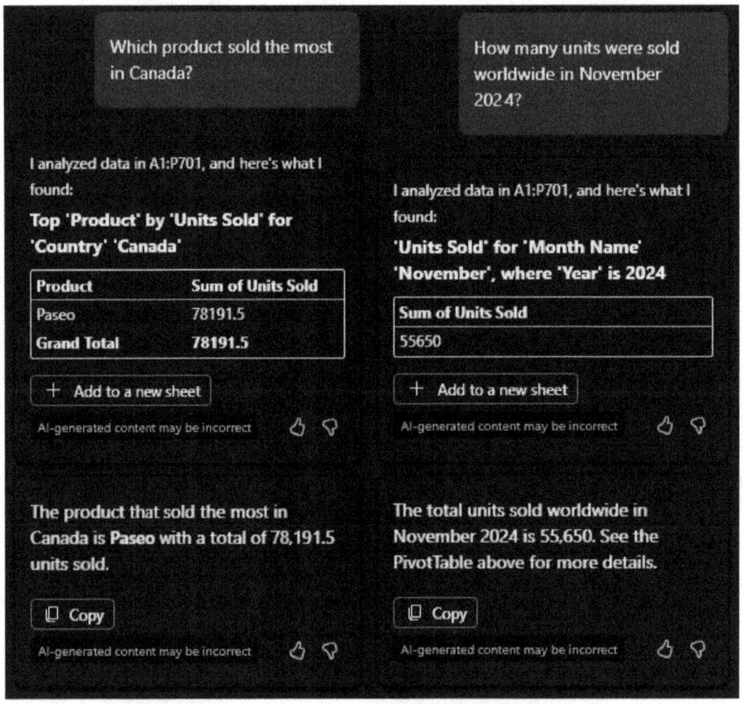

Figure 6.34: Data insights using Copilot in Excel

Additionally, Copilot can help clean your data. Copilot will identify and rectify issues, standardize formats, and ensure that your dataset is prepared for analysis.

Generating formulas

A great feature of Copilot in Excel is its capability to generate complex formulas and functions effortlessly within your table to perform calculations based on existing data. By merely describing the desired outcome, Copilot will formulate the necessary function on your behalf. For instance, a formula column may be used to compute the total cost per product, or a calculated row might sum up the total sales for each quarter. This functionality eliminates the necessity of manually entering calculations for each row or column, thereby streamlining your workflow, ensuring accuracy, and saving time.

Open an Excel workbook stored on OneDrive or SharePoint and select the **Copilot** button on the ribbon in the **Home** tab. Choose **Suggest a formula column** from the Copilot chat panel on the right:

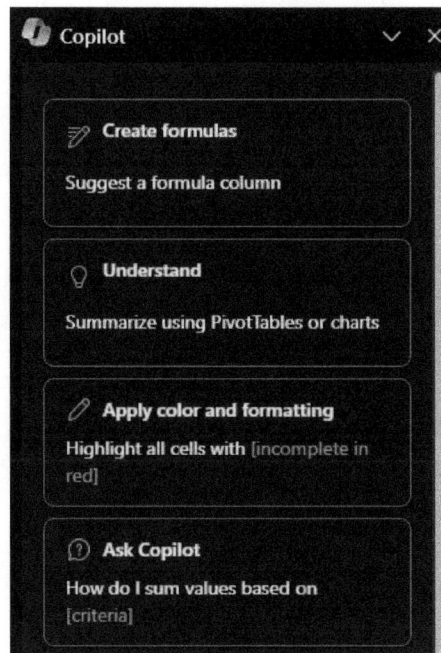

Figure 6.35: Copilot chat in Excel

Copilot provides one or more formula suggestions with an explanation of how each formula works:

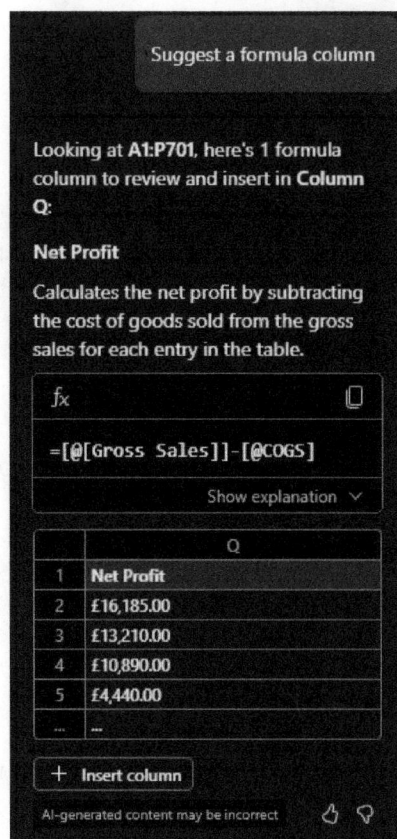

Figure 6.36: Copilot formula suggestion in Excel

If you are happy with the formula, click on **Insert column** to add it to your table.

Alternatively, type your request by explaining what you would like to achieve, and Copilot will try to convert that into a formula. You can even reference columns by their title:

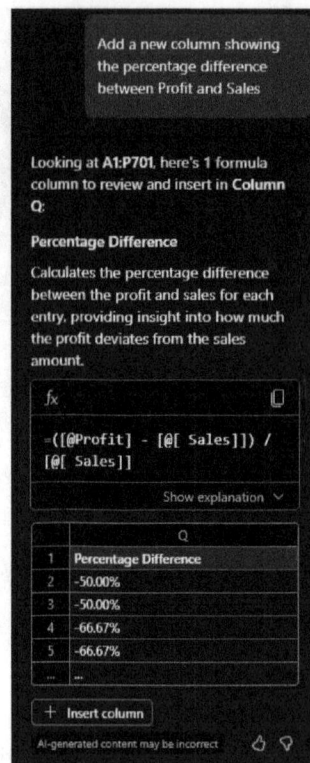

Figure 6.37: Generating formulas using Copilot in Excel

Conclusion

In this chapter, we explored Microsoft Copilot, an AI-driven tool designed to enhance productivity and creativity. We looked at the different versions and uses of Copilot across various Microsoft 365 applications, such as Outlook, Teams, Word, PowerPoint, and Excel, and how Copilot can assist users in managing emails, drafting documents, analyzing data, designing presentations, and facilitating team collaboration overall.

Throughout this chapter, readers have learned about the transformative potential of Copilot and its integration within the Microsoft ecosystem, leveraging large language models to revolutionize user interactions and workflows.

In the next chapter, we will progress into the realm of document and content management with SharePoint Online.

Join our Discord space

Join our Discord workspace for latest updates, offers, tech happenings around the world, new releases, and sessions with the authors:

https://discord.bpbonline.com

CHAPTER 7

SharePoint

Introduction

In this chapter, we will embark on an exploration of SharePoint Online, a pivotal service within the Office 365 suite.

SharePoint Online is not merely a solution for document storage, it is a powerful platform that enhances collaboration and facilitates the seamless distribution of information across an organization. Users can efficiently store and organize their documents, collaborate effortlessly with team members, and create and customize webpages to meet their specific needs.

Additionally, SharePoint Online serves as an invaluable tool for building intranets, enabling organizations to share relevant information and foster a connected and informed workplace.

Structure

This chapter covers the following topics:

- SharePoint overview
- Understanding site types
- Lists and document libraries
- Permissions in SharePoint Online
- SharePoint information architecture
- Search in SharePoint Online
- Site pages

Objectives

By the end of this chapter, you will understand the fundamental concepts and features of SharePoint Online. You will be able to identify and differentiate between the major site types available and their differences. You will gain a comprehensive understanding of SharePoint's information architecture and its significance and learn about lists and document libraries, components that help you boost collaboration and productivity. You will also learn how to manage permissions to ensure data security and compliance. Additionally, you will explore the search functionality in SharePoint Online, enabling you to find relevant information quickly and accurately. Furthermore, you will discover how site pages can help you organize content and enhance communication and information sharing within an organization.

SharePoint overview

SharePoint Online, part of Microsoft 365, is a cloud-based service empowering collaboration and content management. Initially launched as an on-premises tool, SharePoint evolved into a robust online platform, offering seamless integration with Microsoft services like Teams and Outlook to enhance productivity and teamwork.

Licensing in SharePoint Online

To access all core features of SharePoint Online, a minimum requirement is the stand-alone **SharePoint (Plan 1)** subscription. Additionally, SharePoint is included in the following Microsoft 365 subscriptions:

- **Business plans**: Basic, Standard, Premium
- **Enterprise plans**:
  - **Microsoft 365**: E3, E5
  - **Office 365**: E1, E3, E5
  - **Frontline**: F1, F3
  - **Government**: Microsoft 365 G3, Microsoft 365 G5, Office 365 G3, Office 365 G5
  - All nonprofit offers

SharePoint start page access and site creation

Accessing the SharePoint start page from the browser can be achieved by navigating to **https://www.m365. cloud.microsoft**, signing in with your work or school account and selecting SharePoint from the app launcher.

Once the SharePoint start page is loaded, you can easily view the sites you follow and the most frequently visited sites, provided there are existing sites where you have been granted access. Here you can also create a new SharePoint site.

Note: **The ability for an end-user to create a SharePoint site is managed in the SharePoint admin center. If you do not see the option to create a SharePoint site on the SharePoint start page, it means that the self-service site creation feature is disabled at the tenant level, and site creation can only be performed by a SharePoint administrator.**

To create a new SharePoint site, click on **Create site** on the SharePoint start page. You will be prompted to select the type of site you want to create:

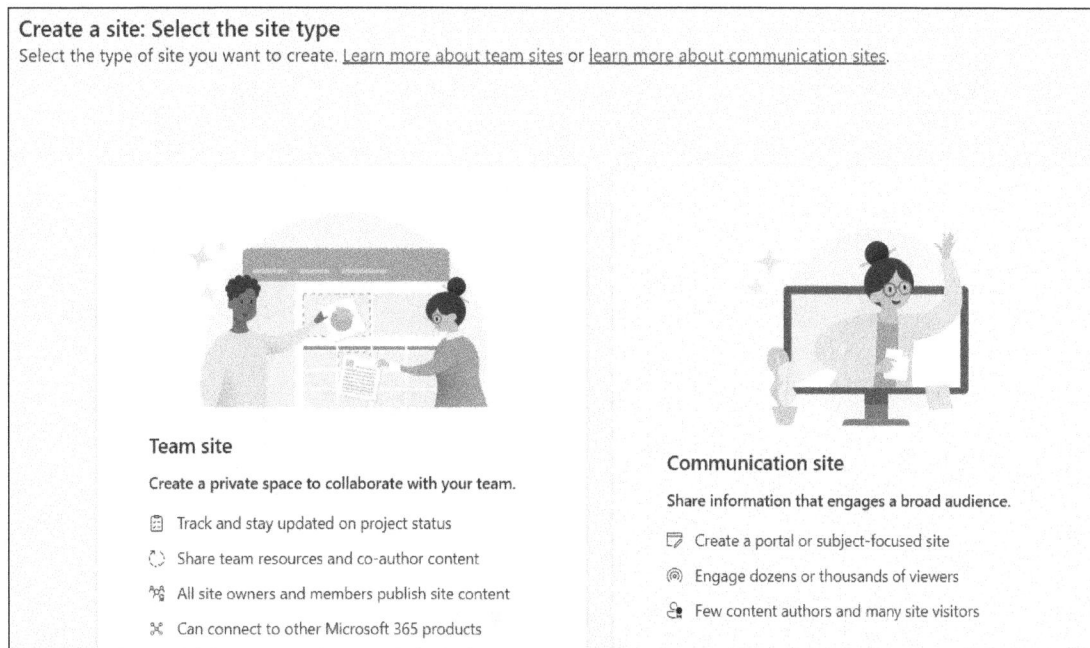

Figure 7.1: *Select the site type*

You can select one of the two options available:

- **Team site**: This site type provides a centralized location for collaboration with your team by sharing documents, information, and resources.

- **Communication site**: This site type is suitable for sharing news, updates, and information with a wide audience within your organization.

In the next section of this chapter, we will cover in detail the differences between these two site types.

For this site creation example, we will create a **team site**.

Next, we need to select a site template. We can choose between templates provided by Microsoft that are customized for different business needs, like *Standard team, Crisis communication team, Employee onboarding team, Event planning*, etc., or select a custom template created and made available by the organization (in case there are available templates that the organization created at the tenant level):

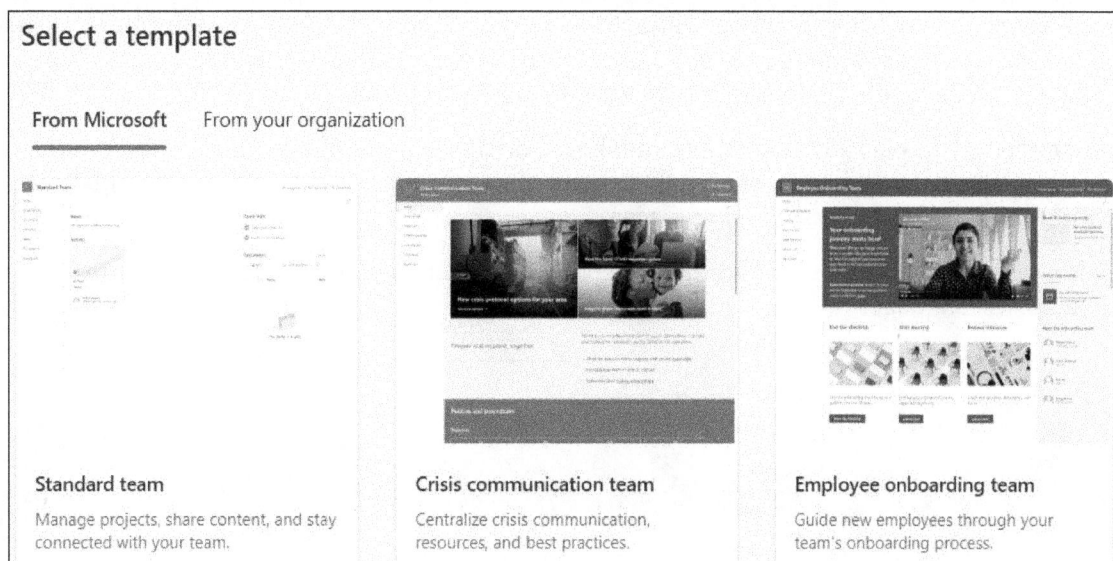

Figure 7.2: *Select a template*

After selecting the site template, you will see details about the site's capabilities, the content included as part of this template (such as the number of pages, lists, and page templates), and a preview of the respective site template. Click on **Use template** if you wish to continue with the template selected.

Next, you need to provide a name for the site and a description (optional). You will notice that based on the site name provided, details like *Group email address* and *Site address* are automatically updated:

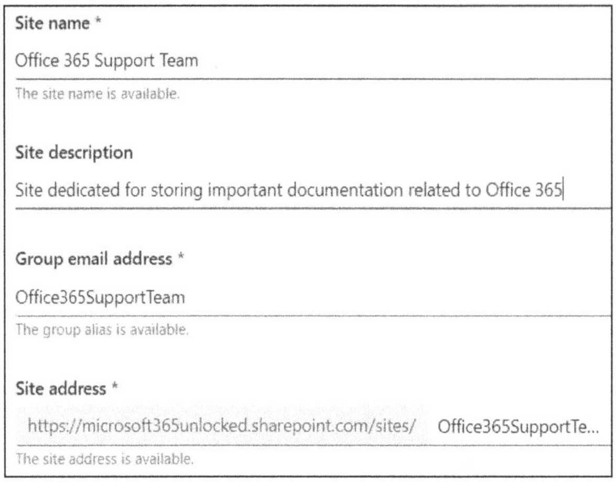

Figure 7.3: Site name and description

These details can be changed to suit your needs, as long as the group alias and site URL are unique (i.e., there is no other Microsoft 365 group with the same alias and no other site with the same URL in the tenant).

Regarding the site URL, only the portion of the URL representing the site name can be changed. Let us break down the site URL to better understand its structure:

- **https://yourorganization.sharepoint.com**: This part represents the URL of your SharePoint tenant, as well as the URL or the root site. It is configured as part of the tenant setup and can only be changed by an administrator. All sites created within the tenant will start with this base URL. In our example, our SharePoint tenant URL is **https://microsoft365unlocked.sharepoint.com**.

- **/sites/**: This represents the managed path under which the site will be created. **Managed paths** in SharePoint help organize multiple sites based on specific criteria, ensuring a logical structure. In SharePoint On-premises, administrators can create multiple managed paths (e.g., **/departments/**, **/projects/**, **/teams/**). However, in SharePoint Online, only two managed paths are available (**/sites/** and **/teams/**), and additional ones cannot be created. Managed paths are controlled by SharePoint administrators; for example, an administrator can configure all team sites to be created under the **/teams/** managed path. End-users cannot modify managed paths.

- **<sitename>**: This part is defined by default based on the name provided for the site. It can be changed as long as there is no other site within the tenant with the same site URL. In our example the site name portion of the URL is *Office365SupportTeam*.

Once the site name and a site description have been provided, the next step is to select the privacy settings and the default site language:

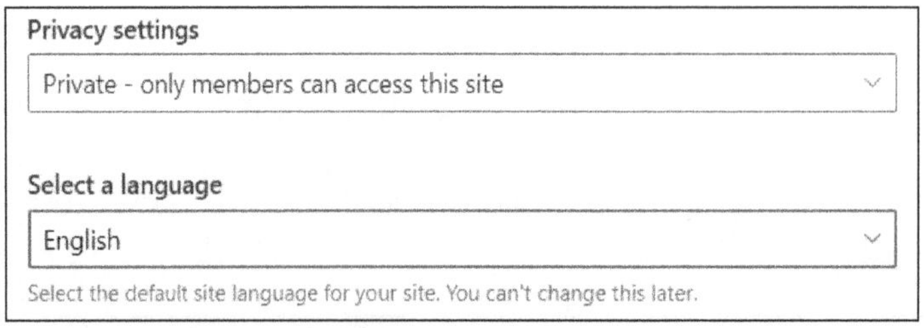

Figure 7.4: Privacy settings and default site language

You can create a site as private, to make sure that only members you explicitly add to the site can access it, or you can choose to create a public site that everyone in the organization will be able to access. The site privacy can be modified after the site creation if needed.

After selecting the site's privacy and language, click on **Create site.** The site creation process will begin, and your site will be available within a few seconds. At this stage, you can also add an additional member or owner to the site:

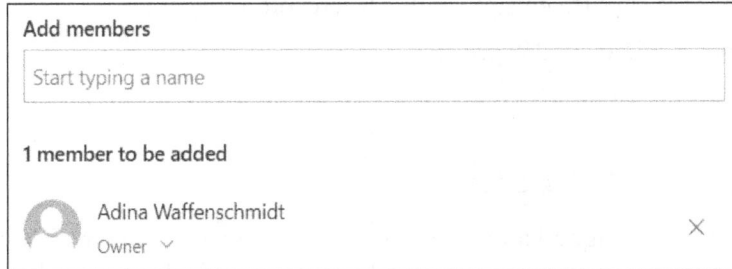

> Add members
>
> Start typing a name
>
> 1 member to be added
>
> Adina Waffenschmidt
> Owner ⌄   ✕

Figure 7.5: Add additional member or owner

By default, the site creator becomes the site owner, but it is recommended to have an additional site owner to help manage the site content. Additional owners and members can be added after the site has been created.

Once the site has been created, you will be redirected to the new site where you can start designing it and create the necessary content as per your requirements.

The process of creating a communication site is similar to the one we have seen for creating a team site. The major differences are:

- The group email address field is missing, as a communication site is a stand-alone site that is not associated with a group.
- The site's privacy field is missing. Communication sites can only be private sites and permissions can be managed at the site level, after the site creation.
- The option to add additional owners or members is missing. This can be done only after the site creation.

Understanding site types

SharePoint Online offers various site types tailored to business needs and requirements. As part of the modern experience, which enhances collaboration and communication within organizations, SharePoint provides two main site types that end-users can create (as we have seen in the previous section):

- Group-connected team sites
- Communication sites

Additionally, there are other site types that can only be created by SharePoint administrators. One important site type that continues to be used frequently for specific use cases is the **Team Site (without a Microsoft 365 group)**.

Other site types that administrators can create include:

- **Document center**: Classic experience site used for centralized document management.
- **Enterprise wiki**: Classic experience site that facilitates knowledge sharing across the organization.
- **Publishing portal**: Classic experience site used for building an intranet portal.

Note: **Classic experience sites are typically used for isolated scenarios or specific business requirements, such as transition or migration cases. The features provided by these site types are covered and enhanced by the modern experience of SharePoint sites and solutions within Microsoft 365.**

Let us explore the major site types to better understand their particularities. We will cover the following site types:

- Group-connected team sites (team sites with a Microsoft 365 group)
- Team sites (without a Microsoft 365 group)
- Communication sites

Group-connected team sites

Group-connected team sites are designed for collaboration among team members. They provide a space where teams can work together on projects, share documents, and communicate effectively.

Being connected with a Microsoft 365 group, these sites provide more than just the usual SharePoint features and the modern experience for pages, lists, and libraries. The group enhances collaboration by enabling integration with other apps and features, such as OneNote, Teams, Planner, Email, and Calendar. Whenever you create a group-connected team site, you get a group mailbox, a shared calendar, a dedicated OneNote Notebook, a Planner board for task management, and the possibility to connect the site with a team in Microsoft Teams.

Team sites can be distinguished primarily by their navigation panel, by default being vertically oriented and located on the left side of the screen.

Site permissions for group-connected sites are typically managed through the associated Microsoft 365 group, allowing multiple members to collaborate on content. Although permissions can be managed directly in SharePoint (outside of the Microsoft 365 group), it is advisable to grant access via the connected group. Managing permissions outside of the group can become complex and overwhelming over time, and it does not provide access to other connected Microsoft 365 services that come with this site type.

This type of site is also created when you set up a team in Microsoft Teams or a Viva Engage Community. Although you do not explicitly create a SharePoint site, Microsoft Teams and Viva Engage use SharePoint for file storage. Therefore, whenever a new team or community is created, an associated group-connected team site is automatically created alongside it.

Stand-alone team sites

These sites provide the same SharePoint experience as the group-connected team sites, but without the additional features that come as part of the connectivity with a Microsoft 365 group.

The recommended approach is to use group-connected team sites whenever possible. However, for certain scenarios, team sites without a connected group are more suitable. For example, when migrating content from file shares or from SharePoint on-premises over to SharePoint Online, these sites are most of the time the right choice, as they provide the necessary SharePoint experience and document management capabilities without the other collaboration features you get as part of the group. The additional features can be overwhelming and difficult to handle for users who are not accustomed to the modern experience, and possibly not needed, so this type of site can be used as part of the transition phase.

Permissions can be managed directly in SharePoint, by granting access to individual users or security groups, which sometimes might be a business requirement.

A great feature is that whenever integration with additional Microsoft 365 features is needed, this site type can be connected with a Microsoft 365 group easily by a site administrator:

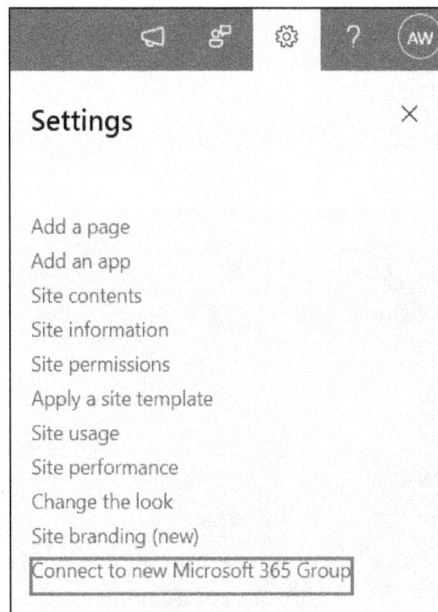

Figure 7.6: Connect a team site to a Microsoft 365 group

Communication sites

Communication sites are designed to share information broadly with a large audience. They are ideal for one-way sharing of information, news broadcasting, reports, and other content to your organization members. They can be used to share important updates and news, publish reports and documents for everyone to see, promote upcoming events and activities, provide access to resources like policies, guidelines, and training materials.

These sites are suitable for creating and configuring your organization's intranet.

Permissions are managed directly in SharePoint, as they are stand-alone sites, and navigation is always horizontally oriented, at the top of the screen.

Creating a communication site does not create anything else but the SharePoint site itself, and this site type cannot be associated with a Microsoft 365 group.

Lists and document libraries

In SharePoint Online, lists and libraries are fundamental components that help you organize, manage, and share information efficiently within your organization.

Lists are versatile tools that allow you to store and manage structured data. They can be used for a variety of purposes, such as tracking tasks, managing contacts, or maintaining inventories. Lists are highly customizable, enabling you to create columns for different data types, set up views to display information in various ways, and apply filters and sorting to find what you need quickly.

Libraries, conversely, are designed for the storage and management of documents and other files. Document libraries, which are the most prevalent type, provide a container for storing, organizing, and sharing files. They offer features like version control, metadata tagging, and co-authoring, making it easy for users to collaborate on documents and keep track of changes.

Both lists and libraries are integral to SharePoint Online, offering powerful capabilities to streamline your workflows, enhance collaboration, and ensure that information is easily accessible and well-organized.

Create new lists

You can create new lists in two ways (from two different locations):

1. Navigate to the SharePoint site where you want to create the list and on the **Home** page, click on **New** and then **List**:

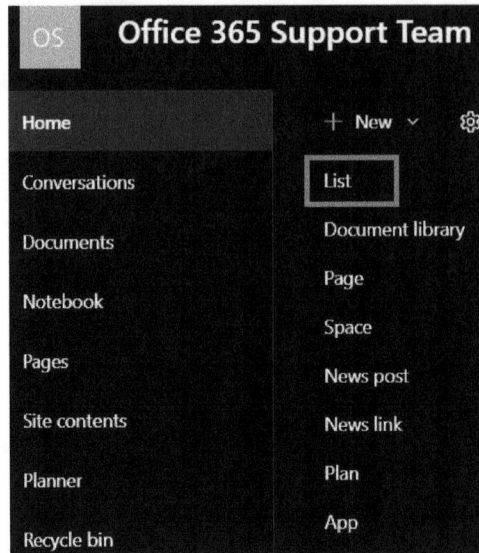

Figure 7.7: Create new list from a SharePoint site

2. Access the **Microsoft Lists** application by searching for **Lists** in the Microsoft 365 app launcher search box. Once in the Microsoft Lists app, click on **New list**:

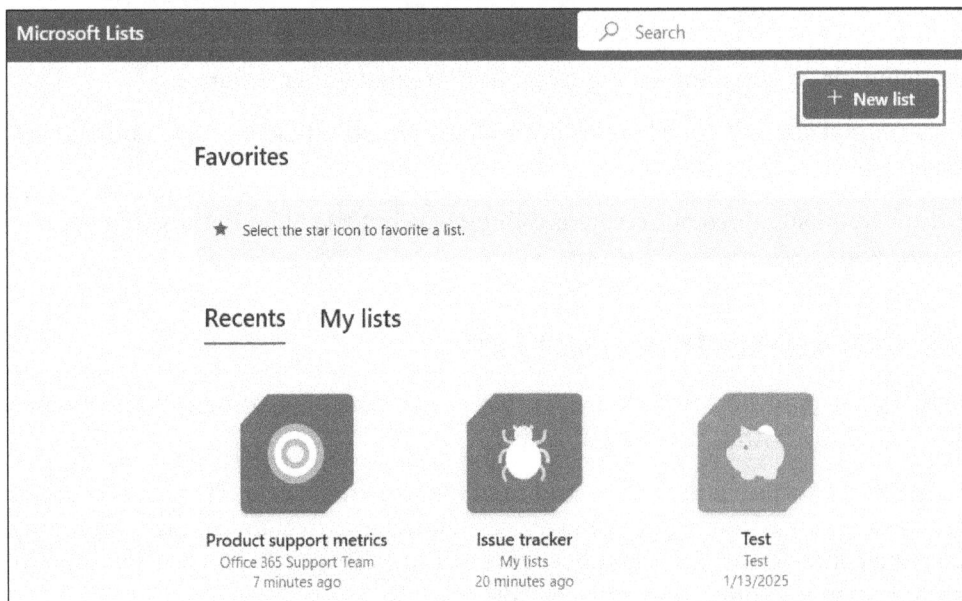

Figure 7.8: Create a new list from the Microsoft Lists app

Depending on the location you wish to start with the list creation (SharePoint site or Microsoft Lists app), you will get a slightly different creation experience.

From both places, the next step is to choose between the following options:

- Create a blank list.
- Use an existing list as a template.

- Create the list from an Excel file or a CSV file. This feature is particularly useful as it imports the existing data and creates the list with the available items you have within the source.

- Select one of the available templates that best suits your requirements. Various templates from Microsoft are available, as well as the option to create a list based on a template provided by your organization (if any has been uploaded).

The next step is to provide a name and a description for your list. If you create the list from a SharePoint site, you can select whether you wish to display the list in the site navigation, and you can then click **Create** to create your list accordingly.

The Microsoft Lists app allows users to select a color and an icon for their list to facilitate identification among other lists in the app. Users can also choose the location where the list will be created, either in an existing SharePoint site, provided they have the necessary permissions, or in their personal OneDrive for Business by selecting the **My lists** option:

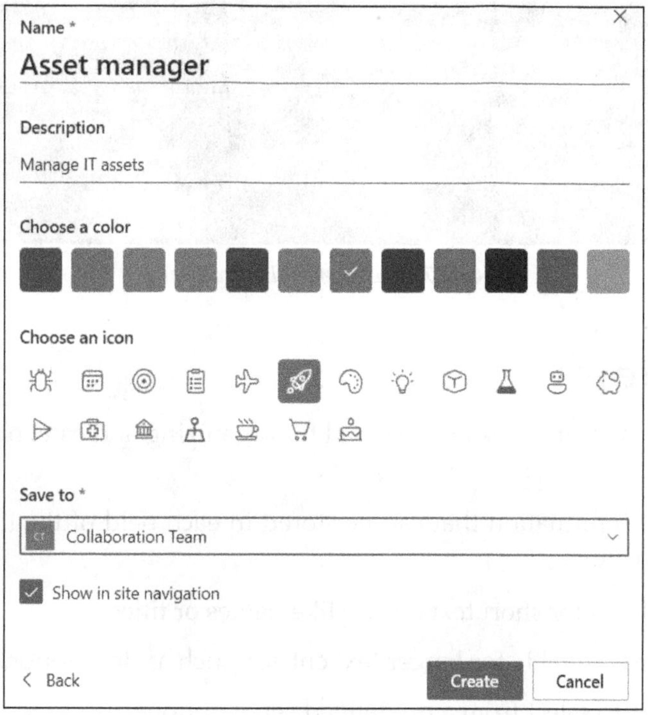

Figure 7.9: List details and location

Create new document libraries

By default, every SharePoint site comes with a document library already created, called *Documents*. It is recommended to organize content in multiple document libraries whenever possible, to improve content management and accessibility. Additionally, organizing content into multiple libraries can enhance performance and streamline collaboration by reducing the number of items in each library.

Creating a new document library is straightforward. Here are the steps:

1. Navigate to the SharePoint site where you want to create the library.

2. On the home page, click on **New** and then **Document library**.

3. Select the option that best meets your needs: create a blank library, use an existing library as a template, or choose from available templates provided by Microsoft or your organization (if available).

4. Give your library a name and a description (optional), choose if you want the library to be displayed in the site navigation, and click **Create**.

Note: If sensitivity labels are configured and enabled within your organization, you will also get the option to select the appropriate sensitivity label that should apply to the Office files within the library.

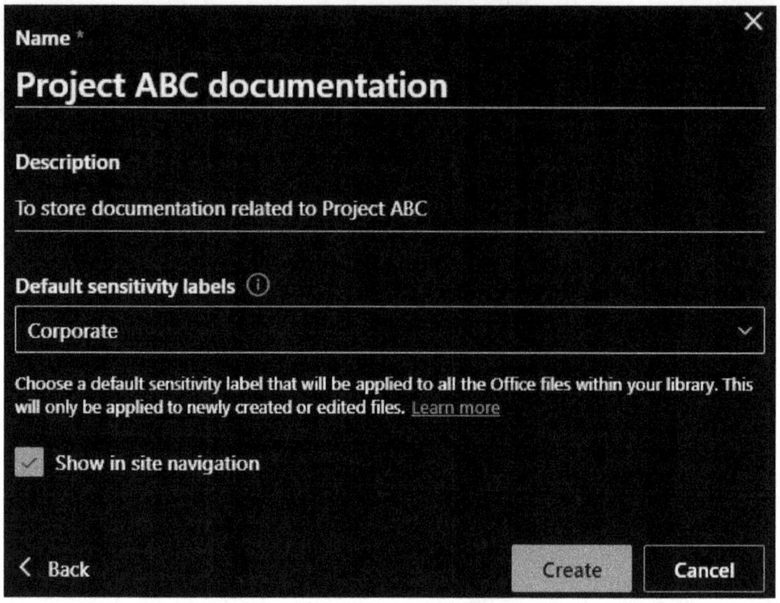

Figure 7.10: Document library details

Columns and views

In SharePoint Online, columns and views are essential for organizing and categorizing data within a list or a library.

Columns define the type of information that can be stored in each field of the list. Here are some common types of columns you can create:

- **Single line of text**: Ideal for short text entries like names or titles.

- **Multiple lines of text**: Suitable for longer text entries, such as descriptions or comments.

- **Choice**: Allows users to select from a predefined set of options, useful for categories or statuses.

- **Number**: Stores numerical data, perfect for quantities or measurements.

- **Date and time**: Captures dates and times, useful for tracking deadlines or events.

- **Currency**: Stores monetary values, ideal for budgets or expenses.

- **Lookup**: Links to data from another list, enabling relational data management.

- **Yes/No**: Represents binary choices, such as true/false or active/inactive.

- **Person or group**: Allows selection of users or groups, useful for assigning tasks or responsibilities.

- **Hyperlink or picture**: Stores URLs or images, useful for linking to external resources or displaying visuals.

- **Calculated**: Performs calculations based on other columns, useful for creating dynamic data.

To add a new column, simply navigate to your list or library and click on **Add column** next to the last column in your list or library, or hover between two existing columns and click on the + sign:

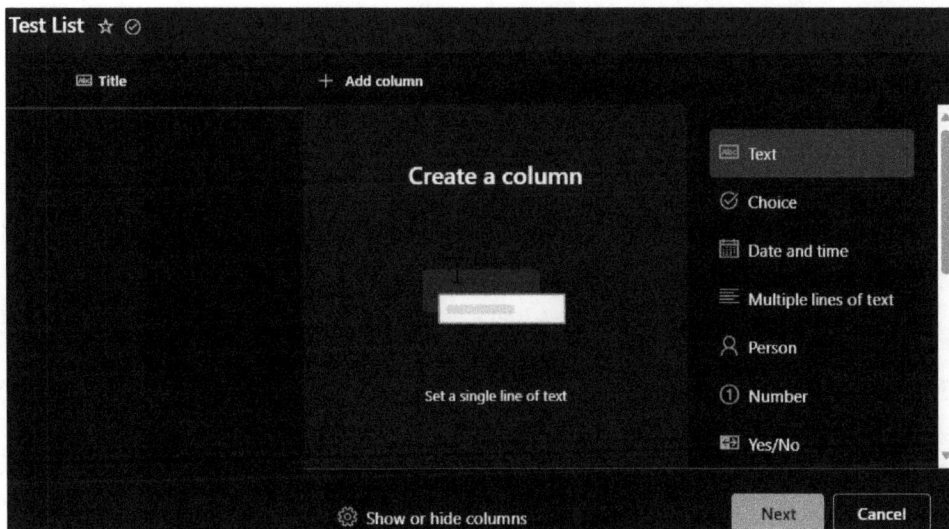

Figure 7.11: Add a new column

Depending on the column type selected, you will get different configurable options. For example, for the **Person or Group** column type, you can choose if selection of groups and multiple selections are allowed or if you want the profile pictures of the users to be displayed:

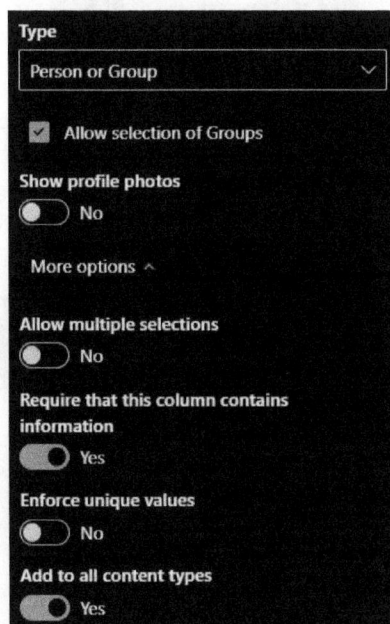

Figure 7.12: Configurable options for Person or Group column

Views provide different ways to display and interact with the data in a list or library. Creating additional views can help users find and manage information more effectively.

Every list or document library you create includes a default view named *All Items* for lists and *All Documents* for libraries.

Here are some scenarios where you might create additional list views:

- **Filtered views**: To display only items that meet specific criteria, such as tasks assigned to a particular user or items with a certain status.
- **Sorted views**: To organize items in a specific order, such as by due date or priority.
- **Grouped views**: To categorize items into groups, such as by department or project.

- **Custom views**: To tailor the display of columns and data to meet specific needs, such as showing only relevant columns for a particular team.

To create a new view, you can follow these steps:

1. **For lists**: In the command bar of your list, click on **Add view**.

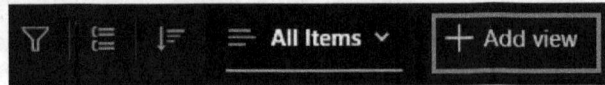

Figure 7.13: Create a new view in a list

2. **For libraries**: In the command bar of your library, expand the **View options** menu (where your current view name is displayed) and select **Create new view**.

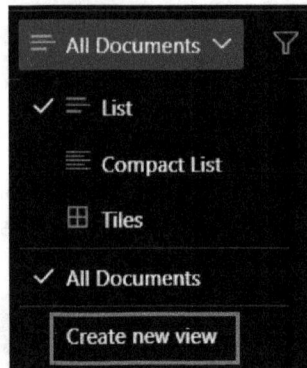

Figure 7.14: Create a new view in a document library

3. In the **Create view** dialog box, provide a name for your view, select the type of view you want to create under the **Show as** section, and choose if you want to make the view public (for everyone with access to the list) or keep it private (only for you):

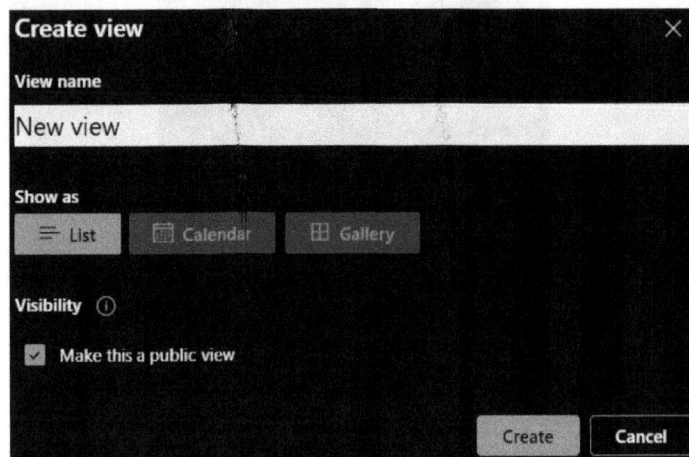

Figure 7.15: Create view options

4. Once you are happy with the options chosen, click **Create**. Your new view will open, and you can start customizing it based on your needs.

To edit an existing view, expand the **View options** menu (where your current view name is displayed) and select **Edit current view**:

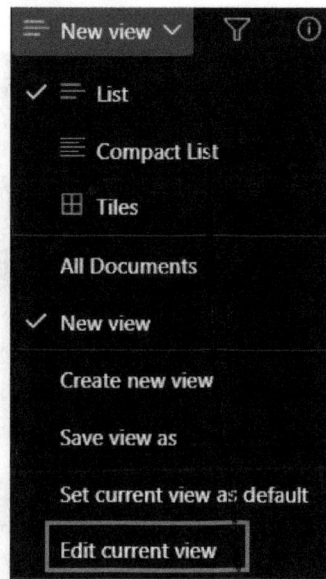

Figure 7.16: *Edit current view*

From the **Edit View** page, you can:

- Change the name of the view and its web address.
- Choose to make the view the default view for your list and library (applies for public views only).
- Select the columns to be displayed as part of the view.
- Sort, filter, and group items based on specific columns and criteria.
- Limit the total number of items returned.

These are just the main options available; there are more features you can explore.

Effectively utilizing columns and views in your lists and libraries can help organize and structure your content. By creating appropriate columns, you can ensure that data is categorized and stored in a structured manner, making it easier to manage and retrieve information. Additionally, customizing views allows you to display data in ways that best suit your needs, whether it is through filtering, sorting, or grouping items. This flexibility not only improves data accessibility but also streamlines workflows and boosts overall productivity within your organization.

Working with large lists and libraries

Lists and libraries in SharePoint Online can store up to 30 million items in a single list or library. However, working with large volumes of data brings challenges, and appropriate management and planning are required to ensure optimal performance and usability.

While lists and libraries can store millions of items, there are practical limits that users should be aware of. One of the most significant thresholds is the **List View Threshold**, which is set at **5,000 items per view**. When this threshold is exceeded, users may encounter performance issues, such as slow loading times, errors when trying to display the view, and difficulties with sorting and filtering data.

You can always check the number of items currently stored within a list or library by navigating to the site where the list or library is stored, clicking on the gear icon located on the top right side on the site bar, and then clicking on **Site Contents**.

From here you can check the current number of items for each list or library on your site:

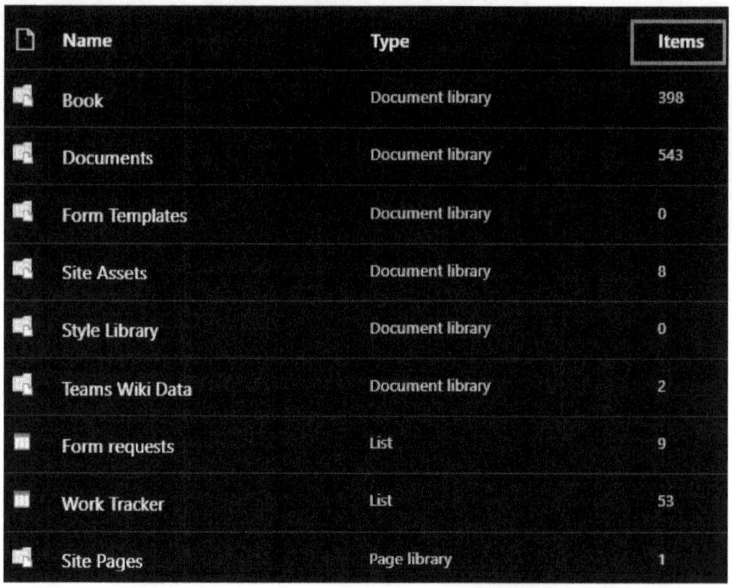

▯	Name	Type	Items
▥	Book	Document library	398
▥	Documents	Document library	543
▥	Form Templates	Document library	0
▥	Site Assets	Document library	8
▥	Style Library	Document library	0
▥	Teams Wiki Data	Document library	2
▤	Form requests	List	9
▤	Work Tracker	List	53
▥	Site Pages	Page library	1

Figure 7.17: Check the number of items for lists and libraries

When the number of items in a list or document library exceeds 5,000, you will see a warning under the **List settings** (for lists) or **Library settings** (for libraries):

List view threshold :   39070 items (list view threshold is 5000).

The number of items in this list exceeds the list view threshold, which is 5000 items. Tasks that cause excessive server load (such as those involving all list items) are currently prohibited.
Learn about managing a large list or library and ensuring that items display quickly.

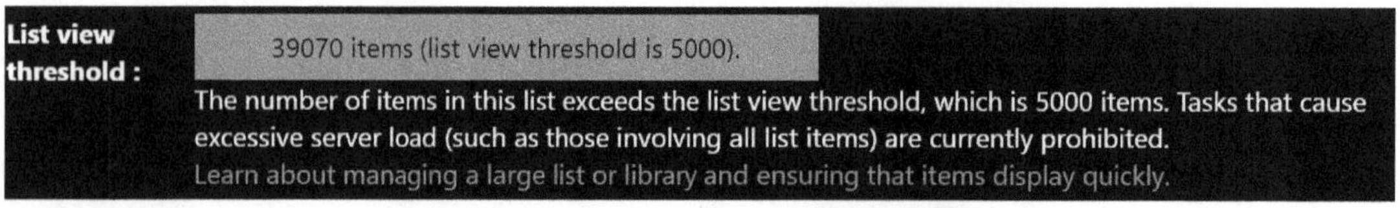

Figure 7.18: List view threshold warning

The best approach to avoid the list view threshold is to use multiple document libraries or lists to organize your documents or items. Opting for this approach whenever possible is recommended, however, there are scenarios where this might not be possible due to specific requirements to keep documents or items within a single library or list.

Creating indexes on columns used in filters is the most efficient step that can be applied to effectively manage large lists and libraries in SharePoint. It is recommended to create indexes as soon as possible, before reaching 5,000 items in a library or list. Here are the steps to create Indexes:

1. Navigate to the respective list or library.
2. Click on the gear icon located at the top right side of the site bar.
3. Select **List settings** (for lists) or **Library settings** and then **More library settings** (for libraries).
4. On the **Settings** page, click on **Indexed columns** and then **Create a new index**:

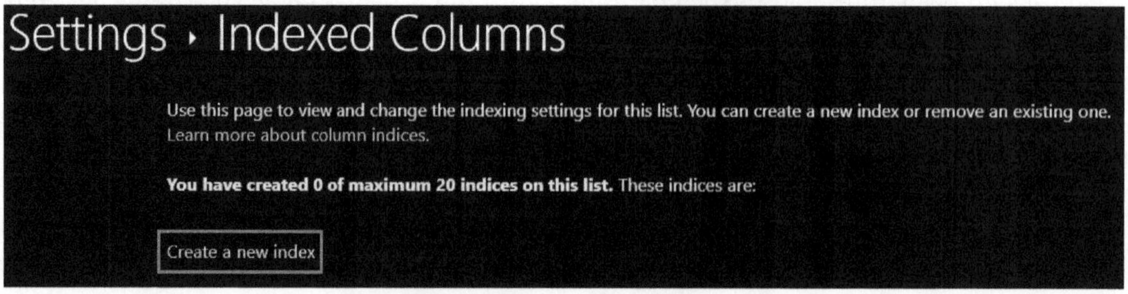

Settings › Indexed Columns

Use this page to view and change the indexing settings for this list. You can create a new index or remove an existing one. Learn more about column indices.

You have created 0 of maximum 20 indices on this list. These indices are:

Create a new index

Figure 7.19: Create a new index

You can create up to 20 indexes for a list or library, but only for the following column types:

- Single line of text
- Choice (single value)
- Number
- Currency
- Date and Time
- Person or Group (single value) (Lookup)
- Managed Metadata (Lookup)
- Yes/No
- Lookup (Lookup)

Other measures that can be applied to work around the list view threshold include:

- **Use filters**: Apply filters to reduce the number of items displayed in a view.
- **Create multiple views**: Break down large lists into smaller, manageable views.
- **Remove sorting, grouping, and totals for the list view**: Set these values to *None* in the view settings.

Managing large lists and libraries in SharePoint Online requires careful planning and strategic implementation of best practices. By understanding the limitations and thresholds, such as the List View Threshold, and applying measures like creating indexes, using filters, and breaking down large lists into smaller views, you can ensure optimal performance and usability. These practices not only help maintain the efficiency of your SharePoint environment but also enhance the overall user experience, making it easier to access and manage vast amounts of data effectively.

Versioning

Versioning is a crucial feature in SharePoint that allows users to track and manage changes to items in lists and documents in libraries. By making use of the versioning feature, you can maintain a history of changes, restore previous versions, and ensure better control over your content.

Versioning settings for document libraries

In SharePoint Online, versioning is enabled by default for both lists and libraries. For document libraries, it automatically saves the last **500 major versions** of a document.

Note: **SharePoint administrators can set the default maximum number of document versions in a library. This limit may be less than 500, managed automatically, or subject to deletion after a certain time. Site administrators and owners can adjust versioning settings for each library as needed.**

To configure versioning settings for libraries, follow these steps:

1. Navigate to the library where you want to adjust versioning settings.
2. Click on the gear icon at the top right corner of the site.
3. Select **Library settings** and then **More library settings**.
4. On the Settings page, click on **Versioning settings**.

When configuring versioning settings, you have several options to choose from:

- **Require content approval**: This option ensures that changes to documents are reviewed and approved before they become visible in public views. This is useful for compliance and quality control.

- **Document version history**: You can choose to create major versions only or both major and minor versions. Major versions are typically used for significant changes, while minor versions can track smaller edits.

- **Version time limit**: You can set a time limit to delete the versions based on their age. The options available are, no time limit (versions are never deleted based on age), automatic (versions are deleted over time based on activity and age), or manual (versions are deleted when they exceed a specified number of days.

- **Limit the number of versions**: To manage storage and maintain performance, you can set a limit on the number of versions retained. For example, you might choose to keep only the last 100 versions of a document.

- **Draft item security**: If content approval or minor versions are enabled, this setting controls who can see draft versions of documents. You can restrict visibility to only users who can edit the items, to users with read permissions or to users who can approve items (including the author).

Versioning settings for lists

Versioning is also enabled by default for lists, and it saves the last **50 versions** of list items. This helps with data loss prevention and ensures that you can track and manage changes to the items effectively.

To configure versioning settings for lists, follow these steps:

1. Navigate to the list where you want to adjust versioning settings.
2. Click on the gear icon at the top right corner of the site.
3. Select **List settings**.
4. On the Settings page, click on **Versioning settings**.

For lists, there are fewer options that can be configured. These include:

- **Require content approval**: This option ensures that changes to documents are reviewed and approved before they become visible in public views.

- **Item version history**: Choose if a version should be created each time an item is edited and if set to *Yes* specify the number of versions that should be kept.

- **Draft item security**: If content approval, this setting controls who can see draft versions of items. You can restrict visibility to only users who can edit the items, to users with read permissions or to users who can approve items (including the author).

Permissions in SharePoint Online

Permissions management is a fundamental aspect of SharePoint that ensures the security and proper management of content within your organization. By configuring permissions and access controls effectively, you can safeguard sensitive information, facilitate collaboration, and maintain compliance with organizational policies.

Understanding permissions

Permissions in SharePoint Online determine what actions users can perform on sites, lists, libraries, and items. These actions include viewing, editing, deleting, and creating content. Permissions are managed through permission levels, which are collections of permissions assigned to users or groups.

SharePoint Online provides several default permission levels, each with a specific set of permissions:

- **Full control**: Users with this level have complete access to all settings and content within the site.

- **Design**: Users can view, add, update, delete, approve, and customize
- **Edit**: Users can add, edit, and delete lists and libraries, as well as view, add, update, and delete items.
- **Contribute**: Users can view, add, update, and delete items in existing lists and libraries.
- **Read**: Users can view pages and items but cannot make changes.

In addition to default permission levels, SharePoint Online allows you to create custom permission levels tailored to your organization's needs. Custom permission levels can be configured by selecting specific permissions that allow the completion of specific actions within the SharePoint site.

Consider a situation where you need to grant access to a group of users within the organization so they can review documents, upload new versions, and actively collaborate on content throughout a SharePoint Online site. However, you want to ensure they cannot delete files, alter existing lists and libraries, or create new lists and libraries. In such cases, assigning one of the default permission levels, like *Edit* or *Contribute*, provides more access than is appropriate for their roles.

Limiting permissions in this manner helps protect important or sensitive information from accidental or unauthorized deletions. It reduces the risk of data loss and maintains the integrity of the organizational content. For example, in a compliance-driven environment, you might want contributors to update files and provide feedback, but only designated administrators should have the authority to remove content.

This is where the flexibility of custom permission levels becomes essential. By creating a tailored permission level, you can precisely define what actions these users are allowed to perform. This granular approach enhances information security and establishes an environment in which users' responsibilities are defined and managed based on organizational requirements.

Note: Permissions and permission levels can be managed by users who have been assigned a permission level that includes Manage Permissions site permission. Typically, these users are site administrators or owners with full control over the site.

To create a new permission level, follow these steps:

1. Navigate to the site where you want to create the new permission level, ensuring that you have the necessary access rights.
2. Click on the gear icon at the top right corner of the site.
3. Select **Site Permissions** and then **Advanced permissions settings**.
4. Select **Permission Levels**. On the *Permission Levels* page, the default permission levels will also be displayed:

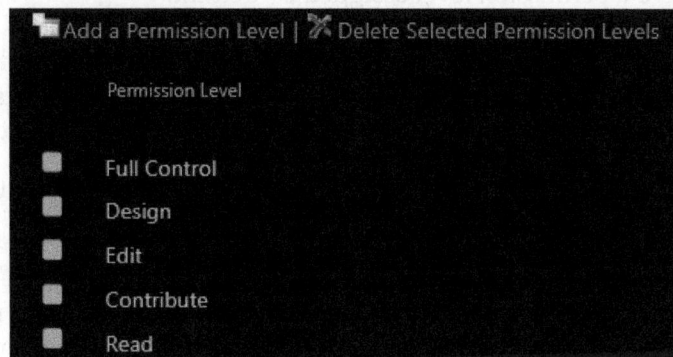

Figure 7.20: Permission Levels

5. Click on **Add a Permission Level.**
6. Type a name and a description, and then select the permissions to include in this permission level.

You will notice that selecting certain permissions automatically selects other dependent permissions in the list. For example, selecting **Approve Items**, automatically selects **Edit Items, View Items, View Pages,** and **Open** permissions.

7. Once you finished the permissions selection, click **Create.** A custom permission level is created that can then be assigned to individual users or groups.

Permissions can be managed at various levels within SharePoint Online:

- **Site level**: Permissions can be set for the entire site, affecting all content within it.

- **List and library level**: Permissions can be configured for individual lists and libraries, allowing for more granular control.

- **Item level**: Permissions can be set for specific items within a list or library, providing the highest level of precision.

SharePoint groups

SharePoint uses groups to simplify the management of permissions. These are SharePoint groups, and not Entra ID or Microsoft 365 groups. These groups are collections of users that share the same permission level. When creating a new SharePoint site, the following groups are created by default within the site:

- **Owners**: **Full Control** permission level assigned.

- **Members**: **Edit** permission level assigned.

- **Visitors**: **Read** permission level assigned.

These groups can be used to grant users different levels of access to the site.

Besides these three groups, SharePoint also provides by default two special dynamic groups used to manage access widely:

- The **Everyone** group includes all users who have access to your SharePoint environment. The group encompasses both internal users (employees within your organization) and external users (guests or partners who have been invited to collaborate).

- The **Everyone except external users** (**EEEU**) group includes only internal users who are part of your organization. External users, such as guests or partners, are excluded from this group. This distinction is crucial for scenarios where you want to share content with all employees but not with external collaborators.

These two groups do not have a permission level assigned by default.

Note: For security reasons, the Everyone group is hidden by default, preventing its use for granting access in SharePoint Online. Only a SharePoint administrator can change this setting. Similarly, the 'Everyone except external users' group may also be hidden if configured by an administrator.

In addition to the default groups, custom SharePoint groups can also be created to tailor permissions and access controls to specific needs within your organization.

For example, within a SharePoint site, we might need to add users in charge of item approval and these users should not be provided with higher privileges. The first step is to create a custom permission level to fulfill this requirement, but then it is recommended to use a SharePoint group to which we can add this permission level and then add the necessary users to the group.

To create a new SharePoint group, follow these steps:

1. Navigate to the site where you want to create the new SharePoint group, ensuring that you have the necessary access rights.

2. Click on the gear icon at the top right corner of the site.

3. Select **Site Permissions** and then **Advanced permissions settings**.

4. In the **Advanced Permissions** page, click on **Create Group**:

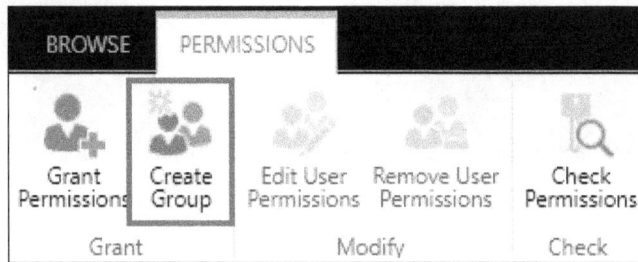

Figure 7.21: Create a SharePoint group

5. Give your group a name and description and add a group owner:

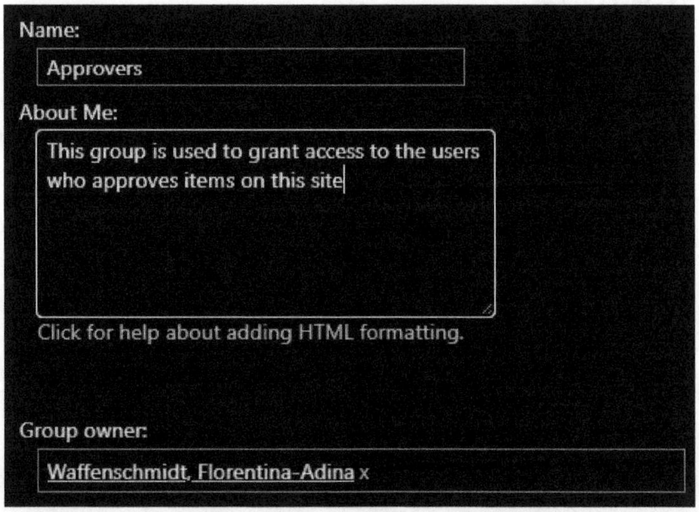

Figure 7.22: Group name, description and owner

6. Under **Group Settings** choose who can view and who can edit the membership of the group:

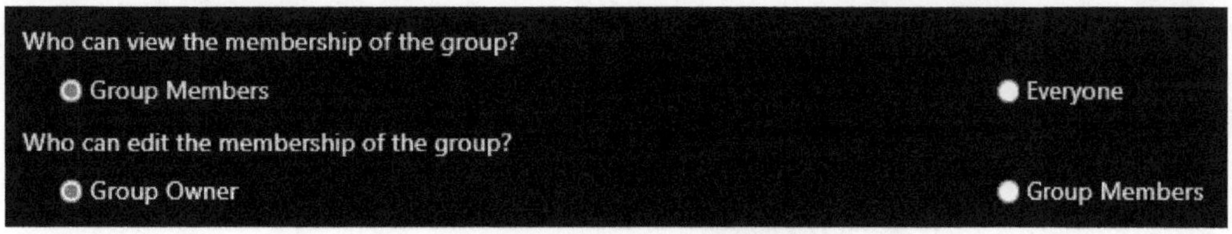

Figure 7.23: Group Settings

7. Under **Membership Requests**, select if you want to allow requests to join/leave this group and whether they should be automatically accepted:

Figure 7.24: Membership Requests

8. Assign the appropriate permission level for the group:

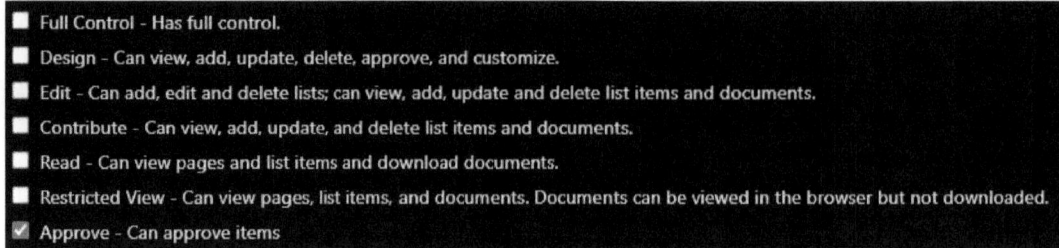

Figure 7.25: Assign permission level for the group

9. Click **Create** to create the group.

Once created, you can grant people access to the site using this group.

Site level permissions

Site level permissions management is dictated by the site type. For example, from a permissions management best practices point of view, access should be granted differently for a group-connected site than for a stand-alone site. In this section, we will be looking at different options to assign permissions to a site based on the site type.

Stand-alone sites

We call stand-alone sites the type of sites that are not connected to a Microsoft 365 group, such as Team sites (without a group) or Communication sites.

Permissions to these sites are managed within SharePoint, either through SharePoint groups or directly outside of a SharePoint group.

To grant Full Control, Edit, or Read access to a stand-alone SharePoint site, follow these steps:

1. Click on the gear icon at the top right corner of the site.

2. Select **Site permissions**. You will be able to see the three default SharePoint groups (*Owners*, *Members*, and *Visitors*) and their membership. From here, you can also manage existing membership by changing the permission level assigned or removing a user:

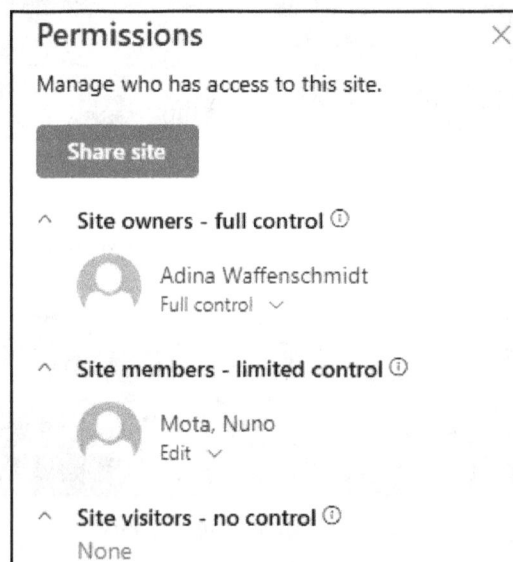

Figure 7.26: Site permissions

3. Select **Share site**.

4. Add the users or groups you want to share the site with and select the appropriate permissions level for each. You can also choose to send an email to the users to let them know they have been added to the site:

Figure 7.27: *Site access*

> **Note: Sharing with external users is also possible if not blocked by your organization's policies and if enabled at the site level by a SharePoint administrator.**

5. Click **Add** to add the users to the site. The users and groups will be added to the default SharePoint groups according to the permission level granted to each (*Site Owners* for *Full Control*, *Site Members* for *Edit*, and *Site Visitors* for *Read*):

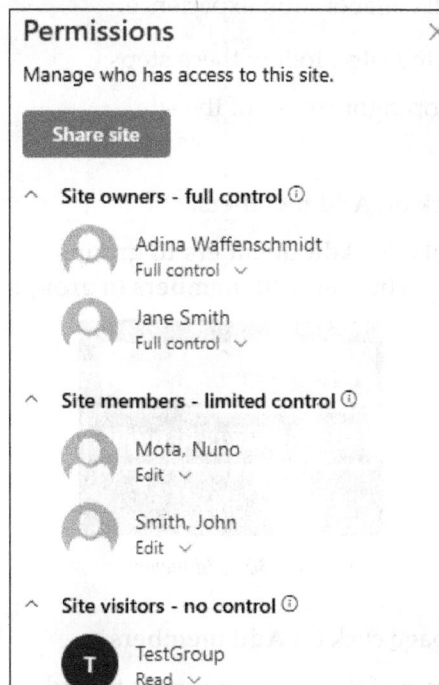

Figure 7.28: *Access granted*

From the **Permissions** page, you can only view and assign permissions through the three default SharePoint groups (*Owners*, *Members*, and *Visitors*).

If you need to assign permissions through a different SharePoint group you might have created within a site, you need to navigate to the **Advanced permissions settings** page. From here, you can grant permissions through different SharePoint groups, or grant access directly by assigning one of the available permission levels:

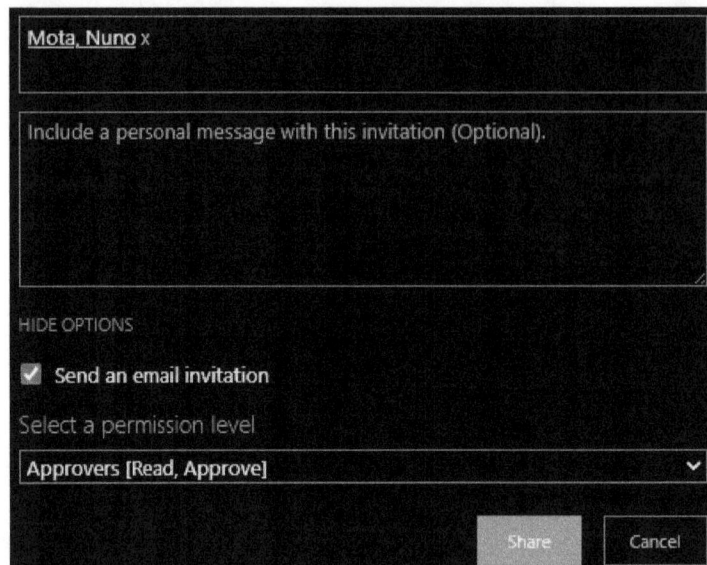

Figure 7.29: Assign permissions via the Advanced permissions settings page

Group-connected sites

While you can manage permissions for group-connected sites as you would do for a stand-alone site, the recommended approach is to grant permissions through the Microsoft 365 group associated with the site. This approach ensures that users are being granted access to the connected Microsoft 365 services, such as calendars and conversations, for a full collaboration experience.

To add members to the group-connected sites, follow these steps:

1. Click on the gear icon at the top right corner of the site.

2. Select **Site permissions**.

3. On the **Permissions** page, click on **Add members.**

4. You will see two options available, **Add members to group** and **Share site only**. To grant access via the connected Microsoft group, click on **Add members to group**:

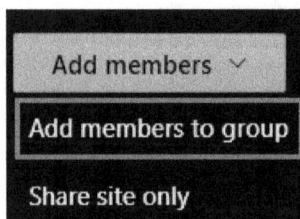

Figure 7.30: Add members

5. On the **Group membership** page click on **Add members**.

6. Type the name or email address of the users you want to add, select the appropriate role (**Owner** or **Member**) and click **Save**:

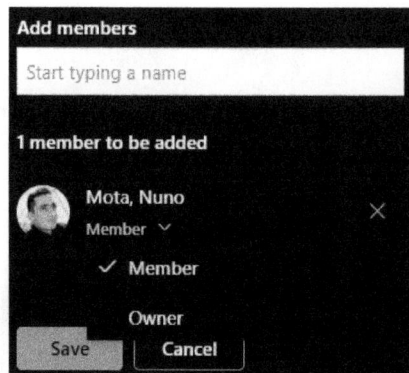

Figure 7.31: Add members to group

In group-connected sites, the individuals designated as Microsoft 365 group owners are assigned the role of site owners within the *Owners* SharePoint group. Likewise, members of the Microsoft 365 group are assigned the role of site members, belonging to the *Members* SharePoint group.

Private vs. public group-connected sites

As we have seen earlier in this chapter, when creating a group-connected team site, we can choose between *public* and *private* site privacy. Similarly, when creating a team in Microsoft Teams or a community in Viva Engage, you can choose private or public settings. This will determine if the related SharePoint site is private or public.

The site privacy can be seen in the right top corner of a group-connected site:

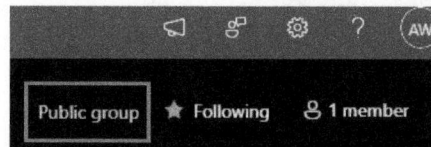

Figure 7.32: Site privacy

Private sites are accessible to users who have been explicitly added as owners or members through Microsoft 365 group membership.

Public sites can be accessed by all users in the organization. For this to be possible, each time a public group gets created or when you change the privacy of a site from *Private* to *Public*, SharePoint adds the EEEU group to the *Site Members* SharePoint group:

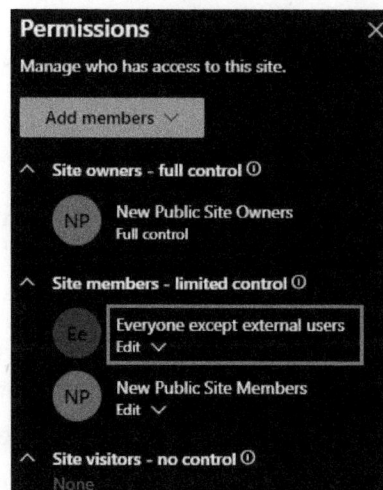

Figure 7.33: EEEU group added to Public sites

This enables everyone in the organization to collaborate on the site, as they are being granted with **Edit** permission level.

Changing the site privacy from private to public, or vice-versa, can be done by following these steps:

1. Click on the gear icon at the top right corner of the site.

2. Click on **Site Information**.

3. On the **Site Information** page change the **Privacy settings**:

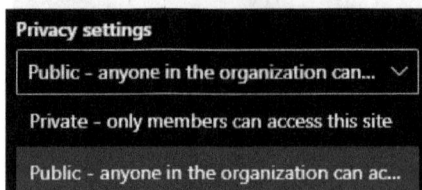

Figure 7.34: Privacy settings

Channel sites

Upon creating a **private** or **shared channel** within a team in Microsoft Teams, a distinct SharePoint Online site is automatically generated for that channel. This site is different from the parent teams-connected group site when the team itself is created in Microsoft Teams.

A channel site is essentially a team site, but what sets it apart is that permissions cannot be managed at the site level. Instead, membership is managed directly within Teams:

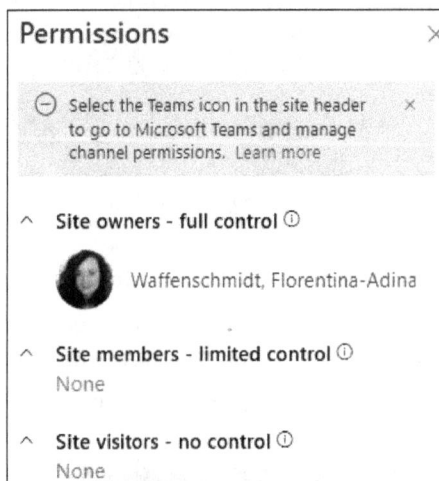

Figure 7.35: Permissions for Channel sites

Inheritance and unique permissions

By default, permissions in SharePoint Online are inherited from the parent site. This means that lists, libraries, and items within a site will have the same permissions as the site itself. However, you can break inheritance to configure unique permissions for specific lists, libraries, or items.

To break permissions inheritance for libraries and lists, follow these steps:

1. Navigate to the list or library where you want to break inheritance.

2. Click on the gear icon and select **List settings** or **Library settings**.

3. Click on **Permissions for this list** or **Permissions for this library**.

4. Select **Stop Inheriting Permissions** and confirm the action:

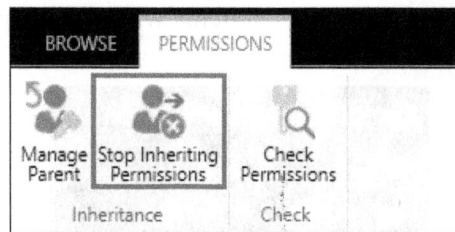

Figure 7.36: Stop Inheriting Permissions

Once inheritance is broken, you can assign unique permissions to the selected list or library.

To break inheritance at a folder or file/item level. Follow these steps:

1. Right-click on the folder/file/item.
2. Click on **Manage access**.
3. Click on **More options (...)** and then **Advanced settings**.
4. Select **Stop Inheriting Permissions** and confirm the action.

Stopping permissions inheritance does not automatically remove existing inherited permissions from the parent. You must manually remove access for existing groups and users, then add different entitlements if this is required.

To restore permissions inheritance, on the **Advanced Permissions** page of the respective list, library, or item, click on **Delete unique permissions**:

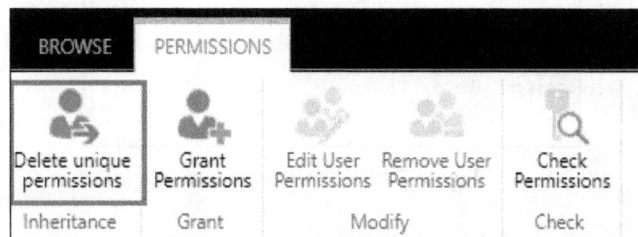

Figure 7.37: Delete unique permissions

Note: **Once you delete unique permissions, any custom permission will be lost and the list, library, or item will start inheriting the same permissions as the parent.**

When a file, folder, item, or list is shared individually, or sharing links are generated for users, unique permissions are established for the respective shared item.

Checking permissions

With so many ways to set permissions in SharePoint, it is important to know how to check what permissions are assigned on your site, see what items are being shared, find out who has access, and understand their level of access.

From the **Advanced Permissions** site page, you can check if there are items with different permissions than the ones established at the site level. In such a case, a notification will appear on the page alerting you that there is content on the site with different permissions:

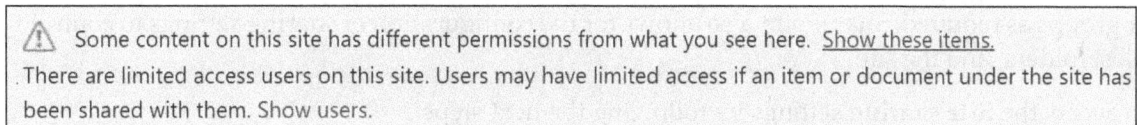

Figure 7.38: Unique permissions warning

Clicking on the **Show these items** link will display all items with unique permissions, allowing you to easily navigate to their respective permissions pages:

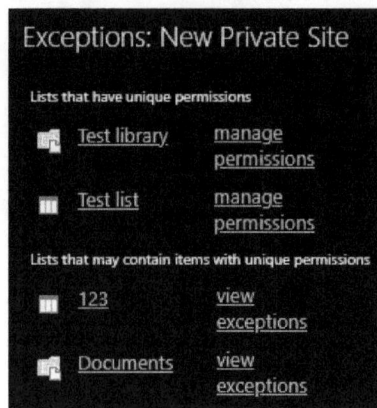

Figure 7.39: Items with unique permissions

Additionally, as seen in *Figure 7.38*, **Show users** link will appear if there are users with limited access to the site. Limited access is granted whenever there are individual items on the site shared with specific users.

On the **Advanced Permissions** page, you can verify the permissions assigned to a user or group by selecting **Check Permissions**:

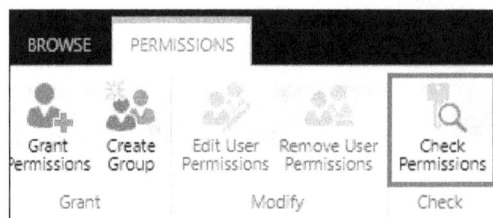

Figure 7.40: Check Permissions

Enter the name or email address of the user or group whose permissions you want to check. You will then be able to see the permissions granted to that user or group:

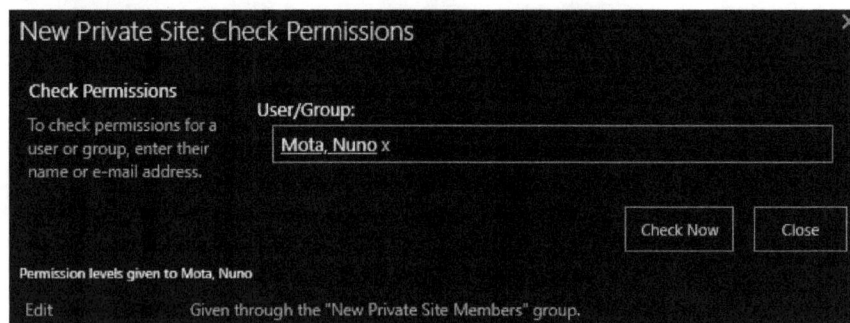

Figure 7.41: Check Permissions granted to user

Sharing settings and access requests

In addition to managing access to the site and content you own through permission levels granted to specific users or groups as required, SharePoint also allows for the configuration of sharing settings to control who can share files, folders, and the site.

You can access the **Site sharing** settings by following the next steps:

1. Click on the gear icon at the top right corner of the site.

2. Select **Site Permissions** and then **Change how members can share** under **Site Sharing**:

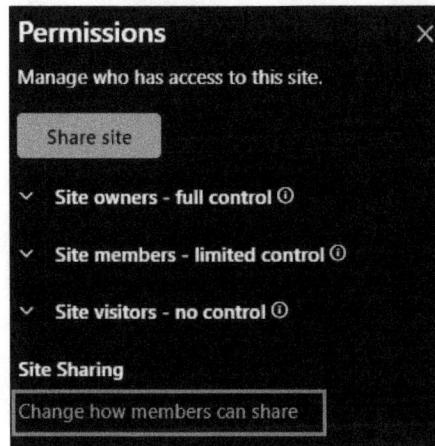

Figure 7.42: *Change how members can share*

3. Under the **Site sharing settings**, select one of the three options available:

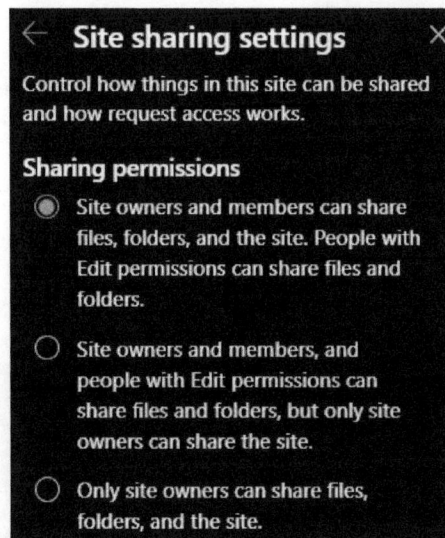

Figure 7.43: *Site sharing settings*

4. Click **Save**.

By default, site owners and members are authorized to share files, folders and the entire site. Individuals with *Edit* permissions can share files and folders. This represents the most permissive setting. Depending on your security requirements, it is possible to limit site sharing exclusively to site owners or further restrict content sharing, including files and folders, to site owners alone, by selecting the appropriate sharing option.

As a site owner, you can also configure the access request settings to receive a notification email whenever someone requests access to the site.

To configure access requests, follow these steps:

1. Click on the gear icon at the top right corner of the site.

2. Select **Site Permissions** and then **Change how members can share** under *Site Sharing*.

3. Under **Access requests**, make sure the toggle for **Allow access requests** is set to **On** (if you want to allow access requests for your site):

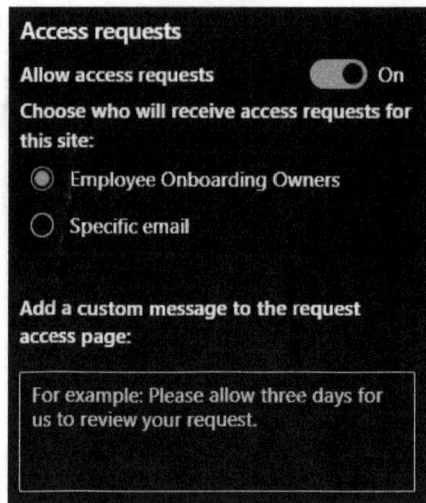

Figure 7.44: Access requests settings

By default, this option is enabled on SharePoint sites. Access requests are directed to users in the *Owners* SharePoint group for communication sites and stand-alone team sites, and to group administrators for group-connected team sites. You can configure these requests to be directed to a specific email address and you can add a custom message that will be displayed on the request access page (optional). If you do not want to allow access requests for your site, you can simply set the **Allow access requests** toggle to **Off**.

4. Once you are happy with the changes, click **Save**.

When access requests are permitted and someone requests access to the site, the owners or the designated email address will receive an email notification, as illustrated in the following figure:

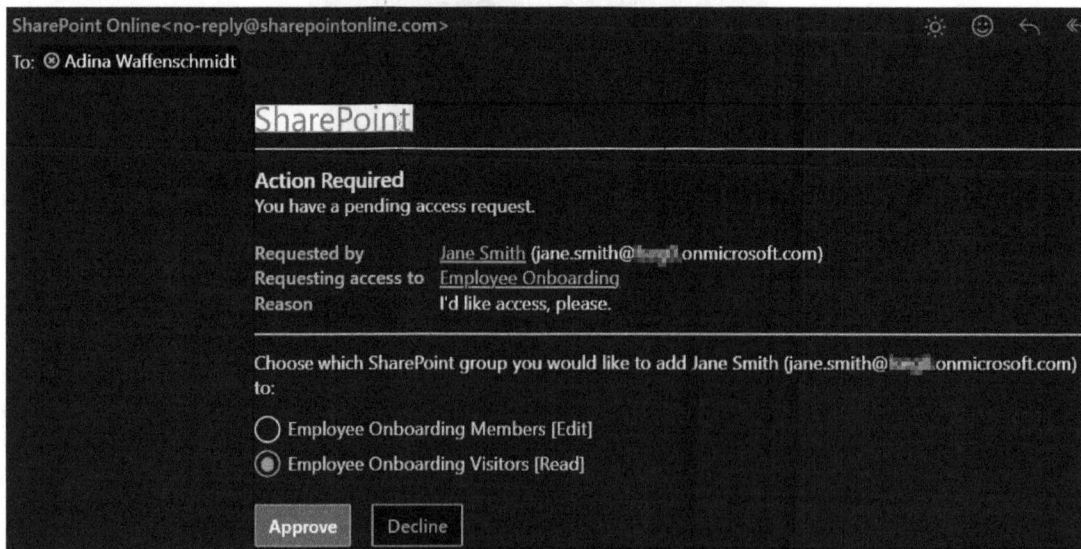

Figure 7.45: Access request email notification

From the email notification, you have the option to either approve or decline the access request. Additionally, before approving, you can specify the level of access: granting *Edit* permissions as part of the *Members* group or *Read* permissions as part of the *Visitors* group.

You can see all the pending access requests and you can approve or decline them directly from the SharePoint site, as follows:

1. Click on the gear icon at the top right corner of the site.

2. Click on **Site contents** and then click on **Access requests** (this button is visible only if there are pending access requests).

3. Under **PENDING REQUESTS**, you will be able to see all the access requests submitted for the respective site, as shown in the following figure:

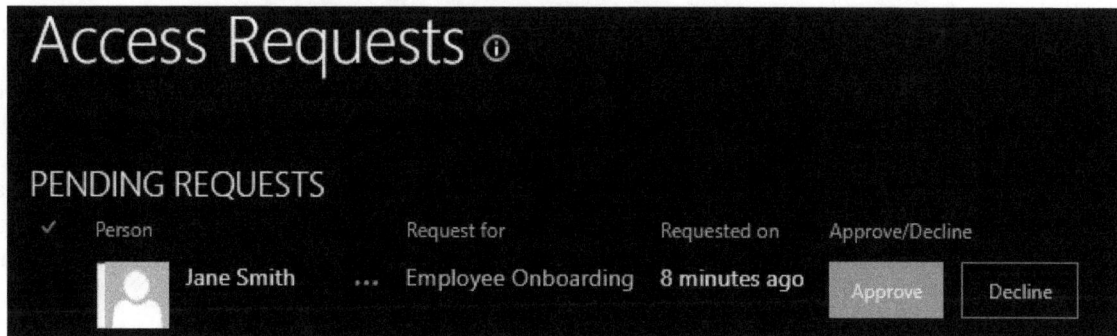

Figure 7.46: Pending access requests

4. You can directly approve or decline the request. By clicking on the ellipses (...), you can also select the permission to be granted to the user (default is *Read* granted through the *Visitors* group) and you can type a message for the requestor before approving the site access request:

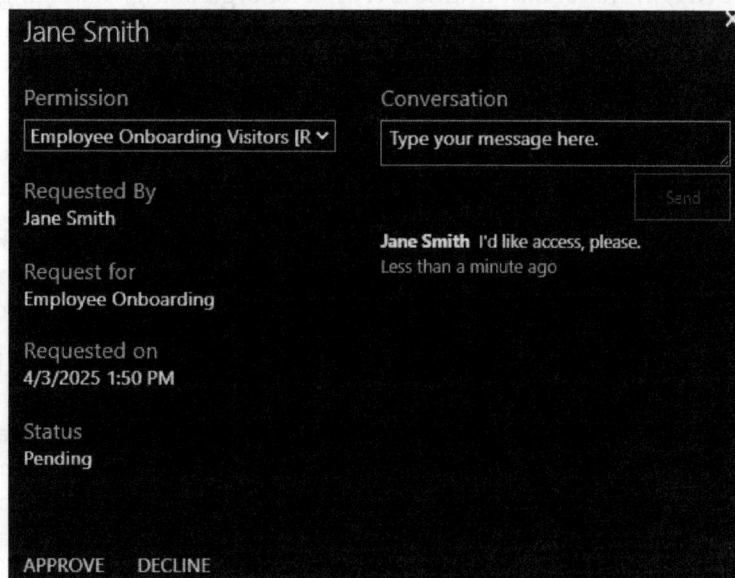

Figure 7.47: Manage pending access requests

5. Once the request has been approved, the user will be granted access to the site accordingly.

Note: If site and content sharing is limited to site owners and access requests are enabled, any attempt by members to share the site or its content will result in an access request being generated for approval by the site owners.

Best practices for permissions management

To ensure effective management of permissions and access controls in SharePoint Online, consider the following best practices:

- **Use groups**: Assign permissions to groups and make use of SharePoint groups instead of grating access directly to individual users of the site. This approach simplifies permissions management and ensures consistency.

- **Adhere to the principle of least privilege**: Provide users with only the minimum access needed to accomplish their tasks.

- **Avoid breaking inheritance**: Unless necessary, make sure you avoid unique permissions, especially at the item level. This can increase the complexity of permissions management over time.

- **Consider the site type**: Manage site permissions in SharePoint based on the site type. It is recommended that permissions for group-connected sites be managed through the associated Microsoft 365 group. Additionally, permissions for a site connected with a team in Microsoft Teams or with a Viva Engage community should be administered via Microsoft Teams or Viva Engage, respectively.

- **Regularly review permissions**: Periodically review and update permissions to ensure that only entitled users and groups have permission to access your site's content and that they are being granted the appropriate permission level. Consider making use of the **Check permissions** option when you want to verify if a particular user or group has access to your site.

By implementing these best practices, you can maintain a SharePoint Online environment that supports collaboration, but at the same time protects sensitive information.

SharePoint Information Architecture

Information Architecture (IA) in SharePoint Online is crucial for organizing, managing, and accessing content efficiently. It involves structuring sites, libraries, lists, and pages to ensure users can find and interact with information seamlessly.

Traditionally, SharePoint's classic experience utilized nested architecture, where sites were organized hierarchically with subsites under parent sites. The top-level site, known as the site collection, could contain multiple subsites, each of which could further include additional subsites, creating a multi-layered structure.

While nested architecture was common in classic SharePoint, it brought challenges like complex navigation, increased management overhead, limited flexibility, performance issues, and cumbersome permissions management. These drawbacks have led to the adoption of flat architecture in SharePoint Online.

In a flat architecture, all sites exist at the same level without subsites, offering simplified navigation, better performance, enhanced flexibility, and easier governance, aligning better with the modern SharePoint practices. Additionally, managing permissions in this architecture becomes more streamlined. With each site operating independently, permissions can be managed at the site level without the complications of inherited or unique permissions cascading through subsites. This clear segmentation makes it easier to assign, monitor, and audit access, ensuring that users only have the permissions necessary for their roles while reducing the risk of accidental overexposure of sensitive information.

Hub sites

Hub sites are a key feature in SharePoint Online, designed to organize and connect related sites within a flat architecture. They provide a centralized way to manage and communicate across multiple top-level sites and are particularly beneficial for enhancing navigation, consistency, and discoverability in large organizations. Hub sites offer several benefits:

- **Unified navigation**: Hub sites enable seamless navigation across connected sites, simplifying access to related content for users.

- **Consistent appearance**: Themes and branding are applied across associated sites.

- **Enhanced search**: Hub sites enhance content discovery by enabling users to search across all associated sites.

- **Centralized information**: Hub sites can aggregate news, activities and events from associated sites, offering a single, consolidating view of essential updates.

- **Permissions management**: While hub sites provide these unifying features, it is important to note that associated sites do not inherit permissions from the hub. Each site manages its own permissions independently, allowing granular control over access to content.

Instead of using subsites, organizations can create multiple top-level sites and associate them with a hub site. This approach maintains the benefits of flat architecture while still providing a way to group related sites.

Figure 7.48 shows the navigation inheritance of a site associated with a hub site:

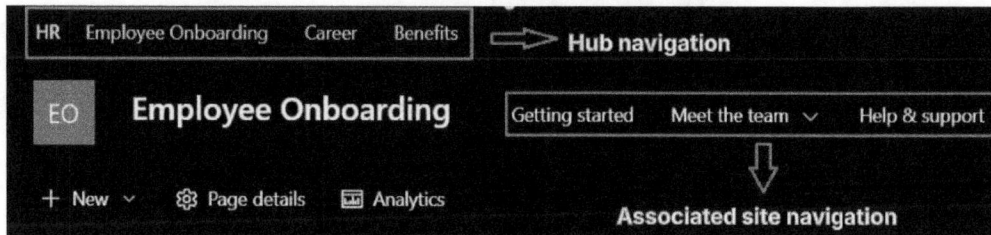

Figure 7.48: *Hub site navigation inherited*

Note: A hub site is a communication or team site designated as a hub by a SharePoint administrator. Site owners can associate their sites with existing hub sites that are available for association and not restricted to specific users. However, only SharePoint administrators can register a site as a hub site.

To associate a site with an existing hub site, follow these steps:

1. Click on the gear icon at the top right corner of the site.
2. Click on **Site Information**.
3. On the **Site Information** page select an existing hub site under **Hub site association**:

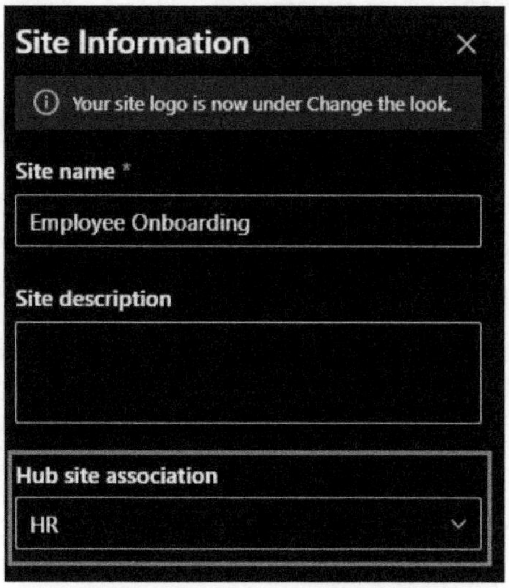

Figure 7.49: *Hub site association*

By leveraging hub sites, organizations can achieve a balance between the simplicity of flat architecture and the need for organized, related content. This modern approach to information architecture in SharePoint Online ensures that users have a streamlined, efficient, and user-friendly experience.

Search in SharePoint Online

SharePoint Online's search functionality is highly advanced, enabling users to easily locate various elements within SharePoint, such as sites, pages, folders, files and much more. The modern search experience, known as Microsoft Search, is tailored to provide a personalized user experience, facilitating the discovery of relevant results. The modern search experience is available to users on the SharePoint start page, hub sites, communication sites, and modern team sites.

A key feature of the search functionality in SharePoint is that search results are displayed according to the user's permissions. Only sites and content accessible to the user will be included in the search results.

Search scope

The search scope is an important aspect of the search functionality in SharePoint. The search box on the SharePoint start page retrieves results from the entire tenant. If users navigate to a SharePoint site, the search scope is limited to that site (unless it is a hub site or a home site). Navigating to a list or library restricts search results to the respective list or library.

The search scope for a hub site extends to all associated sites. Same applies to the site configured as home site by your administrator. Additionally, administrators have the option to configure the site's search scope to apply to the entire tenant.

Next, we will explore the default search experience in different SharePoint locations, such as SharePoint Start page, site, list and document library.

SharePoint start page, tenant level search

The search box on the SharePoint start page can be used to find content within the SharePoint tenant, including pages, files, sites, people, and news. The hint text in the search box, **Search in SharePoint**, indicates its use for searching information across the entire SharePoint tenant:

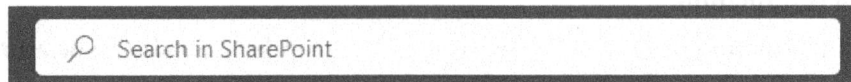

Figure 7.50: Search box on SharePoint start page

The following figure illustrates an example in which we performed a search for the term *employee*:

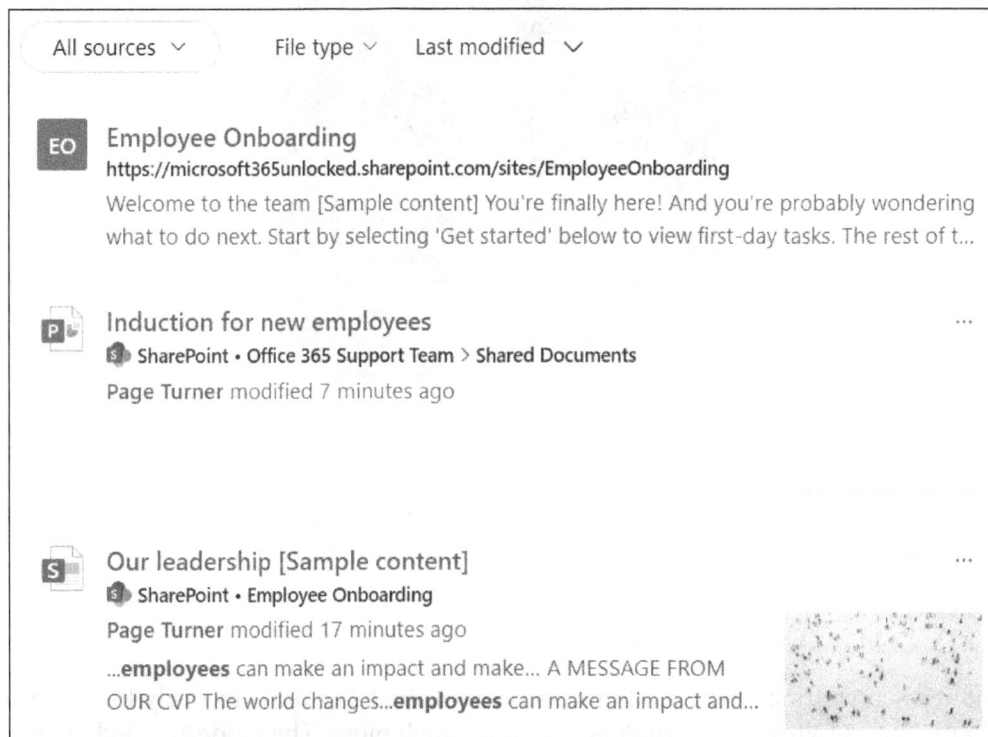

Figure 7.51: Searching across the SharePoint tenant

As seen in our example, all search results include *employee*, either in the title or content. For instance, SharePoint found a site called **Employee Onboarding**, a PowerPoint file titled **Induction for new employees**, and a page without *employee* in the title but within the content. SharePoint searches the content of files and pages to retrieve relevant matches.

Site level search

When navigating to a team site or communication site, the hint text in the search box changes to `Search this site`, as seen in the following figure:

Figure 7.52: Search box on SharePoint site

Search is restricted to the specified site, providing results for items stored within that site. This restriction is applicable if the site is not a hub site or home site, or if the administrator has not configured the search scope to apply to the entire tenant.

In the example below, we conducted a search for the term *department* within a specific site. The figure illustrates the search results from various locations within the site, including a list named **Test list** and two distinct document libraries (**Shared Documents** and **Invoices**). The list and the libraries contain items and documents that include the keyword *department*:

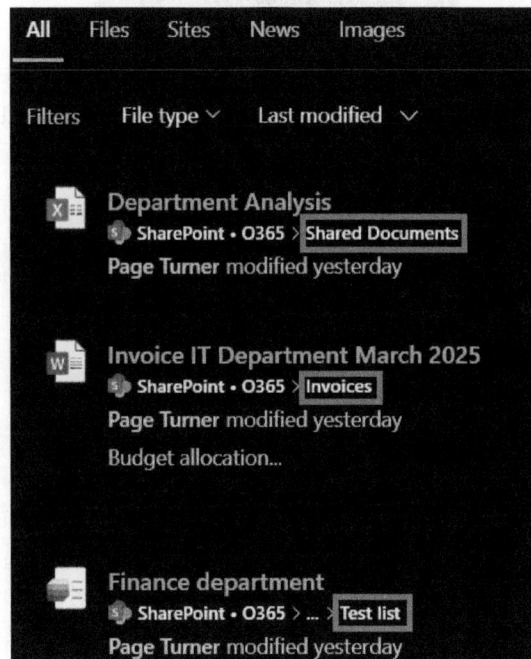

Figure 7.53: Searching within a SharePoint site

List and document library search

Searching at the list or document library level restricts the search to that specific list or library. The hint text displayed in the search box is `Search this library` for document libraries and `Search this list` for lists.

Limiting the search to a specific list or library is particularly useful, as it allows users to quickly find relevant information without sifting through unrelated content. This targeted approach enhances efficiency and productivity by narrowing down the search scope to the most pertinent data.

The following figure illustrates a search example at the document library level. The keyword used was *project*:

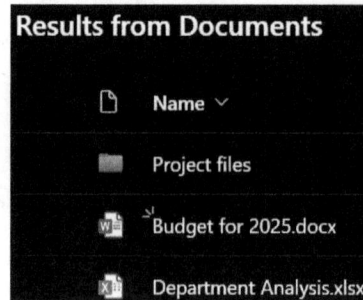

Figure 7.54: Searching within a document library

In our example, the search results retrieved were as follows:

- A folder containing the keyword we used in the folder's name, **Project files**.
- A Word file titled **Budget for 2025**, located within the **Project files** folder:

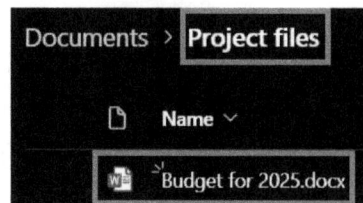

Figure 7.55: Folder content

- An Excel file named **Department Analysis** which includes the relevant keyword within the document:

Figure 7.56: Keyword present in the document's content

This example demonstrates that SharePoint retrieves results if the keyword is present in the title, as well as if it is present within the content of the files. Additionally, SharePoint retrieves files located within a folder that contains the keyword in its title.

Search queries

When working in SharePoint Online, constructing effective search queries is essential for retrieving relevant information quickly and accurately. SharePoint's search functionality leverages the **Keyword Query Language** (**KQL**), a powerful syntax that allows users to create complex search queries using keywords, property restrictions, and operators.

Basic KQL queries

At its core, a KQL query consists of one or more keywords. These keywords can be single words or phrases enclosed in double quotation marks. For example:

- The keyword **budget** returns results containing the word **budget**:

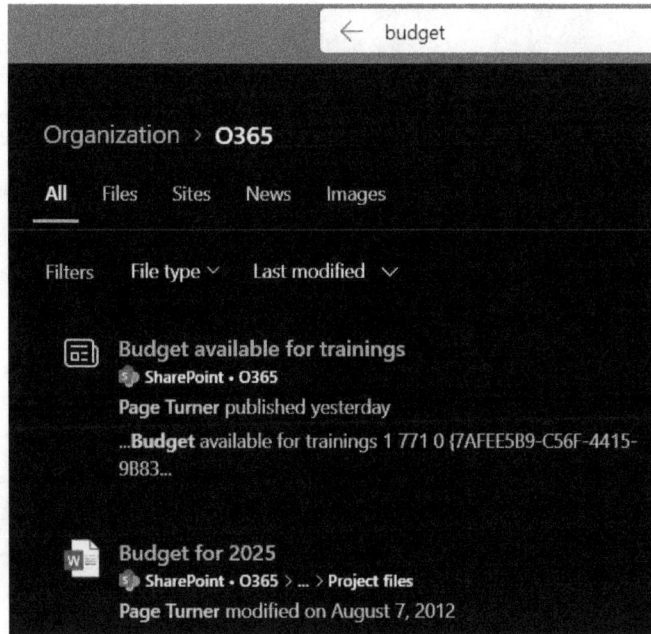

Figure 7.57: Free-text query by word

- **industry landscape continues to evolve** will return results containing the exact phrase:

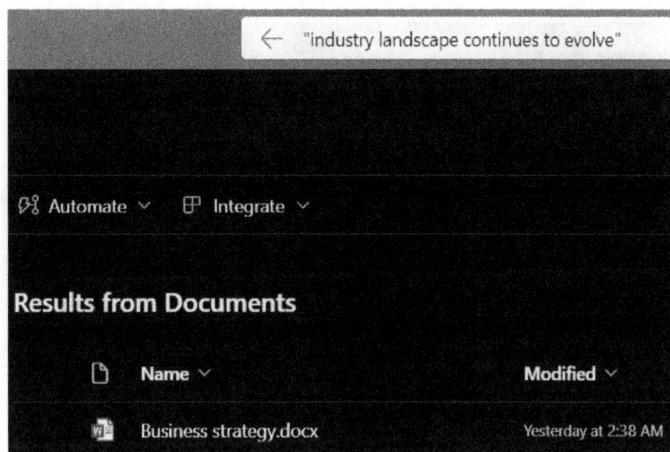

Figure 7.58: Free-text query by phrase

Property restrictions

KQL allows you to refine your search by specifying property restrictions. Property restrictions limit the search to items where a specific property matches a given value. For example:

- *Title:"Budget for 2025"* returns items with the title *Budget for 2025*:

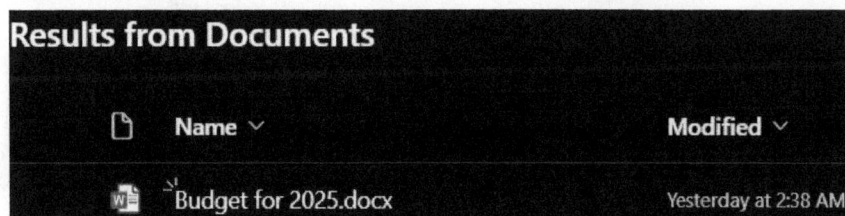

Figure 7.59: Search by title

- *Author:Page Turner* returns items authored by Page Turner:

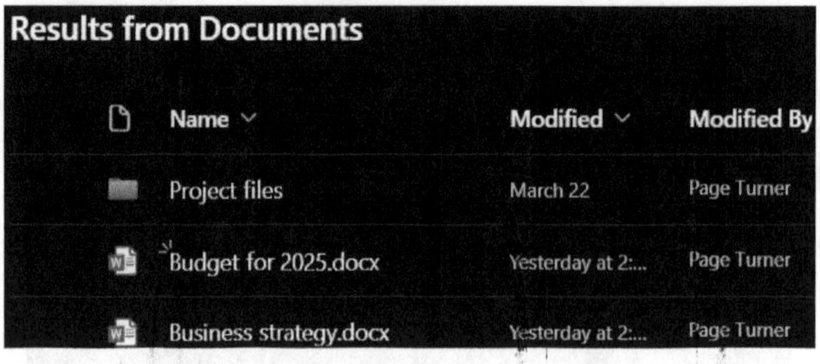

Figure 7.60: Search by author

- *Filetype:xlsx* returns all **.xlsx** files from a specific site or library, depending on the search scope:

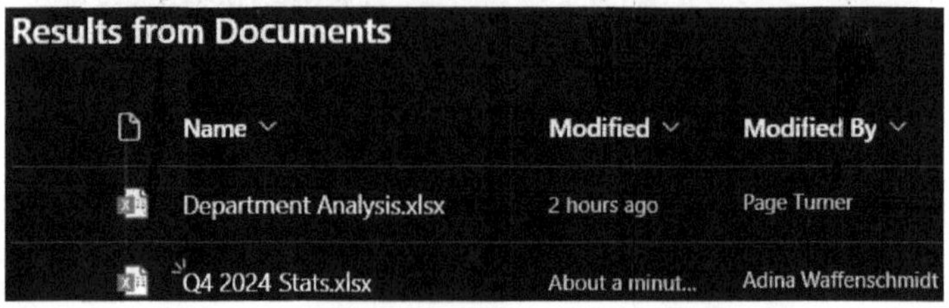

Figure 7.61: Search by file type

- *Lastmodifiedtime=yesterday* returns all items that were last modified yesterday:

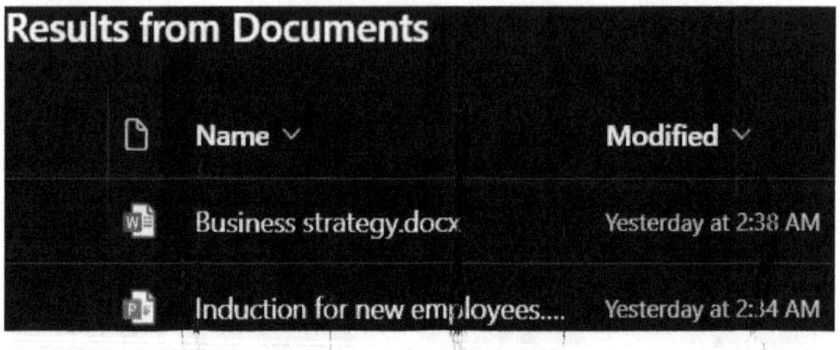

Figure 7.62: Search by last modified time

Combining keywords and property restrictions

You can combine multiple keywords and property restrictions using logical operators such as AND, OR, and NOT. For example:

- *market AND "supply chain"* will return items containing both *market* and *supply chain.*

- *Title:"Budget for 2025" OR Title:"Business strategy"* will return items with either *Budget for 2025* or *Business strategy* in the title.

- *Author:"Page Turner" NOT Title:"Draft"* will return items authored by Page Turner but exclude those with *Draft* in the title.

Using wildcard

KQL queries support the use of wildcards as suffixes. By using the wildcard operator (*), it is possible to use just the beginning portion of a word to facilitate prefix matching. In prefix matching, SharePoint Search returns results that include words containing the specified term followed by zero or more characters. For example:

- *Title:"proj*"* returns items containing in the title words that start with *proj*, such as *project* and *projections*:

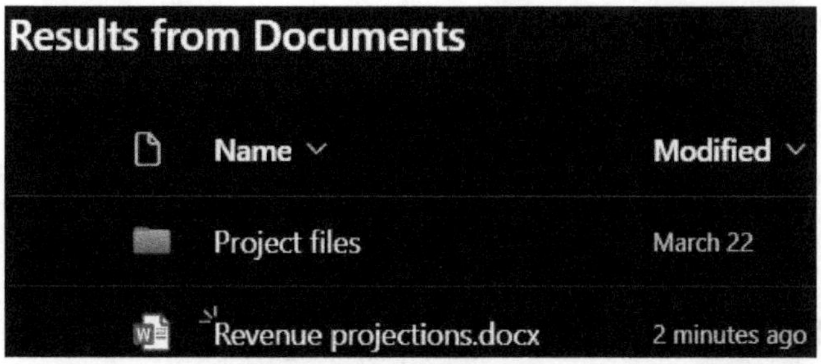

Results from Documents

🗋	Name ∨	Modified ∨
🖿	Project files	March 22
📄	Revenue projections.docx	2 minutes ago

Figure 7.63: Search using wildcard

These are only a few examples of search queries that can be used in SharePoint Online. With KQL you can create precise and efficient search queries that help you find the information you need in SharePoint Online quickly and effectively.

Site pages

SharePoint site pages are essential components of SharePoint Online, enabling users to create, manage, and share content within their organization. These pages can be customized to suit specific needs, making them versatile tools for collaboration, communication, and information sharing.

A SharePoint site page is a web page that can be created within a SharePoint site. It serves as a canvas where users can add and organize various types of content, such as text, images, videos, documents, and more. SharePoint pages are designed to be user-friendly and responsive, ensuring that they look great on any device.

All new SharePoint sites are created with one or more site pages, depending on the chosen site template. For instance, a communication site created using the Blank template contains a single site page that serves as the home page. In contrast, a communication site created based on the *Human Resources* template includes one home page and four additional pages. The number of site pages included with the selected site template is shown during the site creation process.

The following figure provides details about the number of site pages included in the Human Resources site template:

Site capabilities ∧

- Showcase information about compensation and financial wellness
- Highlight career resources for learning and development
- Feature benefits available to employees
- Share the organization's cultural priorities and values

What's included ∧

1 home page
4 additional pages

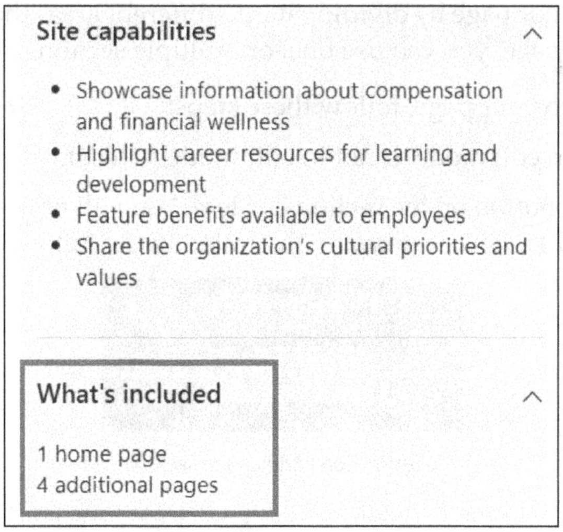

Figure 7.64: Pages included in the Human resources site template

It is important to distinguish between a SharePoint page and a SharePoint site. Much like creating multiple lists or libraries within a SharePoint site, one can also create multiple pages to display relevant content. Essentially, the site serves as the container for these SharePoint pages. For instance, if there is a site dedicated to the Marketing department within an organization, various site pages can be utilized within the site to organize and present content effectively. This might include a home page offering an overview of the department's activities, announcements, and important links; a page detailing marketing campaigns; another page providing updates on ongoing marketing projects, and so forth.

Creating different site pages within a SharePoint site allows for better organization and accessibility of information, enabling enhanced navigation and focused content.

Creating and customizing a site page

To create a new site page, you can follow these steps:

1. Navigate to the home page of your site
2. Click on + **New** and then select **Page**:
3. Select a page template from the list of available templates.
4. Select **Create as a private draft** (optional) if you want to create the page as a private draft, meaning that no one except you and the users you decide to share the page with can see it:

Figure 7.65: Create page as private draft

5. Click on **Create page** button to create the page.

The newly created page will open in edit mode and the next step is to customize it as per your requirements.

By making use of sections and web parts to customize a SharePoint page, users can adjust the content and layout according to their particular needs.

Sections allow you to organize your page by dividing it into different areas that you can then use to customize your page. Within a SharePoint page, you can use one, or multiple sections of different types and columns.

To incorporate a new section into your page, follow these steps:

1. Ensure that the page is in edit mode. If not in edit mode, select **Edit** at the top right of the page.
2. Hover over the circled + button on the section borders. You will notice this will change into + **Section**, with a tooltip stating **Add a new section**, as illustrated in the following figure:

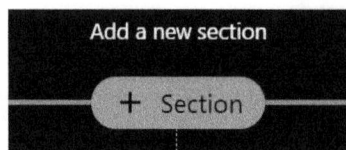

Figure 7.66: Add a new section

3. Click on + **Section**.
4. Select the type of section you need to insert from the options available, as illustrated in the following figure:

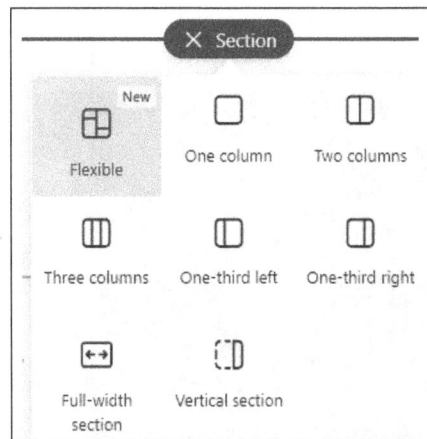

Figure 7.67: Select the section type

Note: Full-width sections are available on communication site pages. On team sites, this section type can only be used at the top of the page with a banner web part.

Web parts are the building blocks of SharePoint pages. They allow users to add different types of content, such as text, images, documents, videos, and more.

Web parts can be added to a page while in edit mode, by hovering the mouse inside an existing section in the location where you want to add the new webpart, and clicking on the + circled button, as shown in the following figure:

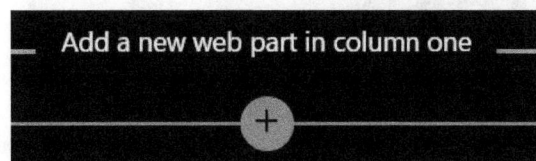

Figure 7.68: Add a webpart

SharePoint offers a variety of pre-built web parts that can be integrated into a page. These range from basic text, media, and content web parts to more advanced options such as code snippet and embed webparts.

The web parts are categorized for convenience, enabling users to filter by category or directly search for a specific web part:

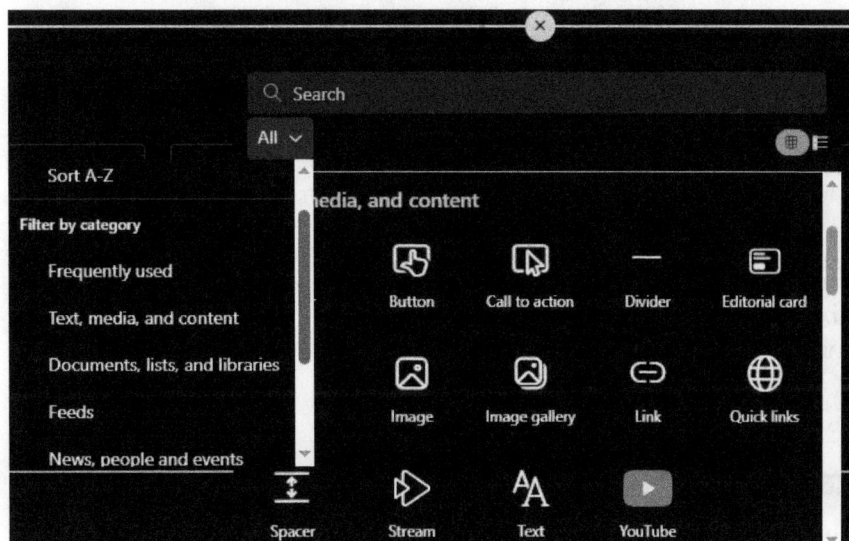

Figure 7.69: Select or search for a web part

When a page is in edit mode, you can also use the **Toolbox** located on the right pane of the screen in order to select and insert new web parts, stock images and section templates:

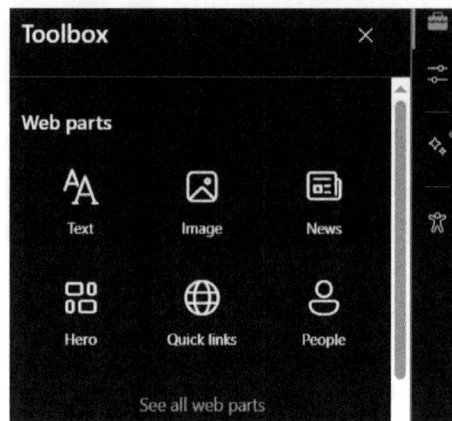

Figure 7.70: Toolbox

Saving and publishing a page

While editing a SharePoint page, any changes you make are automatically saved as a draft. You can also manually save the page as a draft by clicking on the **Save as draft** button:

Figure 7.71: Save as draft

This ensures that the latest version of the page is in a draft state and not yet visible to site visitors. Saving as draft allows you to continue editing and refining the content without making it publicly accessible. This is particularly useful when you need to make extensive updates or review the changes before sharing them with others.

Once you are satisfied with the changes, you can proceed to publish the page or republish it if further modifications are made after the initial publication:

Figure 7.72: Publish a page

Publishing makes the page visible to everyone who can view your site. It ensures that the latest version of the page is accessible to all users, including those with read-only permissions. Publishing is essential for sharing finalized content and updates with your audience.

By understanding the difference between saving as draft and publishing, you can effectively manage the visibility and accessibility of your SharePoint pages, ensuring that your content is shared at the right time and with the right audience.

Manage site pages

All site pages, including drafts, are stored within the *Site Pages* library. To access this library, follow these steps:

1. Click on the gear icon at the top right corner of the site and select **Site Contents**.
2. Under the **Contents** tab, click on **Site Pages**.

In the **Site Pages** library, you can view and manage the version history of a page. Additionally, you can set a different page as the homepage for the site. Both options are accessible by right-clicking on a specific page and selecting **Version history** or **Make homepage**, as illustrated in the following figure:

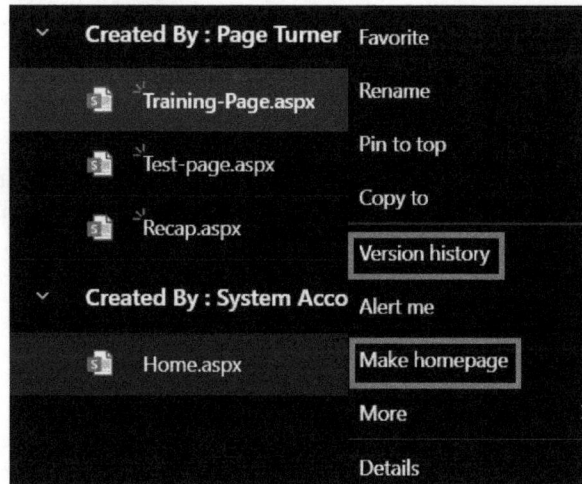

Figure 7.73: Access version history or set a page as homepage

Conclusion

In this chapter, we have looked into the essential aspects of SharePoint Online, including site types, lists and libraries, permissions management, search and site pages.

Overall, this chapter has provided a comprehensive overview of SharePoint Online's core capabilities, empowering you to leverage its features to boost collaboration, productivity, and data security within your organization.

In the next chapter, we will explore OneDrive, a cloud storage service that enables storing, sharing, and synchronizing your files across multiple devices.

Join our Discord space

Join our Discord workspace for latest updates, offers, tech happenings around the world, new releases, and sessions with the authors:

https://discord.bpbonline.com

CHAPTER 8
OneDrive

Introduction

In today's digital age, efficient file management and seamless collaboration are crucial for both personal and professional success. OneDrive offers a comprehensive solution to meet these needs. This chapter delves into the various aspects of OneDrive, exploring its functionalities, benefits, and practical applications. From understanding the basics of OneDrive to mastering advanced features like synchronization and sharing, this chapter aims to equip you with the knowledge to leverage OneDrive effectively.

Structure

The chapter covers the following topics:

- Understanding OneDrive
- Licensing
- Getting started with OneDrive for work or school
- Working with content in OneDrive
- Sharing content and managing access
- Sync your files with OneDrive sync app
- OneDrive mobile app

Objectives

By the end of this chapter, readers will have a comprehensive understanding of OneDrive's functionalities and benefits. They will be able to navigate its features with ease, including creating and uploading files and folders, co-authoring documents, and managing versions. Readers will also learn how to delete and restore content and effectively use the OneDrive synchronization client to sync their files locally. Additionally, they will gain insights into sharing content and managing access, as well as leveraging the OneDrive mobile app for on-the-go productivity. Furthermore, readers will understand the differences between OneDrive for work or school, OneDrive for home, and the OneDrive sync app, and how to utilize each version to enhance their workflow and collaboration.

Understanding OneDrive

OneDrive is a versatile cloud storage service that not only provides a secure place to store your files but also offers a range of features designed to enhance productivity and collaboration. With OneDrive, you can access your files from any device with an internet connection, making it easy to work on the go. The service supports a wide variety of file types, including documents, photos, videos, and more, ensuring that all your important data is readily available whenever you need it.

One of the key advantages of OneDrive is its seamless integration with Microsoft Office applications. This integration allows you to create, edit, and share documents directly from the cloud, with changes being saved automatically. This means you can start working on a document on your computer, continue editing it on your tablet, and finish it on your phone, all without worrying about manually transferring files between devices.

Unlike SharePoint sites, which provide a centralized location for team members to collaborate, OneDrive is your personal space where you can store and work with your files and share only individual files and folders with others, if needed. OneDrive offers robust sharing and collaboration features. You can easily share files and folders with others, set permissions to control who can view or edit your content, and collaborate in real-time on documents. This makes OneDrive an excellent tool for both individual use and team projects, as it facilitates efficient communication and coordination.

Another important aspect of OneDrive is its synchronization capabilities. The OneDrive sync client allows you to sync files between your local device and the cloud, ensuring that you always have the latest version of your files available offline.

Overall, OneDrive is a powerful and flexible cloud storage solution that caters to a wide range of needs, from personal file storage to professional collaboration. Its integration with Microsoft Office, robust sharing features, and reliable synchronization make it an indispensable tool for modern digital life.

Since the name OneDrive is used for different versions of this service, it is crucial to clearly distinguish between them to avoid confusion and ensure that users understand the specific functionalities and features associated with each one. *OneDrive* cloud storage comes in two versions, **OneDrive for work** or school and **OneDrive for home**. Additionally, we have the sync app provided by Microsoft to locally sync files and folders, which is also called *OneDrive*. Let us explore each of them individually to better understand their purposes and functionalities.

OneDrive for work or school

OneDrive for work or school was previously known as **OneDrive for Business**, which is why you may still encounter references to OneDrive for Business in various places, articles, and documentation. This version is part of Microsoft 365 and is designed for organizational use. It offers advanced collaboration features, such as integration with Microsoft Teams and SharePoint, making it ideal for business environments.

With OneDrive for work or school, you have your own personal library where you can store business data you create and edit, without worrying about privacy or security, as these files are by default private to you. Each licensed user in our organization has a personal OneDrive linked to their username.

OneDrive for work or school can be accessed from the Microsoft 365 app launcher, as shown in *Figure 8.1*:

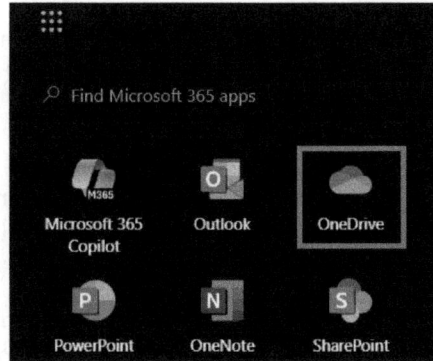

Figure 8.1: *Access OneDrive from the app launcher*

Once you access it, you will notice that the URL for this OneDrive version is **https://yourorganization-my.sharepoint.com**, as in the example shown in *Figure 8.2*:

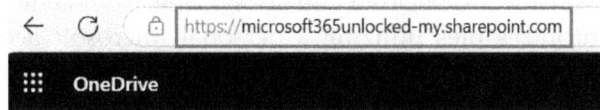

Figure 8.2: *OneDrive for work or school URL*

Let us break down the URL to understand its structure:

- **yourorganization** represents the actual name of your Microsoft 365 tenant. In our example, this is **microsoft365unlocked**.

- The **-my** portion indicates that this is your personal site.

- **sharepoint.com** indicates that OneDrive for work or school is based on SharePoint Online.

Knowing that OneDrive is based on SharePoint Online allows you to better understand the underlying platform and its capabilities. Understanding the URL structure is important because it helps you identify where your accessed resource is hosted. By examining the URL, you can quickly determine the hosting environment and navigate your resources more efficiently.

OneDrive for home

OneDrive for home, also known as **OneDrive Personal**, is intended for personal use. It provides a simple and secure way to store personal files, photos, and videos and share them with family and friends.

This version of OneDrive is available for free by signing up for a Microsoft account. Users can then sign in with this account and access OneDrive for home at **https://onedrive.live.com,** as shown in *Figure 8.3*:

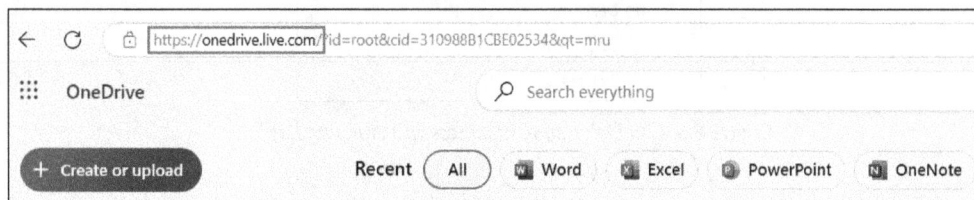

Figure 8.3: *OneDrive for home*

The free version offers 5 GB of cloud storage. Additional storage requires upgrading to a Microsoft 365 Personal or Family subscription.

OneDrive sync app

The OneDrive synchronization application is an essential component that facilitates local file management while ensuring all modifications are mirrored in the cloud, provided internet connectivity is available. This synchronization operates bidirectionally, ensuring any changes made to files or folders in the cloud are also updated locally, and vice versa.

With the sync app, you can manage your synchronized files directly through *File Explorer* and access them even without an internet connection. Once you are back online, any modifications made by you, or others will automatically update.

The OneDrive application is pre-installed on computers running Windows 10 or 11. For Mac or computers running older versions of Windows, the OneDrive application can be downloaded at **onedrive.com/download**.

The OneDrive sync app enables local synchronization of files and folders from OneDrive for home and OneDrive for work or school, as well as from SharePoint Online document libraries.

When synchronization is active, you will observe one or two cloud icons in the Windows notification area on the taskbar, depending on the version of OneDrive you are syncing. The white cloud icon denotes OneDrive for personal use, which synchronizes files utilizing a personal Microsoft account. Conversely, OneDrive for work or school is indicated by a blue cloud icon, which synchronizes business OneDrive files and/or SharePoint Online document libraries.

Figure 8.4 illustrates both cloud icons as displayed on the taskbar:

Figure 8.4: *OneDrive sync app icons*

OneDrive for work or school, OneDrive for home, and SharePoint libraries can all be synchronized on a single device. Here is how these three appear in Windows Explorer:

Figure 8.5: *OneDrive sync instances in Windows Explorer*

SharePoint document libraries are listed under the *Organization name* folder, in our example, is **Microsoft 365 Unlocked**. OneDrive for home or school is labeled *OneDrive – Organization name*, while OneDrive for personal use is labeled **OneDrive – Personal**.

The OneDrive sync app is an essential component of the OneDrive ecosystem. Not only does it keep your files up to date across all your devices, but it also provides confidence by knowing that your data is always secure and accessible whenever you need it.

Licensing

In terms of licensing, **OneDrive for work or school** is included with Microsoft 365 Business and Enterprise subscriptions, which typically offer 1TB of cloud storage per user. For Microsoft 365 E3 and E5 subscriptions, this can be extended to 5TB per user.

OneDrive for work or school licensing model is designed to integrate seamlessly with other Microsoft 365 services. This means that users can enjoy a unified experience across various applications, such as Teams, SharePoint, and Outlook, all while benefiting from the robust storage and collaboration features of OneDrive. This integration not only enhances productivity but also simplifies IT management by providing a cohesive ecosystem for all digital tools.

OneDrive for home is available for free with a Microsoft account, providing 5GB of storage. Users can upgrade to a Microsoft 365 Basic for 100GB of cloud storage or to a Microsoft 365 Personal or Family subscription for 1TB of storage per person.

Getting started with OneDrive for work or school

Going forward in this chapter, we will focus on OneDrive for work or school as part of Microsoft 365. This version of OneDrive is designed to meet the needs of organizations, providing advanced collaboration tools and integration with other Microsoft 365 services. By understanding how to work with content in OneDrive for work or school, you will be able to leverage its full potential to enhance your workflow and achieve your goals.

Once you access OneDrive for work or school either from the Microsoft 365 app launcher or directly by navigating to **https://yourorganization-my.sharepoint.com**, you will reach the OneDrive home page, where you can find your recently accessed and edited content and you can filter it by content type (Word, Excel, PowerPoint, PDF files and more):

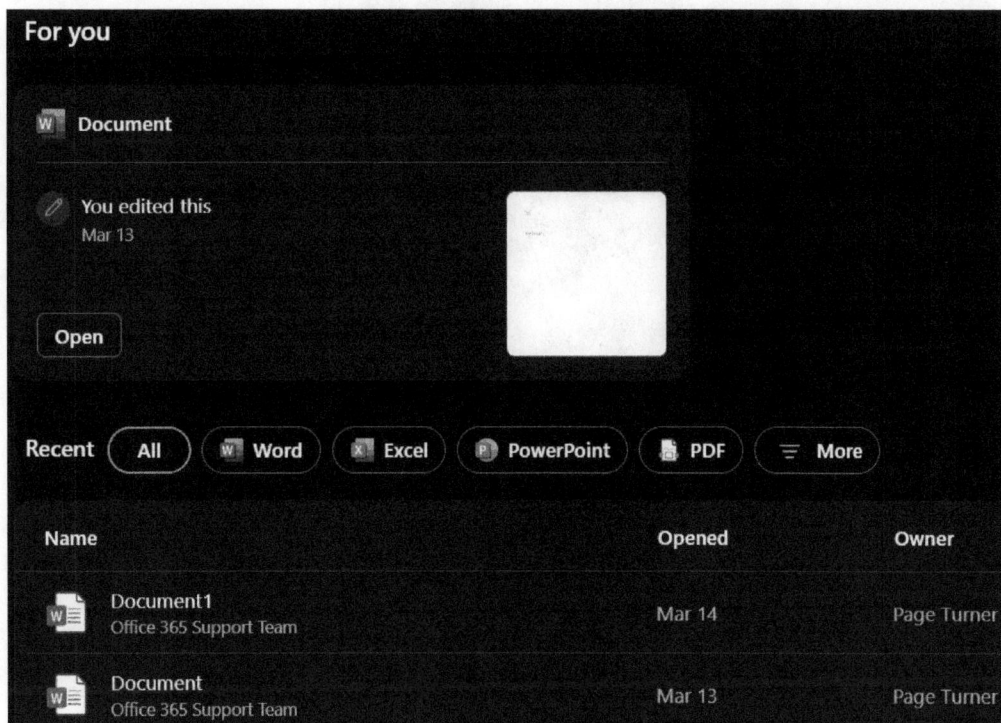

Figure 8.6: *OneDrive home page*

The pane on the left side of the screen provides options to create or upload new content, as well as access existing or deleted content:

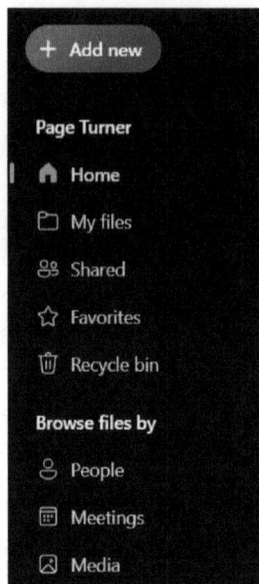

Figure 8.7: OneDrive navigation options

Existing files you have created or uploaded are located under **My files**, while the ones that have been shared with you are located under **Shared**.

Below the options displayed in *Figure 8.7*, there is a **Quick access** menu designed to facilitate navigation to SharePoint Online document libraries from sites you have the necessary permissions to access.

Additionally, you can also view the amount of storage currently utilized against the allocated storage for your account:

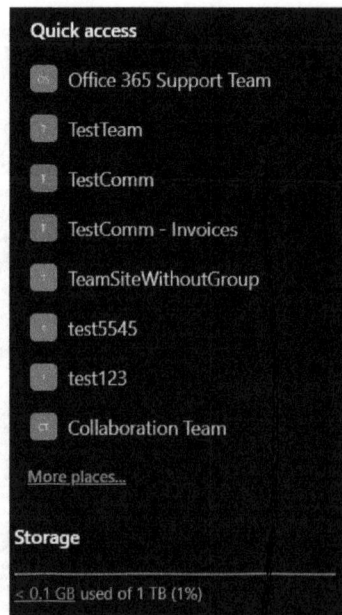

Figure 8.8: Quick access and available storage

Working with content in OneDrive

OneDrive offers a variety of features that allow users to create, upload, share, and manage files effortlessly. Whether you are working on documents, photos, videos, or other types of files, OneDrive ensures that your content is always accessible and up to date across all your devices.

Create and upload content

Creating and uploading content in OneDrive is straightforward. By clicking on the + **Add new** button, you can select one of the available options for content upload or creation. You can create a new folder, upload folders and files, as well as create a new Word document, Excel workbook, PowerPoint presentation, OneNote notebook, and more, as seen in *Figure 8.9*:

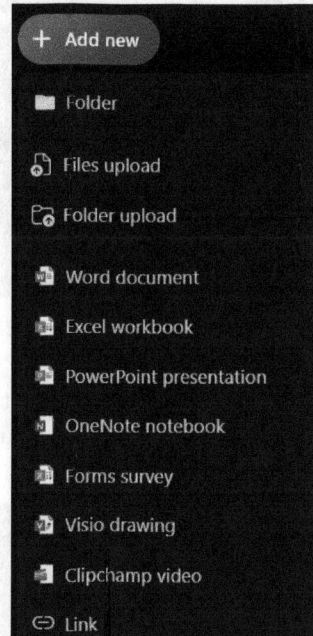

Figure 8.9: Add content

All content that you create, and upload will be available under **My files,** which represents your OneDrive library:

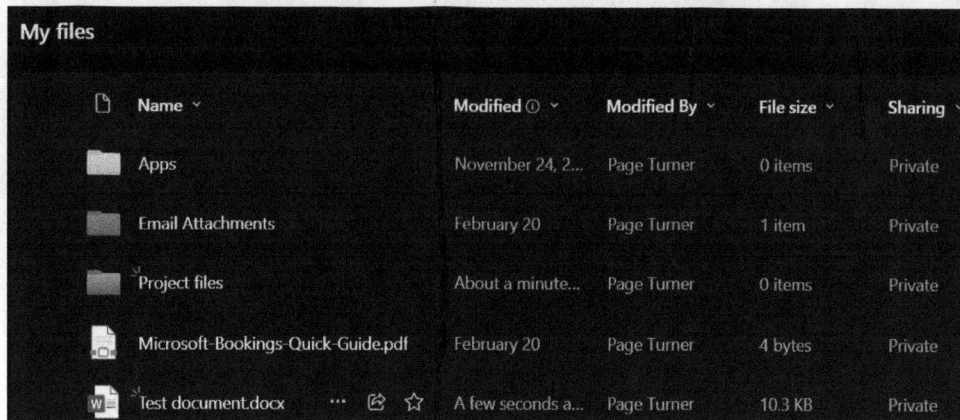

Figure 8.10: My files

To quickly upload content, you can also drag and drop files and folders to the **My files** area.

Copy and move content

In OneDrive, you can easily copy or move content from the original location to a different folder in your OneDrive library or even to a SharePoint Online library.

To accomplish this, navigate to **My files**, right-click on the desired file or folder, and select either **Copy to** or **Move to**, depending on the action you intend to perform:

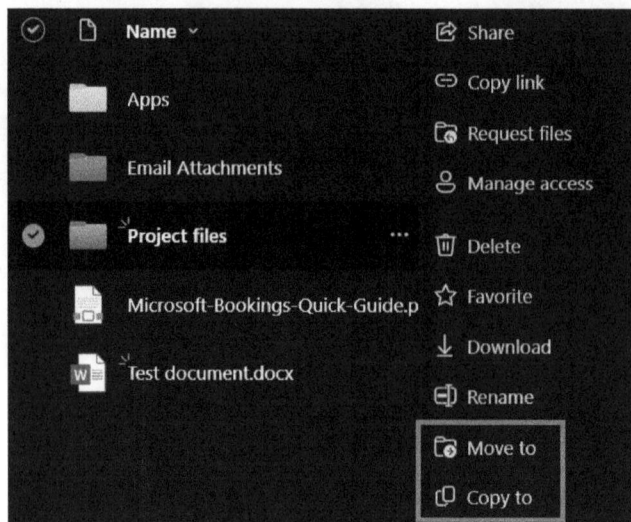

Figure 8.11: Copy or move content

Once the desired option is selected, you will be asked to choose the location where you want to copy or move your file or folder. In the example shown in the following figure, we selected to copy a folder from the OneDrive library to a SharePoint Online document library:

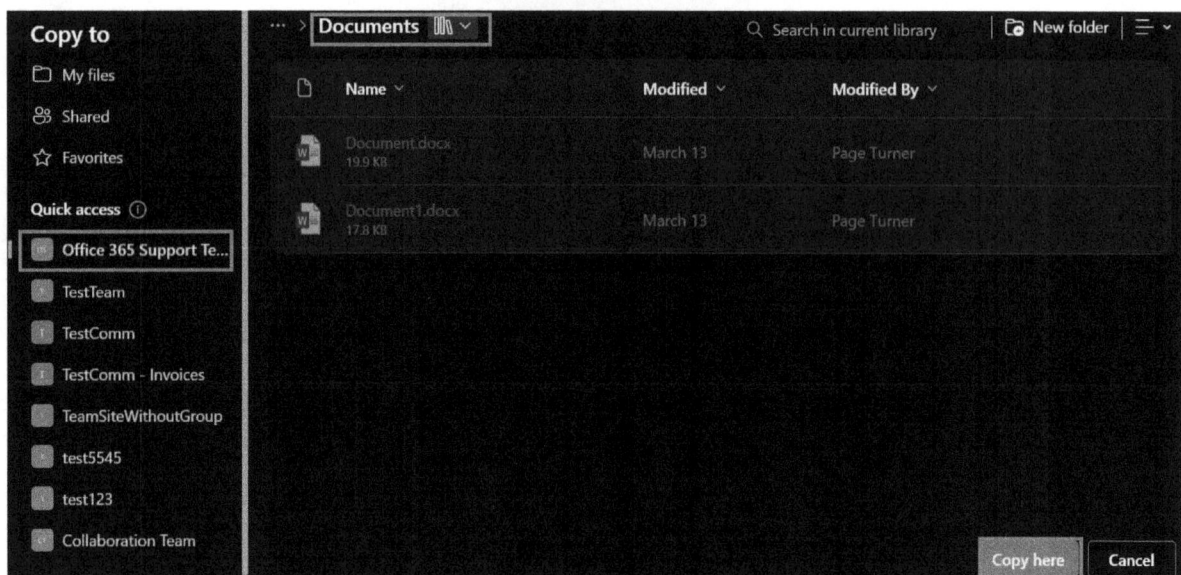

Figure 8.12: Copy content to a SharePoint library

Once copied, we can find the folder in the SharePoint library we selected:

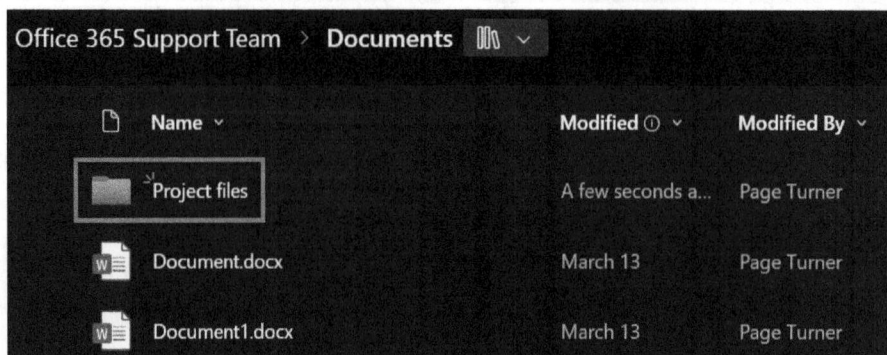

Figure 8.13: Folder copied to a SharePoint library

Collaborating in real-time on documents

Using Microsoft 365 along with OneDrive or SharePoint, several individuals can simultaneously collaborate on Word documents, Excel spreadsheets, or PowerPoint presentations. This simultaneous collaboration is known as **co-authoring**.

Co-authoring allows multiple users to work on the same document at the same time. This feature is ideal for team projects, as it enables real-time collaboration and eliminates the need for sending files back and forth via email.

To collaborate on a document stored in your OneDrive with other users, it is necessary to grant them edit access to the document.

When another person is working on the same document, this will be indicated within the document itself, as illustrated in the following figure:

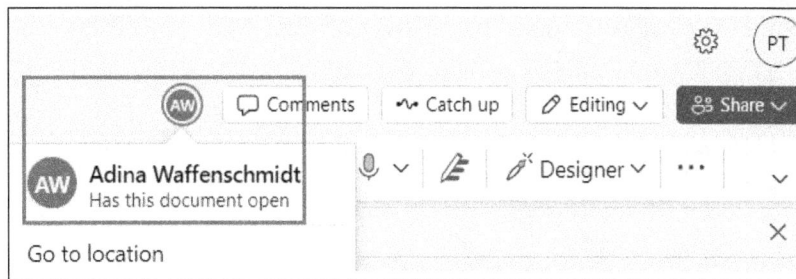

Figure 8.14: Co-authoring a document

When co-authoring a document, you can see the changes made by others in real-time:

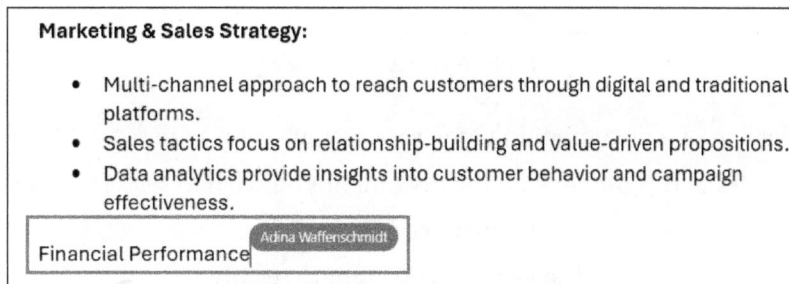

Figure 8.15: View changes in real-time

You can also communicate with your collaborators directly within the document by inserting comments, mentioning individuals, and assigning tasks:

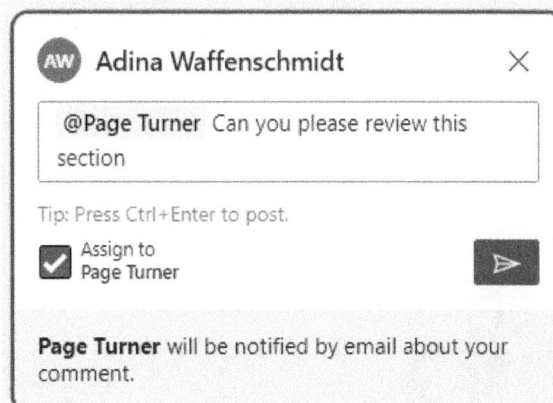

Figure 8.16: Insert comment and assign task

This seamless integration fosters a more efficient and dynamic workflow, as team members can contribute their ideas and feedback instantly.

Real-time collaboration on documents through co-authoring significantly transforms team dynamics. By facilitating concurrent editing, this feature improves productivity, optimizes workflows, and ensures consistency among team members.

Working with versions

OneDrive for work or school document libraries, like SharePoint document libraries, store the last 500 major versions of files by default. Each time a document undergoes a modification or update, a new version is produced, which supersedes the previous version. This helps prevent data loss, particularly when a document is shared among multiple individuals who might make changes that are not intended.

The version history of a file displays the number of versions, the last modification date for each version, the size, and the user who made the modifications, as shown in *Figure 8.17*:

Version history			
Version	Modified	Size	Modified By
5.0	3/24/2025 3:35 PM	12.8 KB	Page Turner
4.0	3/24/2025 3:25 PM	10.5 KB	Adina Waffenschmidt
3.0	3/22/2025 6:26 PM	10.3 KB	Page Turner
2.0	3/22/2025 6:25 PM	10.3 KB	Page Turner
1.0	3/22/2025 6:25 PM	10.4 KB	Page Turner

Figure 8.17: Version history

To restore a previous version of a document in OneDrive, follow these steps:

1. Navigate to **My files** and right-click on the document you wish to restore a previous version of.
2. Select **Version history** from the menu displayed.
3. Click on the ellipsis (...) next to the version you want to restore.
4. Click **Restore**:

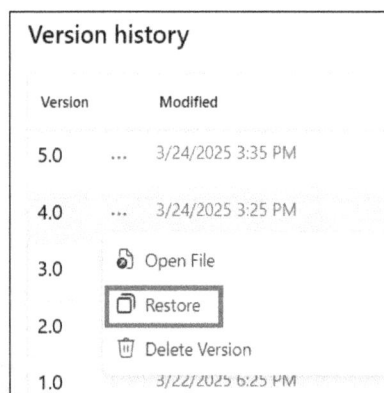

Version history	
Version	Modified
5.0	... 3/24/2025 3:35 PM
4.0	... 3/24/2025 3:25 PM
3.0	Open File
2.0	Restore
	Delete Version
1.0	3/22/2025 6:25 PM

Figure 8.18: Restore a previous version

From this menu, you can open the file to verify the version you wish to restore, or you can delete versions that are no longer required. When you opt to restore a version, a new version identical to the one selected for restoration is created.

There may be circumstances where it is necessary to reduce the version count limit stored in your OneDrive library for storage management purposes, particularly if your documents are frequently updated, and retaining the last 500 versions is not required.

To reduce the version count limit, follow these steps:

1. Click the gear icon on the top right of your OneDrive site and then click on **OneDrive settings**:

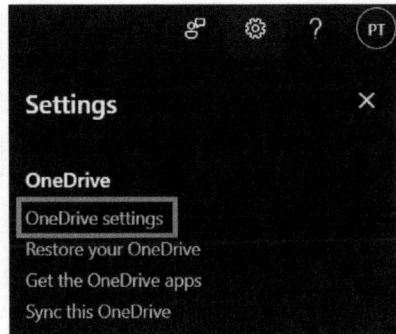

Figure 8.19: OneDrive settings

2. On the left pane, click on **More Settings**.

3. Under **Can't find what you are looking for?** click on **Return to the old Site settings page**:

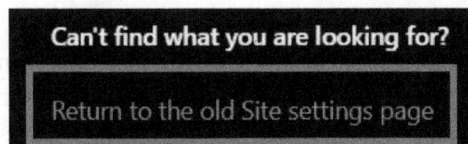

Figure 8.20: Old site settings page

4. On the **Site Settings** page, under **Site Administration**, click on **Site libraries and lists**:

Figure 8.21: Site libraries and lists

5. Select **Customize "Documents"**. *Documents* is the name of your default OneDrive library:

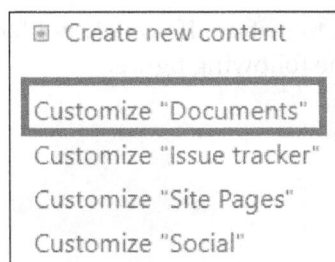

Figure 8.22: Customize "Documents"

6. In the document library settings, under **General Settings**, click on **Versioning settings**:

General Settings

▫ List name, description and navigation
▫ Versioning settings
▫ Advanced settings
▫ Validation settings
▫ Column default value settings
▫ Audience targeting settings
▫ Rating settings

Figure 8.23: Versioning settings

7. Under *Version count limit*, enter the number of versions you wish to keep for the documents in your library. Please note that the minimum number of versions is 100.

8. Click **OK** to save the changes.

Like SharePoint document libraries, the *Versioning settings* page allows you to configure various options. These include creating major and minor (draft) versions, setting version time limits, requiring content approval, and more.

Working with versions in OneDrive provides a robust mechanism for managing document changes and ensuring data integrity. By maintaining a comprehensive version history, OneDrive allows users to easily track modifications, restore previous versions, and safeguard their work against unintended changes. Embracing this feature empowers teams to collaborate more effectively, knowing that their documents are secure, and their progress is always preserved.

Restore content

Whether you accidentally deleted a file or need to restore an entire library, OneDrive makes it simple to restore deleted content.

Restore content from the Recycle bin

When a file or folder is deleted in OneDrive for work or school, it is transferred to the *Recycle bin* and stored for 93 days before being permanently removed. There are two recycle bin stages. Initially, the deleted OneDrive content is sent to the first-stage recycle bin, where it remains for 93 days, unless manually removed. If content is manually deleted from the first-stage recycle bin, it moves to the second-stage recycle bin for the remainder of the 93-day period, unless manually removed from this stage as well.

To restore deleted content from the recycle bin, follow these steps:

1. Navigate to your OneDrive and click on the **Recycle bin** option in the left pane.

2. Locate the file or folder you wish to restore. If you cannot locate the content, check the second-stage recycle bin as well, as shown in the following figure:

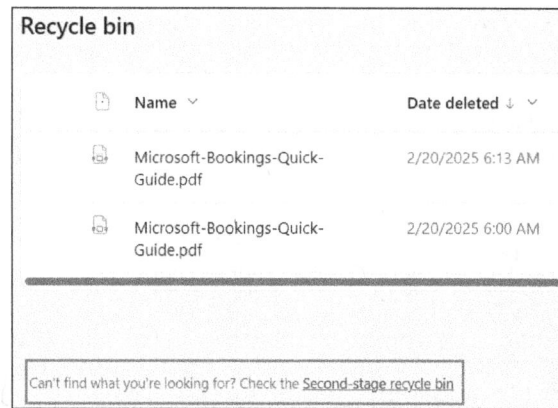

Figure 8.24: OneDrive recycle bin

3. Select the item you want to restore and click on the **Restore** button. The content will be moved back to its original location in your OneDrive.

Restore your OneDrive

In certain situations, it may be necessary to restore the entire OneDrive library to recover lost or deleted files or to revert changes made to the library. Restoring your OneDrive is useful when accidentally deleting multiple files or folders or if something breaks during bulk edits. The *Restore your OneDrive* feature allows you to return your library to a selected point in time, with a maximum restoration period of 30 days.

To restore your entire OneDrive, follow these steps:

1. Go to the OneDrive website and click on the gear icon at the top of the page, then choose the **Restore your OneDrive** option.

2. On the *Restore your OneDrive* page, pick a point in time from the dropdown list, like **One week ago**, or choose **Custom date and time**.

3. Select a change from the activity list. This will highlight the change selected and all the changes before it. The highlighted changes will be the ones to undo. The activity feed shows individual file and folder operations in reverse chronological order. Scroll down to see previous days or use the slider below the daily activity chart to quickly navigate to a specific day:

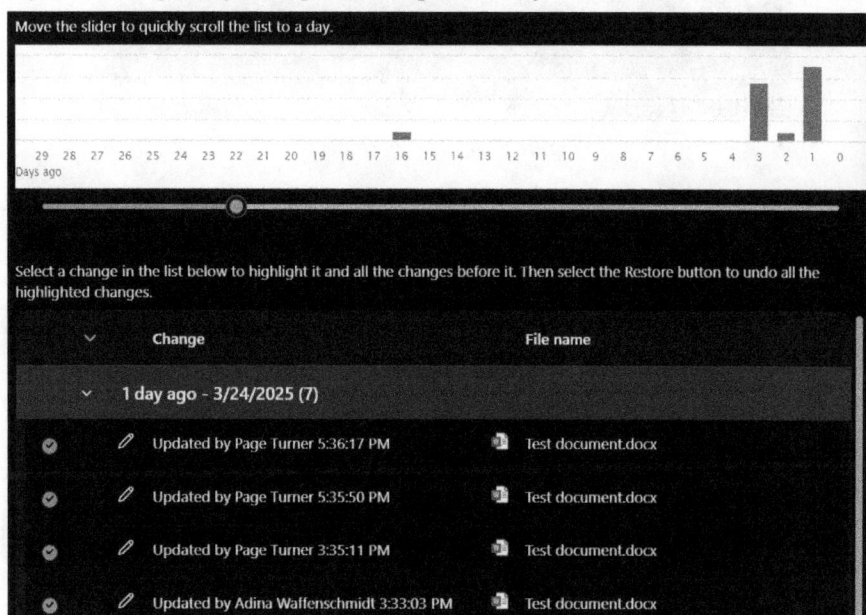

Figure 8.25: Restore OneDrive

4. When you are ready to restore your OneDrive, click **Restore**. This action will undo all the selected activities. Your OneDrive files will be restored to the state before the first activity you selected.

Note: Any files or folders created after the restore point date will be moved to your OneDrive recycle bin. Permanently deleted files from the recycle bin cannot be recovered.

Sharing content and managing access

To collaborate with others on documents and folders in your OneDrive library, or to share a file for viewing or review, you can use OneDrive's sharing feature to share files and/or folders with users and groups.

In OneDrive, you can easily share files and folders from your library with others and grant only the necessary permission level, depending on your requirements.

Sharing content

To share a file or a folder in OneDrive, follow these steps:

1. Navigate to your OneDrive site and go to **My files**.

2. Right-click on the file or folder you want to share and select **Share**.

3. In the sharing dialog window, you can add users or groups by typing their name or email address, and select the appropriate permission level:

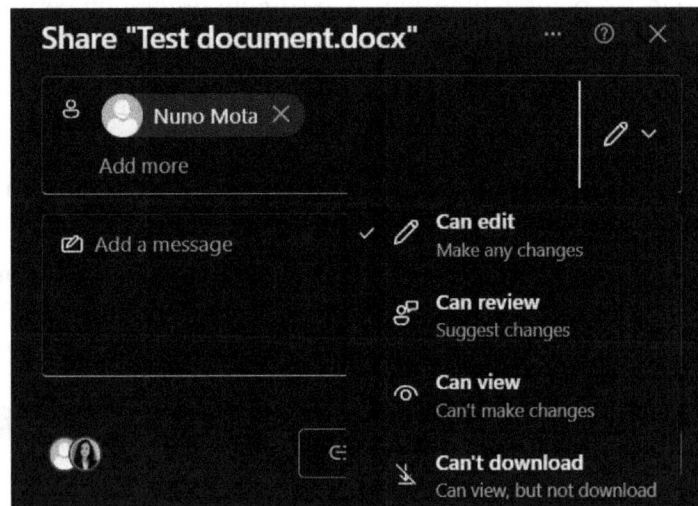

Figure 8.26: Sharing content

When sharing Office documents, the **Can review** permission option will be available for selection, as demonstrated in *Figure 8.26*.

4. Add a message (optional) and click **Send**. This will send an invite in an email to the users you shared the file or folder with.

Alternatively, instead of sharing a file or folder directly and sending an email invitation, you can choose to generate a link to the respective file or folder.

To achieve this, follow the next steps:

1. In the sharing dialog window, click on the gear icon next to the **Copy link** option. This will open the **Link settings** window:

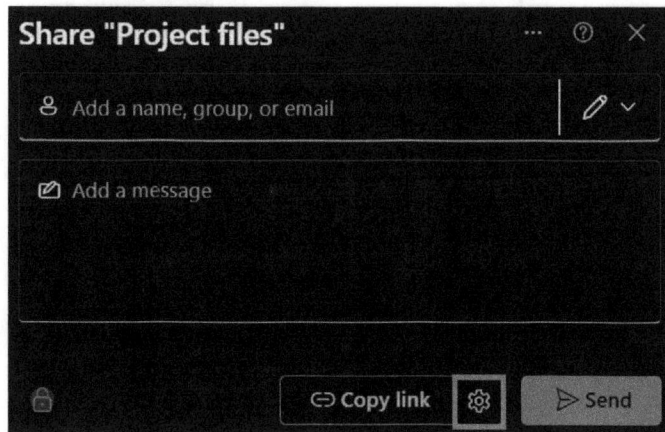

Figure 8.27: Open link settings

2. Under **The Link works for** section, select one of the sharing options available for the link, as shown in *Figure 8.28*:

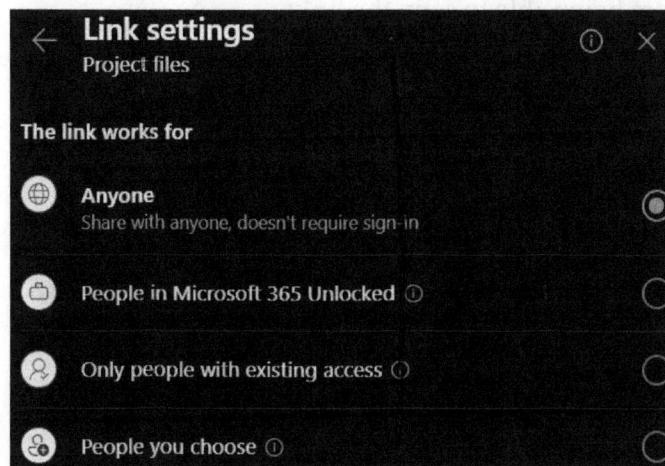

Figure 8.28: Link sharing options

When you share a link with **Anyone**, it grants access to anyone who knows the link, whether they get it directly from you or through someone else. This can include individuals outside your organization. Sign-in is not required to access the content through such a link.

Using **People in <your organization>** with the link allows anyone within your organization who has the link to access the file, regardless of how they received it.

The **People with existing access** option is for those who already have access to the document or folder. It does not alter any permissions and is useful if you just want to send a link to someone who already has access.

Selecting *Specific people* restricts access to only the individuals you specify, although others may already have access. If the sharing invitation is forwarded, only those who already have access to the item will be able to use the link.

Note: **Depending on the configuration made by your administrator at the tenant level, the Anyone option might be unavailable for selection to prevent links from being forwarded outside of the organization.**

3. Under **More settings**, select the permission you want to grant through the sharing link. Optionally, you can also set an expiration date for the link and a password, as shown in *Figure 8.29*. Setting an expiration date is helpful when sharing proposals or temporary files with clients.

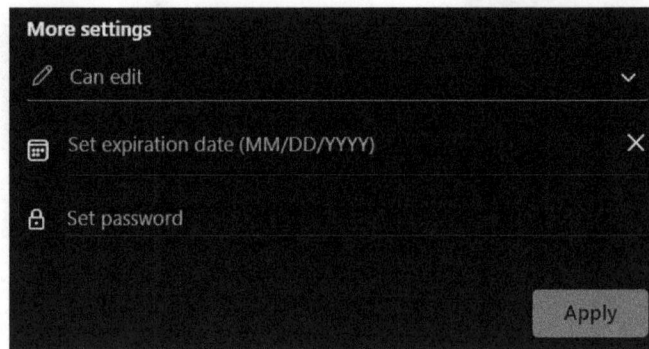

Figure 8.29: Additional settings

4. Once you are happy with the options configured, click **Apply**.

5. Click the **Copy link** in the sharing dialog window. The link will be generated and copied.

   Note: **If you selected the Specific people sharing option, you will also need to add specific users and/or groups before being able to copy the link:**

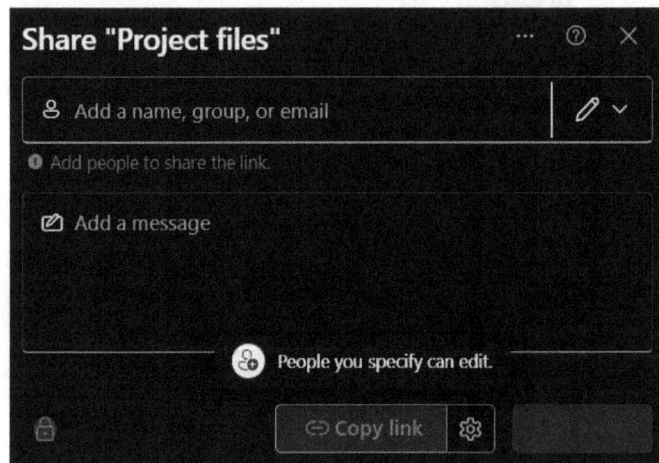

Figure 8.30: Add people to share the link configured for specific users

When a file or folder is shared, the **Shared** column changes from **Private** to **Shared** for that respective item, and the **Activity** column shows the most recent sharing activity:

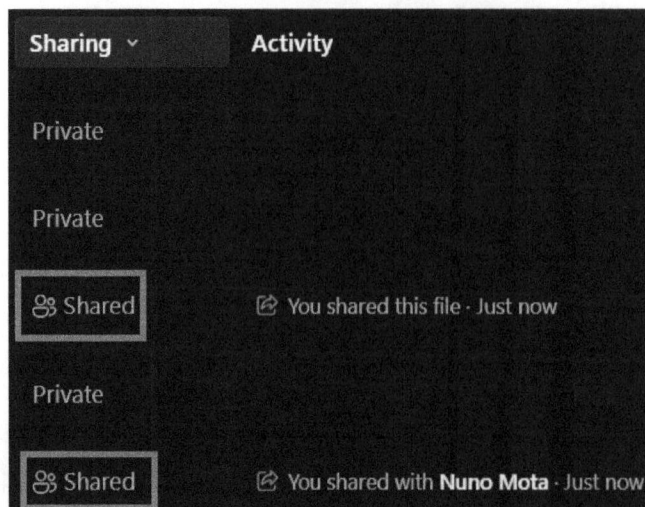

Figure 8.31: Sharing and Activity columns

Managing access

To manage access for a file or a folder in OneDrive, follow these steps:

1. Navigate to your OneDrive site and go to **My files**.

2. Right-click on the file or folder you want to manage access for and select **Manage Access**.

3. In the **Manage Access** window, you can view all individuals and groups with direct access to your file or folder, along with the sharing links. There are three tabs for each, namely **People, Groups,** and **Links**:

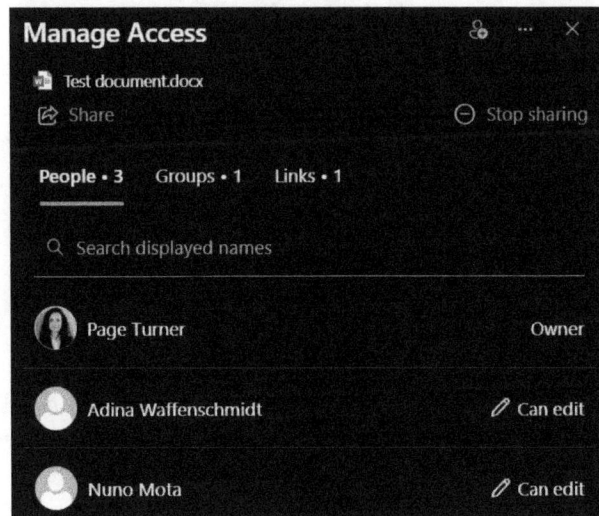

Figure 8.32: Manage access

4. By clicking on a specific individual or group with direct access, you can amend the permission level or remove the access:

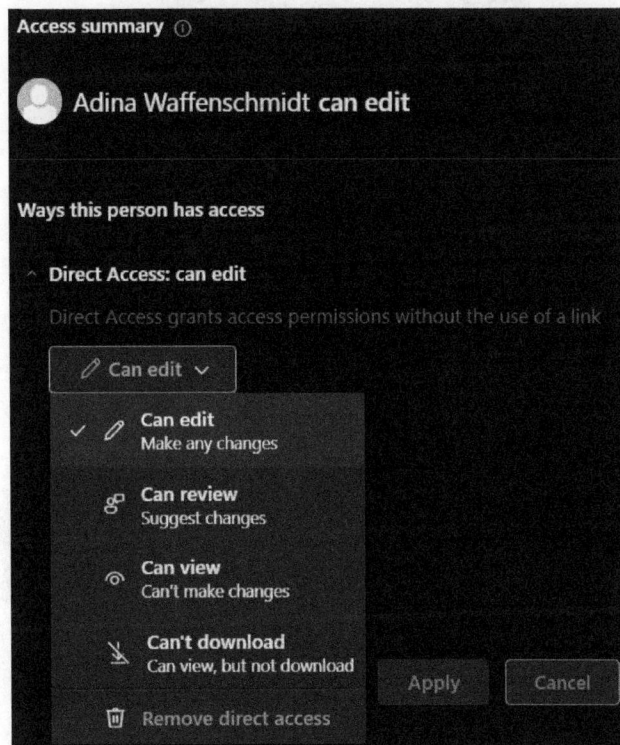

Figure 8.33: Change or remove access

For links, you can set or change the expiration date, or you can remove a link if no longer needed:

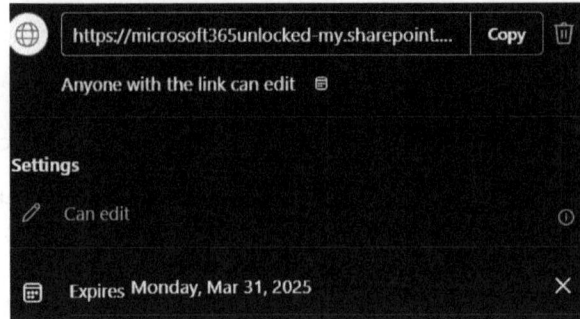

Figure 8.34: Manage access for links

5. Any changes made will be reflected immediately under **Manage Access**.

Effectively managing access in OneDrive ensures that your files and folders are secure and accessible to the right people. By setting appropriate permissions, monitoring access, and regularly reviewing who has access, you can maintain control over your content and foster a collaborative environment.

Sync your files with OneDrive sync app

As we have seen earlier in this chapter, with the OneDrive sync app, you can keep your files synchronized between your local device and the cloud. The sync app allows you to synchronize your OneDrive for work or school library, your OneDrive for home library, as well as SharePoint libraries.

To start synchronizing your OneDrive for work or school, after having the sync app installed, follow these steps:

1. Navigate to your OneDrive site, click on the gear icon at the top of the page, and select **Sync this OneDrive**:

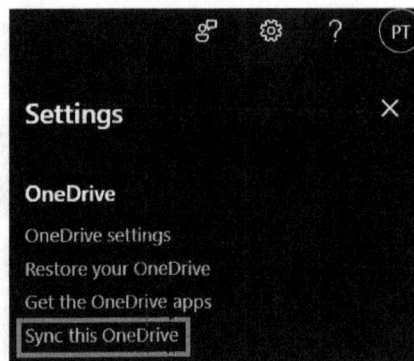

Figure 8.35: Sync this OneDrive

2. If prompted within the browser, select **Open Microsoft OneDrive**:

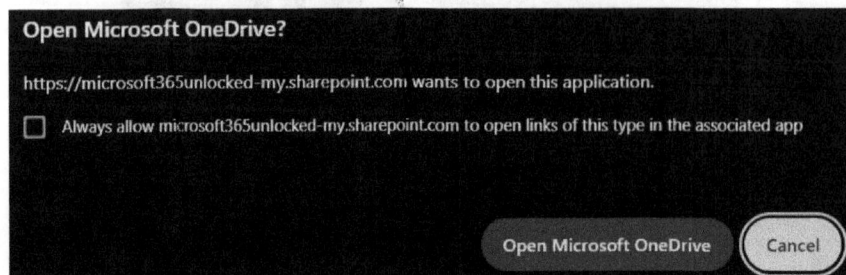

Figure 8.36: Prompt to open the OneDrive app

3. The OneDrive app will open. Click **Sign in** to sign in with your work or school account:

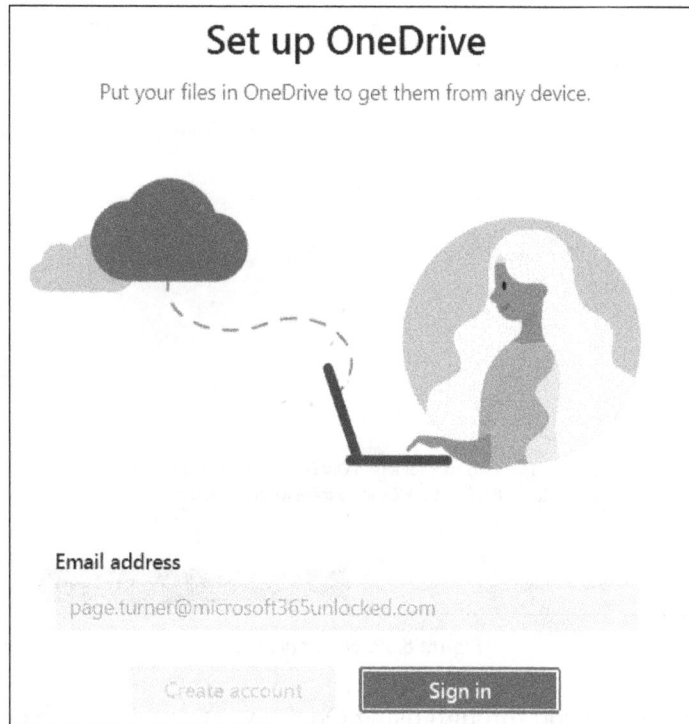

Figure 8.37: *Sign in with your work or school account*

4. Next, a OneDrive folder will be automatically created locally for your synced files. You can opt to change the location where your files are stored, if needed, then click **Next**:

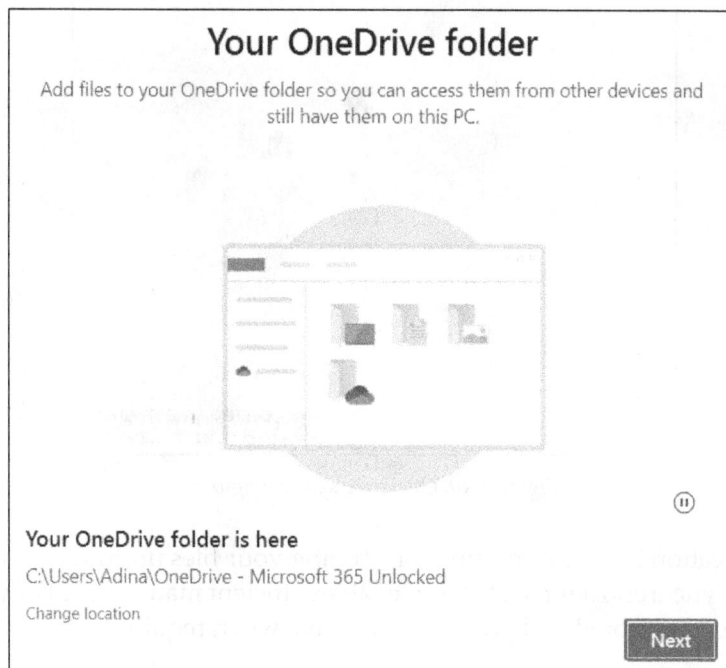

Figure 8.38: *OneDrive folder setup*

5. The next step allows you to select the **Documents**, **Pictures**, and **Desktop** folders for backup. You will be able to back up these folders with your OneDrive for work or school only if folder backup is turned off in your OneDrive Personal account:

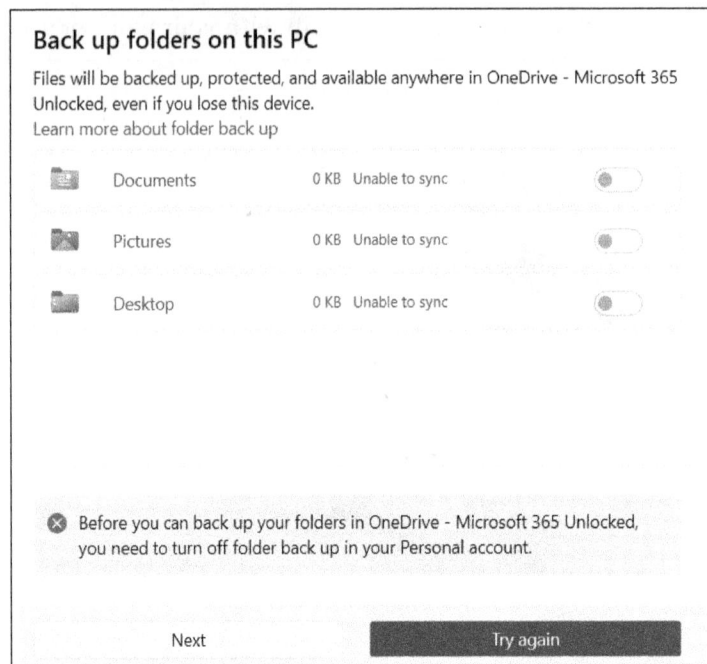

Back up folders on this PC

Files will be backed up, protected, and available anywhere in OneDrive - Microsoft 365 Unlocked, even if you lose this device.

Learn more about folder back up

📄	Documents	0 KB Unable to sync	⬤
🖼	Pictures	0 KB Unable to sync	⬤
🖥	Desktop	0 KB Unable to sync	⬤

❌ Before you can back up your folders in OneDrive - Microsoft 365 Unlocked, you need to turn off folder back up in your Personal account.

Next   Try again

Figure 8.39: Folder backup

6. The wizard will then guide you through using OneDrive. You will also have the option to install the OneDrive mobile app, or you can choose to install it later. After these steps, you will see a message that your OneDrive is ready, with an option to open the folder where files are synced:

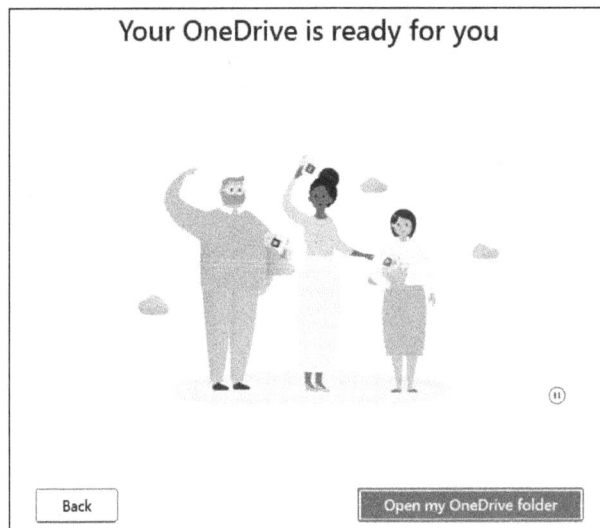

Your OneDrive is ready for you

Back   Open my OneDrive folder

Figure 8.40: OneDrive sync configured

The OneDrive sync application is a great solution for keeping your files up-to-date and accessible on all your devices. Utilizing robust synchronization features, it enables efficient management of your data, ensuring that critical documents are securely stored and promptly available when required.

Files On-Demand

Files On-Demand is a feature in OneDrive that helps you save disk space on your device by allowing you to access all your files stored in OneDrive without having to download them. This means you can see your files in File Explorer as if they were stored locally, but they will not actually take up space on your hard drive until you need them.

This feature is particularly useful as it allows you to keep your files organized and accessible while optimizing your device's performance.

Here is how it works:

- **Online-only files**: With Files On-Demand, all your files in OneDrive appear in File Explorer with a blue cloud icon next to them. These files are online-only, meaning they do not take up space on your device. You can see them and manage them, but they will not download to your device until you open, copy, or move them.

- **Locally available files**: When you open an online-only file, it gets downloaded to your device and becomes a locally available file. These files have a green checkmark icon next to them and can be accessed even when you are offline. If you need more space, you can change the file back to online-only by right-clicking it and selecting Free up space.

- **Always available files**: You can also choose to make certain files or folders always available on your device by right-clicking them and selecting Always keep on this device. These files will have a green circle with a white checkmark icon and will take up space on your device, but they will always be accessible, even when you are offline.

Figure 8.41 shows the status of various files and folders in the OneDrive local folder, based on their availability as managed by the Files On-Demand feature:

Figure 8.41: *File status*

If synchronization conflicts arise, users may be required to resolve them manually through File Explorer.

To set all your files to online-only or download locally all files, you can follow the next steps:

1. Open **OneDrive settings** by selecting the OneDrive cloud icon in your notification area, then select the OneDrive **Help and Settings** gear icon, and then click on **Settings**.

2. On the **OneDrive Settings** page, expand **Advanced settings.**

3. Under **Advanced settings**, you will find the **Files On-Demand** section from where you can choose to set all your files to online-only by selecting **Free up disk space,** or to download all your files locally by selecting **Download all files**:

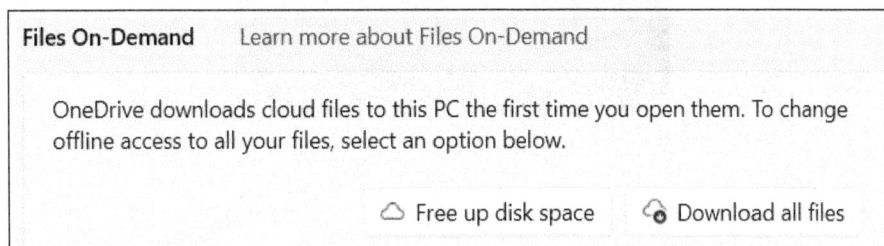

Figure 8.42: *Files On-Demand*

This feature works seamlessly with all your personal and work files from OneDrive, SharePoint in Microsoft 365, and SharePoint Server 2019 team sites.

Note: **Files On-Demand is a feature that requires Windows 10 version 1709 or later, or Windows Server 2019. Starting with OneDrive build 23.066, Files On-Demand is enabled by default. However, it may not be compatible with certain third-party antivirus solutions and is currently not supported when Windows Information Protection (WIP) is enabled.**

OneDrive mobile app

The OneDrive mobile app, available for *iOS* and *Android devices*, is a powerful tool that allows you to store, share, and access your files from anywhere using your smartphone or tablet. It is designed to enhance productivity and collaboration by providing seamless access to your documents, photos, videos, and other files on the go.

The mobile app integrates with Microsoft Office applications, enabling you to create, edit, and share documents directly from your mobile device. This app ensures that your important files are securely stored and easily accessible whenever you need them.

The following figure shows the OneDrive for mobile app home page:

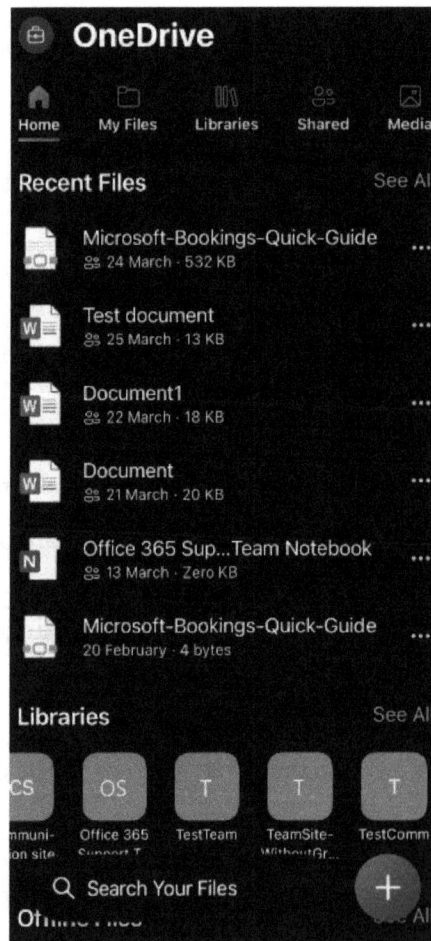

Figure 8.43: OneDrive mobile app home page

The OneDrive mobile app can be used for a variety of purposes, including:

- **Accessing files**: You can open and preview your files, including Word documents, Excel spreadsheets, and PowerPoint presentations, directly from the app.

- **Uploading files**: You can upload new files, photos, and videos to your OneDrive account from your mobile device:

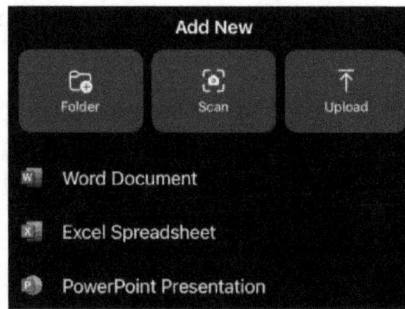

Figure 8.44: Add content using the OneDrive mobile app

- **Sharing files**: You can share files and folders with others, granting the required permission level:

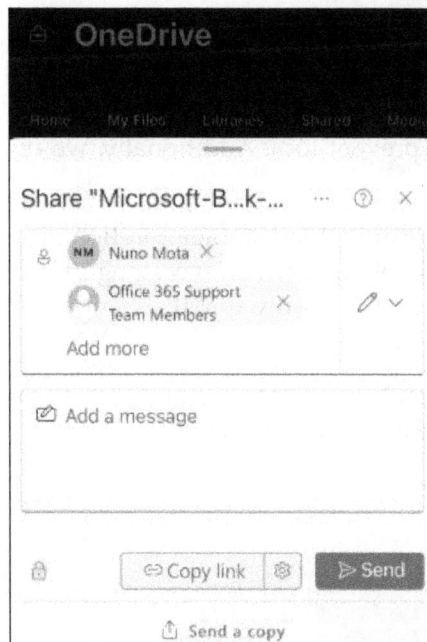

Figure 8.45: Share content using the OneDrive mobile app

- **Offline access**: You can save files offline to view or edit them when you are not connected to the internet:

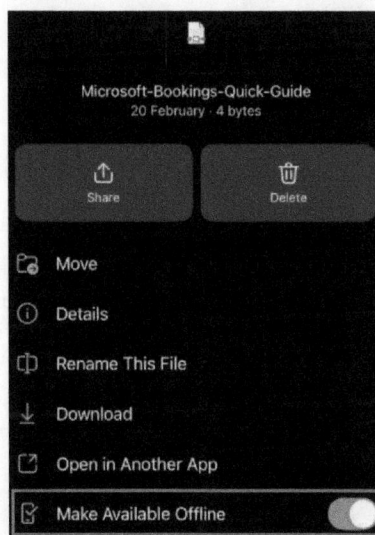

Figure 8.46: Make the file available offline

- **Scanning documents**: You can use the Scan feature to turn documents, whiteboards, or business cards into PDFs that you can then share with others.

By leveraging the OneDrive mobile app, you can enhance your productivity and streamline your workflow, ensuring that your files are always up-to-date and accessible, no matter where you are.

Conclusion

This chapter has provided a comprehensive overview of OneDrive, highlighting its various functionalities and benefits. We began by understanding the basics of OneDrive and its seamless integration with Microsoft Office applications, which allows for efficient file management and collaboration. We explored the differences between OneDrive for work or school, OneDrive for home, and the OneDrive sync app, emphasizing their unique features and use cases.

We looked into getting started with OneDrive for work or school, including how to create, upload, and manage content. The chapter also covered the importance of sharing content and managing access, enabling users to collaborate effectively while maintaining control over their files, as well as managing versions and restoring content to ensure data integrity and prevent loss. Additionally, we discussed the OneDrive sync app and finally the OneDrive mobile app.

Overall, OneDrive is a powerful and flexible cloud storage solution that caters to a wide range of needs, from personal file storage to professional collaboration. By leveraging its robust features, users can enhance their productivity, streamline their workflow, and ensure that their important documents are securely stored and readily accessible whenever needed.

In the next chapter, we will explore OneNote, a versatile digital note-taking app that provides a single place for keeping all your notes, research, plans, and information.

Join our Discord space

Join our Discord workspace for latest updates, offers, tech happenings around the world, new releases, and sessions with the authors:

https://discord.bpbonline.com

CHAPTER 9
OneNote

Introduction

This chapter covers OneNote, Microsoft's versatile note-taking app for efficient organization and information management. OneNote allows users to create, store, and access notes from any location. Whether you are brainstorming for a project, jotting down lecture notes, or planning your next big idea, OneNote provides the flexibility and functionality to keep your information at your fingertips.

Structure

This chapter covers the following topics:

- Getting started with OneNote
- Sections and pages
- Taking notes
- Useful productivity features
- Sharing and collaboration
- Integration with other Microsoft 365 apps

Objectives

By the end of this chapter, readers will gain a comprehensive understanding of OneNote and its features. We will explore the various features that make OneNote a great tool for note-taking, organization, and collaboration. The readers will learn about the core features of OneNote, including note creation and organizing notes. They will also gain knowledge on how to use OneNote for collaboration, how to share notebooks, and collaborate in real-time. Additionally, we will also look at how OneNote integrates with other Microsoft 365 apps, increasing productivity and collaboration.

Getting started with OneNote

OneNote is a versatile tool that can be used for a variety of use cases which involve note-taking. Here are several ways it can be used:

- **Capturing and sharing meetings or class notes**: OneNote allows users to take detailed notes during meetings or lectures, organize them into dedicated sections or pages, and easily share them with colleagues or classmates.

- **Creating to-do lists and checklists**: With built-in checklist features, users can make daily or project-based to-do lists and track progress by checking off completed items.

- **Research and information gathering**: OneNote makes it easy to clip content from the web, such as articles, images, and links. Users can organize their research in notebooks, highlight key points, and annotate materials, making it simple to keep all relevant information in one place.

- **Brainstorming and creative thinking**: The application supports free form drawing and handwritten notes, making it ideal for sketching out ideas and planning projects visually.

- **Travel and event planning**: OneNote helps users plan trips and events by organizing itineraries, confirmations, packing lists, and notes in a single, accessible location. It is easy to attach screenshots or reservation details for quick reference.

- **Personal journals and idea logs**: Individuals can use OneNote as a digital journal or diary, record thoughts, reflections, or inspiration, and revisit previous entries easily. Its search and tagging features make it simple to find past ideas whenever needed.

These diverse capabilities make OneNote a great tool for productivity, creativity, and collaboration across various personal and professional scenarios.

OneNote is available for free to users with a Microsoft account and is also part of Office 365 and Microsoft 365 subscriptions.

OneNote can be accessed online by navigating to **https://www.onenote.com** and signing in with your Microsoft account or your work or school account. It can also be accessed from the Microsoft 365 app launcher, searching for and clicking on **OneNote**. *OneNote Online* is the web-based version of the application that allows you to create and access your notes from any browser without needing to install the app. The following figure shows an example of the OneNote Online view of a user with a Microsoft 365 subscription:

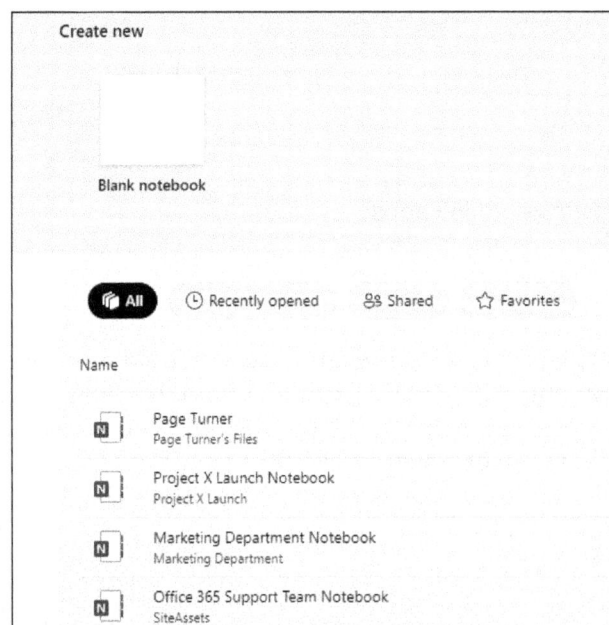

Figure 9.1: OneNote Online

The OneNote desktop application is typically installed along with other Office applications, such as Word, Excel, and PowerPoint, for users with a Microsoft 365 or Office 365 subscription. It can also be downloaded from **https://www.onenote.com** and is available for both Windows and macOS operating systems. The following image illustrates the OneNote desktop application interface after a user has signed in with their Microsoft 365 account:

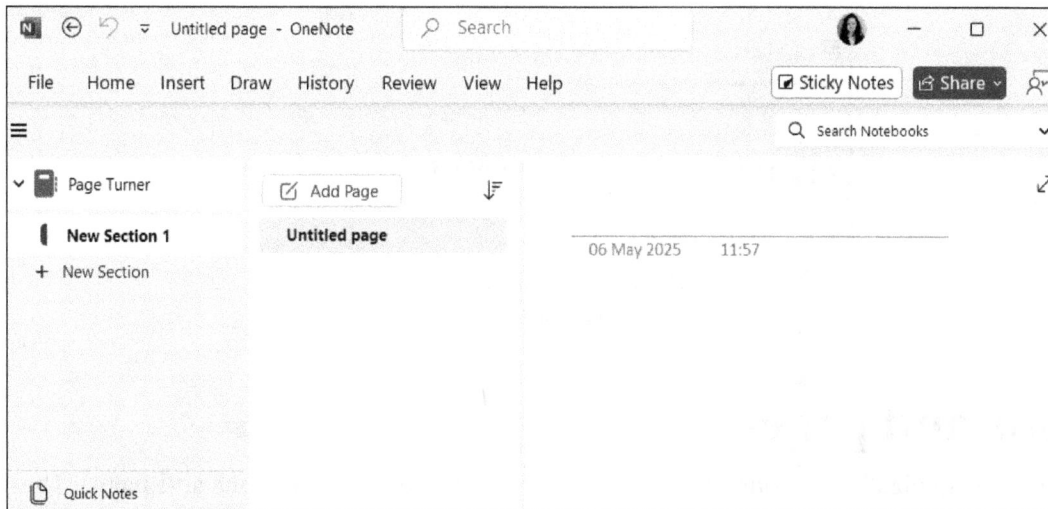

Figure 9.2: OneNote desktop application

In addition to its availability on desktop and online platforms, OneNote can also be installed as a mobile application for both iOS and Android devices. This mobile app ensures that users can seamlessly access, edit, and organize their notes anytime and anywhere, offering great flexibility. The mobile app mirrors many of the functionalities of its desktop and online counterparts, providing tools for note creation, organization, and collaboration, all within a compact and user-friendly interface tailored for smartphones and tablets.

Creating and accessing notebooks

Upon accessing OneNote Online, you have the option to create a new blank notebook or access existing notebooks that you own or those that have been shared with you, as illustrated in *Figure 9.1*. Notebooks created in OneNote Online will be automatically saved to your OneDrive library.

Additionally, using the OneNote desktop application, you can also create new notebooks. To create a notebook in the OneNote desktop app, go to **File**, click on **New**, and choose the storage location for your notebook. You may opt to store your notebook in OneDrive, locally on your computer, or within a SharePoint library, provided you have a Microsoft 365 subscription that includes SharePoint Online:

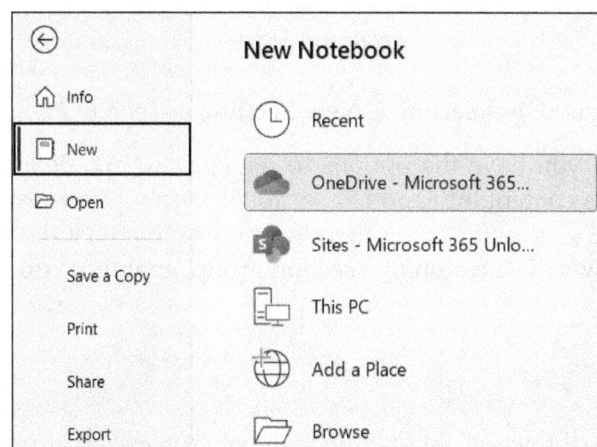

Figure 9.3: Choose location for new OneNote notebook

All existing notebooks are visible and accessible from the left pane in the OneNote application, as illustrated in the following figure:

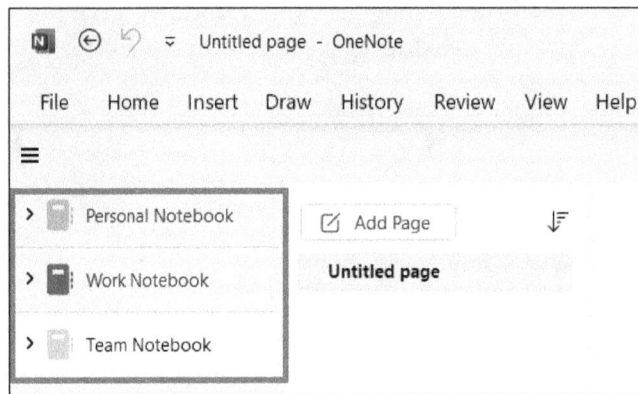

Figure 9.4: *OneNote notebooks*

Sections and pages

In OneNote, the organization of content is facilitated through the use of **sections** and **pages**. These elements are fundamental to structuring your notes in a way that is both intuitive and efficient.

Sections

Sections act as dividers within a notebook, allowing you to categorize notes by project, topic, or any other criteria that suit your needs. Each section can contain multiple pages, providing a hierarchical structure that helps keep your information organized. For example, in a work notebook, you might have sections for different projects, meetings, or departments:

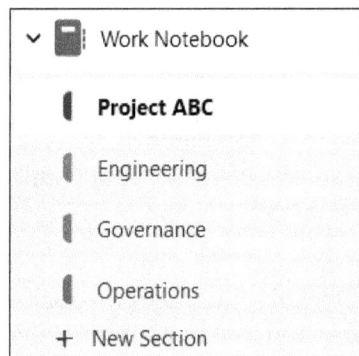

Figure 9.5: *Sections*

A new section can be easily created by selecting + **New Section**, as seen in *Figure 9.5*.

By right-clicking on a section, you have the options to rename, export, delete, move, or copy the section. Additionally, you can merge its content into another section or apply password protection. It is also possible to assign a specific color to the section for better identification or to adjust the position of the section within the list. This menu further allows the creation of a section group, enabling you to organize sections based on particular criteria.

Pages

Pages within sections are where the actual note-taking happens. You can create multiple pages within a section to structure your content as needed. The following figure illustrates an example of pages within a section:

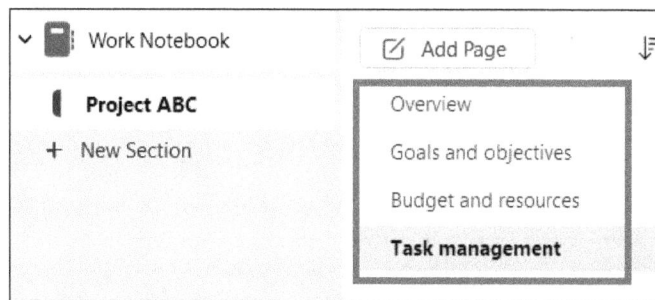

Figure 9.6: Pages

Each page can hold a variety of content types, including text, images, tables, and even embedded files. Pages are flexible and can be customized to fit the specific requirements of your notes. You can create links between pages and use templates to maintain consistency across your notes.

OneNote's design allows for easy navigation between sections and pages. The sidebar provides a clear overview of your notebook's structure, making it simple to switch between different areas of your notes. Moreover, the search functionality allows for efficient retrieval of specific information irrespective of its location within your notebook.

By effectively utilizing sections and pages, you can create a well-organized and easily navigable notebook that enhances your productivity.

Taking notes

Taking notes in OneNote is a seamless and intuitive process designed to enhance productivity and organization. OneNote offers a flexible and dynamic environment where users can capture and organize their thoughts, ideas, and information efficiently.

To create a note in OneNote, simply open a new page within a section of your notebook. You can start typing immediately, and OneNote will automatically save your work.

Every time you start typing or pasting content in OneNote, the content will be included in a note container. Note containers are flexible blocks that can hold various types of content. You can easily move and resize these blocks by clicking and dragging the edges, allowing you to organize your notes in a way that best fits your workflow. The following figure illustrates an example of a note container holding text:

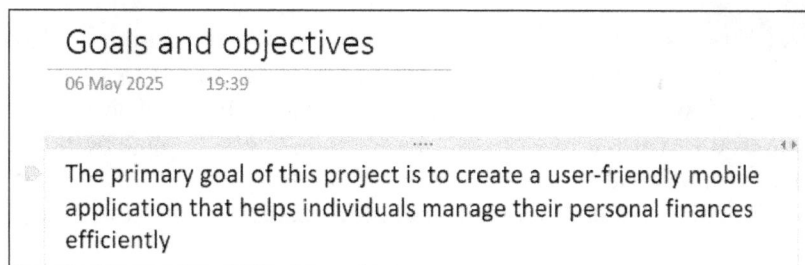

Figure 9.7: Note container

Tip: **Note containers are particularly helpful when organizing meeting notes, to-do lists, and reference content side by side.**

OneNote provides various formatting options to enhance your notes. By selecting the desired text and navigating to the **Home** tab, you can adjust the font style and size, apply bold, italic, or underline effects, and highlight text. Additionally, this tab offers features for creating bullet points or numbered lists, adjusting indentation, and aligning text to the left, center, or right. The following figure shows the various formatting options available in OneNote:

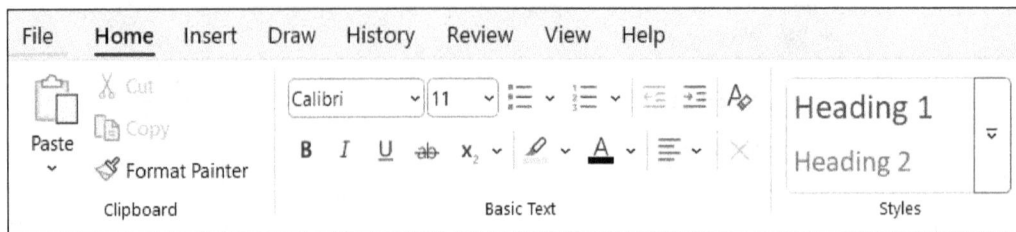

Figure 9.8: Formatting options

Media and file insertion

OneNote offers the capabilities for inserting media and files into your notes, enhancing the richness and utility of your content. You can easily embed images, audio recordings, videos, and various file types directly into your notes.

Images

Inserting images into your notes is straightforward. You can drag and drop images from your computer or use the **Insert** tab to add pictures from your device, online sources, or even use camera to take a photo and insert it in OneNote. You can also use the screen clipping option to take a snapshot of part of your screen and add it to the page. For instance, users can snap an image of a whiteboard in a meeting and easily add it directly to their notes for later reference. Images can be resized and repositioned within your notes, allowing you to create visually appealing and informative pages.

Audio and video

OneNote provides functionality for recording audio and video directly within the application. This feature is useful for recording lectures, meetings, or personal reminders. You can start a recording by navigating to the **Insert** tab and selecting **Record Video** for video recording or **Transcribe** and then **Record Audio** to start an audio recording. Recordings are embedded in your notes and can be played back at any time. You can also insert online videos from various sources such as YouTube, Vimeo, and Dailymotion by navigating to the **Insert** tab, clicking on **Online Video**, and providing the video URL.

Files

You can attach various file types to your notes, including PDFs, Word documents, Excel spreadsheets, and more. This is done by selecting the **Insert** tab and choosing **File Attachment** to insert a file as an attachment. The attached files are stored within your notebook, providing convenient access to documents without needing to exit OneNote. You can also add a pinout of a file to a OneNote page by selecting **File Pinout** from the **Insert** tab. Additionally, you can also add an image of an existing or a new Excel spreadsheet by selecting **Spreadsheet** and then choosing between the **Existing Excel Spreadsheet** or **New Excel Spreadsheet** options.

Draw and sketch

OneNote offers powerful drawing and sketching tools that allow you to express your ideas visually and creatively. Whether you are brainstorming, creating diagrams, or simply doodling, OneNote's drawing features provide a versatile platform for capturing your thoughts. To access the drawing features, navigate to the **Draw** tab in OneNote.

OneNote includes a variety of drawing tools that cater to different needs. You can choose from pens, markers, highlighters, and more, each available in multiple colors and thicknesses:

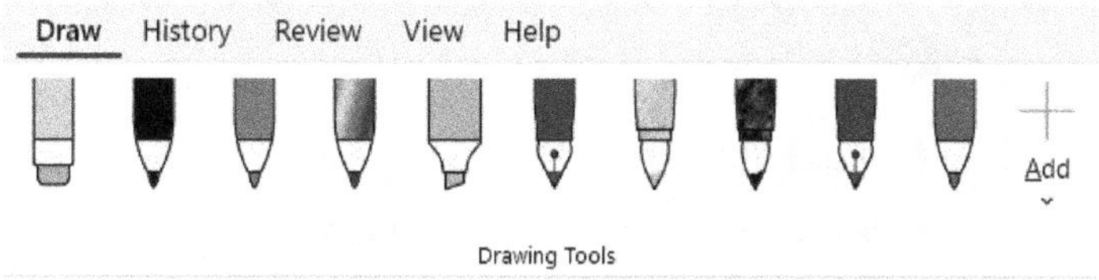

Figure 9.9: Drawing Tools

These tools enable you to create detailed sketches, annotate images, or highlight important information within your notes.

OneNote's drawing capabilities are optimized for touch-enabled devices, such as tablets and smartphones. This facilitates a smooth and user-friendly drawing experience, allowing you to efficiently capture your ideas while on the move. Additionally, OneNote supports digital pens, providing precision and control for detailed sketches.

OneNote's **Ink to Text** feature allows you to convert handwritten notes into typed text. This is particularly useful for those who prefer writing by hand but want the convenience of searchable and editable text. To convert a handwritten note to typed text, select the respective note and click on the **Ink to Text** option from the **Draw** tab.

To enhance your drawings, OneNote provides a selection of shapes. From the **Draw** tab, you can easily insert shapes such as circles, squares, arrows, and lines to create structured diagrams and flowcharts:

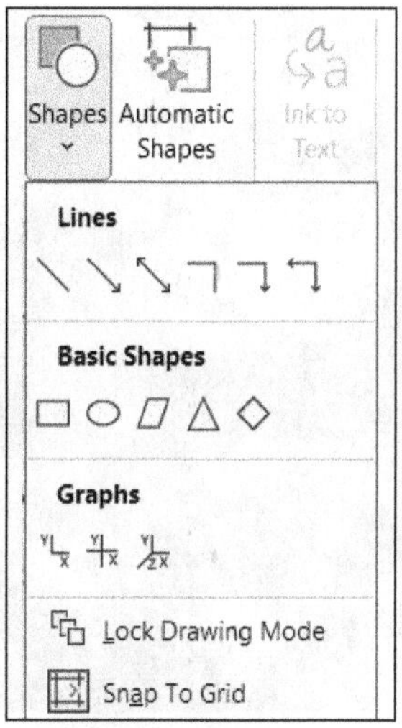

Figure 9.10: Shapes

These shapes can be resized, rotated, and customized to fit your specific requirements.

Useful productivity features

OneNote is packed with features designed to enhance your productivity and streamline your workflow. Here are some of the most useful productivity features that can help you make the most out of OneNote.

Quick Notes

Quick Notes are a convenient way to capture thoughts and ideas on the fly. You can create a Quick note when OneNote is not running by pressing *Windows + Alt + N* on your keyboard, which opens a small OneNote window where you can jot down your note. Quick Notes offer an efficient way to record spontaneous ideas during work, similarly to sticky notes. These notes are automatically saved and can be accessed later from your **Quick Notes** section in OneNote:

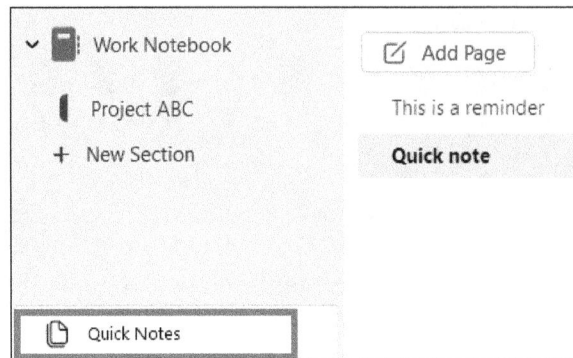

Figure 9.11: Quick Notes

OneNote Web Clipper

The OneNote Web Clipper is a browser extension designed to enable users to efficiently save online content, such as articles and web pages, directly to their OneNote notebook. The extension is available for Edge and Chrome browsers and can be installed from **www.onenote.com/clipper**. Once installed, when you come across an interesting article or a website that you might want to save, you can access OneNote Web Clipper from your browser extensions, and you can easily clip the entire page, a specific region, just the text, or the bookmark:

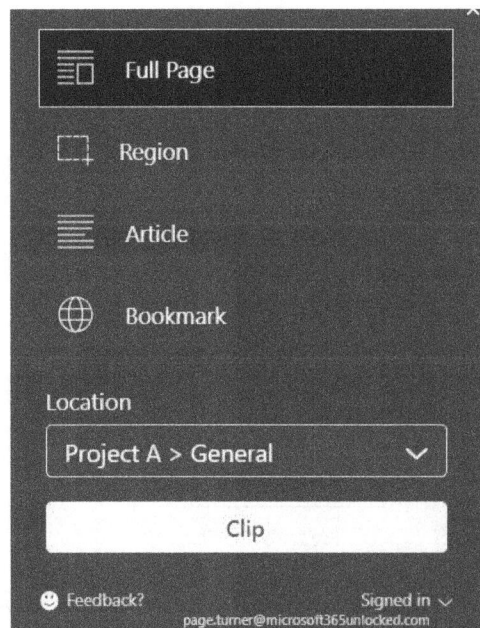

Figure 9.12: OneNote Web Clipper

Page templates

When repeatedly producing similar types of content, such as meeting notes, project overviews, to-do lists, or planners in OneNote, utilizing page templates can significantly enhance time management and efficiency. OneNote provides an array of page templates designed to promote consistency and organization within your notes. These templates cater to various purposes, including meeting notes, to-do lists, and planners. You can access templates by navigating to the **Insert** tab and selecting **Page Templates**. You can also create and save your own custom templates for future use by accessing **Page Templates** and then selecting **Save current page as a template**. Custom templates will be saved within the **My Templates** section. The following figure illustrates the template categories available in OneNote:

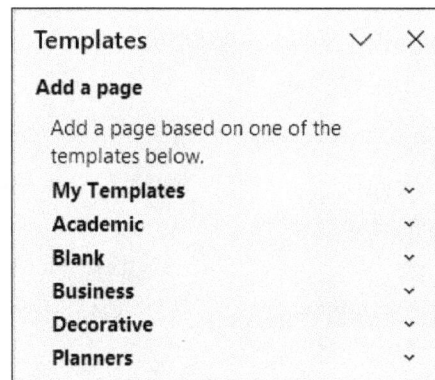

Figure 9.13: Page templates

Tags

Tags serve as an effective way for categorizing and prioritizing your notes. You can add tags to any part of your notes, such as tasks, important information, or questions. To add Tags, navigate to the **Home** tab and under **Tags**, select the tag type you need from the available list. The following figure shows some of the available tags in OneNote:

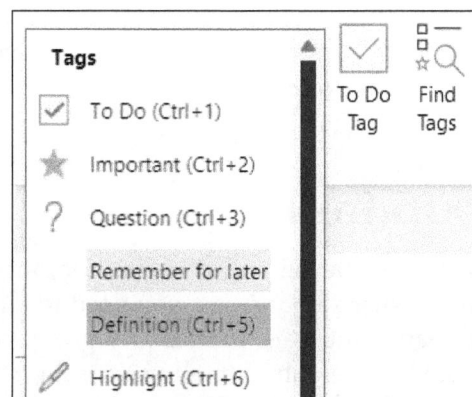

Figure 9.14: Tags

Tags make it easy to find and organize your notes, and you can use the **Find Tags** feature to quickly locate all tagged items across your notebooks.

OneNote search

OneNote's search functionality allows you to quickly locate specific information within your notebooks. Whether you are looking for a particular note, keyword, or tag, OneNote's search makes it easy to find what you need.

OneNote enables you to search across all your notebooks simultaneously. This is particularly useful if you have multiple notebooks and need to find information that may be scattered across different sections and pages. By entering your search query into the search bar, OneNote will show relevant results from all your notebooks. The following figure illustrates a search example, searching for the word **budget**:

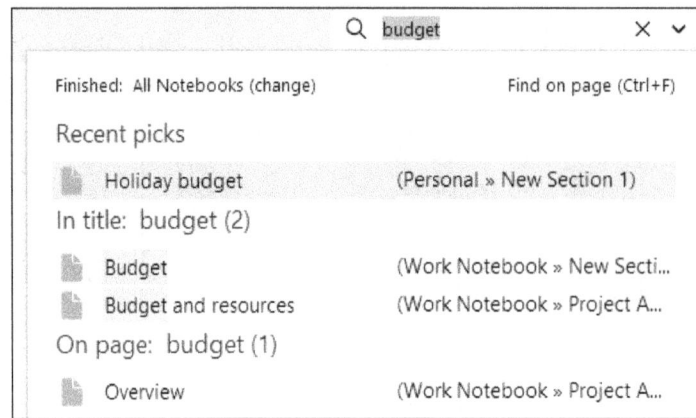

Figure 9.15: OneNote search

You can perform keyword searches to find specific words or phrases within your notes. OneNote highlights the search results, making it easy to identify the relevant content. This feature is especially helpful for locating specific details or references within extensive notes.

OneNote can search not only typed text, but also text in images, being **Optical Character Recognition (OCR)** capable. If you remember a specific term or quote, you can search your entire notebook and OneNote will find the page that contains it, even if it was in a screenshot or a scanned document. For example, searching for *project milestones* will surface the image of a chart you clipped that contains those words in the image. Handwritten notes are also searchable in OneNote, which is especially useful for students or anyone taking notes on the go with a stylus.

Sharing and collaboration

OneNote is engineered to enable seamless sharing and collaboration, making it a great tool for teamwork and collective productivity. To be able to share a notebook, you need to make sure it is stored on SharePoint or OneDrive. Notebooks stored on SharePoint sites, particularly group-connected sites that automatically include a OneNote notebook, are shared by default with all users who have access to the site, based on the permissions granted at the site level. By default, notebooks created and stored in your OneDrive are accessible only to you, but you have the option to share these notebooks with users and groups.

You can share a notebook by selecting the respective notebook in OneNote, clicking on the **Share** button in the top-right corner, and then selecting **Share Entire Notebook**:

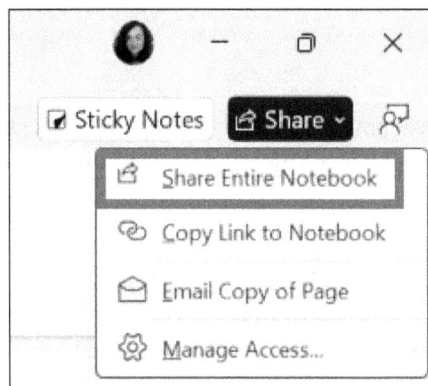

Figure 9.16: Share notebook

In the sharing dialog box, you can add the users and groups you wish to share the notebook with, add a message (optional), and choose the appropriate permission level (view or edit):

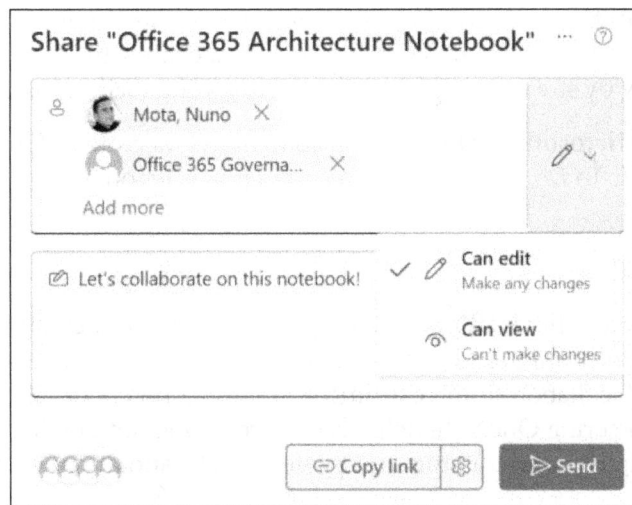

Figure 9.17: *Sharing options*

By clicking **Send**, the notebook will be shared with the specified users and/or groups, and an email invitation will be sent.

Another method for sharing is to generate and copy a link by selecting the **Copy link** button illustrated in *Figure 9.17*. Prior to generating the link, you may configure the link settings to select who the link should work for. Additionally, you can specify the permission level (view or edit) and set an expiration date for the link.

OneNote supports real-time collaboration, enabling multiple users to work on the same notebook simultaneously. Any modifications made by users are immediately visible to others, promoting an environment where ideas can be shared and improved upon in real-time. This functionality is especially useful for brainstorming sessions, team meetings, and collaborative projects.

Integration with other Microsoft 365 apps

OneNote seamlessly integrates with other apps part of the Microsoft 365 ecosystem. This integration enables users to harness the capabilities of multiple applications while maintaining a centralized repository for their notes and information. Essential integrations to boost productivity and teamwork include:

- **Outlook**: This enables users to easily send important emails and meeting invitations from Outlook to OneNote by using the **Send to OneNote** option available in Outlook.

- **Teams**: OneNote's integration with Microsoft Teams facilitates collaboration within the platform. You can add OneNote notebooks to Teams channels, allowing team members to access and edit notes directly within Teams. This integration facilitates communication and makes all relevant information accessible to the team.

- **OneDrive and SharePoint**: OneNote notebooks can be stored in OneDrive, making your notes accessible from any device with an internet connection. OneDrive's cloud storage capabilities provide a secure and reliable location for your notebooks, enabling seamless synchronization and access across multiple devices. OneNote notebooks can be stored and accessed through SharePoint, providing a centralized location for team collaboration. SharePoint's document management capabilities enhance the organization and accessibility of OneNote notebooks, making it easy to share and collaborate on notes with colleagues. This integration helps with automatically saving and syncing notes across devices.

- **Microsoft Loop**: With this integration, you can embed Loop components directly into your OneNote pages, enabling dynamic and interactive content within your notes and collaboration across the Microsoft 365 ecosystem.

- **Microsoft 365 Copilot**: Microsoft 365 Copilot licensed accounts can leverage Copilot within OneNote to efficiently summarize extensive notes, organize ideas, draft action items, and rewrite content. This enhances productivity by streamlining thought processes and facilitating the rapid capture of insights.

- **Outlook Tasks and Microsoft To Do**: Tagging content in OneNote as Outlook tasks syncs them with Outlook and Microsoft To Do, making it simple to manage action items across these apps.

Conclusion

This chapter explored OneNote, Microsoft's note-taking app. We covered creating and accessing notebooks, sections, and pages, different note-taking methods like text, media, files, drawing, and productivity features. We highlighted sharing and collaboration, real-time teamwork, notebook sharing, and integration with other Microsoft 365 apps. Mastering OneNote helps users streamline note-taking, improve organization, and collaborate effectively, making it useful for students, professionals, and anyone needing efficient information management.

In the next chapter, we will explore Microsoft Stream, a powerful video service that allows you to securely upload, share, and manage videos within your organization.

Join our Discord space

Join our Discord workspace for latest updates, offers, tech happenings around the world, new releases, and sessions with the authors:

https://discord.bpbonline.com

CHAPTER 10
Microsoft Stream

Introduction

In this chapter, we will explore Stream, Microsoft's enterprise video platform designed for businesses and organizations. Microsoft Stream allows employees to upload, record, share, and watch videos securely. This can include training videos, meeting recordings, or any other work-related content. Microsoft Stream is a great tool for enhancing learning, communication, and collaboration within an organization.

Structure

This chapter covers the following topics:

- Getting started with Stream
- Video uploading and recording
- Video settings
- Playlists
- Video sharing and access management
- Video analytics
- Integration with other Microsoft 365 apps

Objectives

By the end of this chapter, readers will understand how to utilize Microsoft Stream effectively. They will learn the basics of the platform, how to upload, record, and manage videos, organize content using playlists, and customize video settings. The chapter will also cover video sharing and access management, the use of analytics to monitor performance, and the integration of Stream with other Microsoft 365 apps to enhance collaboration.

Getting started with Stream

Microsoft Stream is fully integrated within the Microsoft 365 suite, serving as a powerful platform for managing and sharing video content across your organization. By utilizing SharePoint as its underlying storage solution, Stream enables users to securely upload, organize, and access videos with ease while benefiting from Microsoft 365's familiar collaboration tools. Stream videos stored in OneDrive or SharePoint are easily accessible on mobile devices using the OneDrive or SharePoint mobile apps, making it convenient for users to watch videos while on the move or out in the field.

Stream is designed to support a wide range of video-related use cases. Here are a few examples:

- **Onboarding and training**: Easily share orientation videos and training modules with new team members to streamline their onboarding experience.

- **Team communications**: Record and distribute internal updates, announcements, or project briefings to keep everyone informed and aligned.

- **Knowledge sharing**: Create concise explainer videos to clarify products, processes, or workflows, making information more accessible to colleagues.

- **Meeting recordings**: Access recordings of important meetings so team members can catch up on discussions they may have missed.

Stream is available to users through Microsoft 365 plans that have SharePoint and OneDrive included. Specifically, Stream is included in the following plans:

- **Business plans**: Microsoft 365 Business Basic, Standard, and Premium.

- **Enterprise plans**: Office 365 E1, E3, E5 and Microsoft 365 E3, E5.

- **Frontline plans**: Microsoft 365 F1, F3.

- **Government plans**: Office 365 G3, G5 and Microsoft 365 G3, G5.

To access Stream, you can navigate directly to **https://m365.cloud.microsoft/launch/stream** and login with your Microsoft 365 credentials or select the **Stream** icon from the Microsoft 365 app launcher.

The Stream home page has been merged with the **Clipchamp** home page. Clipchamp is a comprehensive platform for advanced video editing, which will be discussed in detail in the next chapter. This integration offers a unified platform aimed at enhancing the video experience for users. This streamlined design simplifies navigation, ensuring that users can effortlessly access tools for video creation, editing, and management within a single, cohesive platform. *Figure 10.1* shows the Stream and Clipchamp home page:

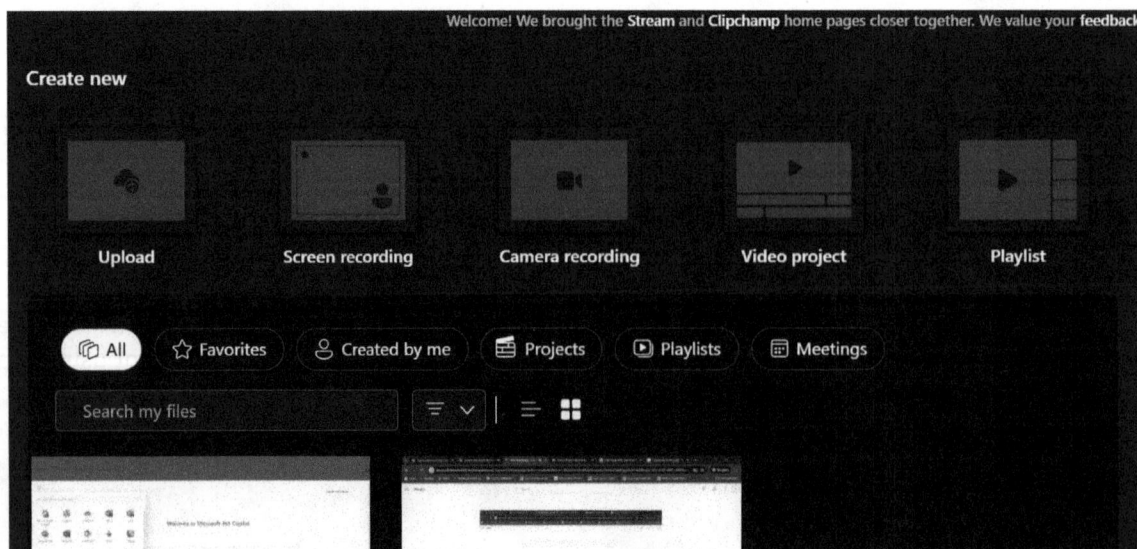

Figure 10.1: Stream and Clipchamp home page

From the homepage, you can upload a new video, create a screen or camera recording, start a video project (which redirects you to Clipchamp), or create a playlist for your videos. Additionally, from the home page, you can access videos you have uploaded, created, or those that have been shared with you.

Video uploading and recording

Uploading or recording a video in Microsoft Stream is designed to be intuitive and user-friendly, suitable for both beginners and experienced users. The platform provides clear options to upload pre-existing videos from your device or to create new content using its built-in recording tools.

To upload a video, simply click the **Upload** option located on the home page. Once you have selected the video file from your device, you can choose to upload it directly to your OneDrive library. Alternatively, you can click **Change location** to select a specific SharePoint library for the video upload:

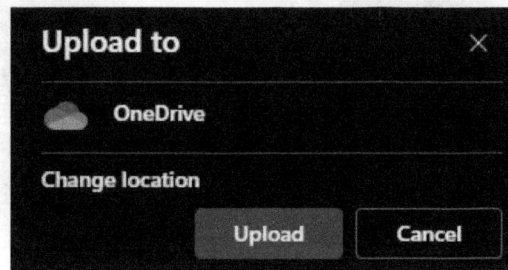

Figure 10.2: Upload a video

To create a new video, users are provided with two options: screen recording and camera recording, as we have seen in *Figure 10.1*. You can record videos up to 15 minutes in length using either the screen or camera recording options provided.

The screen recording feature allows you to capture content from a browser tab, a specific window, or the entire screen, providing flexibility depending on your needs. Furthermore, you can choose to keep your camera enabled, enabling a picture-in-picture effect where your video overlay appears alongside the recorded screen content. This feature is especially useful for creating short tutorials, walkthroughs, or presentations that require a personal touch or additional commentary.

The video recording functionality offers a wide array of features to enhance your content creation process. Users can incorporate and play a pre-written script during the recording, ensuring smooth delivery and consistency. Additionally, various creative effects can be added, such as text overlays, stickers, filters, frames, boards, or photos, allowing for personalization and improved visual appeal.

The screen recording feature is particularly versatile, enabling users to annotate directly on the screen while capturing content. This capability is ideal for creating engaging tutorials, interactive walkthroughs, or presentations that require real-time annotations and emphasis. On the other hand, the camera recording option provides the ability to add a backdrop, allowing users to customize their visual setting to suit the tone and purpose of their videos.

Together, these tools empower users to produce high-quality short video content, catering to a variety of needs.

The following figure illustrates an example of a screen recording session with drawings and effects:

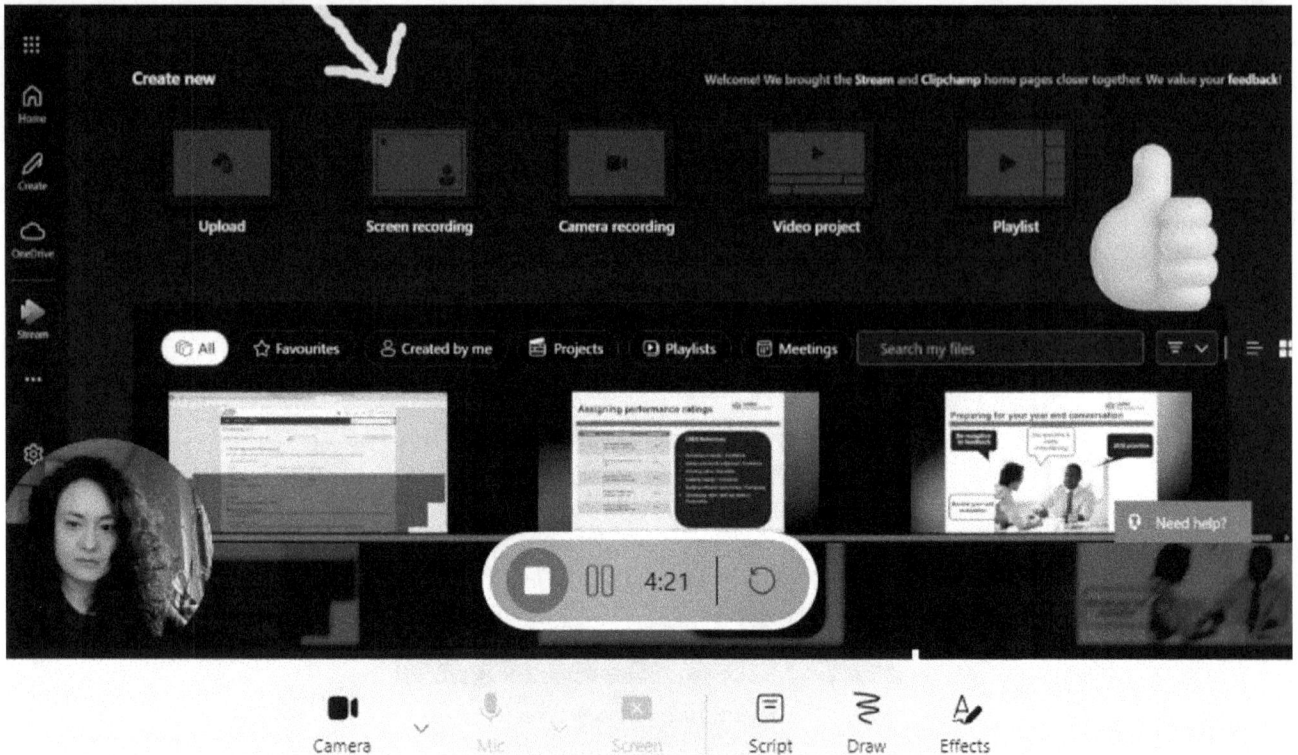

Figure 10.3: Screen recording

Upon completing your video recording, Microsoft Stream offers a variety of options to refine and enhance your content. You can start by trimming unnecessary sections to ensure your video is concise and focused. If needed, you can split your recording into multiple parts and rearrange it for better organization. For videos shorter than the 15-minute limit, additional footage can be recorded and seamlessly integrated. Furthermore, users can elevate the quality of their videos by adding background music, creating an engaging atmosphere that complements the tone and purpose of the content. For those seeking more sophisticated editing tools, selecting the **Open in editor** option allows you to access Clipchamp. The following figure shows the options available upon video recording:

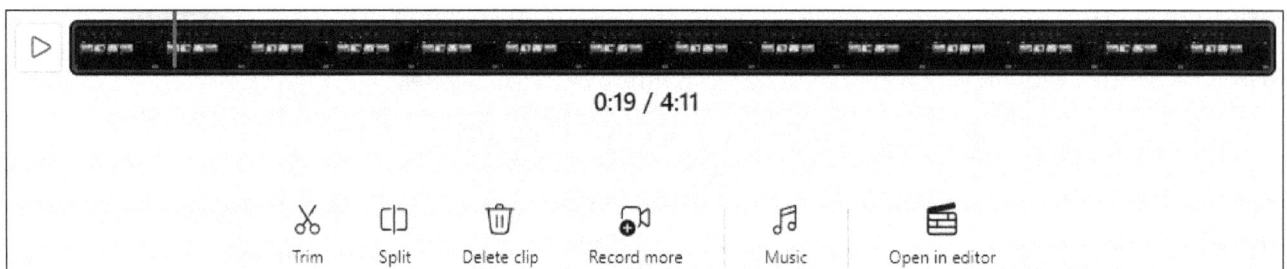

Figure 10.4: Video recording options

Once you have completed editing in Stream, simply click the **Finish** button in the lower-right corner of the screen to save your video to your OneDrive library.

Video settings

When accessing a video in Stream, owners and editors can adjust the video settings that will apply to all viewers. To access and configure the video settings, select **Video settings** on the right side of the video, as shown in the following figure:

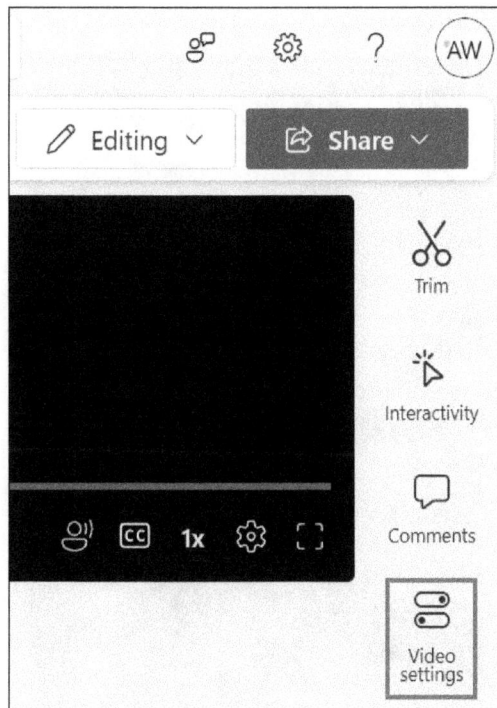

Figure 10.5: *Access video settings*

The Video settings feature offers a variety of options to enhance the viewer experience and manage content effectively. These include:

- **Thumbnail**: Customize the thumbnail to select an engaging image that represents the video.

- **About video**: Turn this setting on to allow users to see information about the video, such as title and description.

- **Transcripts and captions**: Enable accessibility by providing transcripts and captions for those with hearing impairments or for viewers who prefer reading alongside the video. Microsoft Stream supports multilingual transcription. Transcription and closed captioning are generated automatically, and this feature is enabled by default. Administrators at the tenant level can configure this setting.

- **Chapters**: Divide the video into sections for easier navigation and better organization. Chapters can be generated provided there is English transcript available.

- **Interactivity**: Turn on or off the interactivity option, which enables you to add interactive elements like forms and callouts.

- **Comments**: Allow viewers to leave comments on your video.

- **Analytics**: Allow viewers to access video analytics, which help interpret video engagement.

- **Reactions**: Allow viewers to react to your video with likes and emojis.

- **Noise suppression**: Enable noise suppression as default setting for the video. Viewers can turn this on or off within the video player.

- **Audio files**: Upload or replace audio files. These can be used for audio descriptions or language voiceovers that users can select during playback.

The following figure illustrates the video settings available in Stream:

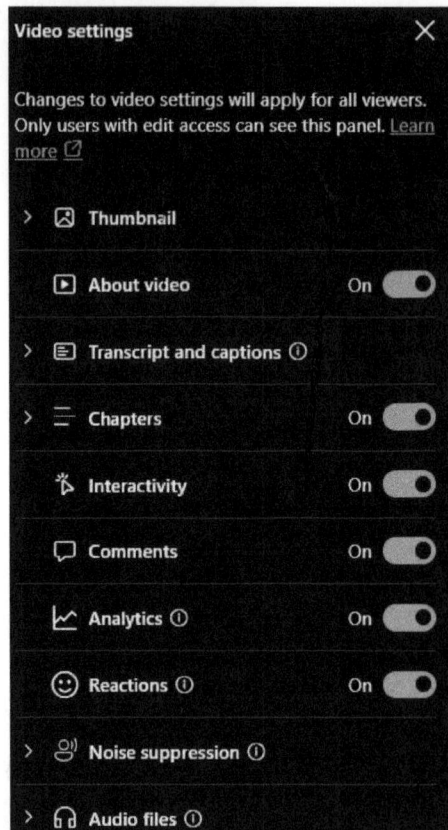

Figure 10.6: Video settings

Playlists

Users can also enhance their experience by creating custom playlists. Playlists allow for a curated viewing journey, whether for educational purposes, entertainment, or collaborative projects. With playlists, viewers can organize content in a way that aligns with their specific needs, making it easier to revisit and share thematic videos.

To create a playlist, select the **Playlist** option on the Stream home page. This will launch the Microsoft Lists app, where you can create a new list for your videos. Provide a name for your playlist, a description (optional), and choose the location where you want to save your list:

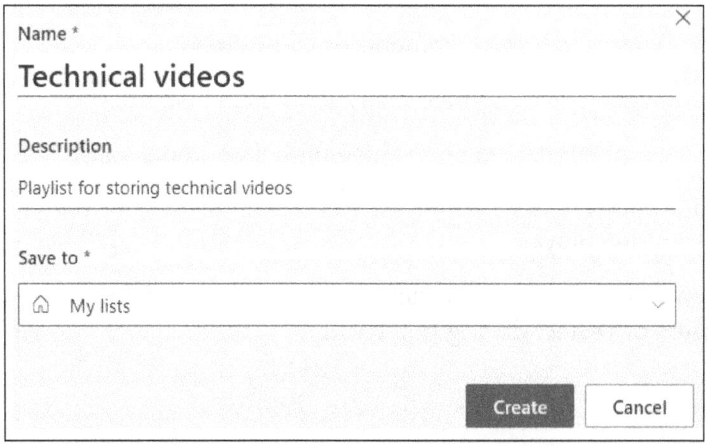

Figure 10.7: Create a playlist

After creating the playlist, click on the **Add new item** button located at the top-left corner of the screen to select and add videos to your playlist. You can choose videos from your OneDrive library or from a SharePoint library you have access to:

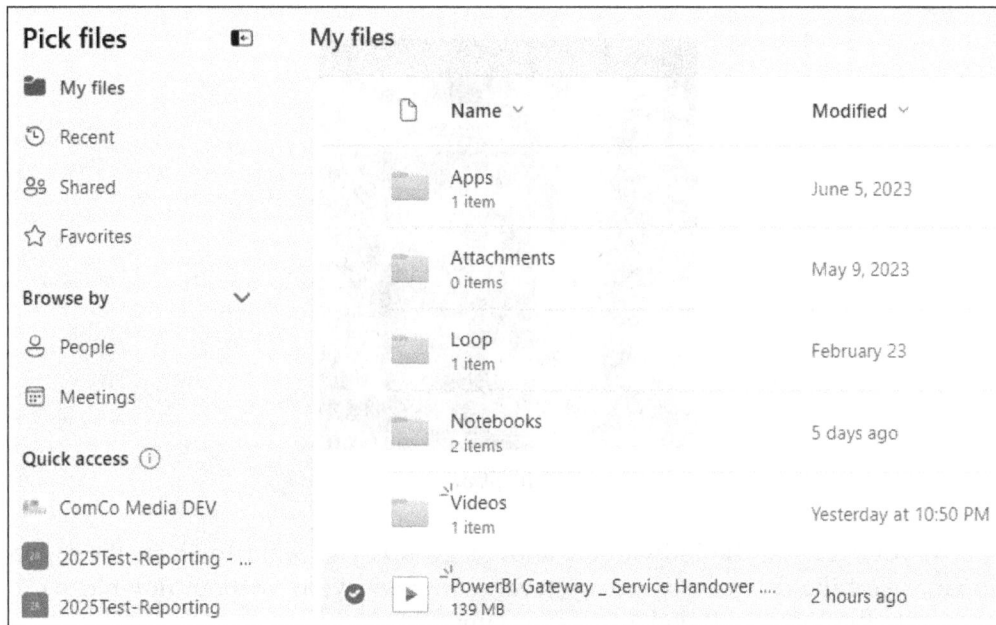

Figure 10.8: Add videos to a playlist

Once the videos are uploaded, they can be viewed and played directly from the playlist. To access your playlist in Stream, select the **Playlists** tab, as illustrated in the following figure:

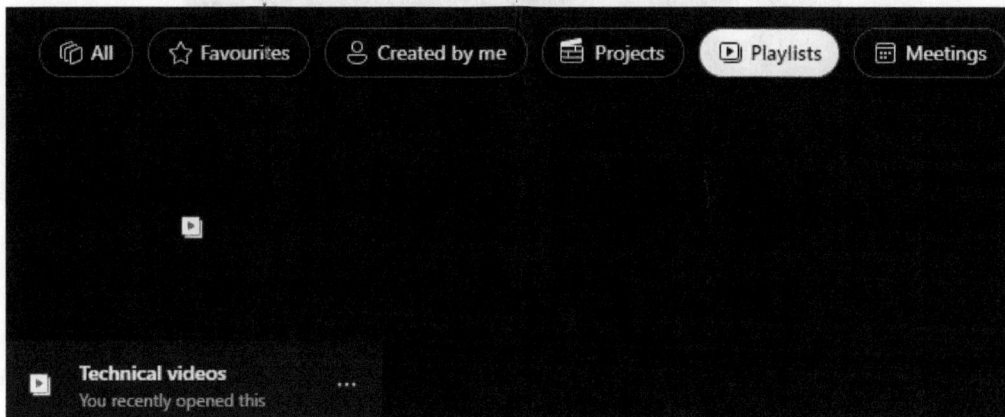

Figure 10.9: Access playlists from Stream

Video sharing and access management

Effectively sharing videos with your audience, coupled with the ability to manage access permissions, plays a pivotal role in ensuring a seamless and secure viewing experience.

Stream uses SharePoint and OneDrive to store videos, meaning that the underlying access permissions granted at the container level also apply to the videos. For instance, if a video is stored in a document library on a SharePoint site, everyone with access to that document library will have access to the video by default, unless permissions inheritance is broken and unique permissions are set for the video.

Sharing a video

To share a video from Stream, click on the **Share** drop-down menu located in the top-right corner of the screen and then select **Share**:

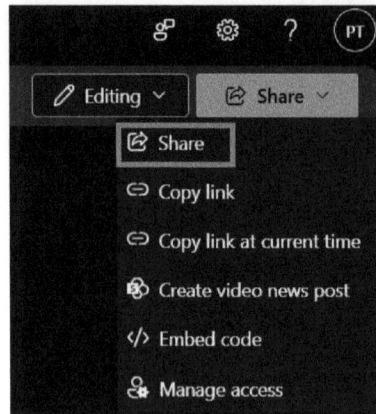

Figure 10.10: Share a video

On the dialog box, you can add the individuals and/or groups you want to share the video with, add a message (optional), select the desired permission level (edit, view, view without download), and then click **Send** to grant access to the video and send an email invite:

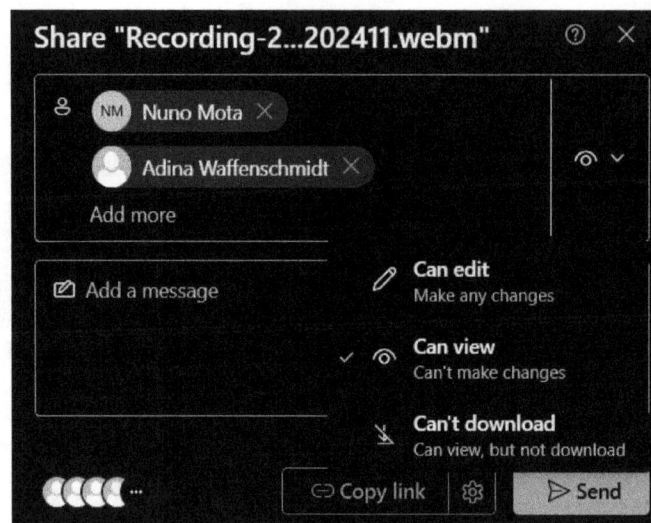

Figure 10.11: Add recipients and send email invite

As an alternative, you can create a shareable link to the video by selecting the **Copy link** option. To customize the accessibility parameters of the link, click on the gear icon located next to the **Copy link** button. This will open the link settings menu, where you can define who will have access to the shared content. The available options typically include settings such as anyone with the link, people within your organization, only people with existing access, or specific individuals. The **Anyone** option might not be available if external sharing is turned off at the tenant level or at the level of the site where the video is stored. Under **More settings**, you can select the permission level to be assigned (edit, view, or view without download) and set an expiration date for the link if required.

By adjusting these options, you can ensure the link is tailored to meet the needs of your audience while maintaining control over privacy and access permissions. The link settings are illustrated in the following figure:

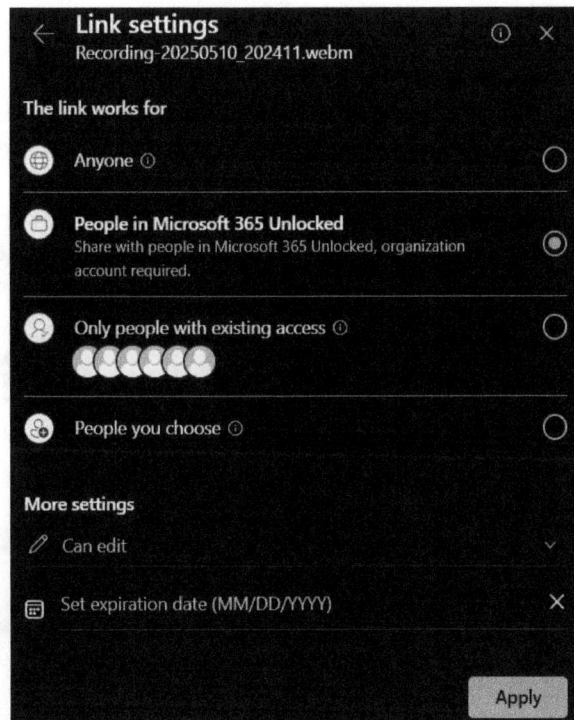

Figure 10.12: Link settings

Managing access

Managing access to your videos in Stream provides an added layer of control to ensure that only the intended audience can interact with the content. By leveraging the permissions model integrated with SharePoint and OneDrive, you can fine-tune the settings to cater to specific needs.

To manage access for a video, click on the **Share** drop-down menu located in the top-right corner of the screen and then select **Manage access**. The following image illustrates the **Manage Access** view in Stream:

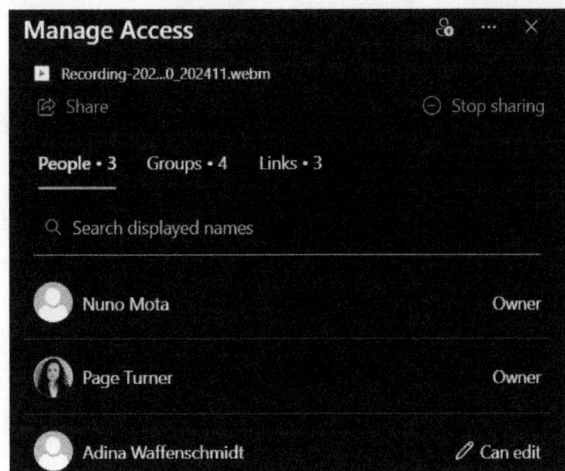

Figure 10.13: Manage access

Within the **Manage Access** window, you can see who has access to the video, including individuals, groups, as well as generated links with their configured settings and you can remove access, delete links and even change permission levels for individuals, groups or links. Permissions for owners, whether individuals or groups, cannot be changed or removed directly from this interface. This restriction ensures that ownership and administrative control remain intact, preventing unintended modifications to essential permissions.

To further manage access effectively, the **Stop sharing** option provides a straightforward way to revoke all access to the video, ensuring that only its owners retain control.

By selecting the ellipsis (**…**) located on the top-right corner of the **Manage Access** window, users can navigate to the **Advanced permissions** page in SharePoint or OneDrive, depending on where the video is stored. This page serves as a powerful tool for managing access and ensuring that the video content is appropriately secured. It offers granular control over permissions, allowing users to modify or revoke access for individuals and groups, establish or delete unique permissions, check the permissions granted to a particular user or group, and tailor permissions to align with organizational policies. The following figure illustrates the **Advanced permissions** page of a video stored on a SharePoint site:

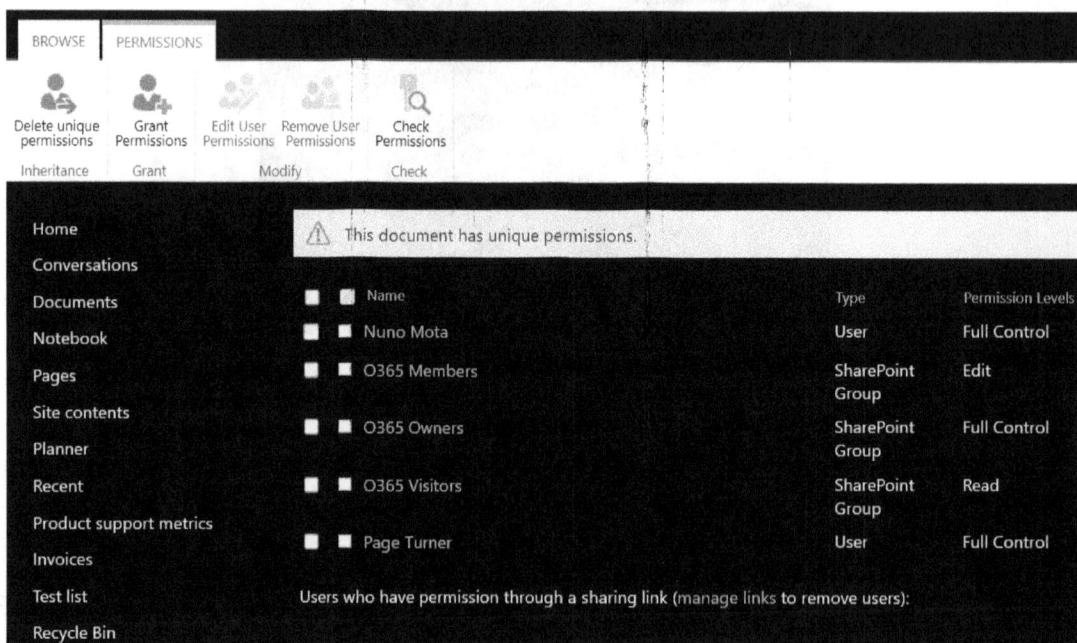

Figure 10.14: *Advanced permissions*

Video analytics

To complement the robust access management features, Stream also offers comprehensive video analytics, empowering users to delve deeper into the performance and engagement metrics of their content.

Microsoft Stream allows video owners and editors to access analytics for each video. These analytics include metrics such as views, viewers, and viewership retention. By selecting the **Analytics** tab, users can view information about how their videos are performing over different periods.

The **All time statistics** section shows the total number of views and viewers since the video was published:

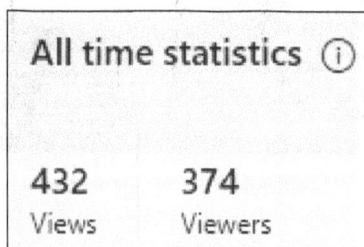

Figure 10.15: *All time statistics*

Under the **Statistics over time** section, users can review data about views and viewer trends over specific periods:

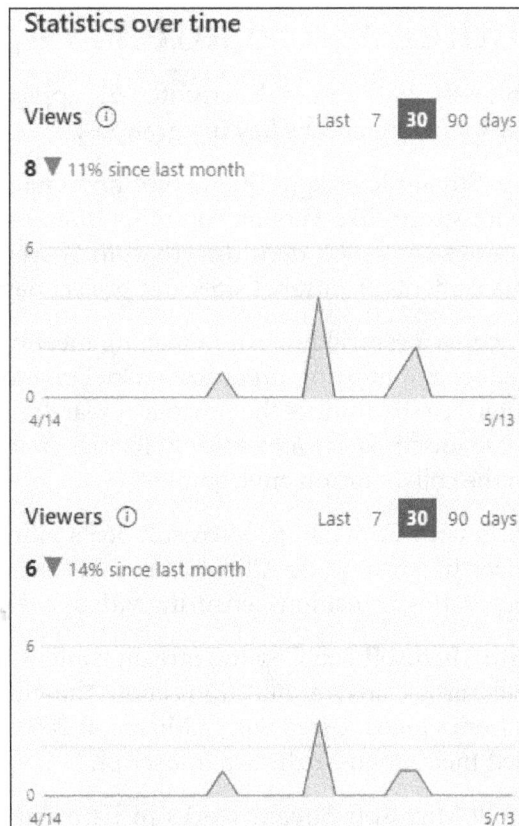

Figure 10.16: Statistics over time

The **Views** metric indicates the total number of times a video has been viewed. This information is essential for assessing the overall reach of your content. You can analyze trends in unique views over the past 7 and 30 days.

Note: The trend of views data for the 90-day period is not available; only the total view count for this duration is provided.

The **Viewers** metric indicates the total number of individual viewers who have watched the video. This helps in identifying the breadth of your audience. Similar to views, unique viewer trends can be reviewed for the last 7 and 30 days, but not for 90 days.

Viewership retention is a video-only metric that tracks how viewers engage with your content throughout its duration. It highlights the moments that receive the most engagement and where viewership drops off. This metric is expressed as a percentage of the peak viewership across the video's duration, with the point of highest views marked as 100%:

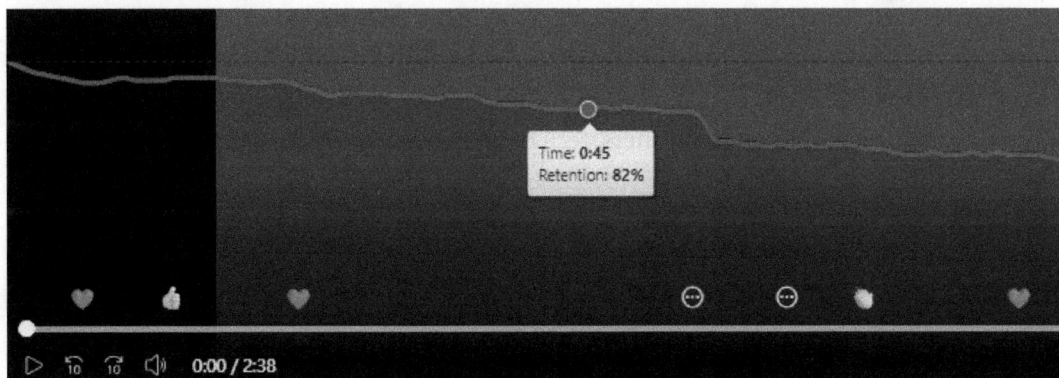

Figure 10.17: Viewership retention

Integration with other Microsoft 365 apps

Microsoft Stream integrates seamlessly with other Microsoft 365 apps, enhancing video management, accessibility, and collaboration. The following are the key integrations:

- **SharePoint and OneDrive**: Stream leverages SharePoint and OneDrive for video storage, offering robust content management features like version control and sharing permissions. Additionally, the Stream web part allows users to embed videos directly into SharePoint pages, making it simple to create engaging multimedia content for intranet sites and project pages.

- **Microsoft Teams**: Stream acts as a central hub for managing meeting recordings in Microsoft Teams. Recordings are stored in either the meeting organizer's OneDrive or the SharePoint site tied to the Teams channel. Stream's interface streamlines the process of searching and retrieving meeting content. Additionally, Stream can be added as an app within Teams, enabling users to watch, share, and organize videos directly in the collaboration environment.

- **Clipchamp**: Stream connects with Clipchamp, Microsoft 365's video editing tool, allowing users to edit and enhance their videos before sharing. Clipchamp offers intuitive features, such as trimming, adding overlays, and incorporating transitions, ensuring videos are polished and professional.

- **Microsoft 365 Copilot**: With Microsoft 365 Copilot, Stream content becomes more powerful. Copilot can summarize meeting recordings, answer questions about the video, list action items, suggest key moments and get insights from videos. Users with a Microsoft 365 Copilot license can access Copilot features in Stream, provided their videos include a transcript.

These integrations demonstrate how Microsoft Stream works in harmony with the broader Microsoft 365 ecosystem to simplify video workflows and maximize productivity.

Conclusion

In this chapter, we looked into the capabilities of Microsoft Stream, a dynamic enterprise video platform designed to foster enhanced learning, effective communication, and seamless collaboration across organizations. We covered essential aspects of Stream, including video uploading and recording, video settings, playlists, video sharing and access management, and video analytics. Additionally, we discussed how Stream integrates seamlessly with other Microsoft 365 apps, such as SharePoint, Teams, and Clipchamp, to provide a comprehensive video management and editing experience. By leveraging Stream, organizations can create, manage, and analyze video content effectively, ensuring a better user experience and improved engagement.

In the following chapter, we will shift our focus to Clipchamp, a robust video editing tool that complements Stream's capabilities by providing an array of features to transform raw footage into compelling content.

Join our Discord space

Join our Discord workspace for latest updates, offers, tech happenings around the world, new releases, and sessions with the authors:

https://discord.bpbonline.com

CHAPTER 11

Clipchamp

Introduction

In the ever-evolving landscape of digital media, video content has become a pivotal medium for communication, storytelling, and marketing. Recognizing the growing demand for accessible and powerful video editing solutions, Microsoft introduced *Clipchamp*, a versatile platform designed to empower users of all skill levels. Whether you are crafting professional presentations, educational materials, or personal projects, Clipchamp offers an intuitive and efficient way to produce high-quality videos. By the end of this chapter, readers will have gained a comprehensive understanding of how Clipchamp works, its capabilities, and how it stands as a powerful tool for modern content creation.

Structure

This chapter covers the following topics:

- Microsoft Clipchamp client
- Licensing
- Camera and screen recording
- Captions and subtitles
- Text, stickers, and annotation visuals
- Trim, split, and crop a video
- Transitions
- Video enhancing
- Resizing and exporting

Objectives

This chapter aims to provide readers with a thorough understanding of the capabilities and applications of Microsoft Clipchamp. By the end of this chapter, readers will have a clear understanding of what Clipchamp is, how it functions, insights into the practical applications and benefits of using it, and knowledge of how to enhance creativity with Clipchamp's versatile video editing features.

Microsoft Clipchamp client

Clipchamp is a versatile video editing tool designed to cater to the needs of both novice and experienced users while providing a user-friendly platform.

To use Clipchamp, and assuming you have one of the required licenses described in the next section, open your browser and navigate to **https://m365.cloud.microsoft/launch/clipchamp**. You will be presented with the following screen with several options to get you started with Clipchamp:

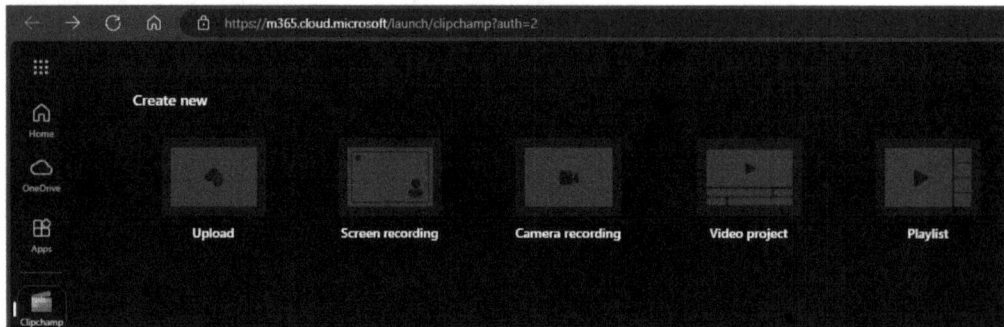

Figure 11.1: Clipchamp web client

Alternatively, download the Clipchamp app from the Microsoft Store for a seamless experience on your desktop or mobile device:

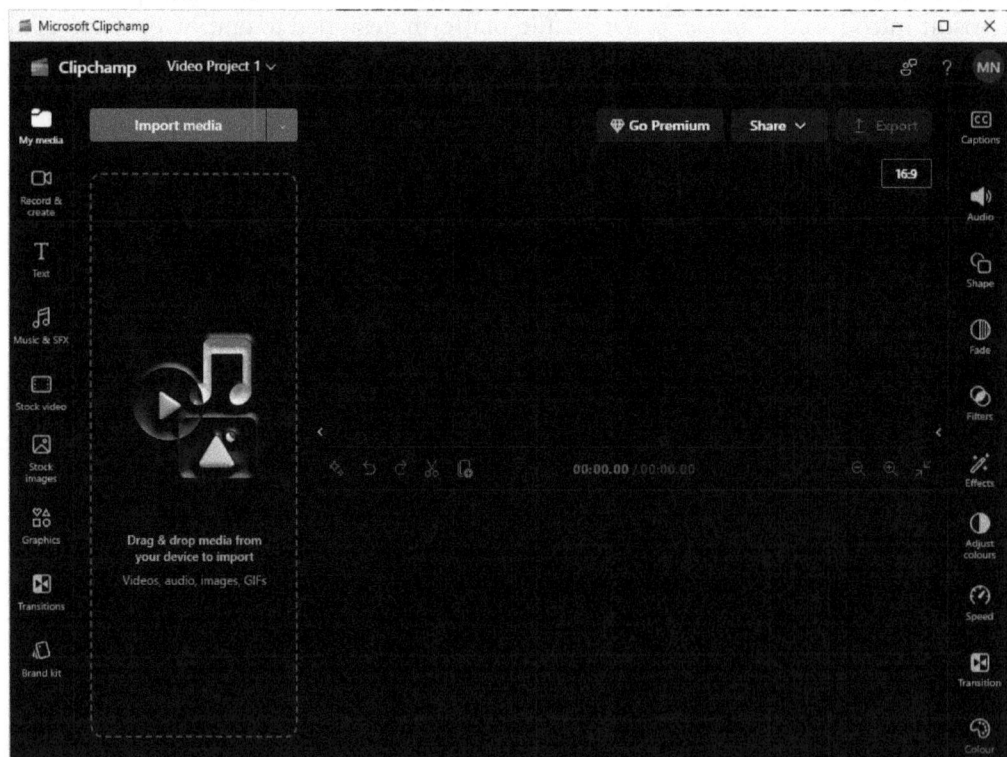

Figure 11.2: Clipchamp desktop client

The web client and desktop app of Microsoft Clipchamp are very similar in functionality, however there are a few subtle differences worth noting, especially in how they are accessed and how they behave under the hood, as follows:

- **Web cient:**
  - o **Runs in-browser** with no installation required.
  - o Accessible on any device with internet and a supported browser.
  - o **Always up to date**: you are using the latest version automatically.
  - o Ideal for those users or organisations who prefer not to install software.
  - o Requires a stable internet connection to function properly.

- **Desktop app:**
  - o Available for **Windows 10 and 11**.
  - o Technically a **Progressive Web App (PWA)**, so it is still web-based under the hood.
  - o Offers a more native feel with a shortcut on your desktop or taskbar.
  - o May offer slightly faster startup and smoother performance due to local caching.
  - o Still requires internet access to function as it is not a fully offline editor.

Both versions support the same core editing tools, AI features (like text-to-speech and auto-cut), and cloud integrations (OneDrive, Google Drive, etc.). Projects are synced across both platforms, so you can start on one and finish on the other.

Licensing

Microsoft Clipchamp is available as two standalone subscriptions:

- *Clipchamp Standard* (sometimes referred to as **Free**) is available for home users for free (for one person) and as part of a *Microsoft 365 Family* or *Microsoft 365 Personal* subscription. For businesses, it is included in the *Microsoft 365 Business Standard* and *Business Premium* plans, and *Enterprise E3* and *E5* plans.

- *Clipchamp Premium* adds 4K resolution, premium stock content, and advanced video analytics to the Clipchamp Standard subscription. Clipchamp Premium is available to home users at a cost and as an add-on for enterprise users.

The following table shows the main additions that the Premium version brings to Clipchamp Standard:

Feature	Free	Premium
Watermark-free exports	✓	✓
Export resolution	Up to 1080p HD	Up to 4K UHD
Audio, image and video stock	Free stock	Premium stock
Filters and effects	Free filters & effects	Premium filters & effects
Brand kit (Logos, colors, and fonts)		Single brand
Content backup		✓

Table 11.1: Clipchamp Standard vs. Premium

Camera and screen recording

Clipchamp offers robust camera and screen recording features, making it an all-in-one tool for creating engaging video content. With Clipchamp's camera recording feature, users can easily capture high-quality video directly from their webcam. This is particularly useful for creating video blogs, tutorials, presentations, and other content that requires a personal touch. The platform supports various resolutions, ensuring that the recorded video meets the desired quality standards.

The screen recording feature allows users to record their computer screens, capturing all on-screen activities. This tool is invaluable for creating software demos, instructional videos, and any other content requiring step-by-step visual guidance. Users can record the entire screen or select a specific area to focus on, providing flexibility in content creation.

To record your screen and/or camera in Clipchamp, click on **Record & create** and then select your desired option:

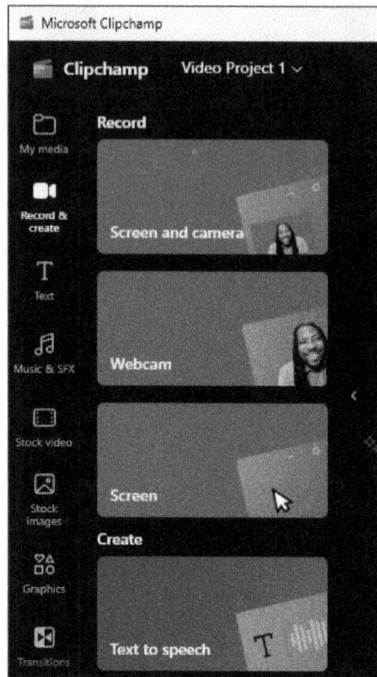

Figure 11.3: Record options

Next, select your microphone and camera sources (you can also choose to record system audio), and choose a tab, window, or entire screen to start recording. It is that simple!

Once you are done, preview the recording and click on **Save and edit** to save your recording to the timeline, as shown in the following figure:

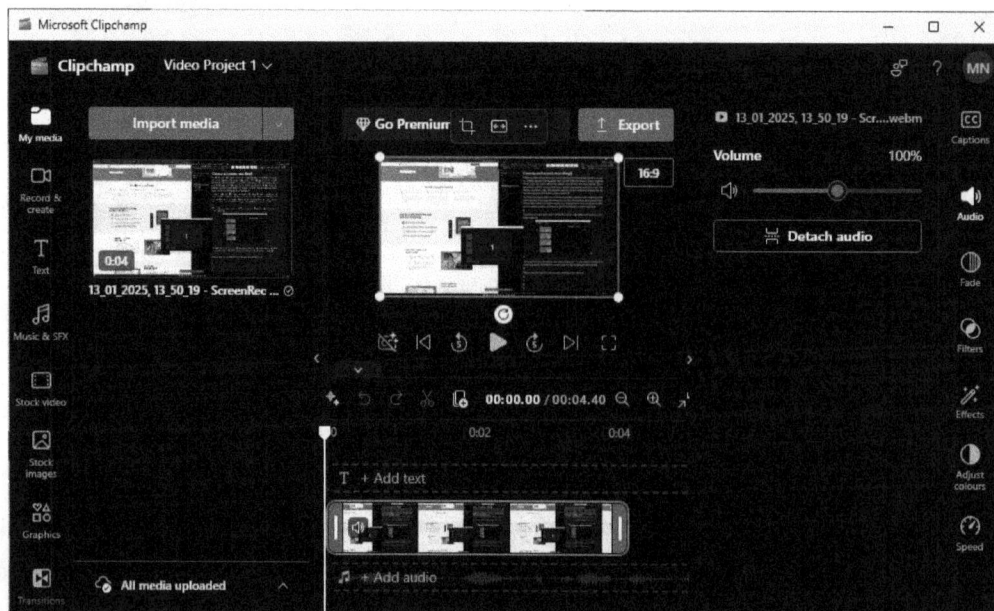

Figure 11.4: Screen recording saved into the timeline

These types of recordings can be extremely useful. For example, you can create **screen recording tutorials**, which are very effective for demonstrating software and on-screen activities, allowing viewers to follow along easily. Viewers see the exact process, simplifying complex tasks, and visual aids like animated arrows and cursor highlights can enhance understanding. Another useful type of video is a **talking head videos** (achieved by overlaying both videos) where the desktop and the presenter are both visible in the video, fostering a personal connection and clear communication. This increases engagement through relatable, humanized content and establishes the speaker as a credible and knowledgeable source.

To use **picture-in-picture overlay** in Clipchamp, start by importing your videos by clicking on the **import media** button in the **My media** tab on the toolbar or adding free stock media like video clips by clicking on the **Stock video** or **Stock images** library tabs.

Drag and drop the files from the media tab into the timeline, making sure the videos are arranged vertically. The one intended for the picture-in-picture effect should be positioned above the other video on the timeline. To overlay your video, select it on the timeline. Click the three dots on the toolbar, then choose the picture-in-picture button, and finally select **Top left**, **Top right**, **Bottom left**, or **Bottom right**, as shown:

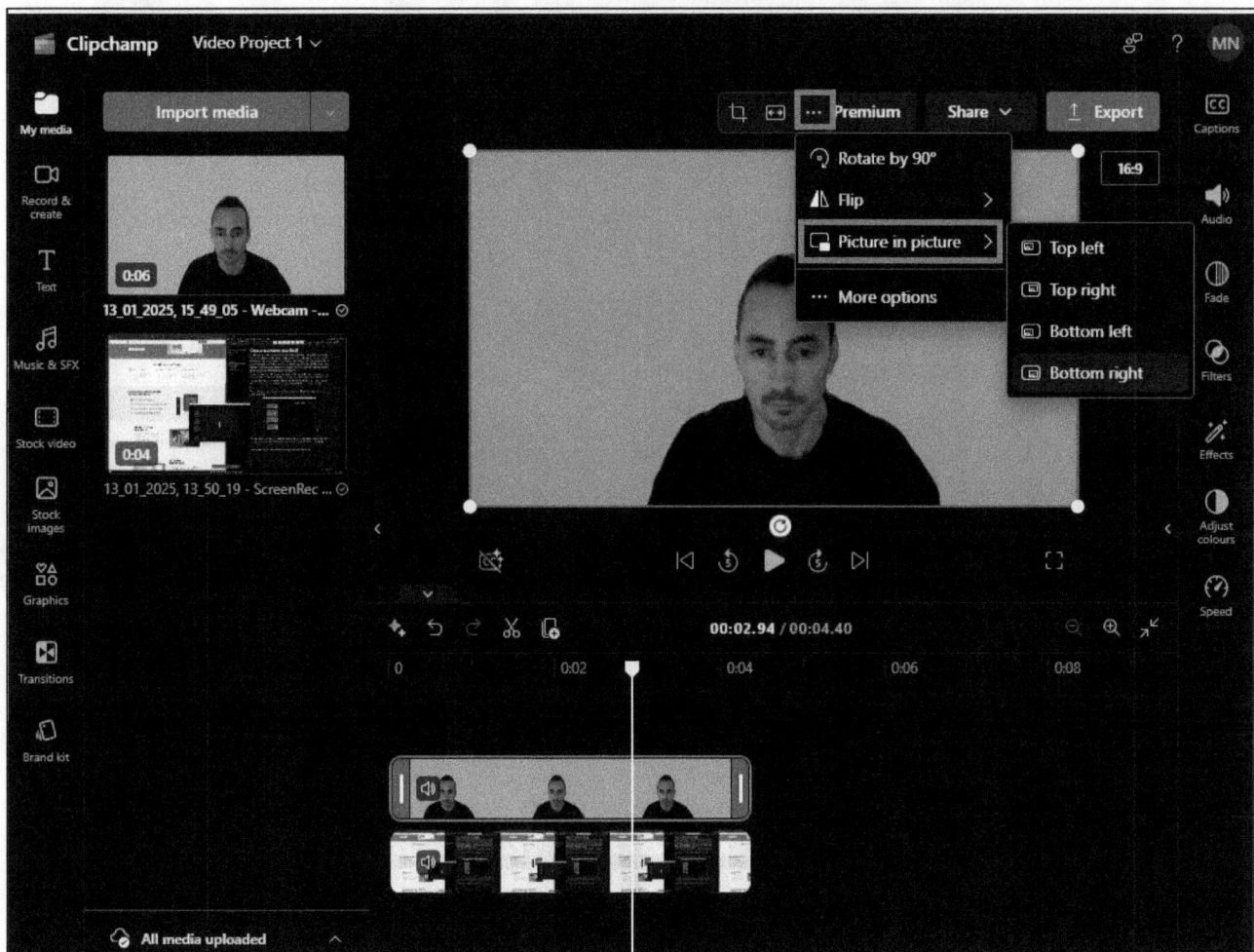

Figure 11.5: Picture-in-picture overlay in Clipchamp

You can then freely adjust the video clip and reposition it within the video preview.

To add effects to your video, select the video on the timeline and go to the **Effects** tab in the property panel (right-hand side). Various effects are available for you to apply to your videos. Hover over one to preview it, then click to apply it. Since the video was recorded using a green screen, we can apply the *green screen* effect to it to make the background of my talking video transparent and the overall video a lot more professional:

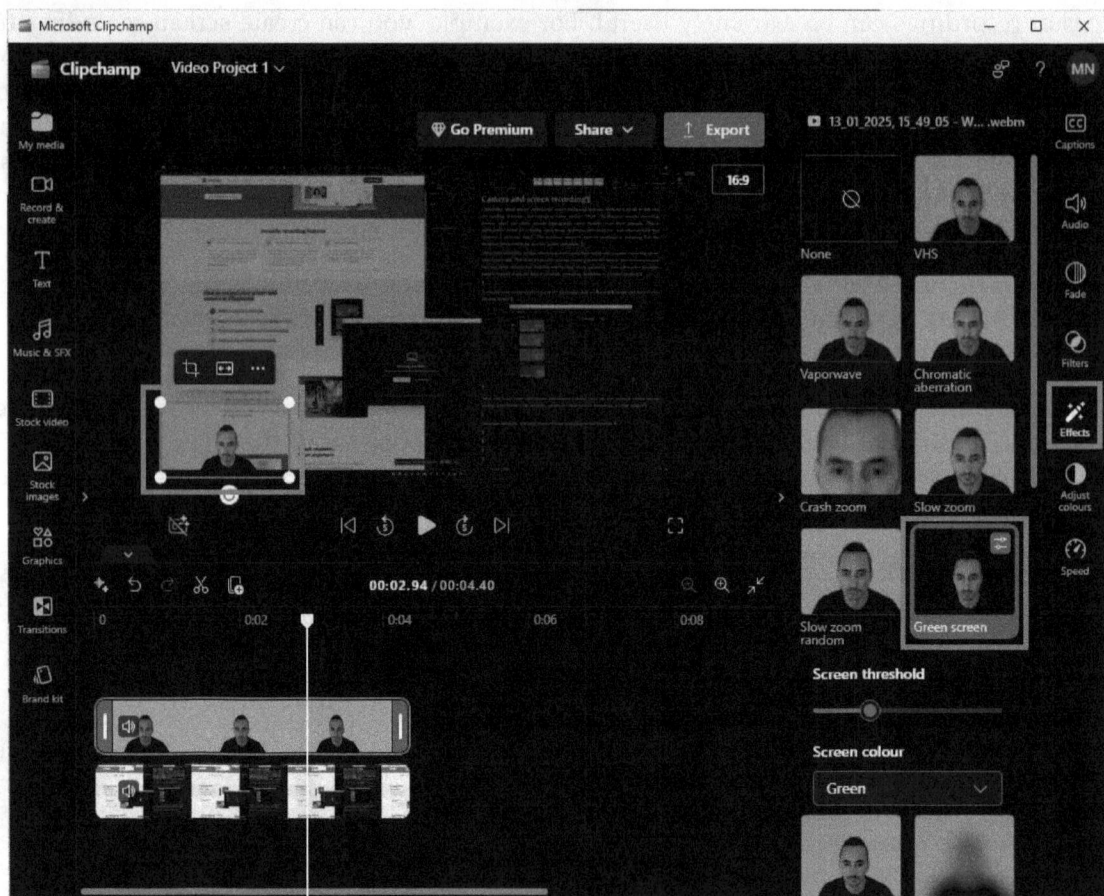

Figure 11.6: Applying the green screen effect to a video

Captions and subtitles

You can improve your videos' accessibility by adding **subtitles** or **captions** and creating inclusive content for audiences like the deaf or hard-of-hearing communities. To do this, navigate to the **Captions** tab on the property panel and click **Try now**:

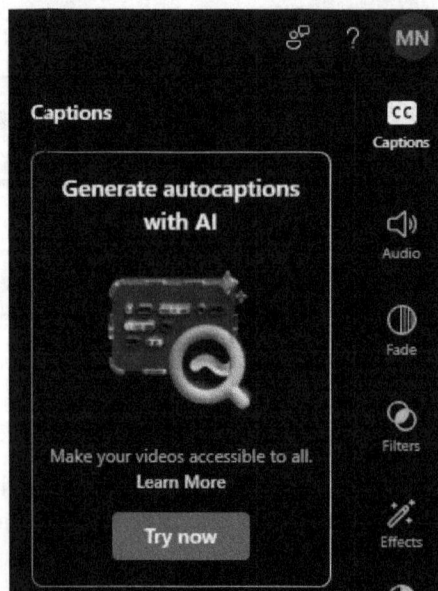

Figure 11.7: Adding captions to a video

A popup window will appear, offering AI transcribing options. You can select your preferred language and filter profanity and offensive language. When ready, click on the **Transcribe media** button to generate your subtitles. Once your subtitles have been generated, they will be displayed as a transcript in the property panel and within the video preview window.

Although Clipchamp is accurate, there is always a possibility that some words may be misspelled. You can easily review the automatic transcript and rectify any misspelled words. The following figure shows the **Transcript** section, where you can review the autogenerated transcript:

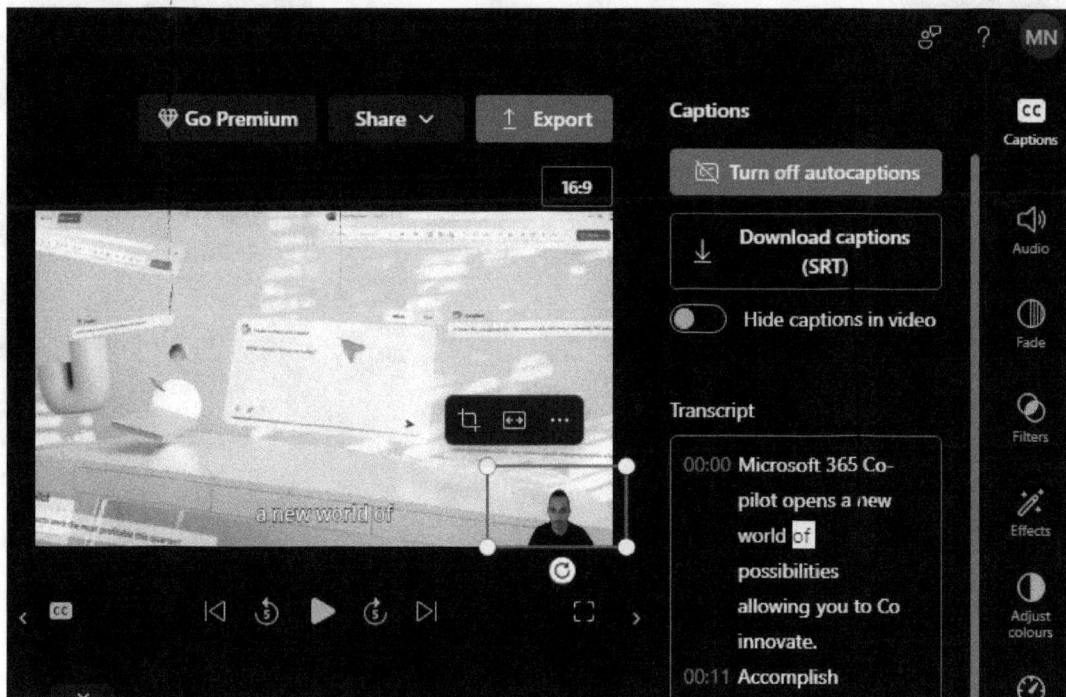

Figure 11.8: Correcting subtitles

To modify the appearance of the subtitles, select the subtitles in the video preview. This action will display various options on the property panel, allowing you to adjust the font, size, alignment, and colors as per your requirements.

In *Figure 11.3*, you might have noticed a **Text to speech** option, which allows you to convert written text into spoken words using advanced AI technology, producing lifelike voiceovers for your videos. This feature offers a variety of voice styles and accents and allows you to select the emotion, vocal pitch, and even pace, enabling you to customize the audio to match the tone and context of your content.

Text, stickers, and annotation visuals

Adding overlays such as text, stickers, backgrounds, frames, shapes, annotations, or GIFs to a video can significantly enhance its visual appeal and effectiveness. Overlays help to emphasize key points, illustrate complex ideas, and provide a visual break that keeps the audience engaged. Annotations, for instance, can direct viewers' attention to specific parts of the video, making it easier to follow along. Similarly, frames and backgrounds can add a professional touch, while GIFs and stickers can inject humor and personality, making the content more relatable and enjoyable. By incorporating these elements thoughtfully, you can create videos that are not only informative but also captivating and memorable for your audience.

To incorporate text into your video, access the **Text** tab located on the toolbar and select a title that aligns with the content of your video. Proceed by dragging and dropping the selected title onto the video. You may then edit your text within the text tab on the property panel and determine when you want it displayed and for how long by adjusting it in the timeline:

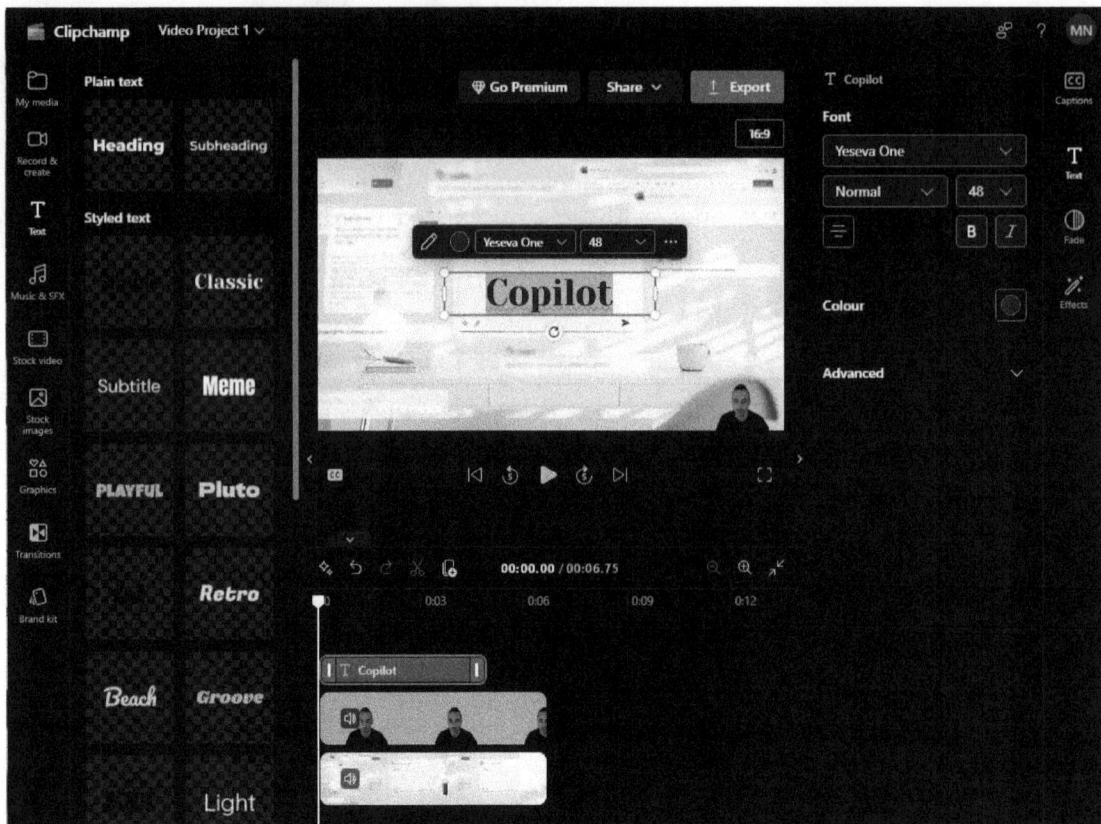

Figure 11.9: Adding text to a video

To incorporate annotations such as circles, arrows, or underlines, select the **Graphics** library tab from the toolbar. Then, search for the type of graphic you want to add and drag and drop it into your video.

The following are a few examples:

Figure 11.10: Example of available visuals

Trim, split, and crop a video

Trimming, cropping, or splitting a video can significantly enhance the final product by removing unwanted sections, focusing on key elements, and creating a more engaging narrative flow. These editing techniques allow you to refine your video, ensuring that it aligns with your intended message and maintains the viewers' attention throughout.

To **trim** the length of your video, select it on the timeline so it is highlighted. Sidebars will be displayed on each end of the video. Click and drag the handles on either side to adjust the length of your video. Drag to the left to shorten or to the right to lengthen the video.

If an excessive portion of your video is trimmed, simply drag the handle back to restore your footage, as highlighted in the following figure:

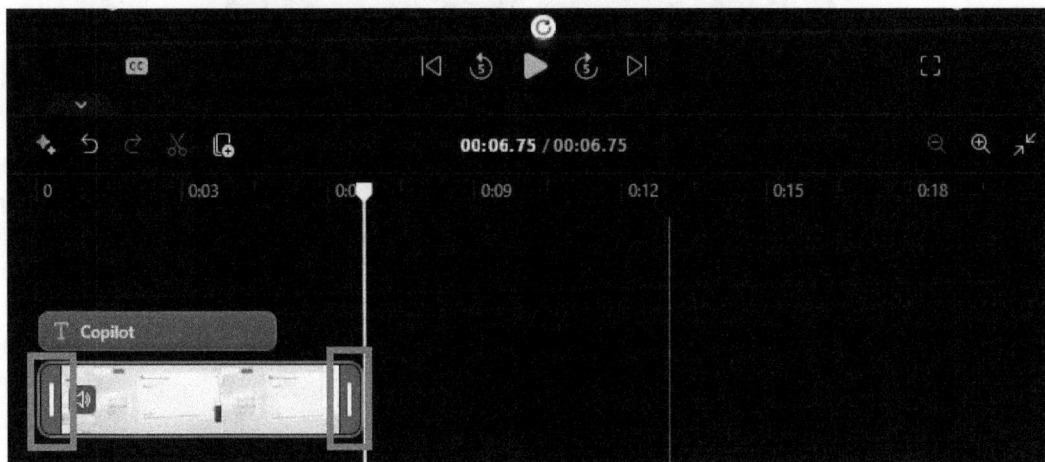

Figure 11.11: *Trimming a video*

To **split** the video into two parts, select it on the timeline. Then, position the seeker (the vertical white line with an arrow at the top) where you want to split the clip. Finally, click the split button on the editing toolbar:

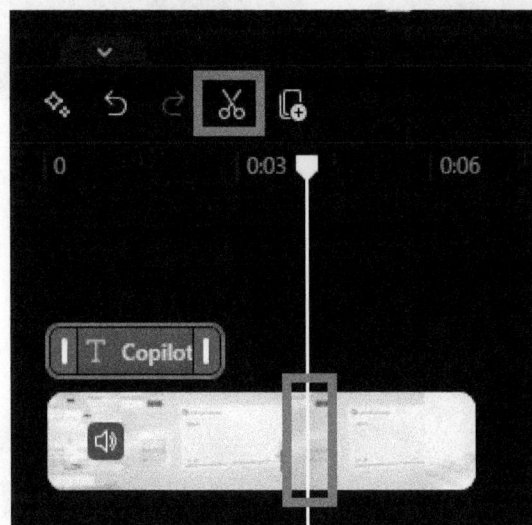

Figure 11.12: *Splitting a video*

To **crop** unwanted areas of your video, use the cropping handles. Select any video on your timeline so it is highlighted, then click the crop button on the floating toolbar. Cropping handles will appear around the video preview window. Adjust the handles to crop the video to the desired size. You can also move your video around the preview window to reposition or recenter it. When finished, click the done arrow button:

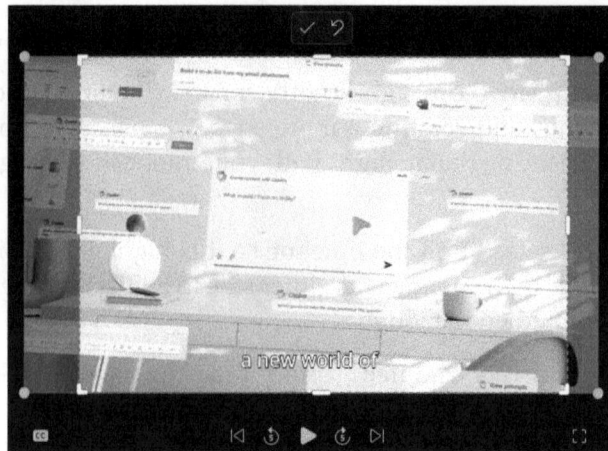

Figure 11.13: Cropping a video

Transitions

Adding transitions to your videos enhances the viewing experience by providing smooth and visually appealing shifts between scenes or segments. Transitions help maintain the flow of your narrative, prevent abrupt cuts that might disrupt the audience's engagement, and add a professional touch to your video. They can emphasize the beginning or end of key sections, create a seamless connection between different clips, and even evoke specific emotions or moods that complement your content.

Connecting your slideshow videos or video clips in montages with transitions could not be easier in Clipchamp. Once you have the videos in your timeline, click the **Transitions** tab on the toolbar. Search through the different transitions available and select the one that best matches the message and tone of your video. To apply the transition, drag it between the clips on the editing timeline.

The + icon will appear between two clips to indicate where the transition will be placed, as you can see next to the number 3 as shown:

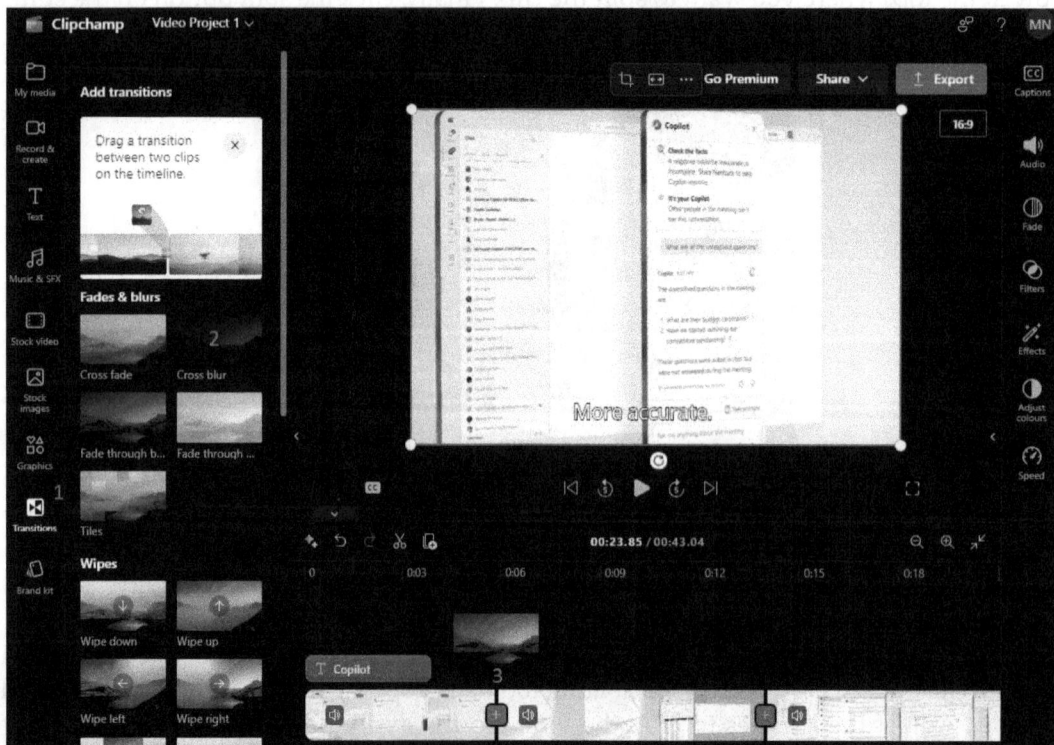

Figure 11.14: Applying a transition between clips

When you click on the transition icon between your media, a property panel will appear on the right side, allowing you to fine-tune your transition. Here, you can adjust the duration of the transition in seconds, which is 2 seconds by default, or select another transition if desired.

Video enhancing

Clipchamp offers various tools to enhance and correct the colors in your videos, ensuring they look their best. Select your video on the timeline, then navigate to the **Adjust colors** tab in the property panel. Here, you can correct the video's colors by using the exposure, contrast, saturation, temperature, and transparency sliders. Adjust the color correction slider to modify the value or intensity. For instance, to increase the brightness of your video, move the exposure slider to the right. Conversely, to decrease the brightness, move the exposure slider to the left. The color correction tool may be used repeatedly as needed.

Refer to the following figure:

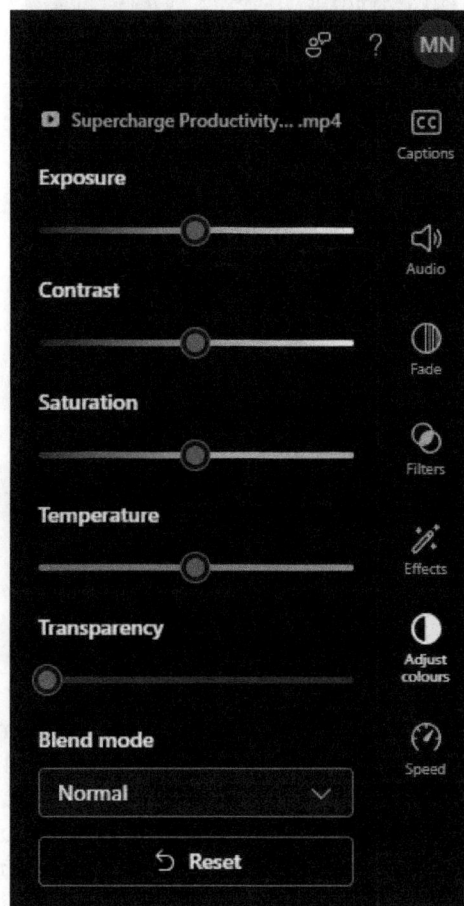

Figure 11.15: Color-correcting a video

If you want to revert your color correction changes, click the **Reset** button, and your video will return to its original state. Alternatively, you can use the undo and redo buttons on the timeline or remove the video and drag the original asset back onto the timeline.

Clipchamp also provides filters that can instantly change the mood and style of your video, from adding a vintage look to creating a modern, cinematic feel. These filters can be used to alter the color of your assets. To do so, select the filters tab in the property panel and hover over a filter to preview it.

Once a filter is selected, click on it to apply the desired changes as follows:

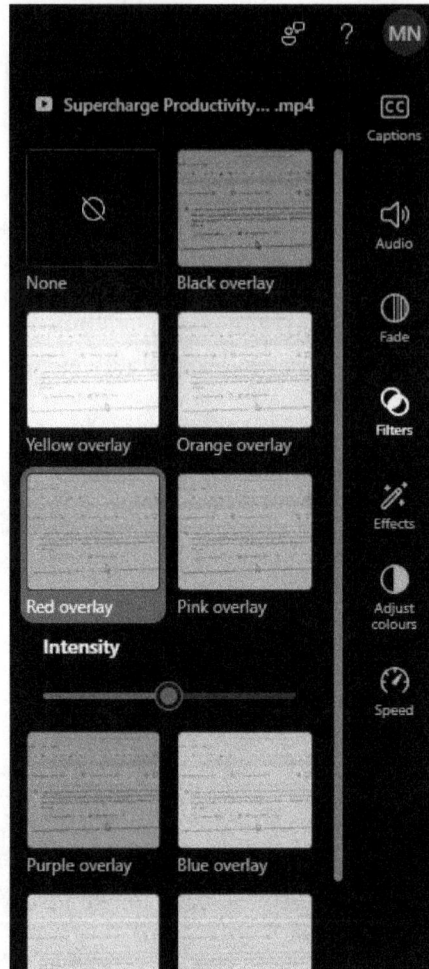

Figure 11.16: *Applying a filter to a video*

Resizing and exporting

Resizing and exporting videos are essential features provided by Clipchamp, allowing users to easily change the video aspect ratios with the online video resizer. This tool is particularly useful for adapting videos to different platforms' requirements, ensuring that your content looks perfect whether you post on social media, embed in a website, or share via email. By adjusting the aspect ratio, you can avoid unwanted cropping or black bars, which can detract from the viewing experience. Additionally, resizing videos helps maintain the quality and integrity of your original content while making it compatible with various devices and screen sizes.

You should use the video resizing feature when you need to:

- Prepare content for specific social media platforms that require unique aspect ratios, such as Instagram or YouTube.
- Ensure your video fits perfectly within the designated space on a website or a presentation slide.
- Optimize the viewing experience for audiences across different devices, from mobile phones to desktop monitors.

Resizing a video in Clipchamp is a straightforward process that can be completed in just a few steps. To adjust the aspect ratio, select the video in the timeline and click on the **16:9** aspect ratio button at the window's top right corner, under the **Export** button. This will open a menu with several preset aspect ratios, such as 16:9,

9:16, 1:1, and 4:5, which cater to different platforms like YouTube, Instagram, and Facebook. Select the aspect ratio that best fits your needs. You can see the ratios available to choose from as follows:

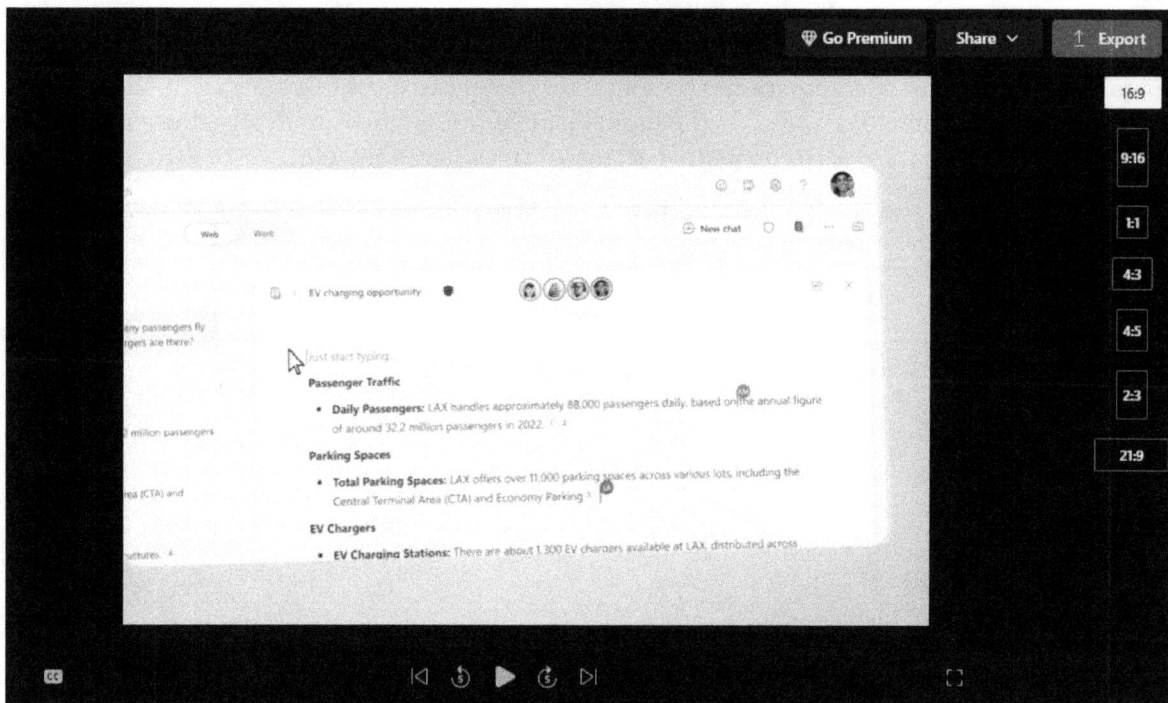

Figure 11.17: Changing the aspect ratio of a video

After choosing the desired aspect ratio, you can further customize the video's dimensions by manually adjusting the crop handles on the video preview. This allows you to fine-tune the framing and ensure that the most important parts of your video remain in view.

Finally, once you are satisfied with the resized video, click on the **Export** button. Choose the desired resolution, such as 720p, 1080p, or 4K, and select the **Export** option to save your video to your computer, as shown:

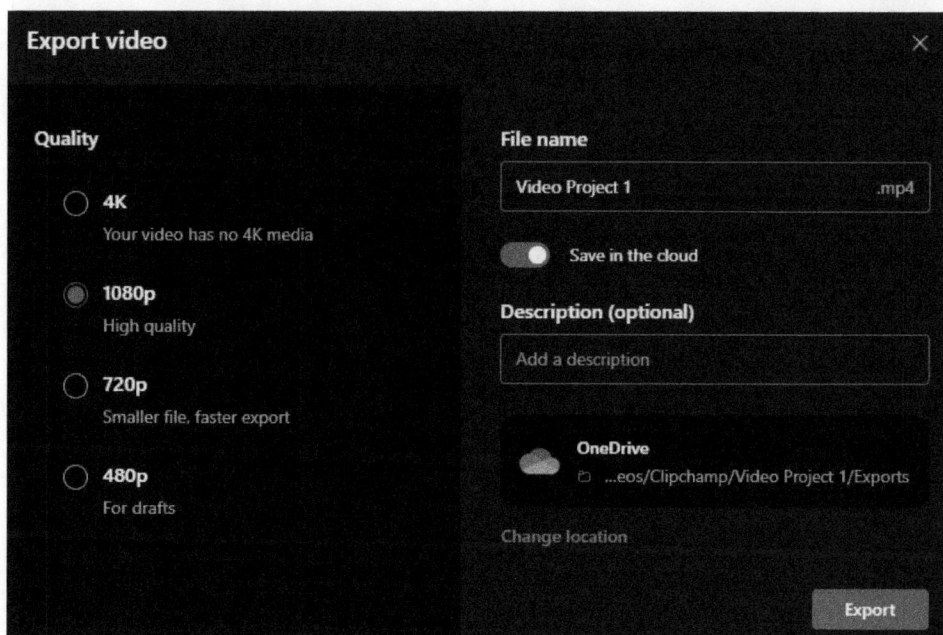

Figure 11.18: Exporting a video

Clipchamp will process the video, and within a few moments, your video will be ready for use.

Conclusion

In this chapter, we explored Microsoft Clipchamp, a powerful suite of tools for video editing tailored to meet the diverse requirements of various social media platforms and presentation formats. Mastering video editing tools like Clipchamp opens many opportunities for content creators to connect with their audiences in engaging and visually compelling ways. As the digital landscape continues to evolve, the ability to produce polished, professional-quality videos efficiently becomes increasingly valuable.

Throughout this chapter, readers have learned how to leverage Clipchamp's features to make their content stand out across various platforms and devices, setting the stage for impactful storytelling and audience engagement.

In the next chapter, we will explore Microsoft Sway, an innovative tool designed to create and share visually stunning interactive reports, presentations, or stories.

Join our Discord space

Join our Discord workspace for latest updates, offers, tech happenings around the world, new releases, and sessions with the authors:

https://discord.bpbonline.com

CHAPTER 12
Sway

Introduction

This chapter looks into Microsoft Sway, guiding readers through its main features and functionalities. From understanding the basics of its intuitive design interface to exploring advanced techniques for integrating multimedia elements, this chapter aims to empower users to create visually cohesive and interactive presentations.

Structure

This chapter covers the following topics:

- Microsoft Sway
- Creating a new Sway
- Storyline
- Adding content
- Customizing your Sway
- Sharing your Sway

Objectives

By the end of this chapter, readers will learn to navigate and utilize the main features of Microsoft Sway effectively. They will gain insights into how to create visually appealing and cohesive presentations by leveraging Sway's intuitive design interface. Through practical examples, readers will understand how to integrate various media elements, such as text, images, and videos, into their projects seamlessly. Ultimately, readers will be equipped to produce professional Sway presentations that stand out for their interactivity and visual impact.

Microsoft Sway

Microsoft Sway, developed internally by Microsoft back in 2014, is an innovative application designed to create and share visually stunning interactive reports, presentations, and stories. Unlike traditional presentation software, Sway emphasizes ease of use and visual impact, making it accessible to users with varying levels of technical expertise. Whether you are an educator looking to create engaging lesson plans, a business professional preparing a dynamic report, or a student creating a project, Sway offers a versatile platform to meet your needs.

This complimentary Microsoft 365 application integrates text, images, video, and other embedded elements to create comprehensive narratives. Sways can easily be shared or embedded within web pages. Additionally, users can view and copy Sways as templates, and the original creator has the capability to track the number of views their Sways receive.

Let us explore some of Sway's key features:

- **Intuitive design interface**: Sway's user-friendly interface allows users to drag and drop content effortlessly. Unlike traditional presentation tools, Sway does not rely on slides but uses a storyline where users can arrange text, images, videos, and other media in a continuous flow. This approach breaks away from the linear slide format, providing a more fluid and natural way to present information.

- **Integrated search**: One of Sway's standout features is its integrated search capability, which allows users to find and insert content from various sources, including Bing, YouTube, and OneDrive, without leaving the app. This feature streamlines the content creation process by providing easy access to a wealth of online resources. For example, if you need a specific image or video to enhance your presentation, you can search for it directly within Sway and add it to your project with just a few clicks.

- **Responsive design**: Sway automatically adapts to different screen sizes and orientations, ensuring that your content looks great on any device, whether it is a smartphone, tablet, or desktop computer. This responsive design feature is particularly useful for users who need to share their presentations with a diverse audience. Whether your viewers are accessing your Sway on a large monitor or a small mobile screen, the content will adjust seamlessly to provide an optimal viewing experience.

- **Sharing and collaboration**: Sway makes it easy to share your creations with others. You can invite collaborators to edit your Sway or share a view-only link with your audience. Additionally, Sway content can be embedded into websites or shared on social media platforms. Users can also control the level of access granted to collaborators, ensuring that sensitive information remains protected.

- **Templates and themes**: To help users get started, Sway offers a variety of templates and themes that can be customized to suit the purpose of the presentation or report. These templates are designed to be visually appealing and professionally structured, saving users time and effort in the design process. Whether you are creating a business proposal, a travel journal, or a school project, Sway's templates provide a solid foundation to build upon. Additionally, users can customize themes by adjusting colors, fonts, and layout options to match their branding or personal preferences.

From an end-user perspective, **Microsoft Sway** and **Microsoft PowerPoint** serve different purposes, even though both are presentation tools.

Sway is designed for creating interactive, web-based content. It is perfect when you want to tell a story or share information in a scrollable, visually engaging format. You do not need to worry much about layout as Sway handles that for you. It is great for digital newsletters, portfolios, reports, or classroom recaps. You simply add your content, and Sway arranges it into a sleek, responsive design that looks good on any device.

PowerPoint, on the other hand, is built for structured, slide-by-slide presentations. It gives you full control over design, animations, transitions, and timing. It is ideal for live presentations, business meetings, lectures, and training sessions. You can work offline, print handouts, and use speaker notes, features that Sway does not offer.

License requirements

Sway is available for use by anyone with a Microsoft Account (Hotmail, Live, or Outlook.com. However, additional features and content options are accessible when using Sway through a Microsoft 365 subscription.

The following table outlines the differences in content limits, per Sway, between the free version and when using Sway in Microsoft 365:

Sway content type	Free limit	Microsoft 365 limit
Headings	20	200
Paragraphs	150	1,000
Images	150	300
Videos	10	40
Audio	10	40
Embeds	10	50
Total Items	200	1,500

Table 12.1: Sway free vs Microsoft 365 content limits

The main difference in Microsoft Sway's user experience comes down to the license type. Free users get the basics, clean layouts, multimedia support, and easy sharing. Microsoft 365 users gain extra features like branding control, password protection, analytics, and better collaboration options, especially useful in business or education settings.

Creating a new Sway

To begin using Sway, navigate to the Microsoft 365 homepage and select **Sway**. Alternatively, you may access it by navigating directly to **https://sway.cloud.microsoft** or **https://www.sway.com** and log in with your Microsoft 365 credentials, assuming you were not logged in automatically. Upon signing in, the Sway dashboard will be displayed:

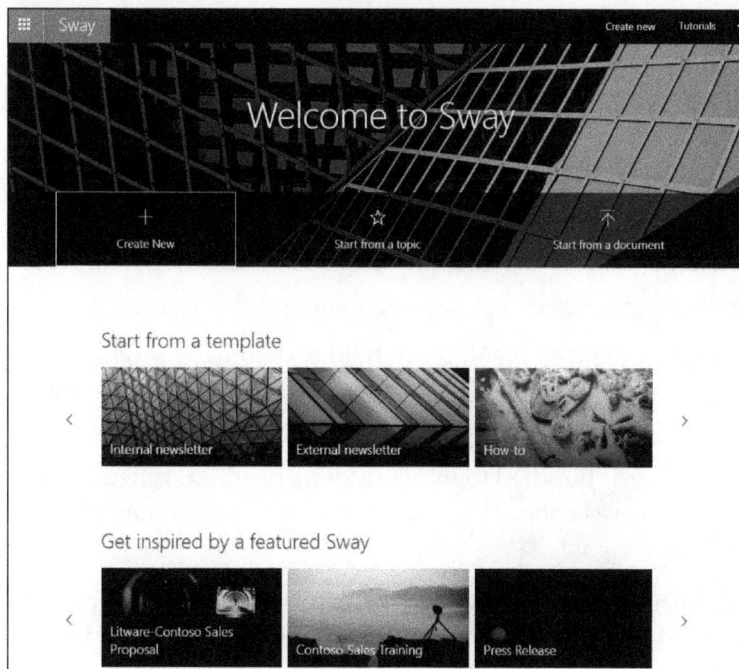

Figure 12.1: Sway's welcome screen

From here, you can create a new Sway in three different ways by using the buttons at the top of the screen:

- **Create New**: Build your Sway from scratch. This option allows you to start with a blank canvas where you can add your content step-by-step, ensuring each element is tailored to your precise needs.

- **Start from a topic**: let Sway generate a base for your presentation by adding content related to a topic of your choice. Simply type your desired topic in the **Enter a topic** box and select **Create outline**. Sway will then automatically generate an outline with suggested headings and content areas, which you can further customize.

- **Start from a document**: import content from an existing file. Browse and select the file you wish to use as the foundation for your Sway, and then click **Open**. Sway will extract relevant content from the document and arrange it into a structured format, which you can edit and enhance.

Once you have chosen your starting point, you can begin building your Sway using cards. These cards act as the building blocks of your digital story, encompassing text, images, embedded videos, tweets, and sound recordings. You can source images and videos from the internet or upload them directly from your computer or mobile device. Additionally, you can rearrange the cards in any sequence to craft a compelling narrative flow.

First and foremost, give your Sway an engaging title. To do this, select the **Title your Sway** placeholder text shown in the first card on the **Storyline**, and type a concise yet descriptive title that encapsulates the essence of your Sway:

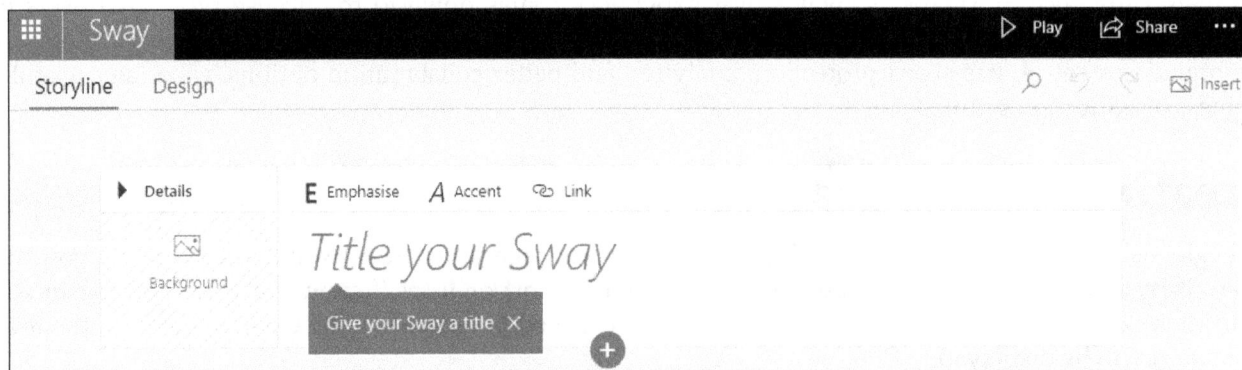

Figure 12.2: Naming your Sway

If you opt to create a Sway based on a topic or document, the title will be automatically generated based on your chosen topic or the file name.

With your title in place, you can focus on the initial card, commonly known as the heading card. This card typically consists of text and may feature a background image for visual appeal. Its main purpose is to introduce and structure your digital narrative into coherent sections, setting the tone for the rest of your presentation.

Cards and **sections** are both building blocks of your content, but they serve different purposes:

- A **card** is an individual content element. It can hold text, images, videos, audio, or embedded content. Think of it like a single slide or block of information. You stack cards in the order you want your story to unfold.

- A **section** is a group of cards bundled together under a heading. When you add a **Heading card**, Sway automatically creates a new section. This helps organize your content into chapters or themes, making it easier for viewers to navigate.

For example, if you are creating a digital travel journal, you might have a section for each city you visited. Inside each section, you would add cards for photos, descriptions, and videos from that location.

Storyline

The heart of Sway is its storyline, which serves as the backbone for organizing and presenting content in a structured, multimedia narrative. It allows users to combine various types of content, including text, images, videos, and documents, into a cohesive and engaging presentation. The storyline is composed of individual cards, each representing a distinct piece of content, which can be easily added, edited, and rearranged to fit the flow of the narrative. In the following figure, you can see an example of storyline with three of its cards visible:

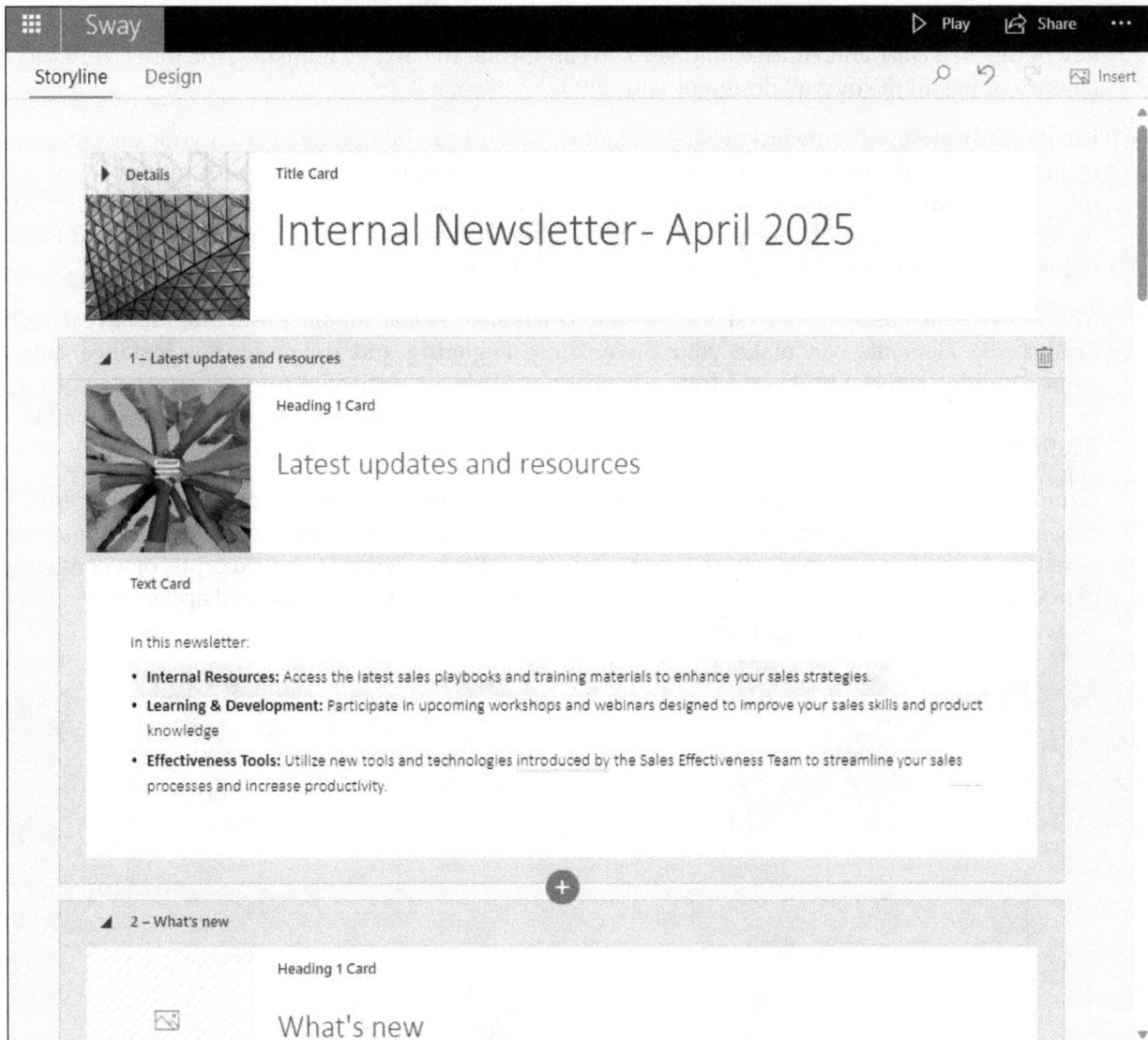

Figure 12.3: *Sway's storyline*

To get started, users add cards to the storyline sequentially, building their Sway piece by piece. Each card can house a specific type of content, such as a block of text, an image, a video clip, or even an embedded Office document. This modular approach offers flexibility, as users can modify the arrangement of these cards at any time, ensuring that the presentation remains dynamic and adaptable to changing needs.

One of the key advantages of the storyline is its intuitive interface, which simplifies the process of creating a multimedia story. The cards within the storyline can be rearranged by dragging and dropping them into the desired sequence. This flexibility enables you to organize your content in a logical and coherent manner. Furthermore, each card can be customized to meet specific narrative requirements. For example, text formatting was modified, images given special focus, and layouts adjusted to enhance the visual appeal of your Sway presentation.

Adding content

Once you have configured your heading card, the next step is to add additional cards and content to those cards. Adding a new card to a Microsoft Sway is a straightforward process. First, click on the + button that appears below an existing card. Next, in the **Cards** pane, you will see different types of cards you can add, which are used to structure and present content:

- **Text cards** are used to add textual content, including headings or paragraphs of descriptive text. These cards are versatile and can be used to introduce sections, provide detailed explanations, or present key points in a clear and concise manner. You can format the text by adjusting the font size, style, and alignment to suit the overall design of your Sway.

- **Image cards** are used to include visual elements. Images can be uploaded from your device, sourced from OneDrive, or found online. These cards help to break up large blocks of text and add visual interest to your presentation. When using Image cards, consider the relevance and quality of the images to ensure they enhance your narrative rather than distract from it. You can also add captions to provide context or additional information about the images.

- **Media cards** are used to embed videos, audio clips, or social media posts such as tweets. These multimedia elements can make your Sway more engaging and dynamic. For instance, you can embed a video tutorial to demonstrate a concept, include an audio clip for background information, or showcase social media posts for real-time updates. Media cards support various formats and platforms, making it easy to integrate diverse content into your presentation.

- **Group cards** are used to organize multiple pieces of content together, such as images or text, in a cohesive layout. These cards are particularly useful when you want to present related information in a structured way. For example, you can create a photo gallery, a series of text excerpts, or a combination of both within a single Group card. This helps to maintain a clean and organized appearance, allowing your audience to easily navigate through the content, as shown:

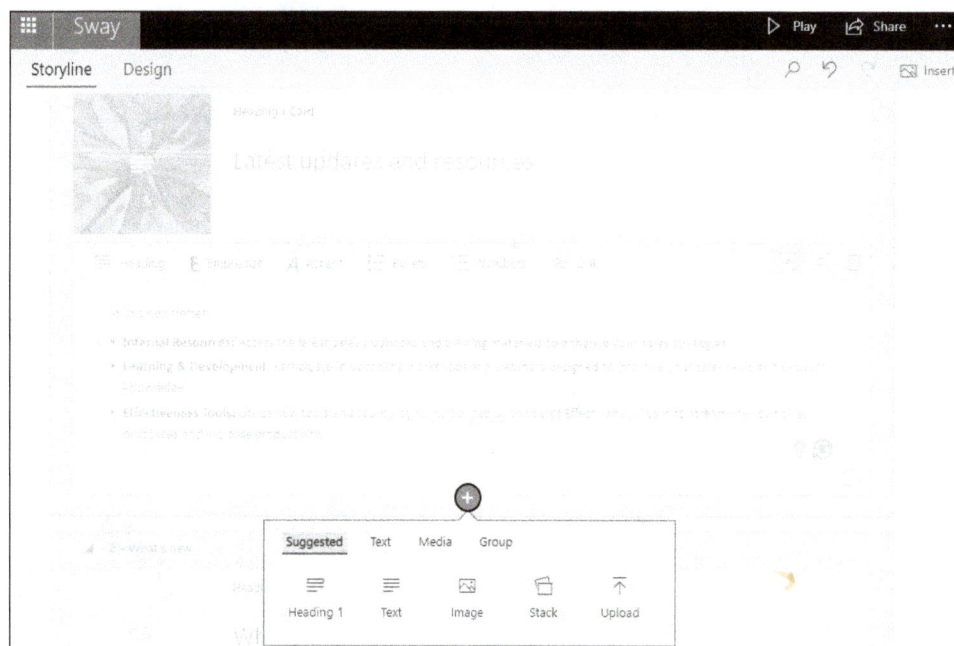

Figure 12.4: Card types in Sway

After selecting the card type, you can start adding your content. For example, if you choose a Text card, you can type your text directly into the card. If you choose an Image card, you can upload an image or select one from the suggested images. Note that each card can have multiple sections. For example, you can have a card with a title, a text section, a video, and a group of images:

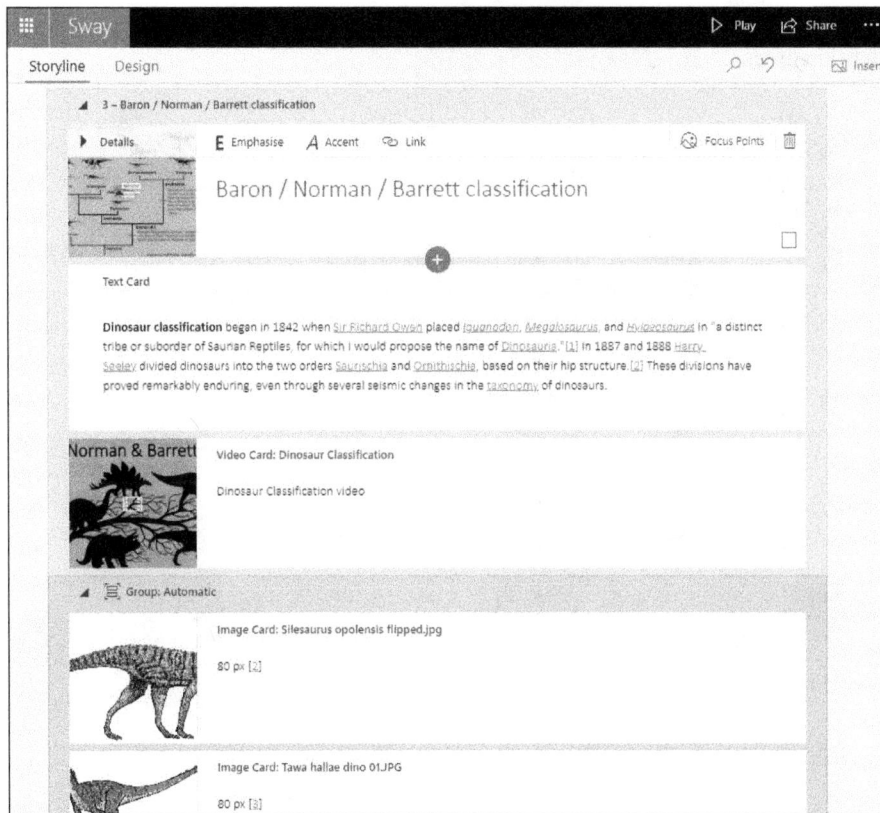

Figure 12.5: *A card with several different sections*

You can think of a card as a single page or slide in your presentation. For example, the above card would look like this on a particular screen size (Sway will adapt the card's layout depending on the screen size):

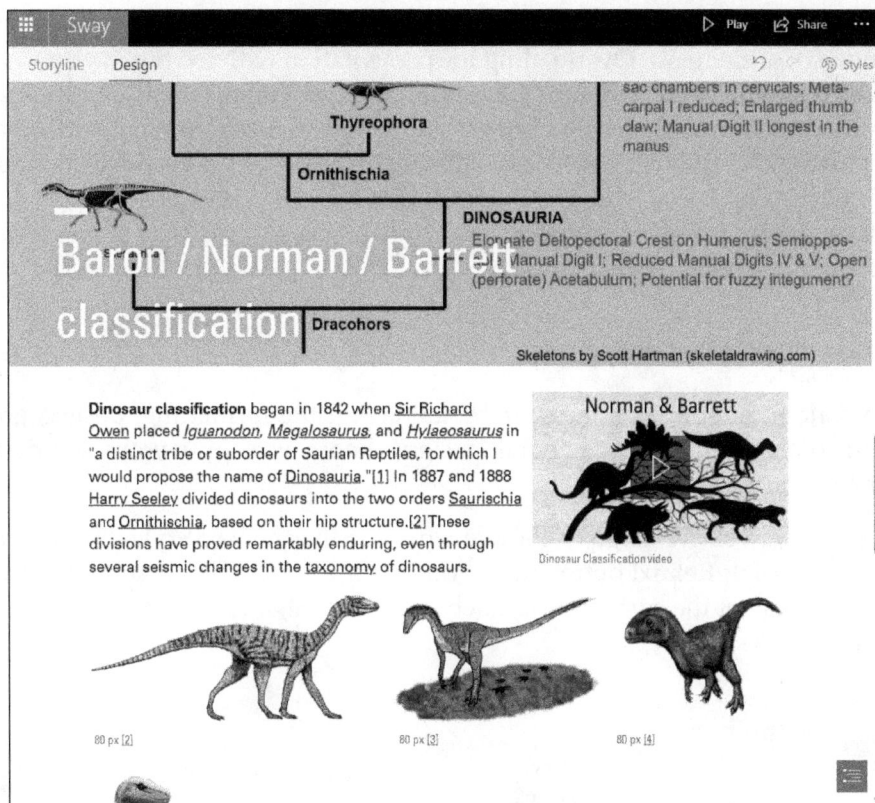

Figure 12.6: *The previous card as visualized by a consumer of the Sway*

Feel free to experiment. You can rearrange the order of your content at any time and customize each card according to your preferences.

Sways provides an easy way to search for and add additional content to your Sway, such as images stored on your device, or the internet for the most relevant content, such as videos. On the menu bar, click on **Insert**, select your preferred content source from the menu, and enter a search keyword or phrase into the **Search** text box:

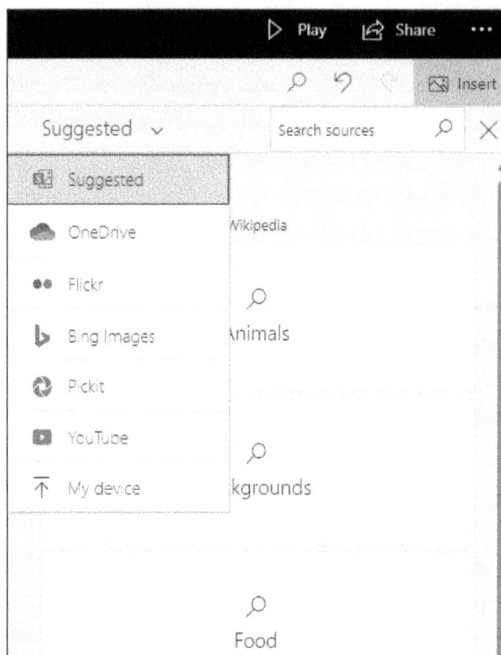

Figure 12.7: Image and video search in Sway

When trying to create a visually appealing and cohesive presentation in Sway, users should be mindful of balancing visual and textual elements. Overloading the presentation with too much visual content can detract from the message and overwhelm the audience. It is important to maintain a clean and consistent layout, using whitespace effectively to avoid clutter. Choose images and media that complement and enhance the narrative rather than distract from it. Additionally, ensure that the text is readable and well-structured, using headings, bullet points, and concise sentences to convey information clearly and effectively. By paying attention to these aspects, users can create a presentation that is not only engaging but also delivers a clear and impactful message.

Customizing your Sway

Sway helps you to concentrate on your message by managing the formatting, design, and layout of your content. You have the option to use Sway's default design, choose and apply your own design, or customize the layout according to your preferences.

To select a style for your Sway, click **Design** on the menu bar and then choose **Styles**. To generate a random look and mood for your Sway, click **Remix!** button until you find a suitable design and layout. Additionally, you can modify specific elements of the current style, such as color, font, and textures, by clicking the **Customise** button in the **Styles** pane, as shown here:

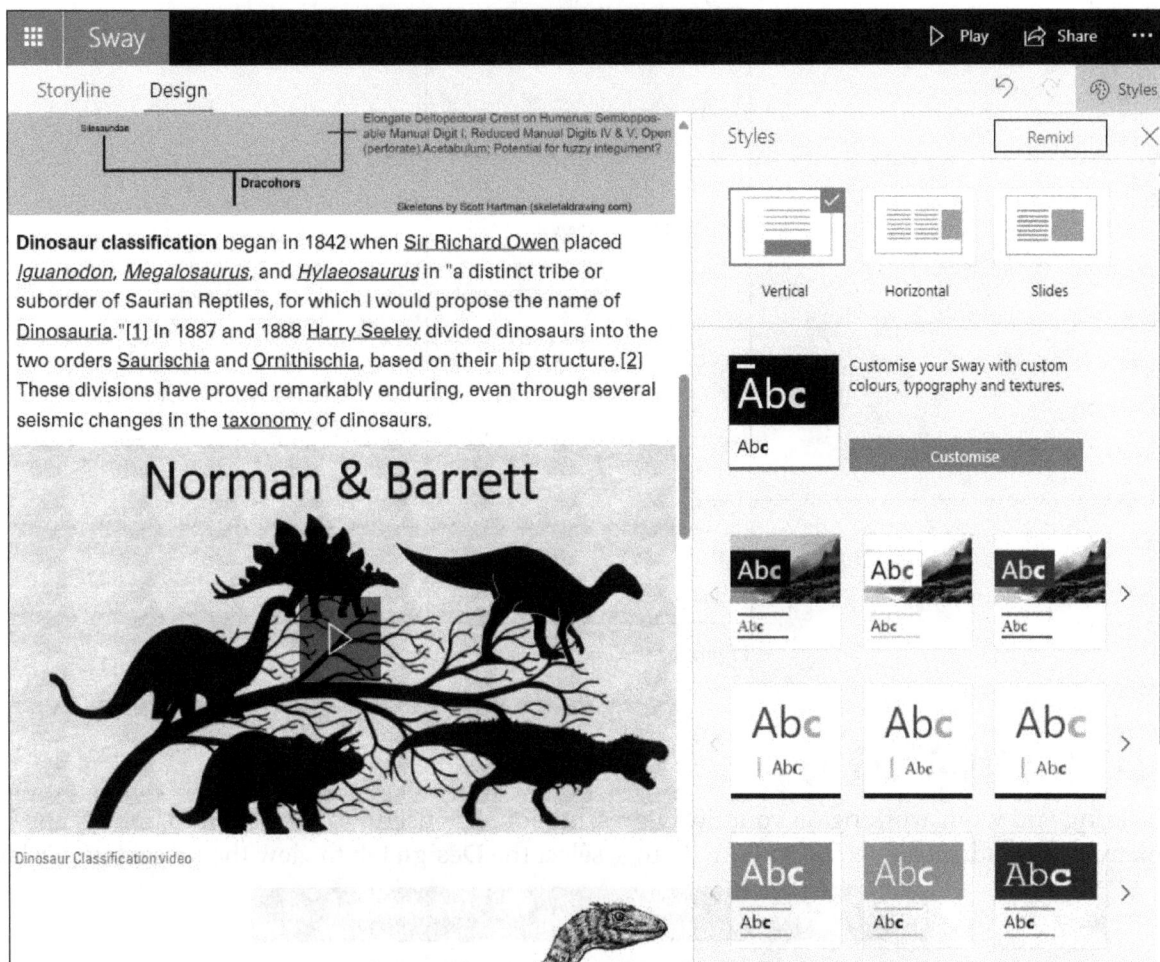

Figure 12.8: Customizing your Sway

To manage how others view and navigate your Sway, choose if the content should scroll vertically, horizontally, or like a slide presentation. This flexibility allows you to tailor the viewing experience to best suit your audience's needs. For instance, a vertical scroll might work well for a blog-style narrative, while a horizontal scroll can mimic a more traditional slideshow. Presentation mode can be ideal for a more dynamic and interactive viewing experience, making it perfect for live demonstrations or speeches.

In addition to customizing the design and layout, Sway offers several settings to enhance your presentation when using the **Play** option:

- **Autoplay settings** allow you to automate the playback of your Sway. This feature is particularly useful for unattended displays or kiosks. You can set the duration for which each card is displayed and choose whether to loop the presentation continuously.

- The **Change layout** feature enables you to switch between different layout modes depending on your presentation style. This includes options like vertical, horizontal, and slide presentation. Each layout mode can be tailored to fit your content's flow and your audience's viewing preferences.

- The **Animations** settings allow you to add dynamic transitions and effects to your Sway. You can choose from a range of animation styles to make your presentation more engaging and visually appealing. This includes options for how text and images appear, move, and disappear within your Sway. The following are some examples of these settings:

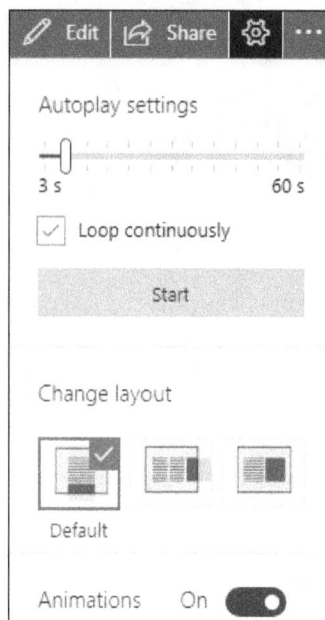

Figure 12.9: Play options in Sway

Sharing your Sway

Before sharing and while working on your Sway presentation, it is useful to preview it to understand how it will look from the audience's perspective. To do this, select the **Design** tab to view the presentation's layout:

Figure 12.10: Previewing a Sway

To return to your storyline when you are done previewing your Sway, click the **Storyline** tab.

Alternatively, select **Play** to see your Sway in full-screen mode and check how it will look to others when shared. To return to editing mode from the play view, click the **Edit** button at the top of the screen.

Once you are happy with the way your Sway looks and are ready to share it, click on the **Share** button on the top menu bar and select how you want to share your Sway. Sway allows you to manage how much you share your creations with others. The sharing options available to you will vary slightly depending on the type of account used to sign into Sway. If you are using Sway as part of a Microsoft subscription, there are three permission levels available for your Sway:

- **Specific people or groups**: Only individuals or groups within your organization with explicit permission can view or edit your Sway. When you share a view or edit link with specific people or groups, they will need to sign in to access your Sway. This setting provides the highest level of security, making it suitable for sensitive or confidential information that should not be shared publicly.

- **Those in your organization with the link**: Only people within your organization will be able to view or edit your Sway. When you send a view or edit link to people in your organization, they will need to sign in to access your Sway. This option is intended for sensitive or confidential information that should only be accessible to people in your organization. Unlike the previous option, any internal user who knows the URL will be able to access your Sway. This is the default setting.

- **Anyone with a link**: Individuals provided with the link to your Sway will have the ability to view or edit it. They are required to sign in only if they have received an edit link. If your Sway does not contain any confidential information, this setting may be appropriate. When this option is selected, additional sharing options will become available, such as sharing to Facebook, X, or LinkedIn.

The following figure shows these three options available when sharing a Sway:

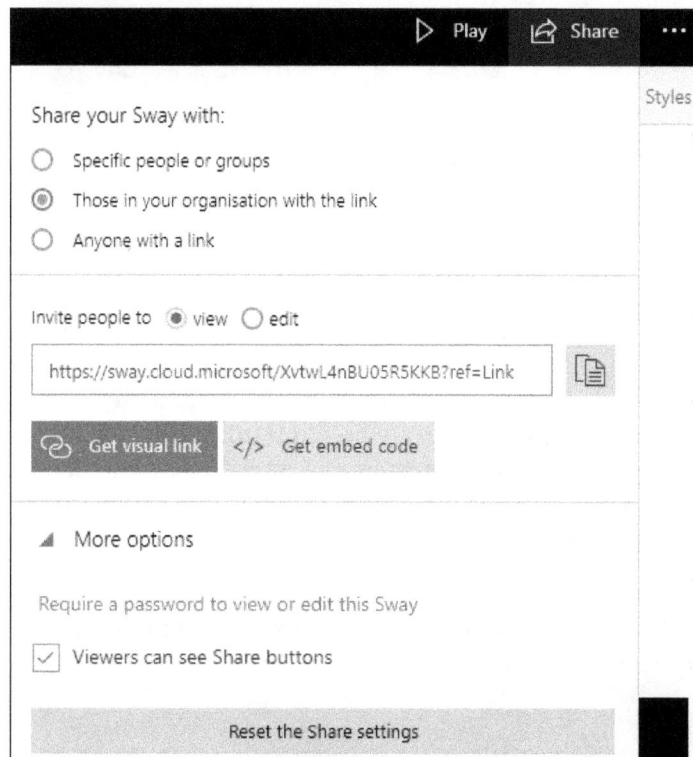

Figure 12.11: Sharing a Sway

An invited author cannot change the share level of a Sway, only the owner has this ability. The list of *Authors* and *Viewers* can be managed by clicking on each person's profile picture. This allows for changing an Author to a Viewer, a Viewer to an Author, or removing the person entirely. An author can be removed at any time by using the **Reset the Share** settings button, which permanently changes the URL of the Sway.

One of the versatile options available when sharing your Sway is the ability to get an embed code. This feature is useful if you wish to integrate your Sway presentation into a website or blog. By selecting the **Get embed code** option shown in the screenshot above, you can generate a piece of HTML code that can be pasted into the HTML editor of your web page. This allows your audience to view the Sway directly on the webpage without needing to navigate away from it.

The embed code can be customized to adjust the width and height of the presentation, ensuring that it fits seamlessly into your web page's design. This is an excellent way to enhance the interactivity and engagement of your website, as visitors can experience the full functionality of the Sway, including its embedded media elements, without leaving your site.

Embedding a Sway can boost the visual appeal and multimedia richness of a website, making it more engaging for visitors. It is also an effective means of disseminating information in a controlled manner, as the embedded Sway retains the sharing permissions set by the creator. Additionally, embedding Sway presentations can enhance storytelling by allowing the integration of interactive and dynamic content directly within articles, reports, or educational material.

Sway also offers some analytics capabilities that can provide insights into how your Sway content is being accessed and interacted with. By accessing the **Analytics** tab in the main dashboard, you can track metrics such as the number of views, the average time spent on each Sway presentation, the average completion, and if readers glanced over the Sway, read it quickly, or read it in depth. These analytics can help you understand your audience's engagement and the effectiveness of your content. The following is an example of these metrics:

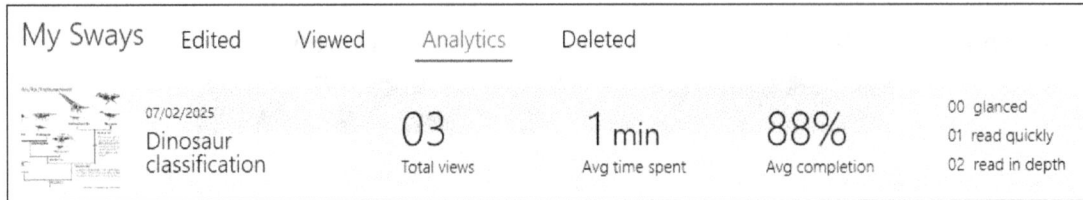

Figure 12.12: *Sway's analytics*

Conclusion

Throughout this chapter, we have delved into the various functionalities and features that make Sway a powerful tool for creating and sharing interactive presentations. Sway's capabilities extend beyond just creating visually appealing presentations. It allows users to embed a range of media, including text, images, videos, and links, making it a robust tool for storytelling and information sharing. The flexibility in sharing settings, from specific people or groups to organizational access to public links, allows users to strike the right balance between accessibility and security. This chapter has equipped you with a comprehensive understanding of how to maximize Sway's features to create captivating and secure presentations tailored to your audience's needs.

In the next chapter, we will shift our focus to Power BI, a dynamic business analytics tool that enables users to visualize and share insights from their data.

Join our Discord space

Join our Discord workspace for latest updates, offers, tech happenings around the world, new releases, and sessions with the authors:

https://discord.bpbonline.com

CHAPTER 13

Power BI

Introduction

In today's world, regardless of the type of business or organization, data plays a crucial role. Without the necessary data, achieving effective decision-making, business efficiency or strategy development becomes a significant challenge. However, merely possessing data is not enough: understanding and interpreting it is equally important. This is where Power BI comes into play. Power BI is more than just a tool, it is a complete solution for data structuring and analysis, helping transform raw data into meaningful insights.

For example, a retail company can use Power BI to analyze sales trends across different regions, identifying which products perform best and where improvements are needed. Healthcare organizations can leverage Power BI dashboards to monitor patient outcomes, manage resources, and track operational efficiency. In the education sector, institutions can use Power BI to visualize student performance data, helping educators make informed decisions to support student success. Financial services firms also benefit from Power BI by monitoring key performance indicators and improving compliance reporting.

These examples illustrate how Power BI empowers a wide range of industries to extract actionable insights from their data, driving better business outcomes.

Structure

This chapter covers the following topics:

- Understanding Power BI
- Power BI Desktop
- Power BI Service
- Power BI Mobile

Objectives

By the end of this chapter, you will understand how Power BI works and how to use its components to start with report creation and data analysis. You will learn the typical workflow for transforming raw data into meaningful reports that can be shared with your team members and co-workers and how Power BI features and tools can help you analyze data.

Understanding Power BI

Before we delve into Power BI and its components, it is important to first understand what **business intelligence** (**BI**) entails. BI is a strategic process that leverages technology and data to enable informed, data-driven decision-making for businesses and organizations. To put it simply, BI functions as an intelligent assistant that aids in understanding your business better. It uses a collection of methodologies and tools to transform available data into meaningful and comprehensive reports and dashboards.

Part of Power Platform, Power BI is the business intelligence solution provided by Microsoft. By leveraging Power BI, organizations can streamline their reporting and data analysis processes, eliminating the need for manual methods and spreadsheets, and adopting a faster and more efficient data processing approach.

Power BI consists of three core components that are in essence connected tools designed to work together, enabling data preparation and comprehensive report creation through **Power BI Desktop**, seamless data collaboration and sharing through **Power BI Service**, and access to reports from mobile devices through **Power BI Mobile**. *Figure 13.1* illustrates the connection between these three tools:

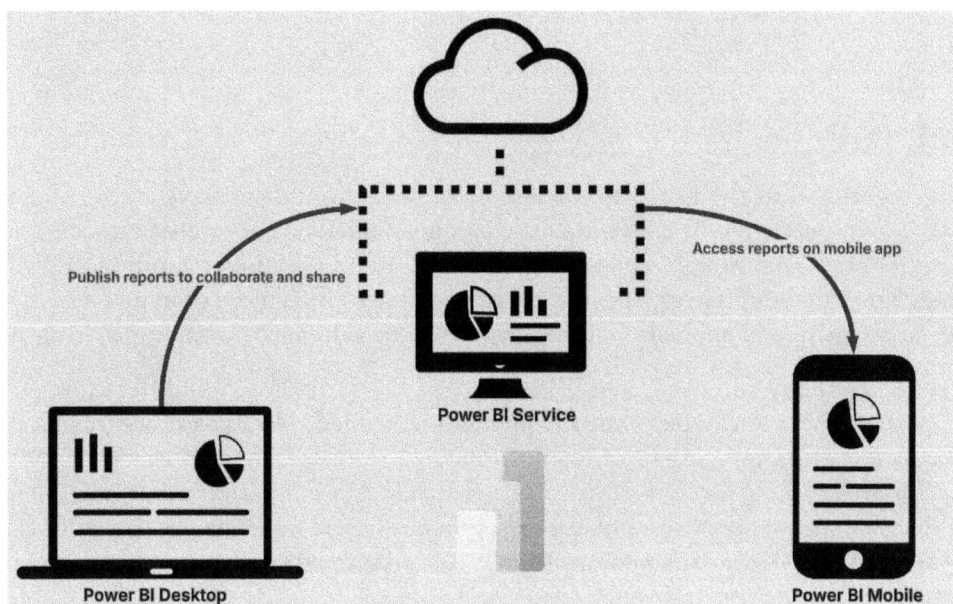

Figure 13.1: Power BI components

This toolset makes Power BI a complete and comprehensive business intelligence solution. In this chapter, we will focus on these core components and will explore each of these three tools to understand their capabilities and how they work together to help users build, share, and access meaningful reports.

Power BI Desktop

Power BI Desktop is the tool where the Power BI workflow typically begins. Within this powerful application, you can connect to various data sources, combine and transform the data from multiple sources, build reports, and visualize data.

Getting started with Power BI Desktop

Power BI Desktop is a free tool that can be downloaded directly from the official Microsoft page at **https://www.microsoft.com/en-gb/power-platform/products/power-bi/desktop**.

By clicking on the **Advanced download options**, you can view information about the tool, including its version and system requirements before downloading it.

Note: **As of the time of writing this book, the Power BI Desktop application is available exclusively for installation on Windows machines.**

After downloading the appropriate executable for your system type (64-bit or 32-bit), you can install the tool by following the straightforward on-screen installation steps.

Once installed, you can start using Power BI Desktop on your machine and begin your reporting and data analysis journey, leveraging the various features this tool offers. *Figure 13.2* shows the Power BI Desktop homepage:

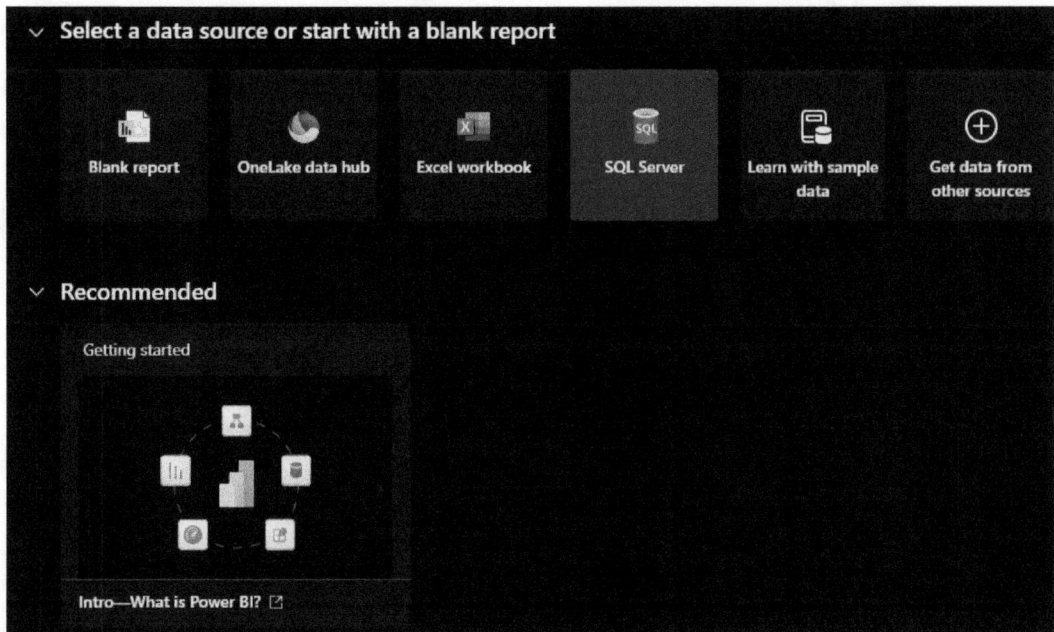

Figure 13.2: Power BI Desktop homepage

From the homepage, you can choose to connect to a data source containing the data needed to build your report, use sample data provided by Microsoft (a great learning option for beginners), or start from scratch by selecting the **Blank report** option.

Additionally, you will find the option to get an introduction to Power BI. By clicking on this tile, you will be redirected to a Microsoft online module that will help you get started, which is ideal for those new to Power BI.

From this point onward in this chapter, to demonstrate how Power BI works and to illustrate common Power BI workflows and features, we will use an example scenario and start from a blank report in Power BI Desktop. Throughout this chapter, we will build this sample report step-by-step as we progress through the content, from connecting to the sources to get the data, to publishing and sharing the report.

Connecting to data sources and load data

With Power BI Desktop, you can seamlessly connect to a variety of data sources, whether they are cloud-based or on-premises. These sources can include files, online services, or databases. Power BI offers the flexibility to connect to one or multiple data sources, allowing you to extract, transform, and load data according to your business needs.

Connecting to a data source in Power BI Desktop is straightforward. Simply click on **Get Data** icon on the **Home** tab, as shown in *Figure 13.3*:

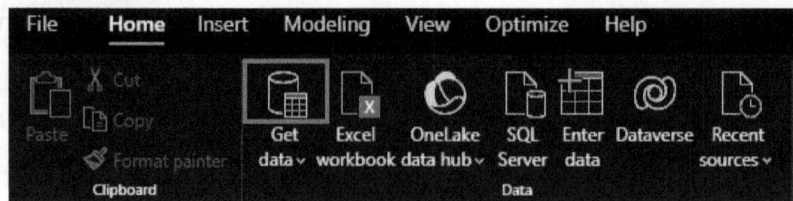

Figure 13.3: Get data

You can search for and select the desired data source type and then follow the prompts to establish the connection, based on the selected data source. *Figure 13.4* shows some of the data source types available in Power BI Desktop:

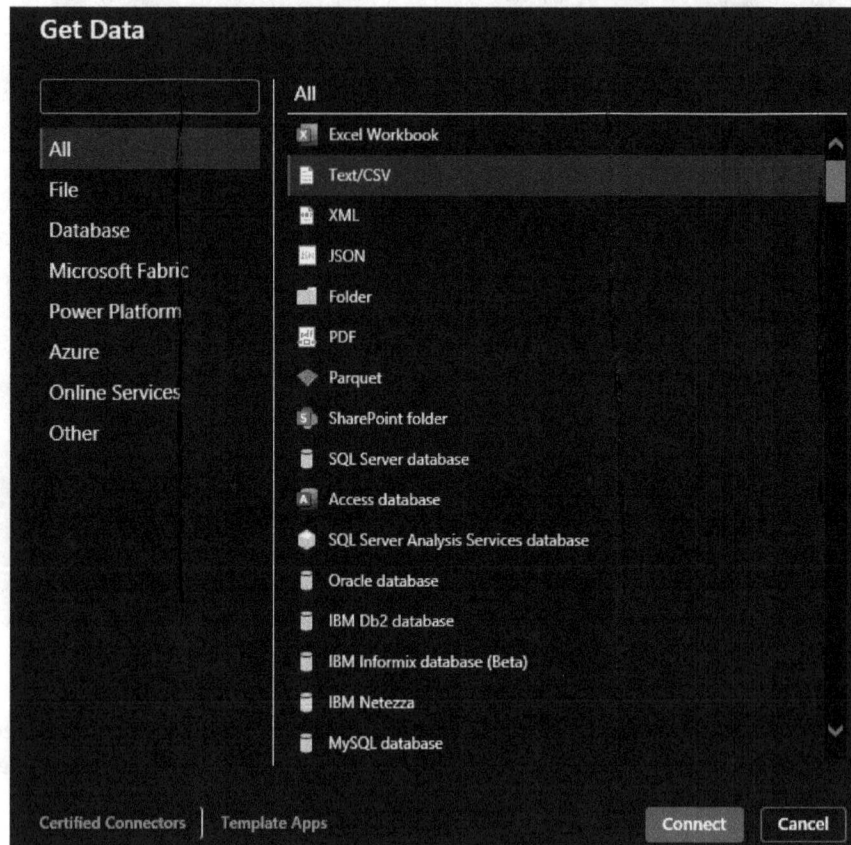

Figure 13.4: Select data source

In our example, we will assume a sales-related scenario where we aim to analyze the relevant information to gain more insights into the sales performance. We will retrieve data from two different sources:

- An Excel file hosted in a SharePoint Online document library. This file contains two tables: one named **Products**, which includes information about products such as product code, category, total cost per unit, and selling price per unit; and another table named **Customers**, which includes information about customers such as customer ID, industry, and country.

- A SharePoint list named **Orders**, that is located within the same SharePoint Online site. This list contains all the orders that have been placed and includes information such as customer ID, product code, quantity ordered, sales representative assigned to the order, status, opened date, and closed date.

Note: The ability to connect to and retrieve data from SharePoint Online depends on having the necessary permissions at the SharePoint site level.

Get data from an Excel file stored in SharePoint Online

We will begin by retrieving the data from the Excel file. Since the file is stored in SharePoint Online, we will use the *Web* source type from the list of available data sources in Power BI Desktop. After selecting *Web* as the data source type, we will be prompted to provide a URL.

To get the URL for the respective Excel file containing the data we need, we follow these steps:

1. Navigate to the SharePoint site where the file is located.
2. Right-click on the file and choose **Details**.
3. Copy the URL found under **Path**.

   Once we have the file URL, we paste it in the *URL* field, ensure the **Basic** option is selected, and click **OK**:

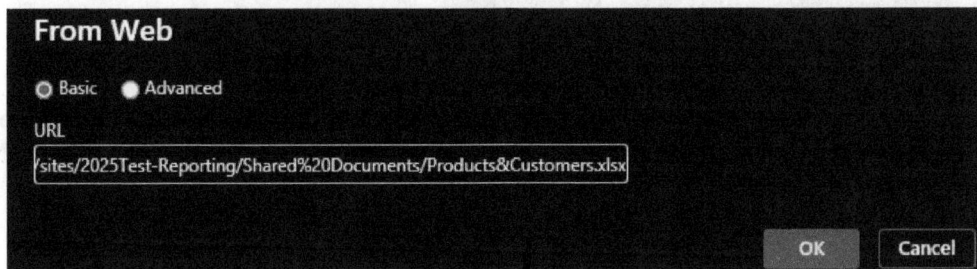

Figure 13.5: Get data from the web

We are then prompted to select the method for accessing the web content. In this case, we select **Organizational account**, choose our SharePoint Online site as the level to apply these settings to, sign in using the Microsoft 365 credentials and then click **Connect**:

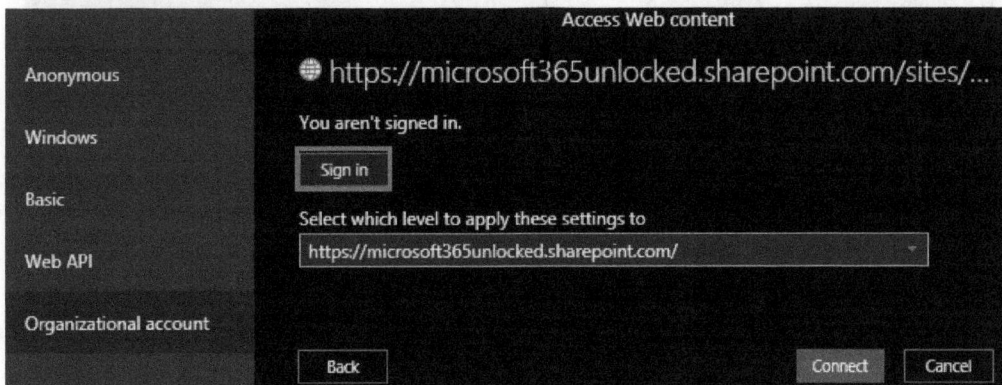

Figure 13.6: Access Web content

The **Navigator** window will open, allowing us to select both the **Customers** and **Products** tables from the Excel file. At this stage, we will load the data in its current form by selecting the tables and then clicking on **Load**. We will also connect to the second source, the SharePoint Online list, to obtain all the required data and afterward we will transform and prepare it for our analysis, using *Power Query Editor*.

Get data from a SharePoint Online list

To get data from the SharePoint Online list, we click on **Get data,** and this time we select **SharePoint Online Lists**.

We then provide the site URL where the list is located. Having the *2.0* implementation selected, under **Advanced options** we choose the **Default View** mode, to retrieve only the columns in the **Default View** of our SharePoint list, as for this example we will not be requiring any additional list columns:

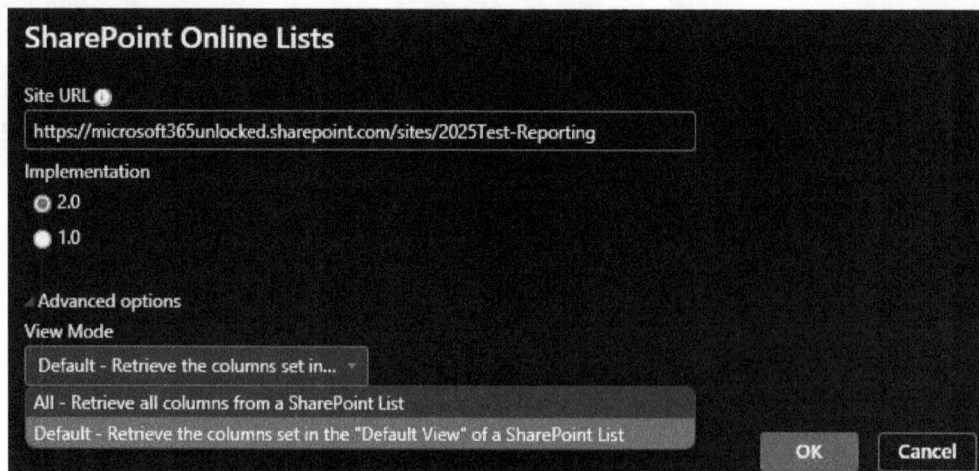

Figure 13.7: Get data from SharePoint Online list

Next, we are prompted to connect to SharePoint Online. To do this, we will select the **Microsoft account** option, choose our SharePoint Online site as the level to apply these settings to, sign in with our Microsoft 365 credentials, and click **Connect**:

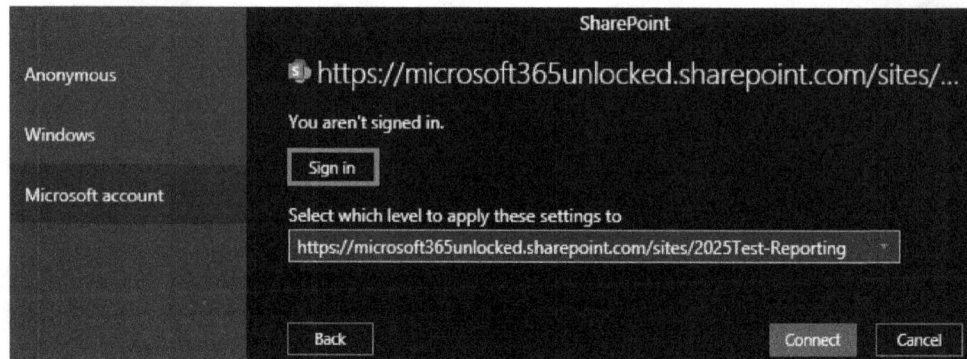

Figure 13.8: Connect to SharePoint Online site

Just like we did previously to load the data from the Excel file, in the **Navigator** window, we select our SharePoint Online list called **Orders** and then click **Load**.

Save the Power BI file

At this point, we have successfully connected to and loaded data from both sources.

Now, let us save our Power BI file by navigating to **File | Save**, provide a name for the file, choose a location to store it, and save it in the `.pbix` format.

Next, we will explore how to prepare our data to ensure it is suitable for the analysis we need to perform.

Data preparation with Power Query Editor

Power Query Editor is a powerful tool within Power BI that functions as a workshop for your data. Imagine having raw materials that require refinement and shaping before they can be utilized to create something remarkable. Power Query Editor is where the process of data cleansing, refining, and shaping takes place.

Using Power Query Editor, we can remove unnecessary data by deleting extra columns or filtering out rows that are not needed for the analysis. We can also rename columns, change data formats, create new columns based on calculations or conditions, apply transformations like splitting columns or aggregating values, combine data from different sources, and much more.

A great feature is that once we have set up our transformations, Power Query Editor can automatically apply these steps every time the data is refreshed, saving time and effort.

Data preparation and transformation can be performed using Power Query Editor even before loading the data in Power BI, by clicking **Transform Data** on the **Navigator** after connecting to a data source.

Going back to our example, we have the raw data we need already loaded and we can now use the Power Query Editor to do the necessary transformations and refinements. To launch Power Query Editor, we click on the **Transform data** icon on the **Home** tab:

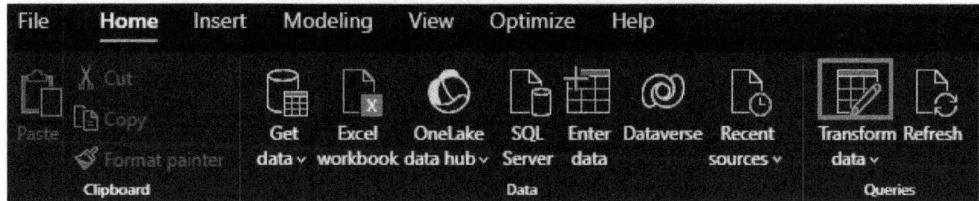

Figure 13.9: Launch Power Query Editor

Once Power Query Editor opens, we see the tables we have previously loaded from Excel and the data from the SharePoint list displayed as queries:

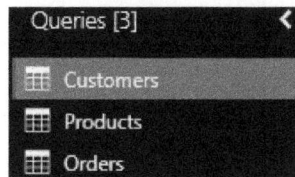

Figure 13.10: Queries in Power Query Editor

We can now proceed with the data cleansing and transformation to shape it in the way we need it for building our report.

Removing and filtering data

It is always recommended to keep only the data needed for your report in Power BI. Having unnecessary data can clutter your workspace, slow down performance, and make it harder to focus on the insights that matter most. By streamlining your dataset, you ensure that your analysis is efficient, and your reports are clear.

The data loaded from the **Orders** SharePoint list in our example contains one column called **Comments** that we will not be needing for our analysis, so we can remove it at this stage. To achieve this, we need to simply select the column that we want to remove and then click on **Remove Columns** on the **Home** tab in Power Query Editor:

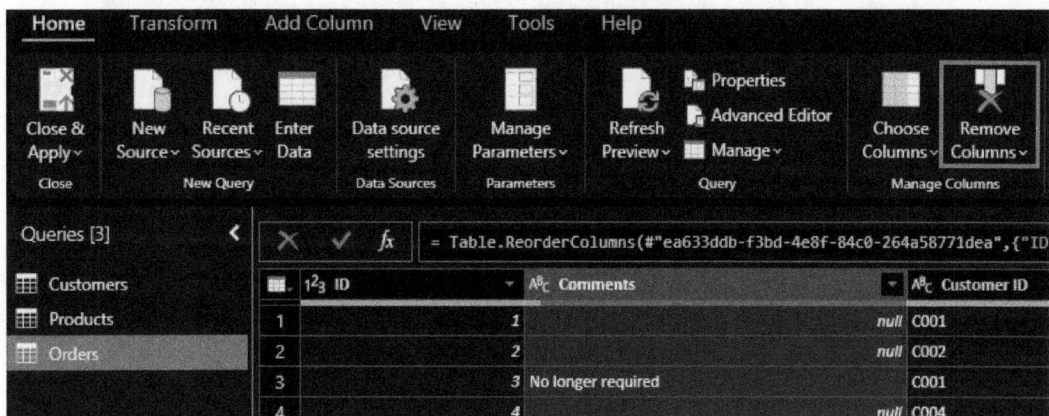

Figure 13.11: Remove columns

The column **Status** from the **Orders** list contains three values: **Cancelled**, **Completed** and **In Progress**. For our analysis and report we will be needing only the completed orders, so we can filter out the orders canceled and in progress, by using the filters in the editor:

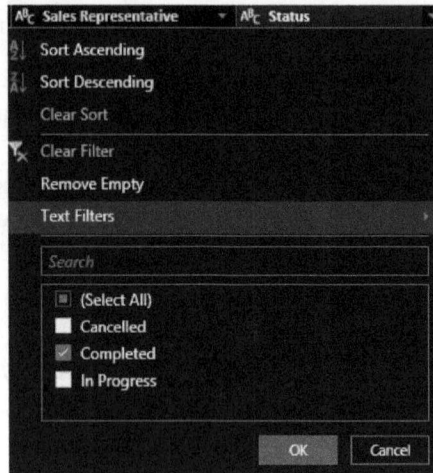

Figure 13.12: Filter data

These steps ensure that we only use the necessary amount of data for analysis and reporting purposes moving forward.

Changing the data type

To ensure accurate calculations and achieve the desired outcomes in our analysis, it is crucial that all columns from our data sources have the correct data types. Typically, the data type of a column is automatically detected based on the source data. However, there are instances where this detection is incorrect, or the data type in the source itself is not suitable for the measures and calculations we need to perform in Power BI.

In our example, the columns **SellingPrice/Unit** and **TotalCost/Unit** in the **Products** table are currently formatted as **Text**, which is how they were loaded from the data source. To perform specific calculations using these columns, we need to change their format.

To change the data type, we just need to select the columns, and on the **Transform** ribbon, choose the desired data type. In this case, we will format the data on these two columns as **Fixed decimal number**.

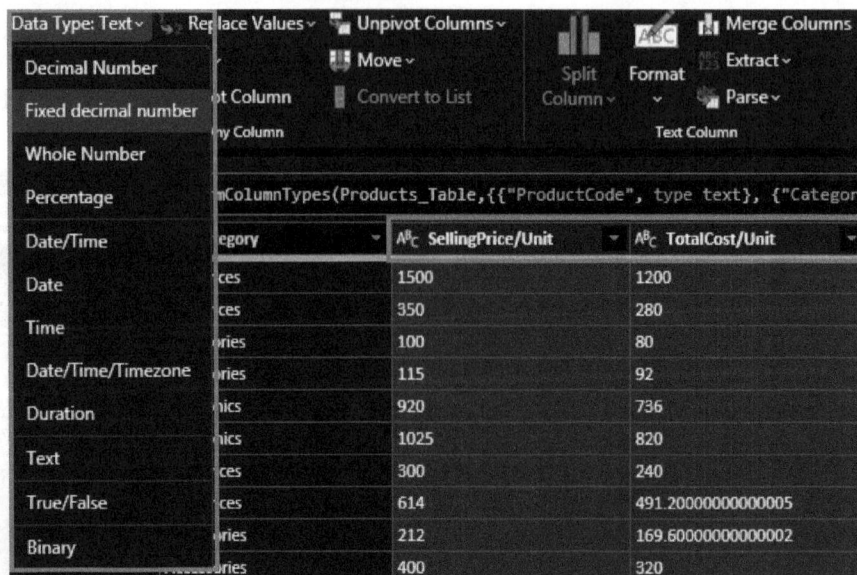

Figure 13.13: Change data type

Renaming columns

Renaming columns in Power BI might be needed for standardization purposes, to improve readability or to bring clarity when combining data from multiple sources with columns having the same name.

To rename a column, we can simply right-click on the respective column, select **Rename** and then change the column's name:

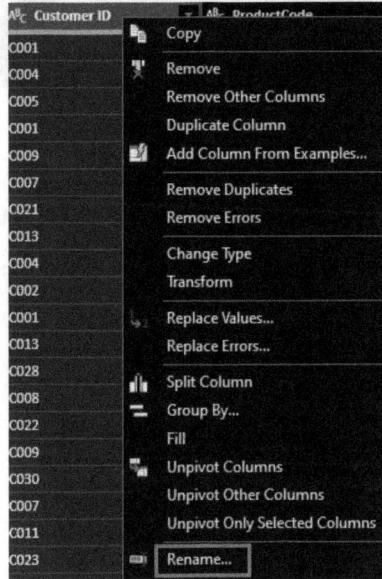

Figure 13.14: Rename column

Custom columns

The custom columns feature in Power BI allows the creation of new columns based on calculated values from existing columns in the dataset.

In our scenario, we create a custom column to calculate the number of days it takes for an order to be completed.

From the **Add Column** ribbon, we click on **Custom Column**. Next, we provide a column name, and a custom formula based on which our values will be calculated.

In this case, we want to subtract the **OpenedDate** from the **ClosedDate** to get the number of days. The existing columns we want to use in our formula can be inserted from the **Available columns** list, helping compose the formula more efficiently and avoid errors:

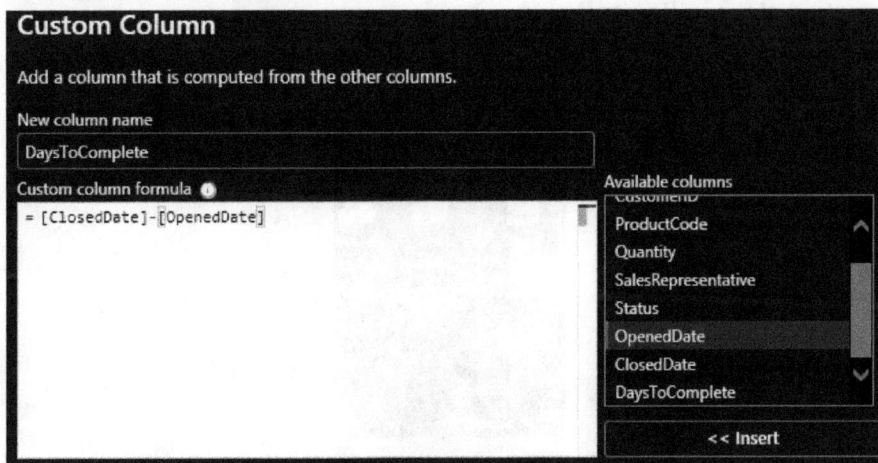

Figure 13.15: Create custom column

After confirming there are no syntax errors, we click **OK**. The **DaysToComplete** column has been added to the table, but its data type is set to **Any**. We simply change the data type to **Whole Number** and the column is now populated with the number of days, as per the calculation:

OpenedDate	ClosedDate	1²₃ DaysToComplete
06/01/2025	06/02/2025	31
09/10/2024	14/10/2024	5
10/02/2024	19/02/2024	9
23/08/2022	31/08/2022	8
12/10/2022	26/10/2022	14
15/05/2023	30/05/2023	15

Figure 13.16: Custom column

Check applied steps and apply changes to the data

Depending on the structure of the source data and the desired analysis outcomes, you may need to apply additional changes to the dataset.

All changes and transformations performed in Power Query Editor are displayed sequentially in the **Applied Steps** list, part of the **Query Settings** pane:

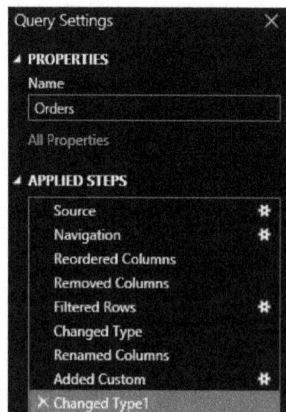

Figure 13.17: Applied Steps

To undo a change or transformation, you can easily remove the related step from the list, as long as there are no subsequent steps that depend on it.

> **Note:** **All data changes performed apply only to the data loaded in Power BI. These changes do not affect or modify the underlying source data. When new data is loaded from the same sources, it will undergo the same transformation steps in Power BI.**

In our example, we have completed the necessary changes and can now apply them by clicking **Close & Apply** on the **Home** tab in Power Query Editor:

Figure 13.18: Close and apply changes

At this stage, we leave Power Query Editor and load our transformed data in Power BI to proceed further with the analysis.

Data modeling and DAX

We have seen how we can clean and transform our data using the Query Editor. Having prepared the data, we can proceed with the data modeling process and afterward start building our report in Power BI.

The data modeling process is typically the next step after data transformation, and it involves structuring, exploring, and inspecting the transformed data. This includes creating and defining relationships, as well as creating calculated columns and measures, with the goal of gaining deeper insights and visualizing the necessary information in a meaningful report.

Understanding relationships

Relationships define how data in one table relates to data in another one. They help Power BI understand how to pull data from different tables to answer specific questions we have related to the available data. Relationships are needed when we have data spread across multiple tables and we want to analyze it together.

In Power BI, there are three main types of relationships that can be created between tables: one-to-one, one-to-many, and many-to-many. Each type of relationship serves a different purpose and helps connect the data in various ways.

A **one-to-one relationship** means that each record in one table is linked to a single, unique record in another table. This type of relationship is less common but can be useful when you have two tables that contain different details about the same set of items.

Example: Imagine you have a table of employee details and another table of employee salaries. Each employee in the details table has a unique ID that matches a unique ID in the salaries table. By creating a one-to-one relationship between these tables, we can combine employee details with their corresponding salaries.

A **one-to-many relationship** is the most common type of relationship in Power BI. It means that a single record in one table can be related to multiple records in another table.

Example: Consider a table of departments and a table of employees. Multiple employees can be part of a single department, but each employee belongs to only one department. By creating a one-to-many relationship between the department ID in the departments table and the department ID in the employees table, we can analyze how many employees there are in each department.

A **many-to-many relationship** occurs when multiple records in one table are related to multiple records in another table. This type of relationship is more complex and is used when there is no clear primary table, and both tables have overlapping data. Some scenarios require the creation of an intermediary bridge table when there is no information available in the existing tables, to be able to create a link between them.

Example: Imagine you have a table of employees and a table of projects. Each employee can be assigned on multiple projects, and each project can include several employees. By creating a many-to-many relationship between these tables, we can analyze which employees work on which project and how many projects each employee is involved in.

Creating and managing relationships

To create and manage relationships in Power BI, click on **Manage relationships** on the **Modeling** tab. From here, existing relationships can be managed, and new ones can be created either manually or using the **Autodetect** feature:

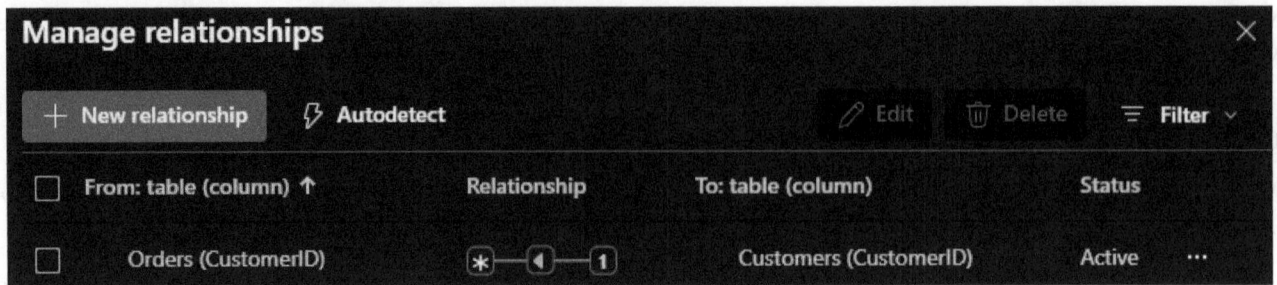

Figure 13.19: Manage relationships

For our sales scenario, we can see in the figure above that there is already a relationship that has been auto-detected, between the **Customers** and **Orders** tables, based on the **CustomerID** column present in both tables.

We need to create an additional relationship between the **Products** table, which contains product information, and the **Orders** table. Each order contains a specific product, but there can be multiple orders for the same product.

We create this relationship manually by clicking on **New relationship**. Then, we select the table **Products** in the **From table** drop-down menu and the table **Orders** in the **To table** drop-down menu. In this case, once we select the tables, the columns needed to establish the relationship as well as the cardinality (one-to-many) and the cross-filter direction (single) are automatically detected by Power BI:

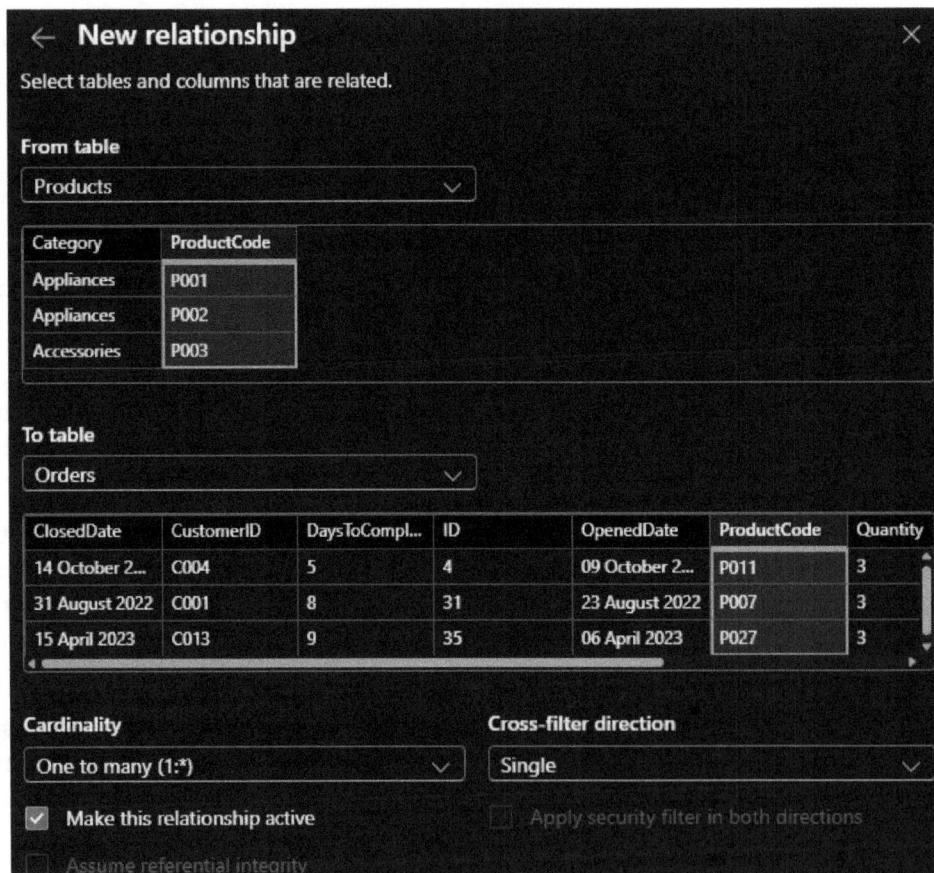

Figure 13.20: Create relationship

Having the necessary configuration in place, we click **Save** to save this relationship.

Additionally, we can manage existing relationships as well as see their graphical representation by accessing the **Model view** in Power BI:

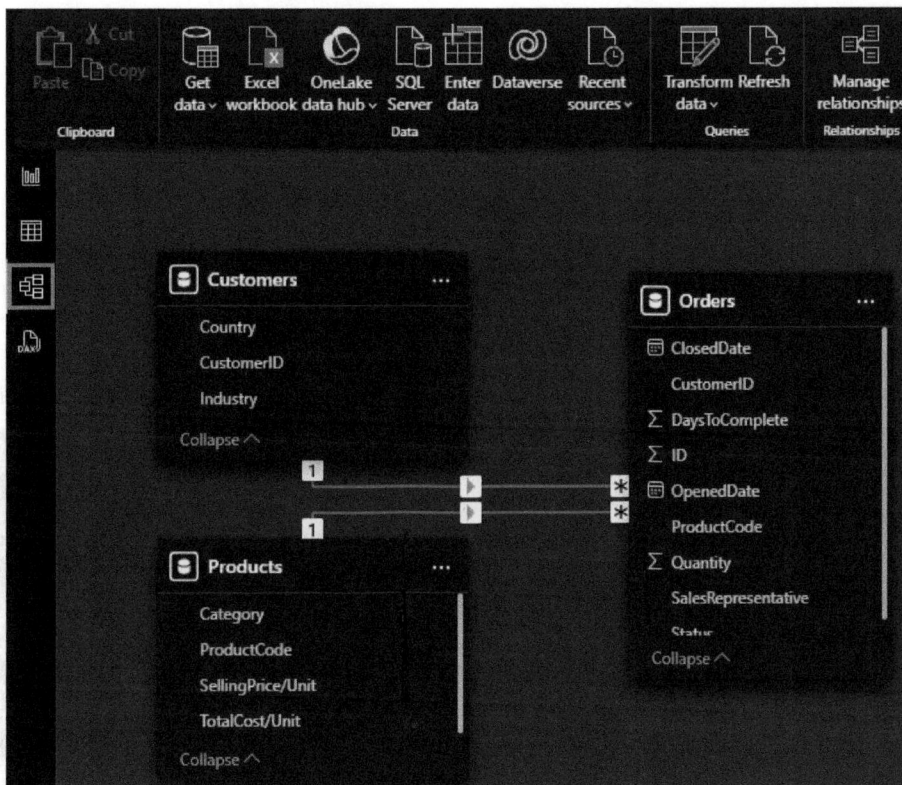

Figure 13.21: Model view

We now have our tables connected effectively through relationships, enabling us to perform comprehensive analysis based on information from more than one table.

Creating measures using DAX

Data Analysis Expressions (DAX), is a powerful formula language used in Microsoft tools like Power BI and Power Pivot in Excel. Think of DAX as the secret sauce that allows you to perform complex calculations and data manipulations.

At its core, DAX is designed to work with data models, enabling you to create custom calculations, aggregations, and measures that go beyond simple arithmetic. It is like having a supercharged calculator that can handle intricate data relationships and provide answers to your most pressing business questions.

DAX includes a rich library of functions that you can use to perform various operations on your data. These functions range from simple arithmetic to complex statistical calculations, giving you the flexibility to analyze your data in countless ways.

Imagine you have a vast amount of sales data, and you want to know the average profit per order, the total sales for each product category, or the year-over-year growth. DAX makes it possible to answer these questions with precision and ease. It allows you to create dynamic calculations that update automatically as your data changes, ensuring your reports are always up to date.

Let us presume that in our sales scenario, the objective is to find out the following information: total sales amount, total cost amount, total profit, profit per year, sales by country and sales by product category. To achieve all this, we need to do additional calculations before being able to reflect all this information in our report through visuals.

Under the **Orders** table, we will create new measures to help us obtain the desired information in the report. Measures are dynamic calculations that are usually created when needing to calculate data across multiple rows at once. Their values adjust based on the data context and filters applied to the report.

To create a new measure, we can select the **Modeling** tab and then click on **New Measure**:

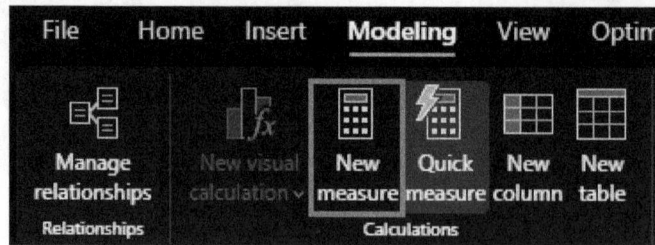

Figure 13.22: *New measure*

The **Measure tools** tab opens, allowing us to create the new measure by using the formula bar:

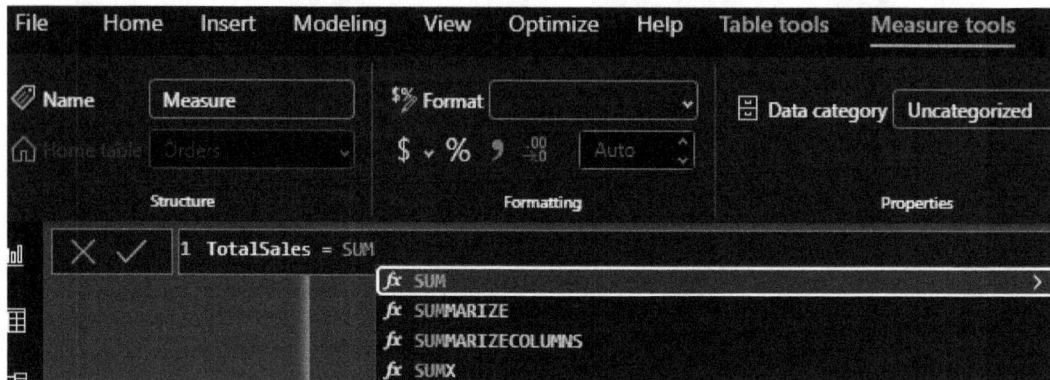

Figure 13.23: *Creating a new measure*

As illustrated in the preceding figure, the measure's formula begins with the chosen name, followed by an = sign. After that, we begin typing the function we need. Power BI is quite user-friendly in this regard, as it provides suggestions once we start typing the first letters of a function. This feature helps us quickly find and select the appropriate function, making the process more efficient and reducing the likelihood of errors.

The first measure we will create is for calculating the total sales amount. For this, we use the following formula:

```
TotalSales = SUMX(Orders, Orders[Quantity] * RELATED(Products[SellingPrice/Unit]))
```

Let us break down the formula to understand how it works:

- The **"Orders[Quantity] * RELATED(Products[SellingPrice/Unit])"** part of the formula calculates the total sales amount for each order, by multiplying the quantity of products ordered (using the *Quantity* column in the *Orders* table) by the selling price per unit value. It uses the **RELATED** function to fetch values from the *SellingPrice/Unit* column in the *Products* table.

- SUMX is an iterator function in DAX that iterates over a table, performing a calculation on each row and then summing up the result. In this case, it iterates over the *Orders* table, performs the above calculation for each order, and sums up the results to get the total sales amount.

The next measure we create is for calculating the total cost amount. The formula is similar to the one we used for the **TotalSales** measure, but this time we will fetch the values from the *TotalCost/Unit* column in the *Products* table. The formula is:

```
TotalCost = SUMX(Orders, Orders[Quantity] * RELATED(Products[TotalCost/Unit]))
```

Having both the total sales and total cost amounts, we can now easily calculate the profit by creating a new measure and using the following formula:

```
Profit = [TotalSales] - [TotalCost]
```

With this formula, we simply subtract the total cost value from the total sales value to obtain the profit figure.

Building visuals and creating the report

We now have the columns and calculations we need to be able to build our report by inserting comprehensive visualizations.

Building visuals in Power BI is as simple as selecting the type of visualization we want to use and then connecting it to the corresponding data from our data model or dragging and dropping the necessary columns for the analysis onto the report canvas.

For instance, to analyze the profit achieved by sales representatives, we begin by dragging and dropping the **Profit** measure from the **Data** pane onto the report canvas. Subsequently, the **SalesRepresentative** column should be dragged and dropped into the automatically generated visualization. If needed, we can then change the visualization type from the **Visualizations** pane:

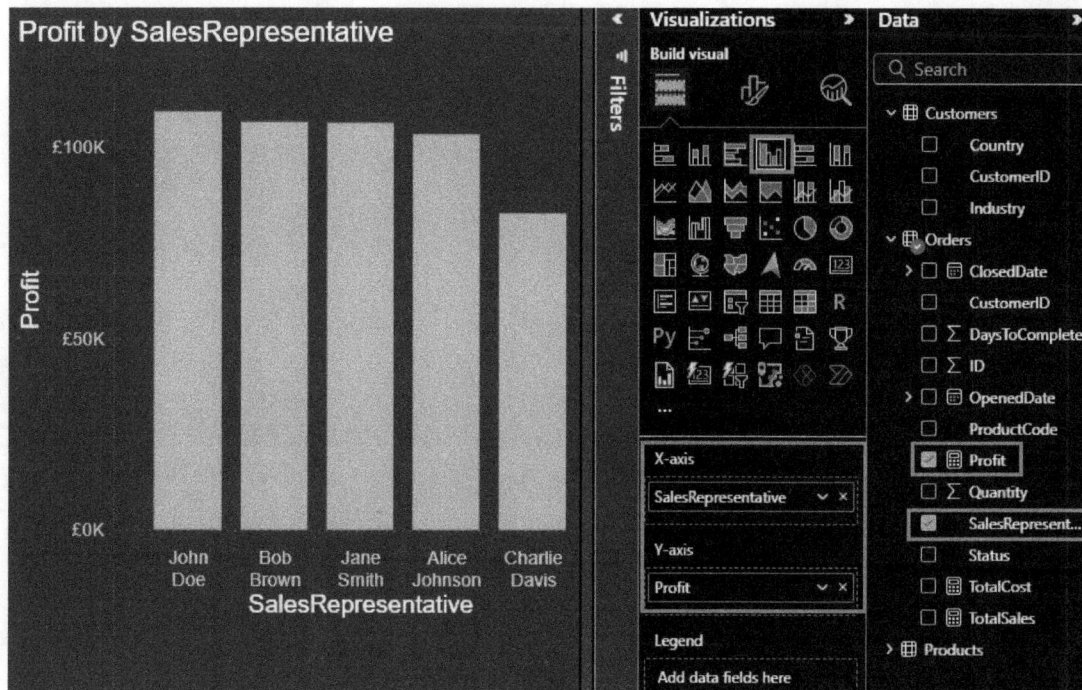

Figure 13.24: Build visual

From the **Format visual** tab, we can customize the appearance of our visuals by adjusting colors, transparency, effects, titles, and much more. Specific settings are available depending on the type of visualization:

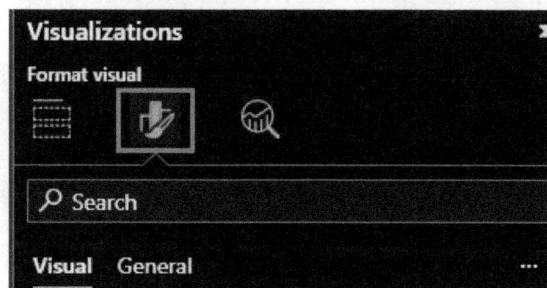

Figure 13.25: Format visual

For our sales report, we have inserted and configured six visuals:

- Two cards to display **Total Sales** and **Profit** values, based on the measures we have created previously.
- A Pie chart to show the sales by product category. For this visual, we used the **TotalSales** measure and the **Category** column from the **Products** table.

- A Treemap to display Sales by Country. We used the **Country** column from the **Customers** table and the **TotalSales** measure for this visual.

- Two column charts: one to display the profit by sales representatives (the visual we created previously, shown in *Figure 13.24*), and another one to show the profit per year. For the latter, we used the **Profit** measure and the **ClosedDate** column from the **Orders** table (displaying only the year value).

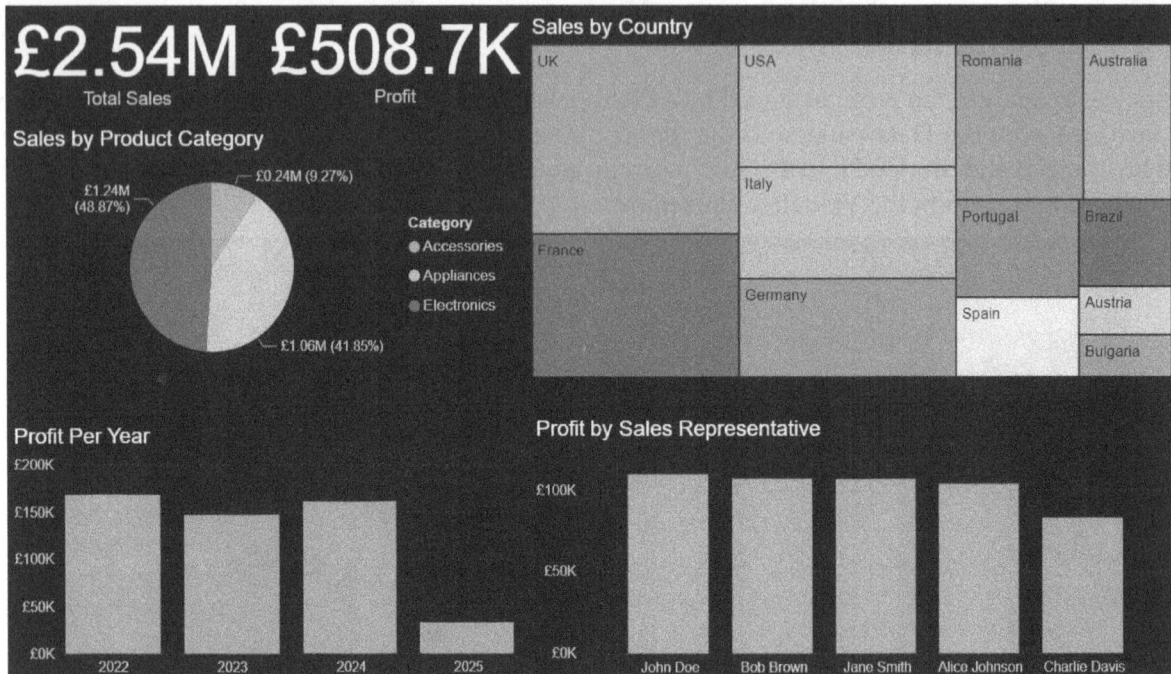

Figure 13.26: Report view

Publishing the report to Power BI Service

Once we are happy with the report built in Power BI Desktop, we can publish it to Power BI Service to share it with others, collaborate on it, and access it from anywhere.

First, we need to ensure all the changes are saved. Then, while in the **Report view**, click on the **Publish** button in the **Home** tab.

If not already signed in, at this stage we are prompted to sign in to Power BI Service. Upon signing in, we need to choose a destination (a workspace in Power BI Service) for publishing the report. In this case, we selected an existing workspace called **Sales Analysis**:

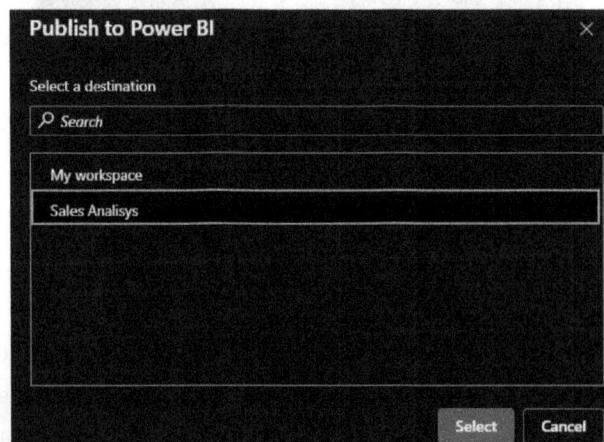

Figure 13.27: Publish report

Once the report has been published, we can open it in Power BI Service:

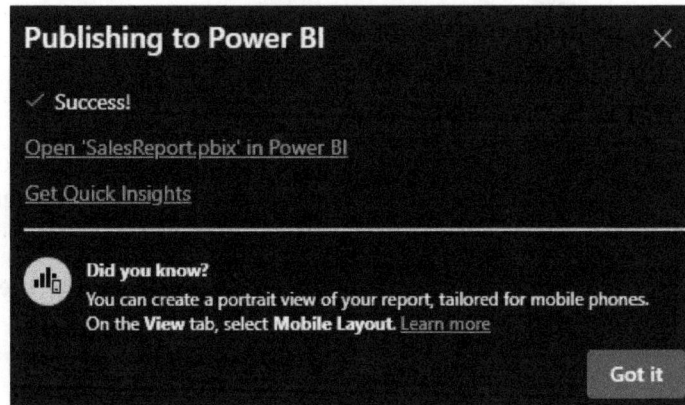

Figure 13.28: Report published to Power BI

Power BI Service

Power BI Service is the cloud-based part of the Power BI solution that enables users to visualize and share insights from their data. It allows for the creation of interactive reports and dashboards that can be accessed from anywhere, providing real-time data analysis and collaboration.

Getting started with Power BI Service

Power BI Service can be accessed by navigating to **https://app.powerbi.com**.

Since this is a cloud service, it is necessary to create an account to access Power BI Service. Additionally, a Power BI Pro or Premium license is required to publish reports for sharing and collaboration purposes. The Power BI Pro license is included with Microsoft 365 E5 and Office 365 E5 subscriptions.

In *Table 13.1*, we can see a comparison between the Power BI Pro and Power BI Premium licensing plans:

Feature	Power BI Pro	Power BI Premium
Publish reports to share and collaborate	Yes	Yes
Advanced AI	No	Yes
Advanced dataflows	No	Yes
Advanced datamarts	No	Yes
XMLA endpoint read/write	No	Yes
Model memory size limit	1 GB	100 GB
Refresh rate for Power BI datasets	8/day	48/day
Maximum storage (native storage)	10 GB/license	100 TB
Data security and encryption	Yes	Yes

Table 13.1: Power BI Pro vs. Premium

Workspaces overview

Power BI Workspaces are collaborative environments within Power BI where you can store, manage, and share your reports, dashboards, and semantic models. Think of them as shared folders where you and your team can work together on data projects. Workspaces are used for:

- **Collaboration**: Team members can work together on the same reports and dashboards.
- **Organization**: Keep all related reports, dashboards, and semantic models in one place.
- **Sharing**: Easily share your work with others in your organization.
- **Security**: Control who has access to your data and reports.

Previously, we observed that when publishing our Sales report to the Power BI Service, we had to select a workspace. This is because, in Power BI Service, every report and its associated semantic model need to be housed within a workspace, which acts as a container for these elements.

In the **Sales Analysis** workspace where we published the report, we can now see both the report and the related semantic model:

Figure 13.29: Power BI workspace content

A semantic model in Power BI is a structured source of data prepared for reporting and visualization, like a blueprint for the data. It defines how the data is organized, how different pieces of data relate to each other, and how calculations are performed. When creating a report in Power BI we also define this underlying semantic model. This model includes tables and columns, relationships, measures, and calculations. When publishing a report to Power BI Service, we are also publishing its related semantic model.

Having these assets published in the cloud, we can now visualize and interact with this report online, create dashboards based on this report, create other reports based on the same semantic model, and share the report individually or even grant access to others at the workspace level for collaboration purposes.

Manage workspace access

Managing workspace access in Power BI is important for maintaining security, collaboration, and efficient data management.

To ensure the right people have the appropriate level of access, Power BI provides these four roles within a workspace: **Admin**, **Member**, **Contributor**, and **Viewer**.

To manage access to a workspace, we follow these steps:

1. In the Power BI Service portal, navigate to the workspace you want to manage.

2. Click on **Manage access** in the upper right corner of the workspace:

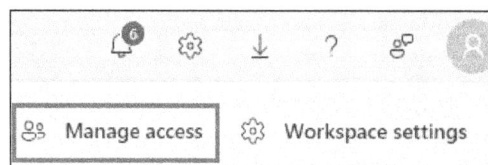

Figure 13.30: Manage workspace access

3. From the **Manage access** list, you can remove existing members or change their roles. To grant access to users or groups, click on **Add people or groups**, enter their name or email address, and select the appropriate role (Admin, Member, Contributor, or Viewer):

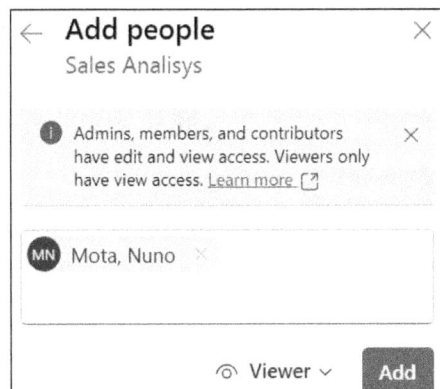

Figure 13.31: Grant access to a workspace

4. Click **Add** to add the new user or group.

For a large number of users, we can consider using groups to manage access. This way, we can manage access for multiple users at once.

> **Note:** **Users who are added to a workspace in a shared capacity must have either a Power BI Pro or Power BI Premium license to collaborate on the dashboards and reports within that workspace.**

My workspace

In Power BI Service, *My workspace* serves as a personal space where you can create, store, and manage your Power BI content. It functions as a private sandbox that allows you to experiment with data, develop reports, and create dashboards without impacting other users. Unlike the collaboration workspaces, this workspace is exclusive to you, and others cannot access it unless you explicitly share content from within this workspace.

One of the main benefits of *My workspace* is that it allows you to work on your data projects independently. You can connect to various data sources, transform data, and visualize it using Power BI's powerful tools. This is particularly useful for testing new ideas or creating prototypes before sharing them with your team.

Additionally, *My workspace* is a great place to learn and practice using Power BI. Since it is a private space, you can explore different features and functionalities without worrying about making mistakes. This can help you become more proficient in using Power BI and improve your data analysis skills.

Reports

Although the typical flow is to build the reports with Power BI Desktop, due to its capabilities for data cleaning, transformation, and modeling, and subsequently publishing them to Power BI Service for sharing and collaboration, it is also feasible to generate quick reports directly within Power BI Service.

While having selected the workspace where you want to create the report, click **Create** on the navigation pane on the left side of the screen to add data and start building the report. You can add data from Excel, CSV (options currently in preview), a published semantic model, or manually enter data:

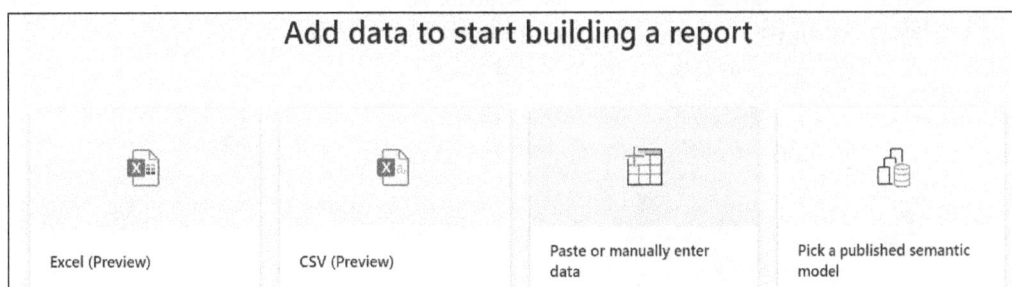

Figure 13.32: Add data in Power BI Service

For example, we are able to pick the published semantic model that we used to create our Sales report previously, and we can use this to create a new report in Power BI Service:

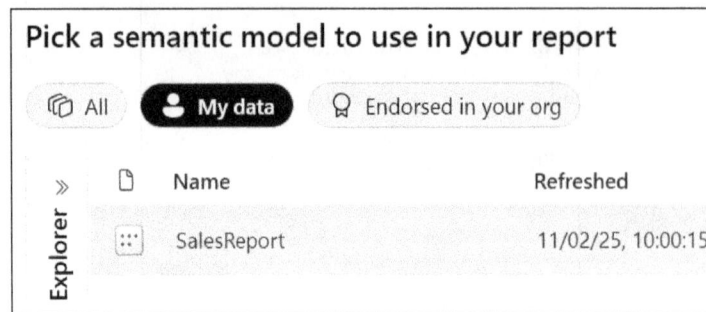

Figure 13.33: Pick a semantic model for building a report

Alter selecting the semantic model, we can choose to auto-create a report, or start from a blank report:

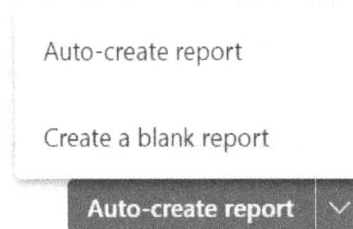

Figure 13.34: Options for report creation

The **Auto-create report** feature will generate a report based on the dataset, with auto-generated visuals connected to the data. You can choose to connect different data from your dataset to the visuals, and they will adapt accordingly. This option is great if you have a well-structured dataset, as it facilitates quick report creation.

The **Create a blank report** option allows you to start from scratch with your report, by selecting the desired visuals and connecting them to the data you need for analysis from your dataset.

Dashboards

Dashboards in Power BI Service are a powerful tool for visualizing and interacting with your data. They provide a single-page, at-a-glance view of your most important metrics and visuals. Each dashboard is composed of tiles, which can display data from different reports and datasets, making it a versatile and comprehensive way to monitor your business.

Dashboards are also highly interactive. Users can click on tiles to drill down into the underlying reports for more detailed analysis. Additionally, dashboards can be shared with colleagues, enabling collaborative analysis and decision-making.

Customization is another strong suit of Power BI dashboards. You can personalize your dashboard by pinning the most relevant tiles, resizing them, and arranging them in a way that best suits your needs. This flexibility ensures that your dashboard is tailored to your specific business requirements.

In Power BI Service, we can create a new dashboard within a workspace by navigating to the respective workspace, clicking on **New item,** and then clicking on the **Dashboard** tile:

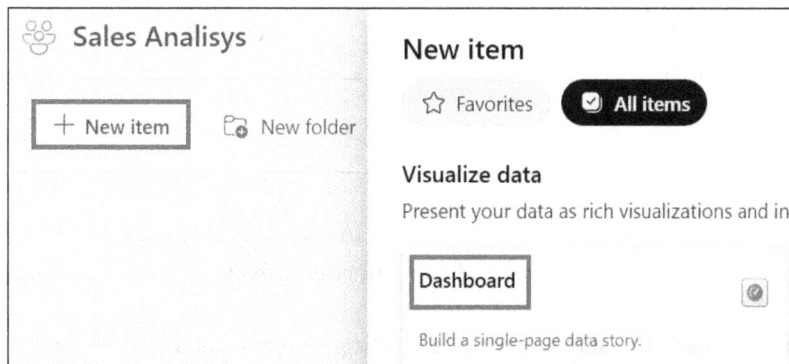

Figure 13.35: Create new dashboard

Alternatively, a new dashboard can be created by clicking on **Pin visual** icon from an existing report and choose to pin it to a new dashboard:

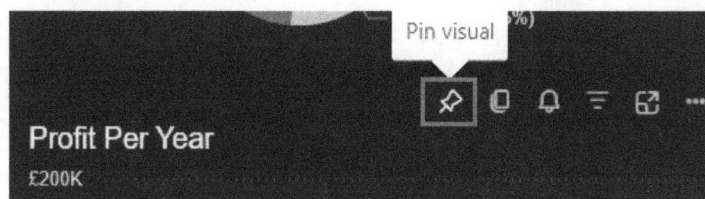

Figure 13.36: Pin visual

Pin it to a new dashboard, as shown:

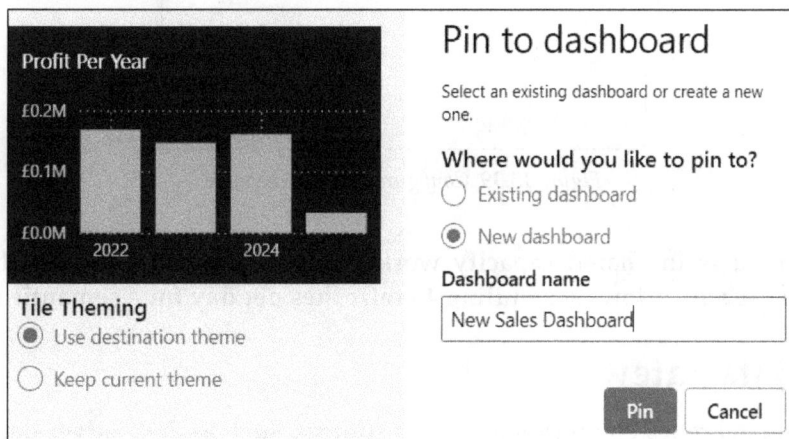

Figure 13.37: Pin to new dashboard

Data refresh overview

To maintain the accuracy and relevance of your visualizations, Power BI offers data refresh capabilities to ensure that your reports and dashboards are based on recent data.

Data refresh in Power BI involves updating your semantic model with the latest information from the original data sources you use to get data for your reports. This can be typically achieved based on a refresh schedule that you define for your semantic model, or on demand - whenever you want to query the data sources to get the most recent data.

To refresh your semantic model on demand or to schedule refresh, navigate to the workspace where the semantic model is stored, select the respective semantic model, and click on the **Refresh now** icon (for on demand refresh) or on **Schedule refresh** to configure a refresh schedule:

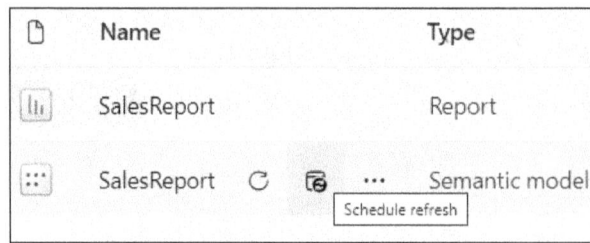

Figure 13.38: Semantic model refresh

By clicking on **Schedule refresh**, the semantic model settings page opens and from there, under the **Refresh** section, you can enable the refresh schedule and set the refresh frequency and time:

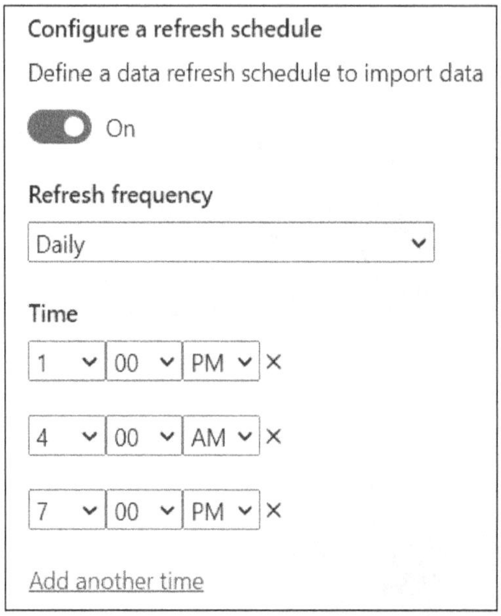

Figure 13.39: Configure a refresh schedule

Note: **For semantic models in shared capacity workspaces, a maximum of 8 daily refreshes can be configured. Premium capacity allows scheduling 48 refreshes per day for a semantic model.**

On-premises data gateway

When your semantic model relies on on-premises data sources, such as SQL Server databases or local Excel files, an extra step is needed before you can schedule refreshes or refresh reports on demand. Since Power BI cannot directly access these sources over a network connection, a bridge is required to connect the on-premises network with the cloud service. This is where the on-premises data gateway comes into play.

The on-premises data gateway is a software provided by Microsoft that you install within your local network. It acts as a secure bridge, facilitating communication between Power BI in the cloud and your on-premises data sources. The gateway ensures that data can flow seamlessly from your local environment to Power BI, enabling you to refresh your datasets and keep your reports up to date.

The detailed installation steps and how to configure a data gateway can be found in the official Microsoft documentation.

By using the on-premises data gateway, you can bridge the gap between your local data sources and Power BI, enabling seamless data refreshes and ensuring that your business insights are always based on recent data.

OneDrive refresh

When you create your semantic models and reports using a Power BI Desktop file, an Excel workbook, or a comma-separated value (`.csv`) file stored on OneDrive or SharePoint Online, Power BI employs a specific type of refresh known as OneDrive refresh. This process is distinct from the typical semantic model refresh, where Power BI imports data from a source into a semantic model.

OneDrive refresh focuses on synchronizing your semantic models and reports with their original source files. Essentially, Power BI checks approximately every hour to determine if any updates or changes have been made to the files on OneDrive or SharePoint Online. If changes are detected, Power BI automatically synchronizes the semantic models and reports to reflect the latest data from the source files.

This synchronization ensures that your reports and dashboards are always up to date with the most recent information from your OneDrive or SharePoint Online files, without the need for manual intervention.

Sharing reports and dashboards

The primary benefit of using Power BI Service for your reports is that it allows you to share your work with others, facilitating collaboration on reports and dashboards and providing access to essential data analytics. By sharing your reports and dashboards, you enable team members and stakeholders to view and interact with the data. This shared access ensures that everyone is on the same page, working with the most current and accurate information. You can share your reports and dashboards with other users inside and outside of the organization.

In addition to collaboration, robust data governance plays a crucial role in managing sensitive information within Power BI, especially when sharing data externally. If enabled on your tenant, sensitivity labels can be applied to semantic models, reports, and dashboards to classify and protect data according to your organization's policies. These labels help ensure that confidential or regulated information is handled appropriately, offering added layers of security and compliance.

> Note: **Sharing content requires users to have a Power BI Pro or Premium Per User license if the content is not located in a Premium capacity. Recipients must also have a Power BI Pro or Premium Per User license to access shared content, unless the content resides in a Premium or Fabric capacity.**

Sharing reports

To share a report in Power BI Service, navigate to the report you wish to share and click on the **Share** button on the top menu of the screen:

SalesReport | Data updated 12/02/25 ∨

□ File ∨   ↦ Export ∨ | 🖻 Share | ⌗ Explore

Figure 13.40: Share a report

Within the sharing dialog, you can select the desired sharing option by choosing between the following:

- **People in your organization**: This option creates a link to the report that can be accessed by anyone in the organization (internal users only) and can be used only if the **Allow shareable links to grant access to everyone in your organization** setting has not been disabled by a Power BI Administrator.

- **People with existing access**: This option does not grant any additional permission and can be used to generate a direct link for those who already have access to the report.

- **Specific people**: This option can be used to share the report with people or groups you specify (internal and guest users in your organization). You will need to enter the names or email addresses of the groups or users you want to share the report with.

In addition to the sharing options, you can configure the settings to be applied through the generated link. This is basically the level of access granted and can be configured for **People in your organization** and for **Specific people** sharing options.

Read permission is included by default once you share a link, but you can also choose to grant reshare permissions to the report and allow users to build content with the data associated with the respective report. You can create the link with both, one, or none of these two permissions selected:

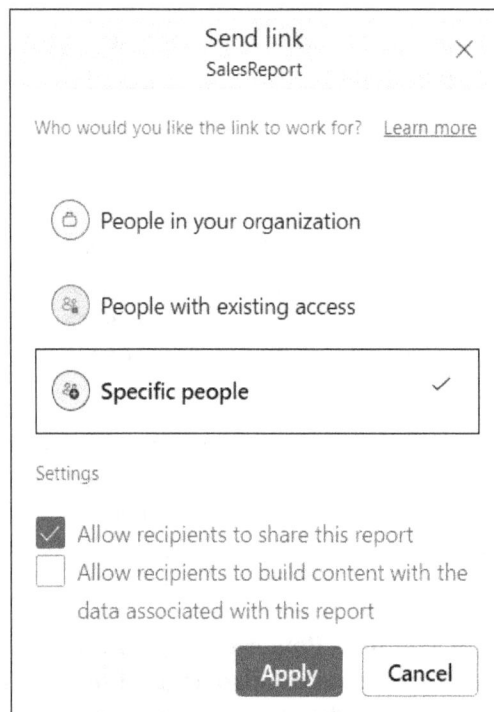

Figure 13.41: Sharing options and settings

Once you have applied the desired sharing option and setting, you can then:

- Send the link (available based on the sharing option chosen). This sends an email notification to the recipients which includes the link to access the report.
- Copy the link.
- Select the **Mail** option to copy the link on a new email that you can compose and send to the desired recipients
- Select the **Teams** option to send the link via Teams.
- Select the PowerPoint option to embed live data in PowerPoint.

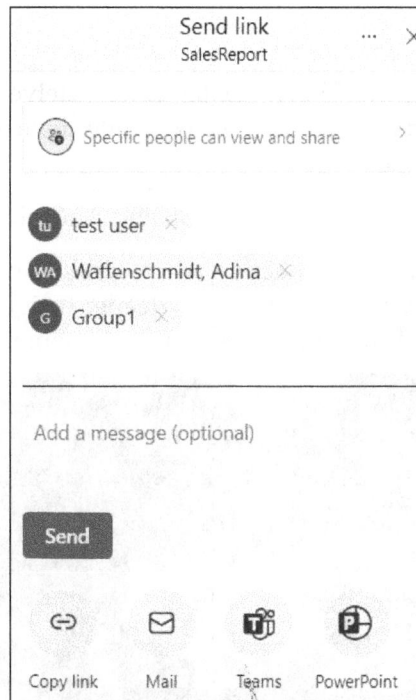

Figure 13.42: Send link

Sharing dashboards

To share a dashboard in Power BI Service, navigate to the dashboard you wish to share and click on the **Share** button on the top menu of the screen.

In the Share dashboard dialog, you can grant access directly to specific users or groups. You can also choose the permissions to grant, similar to report sharing, allowing recipients to reshare the dashboard and build content with the associated data. In addition, you can choose if an email notification should be sent to the users:

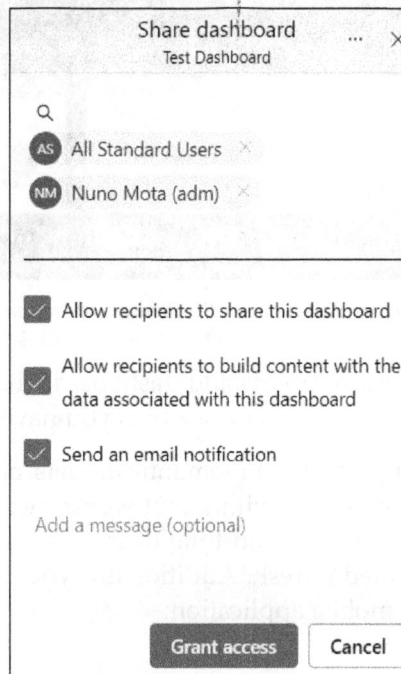

Figure 13.43: Share dashboard

Power BI Mobile

Continuing from our exploration of Power BI Service, let us now delve into Power BI Mobile, the third core component of Power BI which extends its capabilities to mobile devices, ensuring that you can access and interact with your data anytime, anywhere.

The Power BI mobile app is available for download on iOS and Android mobile devices.

The mobile app supports interactive features, enabling you to drill down into data, apply filters, and explore different visualizations. This interactivity helps you gain deeper insights and understand your data better, even on a smaller screen. *Figure 13.44* shows the Power BI mobile home screen:

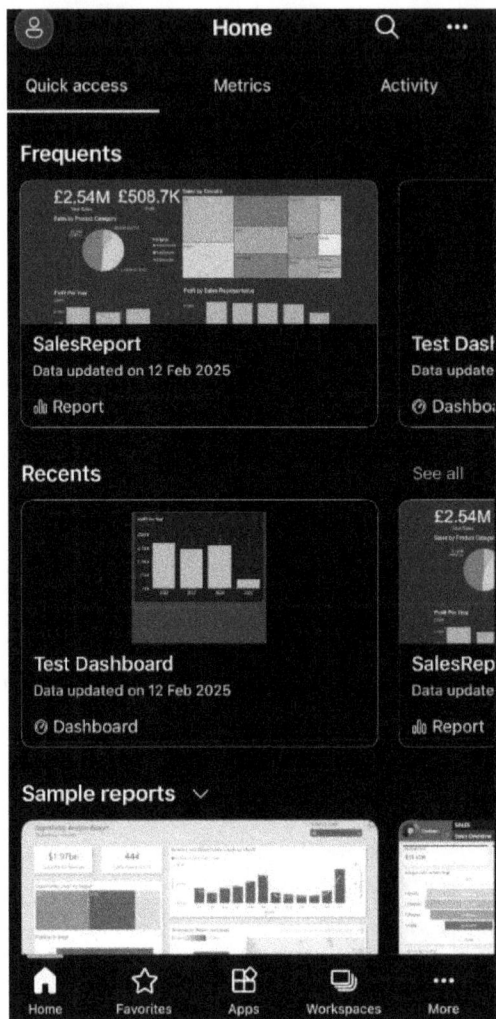

Figure 13.44: Power BI Mobile home screen

From the mobile application, you can access reports and dashboards that you have created or that have been shared with you, as well as applications, workspaces to which you have access, and their respective content.

By navigating to a workspace containing reports and semantic models, and then selecting the **Semantic Model** tab, you can view all available semantic models within that workspace. You may choose a specific semantic model so that you can see details like the date and time of the last refresh and the most recent successful refresh, the owner, and the next scheduled refresh. Additionally, you can perform an on-demand refresh of your semantic model directly from the mobile application:

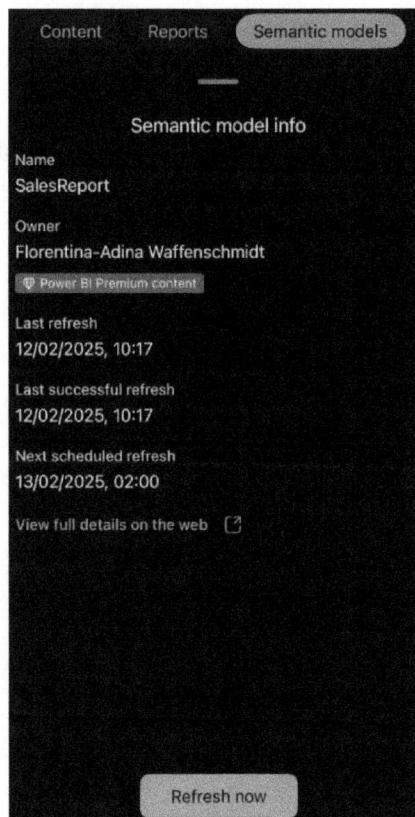

Figure 13.45: Semantic model info

Sharing a report or dashboard is also possible directly from the mobile app:

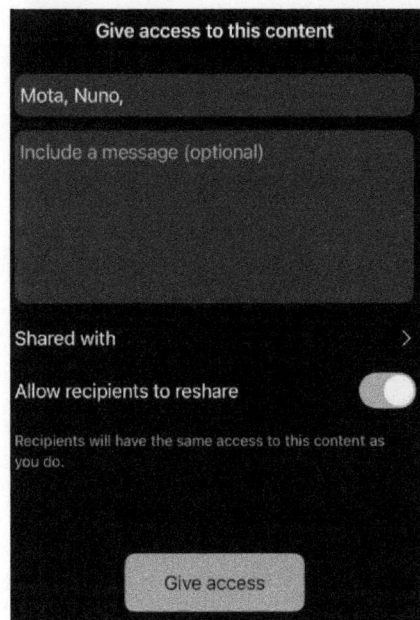

Figure 13.46: Sharing report from mobile app

With Power BI Mobile, your connection to valuable data and insights travels with you. The app empowers you to access and interact with dashboards and reports on your device, ensuring that critical business information is always within reach. Even in situations where you lose internet connectivity, the Power BI Mobile app allows you to view dashboards and reports you previously opened, thanks to its capability to cache up to 250 MB of data for offline use. While offline, your access is read-only and limited to information that has already been loaded onto the app, preserving your ability to stay informed. Once you are back online, Power BI Mobile seamlessly updates its content, restoring full interactivity and access to live data, including real-time changes, refreshed dashboards, and shared reports.

The intuitive design of the app means you can drill down into visualizations, apply filters, explore analytics, and even trigger on-demand data refreshes, all from the palm of your hand. This combination of flexibility and robust functionality ensures that you can make data-driven decisions promptly and respond to business challenges on the go.

Conclusion

In this chapter, we have seen how Power BI can help transform raw data into meaningful insights. By leveraging its core components, Power BI Desktop, Power BI Service, and Power BI Mobile, users can seamlessly connect to various data sources, prepare and analyze data, create interactive reports and dashboards, and access their insights anytime, anywhere.

In the next chapter, we will explore Power Automate, a powerful tool that enables users to automate workflows and streamline repetitive tasks, enhancing productivity and efficiency in various business processes.

Join our Discord space

Join our Discord workspace for latest updates, offers, tech happenings around the world, new releases, and sessions with the authors:

https://discord.bpbonline.com

CHAPTER 14

Power Automate

Introduction

This chapter is dedicated to Power Automate; a versatile cloud-based service originally known as Microsoft Flow. This chapter is designed to equip both beginners and experienced users with comprehensive knowledge about creating automated workflows between various applications and services. Power Automate simplifies repetitive tasks, freeing up valuable time for more critical activities. Readers will gain insights into the licensing options available, understand the tool's capabilities, and learn practical steps to develop their own workflows.

Structure

This chapter covers the following topics:

- Understanding Power Automate
- Licensing
- Creating automated workflows
- Advanced techniques
- Best practices

Objectives

By the end of this chapter, readers will gain a solid understanding of what Power Automate is and what it can do. Readers will acquire the skills to create automated workflows between various services, discovering how to streamline repetitive tasks and integrate different systems for enhanced productivity. Through practical, real-world examples, you will understand the creation and use of effective workflows, ultimately building confidence in developing your own custom workflows to address specific business processes and needs.

Understanding Power Automate

Microsoft Flow launched in 2016 as a tool to automate workflows between different apps and services. In 2019, it was rebranded as **Power Automate** to align with the Power Platform and introduced features like robotic process automation and AI integration. The update reflected a broader, more advanced vision for low-code automation across Microsoft's ecosystem.

Power Automate is a robust automation platform designed to simplify and streamline workflows by connecting various applications and services. It enables users to automate tasks, synchronize files, collect data, and much more, all without requiring extensive coding knowledge. The platform supports a wide range of connectors, allowing seamless integration with popular applications like Microsoft 365 services and even third-party services such as X, Facebook, Dropbox, or Google Drive. Additionally, Power Automate enables advanced functions like conditional logic, loops, and error handling, which allow for the creation of sophisticated workflows tailored to specific business processes.

Note: It is important to note that throughout this book, the terms flow and workflow will be used interchangeably. Both terms refer to a Power Automate workflow, which is the sequence of automated tasks designed to streamline one or more processes.

Before we start creating our first flow, it is essential to understand the main components of a Power Automate flow, which can include:

- **Triggers** are events that initiate the flow. They can be based on various actions or conditions, such as receiving an email, a new item being added to a SharePoint list, or a specific time of day. A trigger is always required.

- **Actions** are the tasks that the flow performs once it is triggered. These can include sending an email, creating a record in a database, posting a message in a Teams channel, among many others. Multiple actions can be chained together to create a comprehensive workflow. One or more actions are required, otherwise the flow will not do anything.

- **Conditions** allow you to set rules that determine the path the flow will take based on specific criteria. For example, you might want the flow to perform different actions based on the contents of an email or the value of a field in a database.

- **Connectors** provide a way for users to connect their data and leverage a set of pre-built actions and triggers to build their applications and workflows. There are several types of connectors:
  - **Standard connector**: Data sources within the Microsoft 365 ecosystem, such as Excel, Outlook, Teams, SharePoint, and so on.
  - **Premium connector**: Certain business systems beyond Microsoft 365, like DocuSign, Zendesk, or Jira Software.
  - **Custom connector**: To support more tailored scenarios, users can build custom connectors with their own triggers and actions. These connectors are function-based, and data is returned based on calling specific functions in the underlying service.
  - **On-premises connector**: Accesses on-premises data, such as Microsoft SQL for example, using a gateway.

- **Variables** are used to store and manipulate data within a flow. They can be utilized to hold values that can be referenced and modified as the flow progresses.

- **Loops** allow you to repeat actions multiple times within a flow. This is useful for scenarios where you need to process several items, such as looping through a list of email recipients or iterating over several rows in an Excel table.

- **Expressions** provide a way to perform calculations, manipulate strings, and evaluate logical conditions within a flow. They are used to create dynamic content and make decisions based on the data available in the flow.

These components work together to create powerful and flexible automated workflows that can streamline business processes, improve efficiency, and reduce the need for manual intervention.

To help readers understand the practical applications of Power Automate, this chapter includes two real-world examples:

- Workflow 1 will automatically save attachments of incoming emails to a specific OneDrive folder.

- Workflow 2 will send a notification when a new file is added to a specific SharePoint folder and trigger an approval flow.

These examples not only showcase the capabilities of Power Automate but also provide readers with the confidence to develop their own custom workflows.

Note: **Flows in Power Automate run on top of Azure Logic Apps. This is relevant because they both use all of the same functions. Because of this, when searching the internet for solutions or reading documentation about Power Automate functions, it is common to encounter Logic Apps documentation.**

Power Automate target audience

No matter a user's expertise, Power Automate offers valuable benefits. Here are some examples of how different users can take advantage of this powerful tool:

- **Business users**: By automating routine tasks such as data entry, notifications, and approvals, business users can save significant time and reduce human error, thus enhancing overall productivity and allowing them to focus on more strategic activities.

- **IT professionals**: IT professionals can create complex workflows to integrate and synchronize disparate systems, ensuring efficient data management. This can lead to improved data accuracy, better system performance, and more seamless operations across different platforms.

- **Developers**: Developers can leverage advanced features and custom connectors in Power Automate to build sophisticated automation solutions. This allows for the creation of highly tailored workflows that can address unique business needs, providing greater flexibility and innovation.

- **Organizations**: Organizations as a whole can benefit from streamlining business processes, which improves collaboration and reduces operational costs. By automating repetitive tasks, organizations can allocate resources more effectively, leading to increased efficiency and competitiveness in the market.

Power Automate capabilities

Power Automate offers a vast range of capabilities to streamline and automate various tasks and processes. The following are just a few examples:

- **Data collection and management**: One of the primary capabilities of Power Automate is its ability to automatically collect, process, and store data from multiple sources. This not only saves time but also ensures data accuracy and consistency across different platforms.

- **Notifications and alerts**: Power Automate can send automated notifications and alerts based on specific triggers and conditions. This functionality is crucial for keeping teams informed and responsive to changes or critical events. Whether it is an email alert for a completed task or a push notification for an urgent issue, automated alerts help maintain seamless communication and prompt action.

- **Approvals and workflows**: Streamlining approval processes is another significant advantage of Power Automate. Users can create automated workflows for document reviews, requests, and other approval processes. This not only accelerates the approval cycle but also reduces errors and ensures compliance with organizational policies.

- **Report generation**: Automatically generating and distributing reports based on predefined criteria is another key feature of Power Automate. This functionality helps in delivering timely and accurate reports to stakeholders, aiding in informed decision-making. Users can set up automated workflows to compile data, generate reports, and send them to the relevant recipients without any manual intervention.

- **API integration**: Power Automate can call external APIs and receive their output, thus making its capabilities almost endless. This feature allows users to connect with a wide array of services and applications, enabling seamless data exchange and process integration. Whether pulling data from a web service or pushing updates to an external system, API integration ensures that Power Automate can interact with virtually any platform, extending its functionality and adaptability.

Cloud flows vs. desktop flows

Cloud flows and desktop flows are two distinct types of workflows available in Power Automate, each designed to cater to different automation needs and environments.

Cloud flows are designed to automate processes that run in the cloud. They can connect to various cloud-based services, such as Microsoft 365, Dynamics 365, and third-party services like Salesforce, Dropbox, and Twitter. Cloud flows are particularly useful for scenarios involving data exchange between cloud systems, real-time notifications, automated approvals, and integration with cloud-based applications. They can be triggered by events such as receiving an email, adding a new item to a SharePoint list, or a specific time of day. Cloud flows are highly scalable and can handle complex workflows that span multiple systems and services.

On the other hand, **desktop flows**, formerly known as UI flows, are designed to automate tasks on a local machine. They can interact with desktop applications, legacy systems, and manual processes that are not accessible through cloud-based APIs. Desktop flows use **robotic process automation** (RPA) to simulate human actions, such as clicking buttons, entering data, and navigating through software interfaces. They are ideal for automating repetitive tasks, data entry, and processes that require interaction with desktop applications. Desktop flows can be triggered manually or scheduled to run at specific times, ensuring that routine tasks are performed consistently and efficiently.

By combining cloud flows and desktop flows, users can create comprehensive automation solutions that integrate both cloud-based and on-premises systems. This hybrid approach enables businesses to streamline operations, improve data accuracy, and reduce the burden of manual tasks, ultimately leading to enhanced productivity and operational efficiency.

The following table compares cloud floes with desktop flows in Power Automate:

Feature	Cloud flows	Desktop flows
Execution environment	Runs in the cloud	Runs on a local or virtual machine
Use case	Automates cloud-based services and apps	Automates desktop and legacy applications
Trigger types	Automated, instant, or scheduled	Typically triggered manually or via cloud flow
Technology	**Digital process automation (DPA)**	**Robotic process automation (RPA)**
Connectivity	Uses over 500 cloud connectors (e.g., Outlook, SharePoint)	Interacts with UI elements, files, and local apps
Platform	Web-based (Power Automate portal)	Power Automate Desktop app
Best For	Cloud-first workflows and integrations	Repetitive tasks on Windows apps or legacy systems

Table 14.1: Cloud flows vs. desktop flows

Licensing

Understanding the different Power Automate licensing options is crucial for maximizing the tool's potential within your organization. By selecting the right plan, you can ensure that your team has the necessary capabilities to automate workflows efficiently and effectively. Whether you are a small team looking to explore automation or a large enterprise with complex needs, Power Automate offers a licensing plan to suit your requirements. Here are some guidelines to help you make an informed decision:

- **Assess your automation needs**: Determine the scope and complexity of the workflows you intend to automate. For basic automation tasks, the Microsoft 365 Plan might suffice. However, for more advanced and high-volume workflows, consider the per-user or per-flow plans.

- **Evaluate user requirements**: Consider the number of users who will be creating and running workflows. If individual users need extensive automation capabilities, the per user plan is suitable. For team-based automation with shared flows, the Per Flow Plan offers a cost-effective solution.

- **Budget considerations**: Analyze your budget and compare it with the features and benefits of each plan. While the Microsoft 365 Plan offers basic automation at no additional cost, the per user and per flow plans provide more extensive capabilities at a higher price point, for example.

This section will cover the most common types of Power Automate licenses, helping you determine which plan best suits your and your organization's needs.

Power Automate Premium

Power Automate Premium spans modern and legacy applications, enabling licensed users to create and run unlimited cloud flows using DPA, plus automate legacy applications with desktop flows through RPA in attended mode. This offer includes full process mining desktop functionality and a limited amount of process mining data capacity (50 MB that can be pooled to a max of 100 GB per tenant). Additionally, Power Automate Premium includes access to AI Builder capacity in support of scenarios like forms processing, object detection, prediction, text classification and recognition, and provides the ability for a user to run an attended RPA bot on a workstation.

> Note: **Running an RPA bot in an unattended scenario requires the addition of the Power Automate Hosted Process license.**

Power Automate Process

The Power Automate Process license can be used to license a single autonomous bot that can be used for unattended Robotic process automation (unattended RPA), independent of a user, or a critical business process that can be accessed org-wide without licensing individual users. Power Automate Process also includes access to AI Builder capacity in support of scenarios like form processing, object detection, prediction, text classification, and recognition.

Power Automate Hosted Process

Licensed per bot, Power Automate Hosted Process is a superset of Power Automate Process, providing the same functionality, but also includes a virtual machine for running unattended automation with zero infrastructure. Each Hosted Process license provides capacity for a single Microsoft-hosted machine.

Power Automate Process Mining

Process mining is a capacity-based, add-on license that enables rapid ROI for customers by identifying critical optimization opportunities and improving existing processes. There are no limits to the number of users per tenant. Capacity should be purchased for peak utilization over a 12-month contract period.

Power Automate per user

Power Automate per user equips individual users to create and run unlimited workflows and business processes based on their unique needs. The per user license is intended to support the broad adoption of an automation culture in an organization. Should the entire organization be licensed with the Power Automate per user, admins will have minimal overhead with tracking how many flows are being activated and used within the organization.

Power Automate per flow

Power Automate per flow is licensed by top-level flow and allows customers to implement critical business processes with capacity that serves teams, departments, or the entire organization without individually licensing each end user that triggers the licensed flow.

Power Automate unattended RPA add-on

The Power Automate unattended RPA add-on extends desktop-based automation by enabling a bot to run autonomously, i.e., independent of a user. Unattended bots can be deployed on a local, remote desktop, or other virtualized environment. Power Automate Premium or Power Automate per flow qualifies as a base license for the unattended RPA add-on. The Power Automate unattended RPA add-on is licensed by the bot. Concurrent instances of a singular process require an additional unattended bot for each instance. Power Automate.

Microsoft 365 Plan

The Microsoft 365 Plan offers basic automation with access to standard connectors. This plan is suitable for organizations already using Microsoft 365, providing an integrated solution for automation within the existing subscription.

With the Microsoft 365 Plan, users can create cloud flows to automate repetitive tasks, integrate with Microsoft services such as SharePoint and Outlook, and streamline their daily operations with ease. While it might not offer the extensive features of the premium plans, it provides a solid foundation for those looking to enhance productivity through automation.

The Microsoft plans that include this license are:

- Microsoft Business Basic, Standard, and Premium
- Microsoft 365 E3 and E5

Checking the assigned license

To check which Power Automate license is assigned to your account, follow these steps:

1. Open the Power Automate portal by navigating to **https://make.powerautomate.com**.

2. Once in the portal, click on the gear icon located in the upper right corner to access the settings menu. From the settings menu, select **View my licenses**. This will display a detailed summary of your assigned licenses, as shown in the following figure:

Licenses	✕	Licenses	✕

My licenses

▣ Power Automate for Office 365
⊠ PAD for Windows
⊠ Power Automate Free
⊠ Power Automate For CCI Bots
⊠ Power Automate Free
⊠ Power Automate Per User Plan
⊠ Power Automate for Project

Environment capacities

⊠ Per-flow plan capacity

Capabilities

✓ Standard connectors
✓ Premium connectors
✓ Custom connectors
✓ On-premise connectors
✕ Robotic process automation (RPA) - attended
✕ Robotic process automation (RPA) - unattended
✕ Robotic process automation (RPA) - hosted
✓ Business process flows
✕ AI Builder
✕ Process mining
Learn how to add capabilities

My licenses

⊠ Power Automate Free
▣ Power Automate for Office 365

Capabilities

✓ Standard connectors
✕ Premium connectors
✕ Custom connectors
✕ On-premise connectors
✕ Robotic process automation (RPA) - attended
✕ Robotic process automation (RPA) - unattended
✕ Robotic process automation (RPA) - hosted
✓ Business process flows
✕ AI Builder
✕ Process mining
Learn how to add capabilities

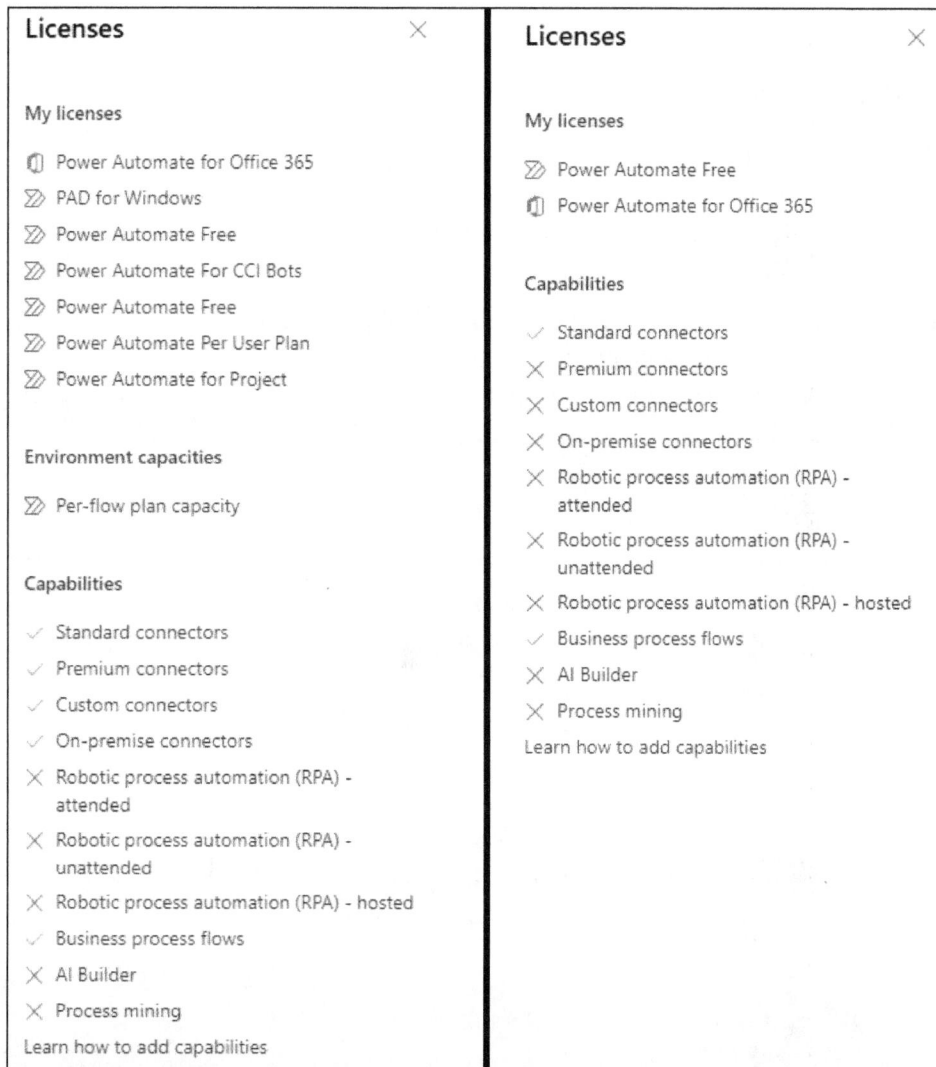

Figure 14.1: Two examples of Power Automate license assignments

In this screen, you will see three sections:

- The **My licenses** section shows the user licenses assigned to your account. It lists the specific Power Automate licenses you have, such as the per user plan, the Microsoft 365 Plan, or Power Automate Premium for example.

- The **Environment capacity** section displays the capacity licenses and any capacity add-ons available to your account for the currently selected environment. This section might not be visible if no capacities are available.

- The **Capacities** section will show a green check on each user entitlement in the context of environment capacities, confirming what specific features and capabilities you can access with your current license.

Creating automated workflows

Creating workflows in Power Automate is a straightforward process, thanks to its user-friendly interface and the vast number of pre-built templates available at **https://make.powerautomate.com**. Users can start with a template or build a custom workflow from scratch. With the drag-and-drop interface, users can easily add, remove, and rearrange elements to create a workflow that meets their needs as we will shortly see.

For our first flow, let us start with a template.

Templates

Templates in Power Automate are pre-built workflow solutions designed to address common business scenarios and automation needs. These templates provide a quick and easy way to get started with creating automated workflows without having to build them from scratch. They are designed by experts and cover a wide range of use cases, helping users save time and effort while ensuring best practices are followed. These are offered across various categories, catering to different business functions and industries, such as approval processes, email management, data collection, social media, productivity, and more.

Using a template in Power Automate is straightforward: from the Power Automate dashboard, access the **Templates** library to browse the extensive library of templates:

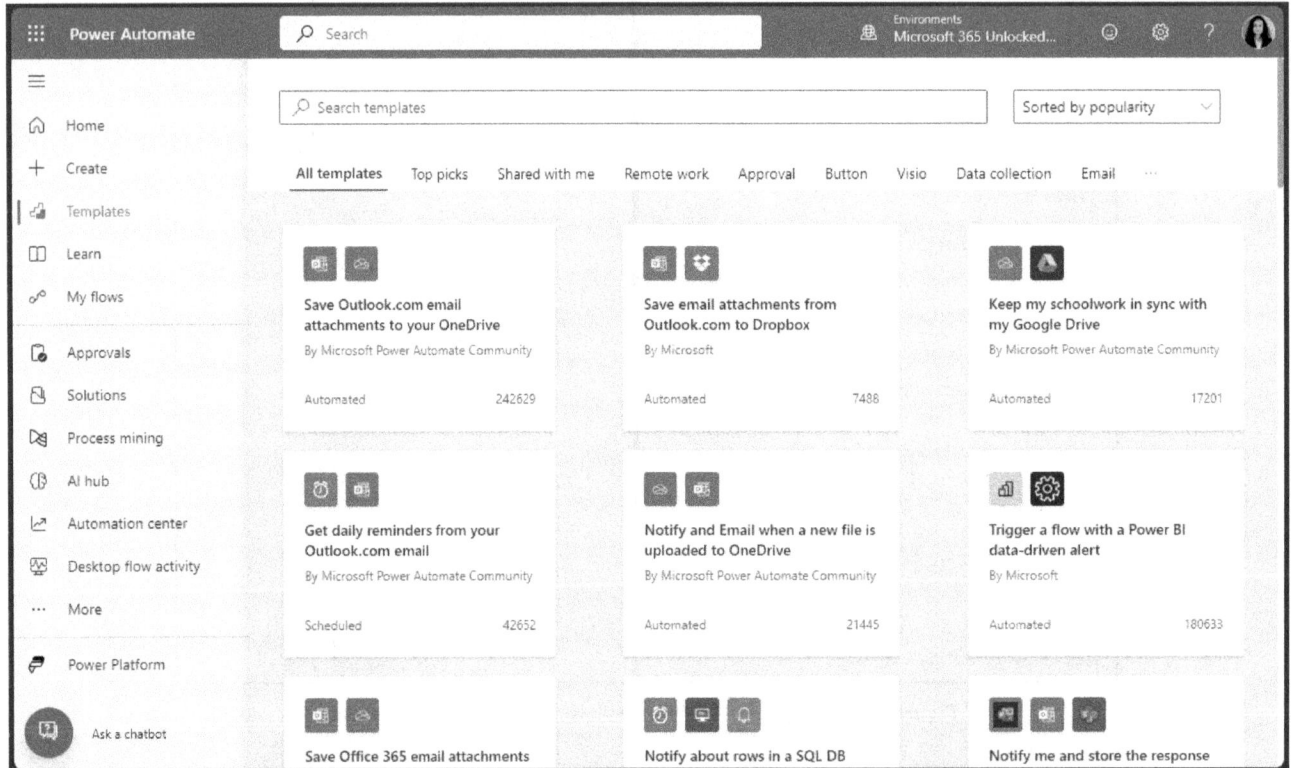

Figure 14.2: Power Automate template library

Here, you can search for templates based on keywords, categories, or popularity. For example, to create our Workflow 1 from a template, let us search for *save email attachments*. You will see some templates reference *Outlook.com* and others reference *Office 365 email* for example. This is because Power Automate can work with both the public consumer version of Outlook.com and its enterprise version of Exchange Online. Similarly, some templates will reference the consumer *OneDrive* while others the enterprise counterpart *OneDrive for Business*. For Workflow 1, we will use the **Save Office 365 email attachments to specified OneDrive for Business folder** template:

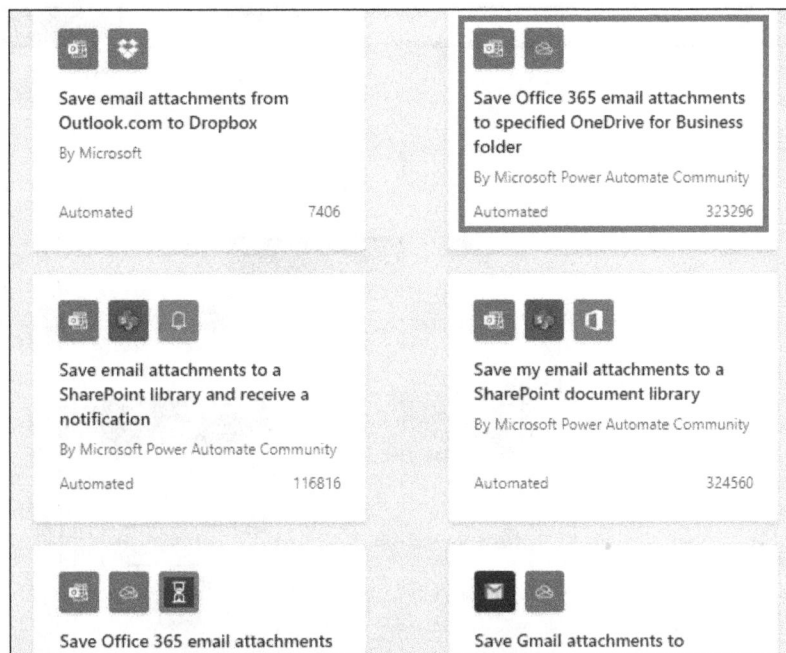

Figure 14.3: Template chosen for our first flow

To use it, we click on this template and further details are shown, including a description of the workflow, the services it connects to, and any prerequisites:

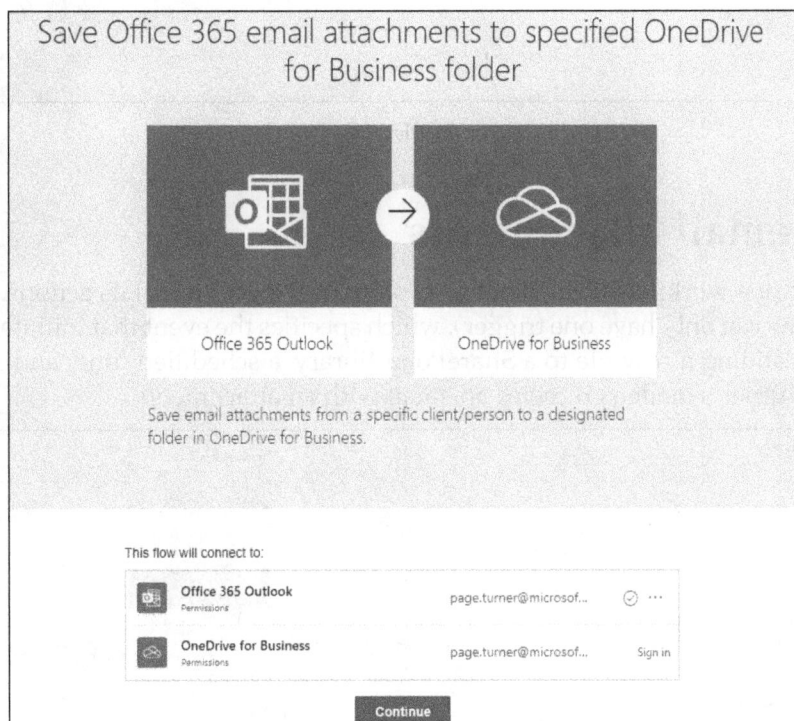

Figure 14.4: Power Automate not signed in to OneDrive

As we have never used the **OneDrive for Business** connector with this account, Power Automate cannot yet connect to it. All we have to do is click on **Sign in** next to **OneDrive for Business** and it will use the current account details to connect to OneDrive. Next, we click **Continue** to create the flow so we can customize it to fit our specific requirements. This may involve modifying triggers, actions, conditions, and other elements within the workflow. Once we click **Continue**, we are taken to our flow as shown in the following figure (we will explore it in detail in the next section):

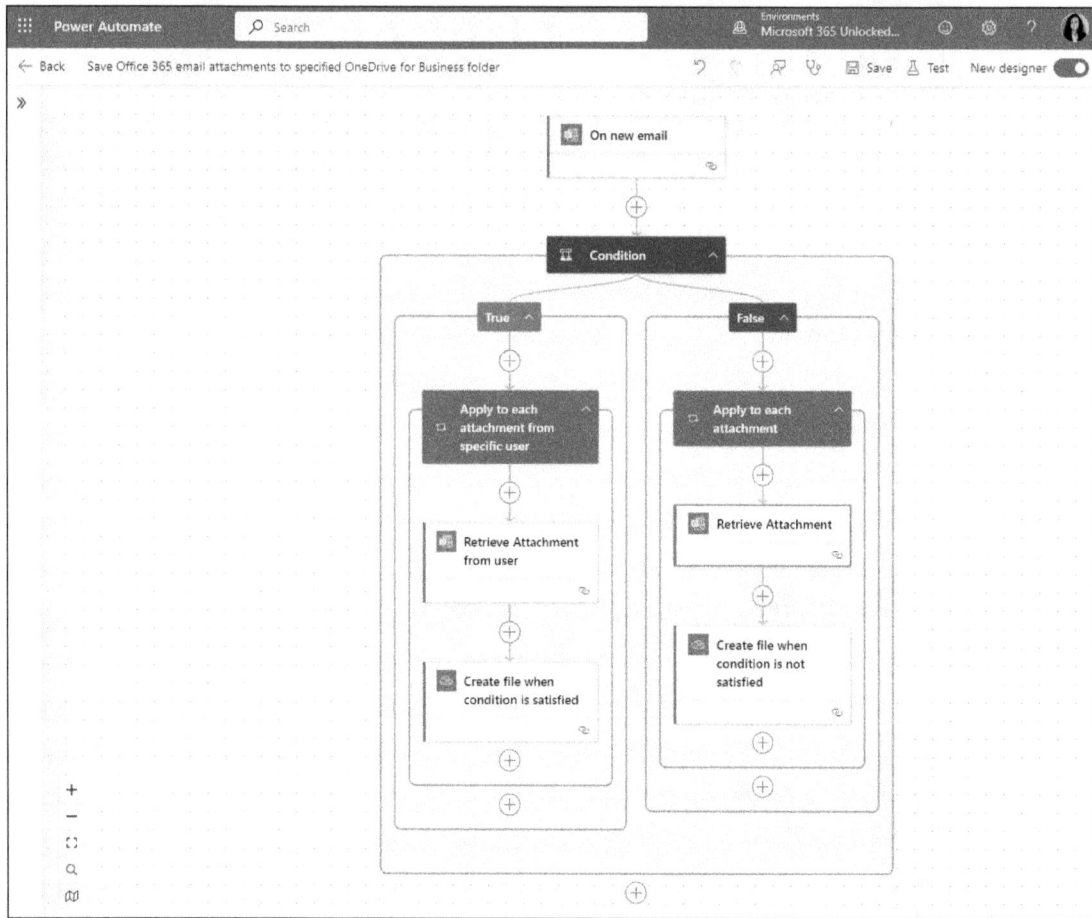

Figure 14.5: Our first flow based on a template

Workflow 1, email attachments

Now that we have our first workflow created, let us explore its trigger and all its actions. The first step of any flow is its **trigger** (a flow can only have one trigger), which specifies the event that initiates the workflow, such as receiving an email, adding a new file to a SharePoint library, a scheduled time, and so on. Our flow gets triggered when Page Turner's mailbox receives an email with an attachment:

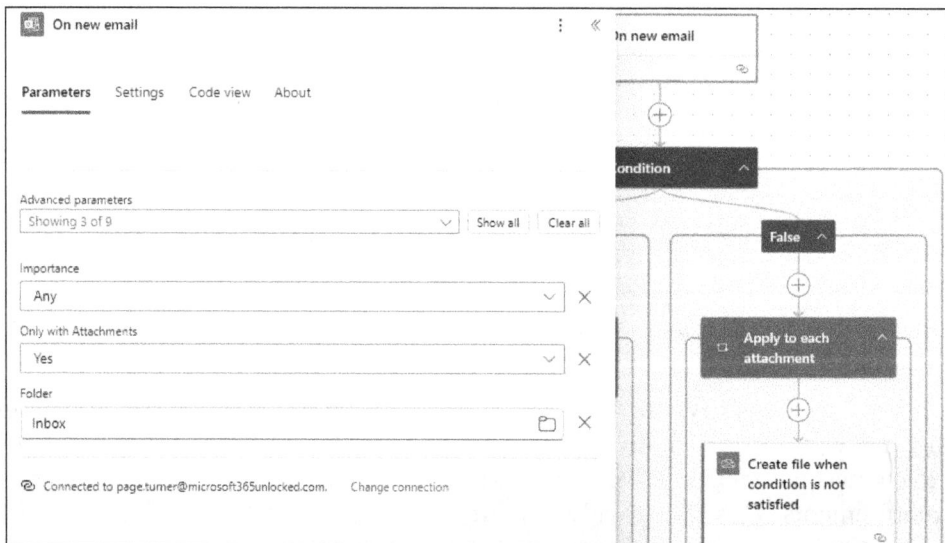

Figure 14.6: The trigger for our first flow

Next, we have a **Condition**. Conditions in Power Automate are used to create branching logic based on the evaluation of specified criteria. Essentially, they act as decision points within the workflow, determining the subsequent actions based on whether the condition is met (true) or not (false).

In this example, the condition evaluates if the email was sent by a particular sender that we enter in the **Choose a value** text box, as shown:

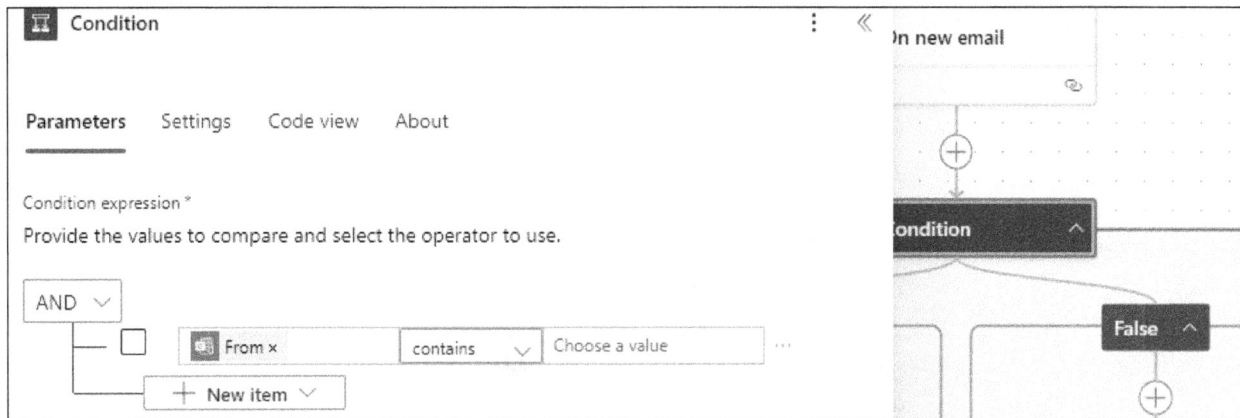

Figure 14.7: A condition checking the email sender

If the condition is true, one set of actions is executed; if false, an alternative set of actions is triggered.

Next, we have our first **action** inside the *true* side of our condition, which retrieves the attachment from the email. As an email can have several attachments, this action is inside a **ForEach** statement that will iterate through every single attachment sequentially:

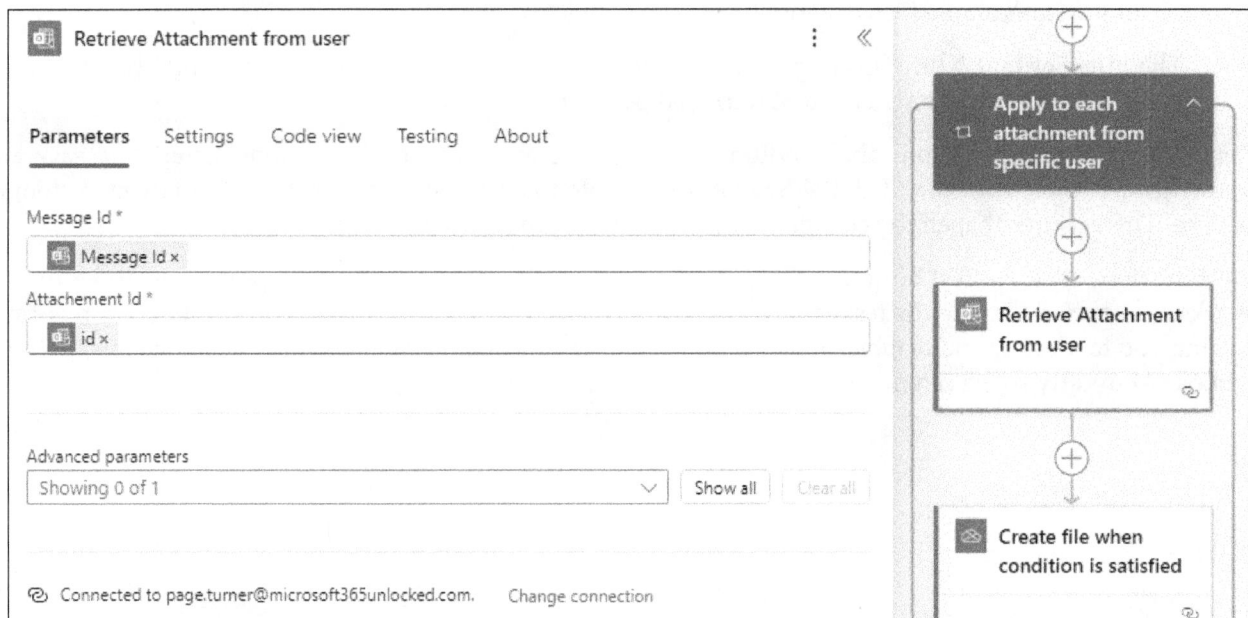

Figure 14.8: Action to retrieve an email attachment

Once the attachment is retrieved, another action saves it into the OneDrive folder we specify:

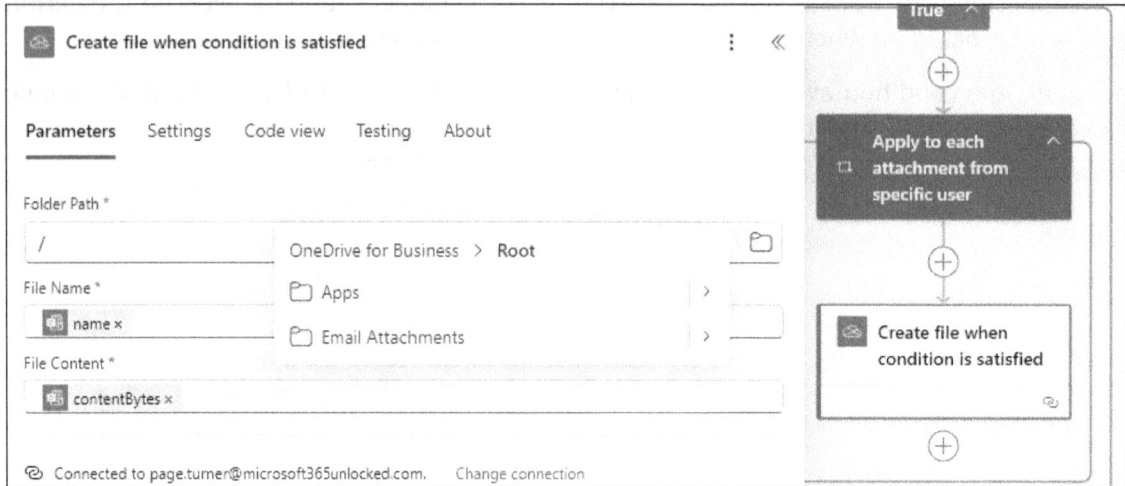

Figure 14.9: *Action to save the attachment in OneDrive*

Within our action, three settings must be configured:

- The **Folder Path** setting allows you to specify the exact location within your OneDrive where the file will be saved. This ensures that all files are organized and stored in the correct directory, making it easy to locate them later.

- The **File Name** setting is used to define the name of the file that will be created. This can be a static name or dynamically generated using expressions and variables, which is particularly useful when dealing with multiple files to avoid overwrite issues.

- The **File Content** setting is where you specify the actual content that will be put into the file. In this case, this is the attachment content retrieved by the previous action.

After configuring all the actions and conditions in your Power Automate flow, the next step is to save and test the flow. To save the flow, click the **Save** button located at the top-right corner of the Power Automate interface. This ensures that all the changes made to the flow are securely stored.

To test the flow, click the **Test** button next to the **Save** button. This initiates a test run of the flow to verify that it works as expected. During the test, you can monitor the execution of each action and condition in real-time, allowing you to identify and troubleshoot any issues promptly. Because we have never run this flow, we need to choose **Manually** so we can manually trigger and test the flow:

Figure 14.10: *Testing our flow*

Once the flow is running, we can perform the action to trigger the flow. In this case, send an email to Page's mailbox:

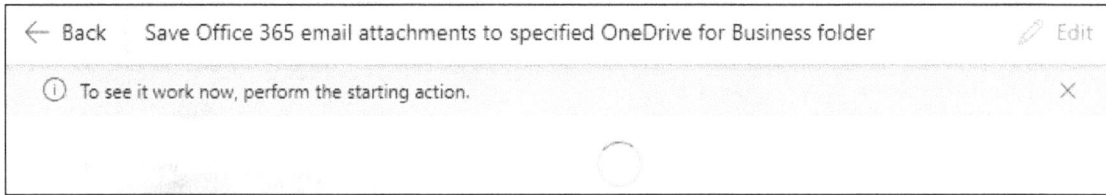

Figure 14.11: Waiting for the flow to get triggered

Once an email is received, Power Automate will automatically show us the result of every step of the flow, where we can check for errors and see exactly what was done:

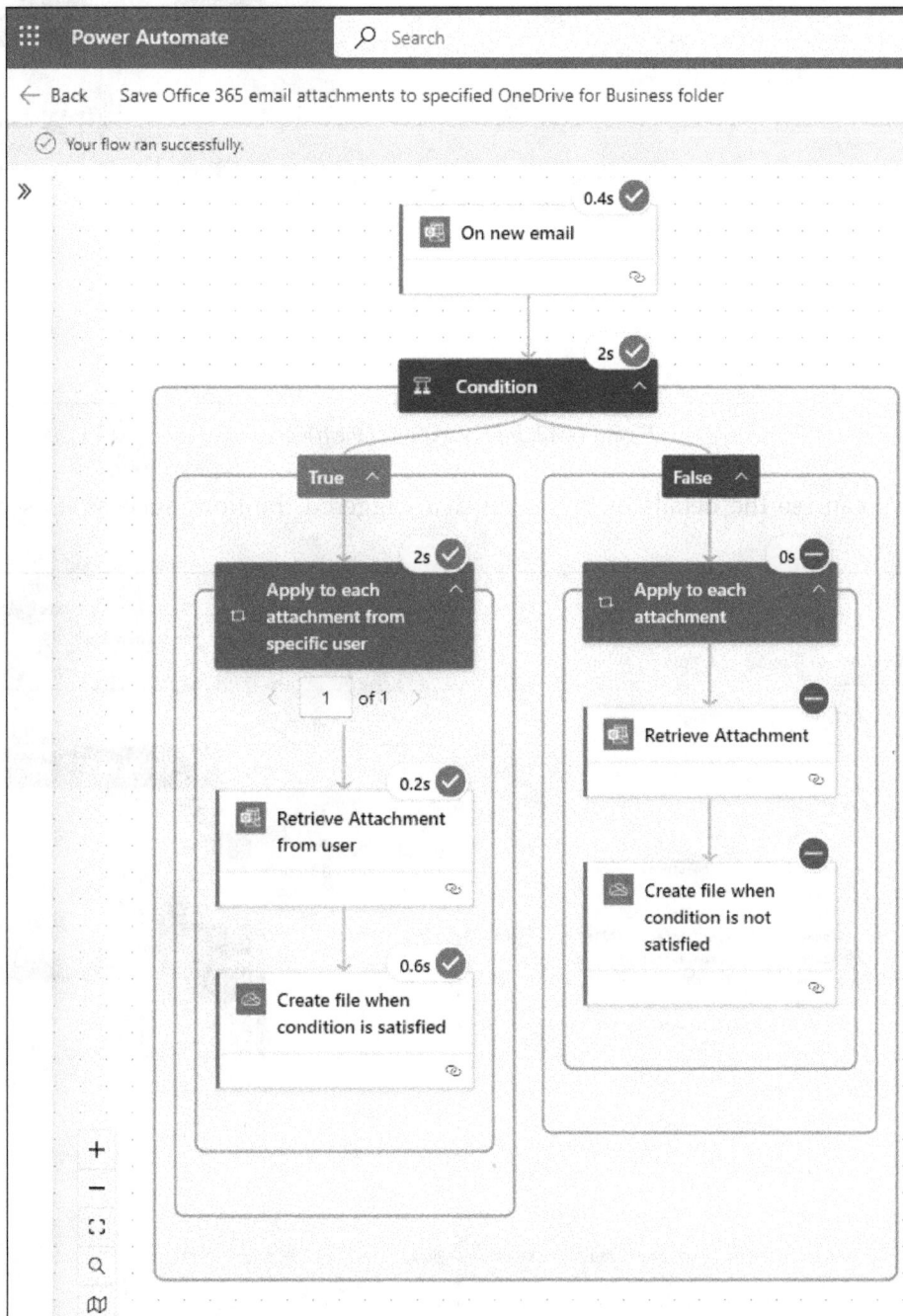

Figure 14.12: All the steps performed by flow

If we click on the trigger, we can see the parameters we specify for our trigger earlier, as well as additional information under **INPUTS**:

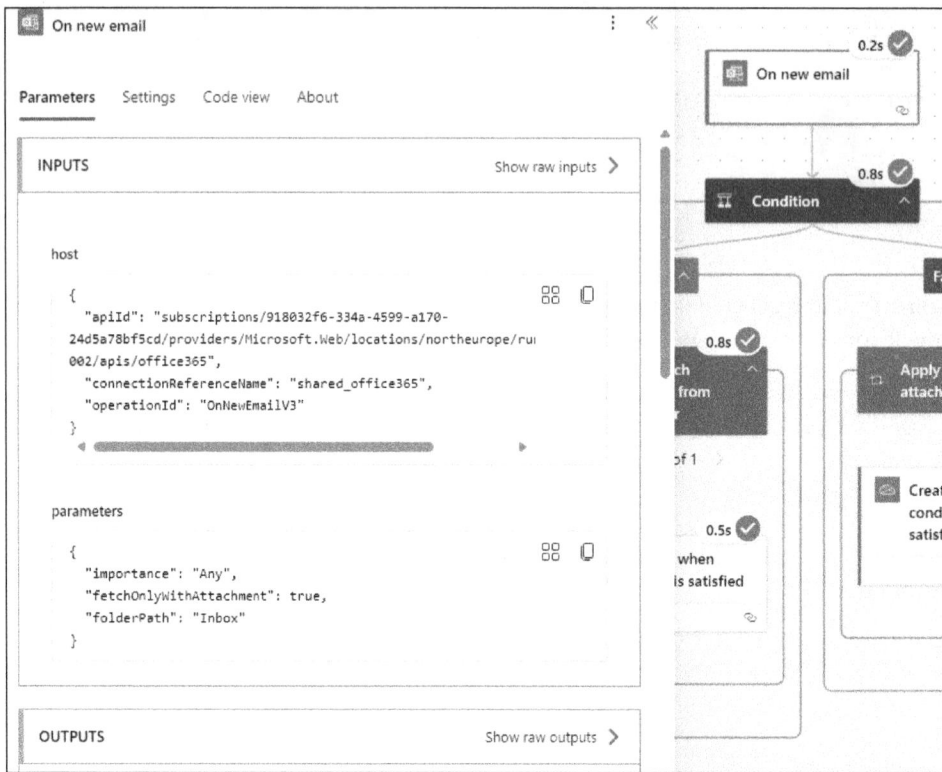

Figure 14.13: Inputs section of the trigger

Under **OUPUTS**, we can see the details of the email that triggered the flow, such as its sender, recipients, attachments, etc:

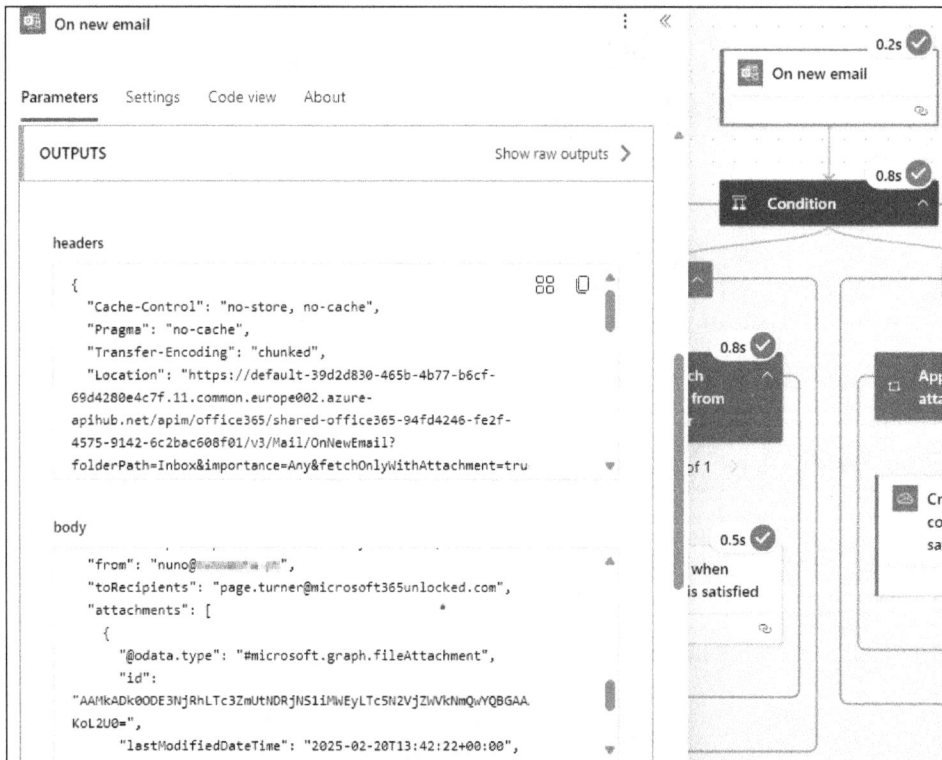

Figure 14.14: Outputs section of the trigger

Next, we can see that our condition evaluated to **true**, meaning the sender was the one we specified:

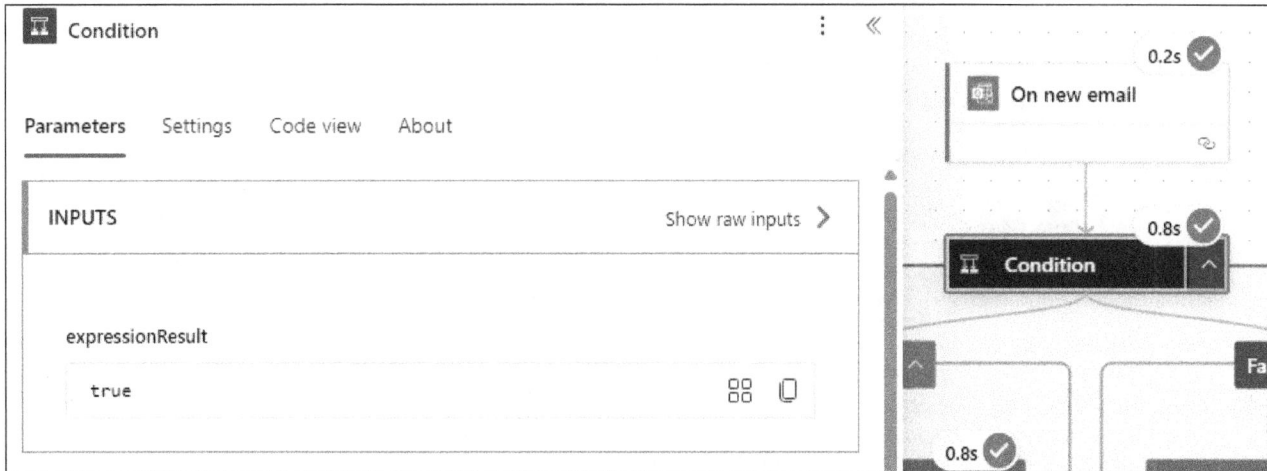

Figure 14.15: Condition result

The flow then retrieves the attachment in the email, a PDF named `Microsoft-Bookings-Quick-Guide` in this case:

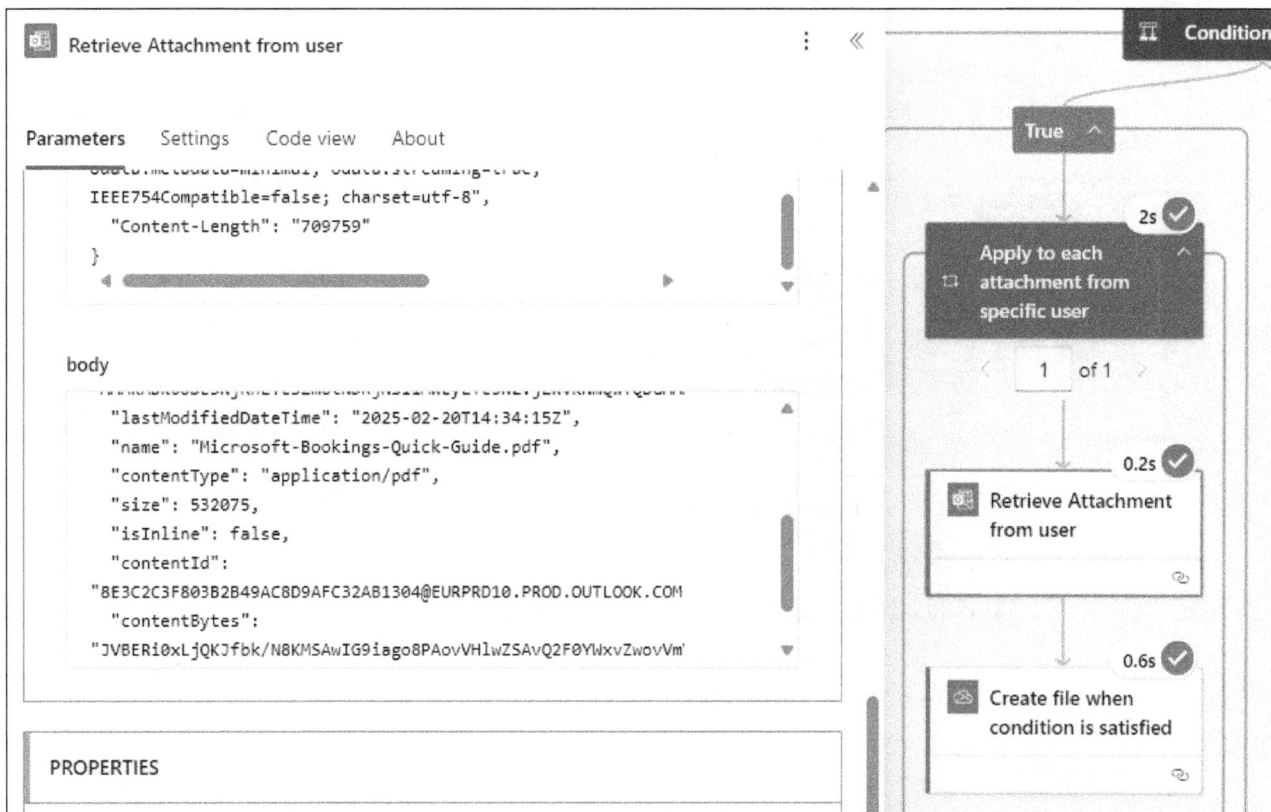

Figure 14.16: Retrieving the attachment result

And finally, the last action saves the attachment in the OneDrive folder named `Email Attachments`:

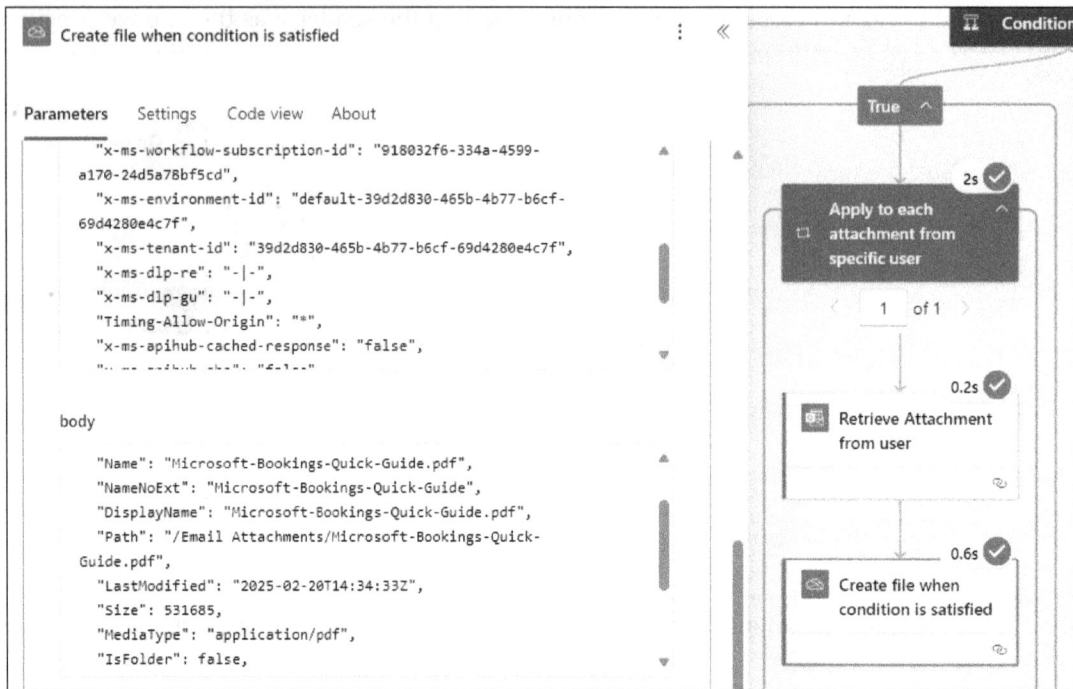

Figure 14.17: Saving the attachment result

If we navigate to the folder, we can see that the attachment was indeed successfully saved into our OneDrive folder, as follows:

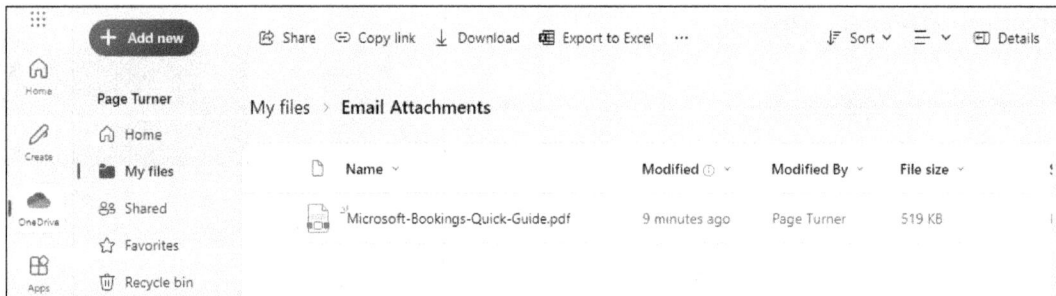

Figure 14.18: Attachment saved into OneDrive

Workflow 2, notifications, and approvals

In this workflow, we will send a notification when a new file is added to a specific SharePoint folder and trigger an approval flow for that file. For this, we have created a dedicated folder in a SharePoint library, as shown:

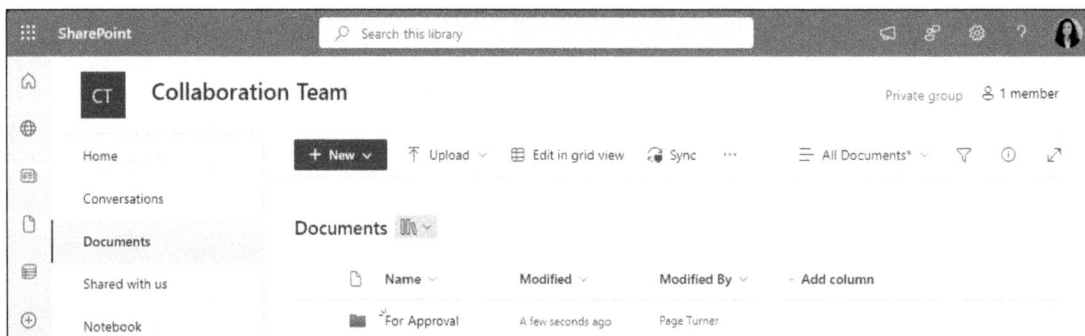

Figure 14.19: SharePoint folder used for approvals

The flow will trigger only when a file is uploaded to this folder, i.e., created, not modified.

This flow will be created from scratch, so the first step is to click on **Create** from the Power Automate portal and then select **Automated cloud flow,** since we want our flow to get triggered automatically when something specific (our trigger) happens, as shown:

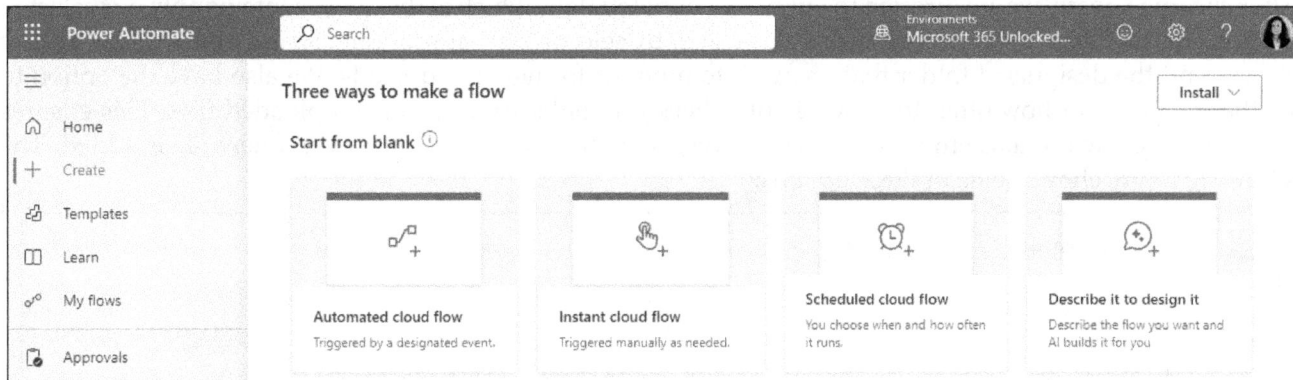

Figure 14.20: Creating a new flow from scratch

Let us take a moment to understand the differences between these flow types. An **automated cloud flow** is designed to perform actions automatically when a specific event or trigger occurs. For example, it can save email attachments to a OneDrive folder as soon as they arrive just like we saw in our previous example.

In contrast, an **instant cloud flow** requires manual activation. Users trigger these flows on-demand, typically from their devices, whenever they need to perform a task immediately, such as copying files between locations.

Lastly, a **scheduled cloud flow** runs at predetermined intervals. Users set specific times and frequencies for these flows to execute, making them ideal for routine tasks, such as daily data backups or weekly report generation.

Next, we give our flow a name and pick our trigger. For this example, we will choose the `when a file is created (properties only)` trigger you can see selected here:

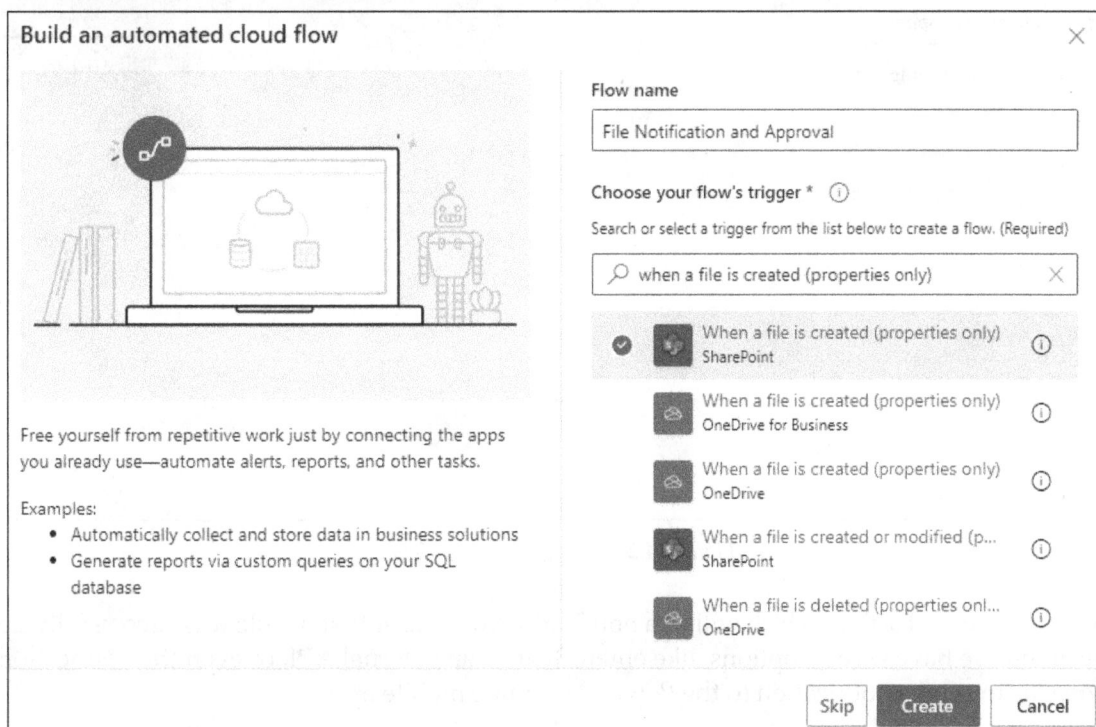

Figure 14.21: Selecting the trigger to our flow

This trigger activates the workflow when a new file is added to a specified SharePoint folder. Unlike similar triggers that respond to both file creation and modification, this trigger focuses solely on newly created files. This means the flow will only initiate actions when a file is first uploaded to the folder, not when it is subsequently edited.

After clicking **Create**, we are directed to our newly initiated flow, which at this stage contains only our selected trigger. The next step involves configuring the trigger by selecting the appropriate SharePoint site, the specific library, and the designated folder that we wish to monitor for new file uploads. We also have the option to set the frequency of how often the flow should check the folder for any newly uploaded files. This ensures that the workflow remains efficient and responsive, activating promptly whenever a new file is added. The following figure shows some of these options:

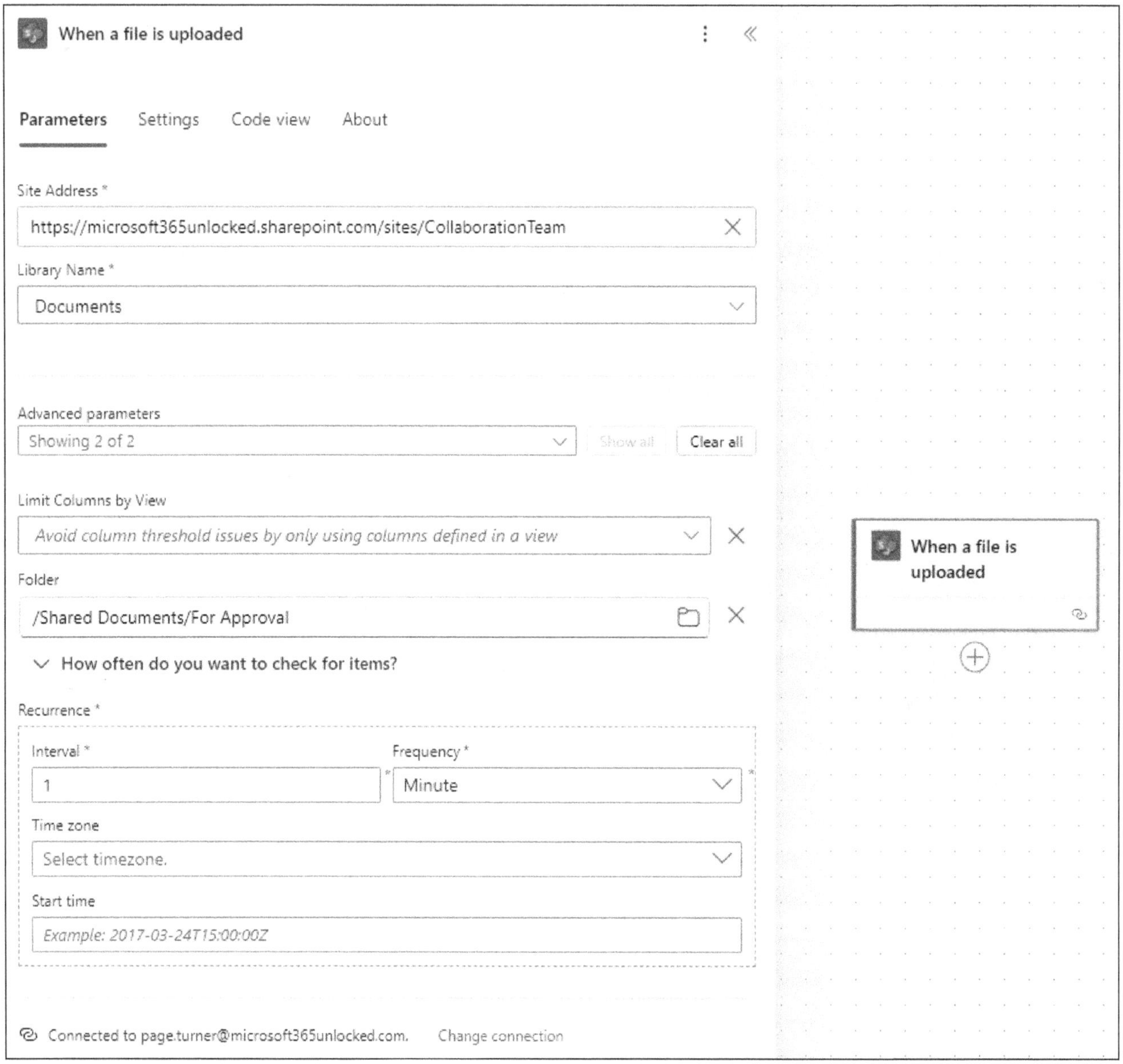

Figure 14.22: Configuring our trigger

Now we can add our first action, which will be a notification to the user that the file was successfully uploaded. For notifications, we have several options, like email, Teams, an external API, or even the notification service which allows us to send a notification to the Power Automate mobile app:

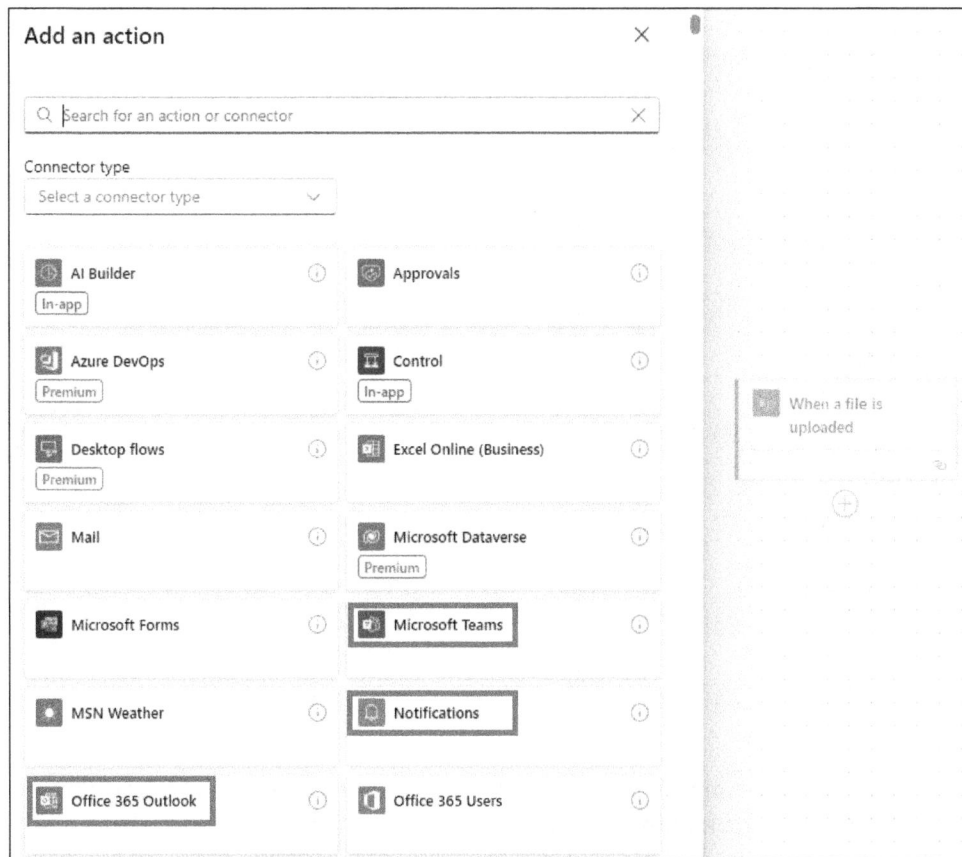

Figure 14.23: Example of notification actions

As an example, a useful action for a Teams notification is posting a message to a chat or channel. With Power Automate, this process is extremely easy. You simply select the **Post message in a chat or channel** action, choose the appropriate chat or channel, and customize your message. The intuitive interface of Power Automate guides you through each step, ensuring that even users with minimal technical experience can set up seamless notifications, making Power Automate an invaluable tool for integrating various services and automating routine tasks efficiently. The following figure shows an action we could use to send a message over Teams:

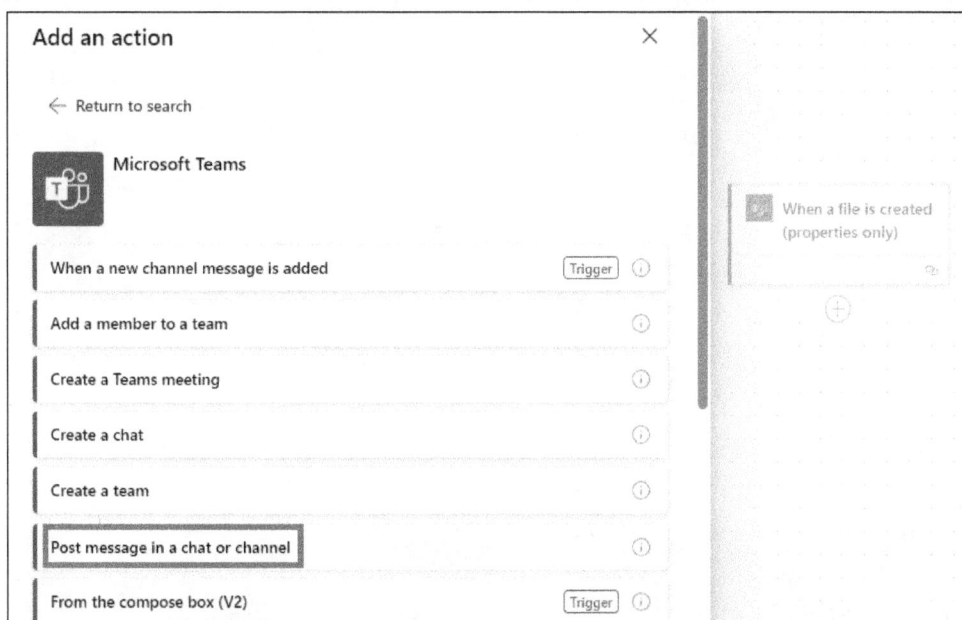

Figure 14.24: Sending a Teams message through Power Automate

For this particular notification, we will send the user an email, so we pick **Office 365 Outlook**, since we are using a corporate Exchange Online, and the **Send an email (V2)** action:

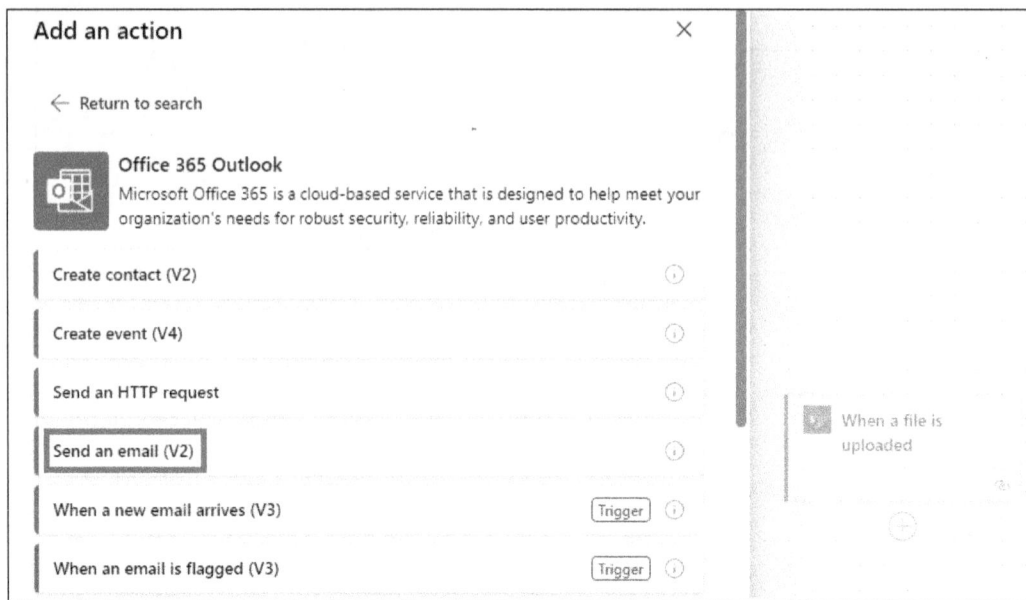

Figure 14.25: Sending an email action

By default, we can enter a corporate user's email address or name in the **To** field, and Power Automate will search Entra ID for a matching user, making it easy to ensure a valid internal recipient is selected. Alternatively, we can click on **Switch to Advanced Mode** and use expressions or a value from a previous step in the flow. Since we want to notify the person to whom we uploaded the file, we could use the **Created by Email** property that gets passed on from our trigger.

You can see some of the main options available when sending an email through Power Automate, with six other advanced parameters not visible, as follows:

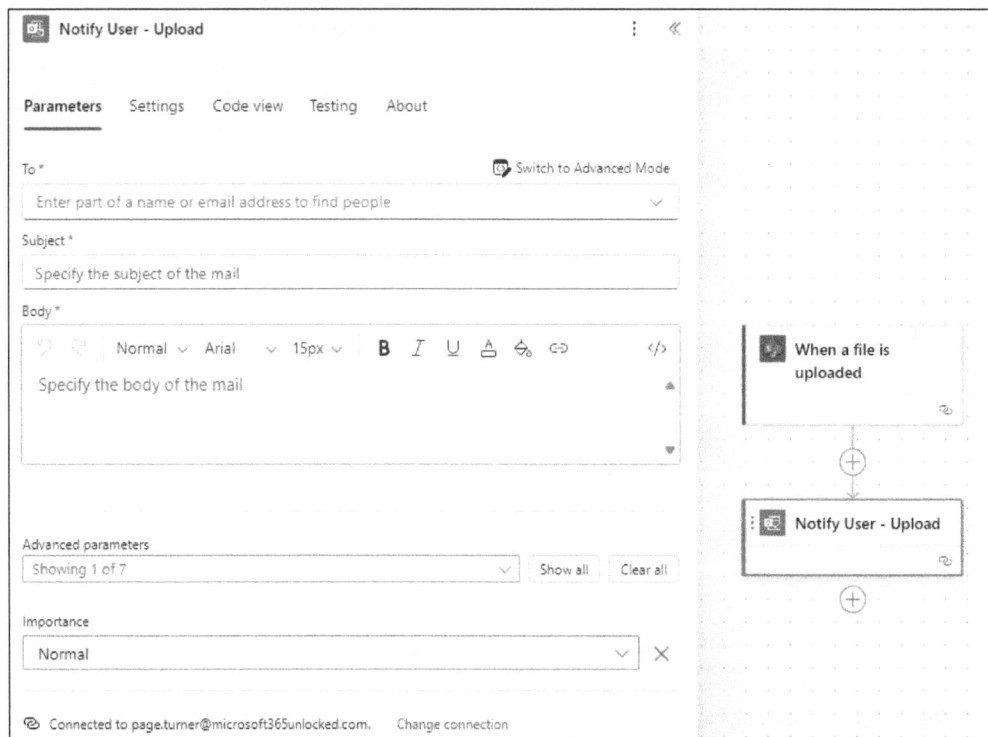

Figure 14.26: Configuring our notification email

Under **Subject**, we can click on the lightning icon to add a property passed on from the trigger:

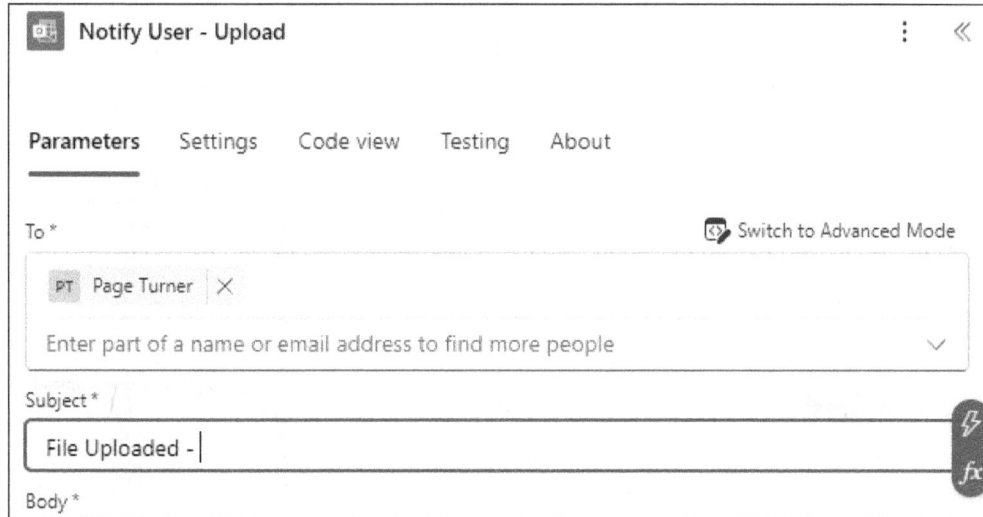

Figure 14.27: Using properties from previous steps

Power Automate will only display the first few properties by default, so to view all the properties passed by our trigger, we need to click on **See more (46)**. This expands the list to show all 46 properties. For this example, we will choose the **Name** property to ensure that the subject line of our notification includes the name of the uploaded file. Adding meaningful details in the subject line helps the recipient quickly identify the email's purpose and take necessary actions without delay.

In the following figure, you can see some of the dynamic properties we can add based on previous steps in the flow:

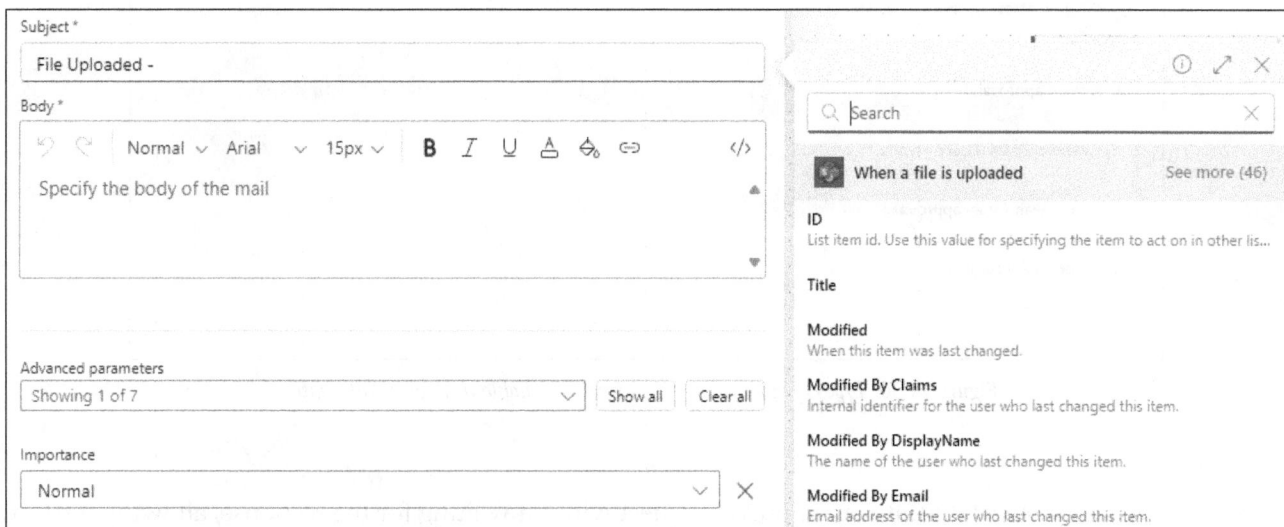

Figure 14.28: Selecting a property from a previous step

For the body of the notification, we can add additional details regarding the file uploaded, such as the full name including the extension of the file, and the path where the file was uploaded to:

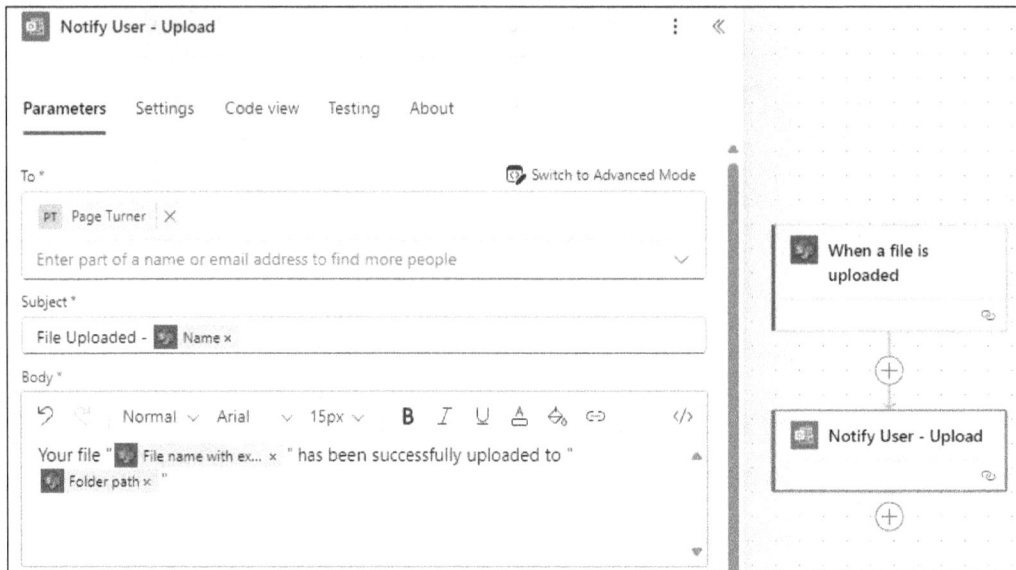

Figure 14.29: Adding meaningful information to our notification email

Next comes the approval flow. For this, we create a new action and search for **Approvals**. Power Automate offers four types of approval actions that facilitate decision-making and streamline workflows, as shown:

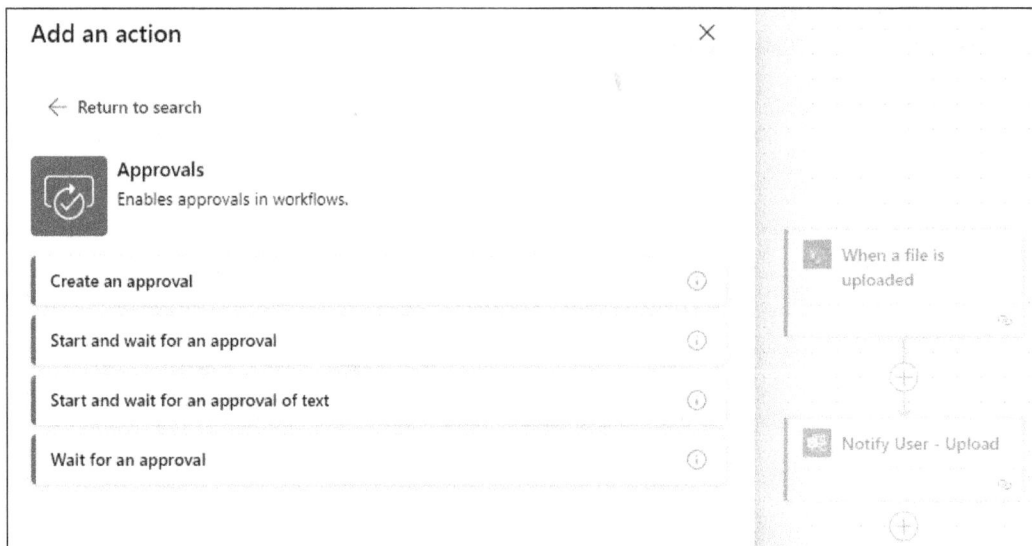

Figure 14.30: Types of approval flows natively available in Power Automate

These are:

- **Create an approval**: Initiates an approval request without waiting for the response, allowing the flow to continue executing other tasks.

- **Start and wait for an approval**: Sends an approval request and pauses the flow until a response is received, ensuring subsequent actions depend on the approval outcome.

- **Start and wait for an approval of text**: Similar to the standard approval action but includes a text response, useful for collecting comments or detailed feedback.

- **Wait for an approval**: Pauses the flow until an approval response is received, typically used in conjunction with a previously created approval request.

Understanding these different types of approval actions is crucial for designing efficient workflows, ensuring processes run smoothly, and capturing decisions accurately.

In our example, we want the flow to wait for a response, so we select the **Start and wait for an approval** action. Since our approval will always go to the same person, and no one else needs to also approve it, we select the **Approve/Reject – First to respond** approval type:

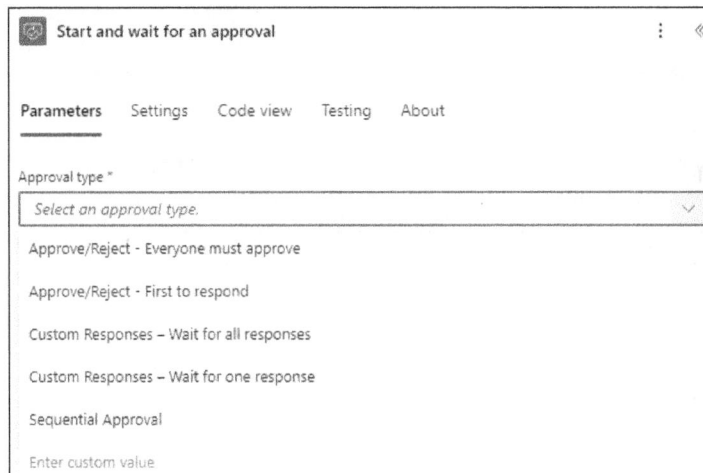

Figure 14.31: Selecting the approval type

Next, we compose our message that will be sent to the approver, ensuring it includes as much useful information as possible so they can make an informed decision. This message should detail the nature of the task, the document being approved, any relevant deadlines, and any additional context necessary for the approver to fully understand the implications of their decision, such as in this example:

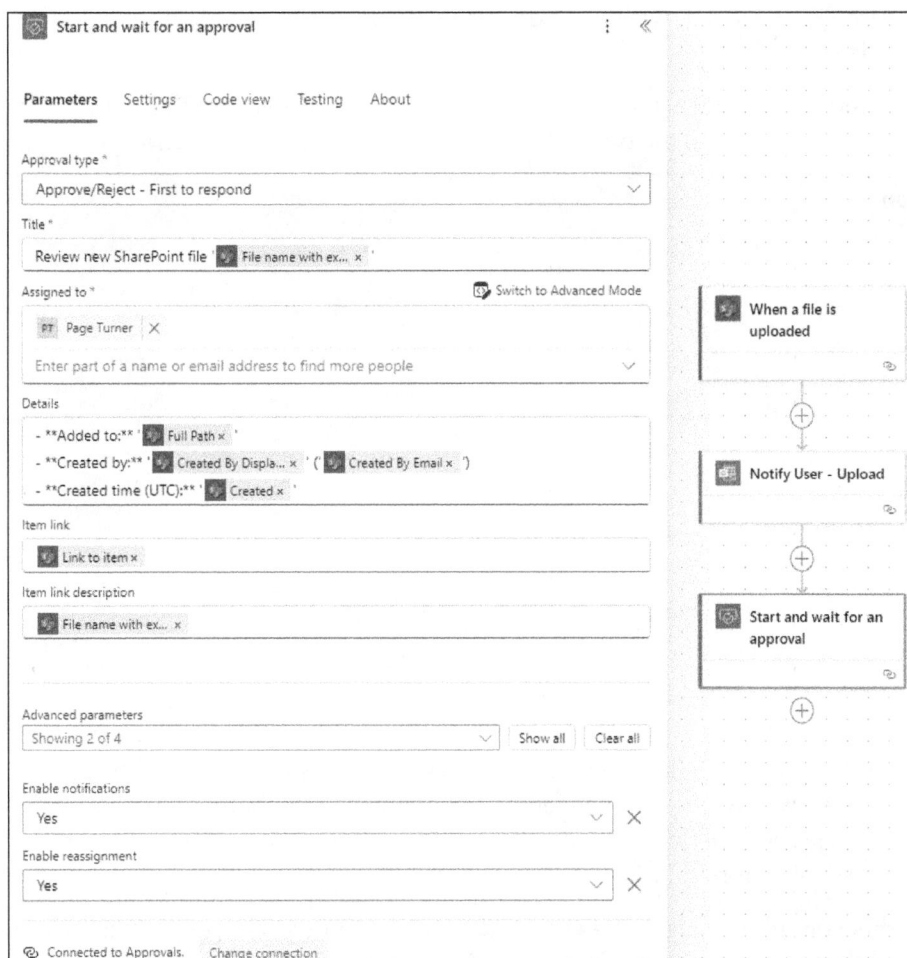

Figure 14.32: Composing our approval message

By providing comprehensive and clear information, we facilitate a smoother and more efficient approval process, reducing the likelihood of delays or misunderstandings. It is also prudent to include instructions on how the approver can give their feedback, whether through comments or by selecting **Approve** or **Reject** with additional remarks.

Note: The body of the message can be formatted using markdown language. For more details, please visit aka.ms/approvaldetails.

Under the **Settings** tab of our approval action, we use the **Action timeout** field to specify how long the flow will wait for a response before timing out:

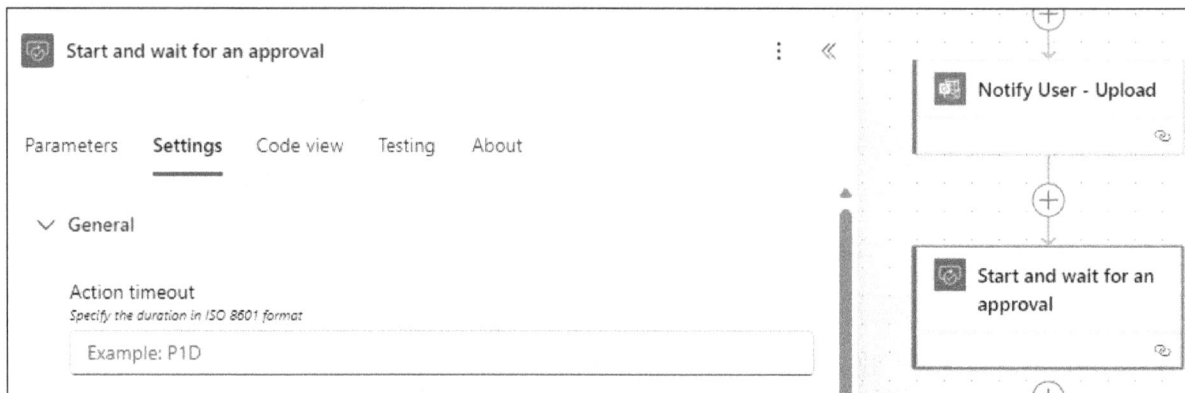

Figure 14.33: Configuring how long the flow will wait for a response

This is specified in ISO 8601 format, with a maximum of 28 days, such as *PT60S* for 1 minute, *PT24H* for 24 hours, or *P7D* for 7 days.

Next, we need to determine whether the approver has approved or rejected the request. To achieve this, we insert a **Condition** action, similar to the one used in our previous flow, as follows:

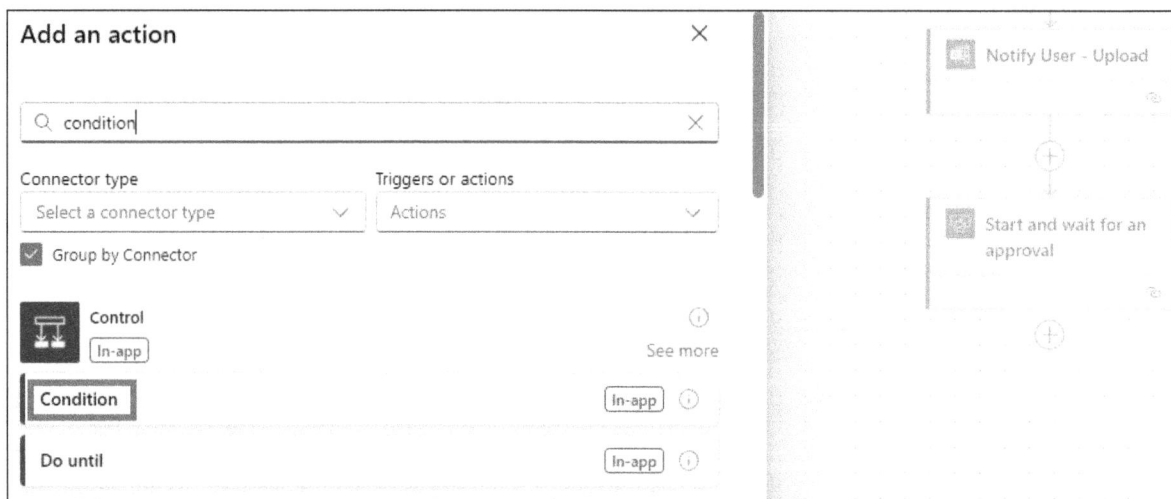

Figure 14.34: Adding a Condition action to our flow

This step is crucial as it enables the flow to branch into different paths based on the approval outcome. If the request is approved, the flow can proceed to execute subsequent tasks that rely on this approval. On the other hand, if the request is rejected, the flow can take an alternative route, such as notifying the relevant parties or triggering a different set of actions.

By incorporating this conditional logic, we ensure that the workflow adapts dynamically to the approver's decision, providing a robust and responsive automation process that handles approval scenarios effectively and efficiently.

To determine if the approval request has been approved, we need to check the **Outcome** property of the approval step, which indicates the approver's decision, as follows:

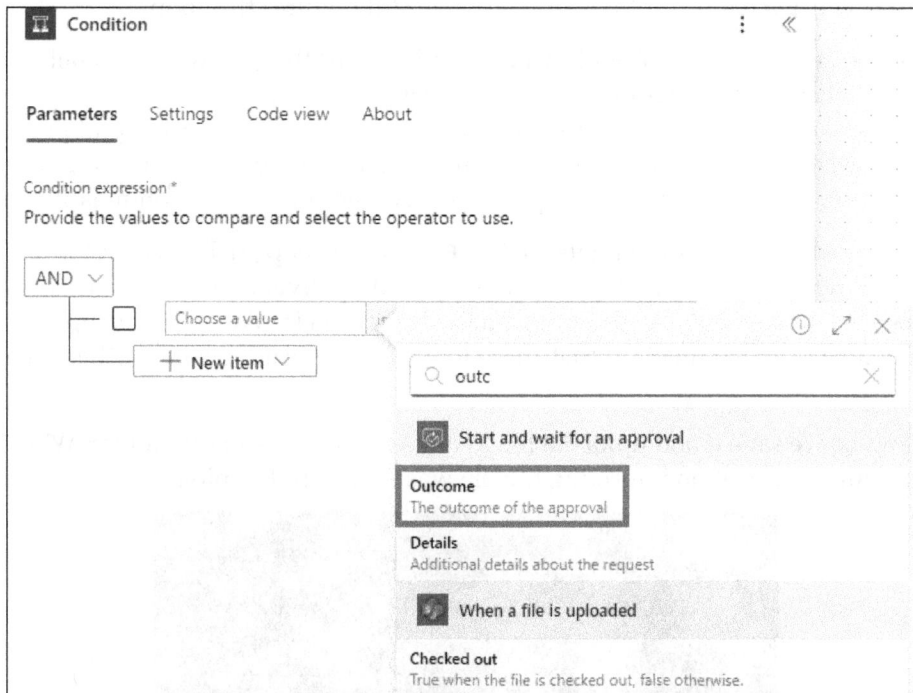

Figure 14.35: Determining if the request was approved

We then select **is equal to** from the drop-down menu and type **Approve** in the field. This configuration ensures that the condition will verify if the approver's response was an approval. If we had specified a custom response instead, we would enter the value of that response to check against it.

Finally, we configure one last action to notify the user that the file was approved, as shown:

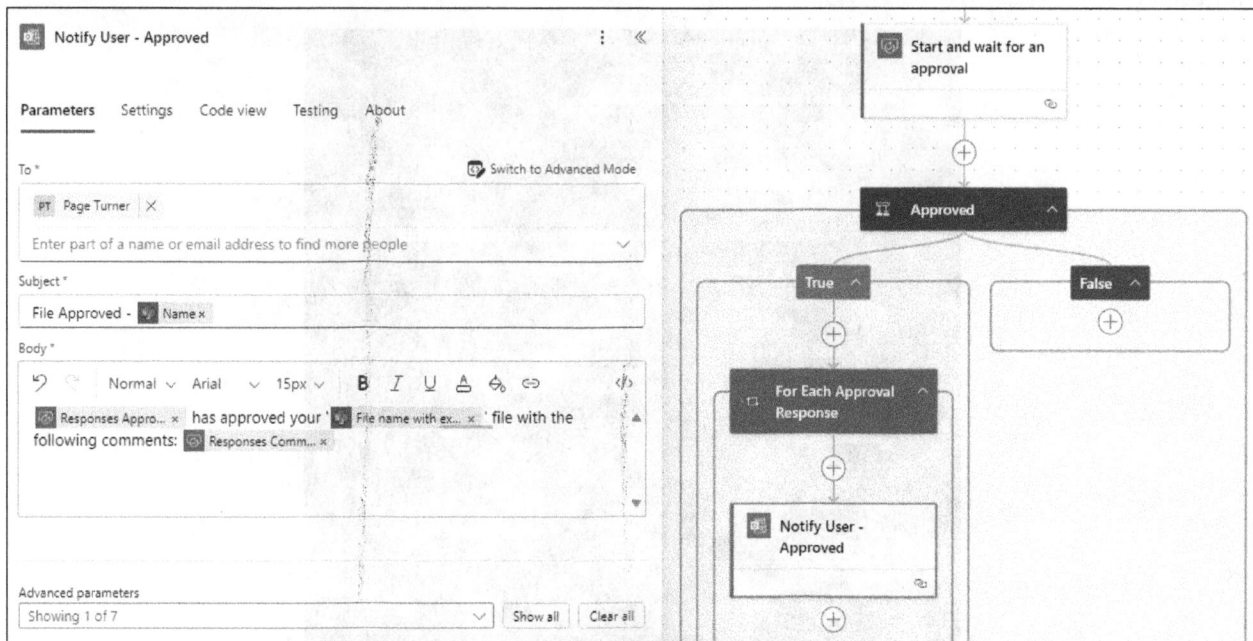

Figure 14.36: Sending a completion notification to the user

As you set up the approval flow, you will notice that a **For Each** loop is automatically created. This occurs because we selected the display name of the approver in the email notification. Since an approval request can be sent to multiple users, Power Automate needs to iterate through all the responses. In our specific case, the approval flow is designed to halt as soon as the first user responds, ensuring that only one response will be processed within this **For Each** loop, but Power Automate still requires this loop.

The **For Each** loop is a powerful tool within Power Automate that allows for detailed management of responses, especially when dealing with multiple approvers. By iterating through each response, it ensures that no input is overlooked, providing a comprehensive mechanism for capturing and processing approvals efficiently. This feature becomes particularly useful in more complex scenarios where approvals from several individuals are required, as it maintains the integrity and accuracy of the decision-making process.

Understanding the functionality and benefits of the **For Each** loop in Power Automate is essential for designing robust approval workflows that are capable of handling diverse and dynamic approval scenarios. It not only streamlines the process but also provides a reliable method for ensuring that approvals are managed accurately and effectively. Not to mention that these loops can be used in many other scenarios outside of approvals.

Time to test our flow, so we save it and upload a file to our specified SharePoint folder. Within a few seconds, we receive the first email notification informing the file was successfully uploaded:

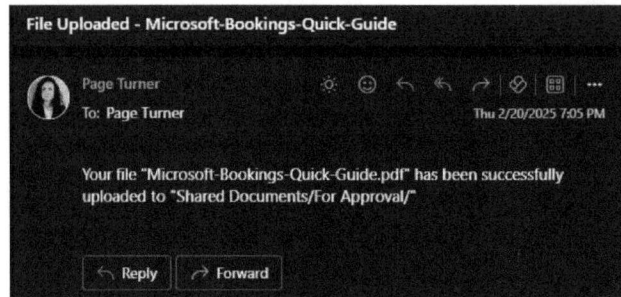

Figure 14.37: First email notification

Straight after, the approval is triggered, and we soon receive an approval request containing all the details we configured as follows:

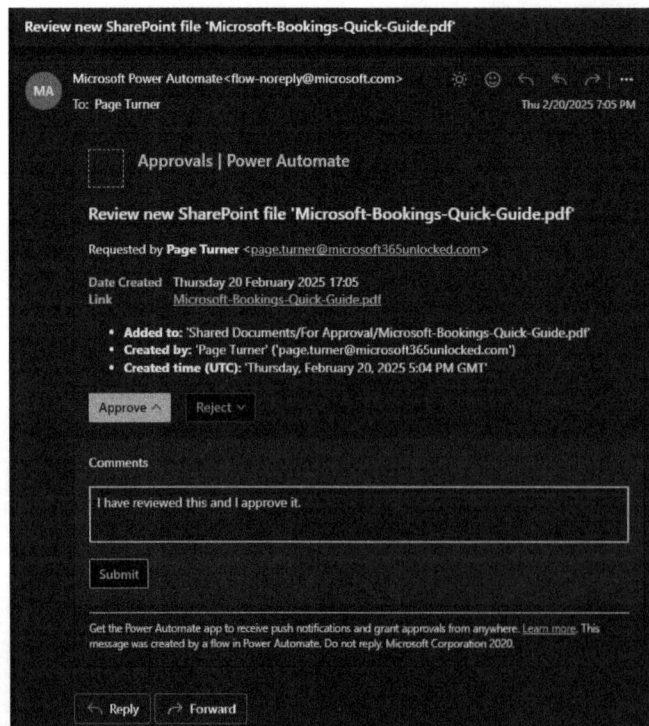

Figure 14.38: Approval request message

The user can click on either **Approve** or **Reject**. Upon doing so, a text box appears, enabling the approver to provide additional comments. These comments can be invaluable in certain cases as they offer insight into the reasoning behind the decision, especially useful for rejections. Besides responding to the request by email, users can also navigate to the **Approvals** section in the Power Automate portal, where they will find all their approval requests as shown:

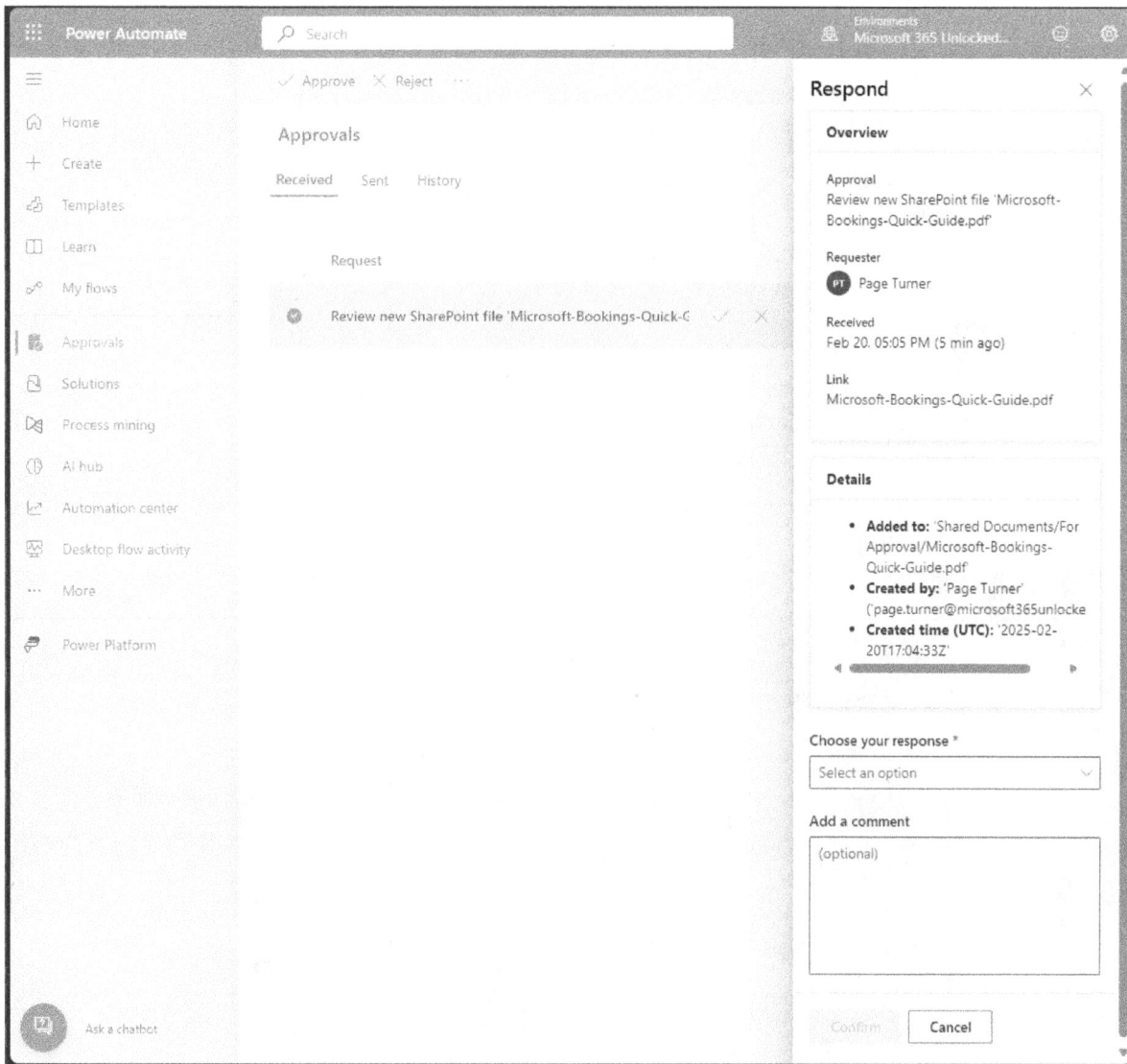

Figure 14.39: Reviewing a request in the portal

Once the response is submitted, the flow continues. Since we approved the request, the user receives a notification informing them of the file's approval, as follows:

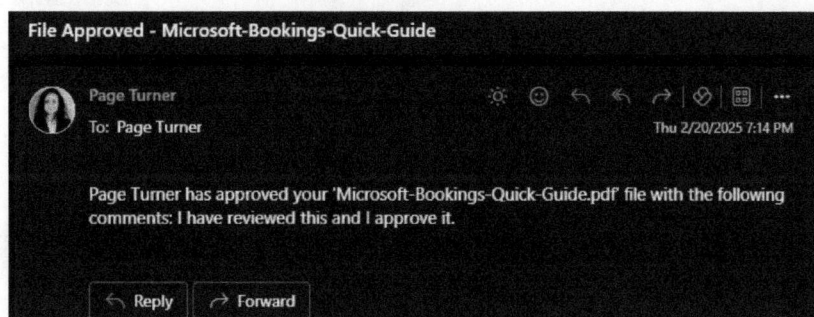

Figure 14.40: Final email notification

This notification is a key step in keeping users informed about the status of their submissions, fostering transparency and prompt communication.

The next steps involve configuring the actions that the flow would take if the request were rejected and adding error handling mechanisms to ensure the process runs smoothly even when issues arise, which we will be covering next.

Please do keep in mind email throttling if your flow will trigger thousands of emails in a short period of time.

Advanced techniques

This section explores advanced techniques that can be used to maximize the efficiency and capabilities of your Power Automate workflows. These techniques will enable you to optimize flow performance, enhance data handling, and implement more complex automation scenarios with precision.

Run history

Run history, or flow history, in Power Automate, is a log of all the executions of a flow, which helps monitor, debug, and optimize workflows. Each time a flow is triggered, detailed information is recorded, including start time, end time, status, actions taken, and their result.

To access it, navigate to the Power Automate portal, select the flow you want to review and find the **Run history** section in the details pane:

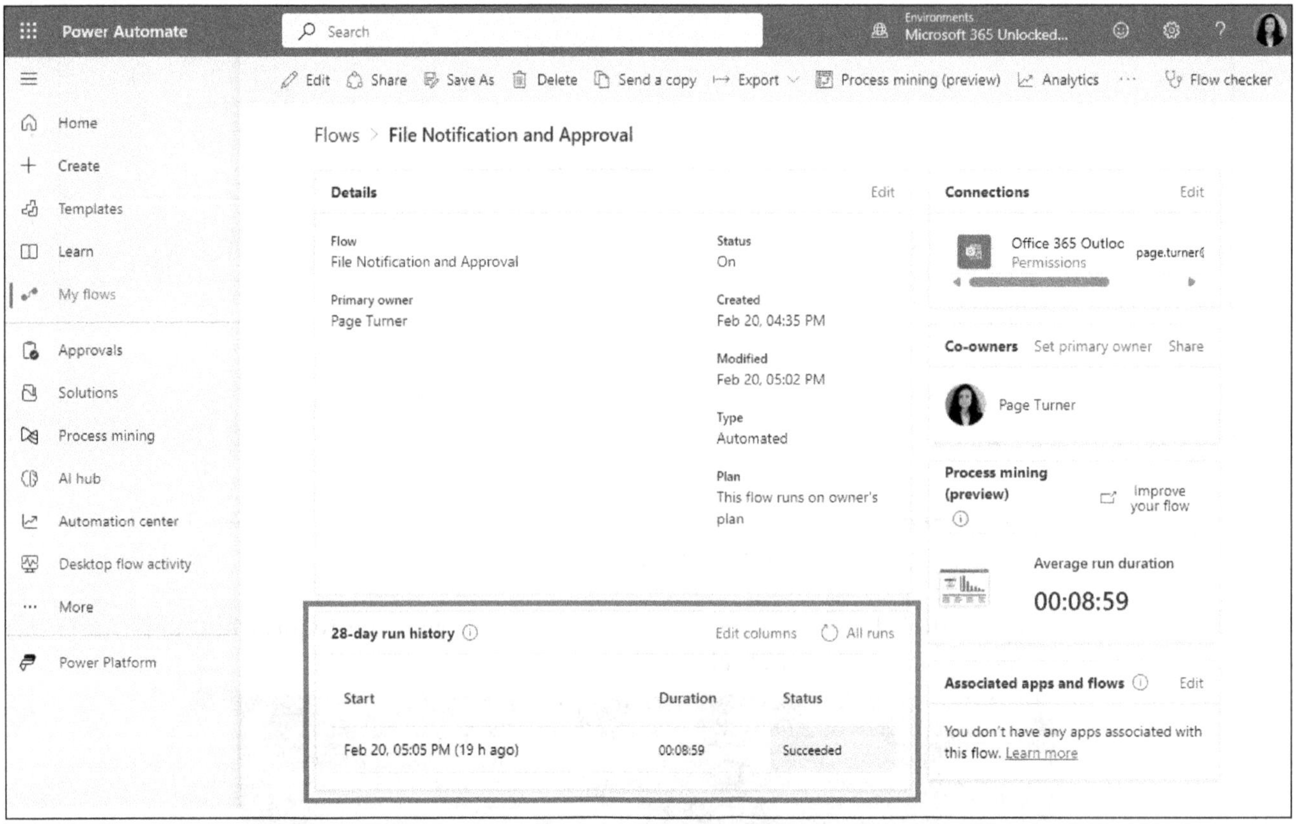

Figure 14.41: A flow's run history

Straightaway, you can see some of the last runs for this flow in the last 28 days, including their start date and time, their duration, and their status. By clicking on **All runs**, you can easily filter by different flow runs, such as all the failed runs, canceled runs, etc.:

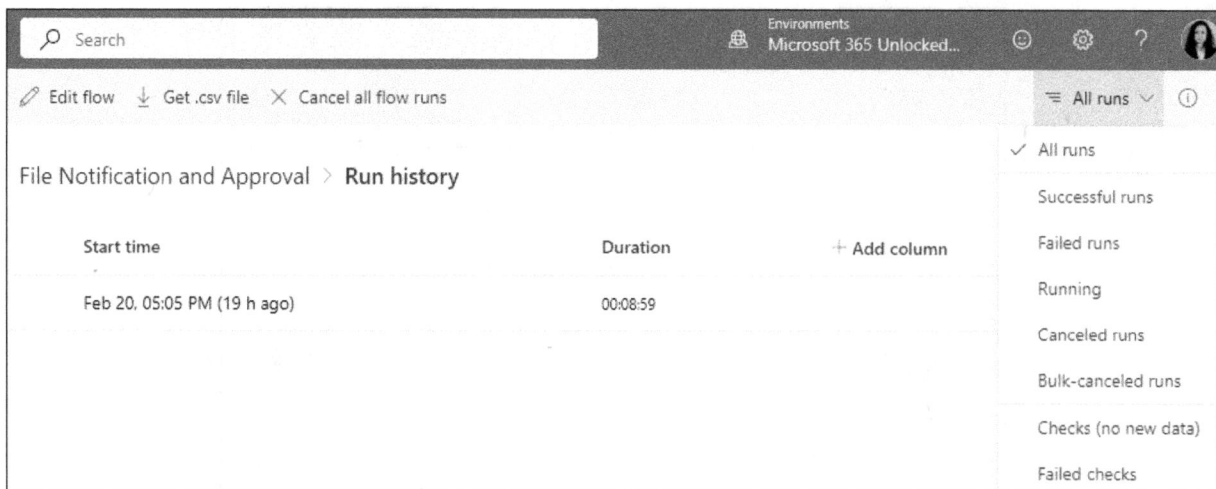

Figure 14.42: All runs of a flow in the last 28 days

A flow's run history is primarily useful for debugging and troubleshooting. By clicking on the **Start time** of any run, you can see all the steps the flow went through, including exactly what was done in each step as we saw when testing our previous flows.

Additionally, you can use the run history to track flow usage, performance, and success rates over time, as well as maintain a record of all actions for accountability and traceability.

Note: **Power Automate will only keep 28 days' worth of runs. You can, however, manually export their results to a CSV file.**

Variables

In Power Automate, variables are fundamental components that enable the storage and manipulation of data within your workflows. They can hold various types of information such as numbers, text strings, arrays, and objects, making them versatile tools for dynamic automation scenarios. Variables are crucial for intermediate storage and for tracking the state of data as you progress through your workflow. They allow for greater flexibility in handling data, enabling you to reference and manipulate information multiple times without resorting to external data sources. This can simplify complex workflows by reducing the need for redundant actions and enhancing manageability. Variables retain their values throughout the workflow, ensuring consistent availability of data across different triggers and actions. They allow for conditional logic and loops based on variable values, facilitating more precise control over workflow execution.

By storing repeated values in variables, you can minimize redundant actions, leading to cleaner and more efficient workflows. Variables enable advanced data manipulation techniques such as concatenation, splitting, and mathematical operations, expanding the functional capabilities of your workflows. However, overuse of variables can lead to increased complexity in workflow design, making it harder to maintain and troubleshoot. Storing large amounts of data in variables can consume significant memory, potentially impacting performance. Incorrect handling of variables can lead to data integrity issues, especially in workflows involving multiple concurrent runs.

Creating a variable is straightforward. If we search for **variable** when creating a new action, we can see all the options we have around variables:

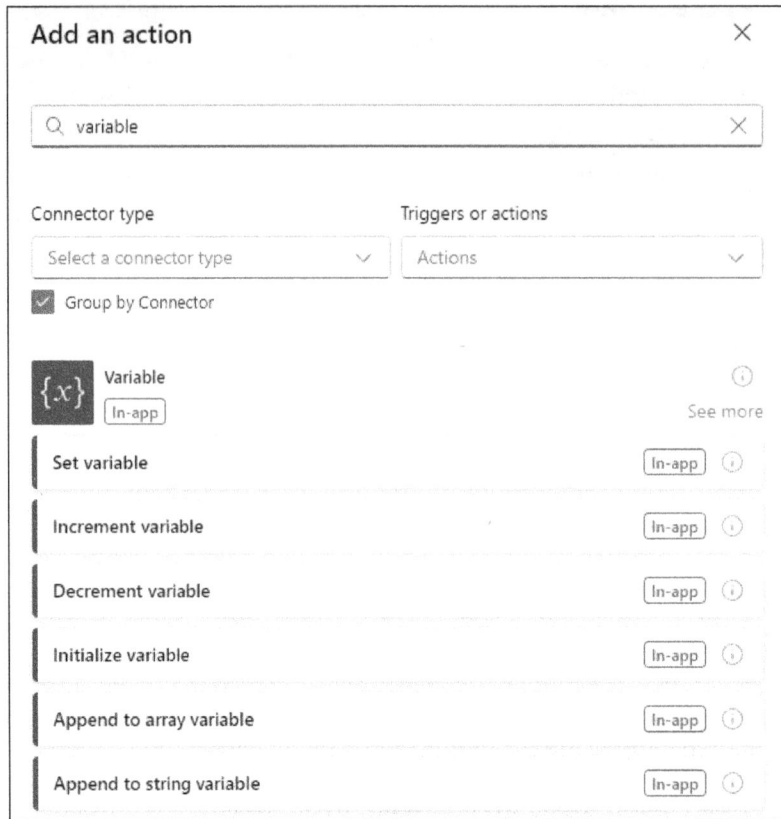

Figure 14.43: Variable actions

To start with, we use the **Initialize variable** action. Next, we name the action, name our variable, and choose the type of data it will hold (Boolean, Integer, Float, String, Object, or Array) and the value we want to store. The value can be something from any previous step in the flow or something defined by us. In this example, we use the expression `utcNow()` to store the current date and time in UTC format:

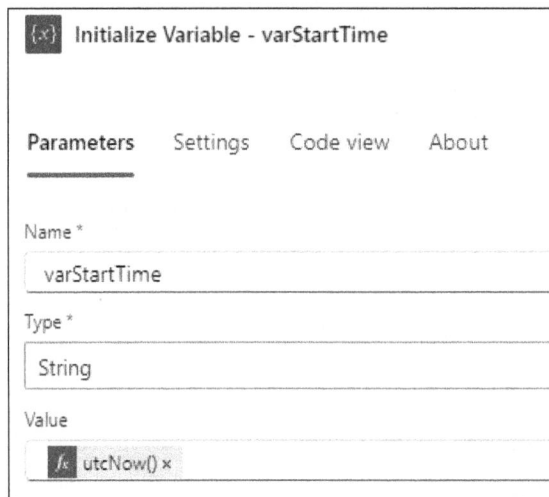

Figure 14.44: Initializing a new variable

If we run a quick test, we can see that the value was correctly stored in the variable. Now, we can use this variable wherever we want in the flow, such as recording in a SharePoint list the time the flow started:

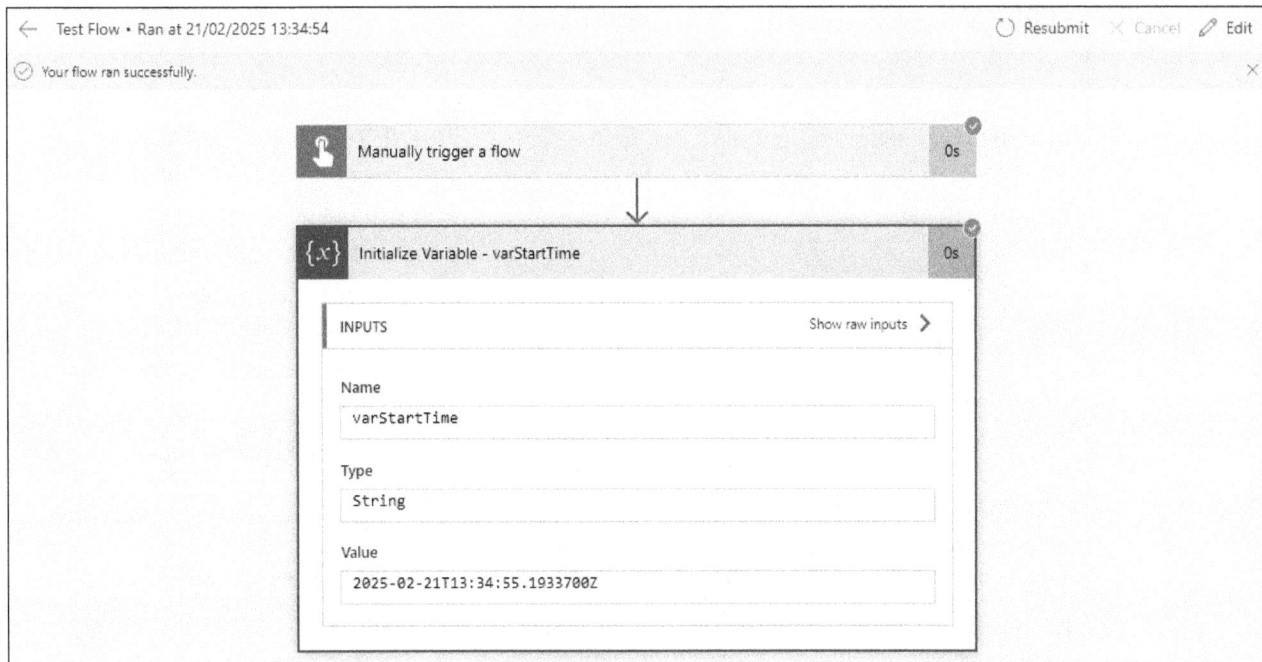

Figure 14.45: Testing the variable action

Expressions

When building a flow in Power Automate, you can easily start adding a trigger and actions, and then passing data between them using dynamic content. However, in many cases, more complex operations are required. This might include performing calculations, transforming data, or accessing, converting, and comparing values. To achieve these tasks, **expressions** can be utilized.

In Power Automate, expressions are a collection of functions designed to facilitate data retrieval and manipulation. By leveraging expressions, you can create dynamic and flexible workflows that adapt to various scenarios. Expressions can be used for a wide range of purposes, such as extracting specific data from a string, performing mathematical calculations, transforming data formats, and making decisions based on conditional logic. Expressions enable you to create highly customized workflows that can handle a variety of data manipulation requirements, ultimately enhancing the functionality and capability of your automated processes.

However, be careful when using expressions. Overuse or misuse of expressions can lead to increased complexity in your workflow design, making it harder to maintain and troubleshoot. Additionally, complex expressions can be difficult to understand and manage, especially for those who are not familiar with the syntax and logic used in Power Automate. Proper documentation and clear naming conventions are essential to ensure that your expressions are easily understandable and maintainable.

To get started with expressions, you first need to understand the basic syntax and structure of expressions. Start by identifying the specific data manipulation or transformation you need in your workflow. For instance, if you need to format dates or perform calculations, you can use date and time functions such as **formatDateTime()**, **addToTime()**, or **subtractFromTime()**. These functions allow you to adjust and format date values dynamically, enabling more precise control over date-related data within your workflows.

Here are a few examples of logical expressions you can also use:

Expression	Description	Example
and	Takes two arguments and returns *true* if both arguments, which must be Booleans, are true.	This expression returns **false**: `and(greater(1, 10), equals(0, 0))`
or	Takes two Boolean arguments and returns **true** if either is true.	This expression returns **true**: `or(greater(1, 10), equals(0, 0))`
equals	Returns **true** if two values are equal.	For example, if parameter1 is **someValue**, this expression returns **true**: `equals(parameters('parameter1'), 'someValue')`
less	Takes two arguments and returns **true** if the first argument is less than the second argument. The supported types are integer, float, and string.	This expression returns **true**: `less(10, 100)`
lessOrEquals	Takes two arguments and returns **true** if the first argument is less than or equal to the second argument.	This expression returns **true**: `lessOrEquals(10, 10)`
greater	Takes two arguments and returns **true** if the first argument is greater than the second argument.	This expression returns **false**: `greater(10, 10)`
greaterOrEquals	Takes two arguments and returns **true** if the first argument is greater than or equal to the second argument.	This expression returns **false**: `greaterOrEquals(10,100)`
empty	Returns **true** if the object, array, or string is empty.	This expression returns **true**: `empty('')`
not	Returns the opposite of a boolean value.	This expression returns **true**: `not(contains('200 Success', 'Fail'))`
if	Returns a specific value if the expression results in **true** or **false**.	This expression returns **"yes"**: `if(equals(1, 1), 'yes', 'no')`

Table 14.2: Examples of logical expressions in Power Automate

Date and time functions

Here is an example to illustrate how to use an expression in Power Automate. Suppose we want to calculate the date two weeks from today and format it in **day/month/year** format. In this example, let us use a variable named **var2Weeks**. We configure it as a **String**, and under **Value**, we click on **fx** so we can enter our expression:

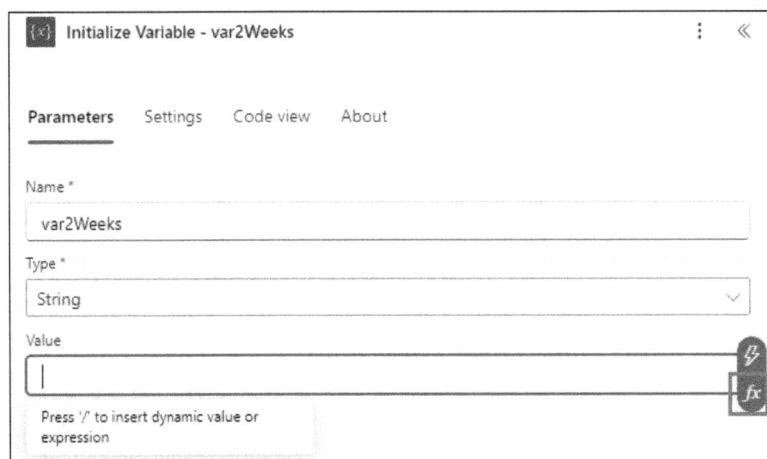

Figure 14.46: Using an expression as he value for a variable

The expression composer window opens, and it provides a user-friendly environment that helps streamline the process of building and testing expressions:

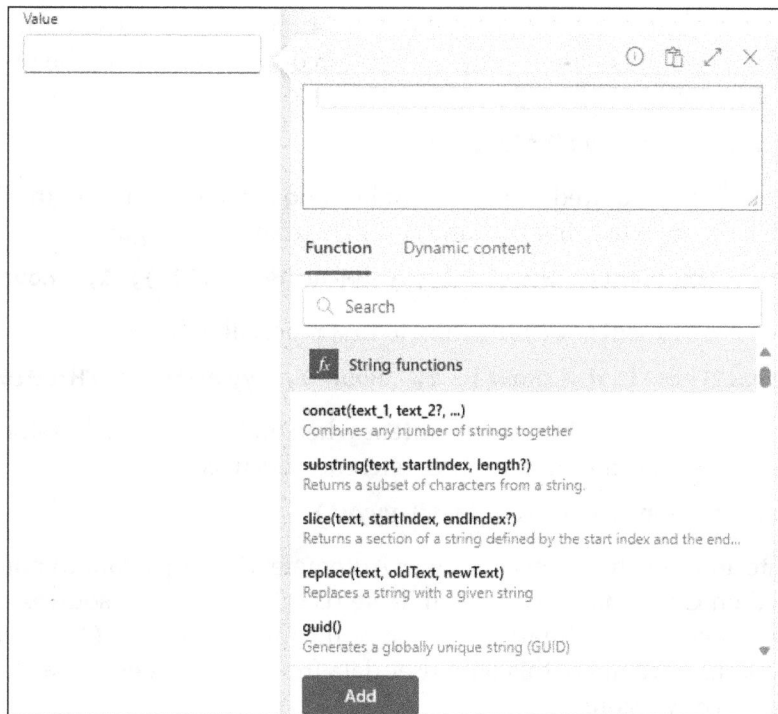

Figure 14.47: Expression composer window

The window is divided into several sections to help users efficiently create and understand expressions. The top text box is where you write or paste your expression. Below this, tabs for **Functions** and **Dynamic content** offer a comprehensive library of available functions and elements to incorporate into your expression. Using the **Function** tab, you can browse through different categories of functions like string manipulation, date and time, logical operations, and more. When you enter a function in the formula bar, you see a pop-up with syntax suggestions. It tells you all the parameters it expects, their format, and if they are mandatory or not:

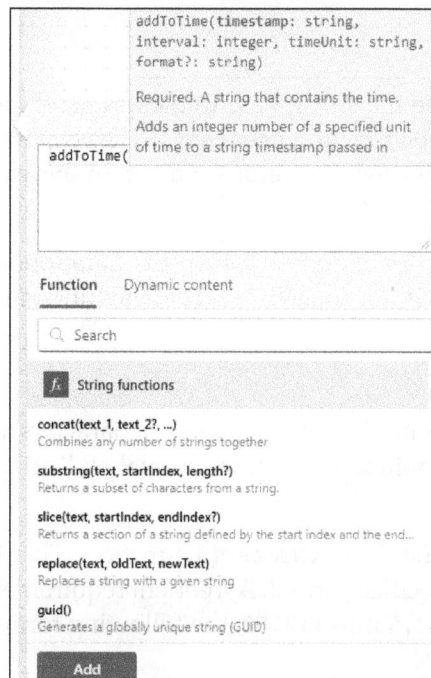

Figure 14.48: Expression syntax helper

The **Dynamic content** tab helps incorporate elements from previous steps in the flow, ensuring that expressions are dynamic and responsive to the data being processed.

For this example, we use the following expression to add 14 days to the current date and then format the result in the specified date format. Looking at the description of this function in the previous screenshot, we can build our function as follows:

```
addToTime(utcNow(), 14, 'Day', 'dd/MM/yyyy')
```

Since the format parameter is not required, we can exclude it and format our date in the timestamp parameter. In the following example, we are retrieving the time and date from 1 hour ago:

```
subtractFromTime(formatDateTime(utcNow(), 'yyyy-MM-ddTHH:00:00'), 1, 'Hour')
```

We could also move the **formatDateTime()** function to first place, like this:

```
formatDateTime((subtractFromTime(utcNow(), 1, 'Hour'), 'yyyy-MM-ddTHH:00:00')
```

To reference other variables, we use the **Dynamic content** when building our expression, or we can manually type their name in the expression using the variables reference, such as:

```
formatDateTime(variables('var2Weeks'), 'dd-MM-yyyy')
```

When working with date and time functions in Power Automate, it is important to note that these functions frequently operate based on Coordinated **Universal Time** (**UTC**). Many data sources exchange information with Power Automate using the UTC format. Additionally, the function **utcNow()** returns the current time in UTC format as we have seen. To compare this with user data from the **Eastern Time Zone**, you must employ an appropriate formula for conversion:

```
convertFromUtc(utcNow(), 'Eastern Standard Time', 'dd-MM-yyyy hh:mm tt')
```

Logical functions

These functions are employed for handling conditions, comparing values, and performing other logic-based evaluations. They are commonly referred to as **If** statements. In the following example, an expression evaluates whether **15** is greater than **9** and outputs the corresponding string. This example also demonstrates the use of multiple functions within a single expression, specifically combining the **if()** and **greater()** logical functions.

```
If(greater(15, 9), 'Yes', 'No')
```

The outcome of this expression will be the string **Yes**. To comprehend the expression, it is crucial to analyze it from the innermost part outward. The function **greater(15, 9)** evaluates whether **15** is greater than **9** and returns **true** if the condition is met; otherwise, it returns **false**. In this case, since **15** is indeed greater than **9**, the function returns **true**.

Given that the answer is **true**, the **If** function will return the data following the first comma, which in this instance is the string **Yes**. Conversely, if the answer is **false**, the function will return the string **No**.

String functions

String (text) functions are utilized to modify strings, locate characters within a string, format strings, and perform other operations. Text manipulation is a fundamental skill frequently employed to format or alter data received from other sources.

An example of a string function is the **formatNumber()** function. This function is capable of converting a number into a string according to a specified format. A frequent requirement is to format a number as currency. For instance, to convert the number **12.5** into **$12.50**, the following formula can be utilized:

```
formatNumber(12.5,'C')
```

The **C** represents the currency numeric format string. We can also use **C2** instead where the number denotes the number of decimal places to return. If you wish to display the number as currency using the US Dollar symbol, there is an optional parameter that allows the locale to be specified:

```
formatNumber(12.5637,'C2','en-US')
```

This formula returns **$12.56**.

Next, consider using expressions to handle string manipulations. For example, you might need to extract a substring from a text value or concatenate multiple strings together. Functions such as **substring()**, **concat()**, and **replace()** can help you achieve these tasks effectively.

When incorporating text into a Power Automate expression, it is necessary to utilize single quotation marks (**'**) at both the beginning and end of each string. For instance, if you wish to concatenate the string **Today is** with the value from a variable that returns a date, we would employ the **concat()** function as follows:

```
concat('Today is ', variables('varToday'))
```

Paying attention to these nuances enhances your efficiency when dealing with expressions.

Math functions

Math functions let you add, subtract, multiply, and more. They can find the smallest or largest number in a set or generate a random number within a specified range. For example, to get a random number from **1** to **100**, use this expression:

```
rand(1, 100)
```

It is important to note that there are separate functions for adding numbers (**add()**) and subtracting numbers (**sub()**). Unlike many formula languages that use negative numbers for subtraction, Power Automate does not. To add two numbers together, the following expression is used:

```
add(15, 9)
```

This operation will yield a result of 24. Should you wish to add three numbers, an additional function must be incorporated as follows:

```
add(add(15, 9), 72)
```

As previously demonstrated, nesting functions help achieve desired results but can make expressions harder to read, understand, and troubleshoot.

Error handling

Error handling in Power Automate is a critical aspect of creating robust and reliable workflows. It involves implementing mechanisms to manage exceptions and ensure that workflows run smoothly even when unexpected issues occur. Error handling can be used to catch errors, log them, notify relevant stakeholders, and take corrective actions to prevent workflow failures. By incorporating error handling, you can improve the resilience of your workflows, making them more dependable and less prone to interruptions.

Using error handling in Power Automate is essential for several reasons. Firstly, it helps maintain the integrity of your workflows by addressing potential issues that could disrupt the process. This is particularly important in complex workflows involving multiple steps and dependencies, where a single error can have a cascading effect. Secondly, error handling enhances the user experience by providing clear and actionable feedback when something goes wrong, allowing users to quickly identify and resolve issues. Finally, it contributes to the overall efficiency of your automated processes by reducing downtime and minimizing the need for manual intervention.

The advantages of using error handling in Power Automate are numerous. It ensures that workflows continue to operate smoothly in the face of errors, thereby maintaining productivity and minimizing disruptions. Error handling also provides a structured way to manage exceptions, making it easier to debug and troubleshoot workflows. Additionally, it allows you to implement fallback mechanisms and alternative actions, ensuring that critical tasks are completed even if the primary approach fails. This level of robustness is crucial for mission-critical workflows that must operate reliably under all conditions.

Going back to our workflow of approving a new document uploaded to a SharePoint library, what happens if the **Start and wait for an approval** action fails? We will not know about it until we receive an email from Power Automate stating our flow has failed, which might take a day or more.

The following figure shows our flow before error handling is added:

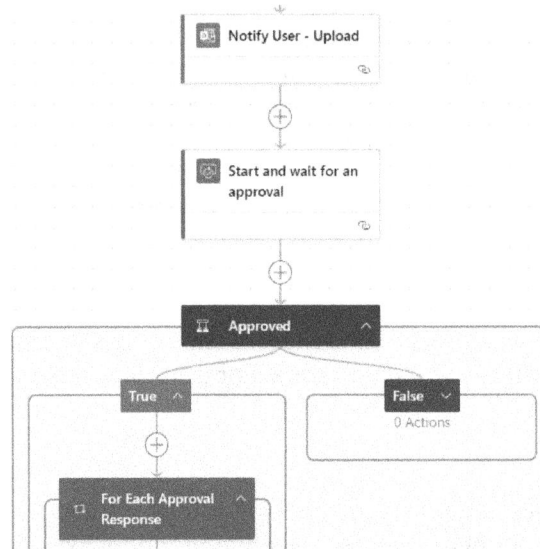

Figure 14.49: Flow without error handling

To add error handling to this action, we click on the + button right after the approval action to add a new action which will be our notification. As before, we could send a mobile notification, a Teams message, send an **HTTP POST** request to another application, etc. For this example, we will be sending an email notification, so we build that action and compose the email with as much detail as we want:

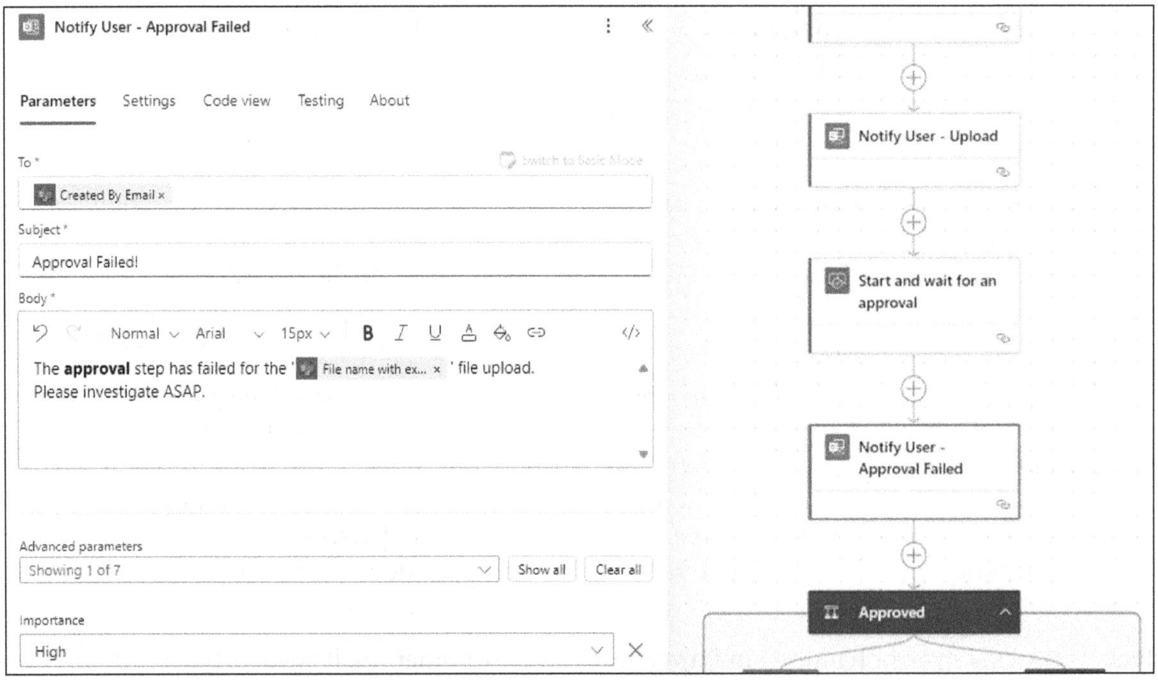

Figure 14.50: Adding a notification for failures

However, as is, the email notification will be sent only if the approval step is successful, as that is what Power Automate does by default. To validate and change this, we need to go to the **Settings** tab of our notification action. As you can see, this action only runs after and if the approval action is successful:

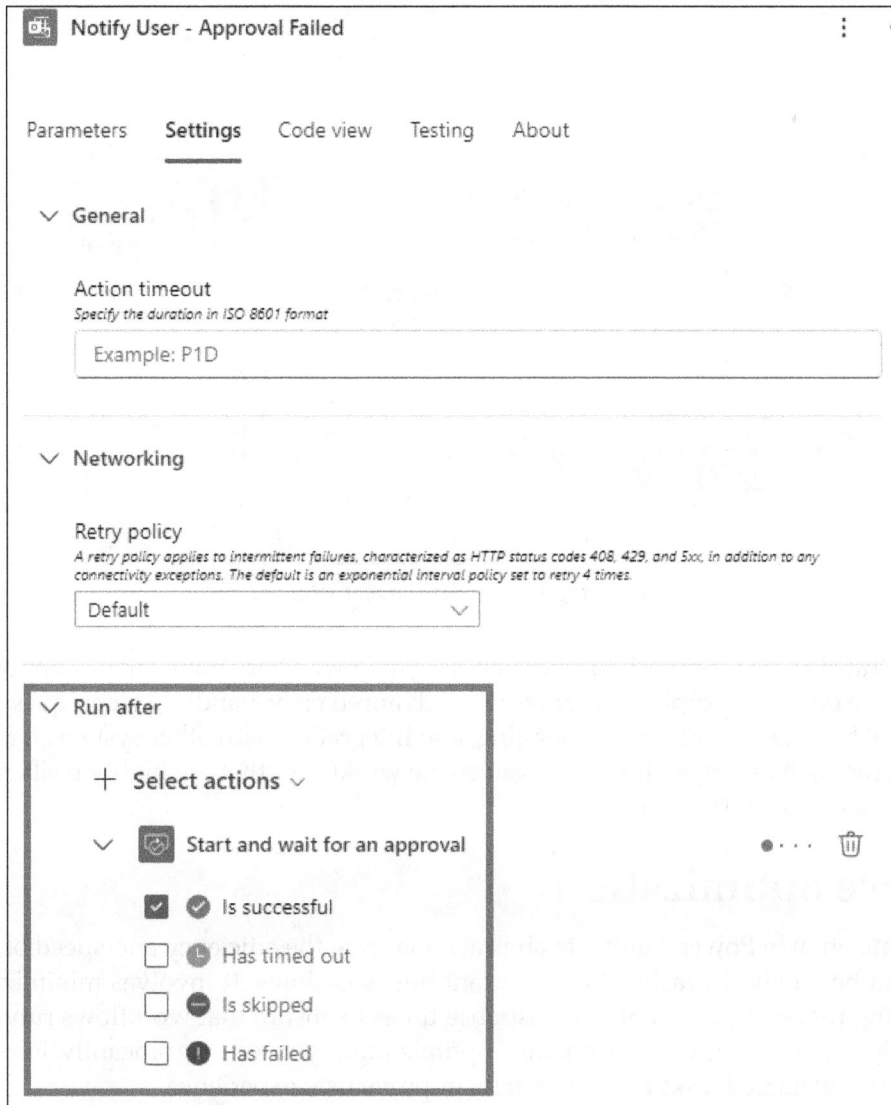

Figure 14.51: Configuring when to send the notification

This is not what we want. As such, we select both **Has timed out** and **Has failed**, and unselect **Is successful**. Now, in the flow, you will notice that this action is on its own branch with a yellow and red circle above it indicating that it only gets triggered if the approval action fails or times out for whatever reason:

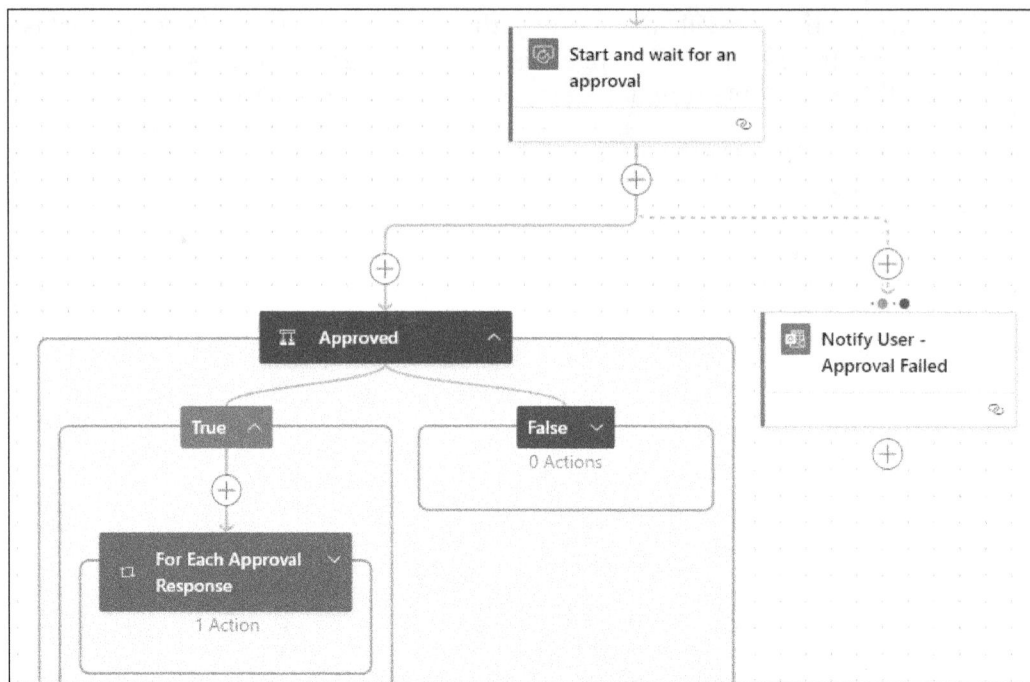

Figure 14.52: Email notification for failures

This example illustrates a basic approach to error handling in Power Automate, but it is important to note that error handling can be far more complex and powerful. Advanced error-handling techniques can include retry policies, conditional branching, custom error logging, and integration with other systems for automated issue resolution. By leveraging these capabilities, you can create workflows that are highly resilient and capable of handling a wide range of potential issues.

Performance optimization

Performance optimization in Power Automate aims at enhancing the efficiency and speed of your automated workflows and can be a critical practice for important business flows. It involves minimizing unnecessary actions, streamlining processes, and reducing response times to ensure that workflows run as smoothly and quickly as possible. By focusing on performance optimization, you can significantly improve the overall productivity of your automated tasks and potentially improve user experience.

One of the primary uses of performance optimization is to ensure that workflows execute within acceptable timeframes, particularly for processes that require real-time responsiveness or handle large volumes of data. Optimizing workflows can prevent bottlenecks and delays, ensuring that tasks are completed promptly and efficiently, potentially improving user experience. Additionally, performance optimization reduces the risk of timeouts and failures, which can disrupt business operations and require manual intervention.

Here is an example: suppose we have a table in an Excel file with 50,000 users in our company with all their details like name, department, email address, username, manager, and so on. Now, let us assume we need to retrieve all the users in the United Kingdom so we can send them all an email. We could load the entire list into Power Automate, then iterate through all the retrieved rows in the table and send an email to those users that match our criteria. However, this has two issues from a performance perspective:

- We are retrieving all the users from the list into Power Automate, instead of just those in the UK

- We are retrieving the entire list of attributes the table holds for each user instead of just the email address

By performing this filter instead of having Power Automate process unnecessary records, we could save a considerable amount of time and resources. So how do we achieve this? That will depend on the connector used and the data source. For this example, we use the **Filter Query** section to create an ODATA filter query that restricts the entries returned (based on the name of a table column and its value) and the **Select Query** section to specify which user properties (in this case table columns) we want to be returned:

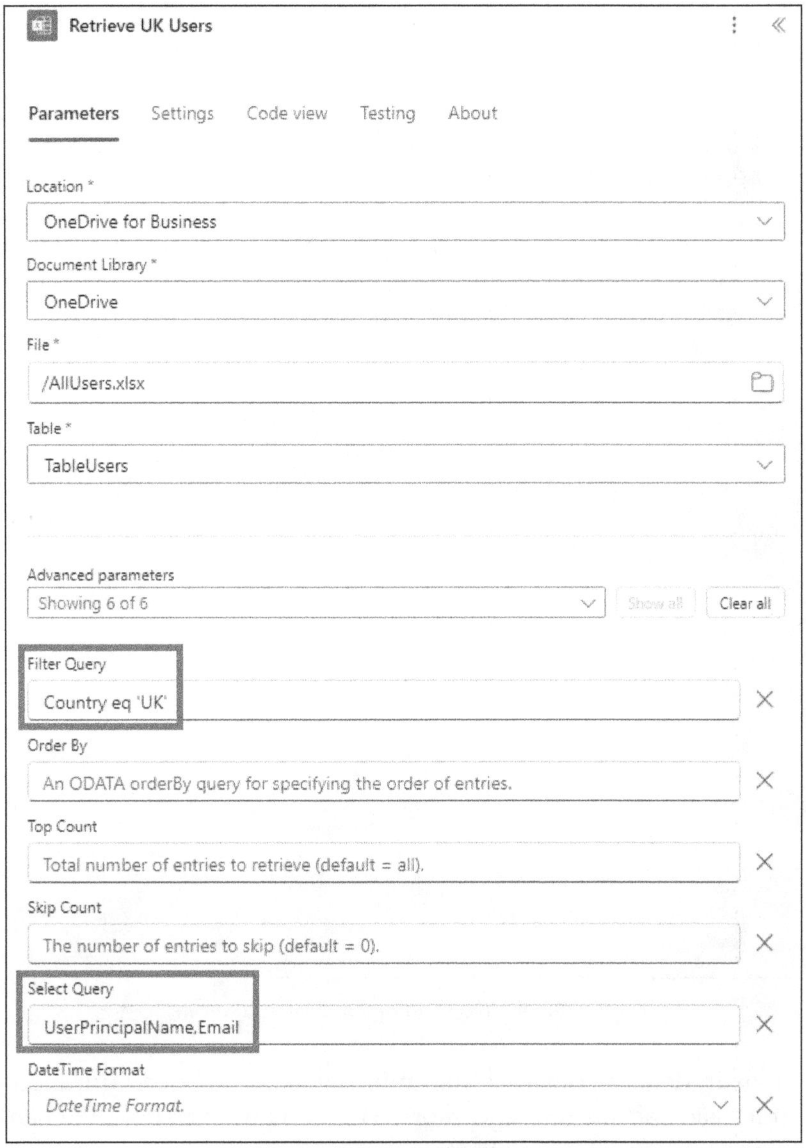

Figure 14.53: Filtering and selection queries

Another way of optimizing a flow is by using the **process mining** feature in Power Automate which tells you what actions in your flow are executing the most and what actions are taking the most time in order to gain insights to improve your flow. By leveraging process mining, you can visualize your flow, identify patterns, pinpoint inefficiencies, and uncover opportunities for optimization. This feature enables you to map out the entire flow lifecycle, from start to finish, providing a comprehensive view of how tasks are performed and where bottlenecks may occur. These insights are generated based on your flow runs in the last 28 days.

In the following figure, we can see all the steps involved in the flow we created earlier the number of times each step ran (in this case they are all 1 since all steps run in sequence and there are no other paths with different actions), the average duration, and much more:

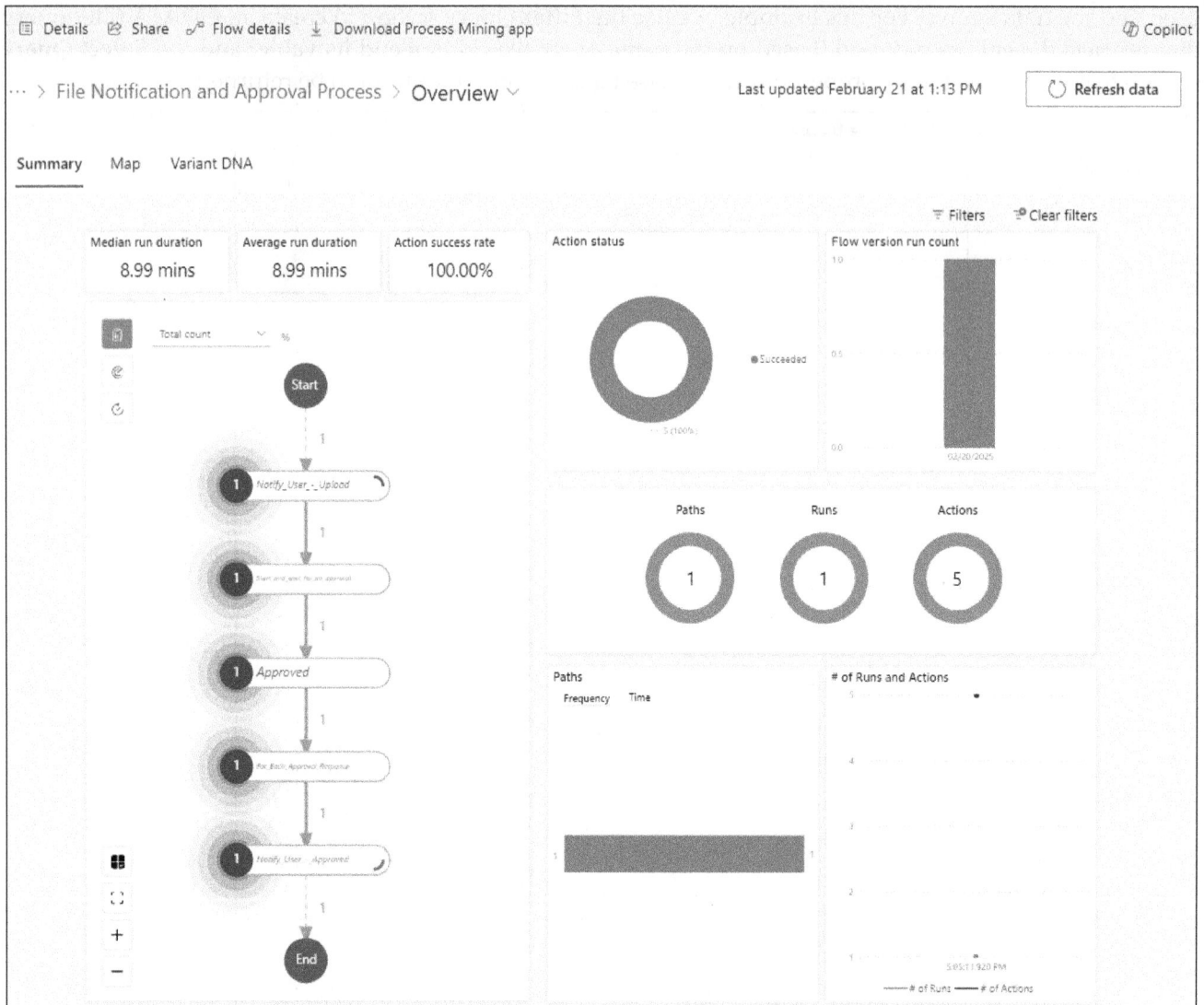

Figure 14.54: Process mining in Power Automate

The map allows us to look in detail at the total/minimum/maximum/mean duration of each action in our flow, the number of times each action ran, and more. With this information, we can easily identify what actions are taking the longest to run so we can try to optimize them for the flow itself, as shown:

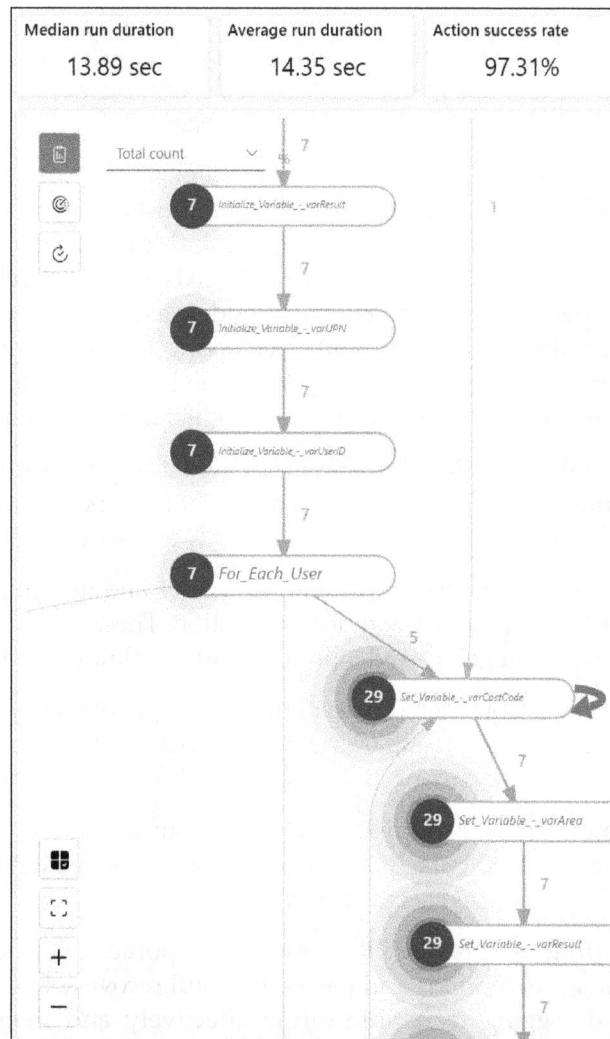

Figure 14.55: Process mining map

Another key technique for optimizing workflow performance is **parallel processing**, which involves executing multiple actions simultaneously, rather than sequentially. This technique can significantly reduce overall workflow execution time, especially for tasks that are independent of each other.

First, you need to identify independent actions, those actions or branches of your workflow that can run in parallel without dependencies. Examples include data retrieval from different sources or parallel approval processes. Then, configure parallel branches by using the **Add a parallel branch** option (instead of **Add an action**) to create multiple branches within your flow. Each branch can contain actions that will be executed simultaneously. Finally, ensure that parallel branches are synchronized, if necessary, by making sure the action after the branches waits for all branches to complete before executing.

For example, suppose you need to retrieve data from multiple APIs. You can:

- Create parallel branches, each responsible for calling a different API.
- Process the data retrieved from each API independently within their respective branches.
- Use a *join* action to combine the results and continue with the next steps in your workflow.

Best practices

To make the most of Power Automate, it is essential to follow best practices when creating workflows. Adhering to these guidelines will help ensure that your workflows are efficient, maintainable, and scalable, as follows:

- **Clear naming conventions**: Use descriptive and consistent naming conventions for flows and actions within your workflows. A clear naming structure makes it easier to understand the purpose and functionality of each component, especially when collaborating with team members or revisiting a workflow after some time.

- **Documentation**: Documentation is a crucial aspect of building Power Automate flows as it provides a clear understanding of the workflow's purpose, structure, and functionality. Proper documentation acts as a comprehensive guide, detailing each step and decision made during the flow creation process. This practice not only aids in maintaining clarity and consistency but also facilitates troubleshooting and modifications. When team members or new users need to review or update a flow, having well-documented workflows ensures continuity and reduces the time spent deciphering complex logic. Moreover, documentation serves as an invaluable resource for training, onboarding, and knowledge transfer within an organization, ultimately contributing to the overall efficiency and scalability of automated processes.

- **Regular testing and monitoring**: Regularly test your workflows to ensure they run smoothly and as expected. Implement monitoring tools to track the performance and identify any issues that may arise. This proactive approach helps in maintaining the reliability and efficiency of your automated processes.

- **Utilize templates and patterns**: Leverage existing templates and design patterns available within the Power Automate community and Microsoft documentation. These resources provide valuable insights and examples that can help you get started, optimize your workflows, and avoid common pitfalls.

- **Optimize for performance**: Consider the performance implications of your workflows, especially when dealing with large volumes of data or complex processes. Use parallel processing, filtering, and other optimization techniques to enhance the efficiency of your workflows.

- **Secure and manage connections**: Ensure that all connections to external services and applications are secure and properly managed. Regularly review and update connection credentials, and limit access to sensitive data by using role-based access controls.

- **Implement error handling**: As previously covered, incorporate error-handling mechanisms within your workflows to manage exceptions and ensure graceful recovery from failures. Use retry policies, error notifications, and logging to handle errors effectively and maintain the integrity of your automated processes.

- **Leverage the Power Automate community**: Engage with the Power Automate community to share knowledge, ask questions, and learn from the experiences of others. The community is a valuable resource for discovering new techniques, troubleshooting issues, and staying updated with the latest features and best practices.

- **Regularly review run history**: Periodically reviewing the run history of your flows is crucial to ensure that they are functioning as intended. This practice allows you to identify and resolve any issues or inefficiencies promptly. It also provides insights into how often flows are being triggered, their success rates, and any potential bottlenecks in the process.

By following these best practices, you can create robust and reliable workflows that enhance productivity and streamline business processes. Power Automate's flexibility and extensive capabilities allow you to automate a wide range of tasks, making it a powerful tool for modern organizations.

Conclusion

In this chapter, we have explored the vast potential of Power Automate within Microsoft 365. From understanding licensing options to creating and optimizing workflows, you now have the knowledge and tools to start harnessing the power of automation. By implementing Power Automate, you can streamline processes, enhance productivity, and drive efficiency across your organization.

In the next chapter, we will continue our journey by diving into Power Apps, a versatile tool that allows users to build custom applications for their business needs without extensive coding knowledge.

CHAPTER 15

Power Apps

Introduction

In this chapter, we will explore the fundamentals and core functionalities of Power Apps, a powerful tool that allows users to build low-code custom applications suitable for their business requirements. The content in this chapter is meant to equip the reader with the essential knowledge and skills to begin unlocking the full potential of Power Apps.

Structure

This chapter covers the following topics:

- About Power Apps
- Getting started with Power Apps
- Environments overview
- Application types
- Model-driven apps
- Canvas apps

Objectives

By the end of this chapter, readers will have a clear understanding of Power App functionality and what it can be used for, the differences between the types of applications and environments, be able to effectively create a simple canvas application leveraging Power Apps capabilities.

About Power Apps

Part of Power Platform, Power Apps is a powerful tool and a data platform that enables users to build custom apps tailored to specific needs. The creation of applications that run seamlessly on web browsers, mobile devices, and tablets is possible with Power Apps without the need to have extensive coding knowledge.

Power Apps integrates with other components of the Power Platform, such as Power BI and Power Automate. By connecting Power Apps with Power BI, users can embed interactive dashboards and analytics directly within their applications, empowering decision-making with real-time data insights. Integration with Power Automate allows users to automate workflows and business processes, enabling apps to trigger actions, approvals, and notifications across various services and platforms. This synergy between Power Apps, Power BI, and Power Automate enables organizations to build comprehensive, data-driven solutions that streamline operations and foster greater collaboration.

At its core, Power Apps offers two main types of applications: canvas apps, an application type that focuses on design and user interface, and model-driven apps, an application type that focuses on data and processes. Choosing the right application type for your development depends on the data source to be used, the business requirements, and the desired outcomes.

An important feature of Power Apps is the ability to connect to various data sources. Data from multiple sources can be integrated into a single application, providing a unified view of information and making it easier to manage and utilize data effectively.

Power Apps also includes a powerful formula language, similar to Excel, which allows the addition of logic and functionality to apps.

The use cases for Power Apps are vast. It can streamline business processes, boost productivity, and improve collaboration within an organization. For instance, a custom CRM system, a project management tool, or an expense tracker application can be created using Power Apps. The flexibility and ease of use make Power Apps a valuable tool for businesses of all sizes, helping them adapt quickly to changing needs and drive innovation.

At the time of writing this book, Microsoft provides access to Power Apps through the following Office 365 and Microsoft 365 subscriptions:

- **Office 365:** E1, E3, E5, G3, G5
- **Microsoft 365:** E3, E5, F3, G3, G5

Power Apps capabilities for Microsoft 365 help in extending the Office experience, as users can create applications based on Microsoft 365 data, using standard connectors.

It is important to mention that the Power Apps for Microsoft 365 plan does not provide the ability to use premium or custom connectors. It also provides limited access to Microsoft Dataverse (the built-in Power Platform data storage solution where you can store securely and manage data that is used by business applications).

Microsoft offers dedicated Power Apps licensing plans, such as Power Apps Premium, granting the ability to use premium and custom connectors.

Power Apps use rights are also included with select Dynamics 365 licenses.

Getting started with Power Apps

Power Apps platform can be accessed through the Power Apps website at **https://make.powerapps.com** or directly from the Microsoft 365 app launcher, at **https://www.microsoft365.com**, signing in with your Microsoft 365 credentials.

Once logged in, the Power Apps home screen provides a user-friendly interface where new apps can be created, and existing apps can be managed:

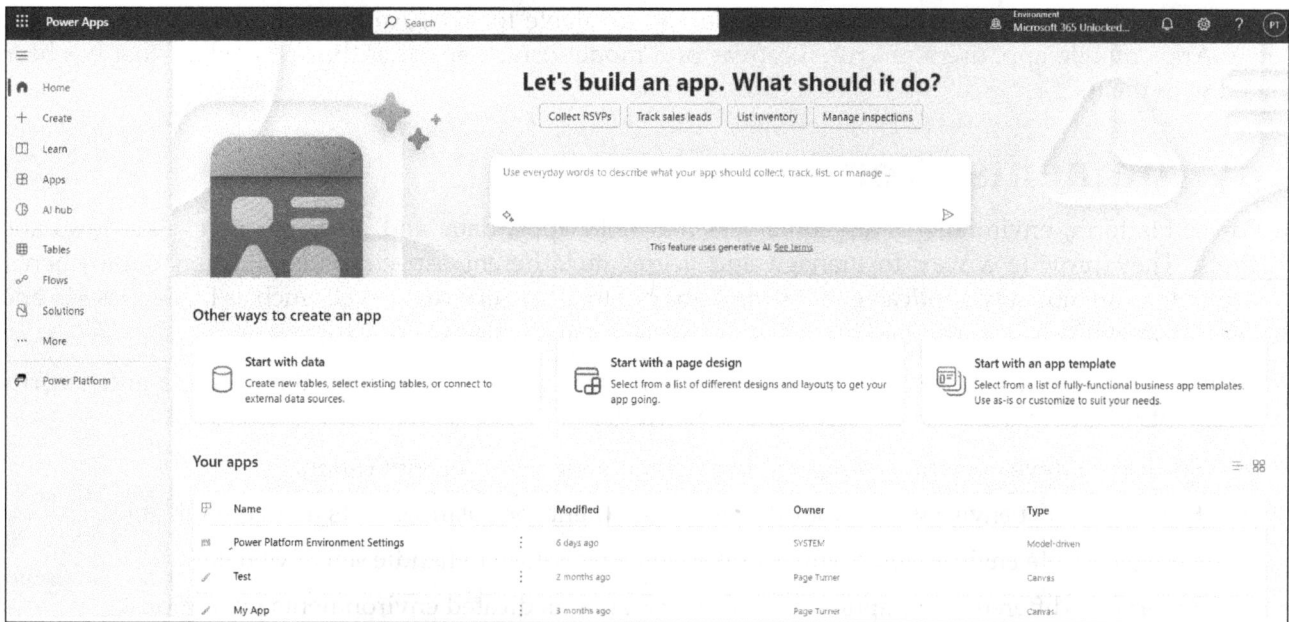

Figure 15.1: *Power Apps home page*

By clicking **Create** on the left-hand side menu of the screen, you will be presented with multiple options to start with our app creation, as shown in the following figure:

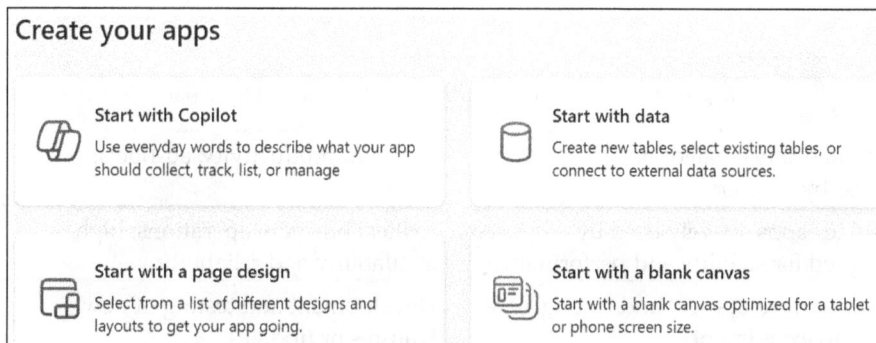

Figure 15.2: *App creation options*

Alternatively, you can start creating an application based on a predefined template provided by Microsoft:

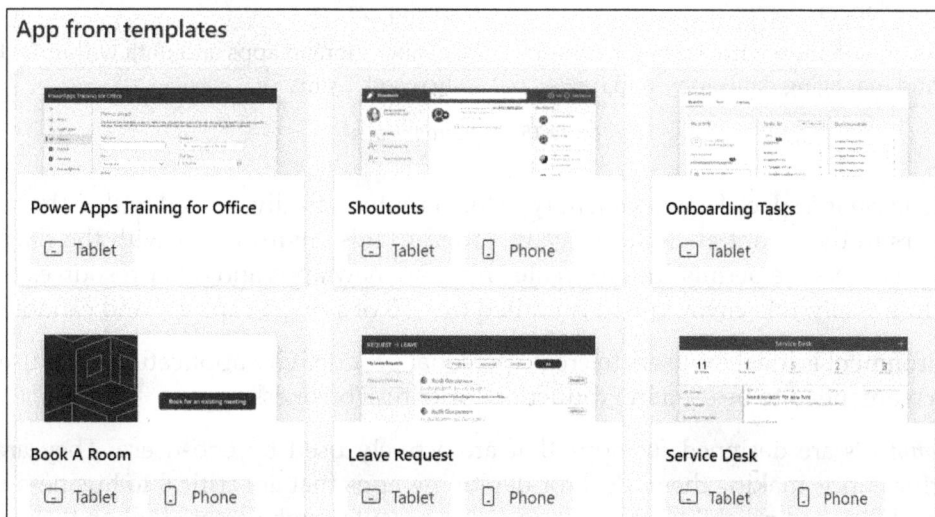

Figure 15.3: *App creation based on a template*

Power Apps can also be accessed via the mobile app available for iOS, Android, and Windows. With the Power Apps mobile app, users can run a canvas or a model-driven app that they created, or that has been shared with them.

Environments overview

In Power Platform, environments are containers that hold apps, data, and other resources like flows and chatbots. They provide a way to manage and segregate different aspects of application deployments. Environments are not only applicable to Power Apps but to other services as well, such as Dynamics 365 and Power Automate.

Environments can be used for multiple use cases and scenarios, depending on the business and security requirements of an organization. Typical scenarios include:

- Separating development, testing, and production versions of an application.
- Having distinct environments for different departments or business units in an organization.
- Using separate environments with appropriate permissions to handle sensitive data.
- Separating different geographical regions by creating dedicated environments per region.

Environment types

Understanding the different types of environments and their particularities is important for effective app management and governance. The following table lists the environment types currently available in Power Platform:

Environment type	Description	Use case	Environment lifespan
Default	Automatically created for each tenant, shared by all users	Personal productivity, ad-hoc app creation	Permanent
Production	Used for apps actively used by end-users, designed for stability and performance	Critical business operations, high availability and reliability	Permanent
Sandbox	Used for development and testing, safe space to experiment	Development and testing of new features or updates	Permanent
Trial	Temporary environment for exploring Power Apps features and Dataverse	Evaluation of Power Apps features	30 days
Developer	Dedicated space for individual developers	Building and testing apps by individual developers	Permanent
Dataverse for Teams	Team-specific environment for storing and managing data, apps, and flows	Collaboration on apps and data within Microsoft Teams	Permanent

Table 15.1: Environments

The *Default environment* is a special environment type that is automatically created within the tenant by Power Apps, and all users in the tenant are automatically added to this environment with the *Environment Maker* role. This role grants users the permissions to create and share new apps and other resources within the same environment. Additionally, this environment is limited to 1 TB of storage capacity and cannot be deleted.

The Default environment is ideal for users to create personal productivity applications that use Microsoft 365 tools. It is not recommended to be used in Production for critical business apps.

Production environments are designed for apps that are actively used by end-users. They are intended for stability and performance, making them ideal for deploying apps that are critical to business operations and require high availability and reliability. Production environments can be created when there is at least 1 GB database capacity available.

Sandbox environments are used for development and testing purposes. They provide a safe space to experiment and make changes without affecting production data. This is perfect for developers and testers to build and test new features or updates before deploying them to production. As in the case of Production environments, Sandbox environments can be created when there is at least 1 GB database capacity available.

Trial environments are temporary environments that allow users to explore Power Apps features and capabilities. They have a limited lifespan of 30 days and are intended for evaluation purposes. This is useful for users who want to try out Power Apps or evaluate new features without committing to a full deployment. Trial environments offer a risk-free way to explore the potential of Power Apps.

Developer environments are designed for individual developers to build and test their apps. They come with a set of tools and resources tailored for development activities. This type of environment can be created by users who have Developer license assigned.

Dataverse for Teams environments are used to store, manage, and share team-specific data, apps, and flows. Each team in Microsoft Teams can have one environment, and it is automatically provisioned when an app or bot is created in the respective team for the first time.

By using the appropriate environment for each stage of app development and deployment, a clear separation can be maintained between development, testing, and production activities, improving overall governance.

> **Note: The ability to create environments is based on the license assigned, admin role assigned and available storage capacity.**

Environments can be managed from the Power Platform admin center at **https://admin.powerplatform.microsoft.com.**

Application types

Power Apps provides the ability to create two main application types: canvas apps and model-driven apps. *Table 15.2* showcases the differences between these two application types:

	Canvas apps	**Model-driven apps**
Design flexibility	Highly customizable, drag-and-drop elements, unique user experiences	Structured and data-driven, layout generated based on data model, limited customization
Focus	Design and user interface	Data and processes
Data sources	Connect to various sources like Excel, SharePoint, SQL databases	Built on Common Data Service (Dataverse)
Ideal for	Custom interfaces, specific look and feel	Complex business applications, consistency, and standardization
Use cases	Tailored user experiences, unique app designs, custom business apps, mobile-friendly applications	CRM systems, ERP systems, managing large amounts of data in an organized way
Access management	Dependency on permissions at the data source level. Application can be shared, granting permissions for app usage or co-ownership.	Role-based security for sharing

Table 15.2: Canvas apps vs. model-driven apps

Model-driven apps

Model-driven apps are structured and data-oriented applications. They focus on organizing data and benefit from an app design that requires little or no coding.

To gain a deeper understanding of model-driven applications within Power Apps, it is essential to first grasp the concept of Microsoft Dataverse, as these applications rely heavily on it.

Microsoft Dataverse

Previously known as **Common Data Service (CDS)**, Microsoft Dataverse is a cloud-based solution designed for storage and management of data that is used by business applications. It functions as a sophisticated database that not only holds data, but also provides tools to organize, access, and analyze it. Dataverse simplifies the creation and management of data models, ensuring seamless interaction between applications and data. This enables the development of powerful apps that leverage this data, without the complexities of data management.

By making use of Power Apps and Dataverse to create apps, users can benefit from several key components that facilitate data organization, access and analysis, like:

- **Tables:** These are used to store data in a structured format, similar to how tables work in a traditional database.
- **Columns**: These define the data types and constraints for the data stored in tables.
- **Relationships**: These establish connections between different tables, allowing for complex data models.
- **Business rules**: These are used to enforce business logic and apply validations without the need for writing code.
- **Forms**: These provide user interfaces for data entry and interaction within an application.
- **Views**: These allow for customized data presentation and filtering.
- **Charts**: These offer graphical representations of data, making it easier to identify trends and patterns.
- **Dashboards**: These provide visual representations of data, helping to monitor and analyze key metrics.

Practical scenario in a model-driven app

To better understand the benefits of model-driven apps and how they work, let us delve into a simple practical scenario for model-driven app creation.

Note: **The application for this scenario has been created using the Power Apps Developer Plan, which allows the development of a model-driven app using all premium capabilities for free. After sharing a model-driven app, all users that consume the application require a dedicated Power Apps license.**

Scenario: Imagine an organization that needs to manage events, the tasks related to these events, and the volunteers assigned to these tasks, to ensure successful event completion.

Objective: The goal is to create a model-driven app that allows administrators to track volunteer information, manage tasks, and organize events.

Creating the solution

In this example, we started by creating a solution in Power Apps, called *Volunteer Task Management*.

A solution in Power Apps serves as a container for multiple objects related to a particular solution, like apps, flows, tables, and dashboards.

In our example, the objects we created for this app, like the tables, dashboard, and the application itself, are all part of the **Volunteer Task Management** solution:

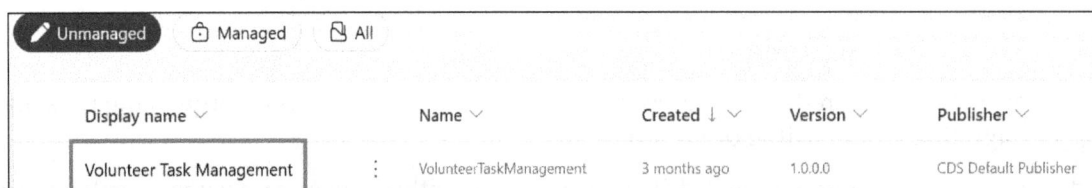

Display name ∨		Name ∨	Created ↓ ∨	Version ∨	Publisher ∨
Volunteer Task Management	⋮	VolunteerTaskManagement	3 months ago	1.0.0.0	CDS Default Publisher

Figure 15.4: Volunteer Task Management solution

Creating tables

Next, we created three custom tables: *Volunteer, Task,* and *Event,* to be able to store the necessary data for the application.

Microsoft Dataverse offers a variety of standard tables for solutions, but custom tables can also be created to meet specific requirements.

In this example, we have chosen to create custom tables:

	Table ↑ ∨		Name ∨	Type ∨	Managed ∨	Customized ∨	Customizable ∨
	Event	⋮	cr650_events	Standard	No	Yes	Yes
	Task	⋮	cr650_tasks	Standard	No	Yes	Yes
	Volunteer	⋮	cr650_volunteers	Standard	No	Yes	Yes

Volunteer Task Management > Tables

Figure 15.5: Custom tables created for the Volunteer Task Management solution

The **Volunteer** table stores information about the volunteers, such as their names, contact details, and availability.

The **Task** table stores information about the related tasks, including the task name, description, due date, status, and the volunteer assigned to the task.

The **Event** table stores information about the events, such as event name, date, location, and description.

Setting relationships

Having the tables and the necessary columns created, we then configured the relationships between tables. The following relationships have been created:

- **One-to-many relationship between Event and Task tables**: Each event can have multiple related tasks, but each task is associated with only one event.

- **One-to-many relationship between Volunteer and Task tables**: Each volunteer can be assigned multiple tasks, but each task is assigned to only one volunteer.

In this case, the relationships were established by creating two lookup columns, **Event** and **Volunteer**, within the **Task** table. The *Event* lookup column references the *Event* table, and the *Volunteer* lookup column references the *Volunteer* table:

Name* ↑ ∨	Description ∨	Due Date* ∨	Event* ∨	Volunteer ∨	+18 more ∨
Collect Food Donations	Set up Collection points and gather...	12/17/2024	Food Drive	Alex Johnson	
Distribute Flyers	Hand out flyers to promote the upc...	1/10/2025	Community Clean-...	John Doe	
Distribute Food Packages	Distribute the packaged food items ...	12/18/2024	Food Drive	John Doe	
Distribute Garbage Collection Supplies	Ensure all volunteers have the nece...	1/12/2025	Community Clean-...	Jane Smith	
Manage Registration Desk	Assist attendees with registration a...	1/20/2025	Charity Fundraiser	Alex Johnson	
Set Up Event Venue	Arrange chairs, tables, and decorati...	1/15/2025	Charity Fundraiser	John Doe	
Sort and Package Donations	Sort the collected food items and p...	12/17/2024	Food Drive	John Doe	
Enter text	Enter text	Enter or pick date	Select lookup	Select lookup	

Task columns and data — Update forms and views — Edit | ∨

Figure 15.6: Lookup columns for table relationships

Relationships can also be created by selecting the table name where the relationship should be established, and then clicking on **Relationships**. The types of relationships that can be created include many-to-one, one-to-many, and many-to-many.

By default, a table has relationships with other standard tables in Dataverse. These default relationships manage values for columns such as **Created By**, **Modified By**, **Owning User**, and other default columns within a table:

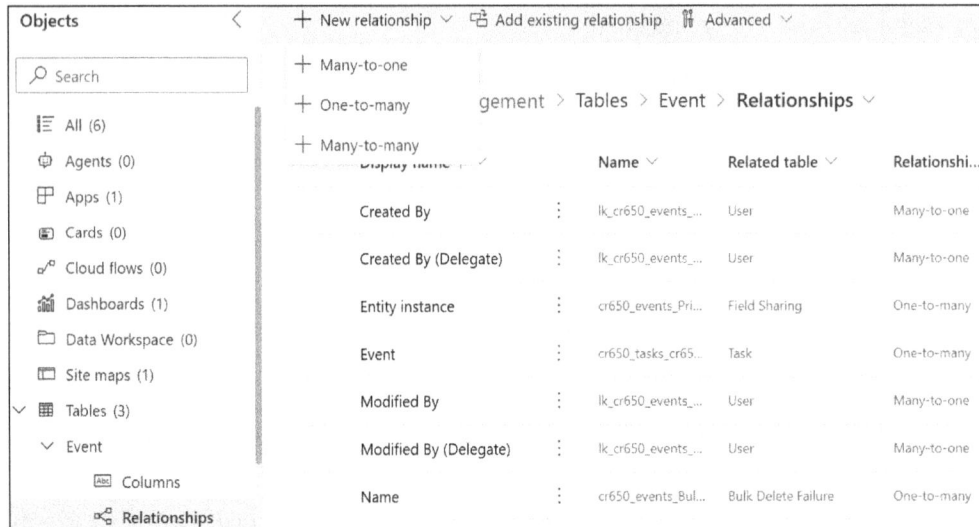

Figure 15.7: Relationships

Creating views and dashboards

After having the relationships established between the tables, we created custom public views within the *Event* and *Task* tables. **Views** define how the list of items in a table is displayed in the application. For this scenario, the following views have been created:

- `Upcoming events in the next 6 months` view created in the *Event* table, to show only the upcoming events in the next 6 months, using relevant filters based on the event date. Items are also being sorted by date:

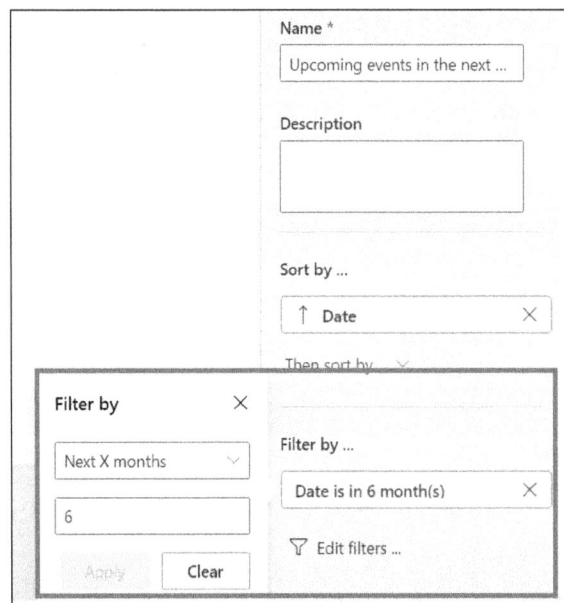

Figure 15.8: Upcoming events in the next 6 months view

- **Past Events** view created in the *Event* table to show only the past events, using relevant filters based on the event date. Items are also being sorted by date:

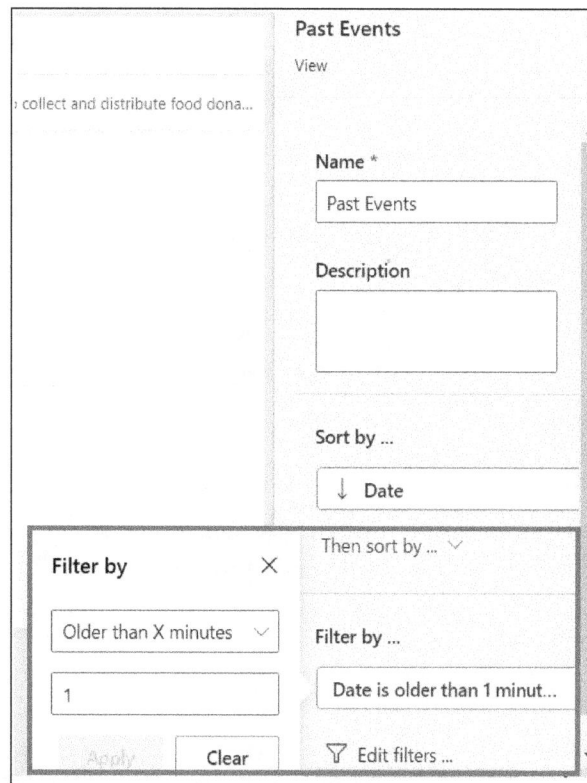

Figure 15.9: *Past events view*

- **All Tasks** view created in the *Task* table, to show all tasks opened and only specific table columns, with items sorted by status:

Figure 15.10: *All tasks view*

- The **Pending tasks** view was created in the *Task* table to show only the pending tasks, filtering out the tasks that have been completed and sorting items by the due date:

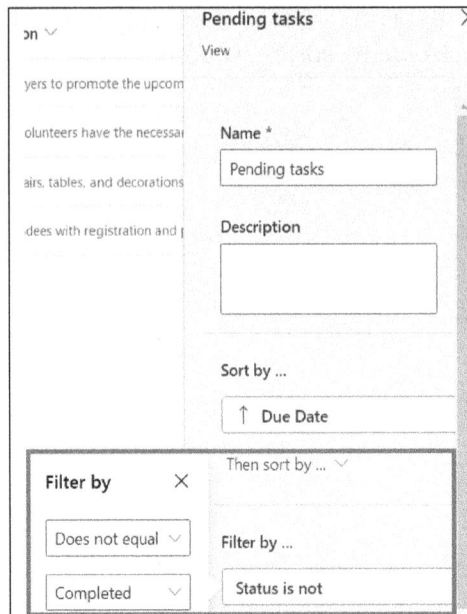

Figure 15.11: Pending task view

We have also created two charts based on the **Task** table, with visuals for tasks by status and by volunteer:

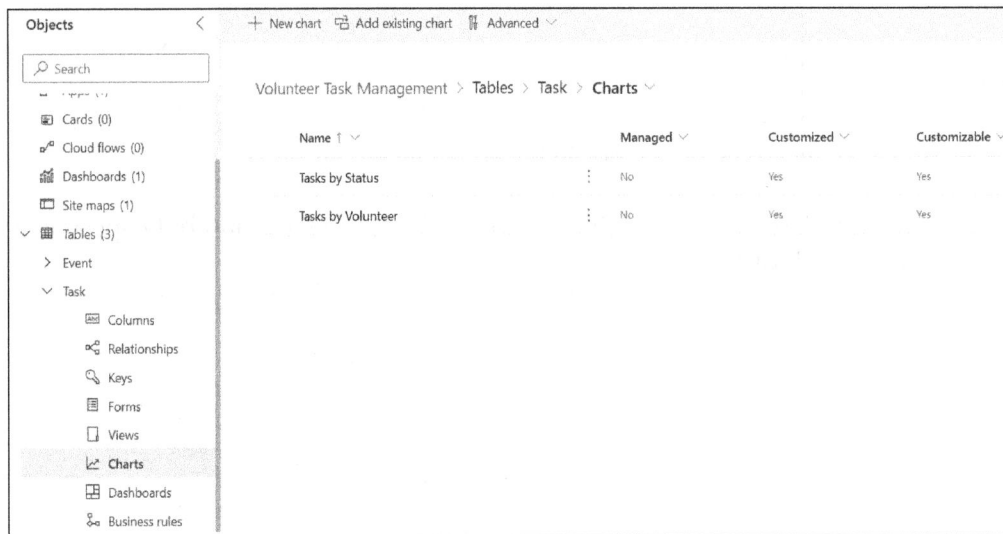

Figure 15.12: Charts

We then created a dashboard called **Tasks Dashboard**, where we added the two charts:

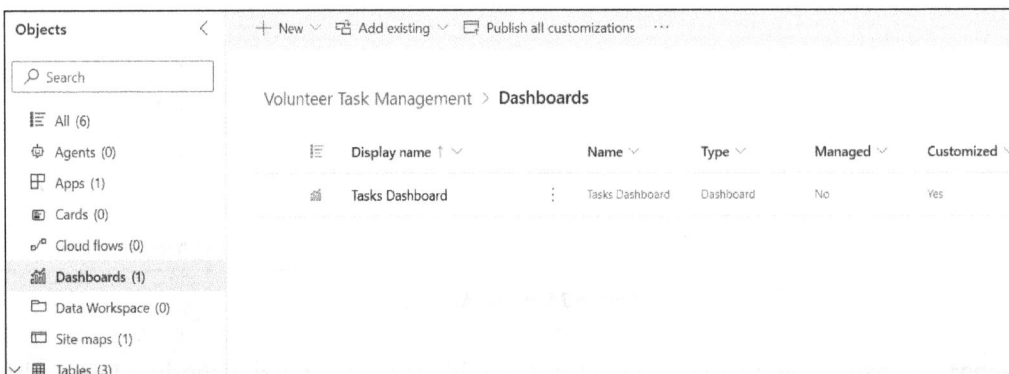

Figure 15.13: Dashboard

The dashboard will appear as follows:

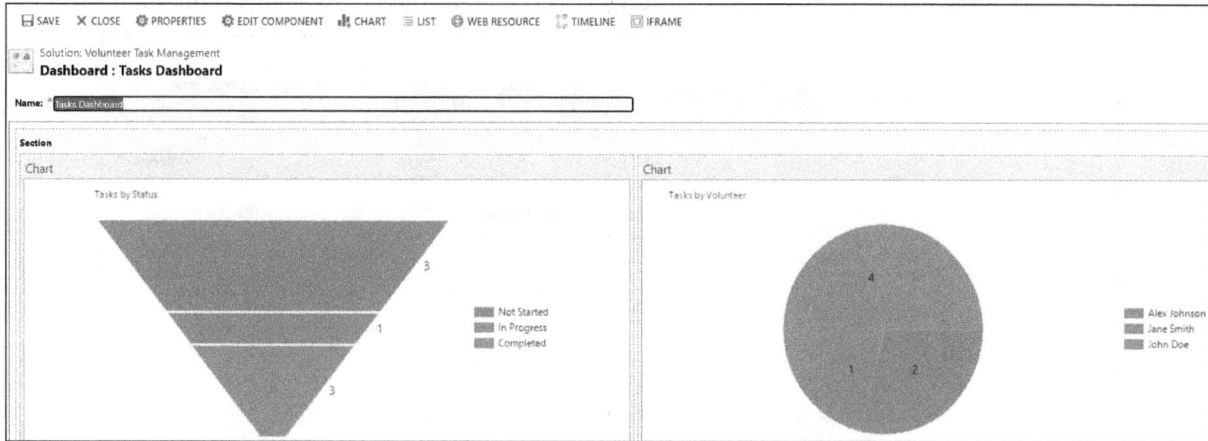

Figure 15.14: Dashboard with added charts

Building the app

After having all the above resources and objects in place, we created the model-driven app called **Volunteer Task Management** within the solution with the same name:

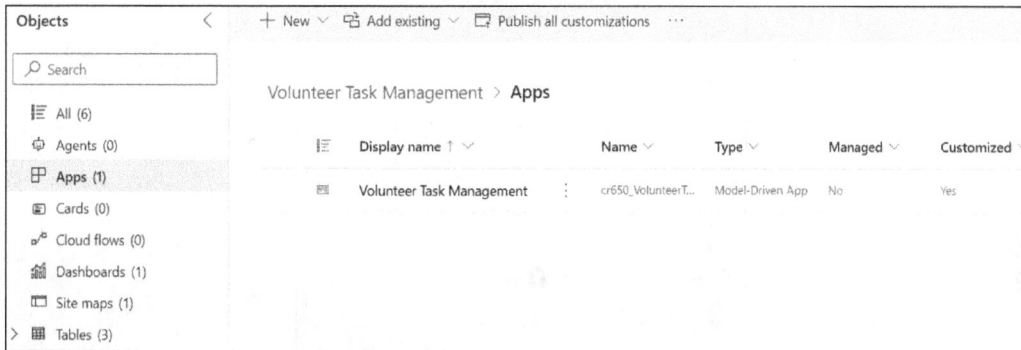

Figure 15.15: Volunteer Task Management app

We have added four pages to the application, three pages to display separately each Dataverse table we previously created, and one page for the **Tasks Dashboard**:

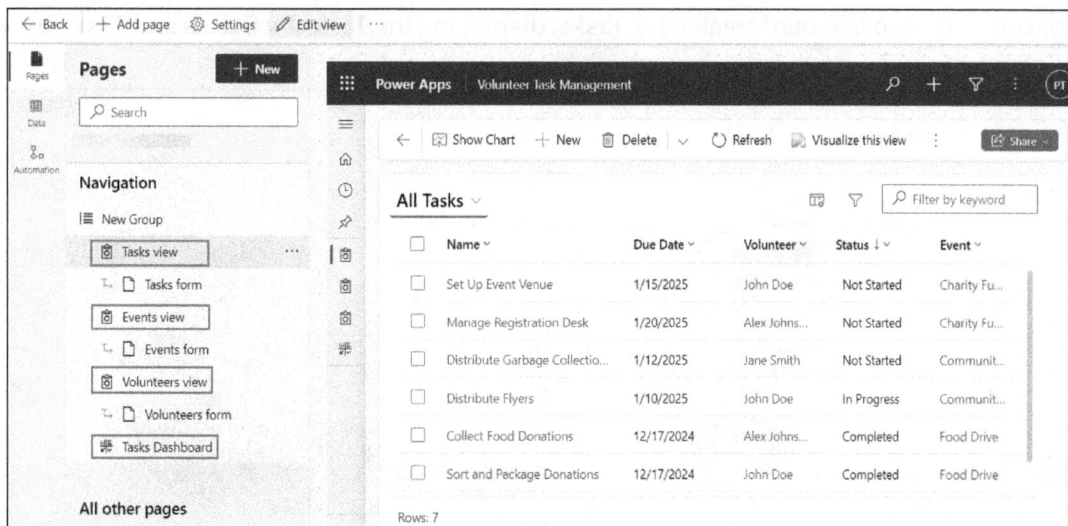

Figure 15.16: Volunteer Task Management app

On the pages displaying data from each respective table, the view displayed is the one that has been set as default within **Views**. However, any of the available views created at the table level can be selected:

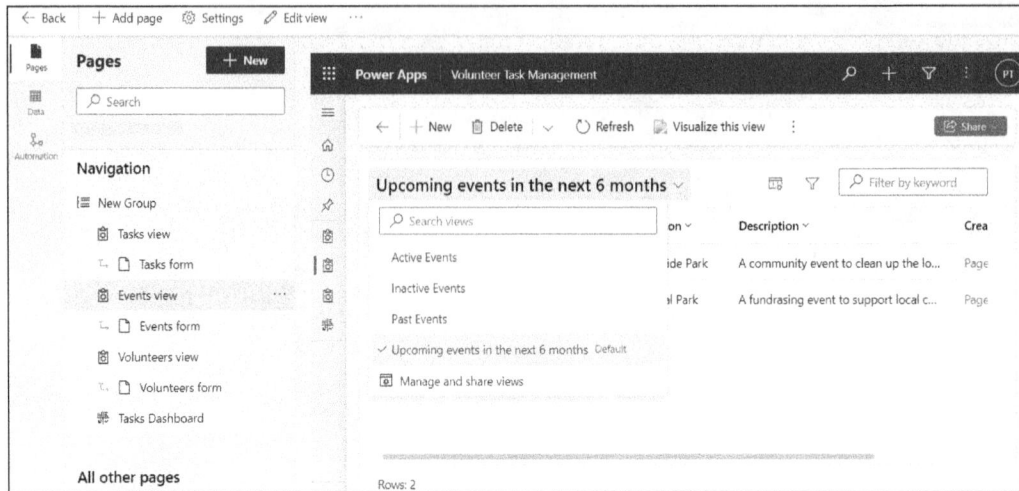

Figure 15.17: Select the view

Each page includes a default form automatically created for each table, enabling users to add new records directly within the tables:

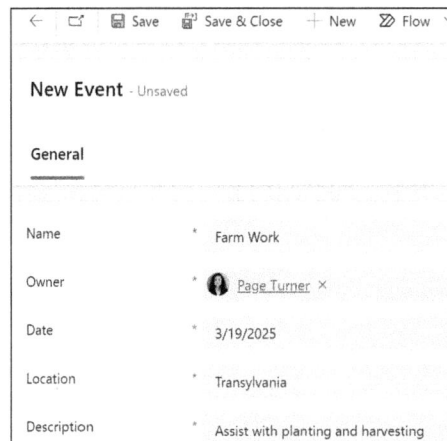

Figure 15.18: Form in Model-driven app

The last page contains the dashboard created for **Tasks**, displaying the **Tasks by Status** and **Tasks by Volunteer** charts:

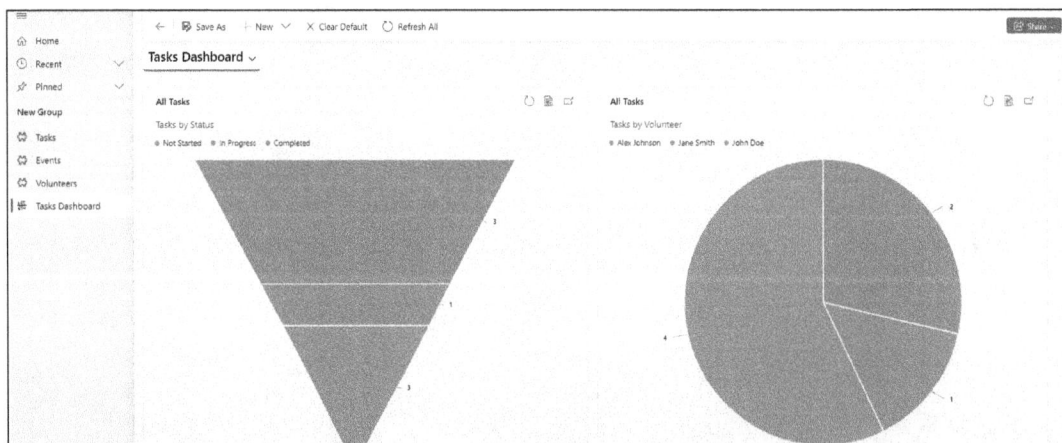

Figure 15.19: Dashboard page

The **Volunteer Task Management** app is designed to streamline volunteer task management by providing a centralized platform for tracking volunteer information, managing tasks, and organizing events. This model-driven app leverages the structured and data-oriented nature of Power Apps to ensure that all relevant data is organized and easily accessible. By creating custom tables for volunteers, tasks, and events, and establishing relationships between these tables, administrators can efficiently manage and monitor all aspects of volunteer activities.

Even though the *Volunteer Task Management* app is a simple example, it demonstrates the essence of how model-driven apps work and their benefits. The app's ability to handle large amounts of data makes it particularly useful for organizations with extensive volunteer programs. Views, charts, and dashboards enable users to visualize and analyze data effectively, ensuring that important information is always at their fingertips. This capability is especially valuable when dealing with large datasets, as it allows for better decision-making and more efficient resource management.

The design of the app was kept simple, making use mostly of the elements and controls already provided by the model-driven application type. This approach eliminates the need for sophisticated app design or the configuration of additional controls, making the development process more user-friendly.

Canvas apps

Canvas apps are designed to allow the creation and customization of applications by inserting or placing elements onto a canvas. Think of it like creating a digital poster where buttons, text boxes, images, and other controls can be placed to design the app. These elements can then be connected to data sources, like Excel or SharePoint, and formulas can be added to set up functions for what these controls should do. This approach provides a lot of flexibility and creativity in how the app looks and works, making it easy to tailor the app to specific needs.

Power Apps Studio

Power Apps Studio is the interface in Power Apps designed for the creation, building, and customization of canvas applications. It offers a user-friendly interface with various components that make app creation and customization more intuitive.

When opting to create a new canvas app or edit an existing one, Power Apps Studio is the platform that opens, enabling the creation or modification of the app. The following figure illustrates the Power Apps Studio interface when initiating the creation of a Canvas app:

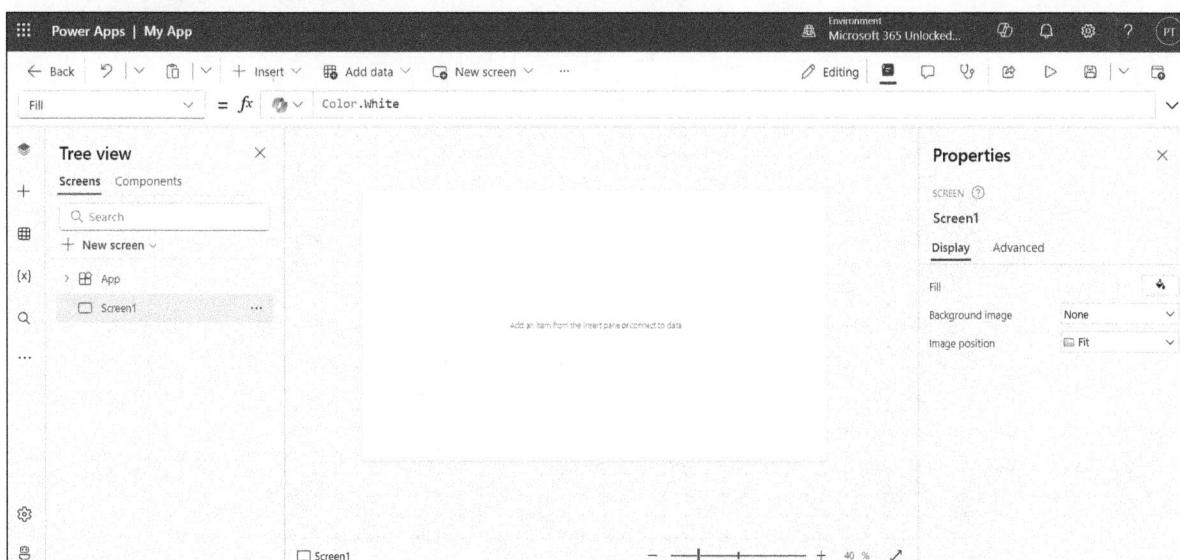

Figure 15.20: Power Apps Studio

The main high-level sections of Power Apps Studio a developer will most likely interact with when building a canvas app are:

- **Modern command bar**: Provides the option to navigate back to the Power Apps hub, to undo or redo the last action, to cut, copy, or paste, and to insert elements and controls like buttons, text labels, icons, galleries, and forms. This bar is dynamic, showing, in addition, different other options and commands based on the object or control selected. The following figure shows the modern command bar highlighted:

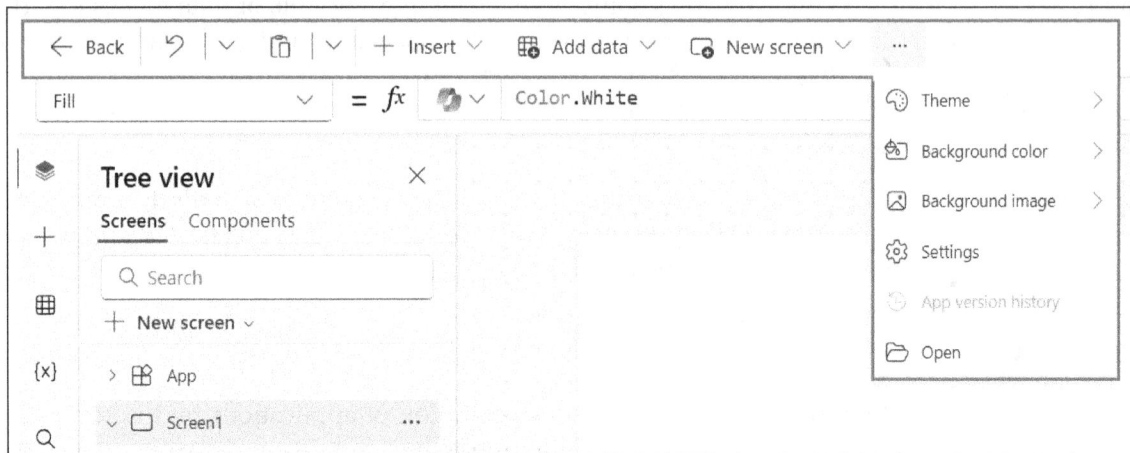

Figure 15.21: Command bar

- **App actions**: This section allows you to open the **Properties** window for the selected object, add comments in the application, use the **App checker** to verify the application's status, and save, publish, run, or share the app:

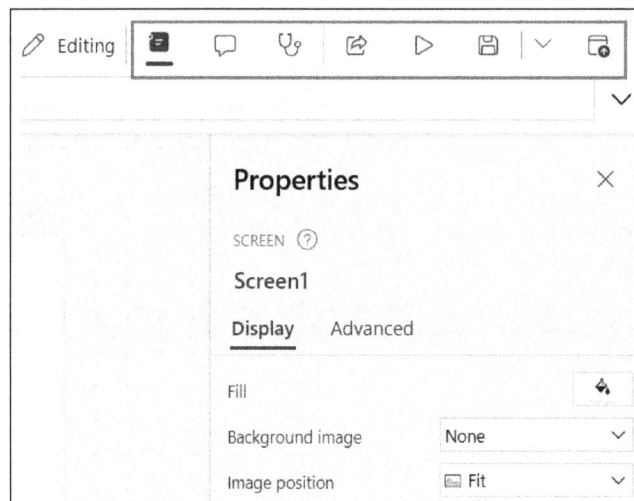

Figure 15.22: App actions

- **Properties list**: This list allows to change properties of a particular control or component. Each control or component added to an app has a set of properties that can be adjusted to change its appearance, behavior, and functionality. For example, properties such as the color, size, visibility, or the functionality that a control should have when selected can be modified. Different properties will be displayed in this list based on the control or component selected. The following figure displays the Properties list for an icon:

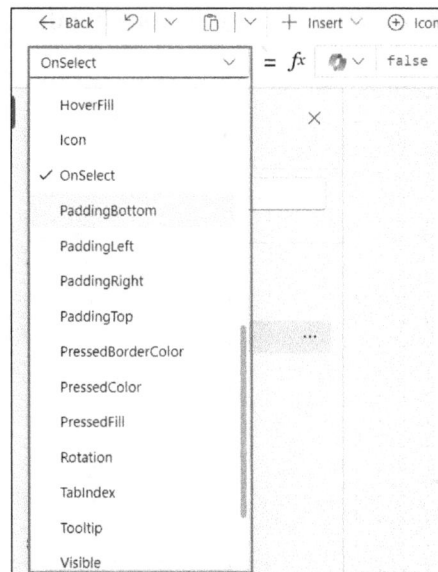

Figure 15.23: Properties list

- **Formula bar**: The formula bar in Power Apps Studio is a powerful tool for defining the logic and behavior of app components and controls. By using the formula bar, it is possible to implement dynamic functionality, such as conditional formatting, data validation, and real-time calculations. For instance, configuring the visibility of an icon can be as straightforward as setting it to *true* or *false*, as shown in *Figure 15.24*, but its visibility can also be configured through more complex formulas based on the value of other controls or components within the application, or based on user actions.

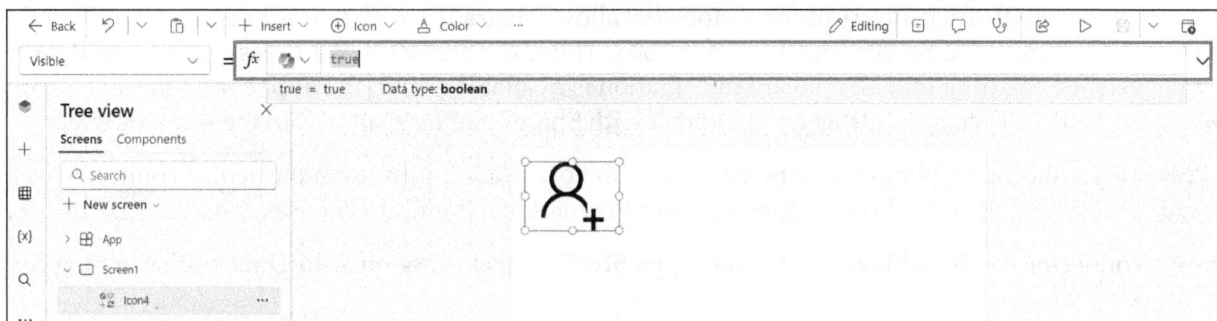

Figure 15.24: Formula bar

- **App authoring menu**: This menu allows switching between multiple options while developing the application, like tree view, insert different controls, add data and connectors, configure variables, search functionality, media, and others:

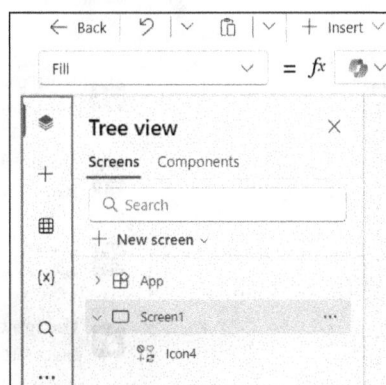

Figure 15.25: App authoring menu

- **Canvas screen**: The actual canvas screen is used for placing the controls and components needed for the application:

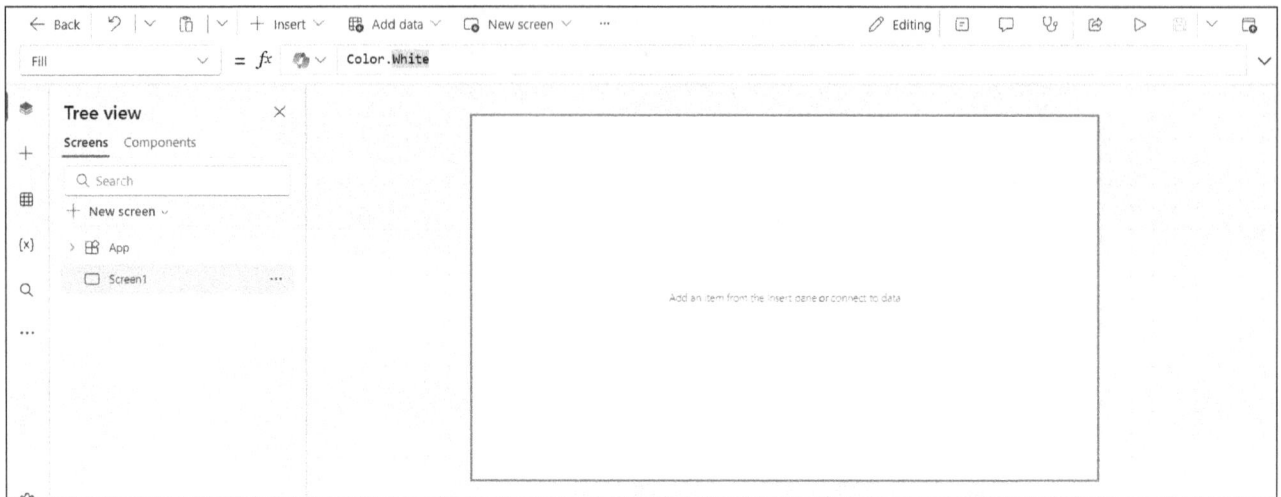

Figure 15.26: Canvas screen

Data sources and connectivity

Canvas apps offer a flexible way to connect to various data sources, enabling the creation of dynamic and interactive applications. One of the key strengths of Canvas apps is their ability to integrate with a wide range of data sources, both cloud-based and on-premises.

Canvas apps come with a rich library of connectors that allow integration with popular services like SharePoint, OneDrive, Dataverse, SQL Server, and Dynamics 365. These connectors make it easy to pull in data from different systems, ensuring that all relevant information is available within the app. For instance, an app can display data from an Excel spreadsheet and interact with SharePoint lists, all within the same interface.

The Power Apps licensing plan should be considered before planning to use a particular connector or data source, as premium and custom connectors require a Power Apps Premium license.

Adding a connector can be achieved in **Power Apps Studio**, by clicking on **Add Data** and searching for the relevant connector:

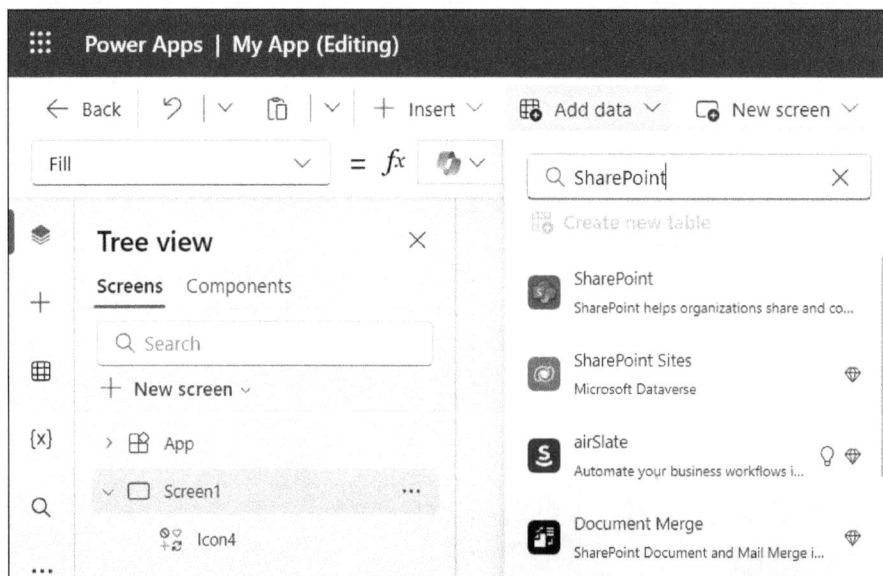

Figure 15.27: Search for connector

Controls

In canvas apps, controls serve as the fundamental elements for building applications. They enable the creation of interactive and dynamic user interfaces that can connect to various data sources and perform a wide range of functions.

Here are some of the key controls and components available in Power Apps:

- **Text Controls** include labels, text input boxes, and rich text editors. These are used to display and capture text data from users. For instance, a label can display static text, while a text input box can capture user input:

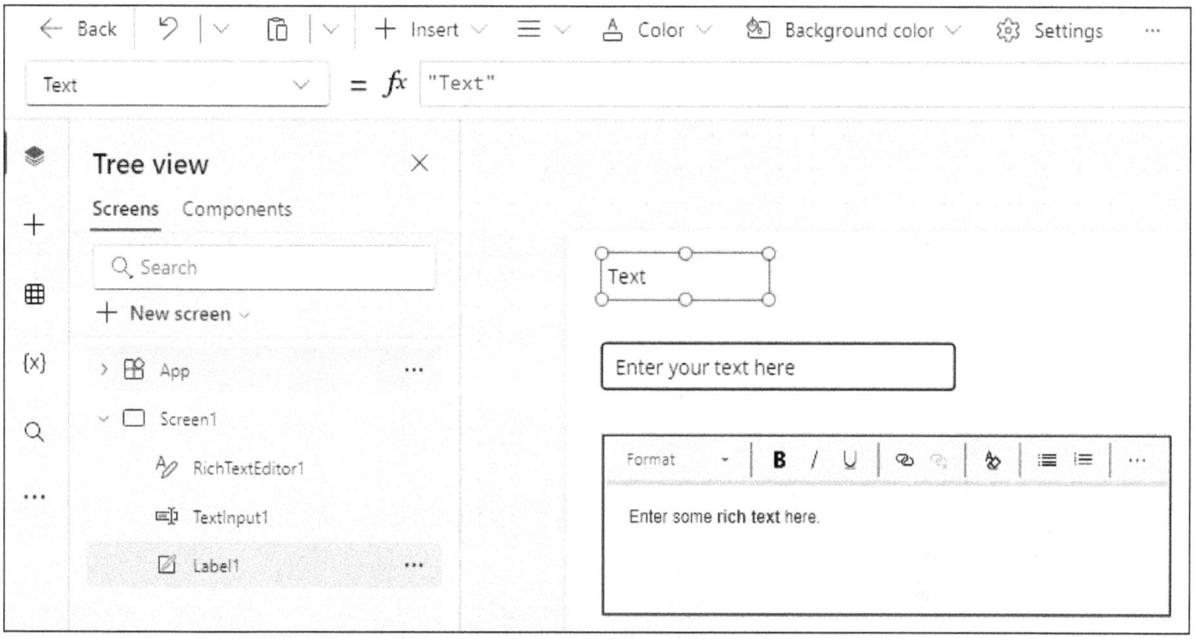

Figure 15.28: Text Controls

- **Icon Controls** include various symbols and images that can be used to enhance the aspect and functionality of the app. Icons can be used for navigation, indicating status, or triggering actions:

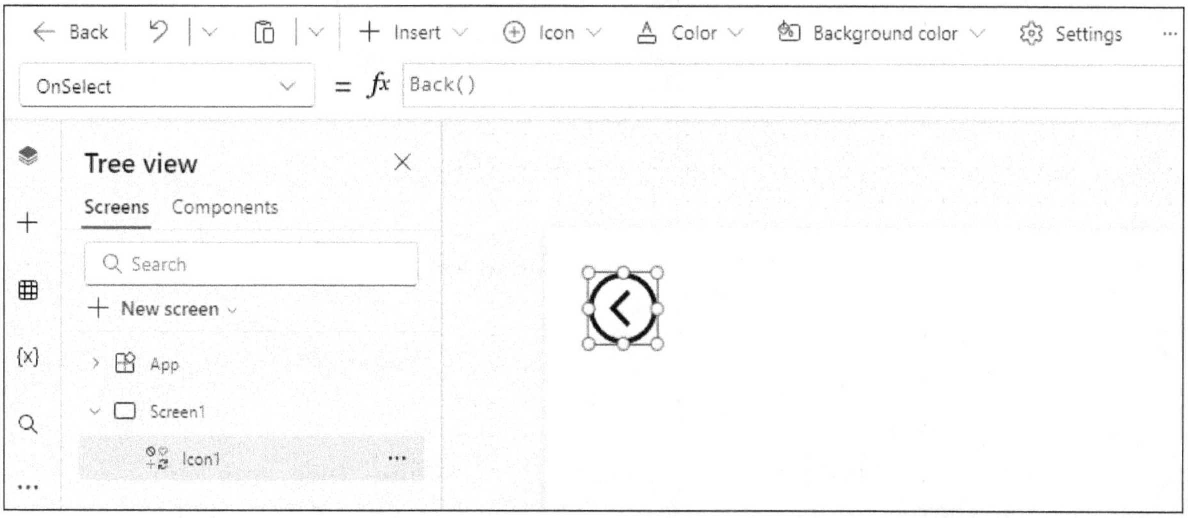

Figure 15.29: Icon Controls

- **Button Controls** are used to trigger actions or events within the app. For example, a button can be used to submit a form, navigate to another screen, or execute a specific function:

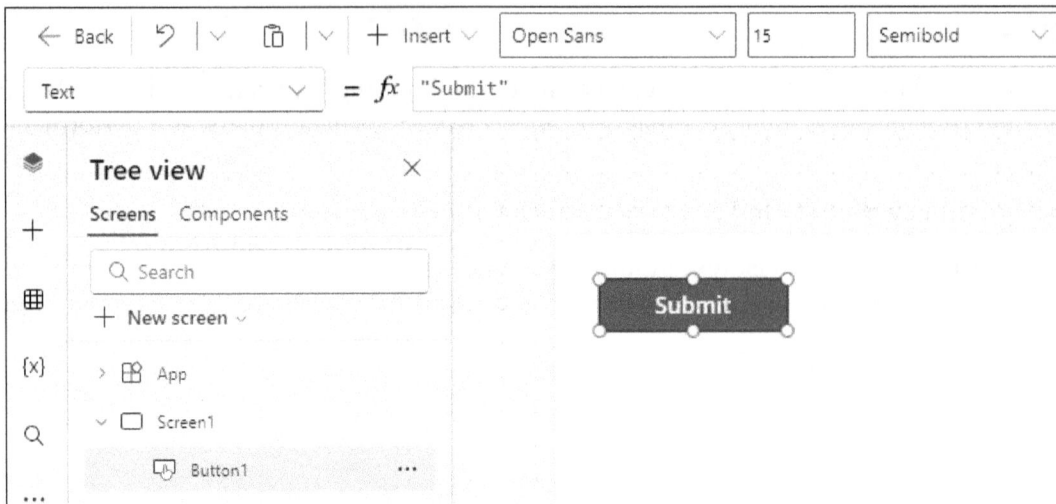

Figure 15.30: *Button Controls*

- **Gallery Controls** display a collection of items in a list or grid format. They are highly customizable and can be used to display data from various sources, such as SharePoint lists, Excel files, or Dataverse tables:

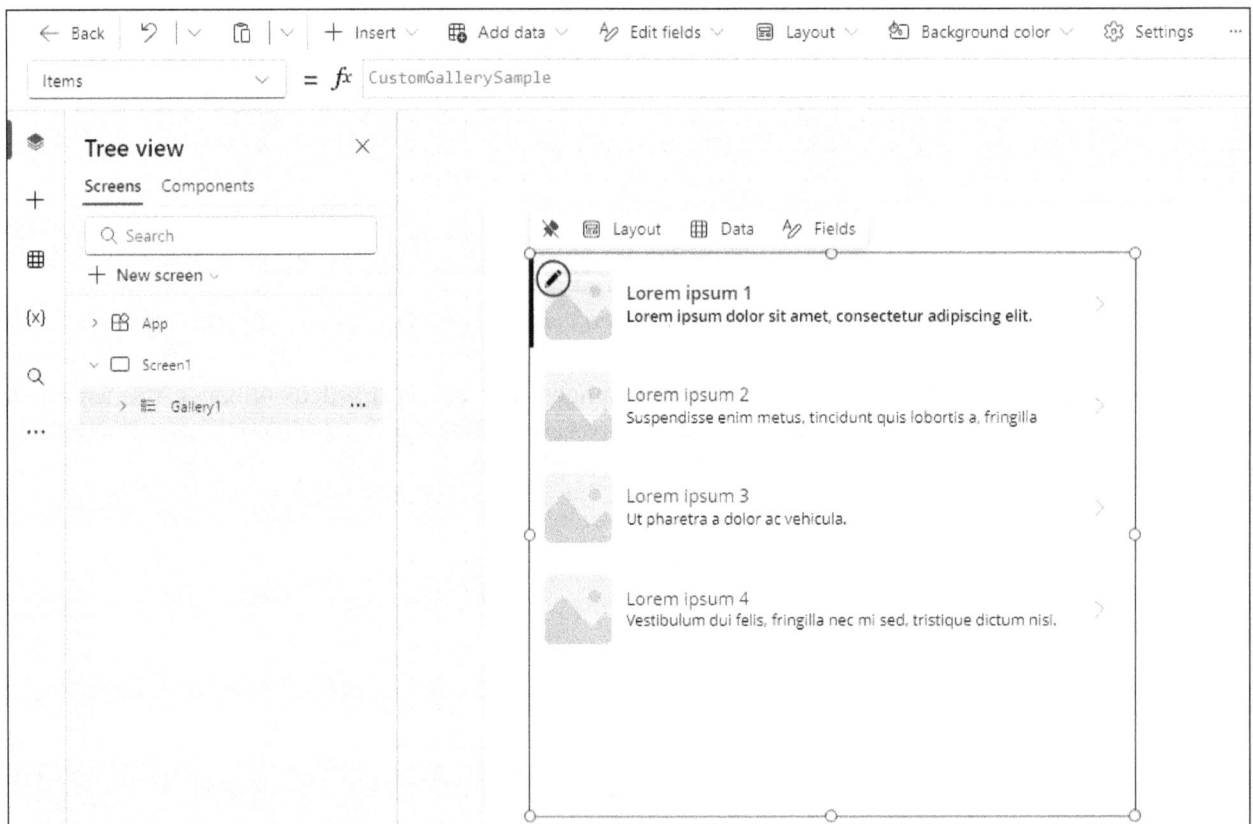

Figure 15.31: *Gallery Controls*

- **Form Controls** are used to display and edit data from a data source. They can be customized to include various input controls, such as text boxes and dropdowns to capture user input. We can insert, for example, an *Edit form* in our canvas app and connect it to an **Issue tracker** SharePoint list, as shown in *Figure 15.32*:

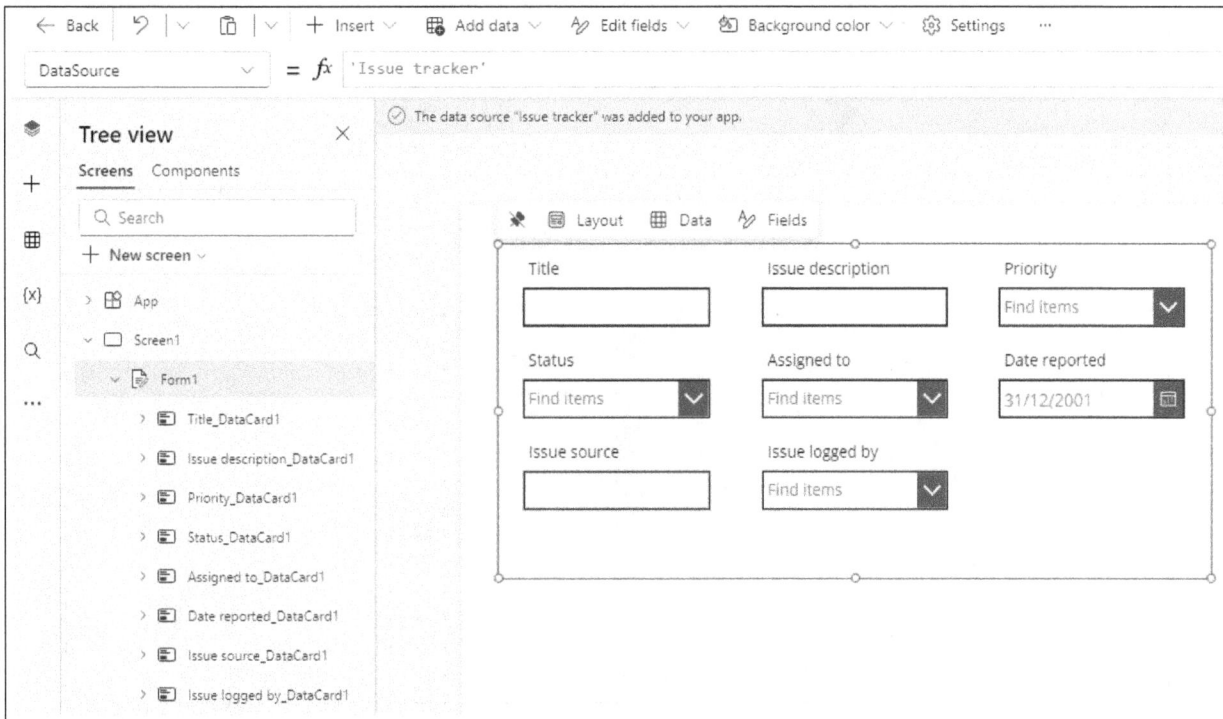

Figure 15.32: Form Controls

- **Media Controls** include image, video, and audio controls. These are used to display multimedia content within the app. For example, an image control can display a picture, while a video control can play a video:

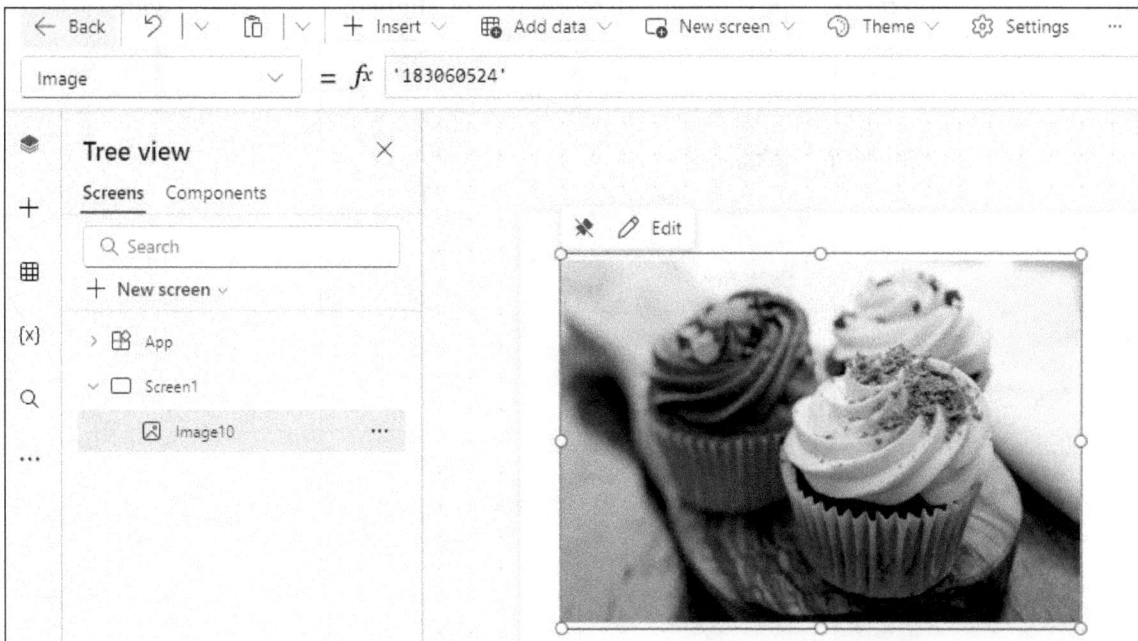

Figure 15.33: Media Controls

- **Chart Controls** are used to visualize data in a graphical format. Power Apps provides various types of charts, such as column, line and pie charts, to help represent data visually:

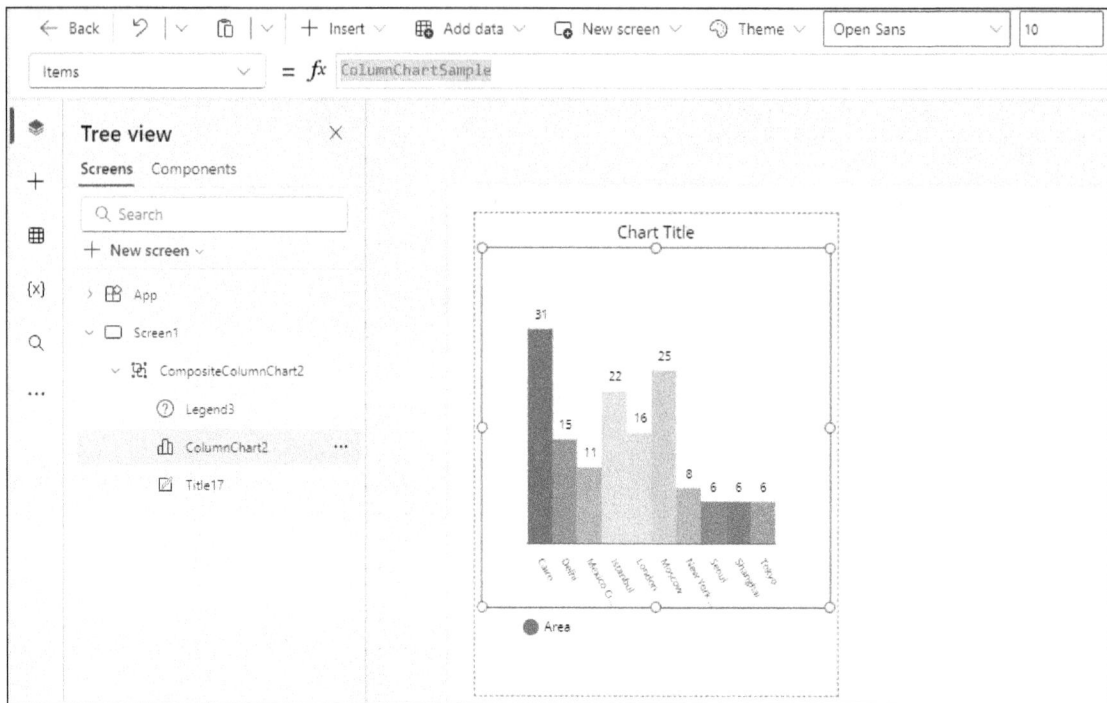

Figure 15.34: Chart Controls

When working with these controls, it is important to consider the user experience and ensure that the app is intuitive and easy to use. Customizing the appearance and behavior of each control to match the app's requirements is essential.

The controls within an app can be copied, renamed, reordered, or aligned, as shown in *Figure 15.35*:

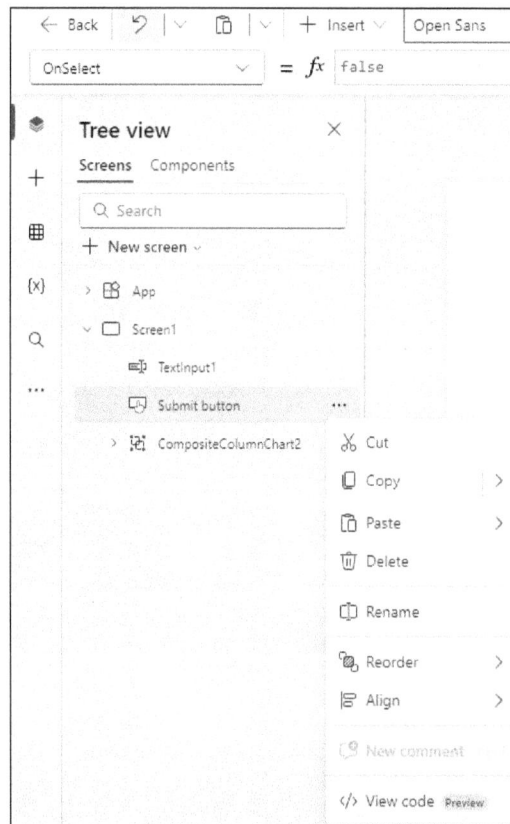

Figure 15.35: Controls options

Components

Components enable the creation of reusable elements that can be utilized within a single app or shared across multiple apps by creating a component library.

Components streamline the development process by allowing developers to build once and reuse multiple times, ensuring consistency and reducing maintenance efforts. For example, a common component that can be created is a custom navigation menu. This menu can include buttons for navigating between different screens, icons for visual appeal, and logic to highlight the current screen. By creating this navigation menu as a component, it can be easily added to any app, ensuring consistent user experience across all applications.

Another example of a component is an application header, which can be used to maintain a consistent format across multiple screens. The following figure shows an example of a header created as component:

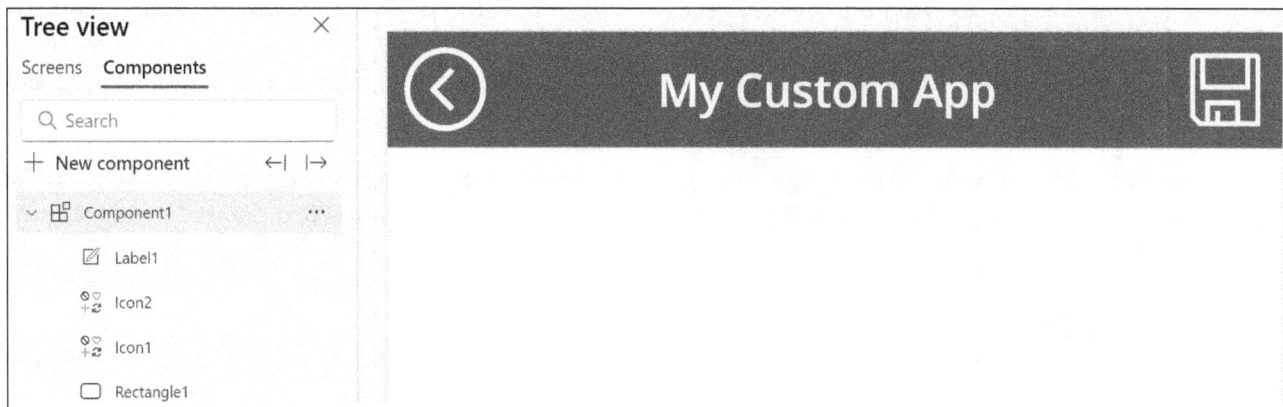

Figure 15.36: Application component

Functions

Power Apps functions are built-in formulas that perform specific tasks, much like formulas in Excel. They help you manipulate data, control the app behavior, perform calculations, and interact with user inputs or data sources. Functions in Power Apps are essential for building interactive, dynamic, and intelligent applications. They are written using Power Fx, the low-code formula language in Power Apps, which is inspired by Excel but tailored for app development. Below, we will explore some of the most commonly used functions in Power Apps and provide examples to illustrate their usage.

Text functions

Text functions are used to manipulate and format text strings. Here are a few examples:

- **Text()**: Converts a value to text.

  Example: `Text(1234)` returns `"1234"`

- **Concatenate()**: Joins multiple text strings into one.

  Example: `Concatenate("Hello, ", "World!")` returns `"Hello, World!"`

- **Left()**: Returns the leftmost characters of a text string.

  Example: `Left("PowerApps", 5)` returns `"Power"`

Date and time functions

Date and time functions help manage and manipulate date and time values. Here are some examples:

- **Now()**: Returns the current date and time.

- **DateAdd()**: Adds a number of units you specify to a date/time value.

  Example: `DateAdd(Today(), 5)` returns the date 5 days from today

Logical functions

Logical functions are used for logical operations. Here are some examples:

- **If()**: Evaluates a condition and returns one value if true and another if false.

  Example: `If(Value(TextInput_Age.Text) >= 18, "Adult", "Minor")` returns **"Adult" if the value entered in TextInput_Age is greater than or equal to 18,** otherwise returns **"Minor"**

- **And()**: Returns true if all arguments are true.

  Example: `And(Value(TextInput_Age.Text) >= 18, TextInput_Country.Text = "USA")` returns **true** if the value entered in **TextInput_Age** is greater than or equal to 18 and the text entered in **TextInput_Country is "USA"**

- **Or()**: Returns true if any argument is true.

  Example: `Or(Value(TextInput_Age.Text) >= 18, TextInput_Country.Text = "USA")` returns **true** if the value entered in **TextInput_Age** is greater than or equal to 18 or the text entered in **TextInput_Country** is **"USA"**

Math functions

Math functions perform mathematical operations. Here are some examples:

- **Sum()**: Calculates the sum of a set of values.

  Example: `Sum(1, 3, 5)` returns **9**

- **Round()**: Rounds a given number to a defined number of decimal places.

  Example: `Round(3.14159, 2)` returns **3.14**

- **Sqrt()**: Returns the square root of a given number.

  Example: `Sqrt(25)` returns **5**

Navigation functions

Navigation functions control the navigation between screens in an app. Here are some examples:

- **Navigate()**: Navigates to a specified screen.

  Example: `Navigate(SuccessScreen)` navigates to the screen named **SuccessScreen.**

- **Back()**: Navigates to the previous screen.

Data source functions

Data source functions interact with data sources. Here are some examples:

- **LookUp()**: Finds the first record in a data source that matches a specified condition.

  Example: `LookUp(Employees, Name = "John")` returns the first record from a data source called **Employees,** where **Name** is **"John"**.

- **Filter()**: Filters records in a data source based on a condition.

  Example: `Filter(Employees, Age > 30)` returns records form a data source called **Employees** where **Age** value is greater than **30.**

- **Collect()**: Adds records to a collection.

  Example: `Collect(TestCollection, {Name: "Page", Age: 20})` adds a record to a collection named **TestCollection.**

These functions are just a few examples of the many powerful tools available in Power Apps. By leveraging functions, users can create dynamic and interactive applications that meet their specific needs. Whether you are manipulating text, performing calculations, or navigating between screens, Power Apps functions provide the flexibility and functionality to bring your app to life.

Building a canvas app from scratch

To better understand how canvas apps work, we will build a canvas app from scratch, using SharePoint Online as a data source. This app will allow users to submit requests for office facilities, such as ergonomic furniture and additional equipment.

Preparing the data source

Before proceeding with the app creation, we need to prepare our data source and the list where the requests will be submitted. For this, we create two lists in a SharePoint Online site:

- **Employee Facilities**: This list has two text columns, **Facility**, and **Category**, and will be the data source for our application. The following figure shows the columns and items created in this list:

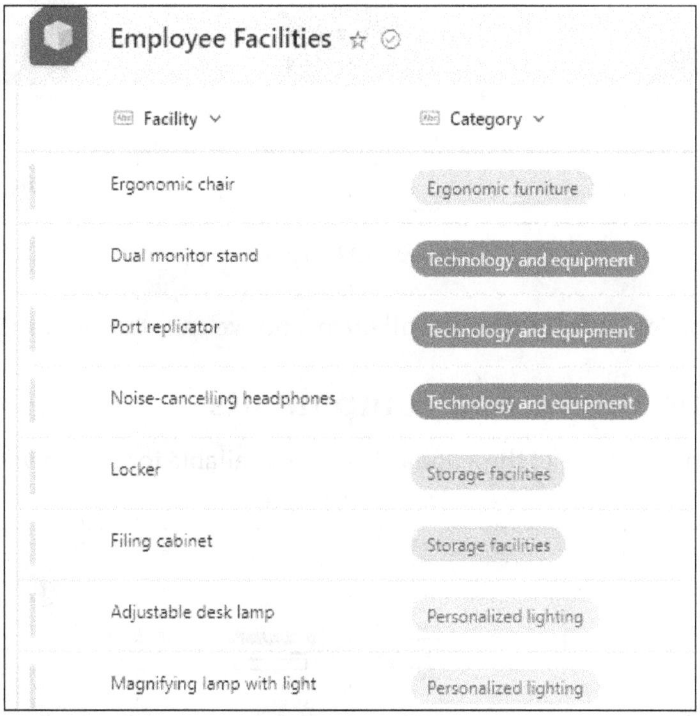

Figure 15.37: Employee facilities SharePoint list

- **Facility request**: This list has nine columns: *Requestor* and *Line Manager* (type: Person), *Priority, Office Location* and *Status* (type: Choice), *Category, Facility* and *Justification* (type: Text), and *Preferred Delivery Date* (type: Date). This is the list we will use for the request form in the app and where the actual requests will be submitted.

Start with the canvas app creation

Now that we have our lists, the next step is to start with the canvas app creation. For this, we access **https://make.powerapps.com** and ensure that we have selected the environment where we want to create this app.

Then we select **Create** from the left-hand side menu, and click on **Start with a blank canvas**:

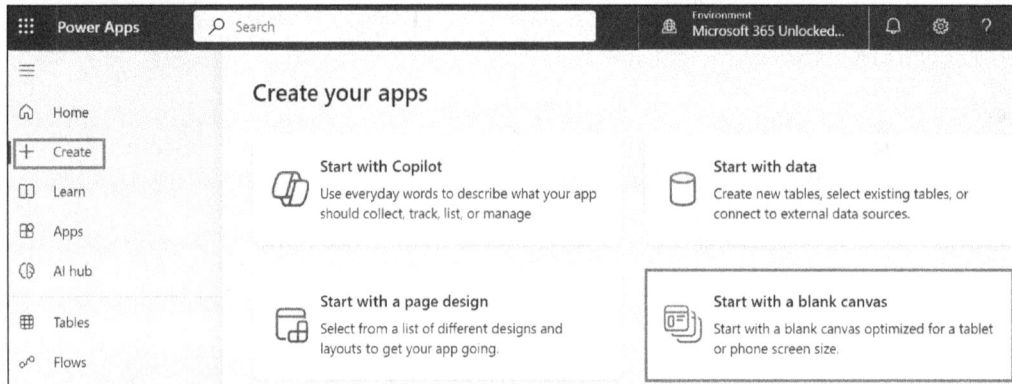

Figure 15.38: Create blank canvas app

We will be prompted to select the size we want to use for our canvas app. In our example, we select **Tablet size**:

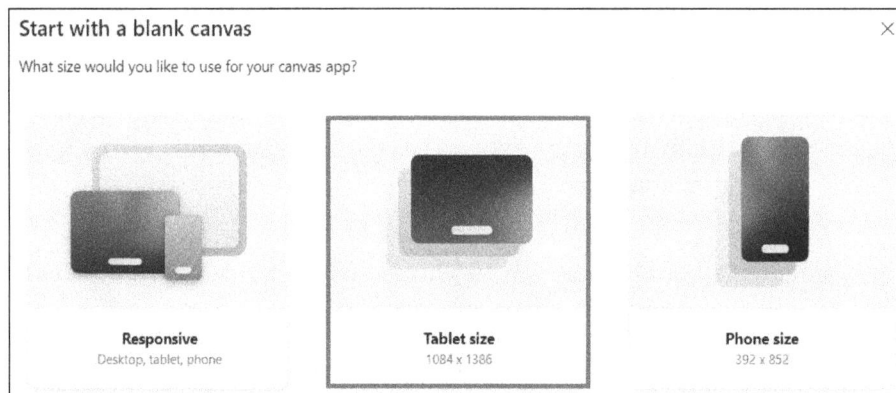

Figure 15.39: App size

After completing this step, **Power Apps Studio** will open, and we can start building the application.

Setting up the app theme and components

We will first choose a theme from one of the standard themes available for the canvas apps, as shown in *Figure 15.40*:

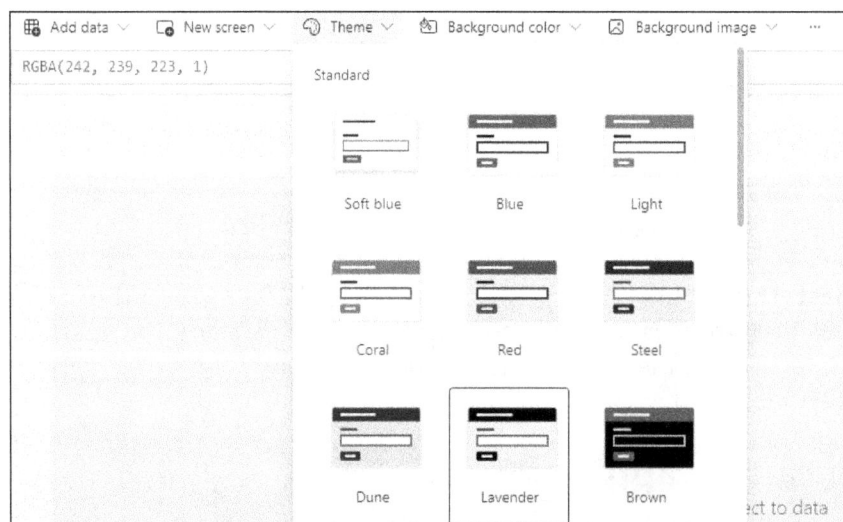

Figure 15.40: Select a theme

We will create a header component that we can add to the screens in our app. In this example, we will use the component on only one screen. However, utilizing components is an important matter in case we decide in the future to further develop the app by adding more screens that need to be designed with this header. Components avoid repetitive actions and provide consistency across the app.

Before adding elements to the components, we must first ensure that the component screen matches the height and width of the screens used in our application, and adjust these values, if needed.

Our component contains a rectangle and a text label that we have added to display the app name. This will serve as our header for the screens which require a header in our app:

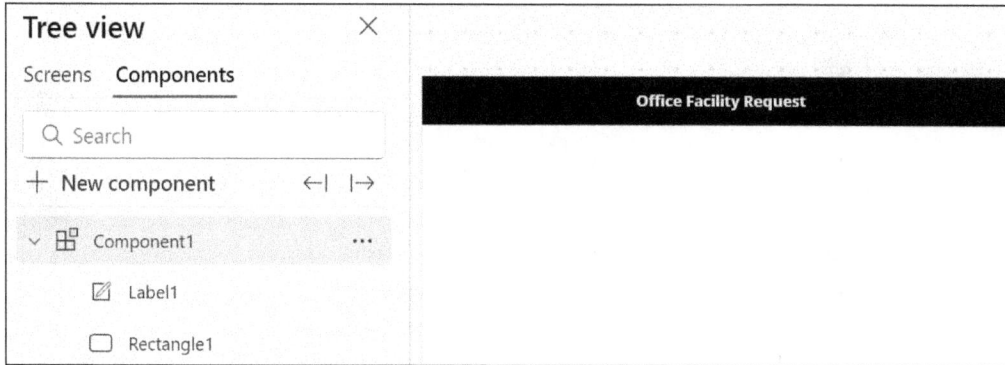

Figure 15.41: Create a component

We have renamed the component created to **Header** and added it to the app screen:

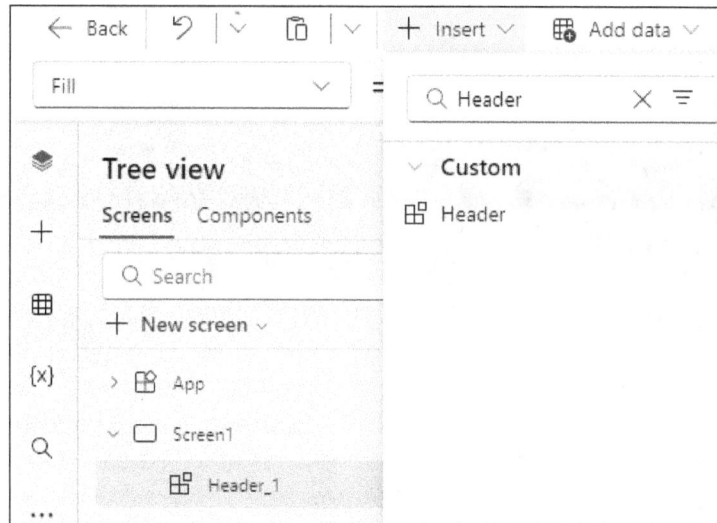

Figure 15.42: Add a custom component

We also renamed the screen to **Request Form Screen** and from the **New screen** option in the command bar, we have inserted two additional screens, selecting from the available screen layouts:

- A blank screen, which we named **Initial Screen**. This will be the first screen of our app.
- A Success Screen, which we named **Success Screen**. This will be the last screen of our app.

These two screens will be used later in the configuration of this application.

At this point, it is a good idea to save our app to ensure we do not lose any changes. Once we save the app, we are prompted to provide the app name. In our example, we named the app *Office Facility Request*. Going forward, regularly saving important updates helps avoid any potential data loss. **Auto-save** option can also be enabled by clicking on **Settings** and then **General** in **Power Apps Studio**.

Adding data to the app

The next step is to add the data we will be using for this application. To achieve this, we will be using the **SharePoint** connector:

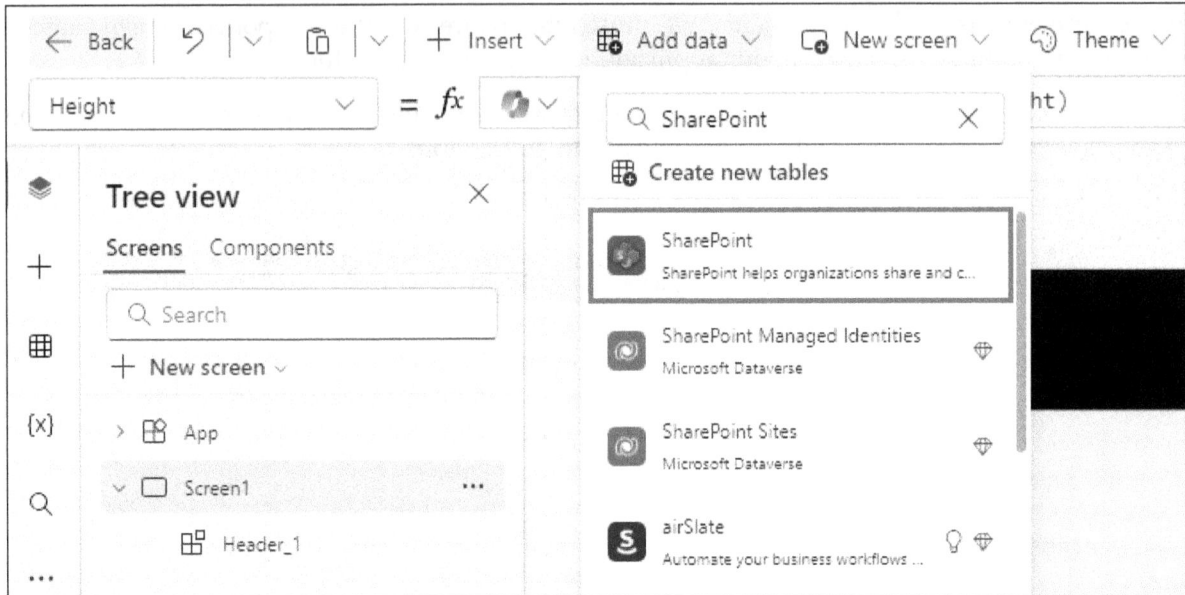

Figure 15.43: Add data

After selecting the connector, we will be prompted to add or select a connection. If this is the first time when using SharePoint Online as a connection in Power Apps, we will need to add it by selecting **Connect directly (cloud services)**:

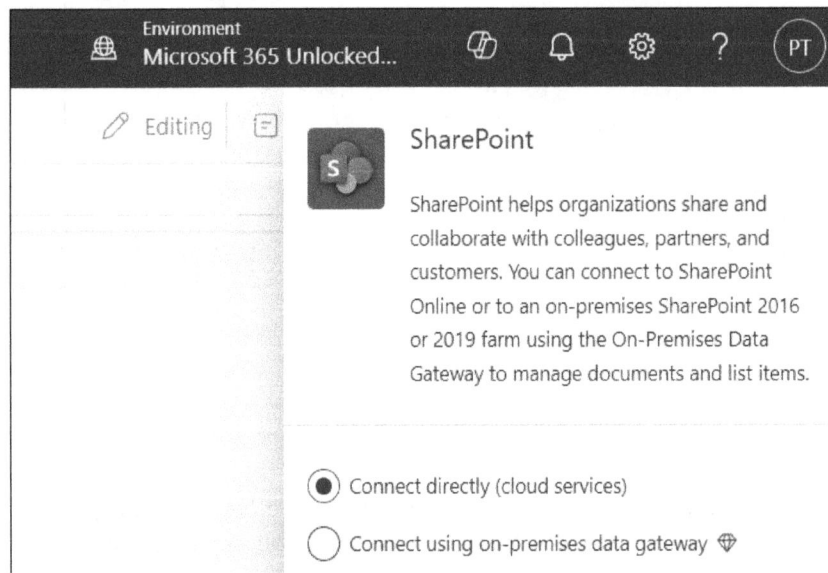

Figure 15.44: Connect to SharePoint Online

Afterward, we will be prompted to connect to a SharePoint site. We can either enter the SharePoint URL for the location of our lists or search and select from **Recent sites**:

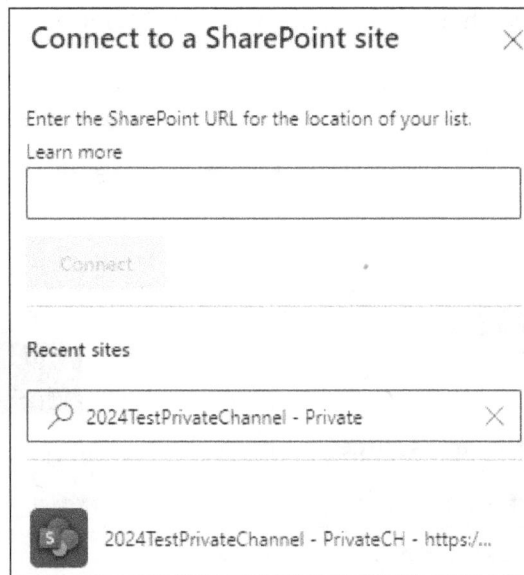

Figure 15.45: *Connect to a site*

Once connected to the SharePoint site, we can now select the lists we have created for this application and click **Connect**:

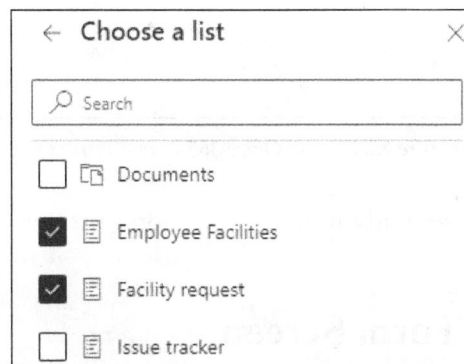

Figure 15.46: *Choose list*

Now, we will be able to see both SharePoint lists under the **Data** tab in our application:

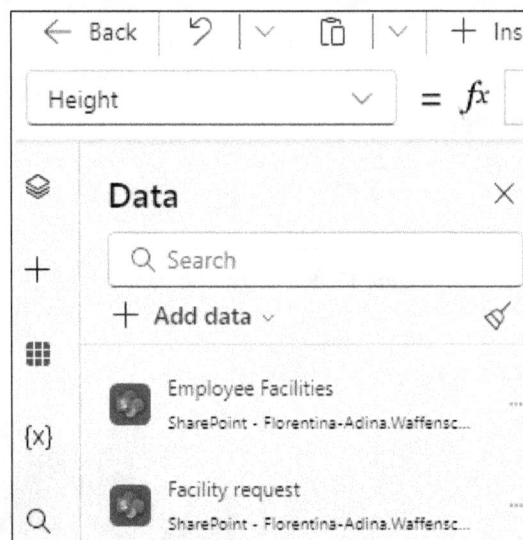

Figure 15.47: *Data*

From the **Data** tab, we will now search for and add the **Office 365 Users** connector, as shown in the following figure:

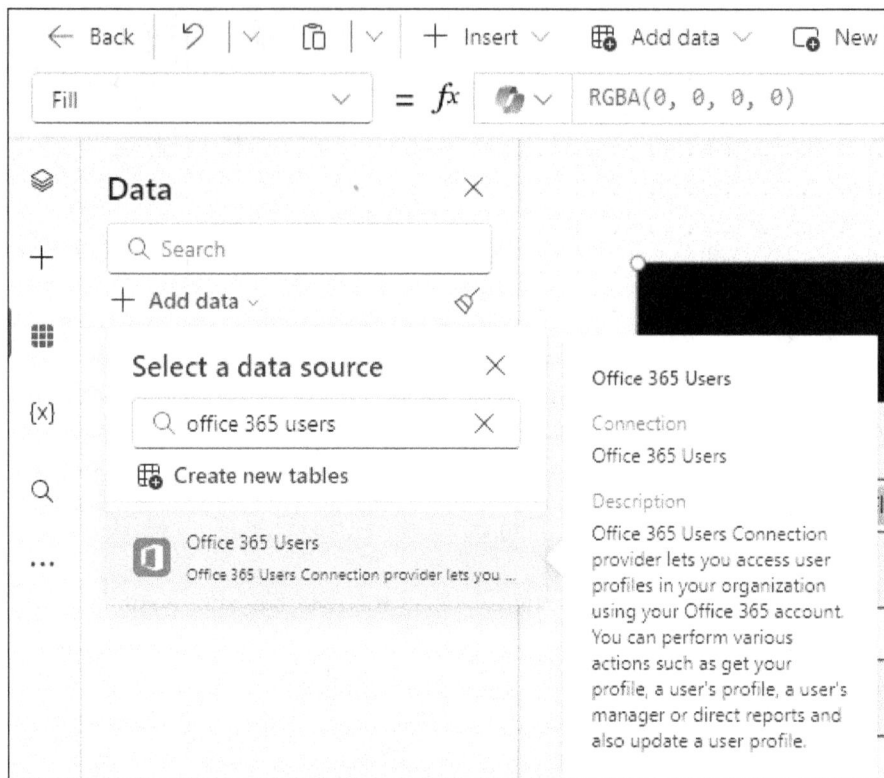

Figure 15.48: Add Office 365 Users connector

This connector will be required subsequently in the application configuration to obtain the profile details of the requestor and the line manager.

Designing the Request Form Screen

The next step is to insert an **Edit form** into the *Request Form Screen* and connect it with the **Facility request** list, as shown in the following figures:

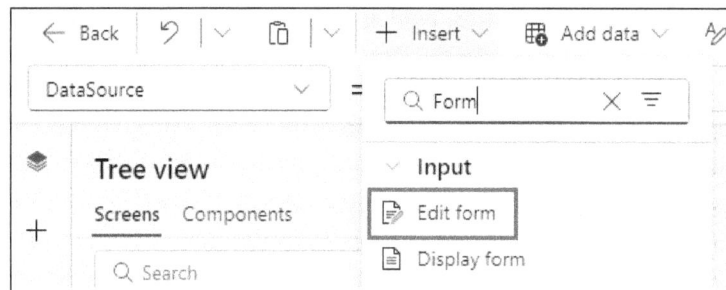

Figure 15.49: Insert an edit form

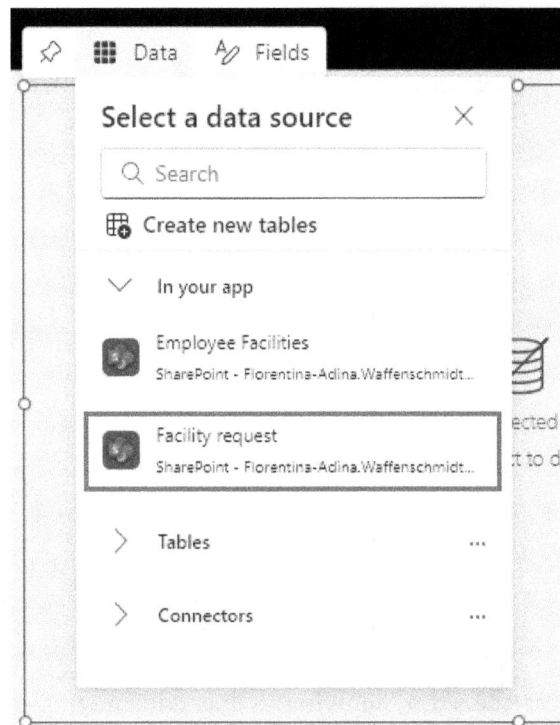

Figure 15.50: Connect a form to a data source

From the **Properties** tab of the form, we can select which fields to be displayed, their order, the number of columns and the layout, as shown in *Figure 15.51*:

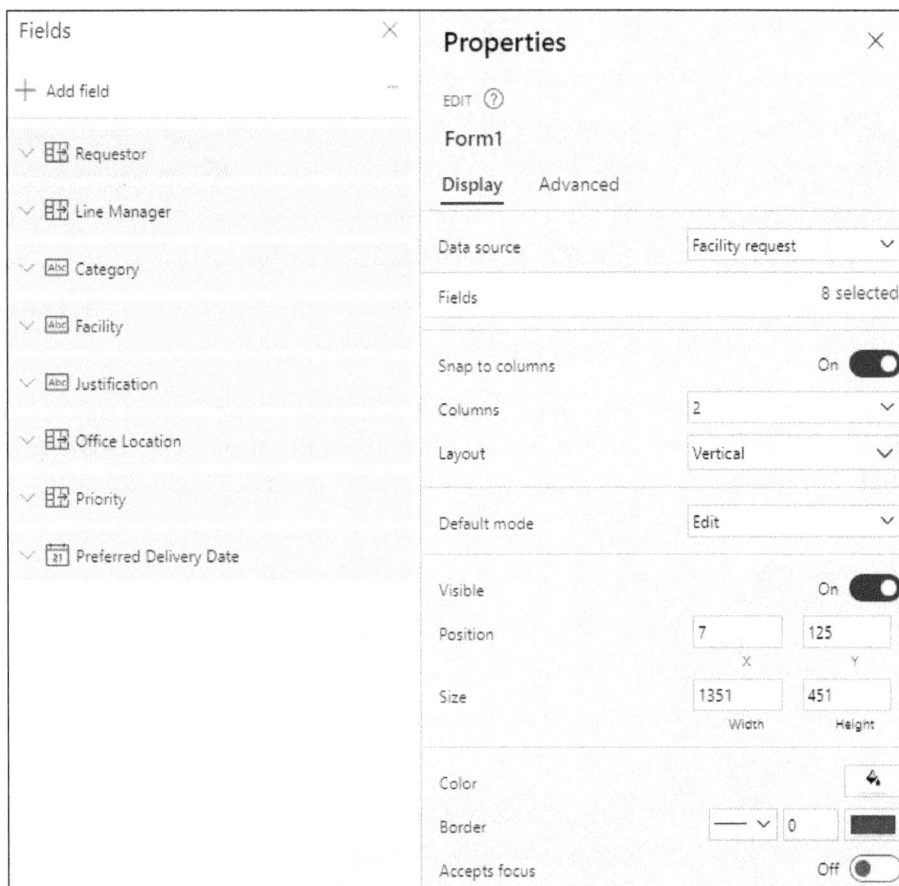

Figure 15.51: Form fields and layout

Under the **Advanced** tab of the form properties, we will set the `DefaultMode` property to `FormMode.New` to allow the creation of a new item once we run the application:

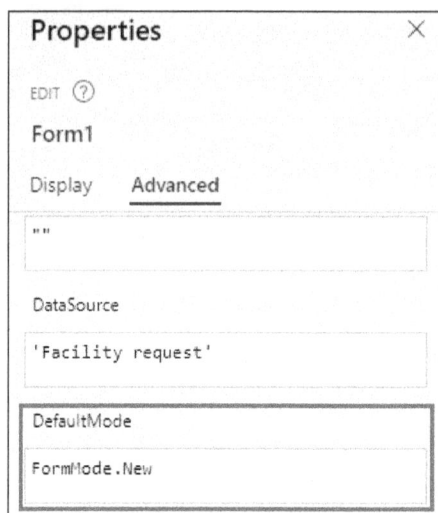

Figure 15.52: Form mode

By default, the mode is set to `FormMode.Edit`, allowing to only edit existing selected items.

We renamed this form to `Request form`:

Figure 15.53: Request form

Next, we will manage the default values displayed for the **Requestor** and for the **Line Manager** fields in our form. In this scenario, we want to display the current user playing the application as the default value for the **Requestor** field, and the requestor's direct manager for the **Line Manager** field. We also want to make sure the user's display name is the value displayed in the fields.

Before being able to edit the properties of any data card, we need to unlock it, as by default all data cards are locked for editing their properties and elements in Power Apps:

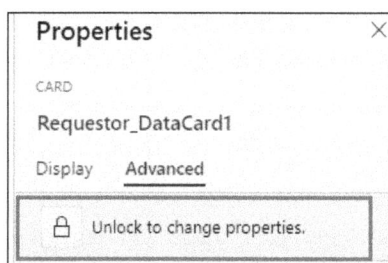

Figure 15.54: Unlock Data Card

With the *Requestor* Data Card being unlocked, we can now change the properties of the combo box where the requestor should be selected.

The first property we will update is the **DisplayFields** property of the control to **["DisplayName"]** value, to ensure the requestor's display name is shown. By default, this value is set to **["Claims"]**.

To do this change, we select the corresponding combo box for the *Requestor* field within the *Requestor* Data Card, search for the **DisplayFields** property in the control's Properties list, and in the Formula bar, we replace the **["Claims"]** value with the **["DisplayName"]** value:

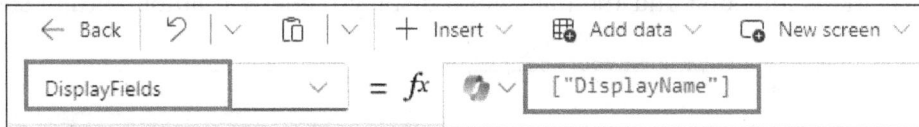

Figure 15.55: Change DisplayFields property for Requestor field

Next, we will change the **DefaultSelectedItems** property for the *Requestor* combo box with the following formula in the Formula bar:

```
{
Claims:"i:0#.f|membership|" & Office365Users.MyProfileV2().userPrincipalName,
DisplayName: Office365Users.MyProfileV2().displayName,
Email: Office35Users.MyProfileV2().mail
}
```

This formula creates a record with three fields: **Claims**, **DisplayName** and **Email** from the Office 365 user profile of the current user. Let us break down the expression to better understand how it works:

- **Claims: "i:0#.f|membership|"** & **Office365Users.MyProfileV2().userPrincpalName**: This concatenates the string **"i:0#.f|membership|"** with the current user's UPN (user principal name). The resulting value is used to update the *Requestor* SharePoint column once a request has been submitted.

- **DisplayName: Office365Users.MyProfileV2().displayName**: This sets the **DisplayName** field to the current user's display name.

- **Email: Office365Users.MyProfileV2().mail**: This sets the **Email** field to the current user's email address.

Once we add this formula, we can see that the **Requestor** field automatically displays the current user's display name:

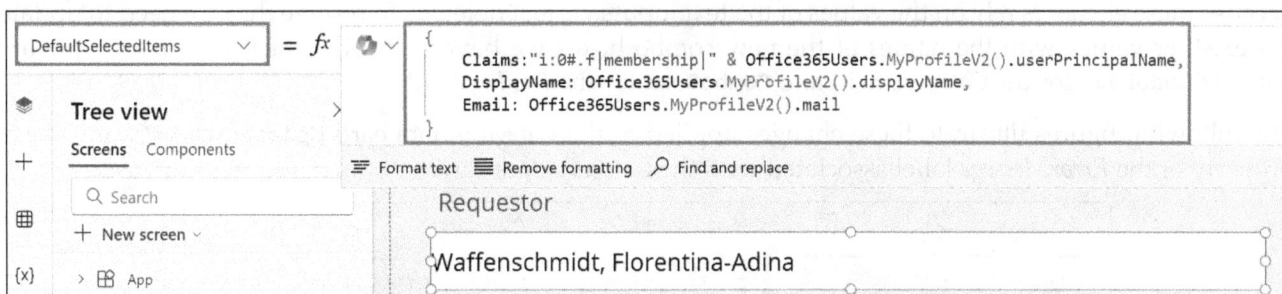

Figure 15.56: Change DefaultSelectedItems property for Requestor field

We will follow the same approach for the **DisplayFields** property of the *Line Manager* combo box, setting it to **["DisplayName"]**, to ensure the manager's display name is the value shown in the field.

In addition, to be able to display by default the current user's manager, we will change the **DefaultSelectedItems** property for the *Line Manager* combo box with the following formula in the Formula bar:

```
{
```

```
DisplayName: Office365Users.ManagerV2(DataCardValue2.Selected.Email).displayName,
Claims: "i:0#.f|membership|" & Office365Users.ManagerV2(DataCardValue2.Selected.Email).
userPrincipalName
}
```

This formula retrieves the *display name* and *claims* of the requestor's manager from the **Office 365 Users** connector, based on the selected requestor's email. In our example, the field holding the value for the requestor is called DataCardValue2.

The formula will work as intended and the manager's display name will automatically show in the **Line Manager** field:

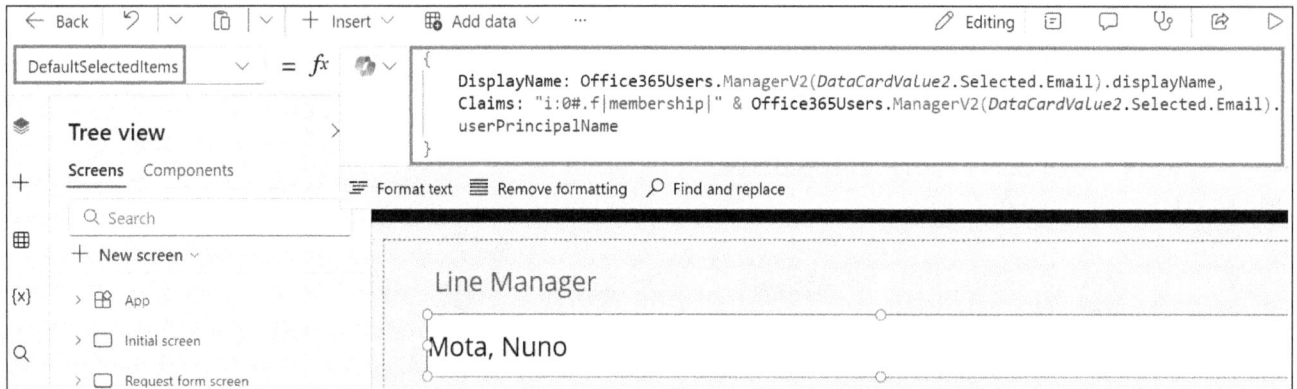

Figure 15.57: Change DefaultSelectedItems property for Line Manager field

Since the requestor and manager fields are now automatically populated with default values based on the user's directory information, it is advisable to lock these fields to prevent users from altering them when submitting a new request. To achieve this, we set the **DisplayMode** property of both *Requestor* and *Line Manager* combo boxes to **DisplayMode.View**.

Next, we will update the *Facility* and *Category* fields. Currently, they are *Text input* controls, but we want to replace them with selection boxes. We will configure these boxes to pull values from the *Facility* and *Category* columns in the *Employee Facilities* SharePoint List. To accomplish this, we will first remove the *Text input* controls associated with the *Facility* and *Category* data cards and replace them with *Combo box* controls.

When we perform the replacements, error messages will appear related to the **Update** property of the data cards for both *Category* and *Facility*, as well as for the **Y** property of the **ErrorMessage** labels. This occurs because these elements rely on the values of the text inputs we just deleted. To resolve this, we need to update the existing values with the names of the new combo boxes we have inserted, which in our example are named **ComboBox1** for the *Category* field and **ComboBox2** for the *Facility* field.

The following figures illustrate these changes applied to the *Category* data card **Update** property and the Y property of the *ErrorMessage* label associated with the *Category* data card:

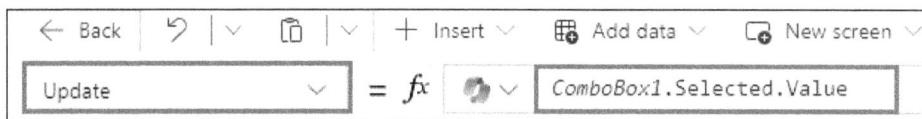

Figure 15.58: Change the Update property of the Category Data Card

The following figure also shows the changes applied:

Figure 15.59: Change the Y property of the ErrorMessage Label

We will also update the *Items* property of the *Category* combo box with the following formula:

```
Distinct('Employee Facilities'.Category,Category)
```

This formula helps to extract a list of distinct categories from the *Employee Facilities* SharePoint list, removing any duplicate entries.

The **Distinct** function is used to return a one-column table that contains the unique values from a specified column in a data source.

In this case, **'Employee Facilities'.Category** refers to the SharePoint list named *Employee Facilities* and its *Category* column. The following figure shows the formula used to update the **Items** property of the *Category* combo box in Power Apps:

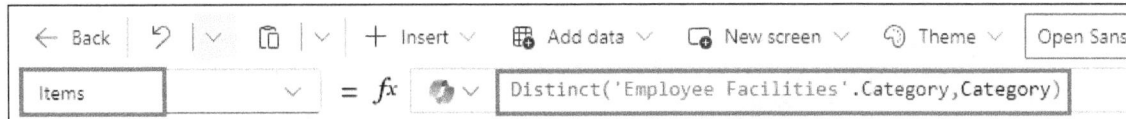

Figure 15.60: Change the Items property of the Category Combo box

To ensure that the **Facility** field shows items only based on the value selected in the **Category** field, we will update the *Facility* combo box **Items** property with the following formula:

```
Filter('Employee Facilities', Category = ComboBox1.Selected.Value).Facility
```

This formula retrieves the **Facility** values from the *Employee Facilities* SharePoint list, where the *Category* matches the value selected in **ComboBox1**:

- **Filter('Employee Facilities', Category = ComboBox1.Selected.Value)**: This part of the formula filters the data source named *Employee Facilities* to include only those records where the *Category* column matches the value selected in **ComboBox1**.

- **.Facility**: After filtering, this part extracts the *Facility* column from the filtered records.

The following figure shows the formula used to update the **Items** property of the *Facility* combo box in Power Apps:

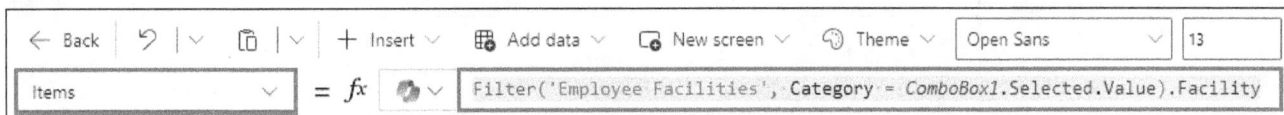

Figure 15.61: Change the Items property of the Facility combo box

After performing this change, we need to update the value of the *Update* property of the *Facility* Data Card, using the formula: **ComboBox2.Selected.Facility**, as shown in *Figure 15.62*. With this, we retrieve the actual value of the **Facility** property from the currently selected item in **ComboBox2**.

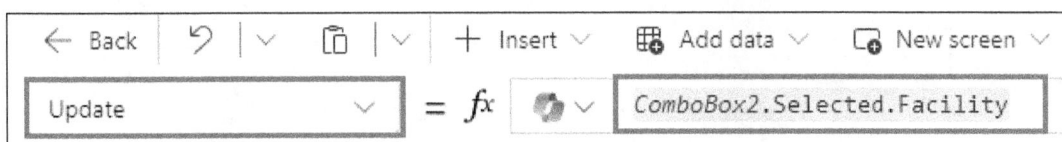

Figure 15.62: Change the Update property of the Facility Data Card

To make sure only one option can be selected in both *Category* and *Facility* fields, we set the **SelectMultiple** property of both combo boxes to **false**.

We also updated the **Width** property of both *Category* and *Facility* combo boxes using the expression **Parent. Width -60**. This sets the controls' width to be 60 pixels less than their parent container, ensuring they match the rest of the data cards and controls within the form.

One final adjustment for these two controls is to ensure that when the value in the *Category* combo box changes, the *Facility* combo box is reset. This allows the requestor to select the appropriate facility based on the chosen category. To achieve this, we need to update the **OnChange** property of the *Category* combo box with the formula **Reset(ComboBox2)**, as shown in the flowing figure:

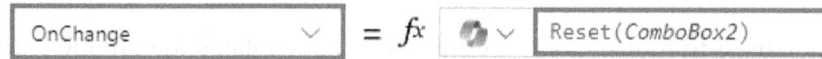

Figure 15.63: Update the OnChange property of the Category Combo box

The next step is to mark all editable Data Cards as mandatory, to make sure that all fields contain values before the request being submitted. This can be achieved by setting the **Required** property of the Data Cards to **true**, as shown in the following figure:

Figure 15.64: Set the Required property

Adding additional controls

On the *Request Form Screen*, we added and configured the following additional controls:

- A *Button*, configured to submit the *Request form* when pressed, using the **Submit('Request form')** formula under the **OnSelect** property of the button:

Figure 15.65: Set the OnSelect property of the Submit button

- A *Back arrow* icon, configured to navigate back to the previous screen (the *Initial Screen*) when pressed, using the **Back()** formula under the **OnSelect** property of the icon:

Figure 15.66: Set the OnSelect property of the Back arrow icon

- A *Reset* icon—configured to reset the *Request form* when pressed, using the **ResetForm('Request form')** formula under the **OnSelect** property of the icon:

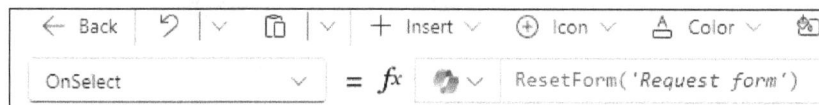

Figure 15.67: Set the OnSelect property of the Reset icon

Additionally, the **OnSuccess** property or the *Request form* had been updated to navigate to the *Success Screen* using the formula: **Navigate('Success Screen')**, as shown in the following figure. This way, the *Success Screen* will be displayed if the form is submitted successfully.

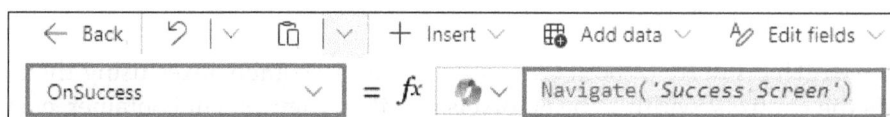

Figure 15.68: Set the OnSuccess property of the form

At this point, we have completed the necessary changes and configurations for the *Request Form Screen*:

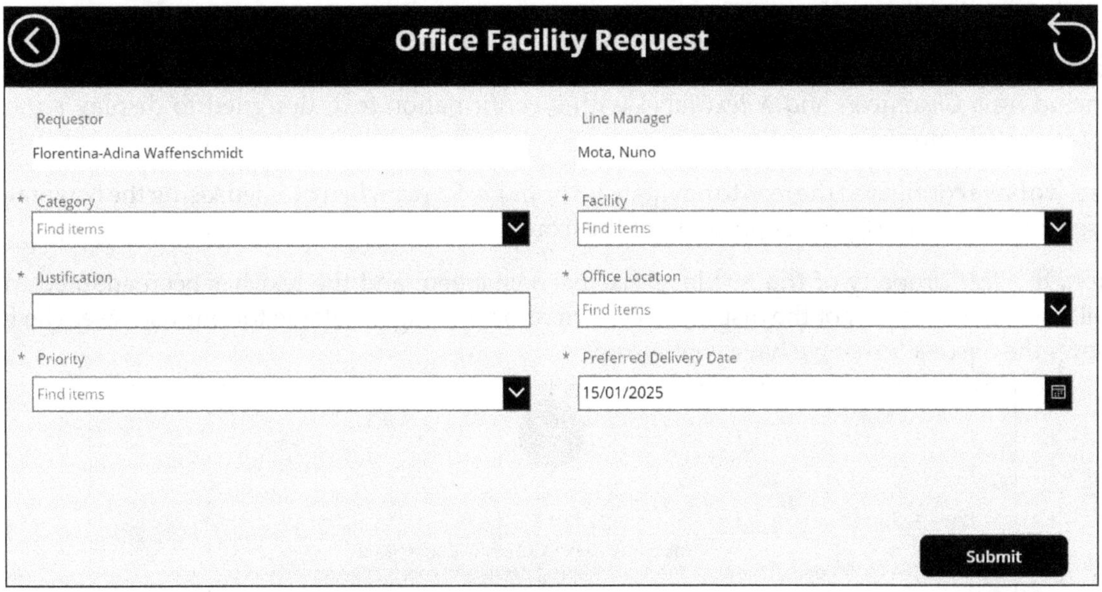

Figure 15.69: Request Form Screen

Designing the Initial Screen

Next, we will design the *Initial Screen,* by adding the necessary controls and configuring the controls functionality.

On the *Initial Screen,* we added the following controls:

- An *Image* from the *Stock images* library, suitable for the application scope.
- A *Text Label*, configured to display the application name
- Another *Text Label*, configured to display information about the application
- A *Button,* configured to navigate to the *Request Form Screen* and reset the *Request form* when pressed. To configure this control, we used the **ResetForm('Request form')** and **Navigate('Request Form Screen')** formulas under the *OnSelect* property of the button.

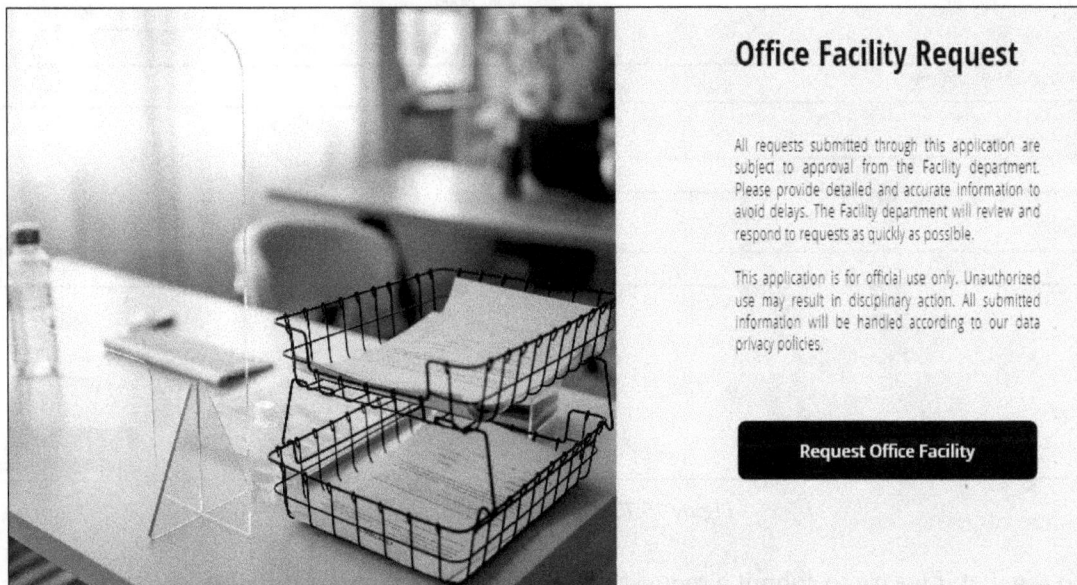

Figure 15.70: Initial Screen

Designing the Success Screen

The last screen to be designed for this sample application is the *Success Screen*. Since this screen has been added to the app using the *Success Screen* layout, this type of screen already comes with specific controls added, including a *Check* icon and a *Text* label with a confirmation text, designed to display a message on successful request submission.

In this case, we have configured the icon to navigate to the *Initial Screen* when pressed, using the **Navigate('Initial Screen')** formula under the *OnSelect* property of the icon.

In addition, the *Text* property of the *Text* label has been changed, and the text has been adapted to provide additional information as part of the displayed confirmation message, suitable for our use case. The following figure shows the *Success Screen* we have configured:

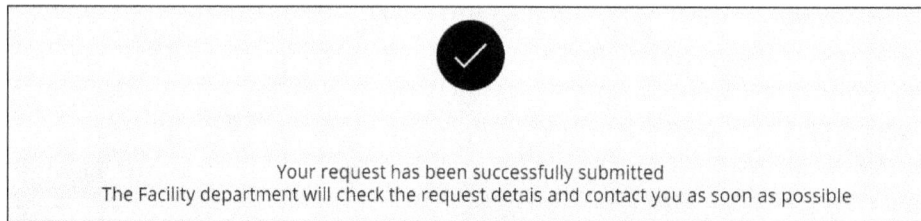

Your request has been successfully submitted
The Facility department will check the request detais and contact you as soon as possible

Figure 15.71: Success Screen

Testing the app

We have now completed our sample application. To check the behavior, we can play the app and submit a new request. This way, we can validate that the navigation between the screens works properly, the form responds as expected and the request can be submitted to the SharePoint list if no error messages are present.

For example, we can see that the corresponding **Facility** options are displayed based on the **Category** selected, validating the field configuration we performed previously:

Figure 15.72: Field selection validation

We can also see that if we try to submit a request without providing values for all the fields in the form, error messages are displayed, and the form is not submitted:

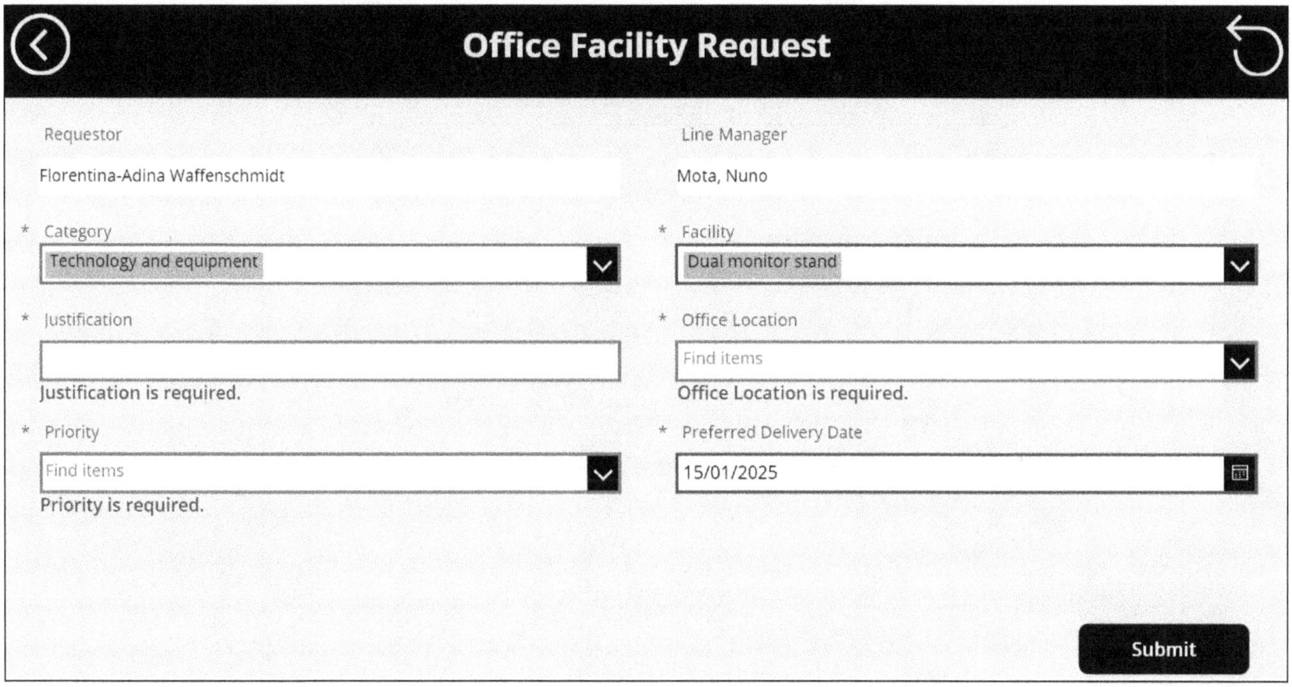

Figure 15.73: Form validation

If a request is submitted successfully, a new item is being created in the *Facility request* SharePoint list, as expected:

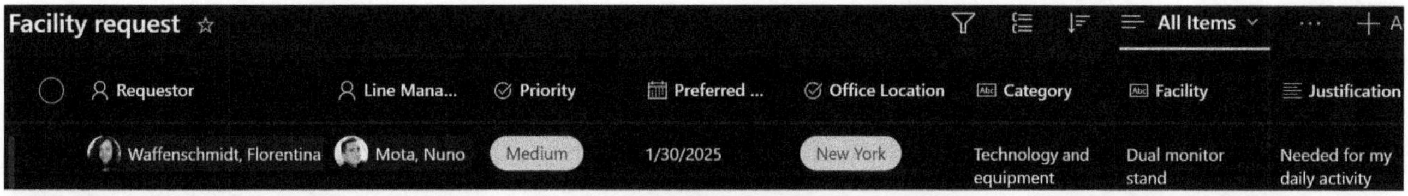

Figure 15.74: Item created in the SharePoint List

The simple canvas app we created in this demo serves as a foundational example of what can be achieved with Power Apps. There is ample room for further development by adding additional screens, controls, and functions to enhance the app's capabilities. This demonstrates the potential for creating more complex and robust applications.

Moreover, an approval flow can be integrated using Power Automate to automatically send approval requests once a submission is made.

Publishing and sharing a canvas application

To make a canvas app available to other users, it must be saved and published. Publishing an application can be done directly from Power Apps Studio, once you are happy with the changes made to the app:

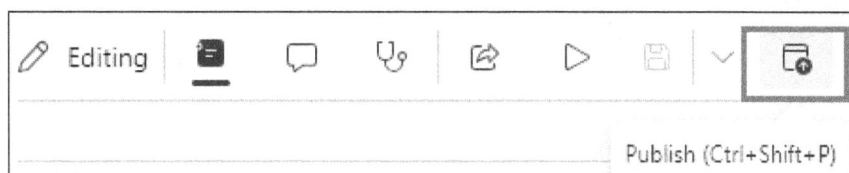

Figure 15.75: Publish app from Power Apps Studio

Once you click on **Publish**, a window will display informing you about the environment where the app will be published, and you can also upload from here an app icon and add an app description before publishing the current app version:

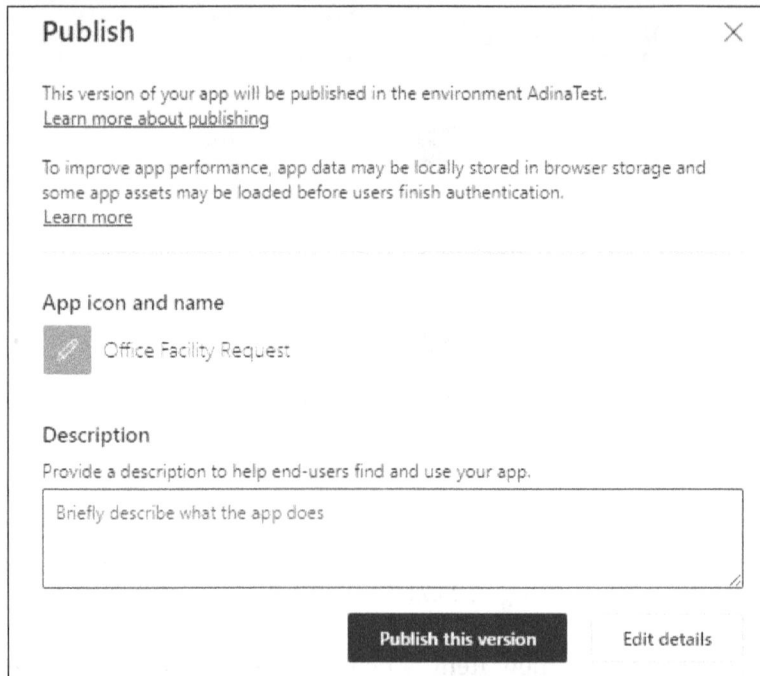

Figure 15.76: Publish current app version

To manage versions or to publish a different app version you need to:

1. Access the **Apps** tab in Power Apps
2. Select the three dots next to the app name
3. Select **Details**
4. Select the **Versions** tab.

Here, you can see the current live (published version) and you can select a different app version for publishing (rollback), if necessary:

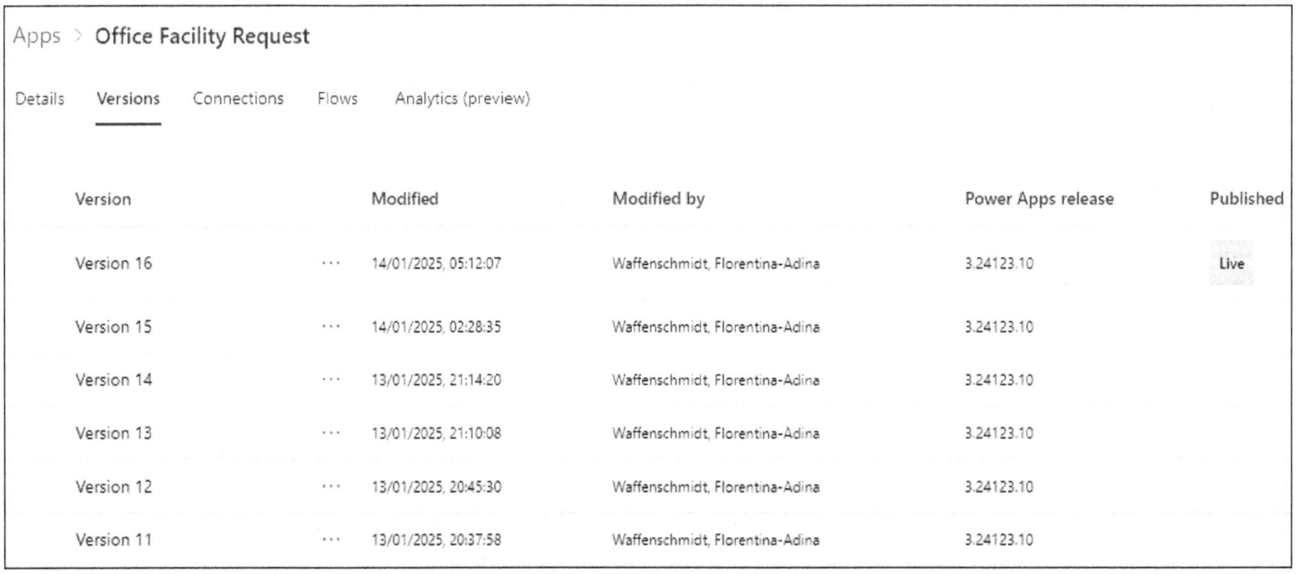

Figure 15.77: App versions

Once the desired app version has been published, the application can be shared either directly from **Power Apps Studio** or by following the next steps:

1. Access the **Apps** tab in Power Apps

2. Select the three dots next to the app name

3. Select **Share**

4. Add the users or groups you want to share the app with

5. Click on the down arrow to select the required permissions for the app

6. Add a message (optional)

7. Click on **Share** to share the application.

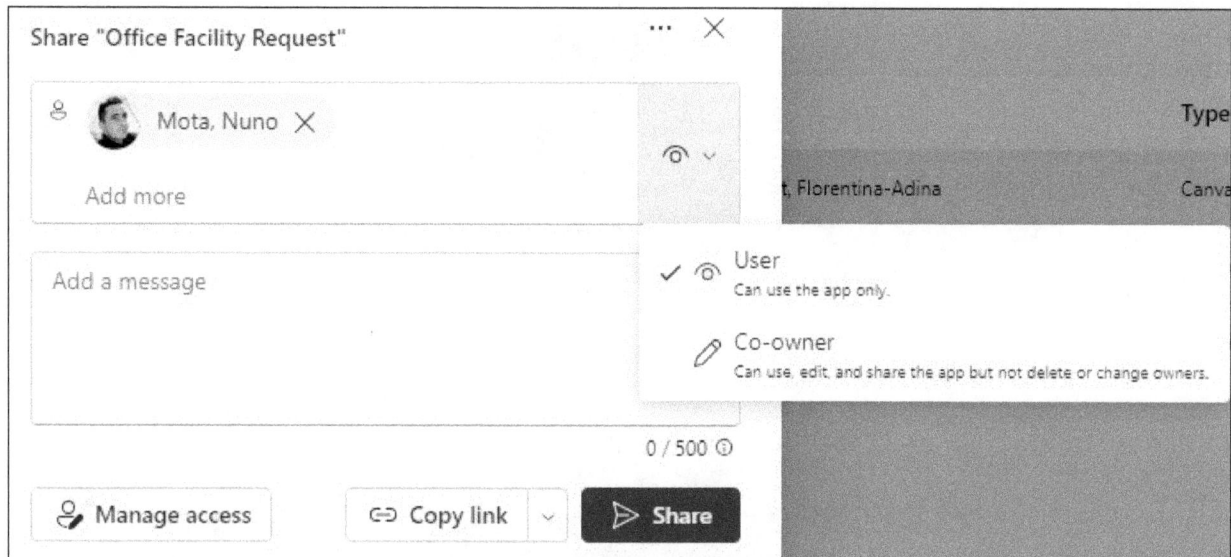

Figure 15.78: Share a canvas app

Canvas apps can be shared with users from the organization, security groups or guest users from a different tenant.

Before sharing an application, it is important to check if additional permissions need to be granted to users at the data source level, for them to be able to play the application.

For example, if your app uses a SharePoint list as a data source, you need to grant the users the necessary permissions at the list level in SharePoint.

Conclusion

In this chapter, we have seen how Power Apps can be a transformative tool within the Microsoft 365 suite, empowering users to create custom applications with ease, even without extensive coding knowledge. We explored the core functionalities of Power Apps, including the differences between canvas apps and model-driven apps through practical scenarios of app creation.

In the next chapter, we will be exploring Power Pages, a powerful tool within the Microsoft Power Platform that allows users to create secure, data-driven websites with ease.

Join our Discord space

Join our Discord workspace for latest updates, offers, tech happenings around the world, new releases, and sessions with the authors:

https://discord.bpbonline.com

CHAPTER 16
Power Pages

Introduction

In the ever-evolving landscape of digital transformation, Power Pages has emerged as a tool that facilitates the seamless creation and management of web pages and applications with minimal coding. As we explore the intricacies of Power Pages in this chapter, you will discover the numerous advantages and applications of this powerful platform.

Structure

This chapter covers the following topics:

- Introduction to Power Pages
- Advantages and disadvantages of Power Pages
- Power Pages architecture
- Getting stared with Power Pages
- Managing sites

Objectives

By the end of this chapter, readers will gain a comprehensive understanding of what Power Pages are and their significance in modern web development. Additionally, readers will follow detailed instructions to create, design, integrate, and manage Power Pages, ensuring a practical understanding of how to build and deploy their own web pages with confidence. This chapter will provide a step-by-step guide that will enable readers to confidently build and deploy their own web pages using Power Pages.

Introduction to Power Pages

Power Pages, previously known as Power Apps portals, is a secure, low-code **software as a service (SaaS)** platform designed for creating, hosting, and administering internal or external-facing business websites. It allows users to build sites using shared business data stored in Microsoft Dataverse, which is also used for creating apps, workflows, virtual agents, reports, and analytics with other Microsoft Power Platform components within an organization. Power Pages allows both low-code makers and professional developers to quickly design, configure, and publish websites compatible with various web browsers and devices.

Here are some common and practical use cases for Power Pages:

- **Customer self-service portals**: Let customers log in to view account info, submit support tickets, or track service requests, reducing the load on your support team.

- **Partner portals**: Enable external partners to register deals, access shared documents, and collaborate on projects securely.

- **Application submission platforms**: Collect and manage applications for things like grants, permits, or job postings with built-in workflows and status tracking.

- **Data dashboards and reporting sites**: Share interactive reports and dashboards (via Power BI) with external stakeholders, like clients or board members.

- **Training and onboarding portals**: Provide new employees or volunteers with access to training materials, forms, and progress tracking.

- **Event registration sites**: Let users register for events, workshops, or webinars with automated confirmations and attendee tracking.

Power Pages integrates seamlessly with other tools within the Power Platform ecosystem, including Power Automate, Power BI, and Power Apps. This integration enables users to create comprehensive web applications that can interact with various data sources, automate workflows, and provide real-time insights. The ability to connect and interact with different components of the Power Platform makes Power Pages a powerful tool for organizations seeking to build dynamic and data-driven web solutions.

One of the key advantages of Power Pages is their ability to support a wide range of applications. Whether you are creating a simple informational website, a complex data-driven application, or an interactive customer portal, Power Pages provides the tools and flexibility needed to bring your vision to life. The platform offers a variety of templates and customization options, allowing users to design pages that align with their specific requirements and branding guidelines.

Power Pages is mainly for business users and developers who want to build secure, data-driven websites with minimal coding, but it is so easy to use that even non-developers can build their own page. Key audiences include:

- **Low-code makers**: People with little to no coding experience who want to create functional websites quickly.

- **Professional developers**: Those who need to build more complex or customized web apps using tools like Visual Studio Code or GitHub.

- **Organizations using Microsoft Dataverse**: Power Pages is tightly integrated with Dataverse, making it ideal for businesses already using the Power Platform.

- **Teams needing external-facing portals**: For customer self-service, partner collaboration, or public-facing sites.

Licensing

Power Pages are licensed based on capacity and offer two types of capacities depending on user type: *Authenticated users per website/month* and *Anonymous users per website/month*.

- Purchase an **Authenticated user capacity** subscription license for the expected number of unique, authenticated users, such as **internal employees** or **external non-employees** accessing a website monthly.

- Purchase an **Anonymous user monthly capacity** subscription license for the expected number of unique, anonymous users who will access a website within a given month.

If you are building a Power Pages website for your (internal) employees who log in using their Entra ID credentials, you can use the *authenticated user capacity* subscription or one of the following types of licenses:

1. **Power Apps per app**: Users can access one Power Pages website which is part of the environment to which Power Apps per app capacity licenses are assigned.

2. **Power Apps per user licensed users**: Users with this license can use unlimited Power Pages websites.

3. **Dynamics 365 enterprise licensed users**: These users can use unlimited Power Pages websites. However, these sites must map to the licensed Dynamics 365 application context and map to the same environment as the licensed Dynamics 365 application.

When selecting a license, organizations should consider several factors. First and foremost, they should assess their usage requirements. This involves determining the number of users and the frequency of site visits to select the most cost-effective plan.

Next, organizations should review the pricing structure of each licensing option to ensure it aligns with their budget constraints. Microsoft provides detailed pricing information on its website, which can help organizations make informed decisions.

Additionally, scalability is a crucial consideration. Organizations should think about future growth and scalability needs, choosing a plan that can accommodate increasing usage and additional visitors without requiring frequent license upgrades.

Finally, integration needs should be evaluated. It is important to determine the necessity of integrating Power Pages with other tools and services within the Microsoft ecosystem. Licensing options that support seamless integration with Power Automate, Power BI, and Power Apps can significantly enhance overall functionality.

Advantages and disadvantages of Power Pages

When considering Power Pages for your web development needs, it is essential to weigh both the advantages and disadvantages of the platform. This balanced perspective will help you determine whether Power Pages aligns with your organizational goals, technical requirements, and budget constraints. The following is an examination of the advantages and disadvantages of using Power Pages.

The advantages are as follows:

- **User-friendly interface**: Power Pages offers an intuitive drag-and-drop interface that enables users of all skill levels to create web pages without the need for complex coding. This user-centric design simplifies the development process and allows for quick modifications and updates, making it accessible to both technical and non-technical users.

- **Seamless integration**: Power Pages integrate effortlessly with other Microsoft tools, such as Power Automate, Power BI, and Microsoft Dataverse. This capability enables users to connect their web pages to various data sources, automate workflows, and visualize data within their web applications. The seamless integration enhances overall functionality and empowers organizations to leverage their existing Microsoft ecosystem.

- **Scalability**: The platform is designed to support a wide range of applications, from simple informational sites to complex, data-driven web solutions. Power Pages can scale to meet the evolving needs of an organization, ensuring that web pages remain relevant and effective as the organization grows. This scalability can make it a versatile choice for businesses of all sizes and industries.

- **Customization**: Power Pages provide extensive customization options, allowing users to modify templates and components to fit specific needs. This flexibility ensures that web pages are unique and engaging, adhering to the branding and objectives of the organization. Users can create personalized experiences for their audience, enhancing user engagement and satisfaction.

- **Security**: Built on Microsoft's robust security framework, Power Pages offers advanced protection features such as user authentication, data encryption, and access controls. These security measures ensure that web applications are secure and compliant with industry standards, safeguarding sensitive information and providing peace of mind to organizations and their users.

The disadvantages are as follows:

- **Dependency on the Microsoft ecosystem**: Power Pages work best within the Microsoft ecosystem, which can limit integration with non-Microsoft tools. While it integrates well with Microsoft products, connecting with third-party tools may be challenging. This reliance on Microsoft's ecosystem can be a drawback for organizations using diverse platforms.

- **Learning curve**: Despite its user-friendly interface, mastering Power Pages can still be challenging, especially for those new to similar tools. Users may need to invest time in learning the features and may require extra training or support to fully utilize its capabilities.

- **Cost**: Licensing and subscription costs can be a concern, particularly for small businesses or individuals. The pricing structure varies based on usage, so organizations must carefully consider their budget and needs to choose the right option.

Power Pages architecture

Power Pages offers a secure, scalable, and highly available platform suitable for building business-critical websites for various use cases. Each production Power Pages website adheres to consistent architecture designed for scalability and high availability. The following figure illustrates the architecture used to host each Power Pages website:

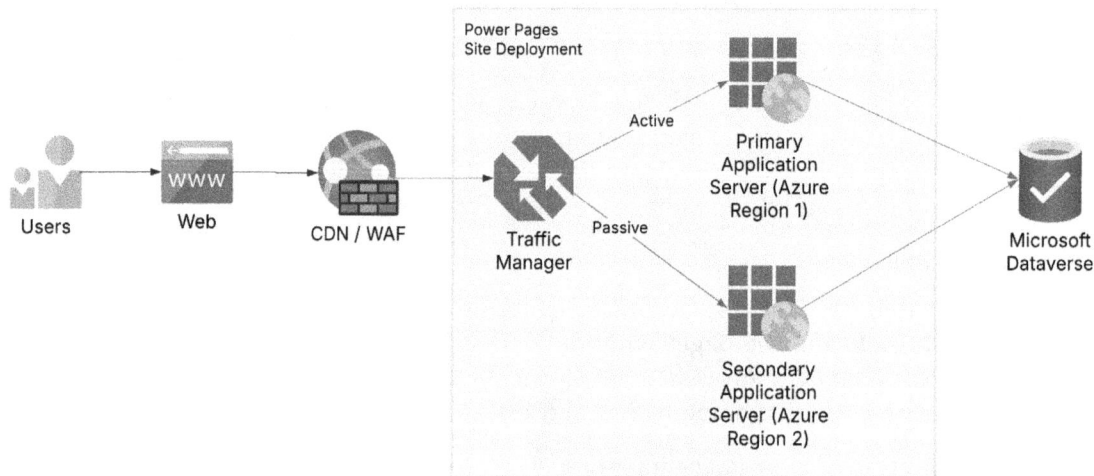

Figure 16.1: *Power Pages architecture*

The explanation of the elements is as follows:

- **Content delivery network**: A **content delivery network** (**CDN**) enhances website performance and scalability by lowering network latency for end users and caching static files, which are then served from an edge network.

    Power Pages includes an out-of-the-box CDN capability that is not enabled by default but can be activated by a site administrator. For those who need more control, Power Pages also supports external content delivery network providers such as Azure Front Door, Akamai, Cloudflare, Imperva, and others that can be configured with your Power Pages website.

- **Web application firewall**: A **web application firewall** (**WAF**) enhances the security of a website by analyzing traffic and protecting it against common attacks such as cross-site scripting, SQL injection, and others. Similar to a CDN, Power Pages offers an out-of-the-box web application firewall that can be enabled by a site administrator. For those who need more control over web application firewall configuration, Power Pages also supports the use of customer-owned web application firewall providers like Azure Front Door, Akamai, Cloudflare, Imperva, and others.

- **Azure traffic manager**: Each Power Pages production website is equipped with an Azure traffic manager instance configured in active/passive mode, directing end-user traffic to the appropriate application server. This functionality ensures both high availability and disaster recovery.

- **Application servers**: Each Power Pages production website consists of at least two application server nodes hosted in different Azure datacenter regions for high availability and disaster recovery. Azure Traffic Manager constantly monitors these nodes and directs traffic to the available node. The location of an Azure datacenter region determines the location of the Power Platform environment to which the site belongs.

  For instance, if the environment location is Europe, application servers will be located in North Europe and West Europe datacenters. The primary region of a site is determined by the primary region of the Power Platform organization to ensure minimal latency between Dataverse and the website. The scaling of these application servers occurs automatically based on the Power Pages licensing capacity assigned to the environment.

- **Dataverse**: Microsoft Dataverse serves as an essential component for any Power Pages website. It functions both as a metadata repository, storing all website configurations such as webpages, content snippets, site settings, and user metadata, among other elements, and as a data store for business data.

Note: **Enabling WAF and/or CDN can only be done by administrators and its implications for governance should be taken into consideration.**

Getting started with Power Pages

This section of the book will guide you through the process of creating a site, from initial setup to advanced tasks like using Dataverse to display data.

Before getting started, however, it is important to explore and understand **environments**, which are foundational to how Power Pages operates as they define the boundaries for your data, security, and customization. Here is how environments come into play:

- **Isolation of content**: Each environment is a separate space with its own Dataverse database, apps, and Power Pages sites. This helps keep development, testing, and production clearly separated.

- **Security and roles**: Permissions (like *system administrator* or *website owner*) are assigned per environment. This means someone can manage a site in one environment but have no access in another.

- **Customization scope**: Any changes to tables, forms, or workflows are scoped to the environment. So, if you customize a table in one environment, it would not affect others.

- **Lifecycle management**: You can move Power Pages sites between environments using solutions, ideal for promoting from dev to test to production.

Think of environments as containers that help you manage governance, security, and scalability. Power Pages supports several types of environments, each designed for different stages of development and deployment within the Power Platform. Here is a quick breakdown:

- **Developer**:
  - o For individual use with the Power Apps Developer Plan
  - o Ideal for building and testing apps solo
  - o Limited to the owner, no sharing with others
- **Trial**:
  - o Temporary (expires after 30 days)
  - o Great for exploring features or short-term testing
  - o One per user, typically not for production
- **Sandbox**:
  - o Non-production environment
  - o Used for development and testing
  - o Supports features like copy/reset
- **Production**:
  - o Meant for live, business-critical workloads
  - o Full access to premium features
  - o Requires proper licensing and capacity
- **Default**:
  - o Automatically created for each tenant
  - o Shared by all users
  - o Limited control, not ideal for structured development
- **Dataverse for Teams**:
  - o Created when building apps inside Microsoft Teams
  - o Limited to Teams users
  - o Best for lightweight, low-code solutions within Teams

Each environment type has its own **security**, **storage**, and **lifecycle characteristics**, so choosing the right one depends on your goals, whether you are experimenting, developing, testing, or going live.

Creating a site

Creating a Power Pages site is a straightforward process that allows you to establish a robust and secure online presence.

This section will guide you through the initial steps of setting up your site, from accessing Power Pages to selecting the appropriate Microsoft Dataverse environment and choosing a suitable template:

1. To start, navigate to **https://make.powerpages.microsoft.com**.

2. Choose the environment where you want to create the site by clicking on **Environment** in the top right corner. It is not recommended to create a site in the default environment, as this environment is shared among all users in the tenant, which may result in unintentional data sharing with other users, as shown:

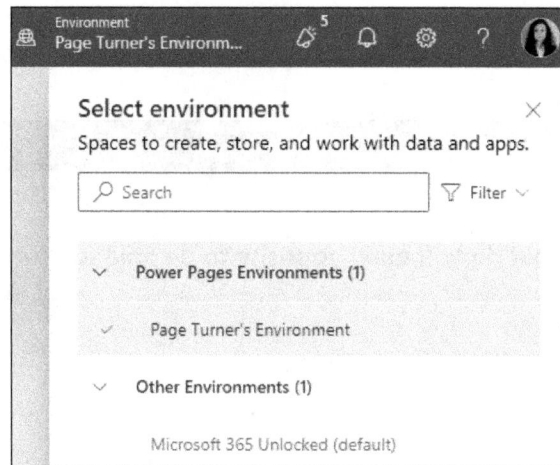

Figure 16.2: *Selecting the environment where to create a site*

3. Now that you have selected the environment where to create the site, you can either manually create your site or use Copilot to help create it for you with the help of AI. Describe the website you want to create, and AI will design it for you. Use natural language processing to build your site by specifying the type of site, intended users, and type of information the site will process. Copilot produces the contextual site name, site address, home page layout, and additional pages using HTML for each page with relevant text and images based on the description. The site includes the home page and the selected additional pages, which are incorporated into the sitemap. After creation, these pages can be refined and edited using Copilot and the WYSIWYG (*what you see is what you get*) editor.

In this example, we click on **Start with a template** to select an initial layout template to construct our site, as follows:

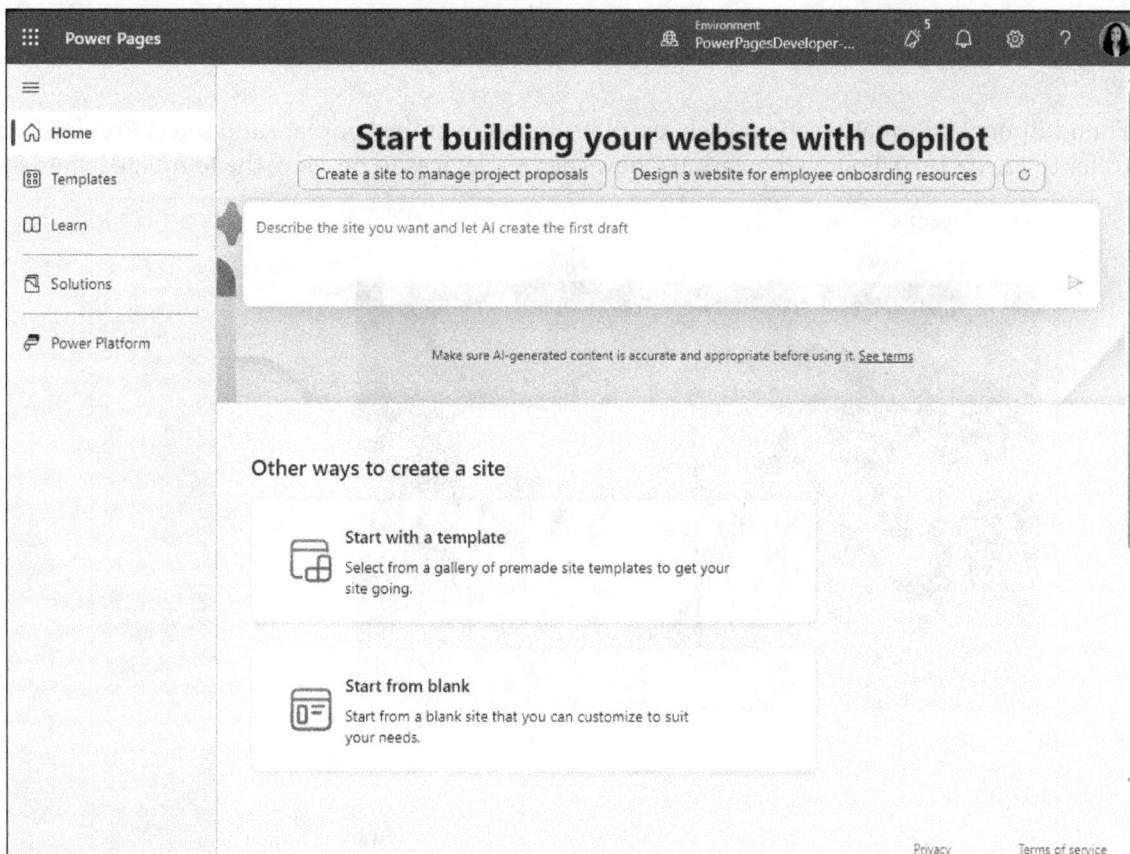

Figure 16.3: *Choosing how to build a site*

Alternatively, we can opt for scenario-based templates to expedite the development process or use the blank page template to create a fully customized website. The following figure shows some of these templates:

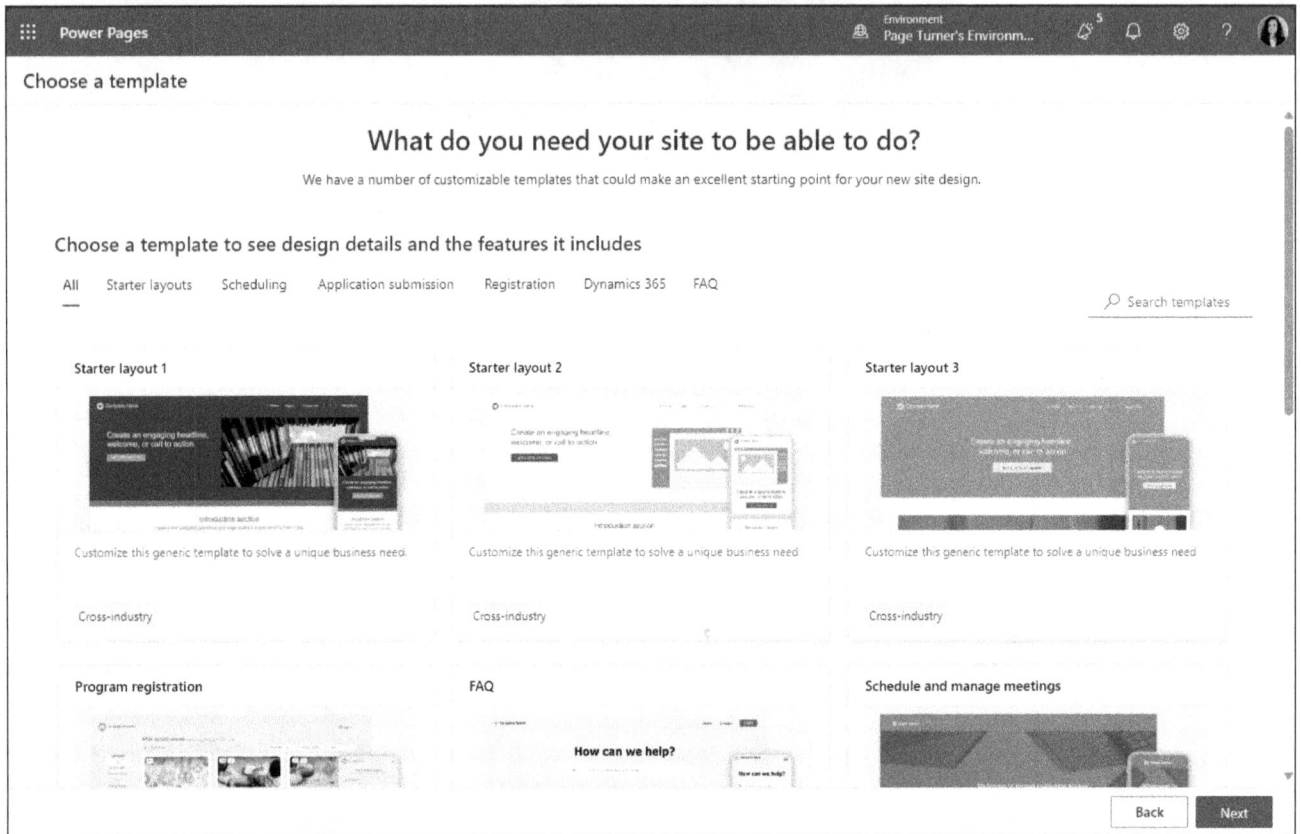

Figure 16.4: Site templates

4. For additional information about each template, hover over the template and select **Preview template** (refer to *Figure 16.5*). Follow the various views across devices to preview the template experience.

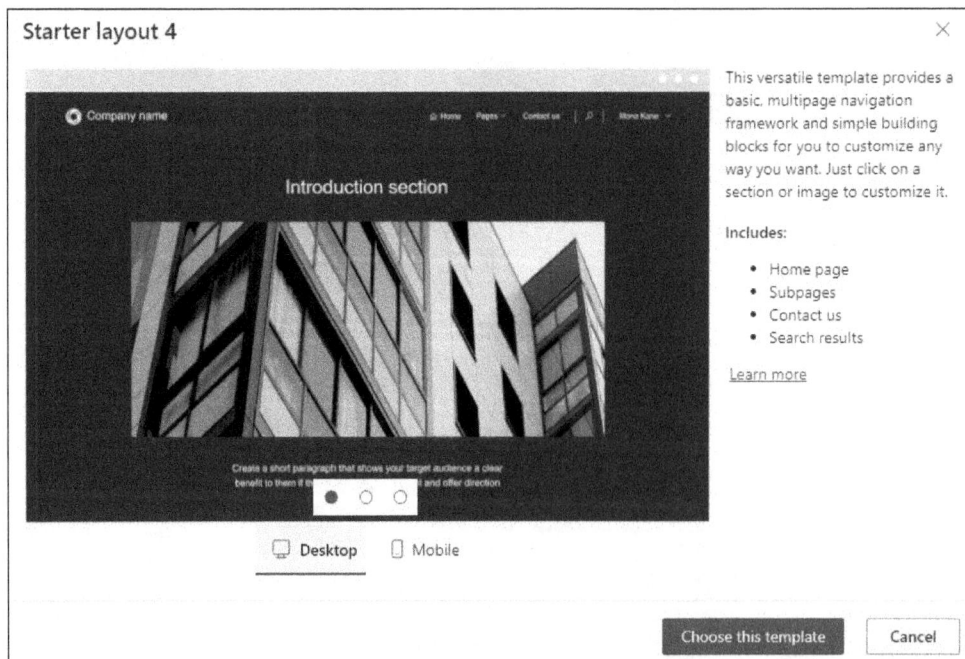

Figure 16.5: Previewing a template

5. Once you have identified the most suitable template for your business requirements, please select **Choose this template**.

6. Confirm the site name and web address (both can be changed later), then click **Done**:

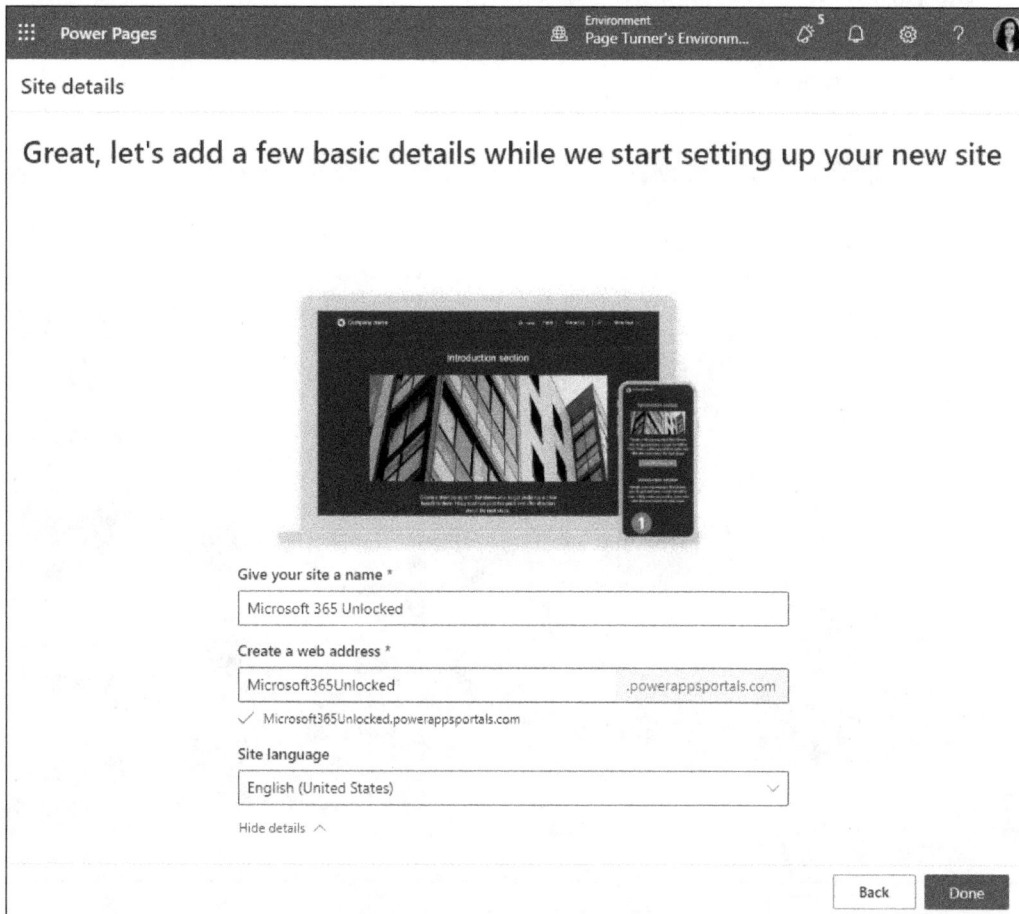

Figure 16.6: *Creating a site from a template*

7. Once the site has been created, which can take a few moments, you may proceed to edit or preview its content:

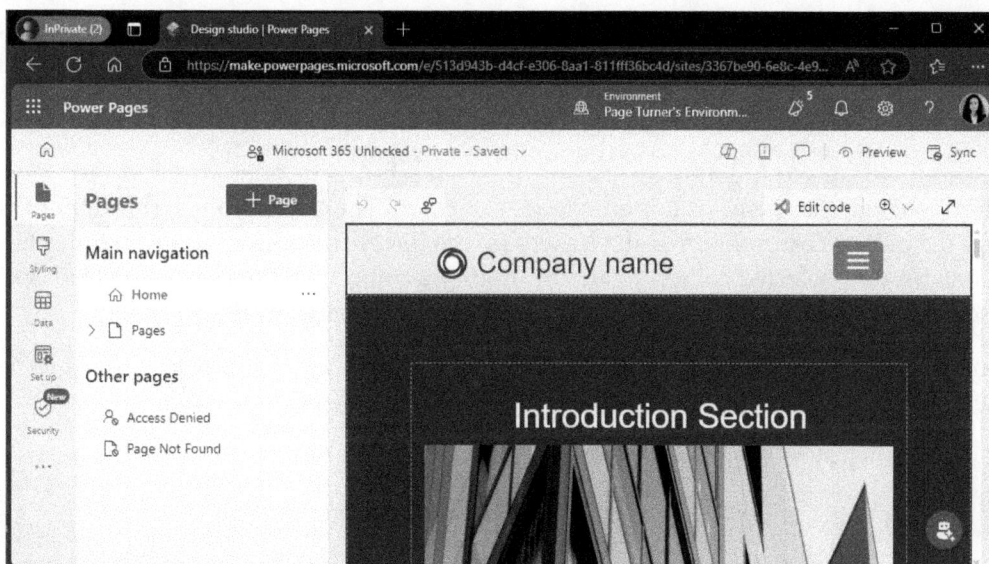

Figure 16.7: *Power Pages editor*

Styling your site

Styling your site is a crucial step in ensuring it aligns with your corporate branding and delivers a cohesive visual experience to your visitors. You should also take responsiveness into account and evaluate how different styling options adapt across different type of devices.

Power Pages offers a comprehensive **Styling** workspace, where you can establish your brand's presence by customizing various aspects of the site's appearance, as shown:

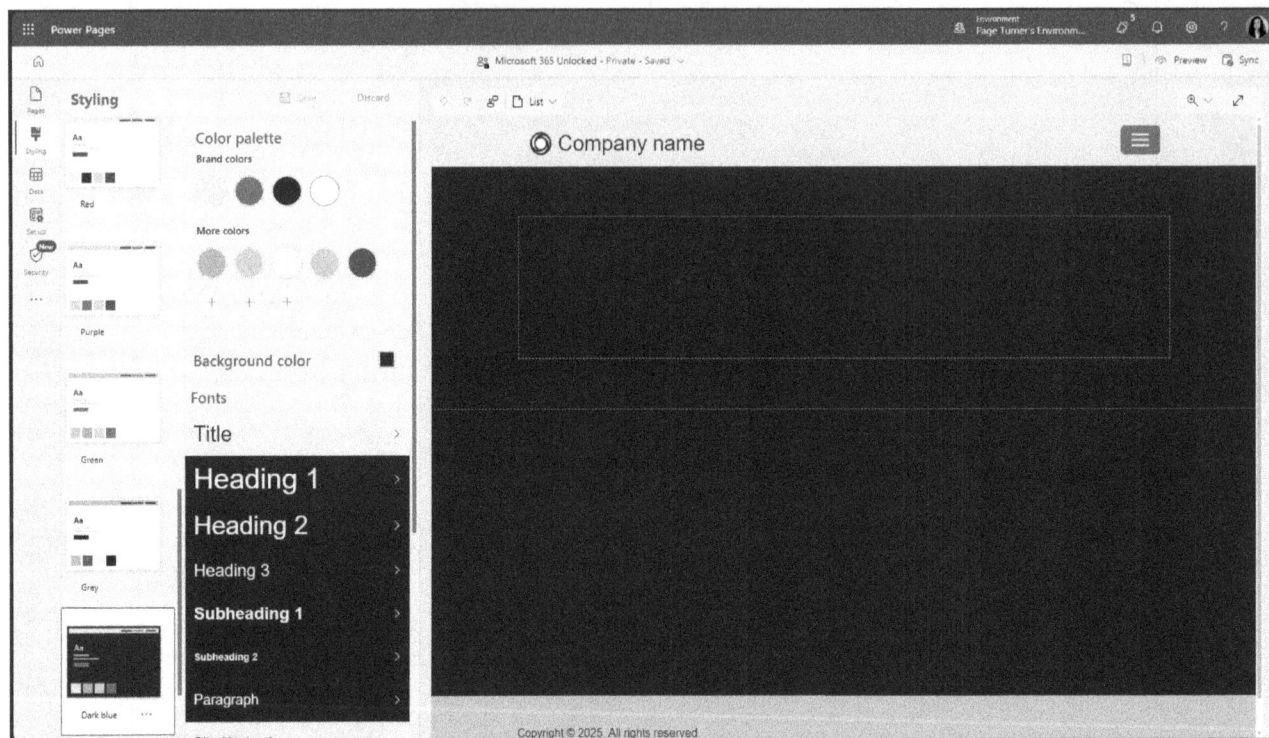

Figure 16.8: Styling workspace

The Styling workspace (*Figure 16.8*) enables the configuration of brand colors, fonts, and design defaults for either the entire site or individual pages. This flexibility allows you to maintain a consistent look and feel across your web presence, reinforcing your brand identity.

You can easily set your brand color palette. For example, consider updating the color palette to include two or three primary brand colors along with neutral complementary tones. These selected colors should be utilized consistently throughout the entire Power Pages site. The steps are as follows:

1. Within the design studio, navigate to the **Styling** workspace.

2. If desired, change the theme and then choose the colors you prefer to use throughout the site. Each color on the palette corresponds to an element on the page. The preset theme includes nine colors and three slots for user-selected colors. To add or modify a color, click the plus sign (+) in the color palette and choose your color using the color picker, hexadecimal value, or RGB values.

3. If at any time you wish to start over, select the ellipses and select **Reset to default** to roll back your changes.

4. When you are happy with the changes, click **Save**, as shown:

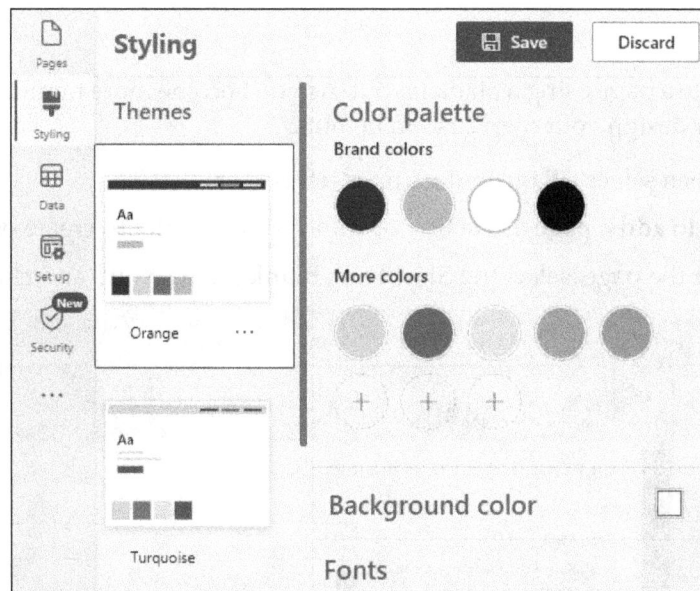

Figure 16.9: Themes and color palettes

Cascading Style Sheets (**CSS**) gives you full control over the site's formatting and styling. Newly created Power Pages sites include **bootstrap.min.css**, **theme.css**, and **portalbasictheme.css** files as part of their initial templates. The style can be modified using the Styling workspace by clicking on the ellipsis (**...**) next to a theme's name and selecting **Manage CSS**. Do keep in mind that overriding these files can affect their corresponding templates. Custom CSS files can also be uploaded to achieve specific design preferences.

Next, we can set up our corporate brand fonts by scrolling down to the **fonts** section. Here we can define the fonts for our headers, sub-headers, paragraphs, buttons, and links:

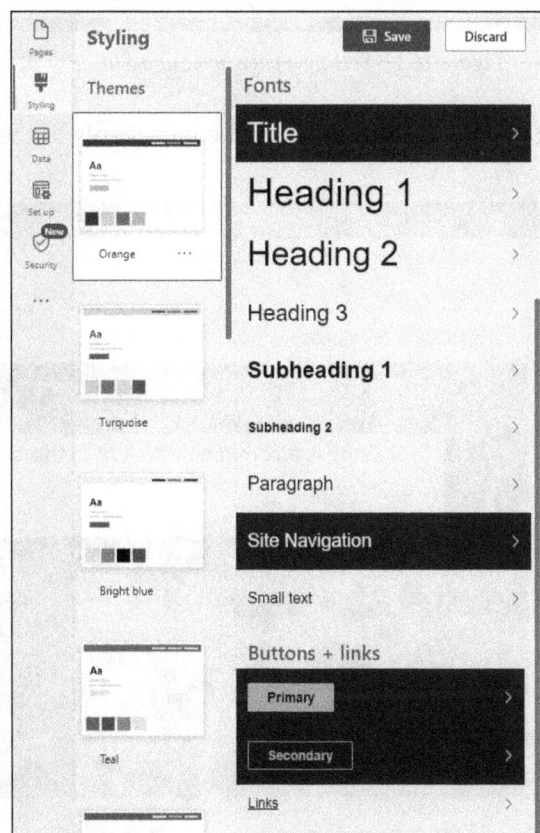

Figure 16.10: Fonts

Adding a page

In these steps, we will create a page using a blank layout. As you become more familiar with Power Pages, you can utilize other layouts or design your own custom layouts:

1. Select **Pages** and then select **+ Page** in the upper-left corner.

2. Select **Other ways to add a page** as we do not want to use Copilot to create our page.

3. Provide a name for the page, select the **Start from blank** page layout, and click on **Add**, as shown:

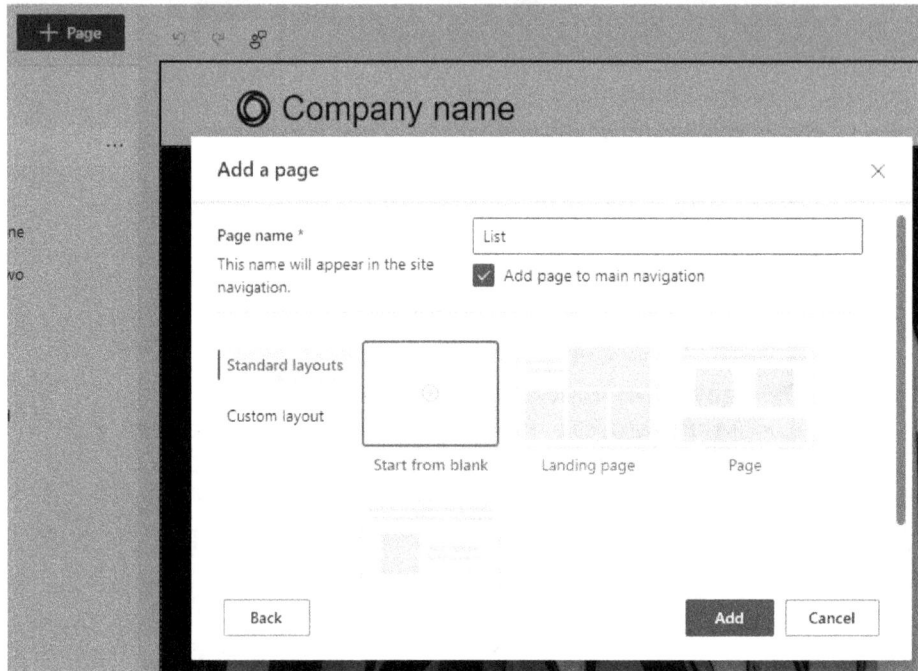

Figure 16.11: Setting a page name and a layout

4. You will soon see a blank page with options to add components to the page as seen below, which we will do next, as follows:

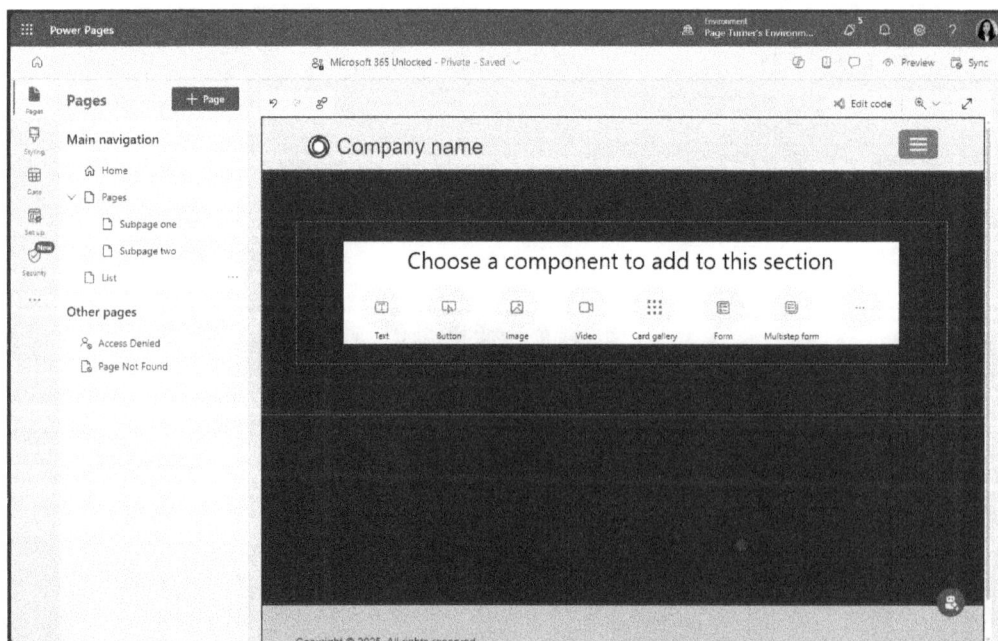

Figure 16.12: Adding components to a page

Designing our page

Designing a web page with Power Pages is a user-friendly process that allows you to create dynamic and interactive content with ease. Whether you are utilizing predefined layouts or crafting custom designs, Power Pages provides a versatile environment that caters to various needs.

You can change the appearance of a page by experimenting with various sections, components, and colors. Specifically, you can add spacers, single-column sections, and button controls to navigate to different pages. You can also center buttons and adjust their appearance. Additionally, integrating dynamic lists and components into the page can further enhance its functionality and interactivity.

Let us start by editing the site header so we can update our company name and logo. To do that, we hover the mouse over the header and click on **Edit site header**:

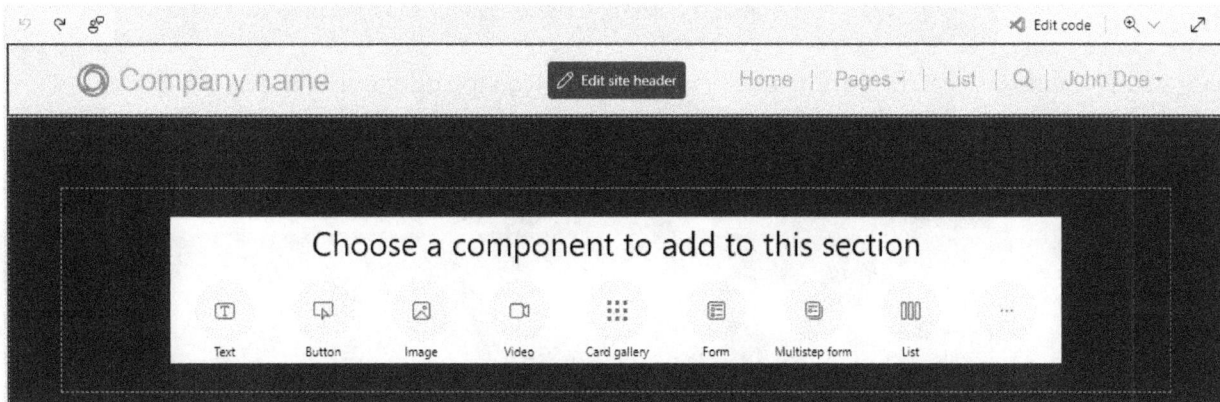

Figure 16.13: Editing a site's header

We select our company name and logo and close the window, as shown:

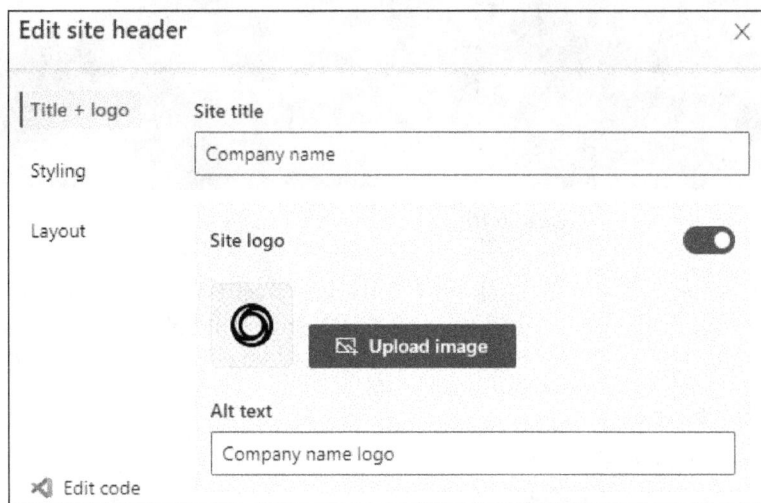

Figure 16.14: Setting the site title and logo

Next, we add some content to our page:

1. Select the **Text** component to add a text box to our page.

2. Enter a name for the page, such as *New Joiners List* for example.

    a. Change the style to **Heading 1**

    b. Click on **B** to make the text bold

    c. Adjust the alignment so the text is centered, as follows:

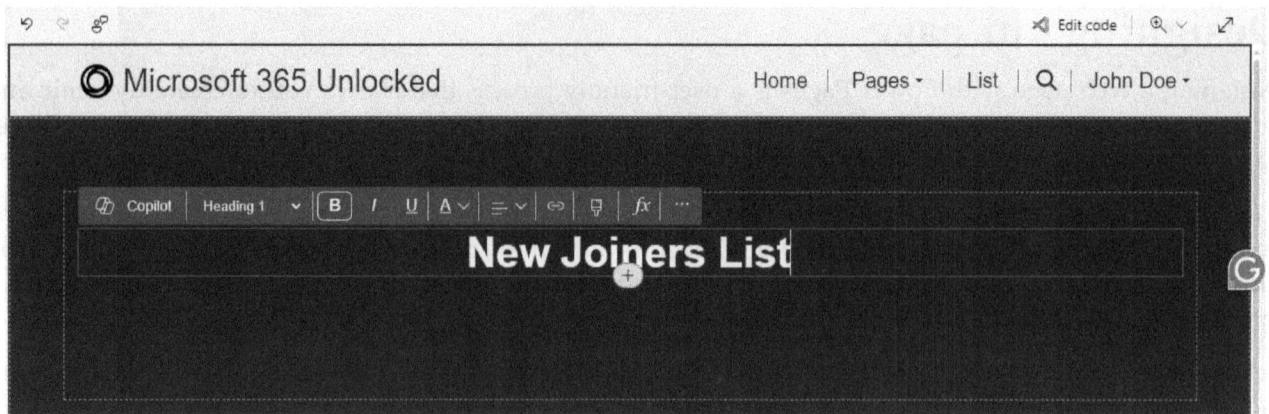

Figure 16.15: Adding a text component

3. Below the text, select the + icon and click the **Spacer** icon to add the spacer component:

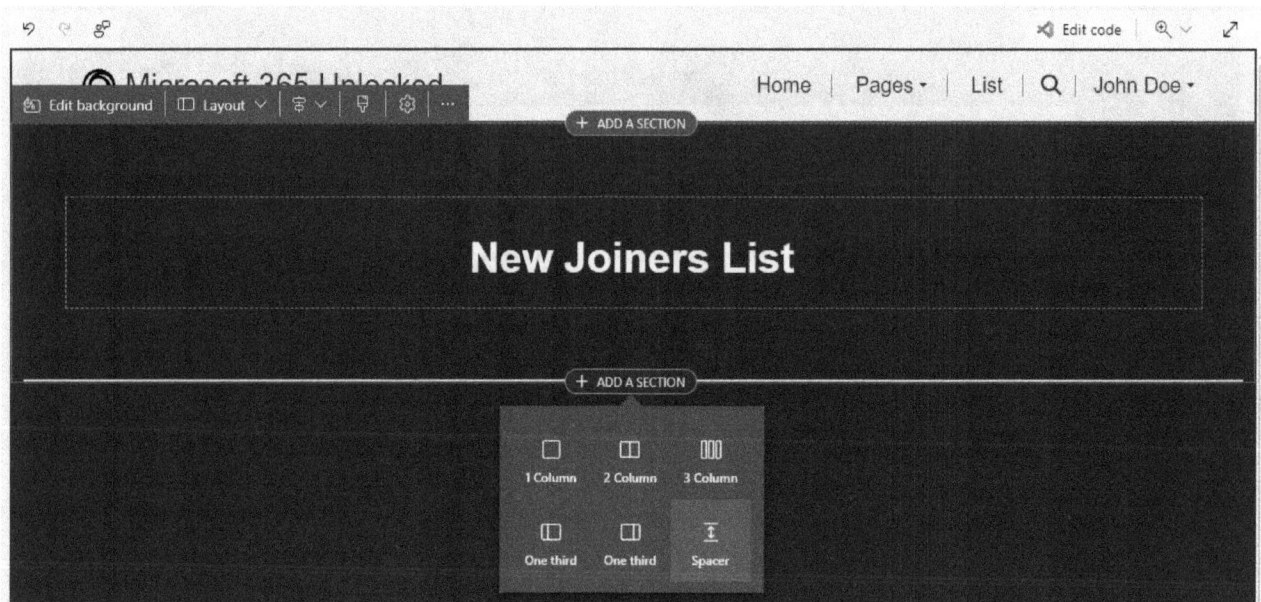

Figure 16.16: Adding a spacer component

4. Below the spacer, select the + icon, click on **1 Column** to add a section that occupies a single column (i.e., the whole width of the page), and then add a **Button** control to take us back to our **Home** page. Configure the following details for the button:

   a. **Button label**: Home

   b. Choose **Link to a page**

   c. Select **Home** page from the dropdown.

   d. Select **OK**

   e. Use the properties menu to center the button

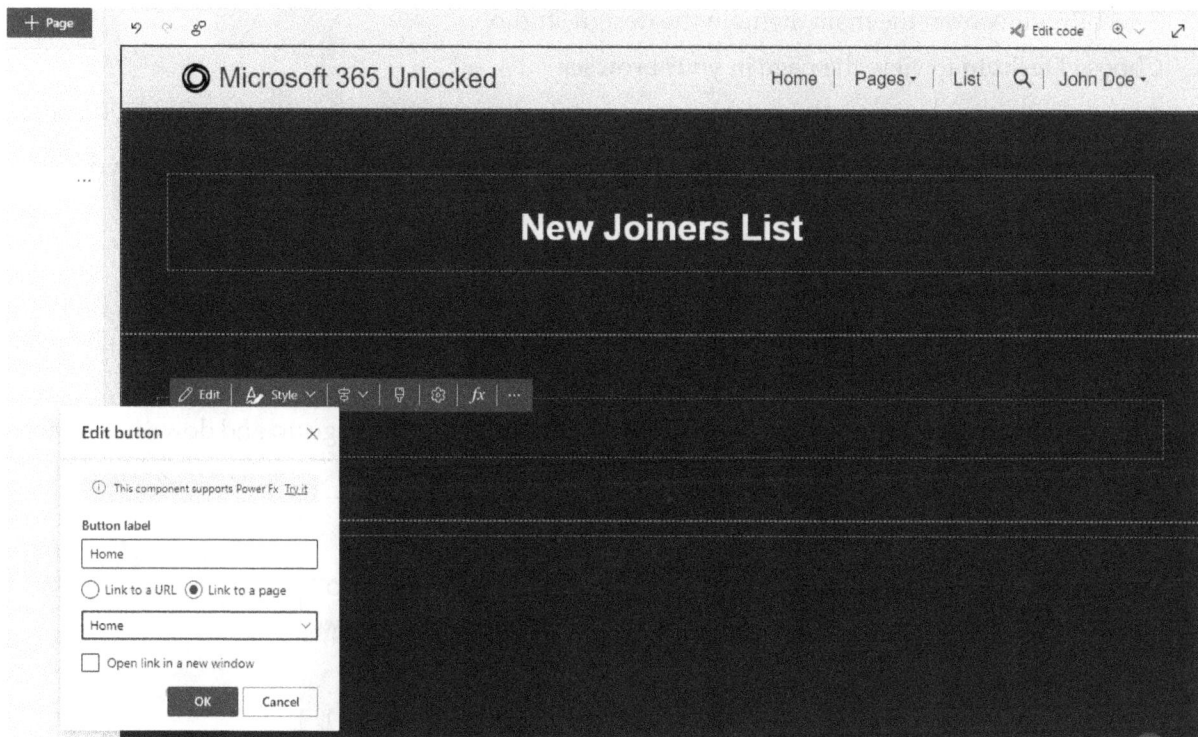

Figure 16.17: Adding a button component

We can also change the button's appearance if required and experiment by adding more sections and components or changing the colors of our page.

Advanced designing

Power Pages offers robust tools for low-code developers and web designers to construct and configure highly functional websites. In some projects though, it can be necessary to enhance the capabilities of the web application through advanced development techniques. The Power Pages platform offers sophisticated tools and technologies designed to enable developers to tackle advanced and complex requirements effectively:

- **Visual Studio Code for the web**: Enables the viewing and editing of HTML, JavaScript, Liquid, and CSS code. Users can modify code on multistep forms, basic forms, content snippets, lists, web files, web pages, and web templates.

- **Visual Studio Code desktop**: Facilitates the viewing and editing of HTML, JavaScript, Liquid, and CSS code. It allows the creation of web pages, web templates, page templates, content snippets, and web files. Users can edit code and website metadata with IntelliSense and generate code using Copilot (please note that Copilot is still fairly new and constantly evolving).

- **Power Pages management app**: Provides capabilities to create Power Pages metadata records. It permits the viewing and editing of HTML, JavaScript, Liquid, and CSS code within the context of a model-driven app.

- **Power Platform CLI**: Allows users to download and upload Power Pages metadata to their local workstation for editing in Visual Studio Code or other editors.

Previewing our page

The **Preview** button allows you to see how your webpage will look on the site at any time during the design process. This feature is essential for ensuring that the design, layout, and content appear as intended on different devices. The steps are:

1. Select **Preview** from the main menu in the design studio.

2. Choose **Desktop** to view the page in your browser.

3. Alternatively, you can view the page on your mobile device by scanning the provided QR code.

This flexibility allows for real-time adjustments and ensures that the page is optimized for both desktop and mobile viewing.

Moving the page in the sitemap

Including the page in the **Main navigation** will automatically add a menu option. The page can be relocated within the site hierarchy using the design studio. The steps are as follows:

1. Under the **Main navigation**, select the ellipse (**...**) icon and move the page up and down in the hierarchy using the **Move up** and **Move down** options as shown:

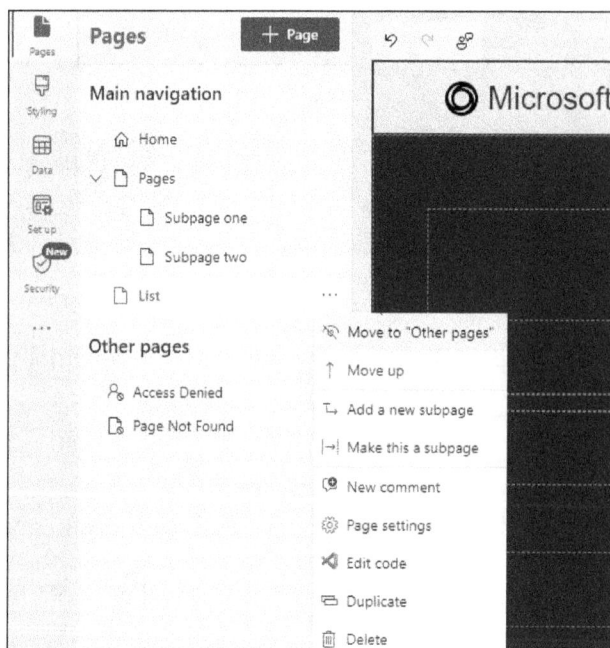

Figure 16.18: Moving a page in the sitemap

2. Alternatively, drag and drop the page underneath the **Pages** link. If you now preview the page, you will notice that the page is a sub-link under **Pages** and also how the URL reflects that this page is now a subpage:

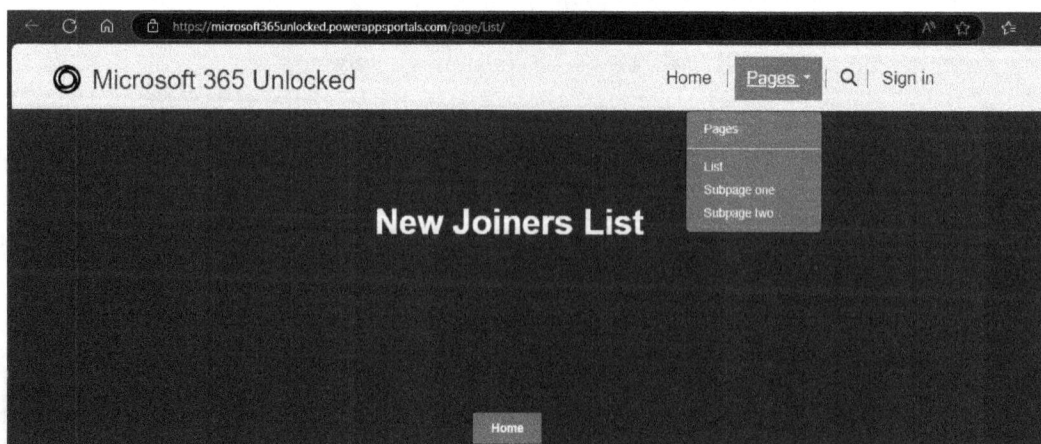

Figure 16.19: Previewing a page's navigation menu

It is important to consider how changes in the sitemap structure could potentially affect your website's **search engine optimization** (**SEO**) and page discoverability.

Adding a list to a page

In this section, we will go through the process of displaying business information from Microsoft Dataverse on a webpage within our site. First, we need to create a table in Dataverse, or select an existing one, to store our business information. Then, configure a view from the table to define the columns and structure of our list. Finally, integrate the list component into a page. For security purposes, users will not be able to access the information until table permissions are defined.

Creating a table

Creating a Dataverse table in Power Pages is a straightforward process that allows you to store and manage business information efficiently. Through a series of simple steps, you can establish a table, define its columns, and populate it with data. This foundational setup is crucial for integrating dynamic lists and other components into your web pages, enhancing the functionality and interactivity of your site. Use the following steps to create a table:

1. Navigate Power Pages at **https://make.powerpages.microsoft.com/**
2. Select the **Data** icon on the left navigation;
3. Click on the **+ Table** button, and select **+ New table**:

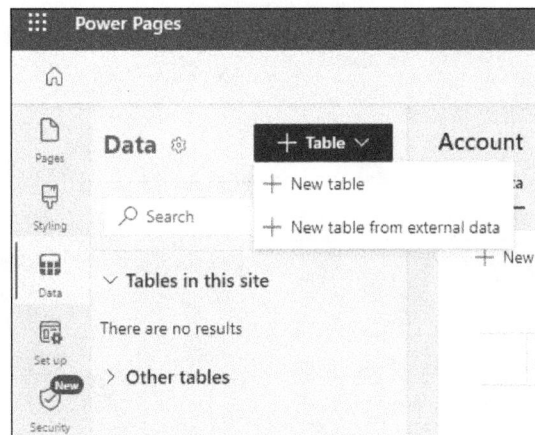

Figure 16.20: Adding a new table

4. Name the table and click on the **Primary column**. Here, we will change the primary column to be *Email* to ensure we have a unique field. When ready, click **Save**:

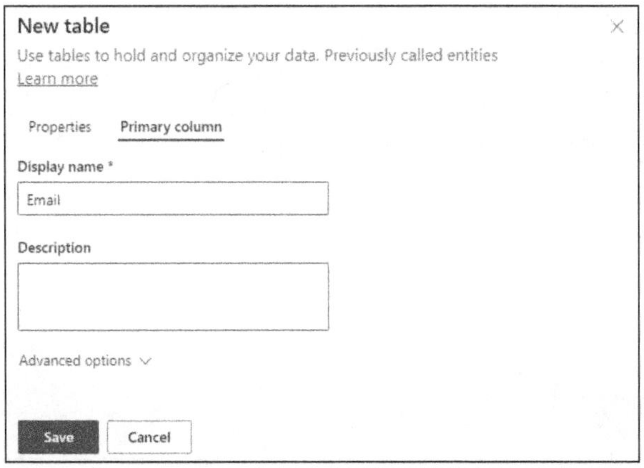

Figure 16.21: Configuring a table's primary column

5. We now have our table with a single column, as well as 17 other default ones like **Created On**, **Create By**, etc. Let us add a few more columns by clicking on **+ New column** as shown:

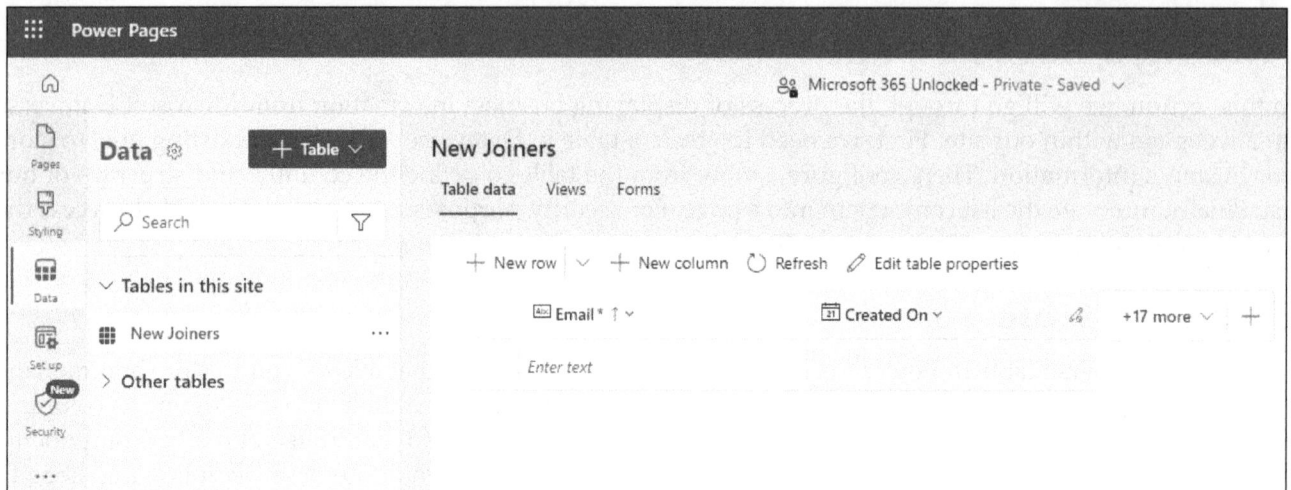

Figure 16.22: *New empty table*

6. Enter a name and a data type, then choose **Save**. For this example, we will add details such as name, job title, department, and so on in the following fields:

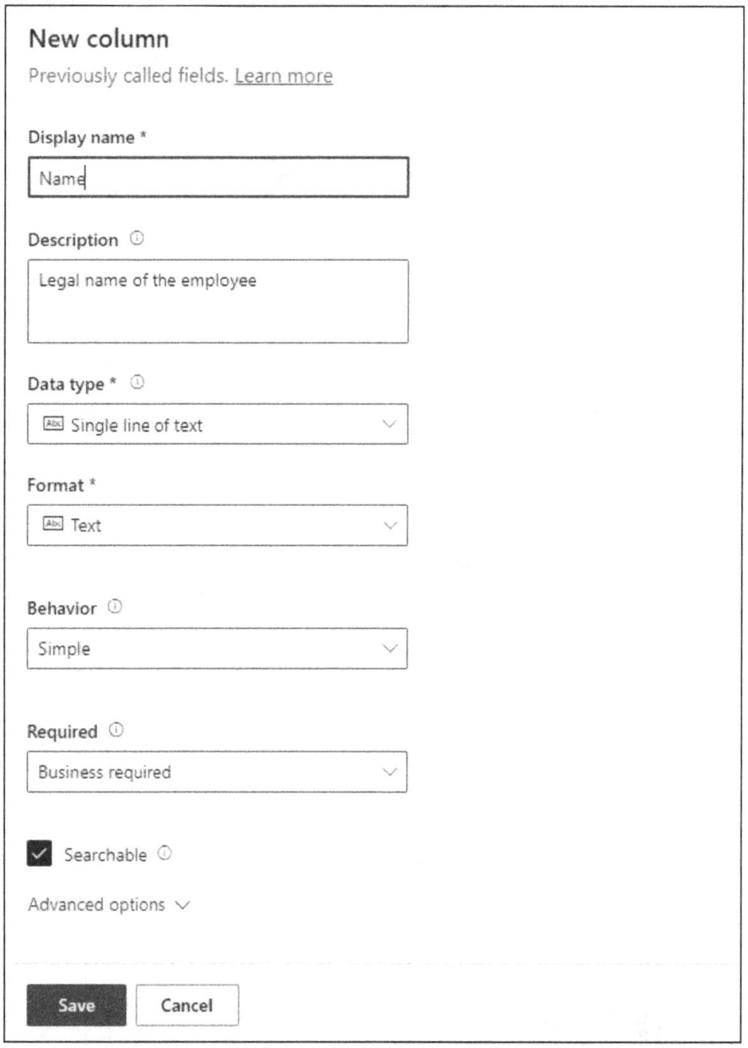

Figure 16.23: *Adding new columns to a table*

7. To enter some sample data, we can select the space under a column and enter our data, as shown in the picture below. We can use the tab key to move to the next column and enter additional data, and also to navigate to the next row and add additional records, as follows:

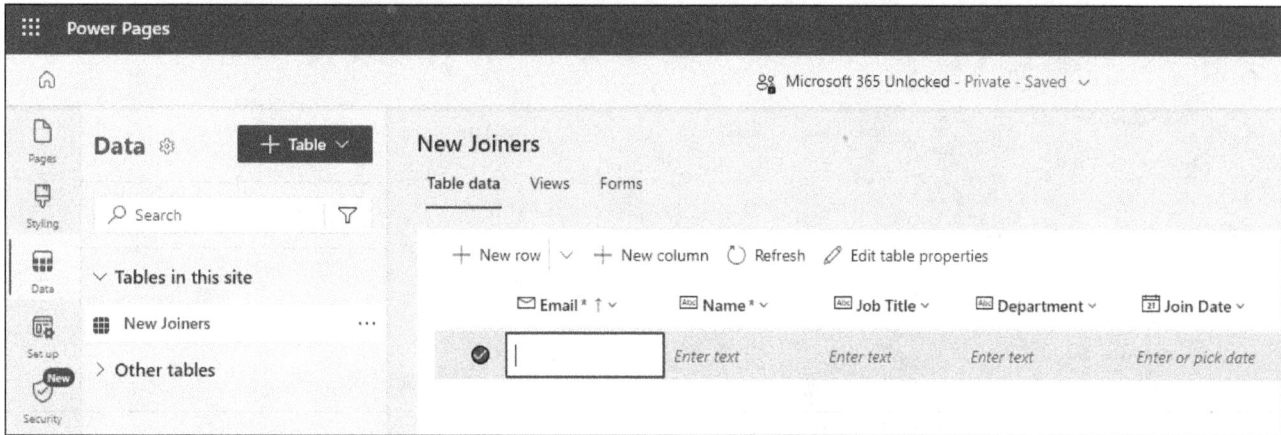

Figure 16.24: Adding records to a table

Creating a view

Using the next steps, we will create a custom view for the table we have just created:

1. Select the table you created in the steps above.

2. Select **Views** and choose **New view**:

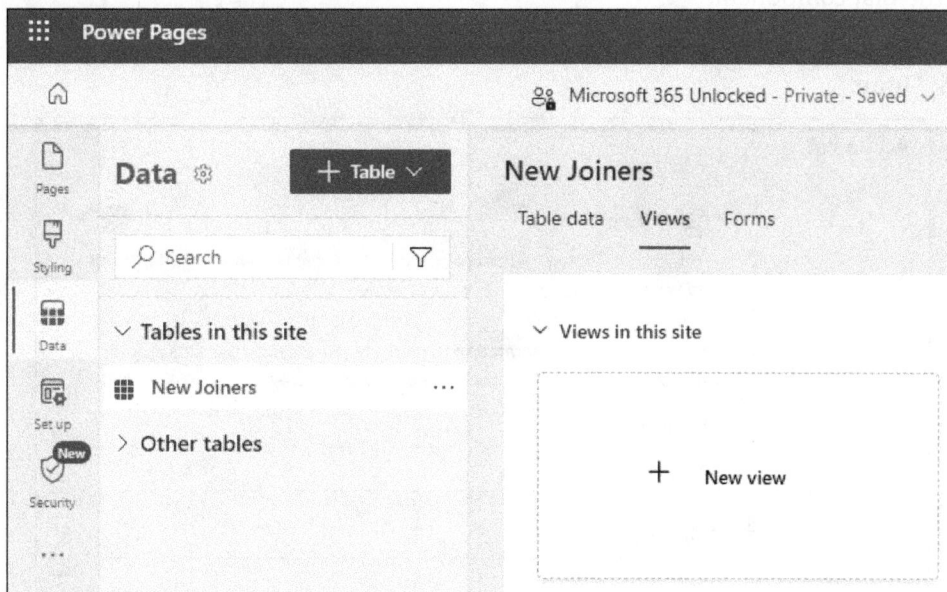

Figure 16.25: Creating a new view for a table

3. Enter a name for the view and click **Create**.

4. Add all the columns we created earlier to the view by clicking on the + **Add column** and then simply clicking on the columns to add:

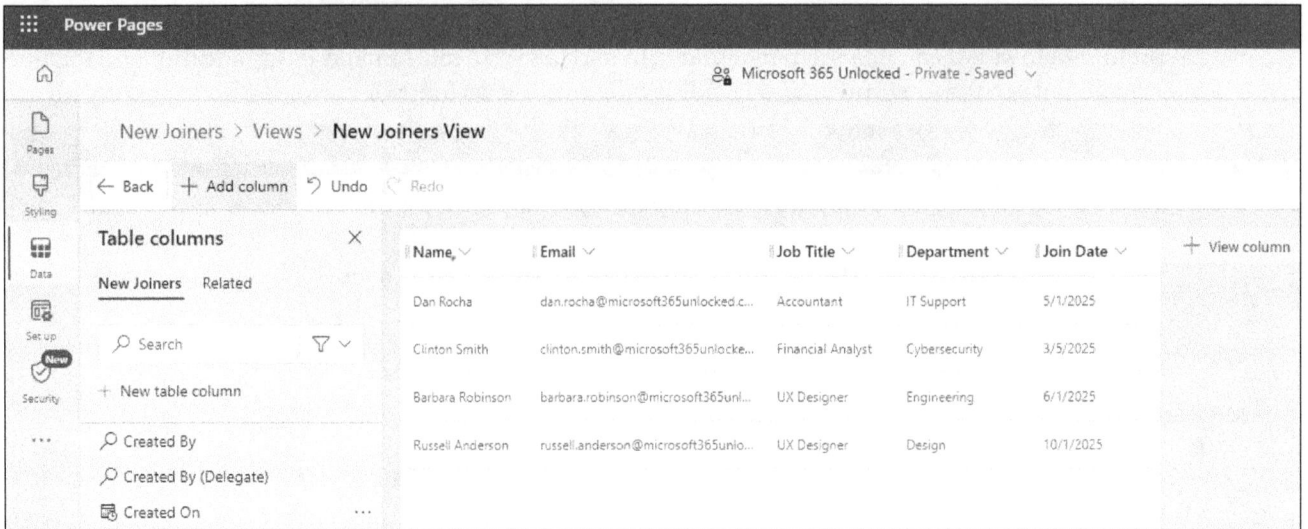

Figure 16.26: Configuring the table columns visible in a view

5. Click on **Save and publish**.

Adding the list to our page

Now that we have our table and a view, let us add it to our page:

1. Navigate to the page to add the list and click on + **Add a Section** to add a **1 Column** section that will contain the **List** component.

2. Fill in the details by selecting the table and the view we have just created from the dropdown menus, and click **Done**:

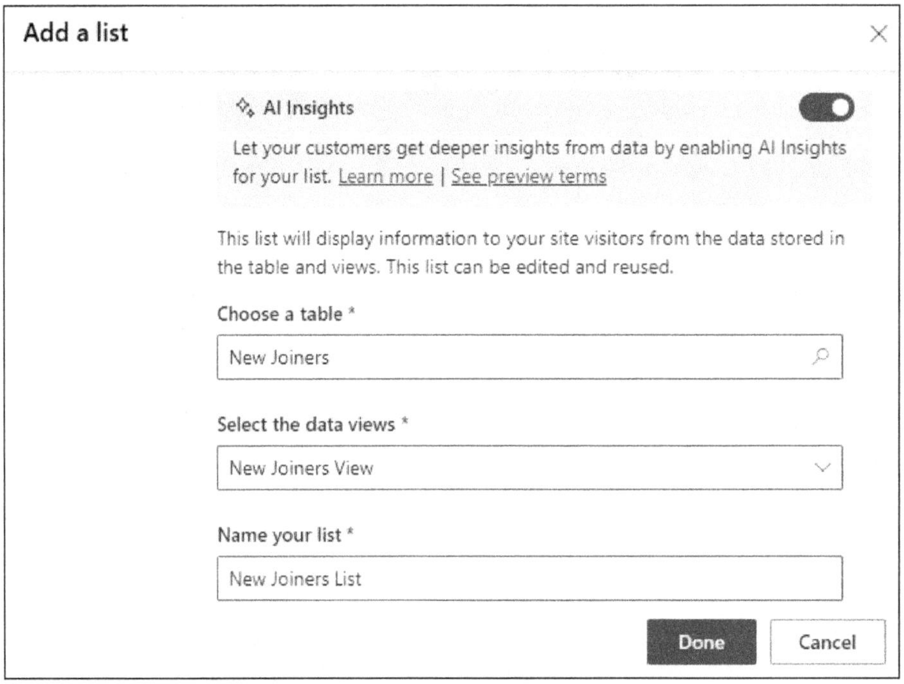

Figure 16.27: Adding a list component

3. You will notice that only sample text is displayed:

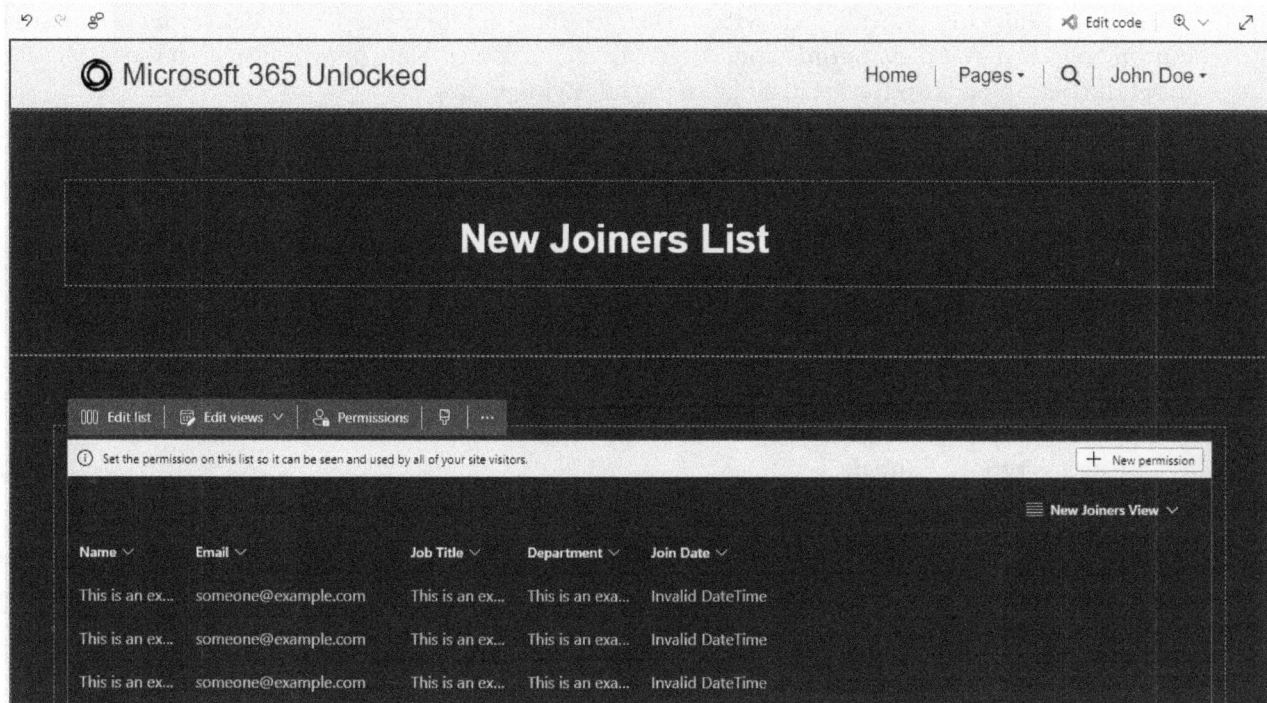

Figure 16.28: List component with sample data

4. And if we preview the page, we get an error stating we do not have permission to view the data:

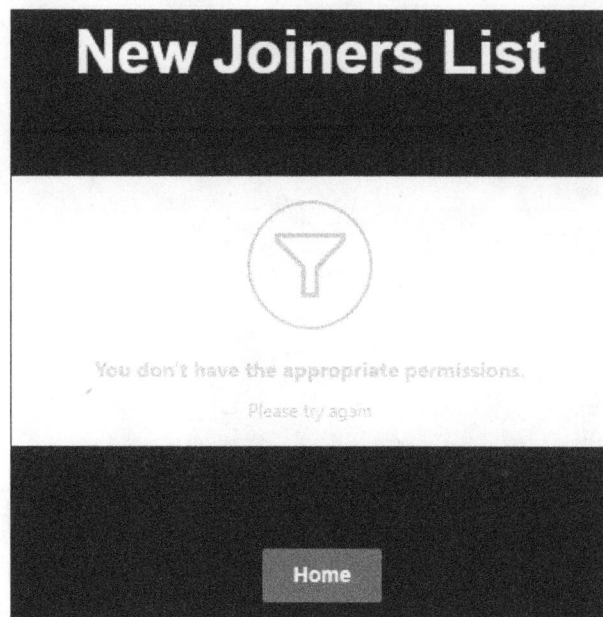

Figure 16.29: Error when viewing the table on the site

This is because Power Pages takes security seriously when building sites. So let us fix this.

Displaying data securely

We now have our page with a list, but users are unable to view any data because Power Pages has security enabled by default to safeguard business data. This section explains how to create table permissions and link them with web roles so visitors to the site can interact with the permitted information only.

First, we need to create a table permission:

1. In the page's workspace, on the page with the list, select the list component and click on the **Permissions** button, followed by + **New permission**. Alternatively, click on + **New permission** if you see a message to set the permissions on the list just like in the following figure:

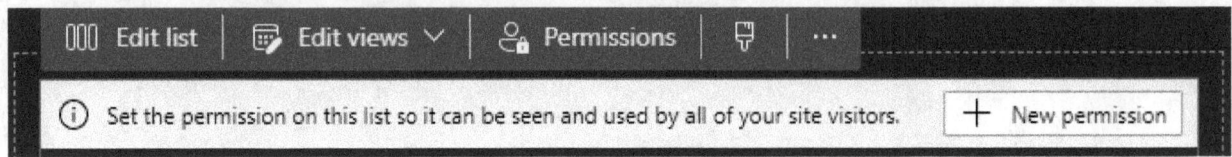

Figure 16.30: Setting permissions on a list component

2. Give the table permission a descriptive name.
3. Select the Dataverse table.
4. Set the access type to **Global**.
5. Set the permissions to **Read**.
6. In this example, to keep things simple, we will add both **Anonymous Users** and **Authenticated Users** roles as you can see in *Figure 16.31*. In a real production page, we would obviously have different permissions for these roles, or block access to anonymous users for example.

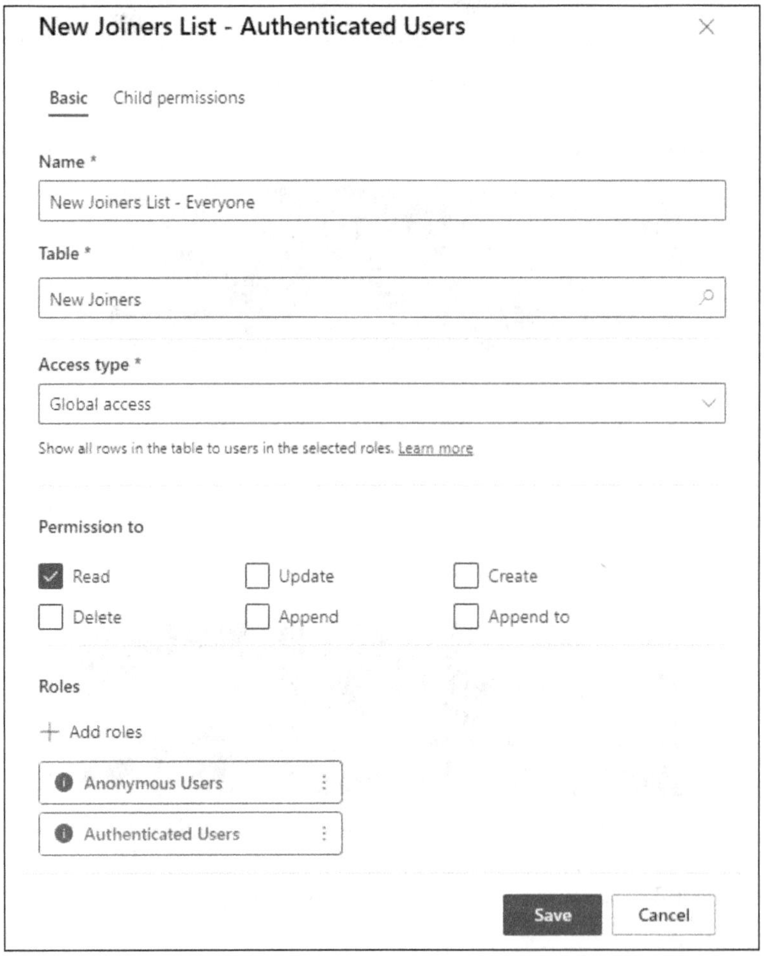

Figure 16.31: Creating a new table permission

7. Click **Save**. Now that table permissions are set, we can preview the page and the data should be visible:

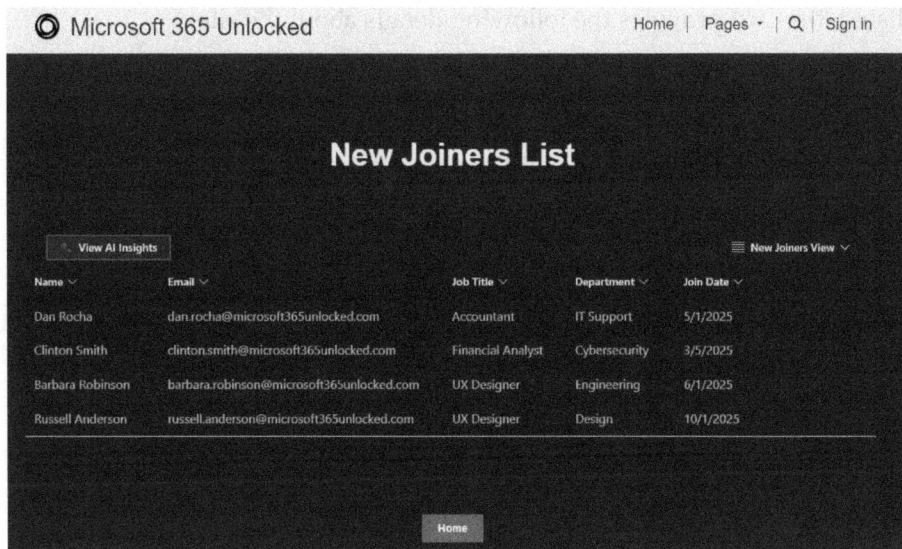

Figure 16.32: List component now visible to users

By utilizing different permissions for various user roles, we can tailor access to sensitive data and functionalities according to the specific needs and responsibilities of each user group. This approach provides several advantages: it enhances security by restricting sensitive information to authorized users only, improves user experience by displaying relevant content, and facilitates efficient management of user roles and permissions.

Managing sites

The Power Pages **Home** section serves as a central hub for managing all your sites. Here, you can view a list of all sites within your selected environment and perform actions for each specific website:

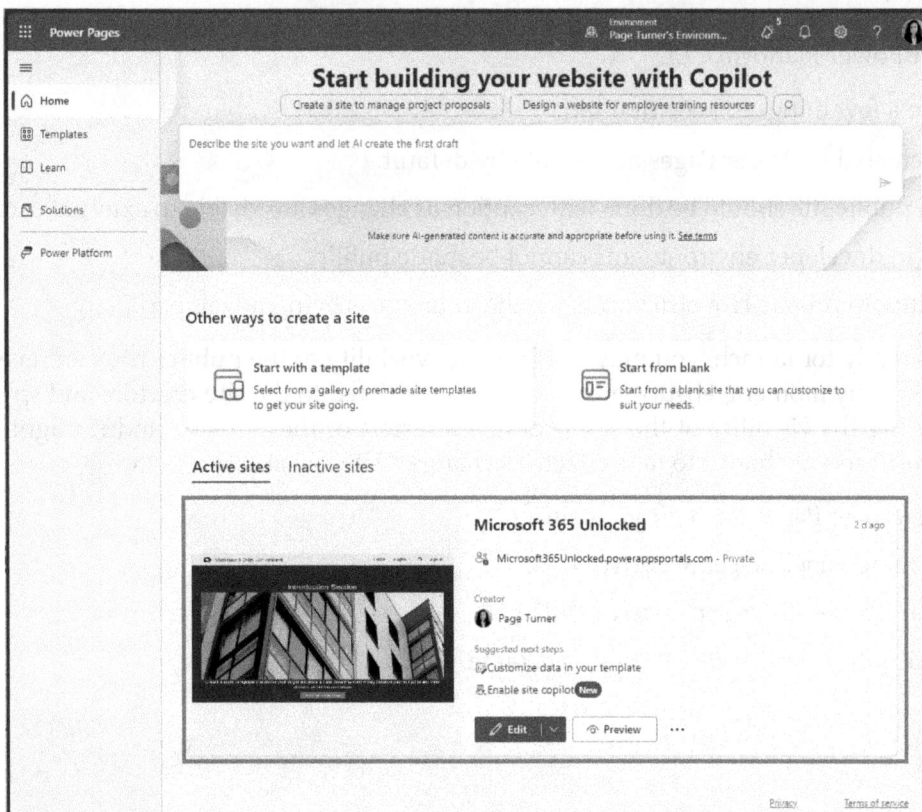

Figure 16.33: Power Pages Home section

For each website listed, the card provides the following details about the site:

- Site name and web address
- Site creator's name
- Suggested next steps, as you build and edit your site
- A thumbnail that captures a snapshot of your site.

Each site card also links to actions by clicking on the ellipsis (**...**) button, such as:

- **Edit**: Redirects to the design studio.
- **Preview**: This shows how users will view the website.
- **Share**: Creates a link for site preview.
- **Details**: Opens the Set up workspace.
- **Portal Management app**: Launches the Portal Management app.
- **Admin center**: Opens the Power Platform admin center.
- **Delete**: Removes the site from the list (please note that deleting a site is a permanent action!).

Changing site visibility

The Power Pages site visibility setting enables control over website access. You can set the site to be:

- **Private**: Websites can be viewed exclusively by site makers and organization users who have been granted access. Site visitors must authenticate using the organization's Microsoft Entra ID identity provider to view the site's contents.
- **Public**: Websites are accessible to anyone, whether they are anonymous users or authenticated through an identity provider. These websites are fully operational for customer use. Notifications appear when editing a public site in the design studio, Portal Management app, Visual Studio Code editor, and the Microsoft Power Platform CLI.

The following are a few things to keep in mind:

- All sites created in Power Pages are private by default.
- Editing a public site should be done with caution as changes are visible to external users immediately.
- Websites in developer environments cannot be made public.
- Set visibility to private to restrict access while your site is being developed.

Once your site is ready for launch, you may configure its visibility to the public. You can revert the visibility setting to private at any moment, ensuring that access is restricted to the site creators and specified users. Be advised that altering the visibility of the site prompts a restart of the website, and it might require several minutes for the most recent change to take effect. To change a site's visibility:

1. Sign in to Power Pages and edit your site.
2. In the left side panel, select **Security**.
3. In the **Manage** section, select **Site visibility**.
4. In the **This site is** card, select **Public** or **Private**.

The screen will be as follows:

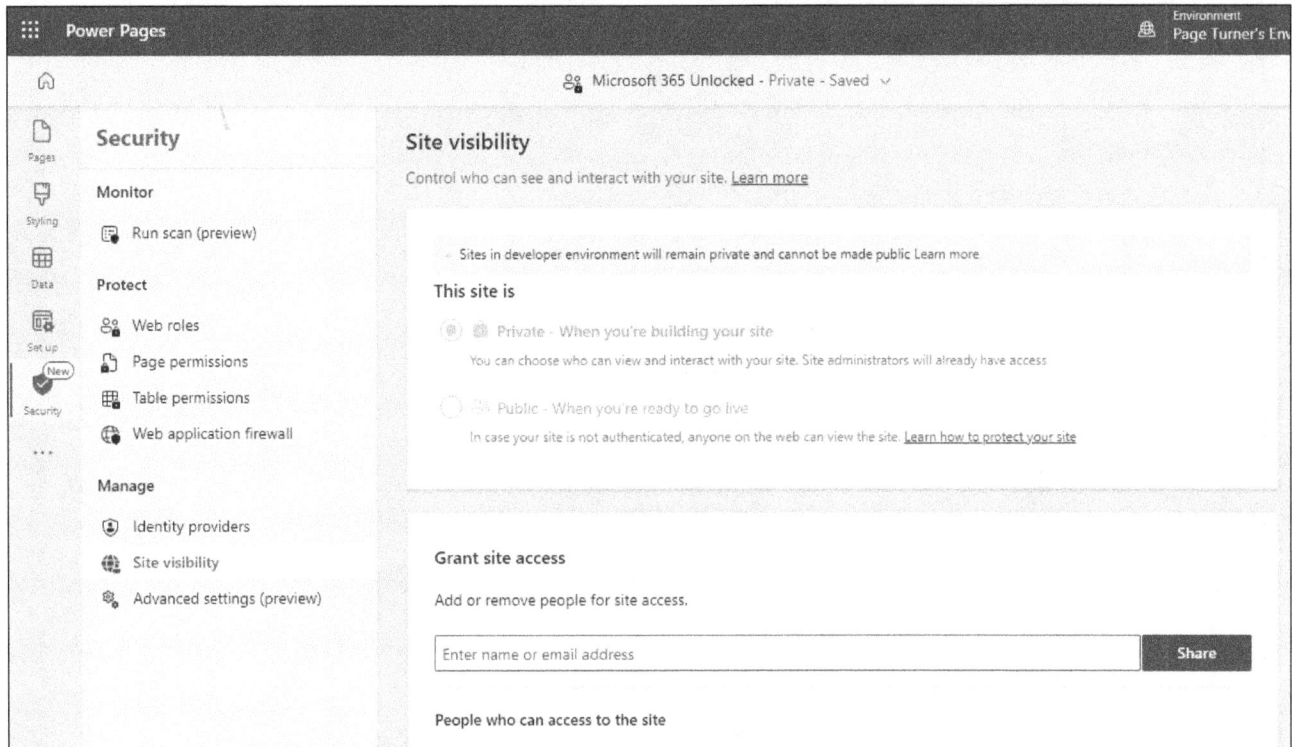

Figure 16.34: Setting a site's visibility

You might have noticed the **Grant site access** option in the previous screenshot. If your site is private, the site visibility page allows you to grant access to other organization users. You may grant access to up to 50 organization users. Users with the *System administrator* role in your site's environment already have permission to view the site by default, so you do not need to grant them access separately.

Configuring authorized access

Power Pages offers integration with various authentication providers to ensure secure access for external users to your site. This feature is instrumental in maintaining the security and integrity of your online presence, allowing site creators to manage user permissions effortlessly.

Let us discuss some of the advantages of this integration:

- **Enhanced security**: By using established authentication providers, you ensure that your site is safeguarded against unauthorized access, protecting sensitive data and user information.

- **User convenience**: External users can reset their passwords and update personal information independently, reducing the need for administrator intervention and streamlining the user experience.

- **Scalability**: The integration supports a growing user base without compromising on security or functionality, making it ideal for expanding businesses and large organizations.

- **Compliance**: Utilizing trusted authentication providers helps ensure your site meets various regulatory and compliance standards, providing peace of mind to both site creators and users.

To implement an external authentication provider, follow these steps:

1. In the design studio, select **Security**.

2. Under **Manage**, select **Identity Providers**. You will see a list of all the available providers to be used in Power Pages:

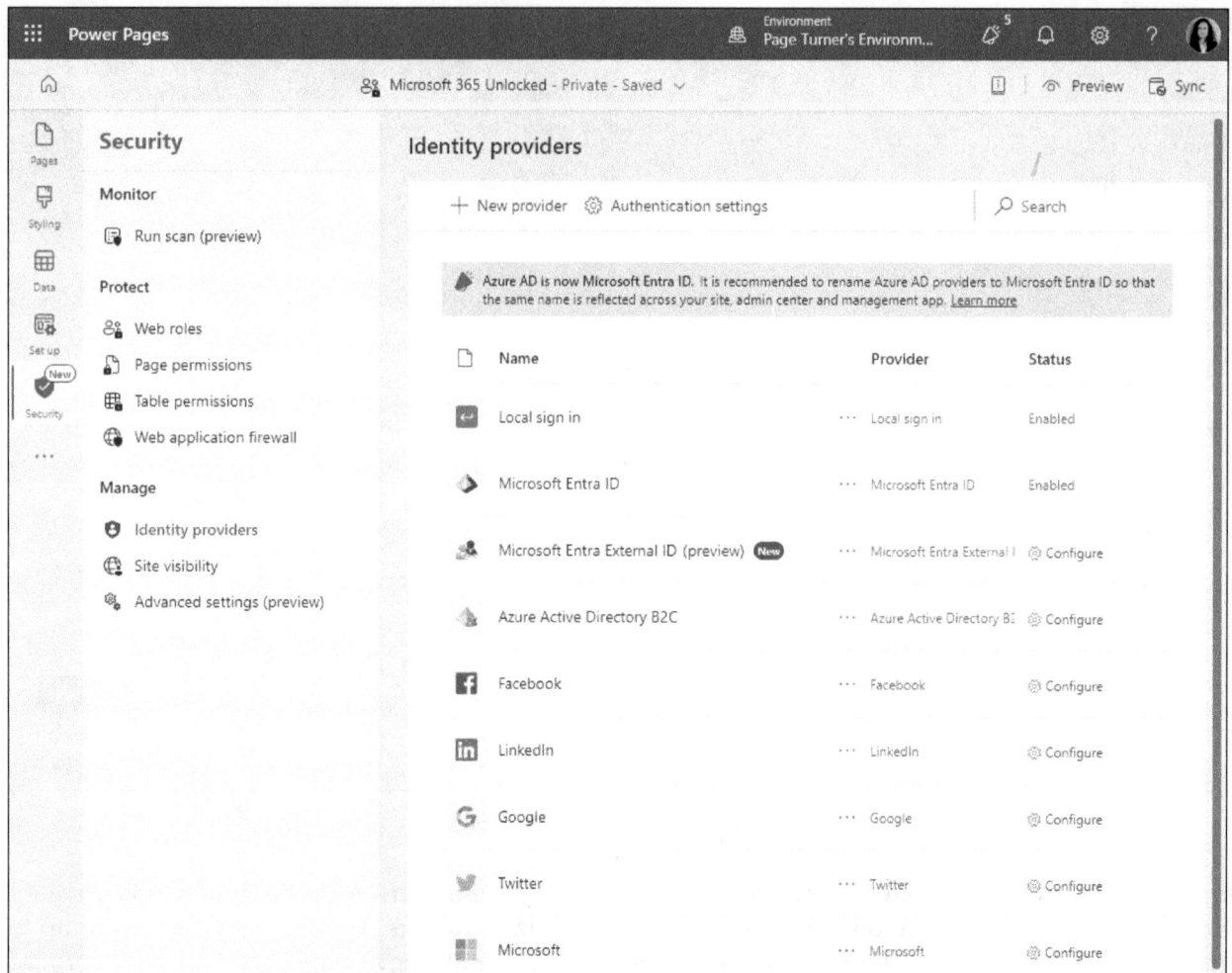

Figure 16.35: Identity providers available

3. Select **Configure** next to the provider you want to use and follow the wizard to complete its configuration.

Once done, your users will have the capability to sign in, register, or redeem an invitation, depending on your chosen provider.

Set up page permissions

When creating a website, you may need to restrict access to certain pages. Page permissions offer makers an additional method to control user access to their Power Pages sites. These permissions can be used to either make content accessible to all site visitors or restrict access to users holding particular roles.

Child pages have the capability to either inherit the permissions of their parent page or establish their own set of permissions. Similarly, web files associated with a page, including downloadable documents, CSS files, or JavaScript files, can either inherit the permissions of the corresponding page or maintain their own distinct permissions.

The following steps describe how to configure page permissions to limit access to a specific page:

1. Select your site, and then select **Edit**.

2. In the page navigation, select the ellipses (...) next to the page you want to update, and select **Page settings**.

3. In the side tab, select **Permissions**.

4. Select **I want to choose who can see this page**.

5. In the list, select the **Authenticated Users** web role.

6. Click **OK**:

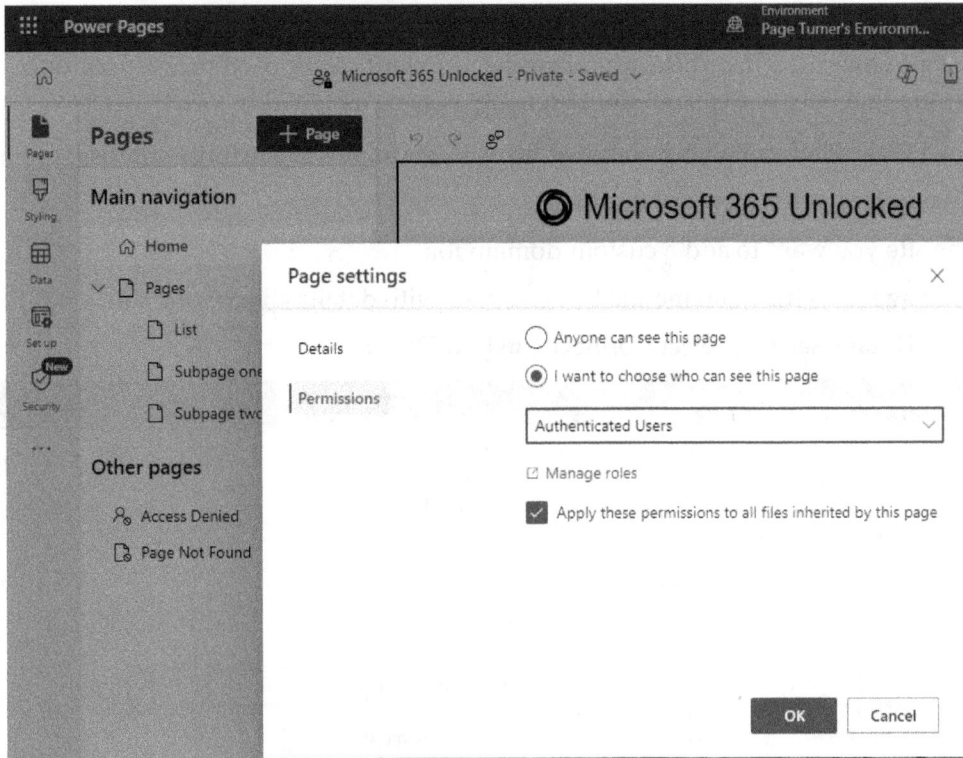

Figure 16.36: Setting page permissions

7. In the design studio, select **Preview** to view your site.

8. If no user is signed in, the protected web page will not appear in the main menu or navigation. Even if we know the direct URL to the page, we cannot access it. The following figure shows the page as expected:

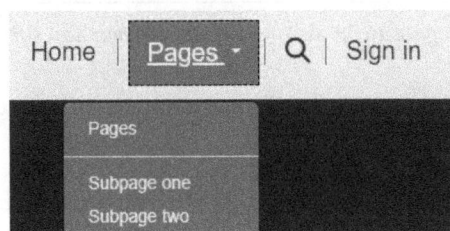

Figure 16.37: Page hidden through page permissions

9. If we now sign in to the site, the link to the protected page will be visible in the main menu and we can see the page:

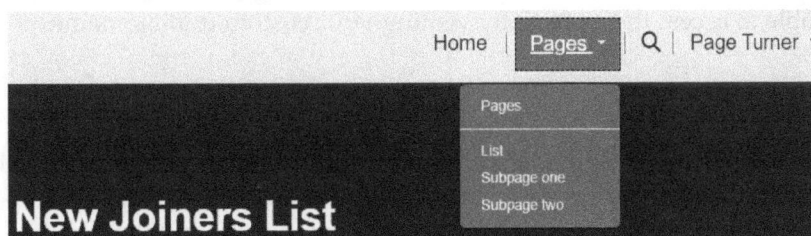

Figure 16.38: Page visible through page permissions

Adding a custom domain name

Power Pages provides a flexible and efficient way to enhance your website's identity by allowing you to add a custom domain. This option can help build brand recognition and create a professional appearance for your site.

After provisioning your website and acquiring a domain name, you must obtain an SSL certificate to establish a custom host name. Once the SSL certificate is acquired, a wizard can be used to link your website to a custom domain. Please note that only one custom domain name may be assigned to a website.

1. Open the Power Platform admin center at **https://admin.powerplatform.microsoft.com**

2. Under **Resources**, select **Power Pages sites**.

3. Select the site you want to add a custom domain for.

4. Select **Manage** from the main menu. A page opens with details about your site.

5. In the **Site Details** section, select **Connect Custom Domain**:

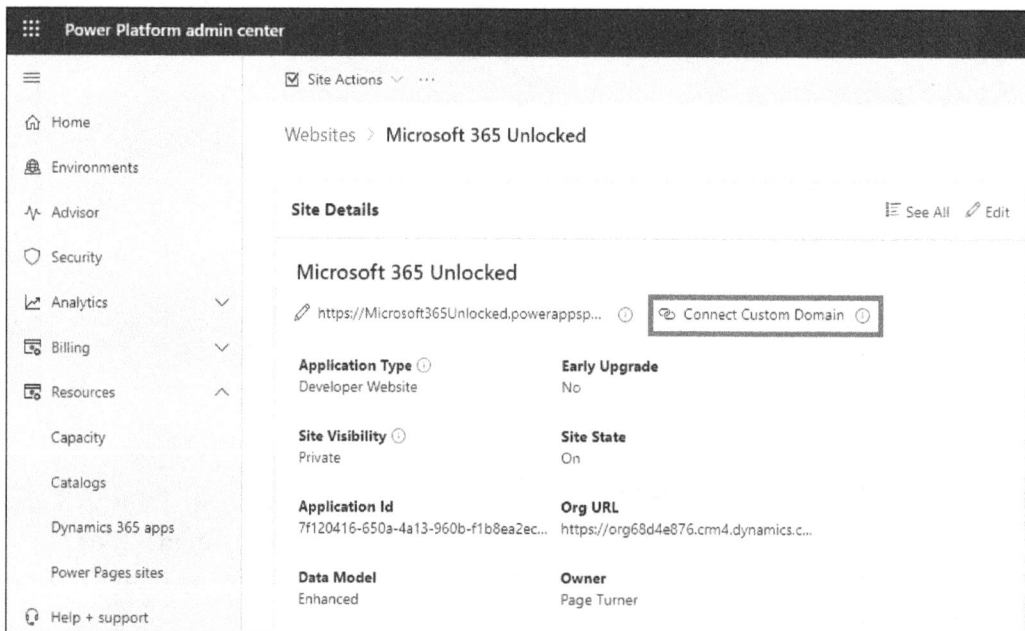

Figure 16.39: Adding a custom domain to a site

6. A side panel appears where you can upload a new SSL certificate or use an existing one.

7. Select **Next**.

8. On the **Choose hostname** section, enter the CNAME you want to use in the **Domain Name** field, such as **www.microsoft365unlocked.com** for example.

9. Select **Next** twice.

10. Review the information and then select **Next** to begin creating the SSL binding.

11. The message `Custom Domain name has been successfully configured` should appear, indicating you are now able to access the website by visiting your custom domain name.

Go live

The **Set up** workspace within the design studio contains a built-in checklist for going live with a website. This checklist is designed to help you prepare your site for launch by providing a step-by-step guide with interactive tasks that ensure all necessary actions have been completed. By following the guided experiences within the checklist, you can view and complete recommended actions to enhance your site's readiness for production use. This ensures that you have considered all aspects of the site's readiness before going live, helps avoid any critical misses that could affect the site's functionality or user experience after launch, and helps improve the overall site experience once it is live.

> **Note: the go-live checklist and supplementary guidance provided in this feature are suggested measures. These recommendations are not required for the site to become operational.**

Note: The following is an example of the checklist as it advances through the various stages:

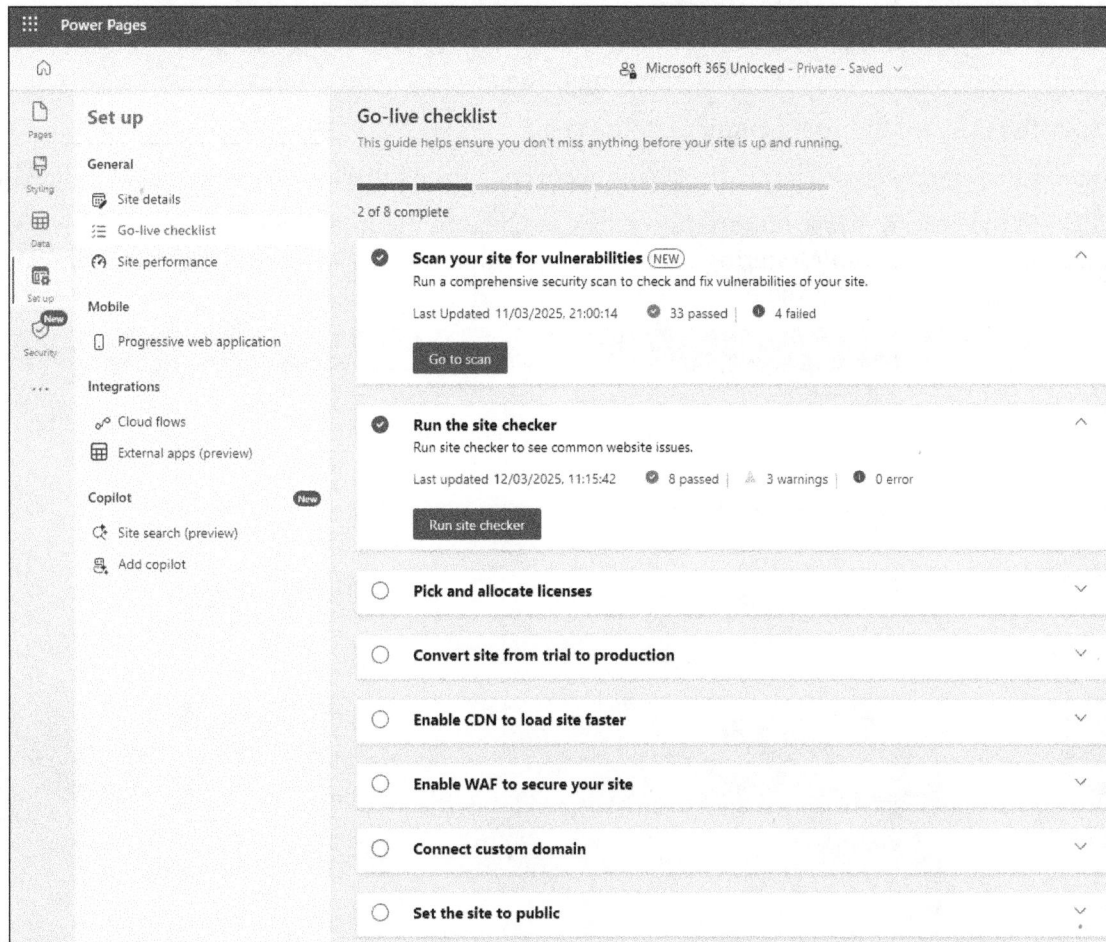

Figure 16.40: Go-live checklist

Completing the go-live checklist assists in preparation and ensures all considerations are addressed before the site becomes operational. Additionally, review the following supplementary go-live guidance:

- Create separate development, testing, and production sites: maintain separate environments to manage the application development lifecycle.

- Configure authentication setup by using a supported identity provider as default and disabling local authentication.

- Test your site performance: enable a CDN and perform load testing for high scalability needs. Consider factors such as the number of daily visitors, traffic volumes at different times, high-traffic pages linked to Microsoft Dataverse, and volume of data stored in Dataverse.

- Finalize your site. Clean up your site by removing sample webpages, text, and placeholder images. Delete or deactivate any unused pages. Set your specific copyright text and add any privacy or other links in the *footer* web template. Protect unfinished pages by using *Page permissions*.

- Manage site visibility: configure site visibility after verifying readiness.

Setting up telemetry monitoring

Telemetry monitoring in Power Pages is an essential feature for tracking and analyzing website traffic. By integrating a telemetry tracking code from your analytics provider, you can gain insightful data on visitor behavior, traffic sources, and trends. This setup allows administrators to monitor site performance, identify potential issues, and optimize user experience.

To implement telemetry monitoring follow these steps:

1. Open the Portal Management app and navigate to the **Content Snippets** section.

2. Create a new content snippet called **Tracking Code** of **Type** = **Text**.

3. Leave the **Content Snippet Language** value blank.

4. Enter the telemetry tracking HTML/JS snippet of code from the telemetry provider into the **Value** box.

5. Click on the **Save & Close** button shown below. Once configured, the telemetry provider will begin monitoring website traffic, offering valuable metrics that can be used to enhance site functionality and user engagement, as follows:

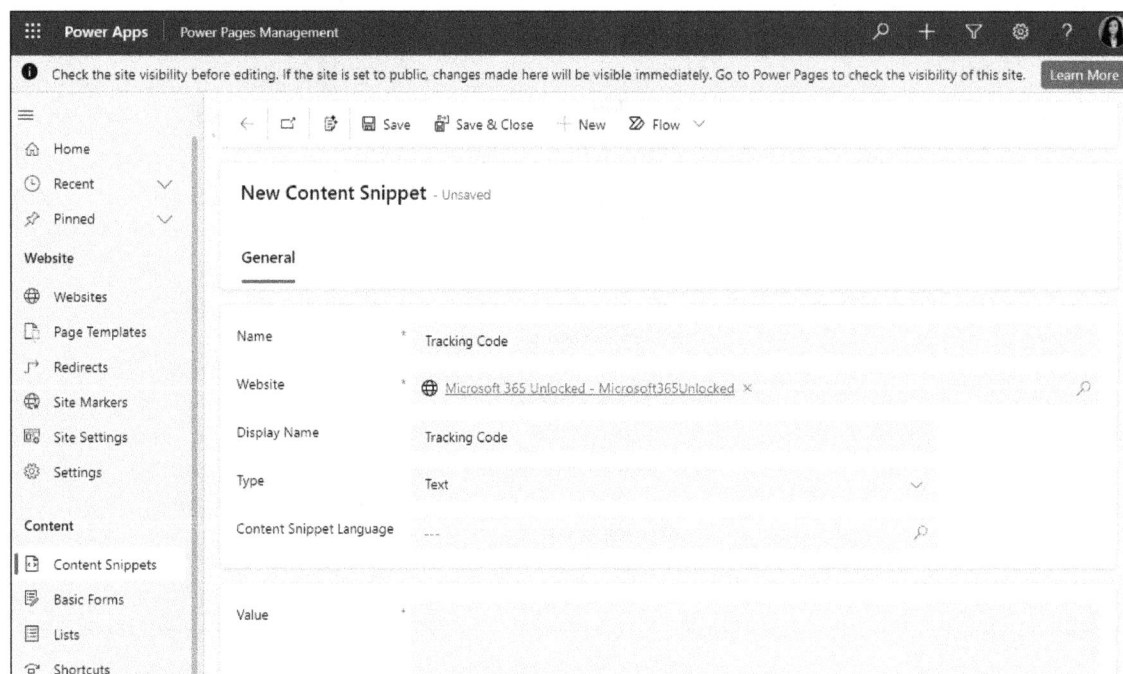

Figure 16.41: Setting up telemetry monitoring

Conclusion

Power Pages offers a powerful and versatile solution for creating and managing websites with minimal coding. By leveraging the capabilities of the Power Platform, users can streamline their development processes, enhance collaboration, and create dynamic, data-driven web solutions. Whether you are a seasoned developer or a newcomer to web development, Power Pages provides the tools and resources needed to bring your vision to life. By following the detailed steps outlined in this chapter, you can gain hands-on experience with Power Pages and unlock their full potential, enabling you to build sophisticated web applications that drive business success.

In the next chapter, we will explore Microsoft Forms, a versatile and user-friendly tool designed for creating surveys, quizzes, and polls, that allows users to collect data and insights efficiently through customizable forms.

CHAPTER 17

Forms

Introduction

Forms are an essential component in the realm of digital documentation and data collection. They serve as a structured method for gathering information, facilitating communication, and streamlining processes across various domains. Organizations in education, healthcare, human resources, customer service, event management, government, and numerous other industries rely on forms for tasks such as surveys, registrations, feedback collection, and data entry. Whether used for classroom assessments, patient intake, employee onboarding, customer satisfaction tracking, or event sign-ups, forms play a pivotal role in capturing information accurately and efficiently.

In this chapter, we will explore the fundamental aspects of Microsoft Forms, a powerful tool that allows users to create quizzes and different types of forms. By leveraging Microsoft Forms, you can enhance your data collection processes and gain valuable insights from the responses.

Structure

This chapter covers the following topics:

- Getting started with Forms
- Creating quizzes and forms
- Sharing forms and collecting responses
- Viewing and analyzing responses
- Integration with other Microsoft 365 apps

Objectives

By the end of this chapter, readers will be able to understand the fundamental aspects of Microsoft Forms and its applications. They will be equipped with the knowledge to create and configure forms and quizzes. The readers will learn how to share forms and collect responses efficiently, as well as analyze the collected data to gain valuable insights. Additionally, they will explore the integration of Microsoft Forms with other Microsoft 365 apps to enhance their data collection and management processes.

Getting started with Forms

Microsoft Forms offers a user-friendly interface and a variety of customization options to suit different needs. Whether you are looking to gather feedback, conduct research, or engage with your audience, Microsoft Forms provides the necessary features to make the process seamless and efficient.

Licensing

Licensing for Microsoft Forms is included in most Microsoft 365 plans, making it accessible to a wide range of users. Whether you are an individual user, a small business, or a large enterprise, Microsoft Forms is available to help you streamline your data collection processes and gain valuable insights from the responses. Microsoft Forms is included in the following plans:

- **Business plans**: Microsoft 365 Business Basic, Standard, Premium

- **Enterprise plans**: Microsoft 365 E3, E5; Office 365 E1, E3, E5

- **Education plans**: Microsoft 365 A3, A5; Office 365 A1, A3, A5

- **Frontline plans**: Microsoft 365 F3

- **Government plans**: Microsoft 365 G3, G5

Additionally, Microsoft Forms is widely accessible to users with Microsoft 365 apps subscriptions and those with personal Microsoft accounts.

Accessing Forms

Microsoft Forms can be accessed by logging in to your Microsoft 365 portal at **https://www.microsoft365.com** and opening **Forms** from the app launcher. Alternatively, navigate directly to **https://forms.office.com** and sign in with your Microsoft 365 credentials.

From the Microsoft Forms home page, you can start with the creation of a new form or quiz from scratch, or choose to start from one of the scenarios presented or from a template in the **Template gallery**:

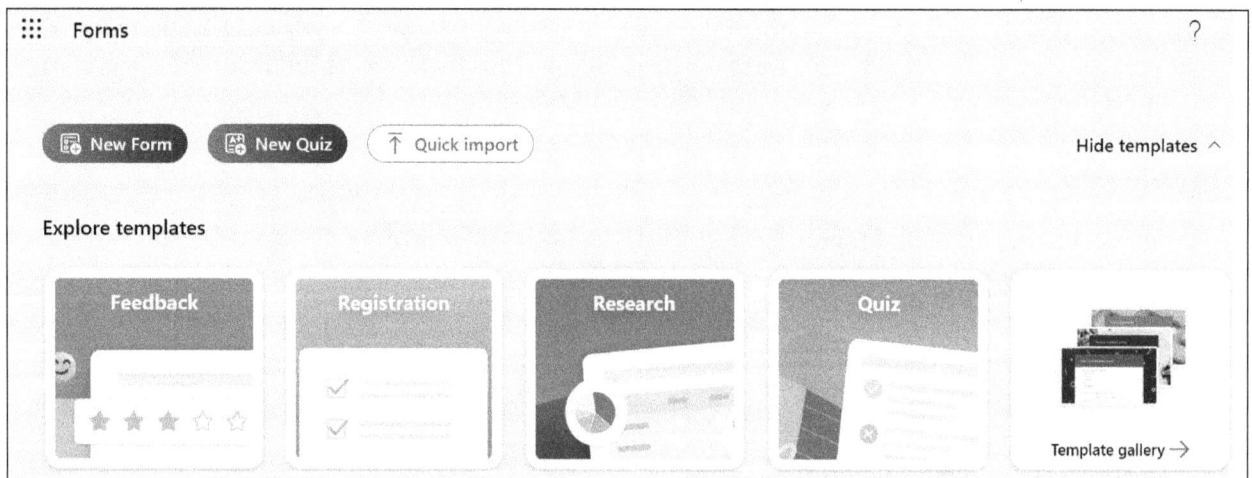

Figure 17.1: Forms creation options

On the home page, you can view and access recent or favorite forms, filled forms, all forms you have created, or forms created by other users and shared with you. These forms are organized by relevant categories, as illustrated in the following figure:

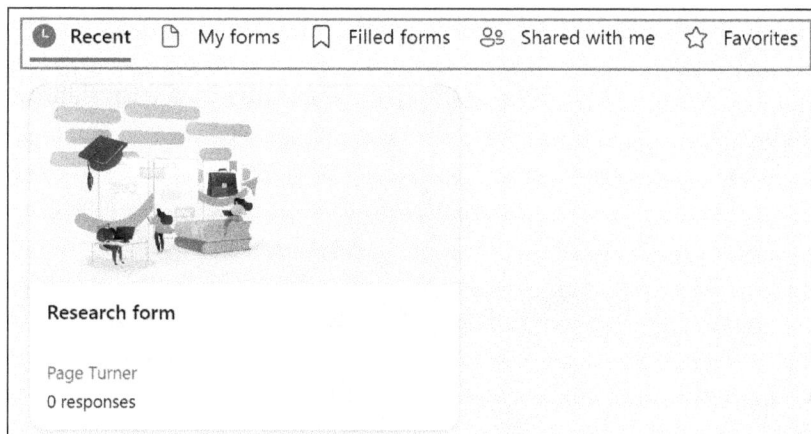

Figure 17.2: *Created forms*

The last section on the Forms home page lists the Microsoft 365 groups you are a member of, and the number of total forms created under each group:

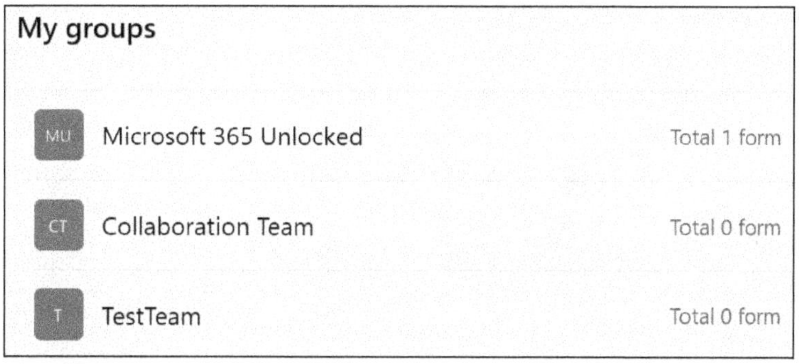

Figure 17.3: *My groups*

From here, you can select a group and start creating a form under the respective group. Creating group forms is helpful from a collaboration and management perspective, as this type of form can be edited and managed by anyone within the Microsoft 365 group.

Creating group forms option is only available for users with a Microsoft 365 subscription that includes access to SharePoint Online.

Creating and configuring quizzes and forms

In today's digital age, quizzes and forms have become indispensable tools for gathering information, assessing knowledge, and engaging with audiences.

Quizzes are primarily designed to test knowledge or skills. They consist of questions that require specific answers, often with a scoring system to evaluate performance. Quizzes can be used in educational settings to assess learning outcomes, in professional environments for training and certification, or even for fun and interactive content on websites and social media.

Forms, on the other hand, are used to collect information in a structured manner. They can include a variety of question types, and they are ideal for surveys, registrations, feedback collection, and data entry. Unlike quizzes, forms do not typically have a scoring system, as their primary purpose is to gather data rather than assess knowledge.

In this section, we will explore the process of creating and configuring both quizzes and forms using Microsoft Forms.

Creating a quiz

To create a quiz, navigate to Microsoft Forms and click on **New Quiz** in the top-left corner of the screen, as shown in the following figure:

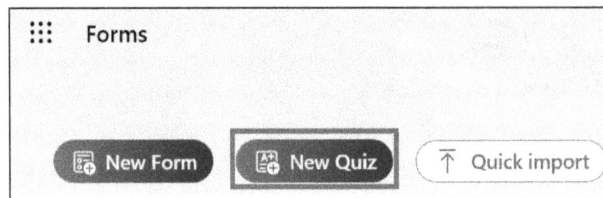

Figure 17.4: New Quiz

Next, you can give your quiz a name, a description, and select a question type from the + **Quick start with** menu. In our example, we named the quiz **General Knowledge Quiz** and started with a **Choice** question type:

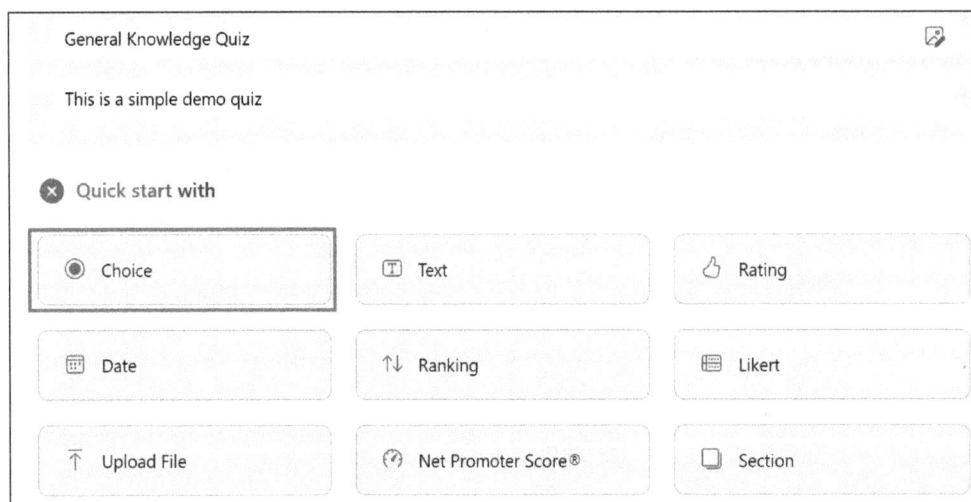

Figure 17.5: Quiz title and start question

A variety of question types can be selected, as illustrated in *Figure 17.5*. For the purposes of our demonstration, we will utilize **Choice** and **Ranking** questions, which are generally well-suited and commonly used for quizzes.

We can now write our first question and the options that will be available for selection for those who fill in the survey. We can also select which one is the correct answer, as shown in the following figure:

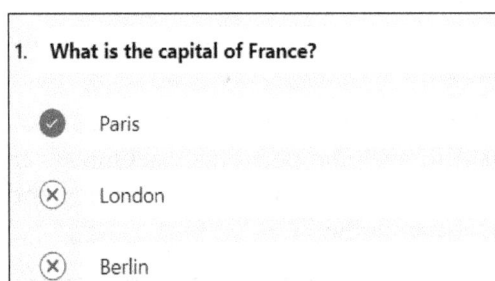

Figure 17.6: Writing the question, the options, and marking the correct answer

Next to each answer option, you will see the option to insert an image. By hovering the mouse over the answer option, additional options will appear, such as writing a message for those who choose the respective answer option, deleting the option, or moving the option up or down:

London ☐ ☐ ☐ ↑ ↓

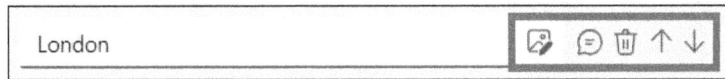

Figure 17.7: Inserting images and additional options for answer choices

Below the question, it is possible to specify the number of points allocated to the question, to enable **Maths** functionality (for questions containing mathematical equations and expressions), activate **Multiple answers** (if more than one answer is correct), and mark it as *Required* (if the question must be answered):

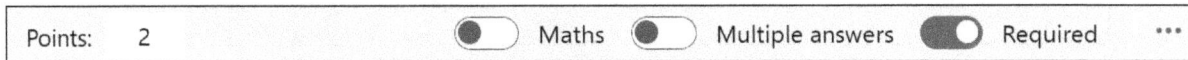

Points: 2   ⬤ Maths   ⬤ Multiple answers   ⬤ Required   •••

Figure 17.8: Allocating points and enabling additional question options

By selecting the ellipsis button illustrated in *Figure 17.9*, various options can be chosen: shuffling answer choices to randomize their order for each quiz attempt, utilizing a drop-down menu to display the answer choices, adding a subtitle to the question, or incorporating branching (explained later in this chapter):

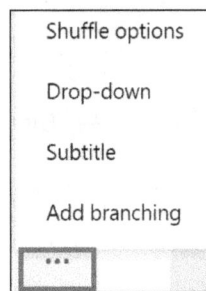

Shuffle options

Drop-down

Subtitle

Add branching

•••

Figure 17.9: Advanced question options

Some of the question options discussed above are available only for **Choice** questions. Other question types will display different options, as they can be configured differently based on their type.

In our demonstration, we have configured our *Choice* question to shuffle its options, and we marked it as a required question.

By clicking on the + **Add new question** button, we included an extra *Choice* question. This question has been made mandatory and configured to shuffle its answers. Moreover, a *Ranking* question was added and set as required. The quiz allocates 3 points for each *Choice* question and 4 points for the *Ranking* question.

For the ranking question, we need to list the options in the correct order as shown in the following figure:

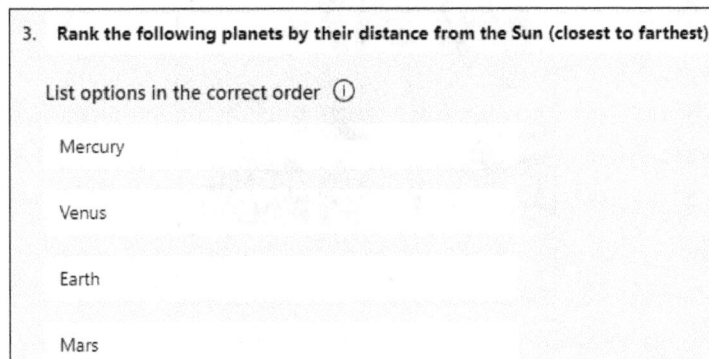

3. **Rank the following planets by their distance from the Sun (closest to farthest):**

List options in the correct order ⓘ

Mercury

Venus

Earth

Mars

Figure 17.10: Ranking question

The options will then appear in a random order for those who will fill in the quiz.

By selecting a question within a quiz or form, we can easily copy it, delete it if no longer required, or change its order by moving it up or down the quiz, as shown in the following figure:

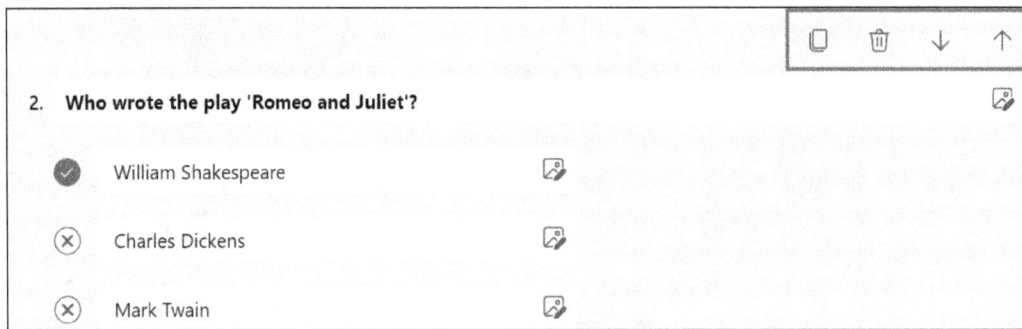

Figure 17.11: Copy, delete, or move question

Once all the necessary questions have been added and configured, we can define the layout and theme of the quiz. This can be done by clicking on the **Style** button, as shown in the following figure:

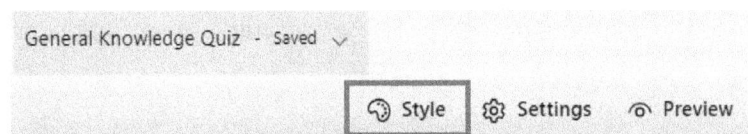

Figure 17.12: Access Style options

We can choose from six layouts and various suggested themes, and even apply background music, as shown in the following figure:

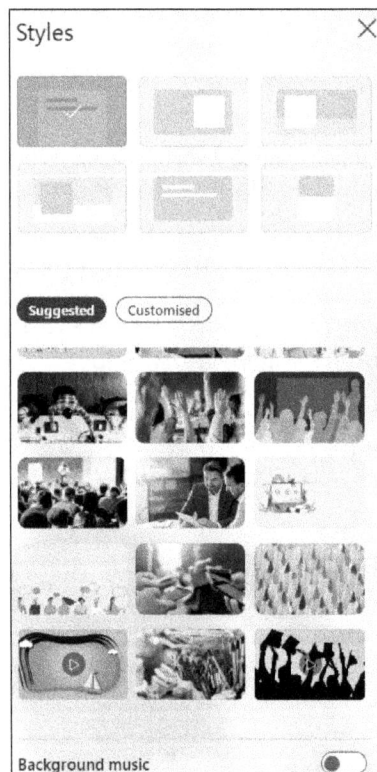

Figure 17.13: Style options

We can also opt for a customized theme by uploading an image or applying a customized color.

At any time, users can view the appearance of the quiz by selecting **Preview**. This allows them to see how it will look for those who access and complete it.

Changes to quizzes and forms are saved automatically.

Creating a form

A form can be created by accessing Microsoft Forms and clicking on **New Form** on the top-left conner of the screen.

To showcase a form creation, as well adding branching and structuring a form into sections, we will take as an example an event registration form.

We start by giving a name to the form, which in this case is the **Event Registration Form**. Then, we create the first section in the form by selecting **Section** from the + **Quick start with** menu:

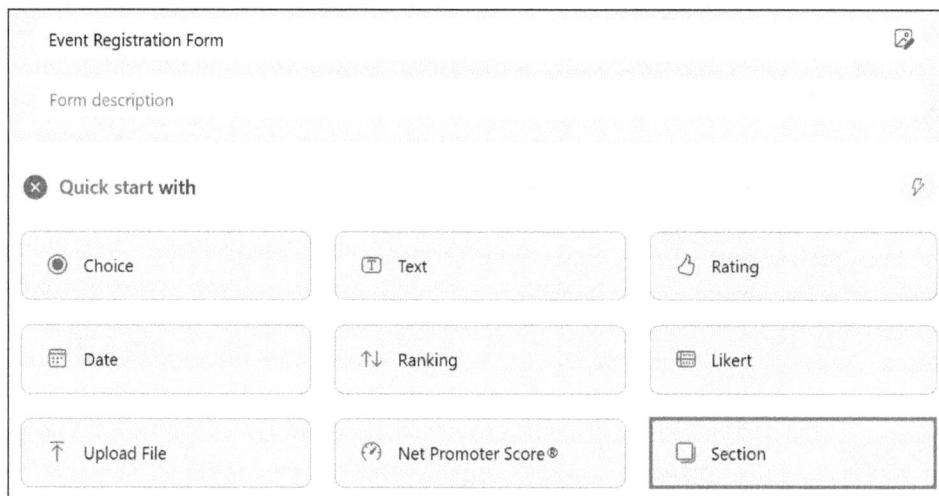

Figure 17.14: Add section

We named this section **Personal Details** and added under it the following questions, both of type *text input*:

- *What is your full name?*
- *What is your email address?*

Sections help structure the form, but they also prevent users from proceeding to the next section if at least one of the questions in the section is mandatory. In our example, both questions from the first section were marked as required.

The question asking for the email address has been configured to restrict the text input to an email address in the following way:

1. Click on the ellipsis button (*More settings for question*) and select **Restrictions**.
2. From the **Restrictions** drop-down menu, select **Email**, as shown:

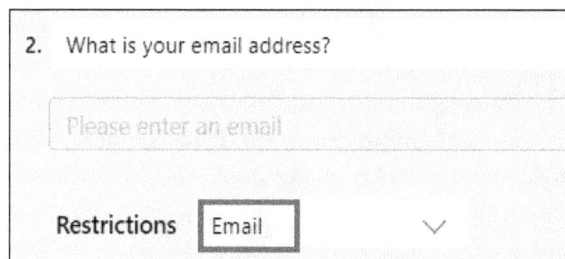

Figure 17.15: Answer restrictions

Next, we added another section that we named *Event Preferences*. This section contains the following questions, all of type *choice*:

- *Which type of event are you interested in?* The answer options for this question are *Workshop* and *Seminar*.

- *Which workshop topic are you interested in?* The answer options for this question are *Data Science, Digital Marketing,* and *Project Management.*

- *Which seminar topic are you interested in?* The answer options for this question are *Leadership, Innovation,* and *Sustainability.*

The current form configuration allows users to answer all questions sequentially. However, the goal is to direct users who select *Workshop* for the *Which type of event are you interested in?* question to only answer the *Which workshop topic are you interested in?* question and then proceed to the end of the form. Similarly, users who select *Seminar* should only provide an answer to the *Which seminar topic are you interested in?* question, which is the last one in our form. To achieve this, we need to add **branching**.

Branching can be added by selecting the question you want to add branching for and then clinking on the ellipsis button and select **Add branching**.

You can then choose the next question or step based on each answer choice. You may select a question from the current section or opt to proceed to a different section after selecting a specific answer. In our case, we selected the questions according to the logic we want to have for our form, as described above. The following figure illustrates the branching selections:

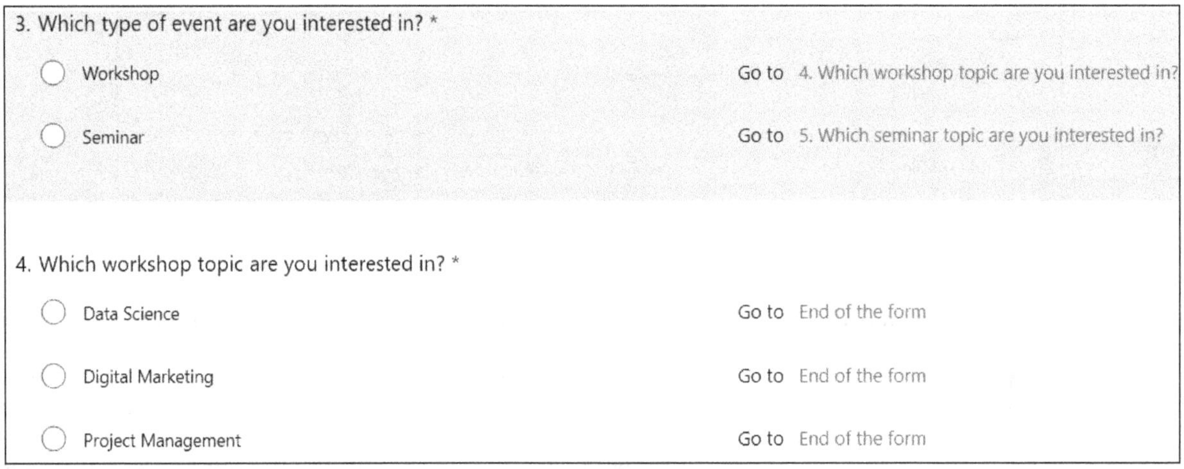

Figure 17.16: Branching

All form questions have been marked as required in our example.

Having configured all essential sections, questions, and logic, we can now proceed to apply a layout and theme in the same manner as demonstrated for the quiz.

Forms, like quizzes, provide the **Preview** option. This feature lets users check how their form will look to the end user whenever needed.

Form and quiz settings

When creating forms and quizzes using Microsoft Forms, it is essential to understand the various settings available to customize and optimize your data collection process.

The form or quiz settings can be accessed and configured by navigating to a form or quiz you own and selecting **Settings**, as shown in the following figure:

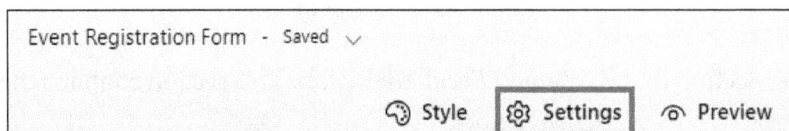

Figure 17.17: Accessing form settings

Most of the configurable options are the same for both quizzes and forms. These include:

- **Who can fill in this form**: This option allows you to configure who should be able to complete the respective form or quiz. The available options are:

  o **Anyone can respond**: This option implies an anonymous response, and sign-in is not required. Selecting this option means that you can share the form or quiz link with anyone in or outside of the organization and it is suitable for public forms.

  o **Only people in the organization can respond**: This option requires signing in to validate access within the organization and is suitable for internal forms that accept responses from anyone within your organization. When this option is selected, you can choose if you want to record the name of the respondent (otherwise it will be anonymous) and if you want to allow only one response per person.

  o **Specific people in the organization can respond**: This option requires signing in to validate access. When this option is selected, you can choose if you want to record the name of the respondent and if you want to allow only one response per person.

- **Options for responses**: This section allows you to configure various settings for your form, such as enabling or disabling form responses, specifying a start and end date for response acceptance, setting a time duration for completing the form, shuffling questions, hiding question numbers, displaying a progress bar (available for multi-page surveys, forms, or quizzes), hiding the option to submit another response (available if multiple responses are permitted), customizing the **Thank you** message after form submission, and allowing respondents to save and edit their responses.

- **Response receipts**: This section allows you to enable receipt of responses after submission, enable email notification of each response and enable smart notification emails to track the response status (available for forms distributed through invitation channel).

In addition to these options, there are additional options that can only be configured for quizzes:

- **Practice mode**: When activated, this feature permits respondents to review questions at their own pace and view the correct answers before submission. If this option is enabled, the time duration setting becomes unavailable.

- **Show results automatically**: Participants will see their results and correct answers right after submitting the quiz.

Sharing forms and collecting responses

Sharing forms and collecting responses is an important step in the data collection process. Microsoft Forms provides several options to share your forms and gather responses efficiently.

To share your form and start collecting responses, navigate to a form or quiz you own and click on **Collect responses**, as shown in the following figure:

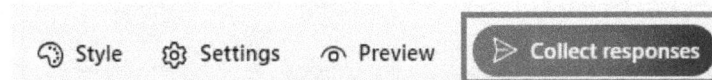

Figure 17.18: Collect responses

The **Send and collect responses** dialog box will open, and from here, you can:

- **Select who can respond to your form**: anyone, only individuals within your organization, or specific people within the organization. This setting can be adjusted under the form settings, as discussed previously. However, when sharing the form, you can further modify this configuration. If you decide to share the form with specific people, you must specify their names or email addresses:

Figure 17.19: Select who can respond to the form

- **Copy the form link**: This link can then be shared via email, chat, intranet page, or social media. You can also get a short form URL by selecting the **Shorten URL** option:

Figure 17.20: Copy form link

- **Send an invitation via Outlook and/or Teams**: This method is particularly useful for targeting a specific group of people. You can also customize the email message to provide context and instructions:

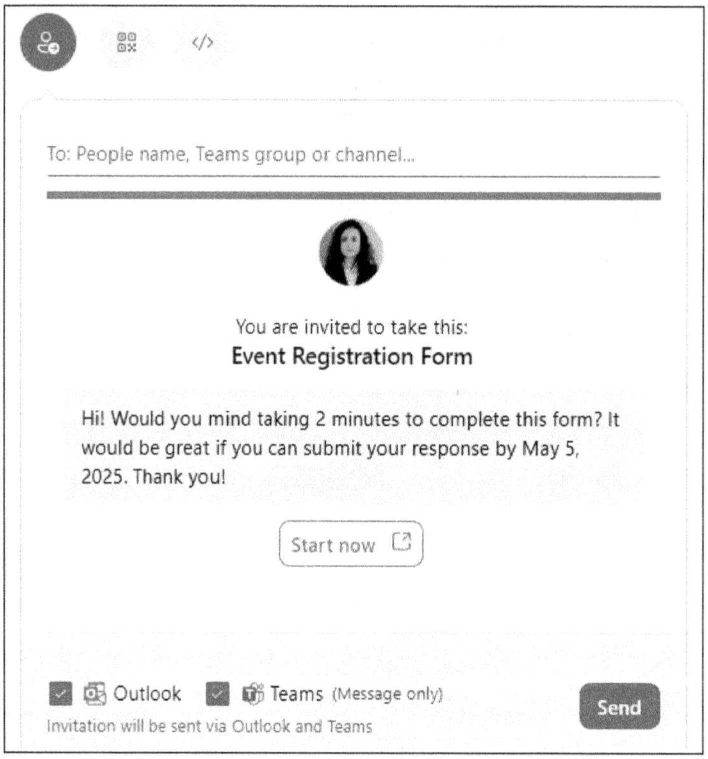

Figure 17.21: Send Outlook and Teams invitation

- **Generate a QR code**: For quick and easy access, you can generate a QR code for your form:

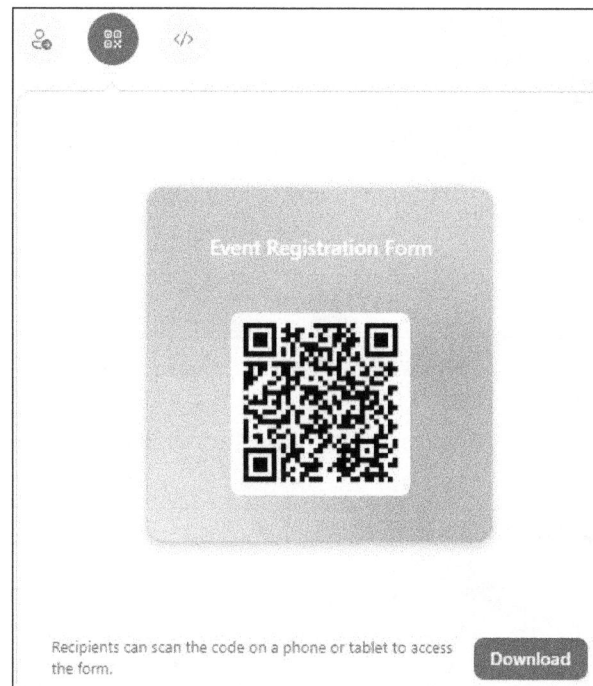

Figure 17.22: Generate a QR code

- **Embed code**: If you want to embed your form directly into a webpage, you can use the embed code provided by Microsoft Forms:

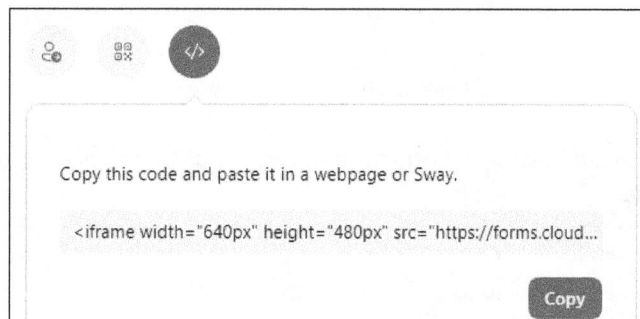

Figure 17.23: Embed code

Once the form has been shared, respondents can complete it and submit the responses as per the form configuration.

Viewing and analyzing responses

Once you have shared your form and collected responses, the next step is to view and analyze the data to gain valuable insights.

Microsoft Forms offers a real-time summary of responses, which includes graphs that visualize the data. This summary helps you quickly identify trends and patterns in the responses. To access the responses summary, navigate to your form and click on **View responses**, as shown in the following figure:

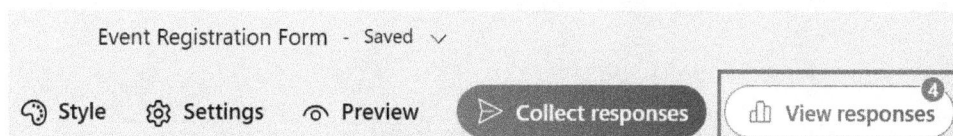

Figure 17.24: View responses

On this page, you will be able to see the responses overview, which will show details like the total number of responses and the average time to complete the form. For quizzes, you will also be able to see the average score, as shown in the following figure:

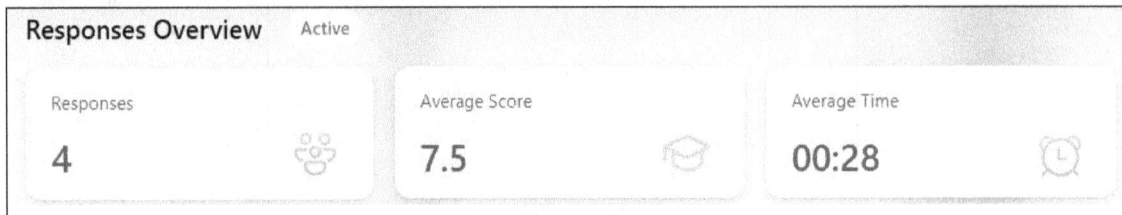

Figure 17.25: Responses overview

Below this information, you can view statistics for each question in the form, as demonstrated in the example shown in the following figure:

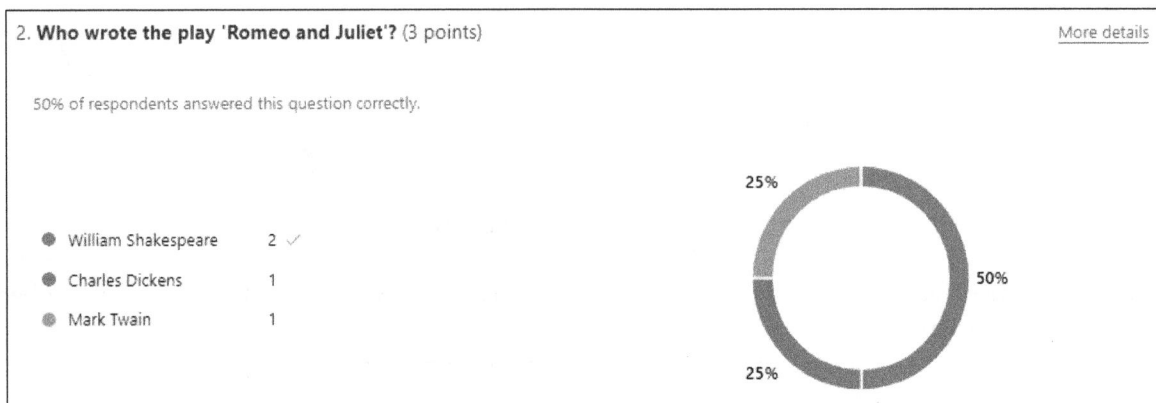

Figure 17.26: Question statistics

Selecting the **More details** option beside the question allows you to see the responses of each individual, as shown in the following figure:

Figure 17.27: Individual responses to a question

Under **Insights and actions** on the responses page, you can check individual answers for all questions by selecting **Check individual results** (for forms) or **Review answers** (for quizzes), as shown in the following figures:

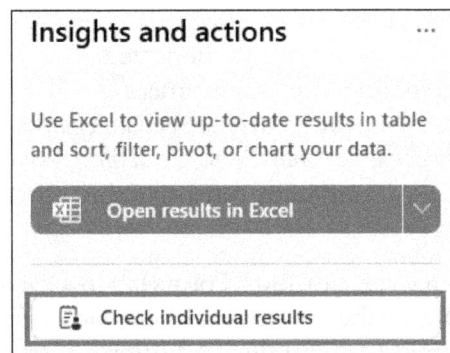

Figure 17.28: Check individual results for forms

The answers can be reviewed as follows:

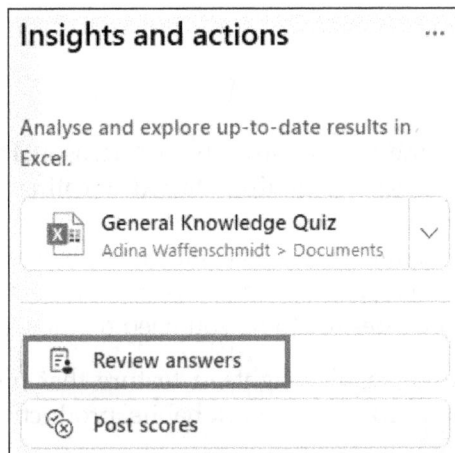

Figure 17.29: Review answers for quizzes

Quizzes also allow you to post scores, as seen in *Figure 17.29*, to grant respondents access to view the feedback and the results of their quiz.

Both quizzes and forms allow you to open results in Excel (online or desktop application). The Excel file is synced with Forms, and new responses can be viewed as soon as they are submitted. You can also download a copy of the file to perform further analysis based on the available responses.

Integration with other Microsoft 365 apps

Microsoft Forms seamlessly integrates with various Microsoft 365 apps, providing users with enhanced capabilities to streamline their workflow. This integration makes it easy to collect, manage, and analyze data across platforms, ensuring that the responses gathered can be effectively utilized. Leveraging these integrations allows for effortless collaboration and optimized productivity.

As we have seen earlier, Forms integrates seamlessly with Excel for response analysis, with Teams for sending invitations directly within the platform, and with Outlook to send form invitations and receive email notifications regarding submissions and responses.

In addition to these services, Forms also integrates with the following apps:

- **SharePoint**: A **Forms** out-of-the-box web part enables users to add a form or quiz to a SharePoint page. This can be set up to collect responses or display form results. Also, the Excel file containing the responses of a group form, along with any other file uploaded as part of a form response, is stored in the SharePoint site linked to the corresponding Microsoft 365 group. The Excel file and files uploaded as part of forms owned by individual users are hosted in the users' OneDrive.

- **Power Automate**: You can create flows that trigger actions such as sending notifications, updating records, or generating reports when a form is submitted. This integration helps you save time and reduce manual tasks by automating repetitive processes. Power Automate provides a variety of templates ready to be used in this regard, such as *Send an email to responder when response submitted in Microsoft Forms, Record form responses in SharePoint, Send form responses for approval, Create a Planner task when a Microsoft Forms is submitted,* and many other templates that you can chose from, based on your requirements.

- **Microsoft Teams**: Within Teams, you can add a Forms tab to a team channel, providing direct access to an existing form. You can configure these forms to either collect responses or display results, depending on the requirements of your project or workflow. Additionally, shared forms can be created to facilitate collaboration among team members, ensuring input and edits can be made without leaving the Teams application. This integration simplifies the process, allowing teams to manage forms effortlessly while staying within the Teams environment, thereby optimizing productivity and ensuring a cohesive workflow.

Conclusion

In this chapter, we have looked into the various aspects of Microsoft Forms, a powerful tool for creating quizzes and forms. We covered the basics of getting started, creating quizzes and forms, sharing them, collecting responses, viewing and analyzing the data, and the integration of Forms with other Microsoft 365 apps. By utilizing Forms, you can streamline your data collection processes, enhance collaboration, and gain valuable insights from the responses you gather. Whether you're conducting surveys, gathering feedback, or organizing events, Microsoft Forms provides the tools you need to make the process efficient and effective.

In the next chapter, we will explore Personal Insights, a feature that provides personalized analytics and insights to help you understand and improve your work habits, productivity, and well-being.

Join our Discord space

Join our Discord workspace for latest updates, offers, tech happenings around the world, new releases, and sessions with the authors:

https://discord.bpbonline.com

CHAPTER 18
Personal Insights

Introduction

Personal insights have become increasingly significant in the modern workplace, providing employees with valuable knowledge regarding their work patterns and productivity. This chapter delves into how Personal Insights harnesses the power of these insights to foster a more efficient and collaborative environment. By analyzing user interactions within various tools, Personal Insights offers personalized recommendations that aim to enhance not only individual performance but also overall well-being.

This chapter will explore the various features and benefits of Personal Insights, demonstrating how this tool can help achieve a balanced and productive work life.

Structure

This chapter covers the following topics:

- Personal Insights and Viva Insights
- Personal Insights in Microsoft Teams and on the web
- Viva Insights Outlook add-in

Objectives

The primary objectives of this chapter are to provide an understanding of Personal Insights and to illustrate how these insights can be applied to achieve a balanced, productive, and collaborative work life. Readers will learn how Personal Insights can be accessed and utilized within Microsoft Teams, Outlook, and web-based platforms to enhance work habits and overall well-being. Additionally, they will learn practical ways to leverage Personal Insights to improve individual work patterns and lifestyle choices.

By the end of this chapter, readers will be equipped with the tools and understanding needed to integrate Personal Insights into their daily routines, ultimately leading to a more efficient, connected, and balanced professional life.

Personal Insights and Viva Insights

Understanding how you spend your time at work is crucial to making informed decisions that lead to improved work habits. **Personal Insights**, part of Viva Insights and previously known as MyAnalytics, helps you understand and improve your work habits and productivity. By analyzing various aspects of how you interact with your tools and colleagues, Personal Insights provides personalized recommendations and actionable insights to enhance efficiency, collaboration, and well-being.

Personal Insights summarizes how you spend your time at work and then suggests ways to work smarter. These personalized insights are provided through elements that you can access in Microsoft Outlook, in Teams, or through your web browser, and are designed to guide you towards smarter working strategies, ensuring that you can maximize your potential while maintaining a healthy work-life balance. It offers several benefits to users:

- **Increased productivity**: By recognizing and refining work habits, users can maximize their efficiency and accomplish tasks more effectively.

- **Better collaboration**: Insights provide information on communication patterns and help users build stronger connections within their teams.

- **Enhanced work-life balance**: Recommendations on taking breaks, managing stress, and scheduling focus time contribute to a healthier and more balanced lifestyle.

- **Data-driven decisions**: The insights are based on real data from the user's interactions, ensuring that recommendations are relevant and actionable.

While Personal Insights is specifically tailored to individual users, **Viva Insights** extends its capabilities to managers and leaders, providing them with advanced insights to help their teams and organizations thrive.

In essence, Personal Insights is a subset of Viva Insights, concentrated on individual productivity and well-being, whereas Viva Insights covers a more comprehensive scope, addressing the needs of both individuals and organizational leaders.

As previously mentioned, Personal Insights consists of several elements designed to boost productivity and well-being, all of which we will be exploring next:

- Viva Insights in Microsoft Teams
- Viva Insights on the web
- Viva Insights Outlook add-in

Licensing

Viva Insights and the entire Viva suite have several different licenses that provide different apps and services. However, some of the elements of Viva Insights, such as Personal Insights, are provided automatically to users of various Microsoft 365 and Office 365 plans as part of **Microsoft Viva in Microsoft 365**:

- Microsoft 365 E3, A3, E5, A5, Business Basic, Business Standard, or Business Premium.
- Office 365 E1, E3, A3, E5, A5.

Note: Viva Insights is managed by IT administrators through Microsoft 365 admin center and Entra ID. As such, if you do not have access to Viva Insights, please contact your IT department.

Viva Insights in Microsoft Teams and on the web

The Microsoft Viva Insights app within Microsoft Teams and on the web is the gateway to Personal Insights. By tapping into data from Microsoft 365 activities such as emails, meetings, calls, and chats, it provides actionable insights to help users develop optimal work habits.

You can access the app on the web by visiting **https://insights.cloud.microsoft** or through the Microsoft 365 app launcher at **https://m365.cloud.microsoft**.

To use the app in the Teams client, follow these steps:

1. Select the ellipsis (**View more apps**) on the left bar in Teams.
2. In the search field, type **Insights**, and then select **Add** next to the *Viva Insights* app, as shown:

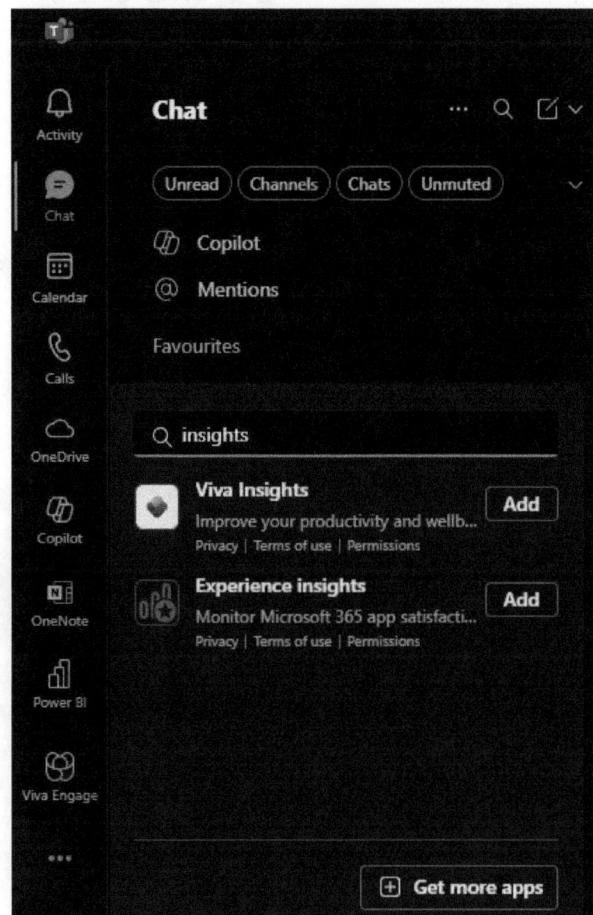

Figure 18.1: Adding the Viva Insights app in Teams

Once installed, you can right-click the app icon in the left bar in Teams and then select **Pin** to keep it visible in the left bar in Teams.

> **Note:** The insights provided by this app are personal and confidential. Only the individual user can view their personal insights; neither managers nor system administrators have access to these insights.

The app consists of four tabs, which will be described in detail next.

Overview tab

The **Overview** tab offers a holistic view of your work patterns and provides a summary of key metrics related to your productivity and well-being. In the following figure, we can see some of these:

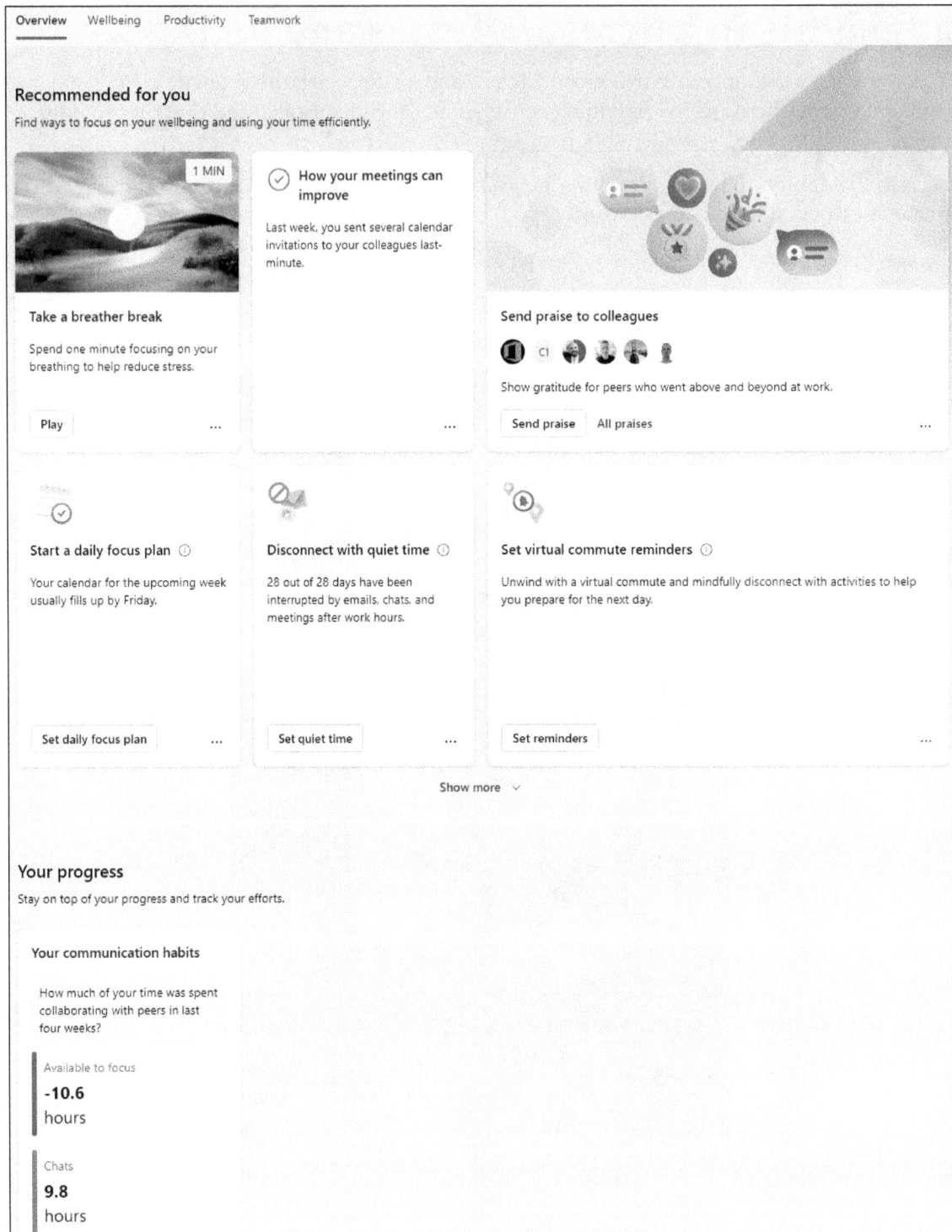

Figure 18.2: Overview tab of the Viva Insights app

It aggregates data from various Microsoft 365 activities, giving you a snapshot of how your time is allocated across tasks such as meetings, emails, and focused work periods. This tab enables you to quickly identify areas for improvement and track your progress towards building more effective work habits.

This tab is subdivided into three sections: *Recommended for you, Your progress,* and *Inspiration library.*

Recommended for you allows you to send praise to your colleagues, book some focus time, set quiet time to temporarily disable notifications, read tips about promoting healthy meeting norms, schedule a team no-meeting day, start a shared focus plan, and more.

The praise option is a feature designed to recognize and appreciate the efforts and contributions of employees and colleagues. It allows you to send praise notifications within Teams, offering flexibility in how these messages are shared. You can choose to send them privately, ensuring a more personal touch, or share them publicly in a Teams channel conversation for broader recognition and encouragement. This feature fosters a positive work environment and promotes a culture of appreciation and gratitude. The following figure is the card used to send praise:

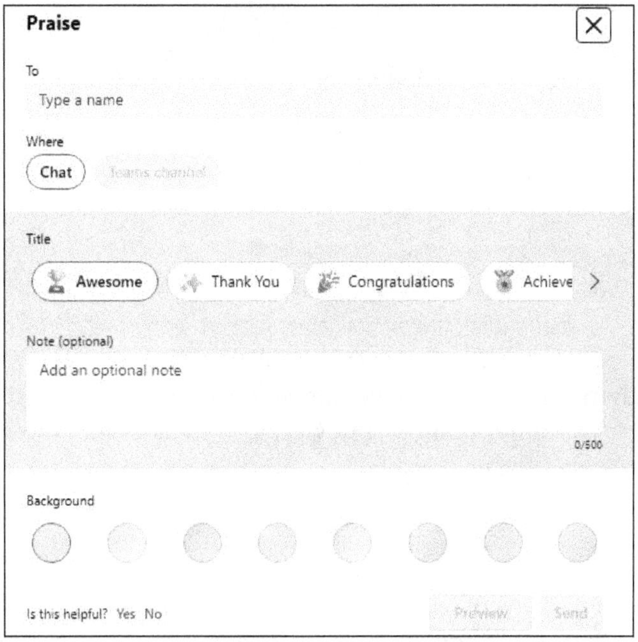

Figure 18.3: Sending a praise

Your progress shows how much time you have had to focus, and how much time you spent on chats, emails, and meetings:

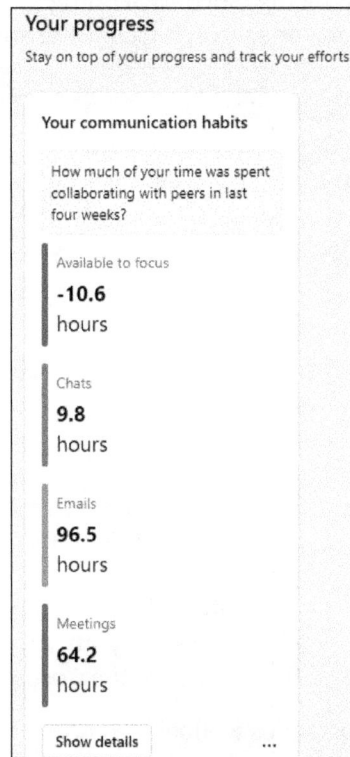

Figure 18.4: Time spent collaborating with others

Finally, the **Inspiration library** provides curated content related to wellbeing and productivity from industry experts:

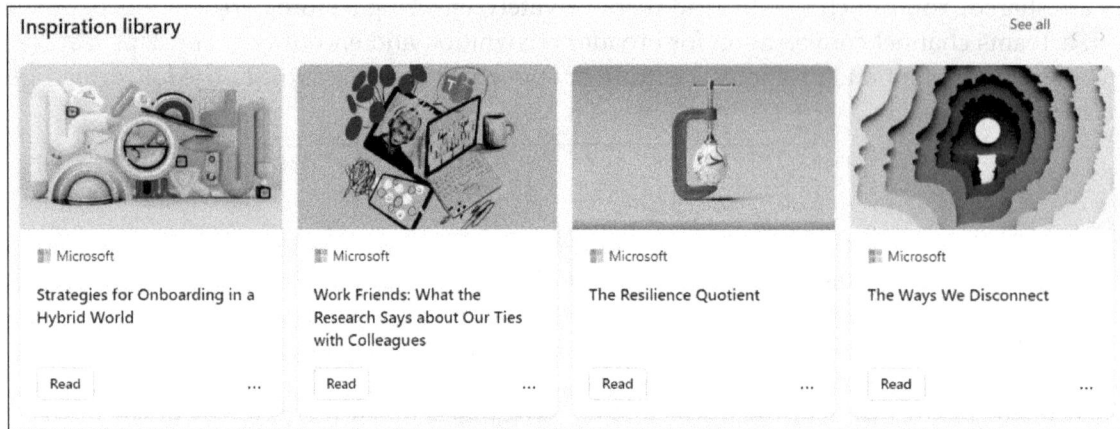

Figure 18.5: Inspiration library with wellbeing content

The library prioritizes displaying articles that have not yet been read. These articles can be accessed through the Teams application on your computer or mobile device, as well as within the Viva Insights app on the web. To read an article, simply select its title.

Wellbeing tab

The Wellbeing tab provides an overview of work habits, assists in time management, and supports maintaining a balance between life and work. You can book focus time, engage in guided meditations, and access wellbeing topics. Within this tab, there are four sections:

- **Take action to improve your wellbeing**: This section provides guidance on how to modify habits, manage your time effectively, and disconnect from work at the end of the day. It offers a selection of actions focused on enhancing wellbeing, such as sending praise to colleagues, starting a daily focus plan, disconnecting with quiet time, or setting virtual commute times, for example:

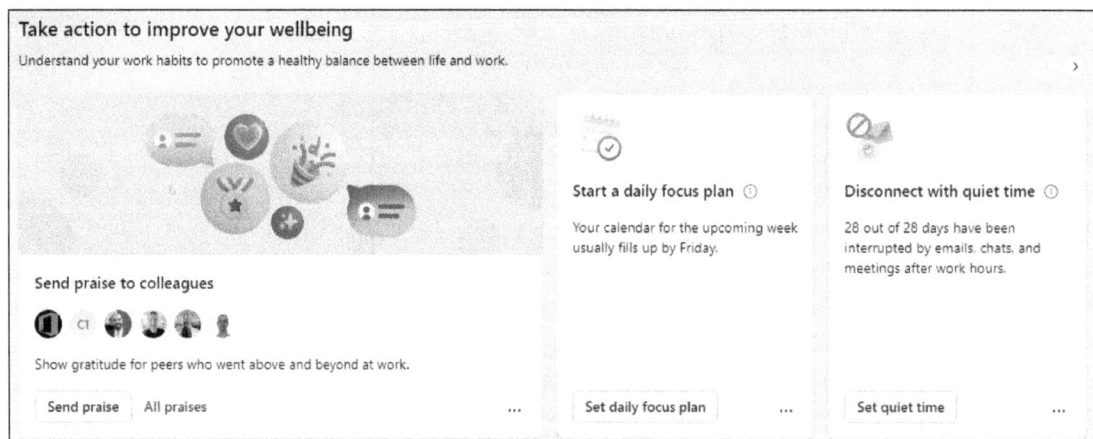

Figure 18.6: Take action section

- **Track your progress**: Once an action is established, Personal Insights provides information on its effectiveness in this section. It offers statistics on your focus time from the past few months and presents a summary of the allocated focus time for the upcoming week.

- **Act with intention**: This section provides wellbeing content. You can use the **Focus** or **Articles** buttons to explore different topics, like doing a breathing exercise, accessing articles about wellbeing, or booking focus time, as shown in the following figure:

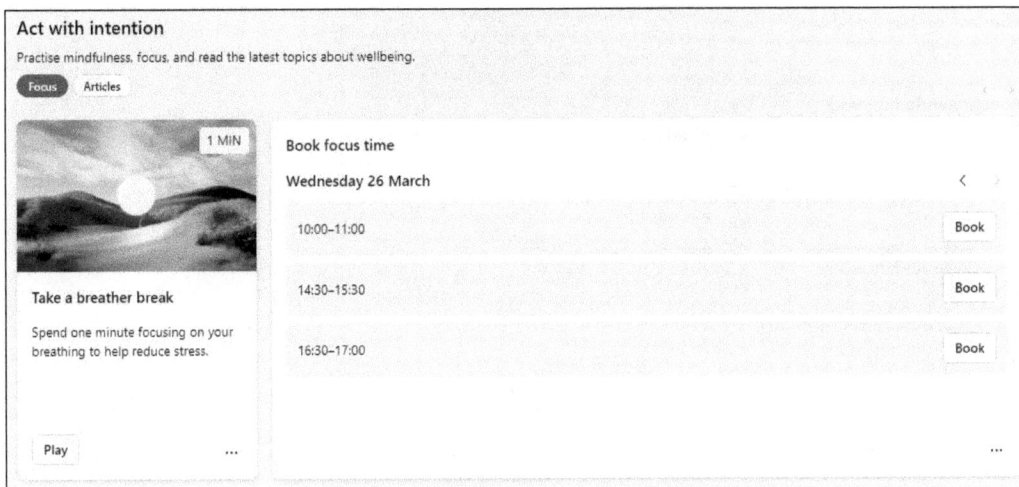

Figure 18.7: Act with intention section

- **Reflect on your emotions**: Here, you can assess your emotions by monitoring your feelings and reviewing your reflection patterns:

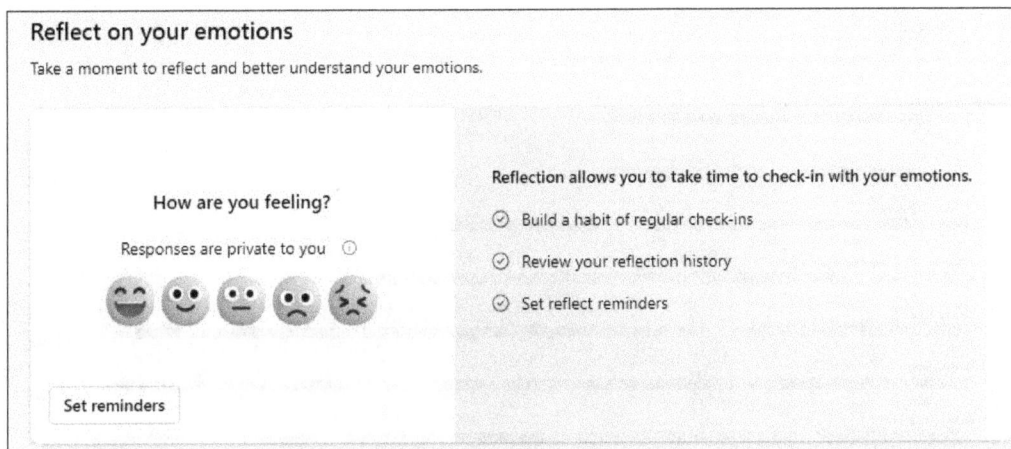

Figure 18.8: Reflect on your emotions section

Focus time is a feature designed to help users carve out time for uninterrupted work. By booking focus time in your calendar, you can ensure that this period is dedicated to completing tasks that require deep concentration and minimal distractions. During focus time, notifications from emails, chats, and other applications are temporarily muted to allow you to work efficiently. This can help boost productivity by minimizing interruptions and helping you stay on track with your goals.

Quiet time, on the other hand, is aimed at supporting mental wellbeing by creating periods of reduced work-related activity. This feature allows you to disconnect from work, either during or after working hours, by silencing notifications and giving you a chance to relax. Quiet time can include activities such as guided meditations, breathing exercises, or simply taking a break to recharge. By incorporating quiet time into your routine, you can prevent burnout and maintain a healthier work-life balance, ensuring that you are mentally refreshed and ready to tackle your tasks.

Productivity

The **Productivity** tab is designed to enhance the effectiveness of your meetings, help you stay on top of your tasks, and streamline your workflow for better efficiency. This section provides tools and insights that enable you to manage your time and tasks more effectively, ensuring that you can achieve optimal productivity throughout your workday. The following is an example:

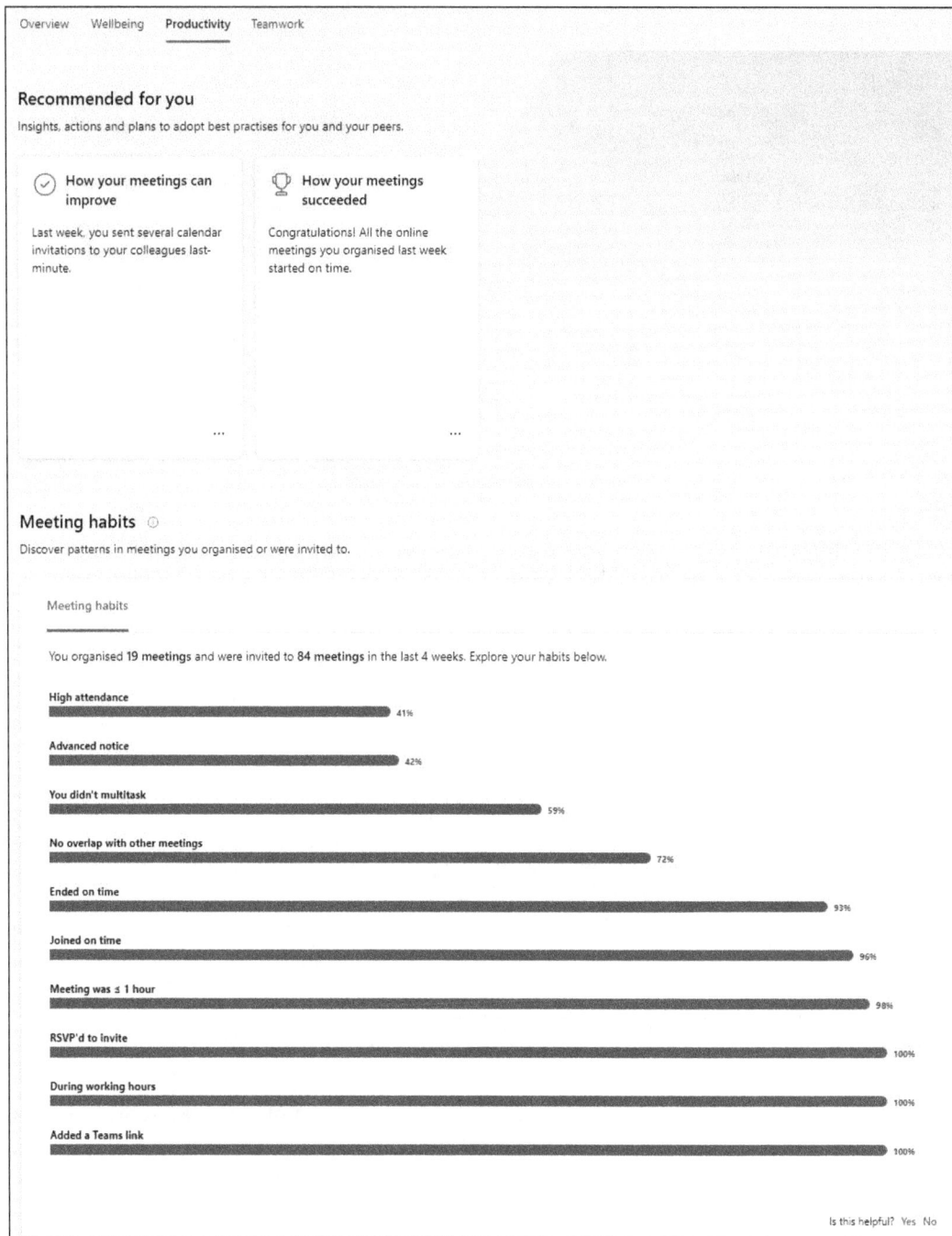

Figure 18.9: Productivity tab

The **Meeting Habits** section emphasizes the frequency with which you organize or attend meetings that demonstrate specific practices. Here is how the habits shown in this section are calculated:

- **High attendance**: Meetings with over 50% response rate
- **Advanced notice**: Invitations sent with over 24 hours' notice
- **You did not multitask**: No emails or chats during meetings
- **No overlap with other meetings**: Meetings without calendar overlaps
- **Ended on time**: Online meetings ended within one minute of the scheduled end
- **Joined on time**: Joined online meetings within five minutes of the start time
- **Meeting was <= 1 hour**: Organized meetings lasting one hour or less

- **RSVP'd to invite**: Accepted or declined meeting invitations
- **During working hours**: Meetings scheduled during working hours
- **Added a Teams link**: Meetings with a Teams link for remote attendees

Teamwork tab

Teamwork is your hub for building and strengthening connections with your team and colleagues. Use this tab to understand who your top collaborators are and how much time you spend collaborating with others. It provides insights on communication patterns, helping you identify opportunities to improve collaboration and recognize the achievements of your team members. By analyzing these patterns, you can foster a more connected and efficient team environment, ultimately enhancing productivity and team morale.

The following figure shows an overview of these patterns:

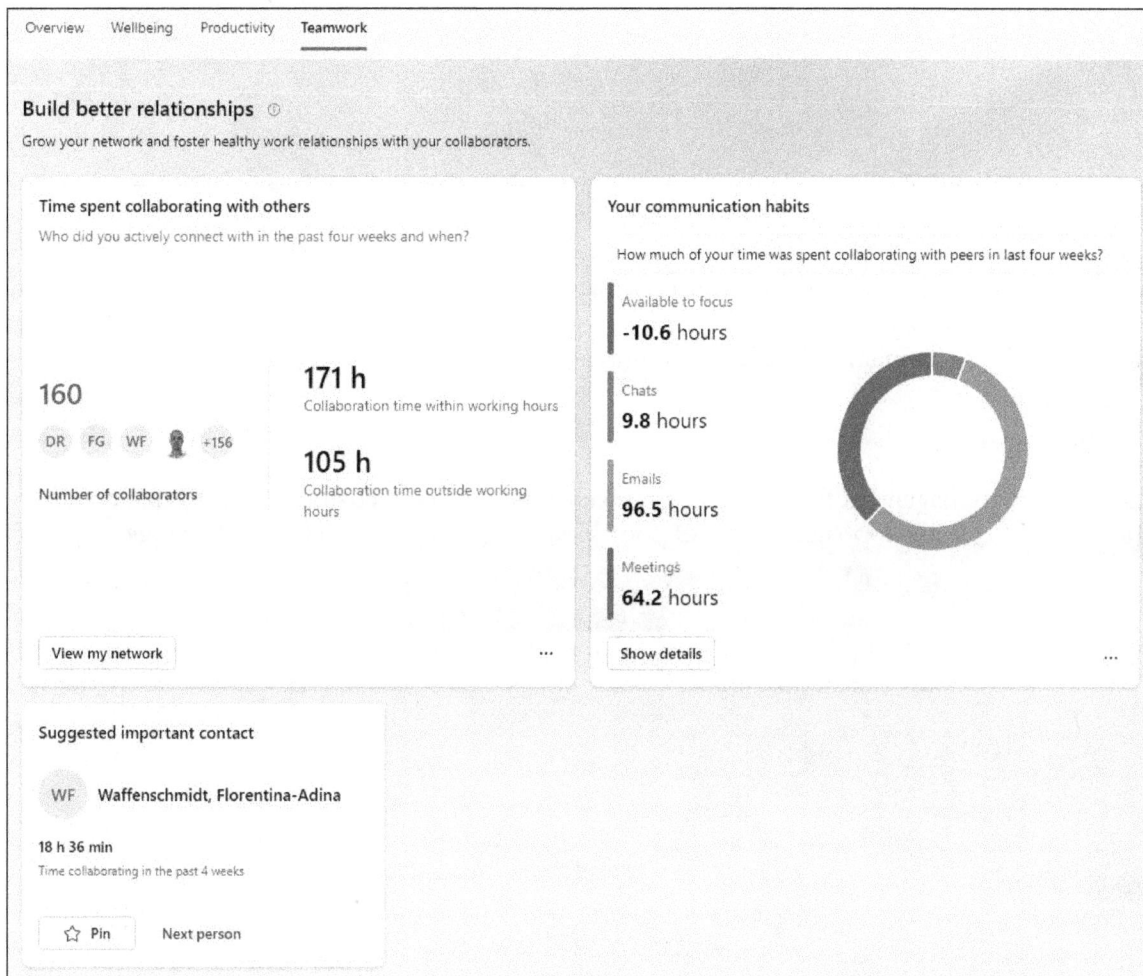

Figure 18.10: Teamwork tab

Time spent collaborating with others reflects the number of individuals you have engaged with over the past month. In this section, *Collaboration time within working hours* denotes your estimated time allocated to meetings, emails, calls, and Teams chats during your designated working hours, while *Collaboration time outside working hours* represents your estimated time involved in those same activities but outside your specified working hours.

Under **Your communication habits** you can see what percentage of your time is available to focus and what percentage of your time is spent collaborating with others. For additional details regarding your communication habits, click on **Show details** and you will see the following chart:

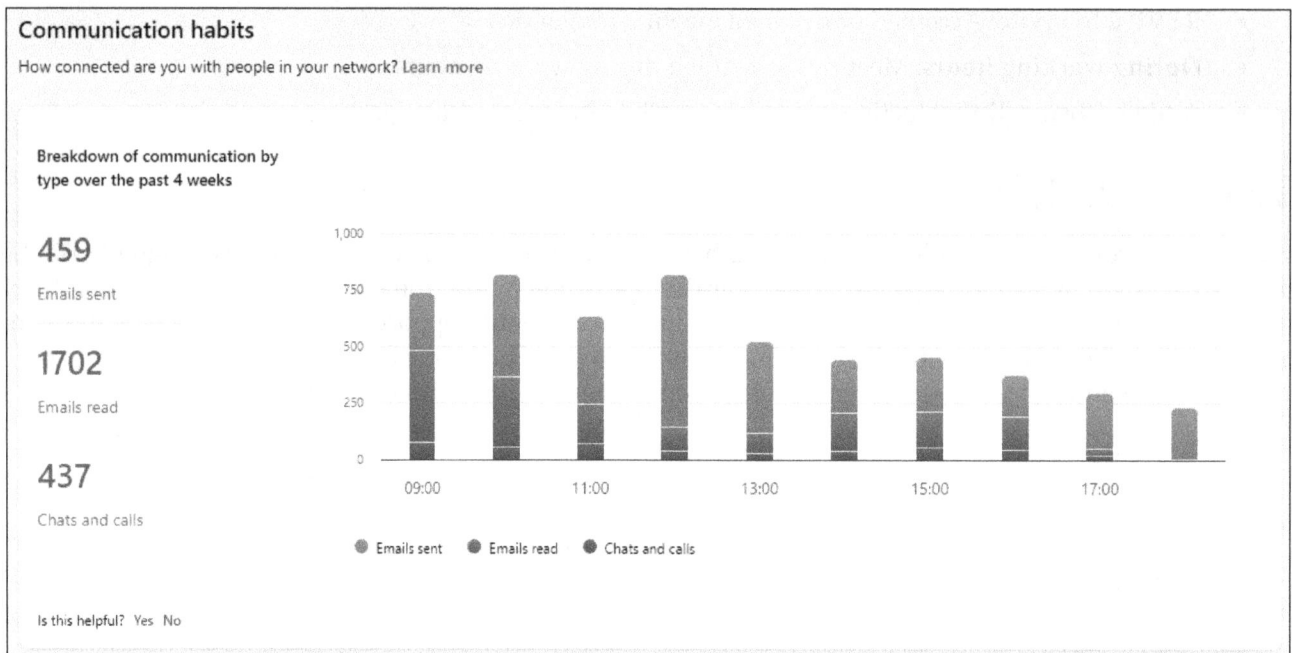

Figure 18.11: Communication habits

The **suggested important contact** feature highlights a contact you have frequently collaborated with and may want to pin as a favorite. By using the *Pin* button, you can mark someone as a favorite, which prompts Viva Insights to remind you to finish tasks and check unread emails from these contacts.

Settings

To access the time management feature settings, including options to customize or disable certain features, select the ellipses (**...**) in the top-right corner of your Viva Insights app, and click on **Settings**:

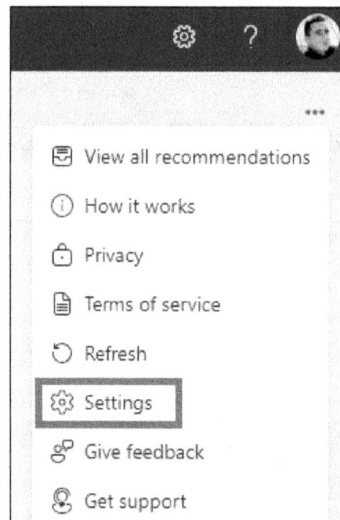

Figure 18.12: Viva Insights app menu

In the **Settings** section, you can find several key options that are particularly significant for managing your work environment. These settings include tools to optimize your working hours, enhance collaboration, and promote a balanced work-life routine.

The **Work Week** setting allows you to define your working hours and days. This customization helps the app provide more accurate insights and recommendations based on your specific schedule. By setting up your work week, you ensure that the app aligns with your personal and professional routines, enhancing its relevancy and usefulness. The following figure shows a typical working hours and days setting:

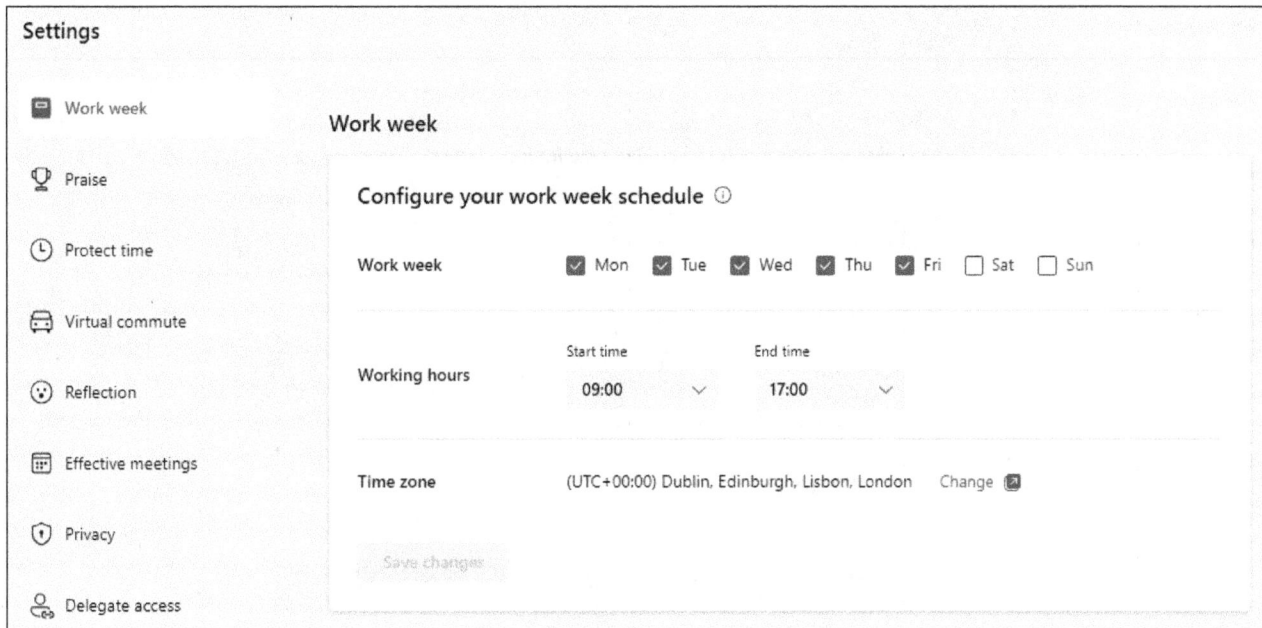

Figure 18.13: Work week settings

With the **Praise** setting, you can designate specific days and times for Viva Analytics to prompt you to recognize and commend your colleagues. This feature ensures regular intervals for acknowledgment and appreciation, fostering a supportive and motivational work atmosphere. By default, this is disabled, as you can see in the following figure:

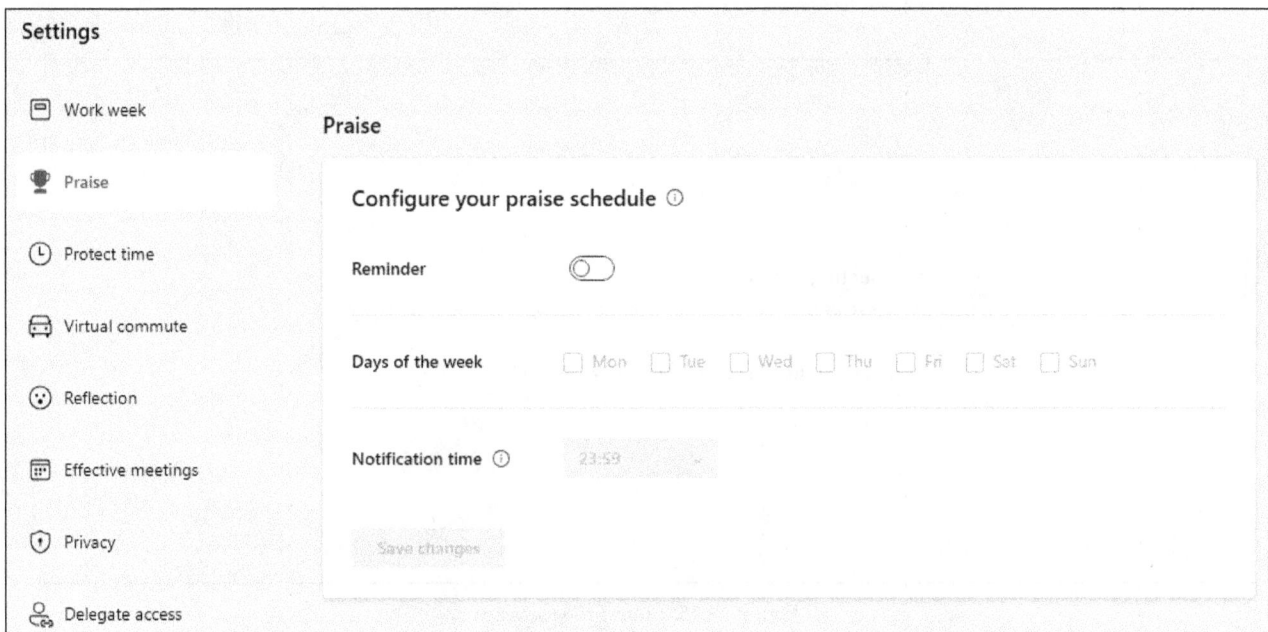

Figure 18.14: Praise settings

The **Protect time** setting allows you to configure your quiet time, configure lunch hours (and even add a recurring calendar event to protect your lunch hours), and configure reminders to clear conflicts on a no-meeting day:

Settings

- ▣ Work week
- ♀ Praise
- 🕐 Protect time
- 🚗 Virtual commute
- ☺ Reflection
- ⊞ Effective meetings
- 🛡 Privacy
- 👥 Delegate access

Protect time

☁ Configure your quiet time ⓘ

Insights can help protect your quiet time from work-related notifications

Set up your quiet time and we'll mute mobile notifications from Outlook emails and Teams.

[Get started]

Productivity inline suggestions

Show inline suggestions on emails and meetings in Outlook to help book focus time, manage tasks, and more.

Productivity inline suggestions   ⬤─ On

Save changes

Lunch hours

Viva Insights uses this setting to improve recommendations for booking focus time and meetings.

My lunch hours are: 12:00 ⌄   to   13:00 ⌄

☐ Add a recurring calendar event to protect this time

Save changes

No-meeting day plan settings

Insights sends reminders before each no-meeting day to cancel conflicting meetings.

Send reminders to clear conflicts on no-meeting days?

◉ Yes ○ No

Save changes

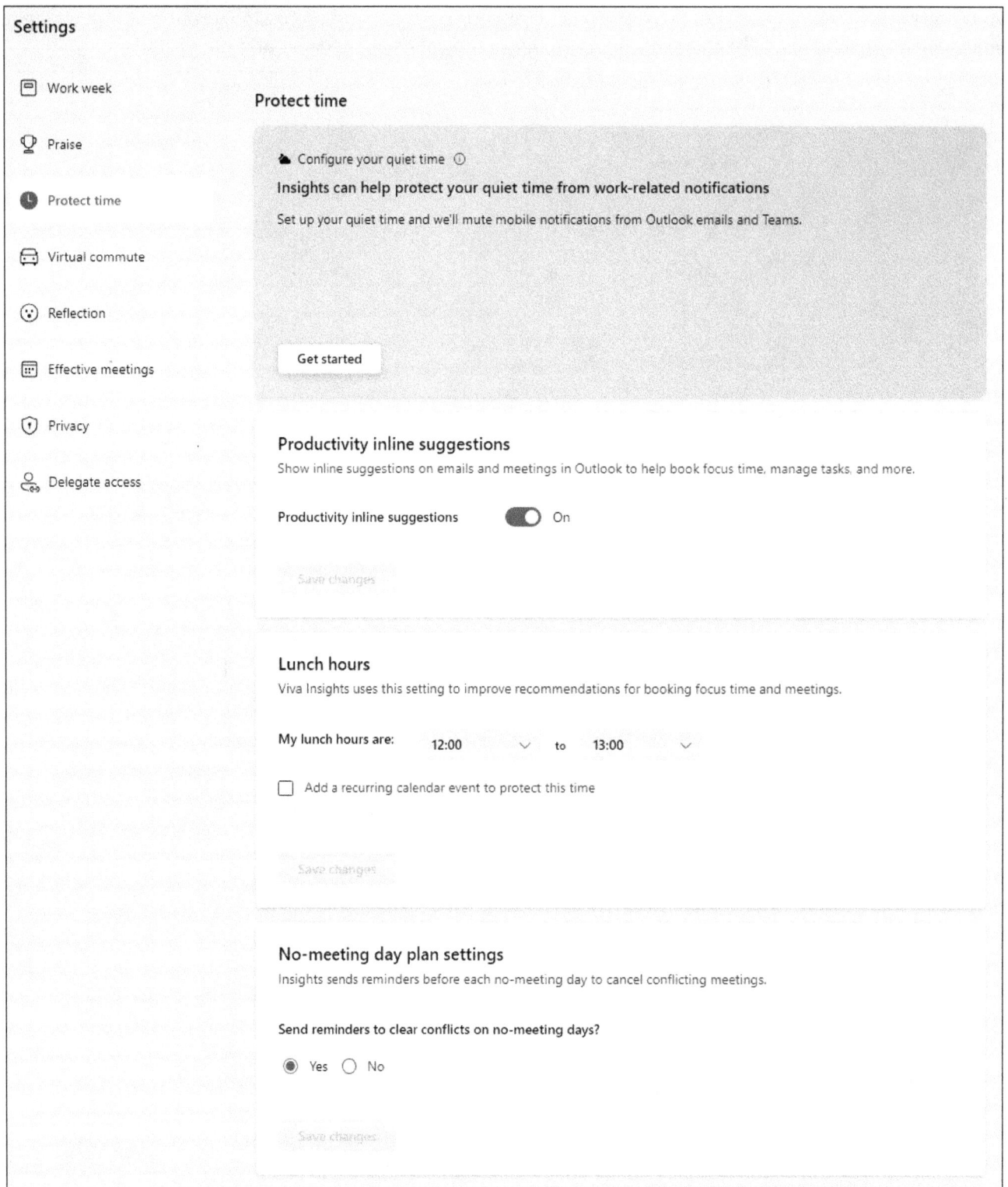

Figure 18.15: Protect time settings

Under **Effective Meetings**, you can optimize your meeting schedule to maximize productivity and minimize fatigue. The **Shorten Meetings** option reduces the duration of your meetings, ensuring they end a few minutes earlier than scheduled. This adjustment allows participants to transition smoothly to their next commitment, enhancing overall efficiency. The **Add Teams Meeting** option automatically includes a Teams meeting link whenever you schedule a meeting. This ensures all participants have direct access to the meeting platform, saving time on coordination. These tools contribute to a more structured and manageable meeting schedule, reducing stress and improving the quality of your interactions with colleagues. The following figure shows the settings that can be configured in this section:

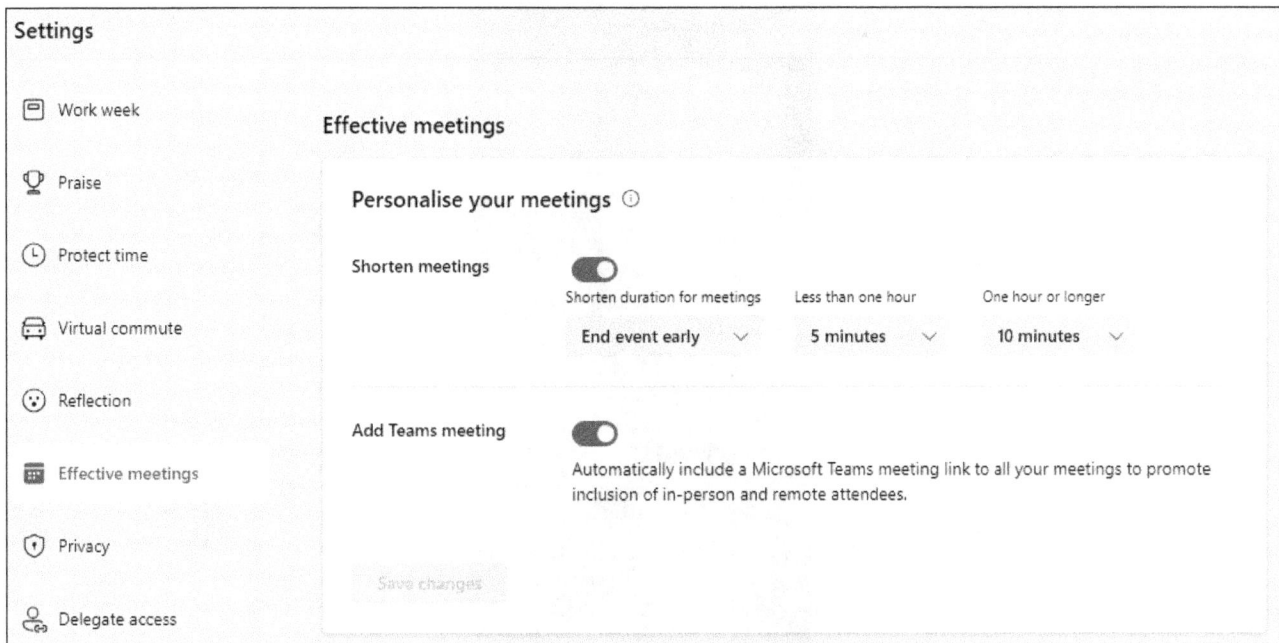

Figure 18.16: Effective meeting settings

Viva Insights Outlook add-in

The Outlook add-in delivers actionable insights that help you stay on top of your tasks and improve efficiency. By embedding these insights directly into your email platform, Viva Insights ensures that you can access valuable recommendations without disrupting your routine. Whether it is prioritizing important emails or scheduling time for focused work, the add-in offers support to enhance your productivity.

Accessing the add-in

To access the Viva Insights Outlook add-in in the desktop app, follow these steps:

1. Open your Outlook application.
2. In the **Home** tab, click on **All Apps**, followed by **Add Apps**.
3. Search for **Viva Insights**, select it, and click **Add**.

Once installed, the add-in will appear in your Outlook toolbar, ready to provide you with actionable insights to boost productivity. If you are unable to install the add-in, it could have been disabled by your IT department.

In Outlook on the web, simply open an email message, select **Apps** in the top-right corner of your email message, and select **Viva Insights** from the list. Now you can pin the add-in to your quick-access pane.

After opening the Viva Insights add-in, you will see multiple cards in the right pane:

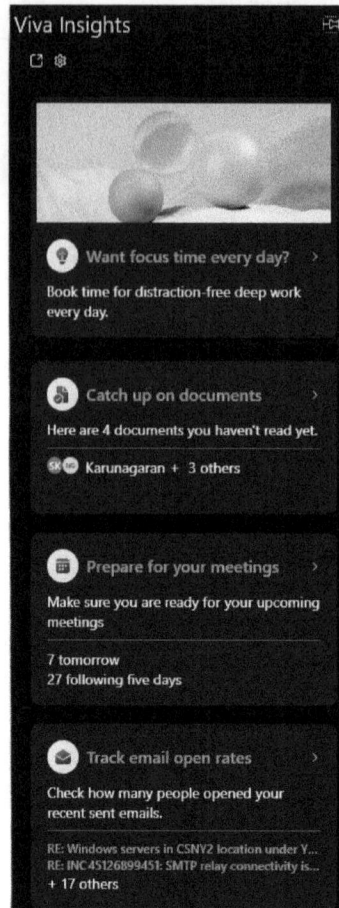

Figure 18.17: *Viva Insights add-in pane*

These cards provide various suggestions aimed at improving focus, preparing efficiently for time away, or managing daily tasks. By offering tailored recommendations, Viva Insights ensures that you are equipped with the tools needed to enhance your productivity and maintain a healthy work-life balance. Whether you need assistance in scheduling your day or prioritizing tasks, these insights are designed to support your professional journey by seamlessly integrating into your Outlook experience.

Let us look at some of these cards.

Prepare for your meetings

Meetings are essential for effective collaboration. Implementing improved meeting practices can enhance productivity, facilitate information sharing, drive innovation, support decision making, and strengthen connections among team members. The **Prepare for your meetings** insight lists upcoming meetings that you have organized or been invited to for the next seven calendar days:

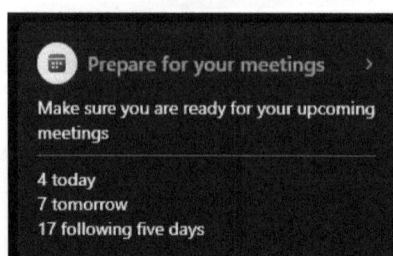

Figure 18.18: *Prepare for your meetings card*

This insight assists you in determining if you are prepared for each meeting. Select **Prepare for your meetings** to view an insight for each of your upcoming meetings. You can filter by **All**, **Organized**, or **Invited** meetings:

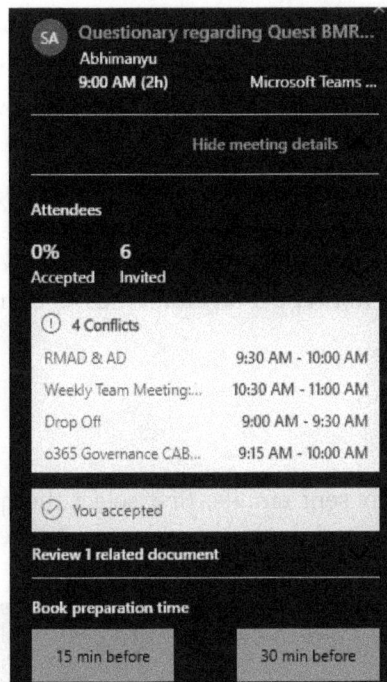

Figure 18.19: Meeting details card

With this insight, you can perform the following actions:

- **Attendees**: Identify the percentage of invitees who have accepted the meeting and the total number of invitees. Select the down arrow to access more detailed information about these attendees.

- **Conflicts**: Obtain a list of all other meetings that conflict with this scheduled meeting, if any.

- **Respond (if you are an invitee)**: Indicate your acceptance or decline of the invitation by responding **Yes** or **No**. If you have already responded, your response will be displayed here. Meetings scheduled outside of your typical meeting hours will be highlighted, providing an option to respond accordingly.

- **Attachments**: Access attachments related to the meeting, along with their titles and storage locations (whether online or local). For online attachments, you can view additional details or open them.

- **Related documents**: Examine documents that may assist in preparing for the meeting.

- **Determine whether the meeting has an online link (if you are the organizer)**: Check whether the meeting includes an online link, indicated by **Yes** or **No**.

- **Book preparation time**: Schedule either 15 minutes or 30 minutes of preparation time before the meeting, if your calendar is free before the meeting. This booked time will appear on your calendar and reference the meeting as *Preparation time for [meeting title]*. You also have the option to cancel or delete the meeting preparation time directly from your calendar.

Track email open rates

With the option to track email open rates, Viva Insights provides valuable details about your sent emails:

- View how many recipients have opened your email.
- Analyze the average time recipients spent reading your email.
- Check how many recipients opened a document you shared within the email, whether as a link or an attachment.

This feature allows you to gauge the effectiveness of your communication, helping you to refine your approach for future correspondence. You can monitor engagement levels and adjust your strategies to ensure your messages resonate with your audience.

Note: After an email message is sent, it may take up to 30 minutes for Viva Insights to provide information regarding it. If the email is dispatched from a delegated mailbox with send on behalf permission, the delegate will be able to view the read statistics.

Statistics for read emails are displayed exclusively for *qualifying messages*. A qualifying message refers to an email sent to five or more qualifying recipients. Qualifying recipients are individuals within the same company as the sender who possess a cloud mailbox. Distribution lists are expanded prior to counting qualifying recipients. However, Viva Insights does not report on email messages in the following categories:

- Email sent from a shared mailbox.
- Email sent more than 14 days ago.
- Email sent to modern groups.

To see and read information about your sent emails, first select the qualifying email. Next, just below the email's body, you should see how many recipients have already opened the email, just like in the following figure:

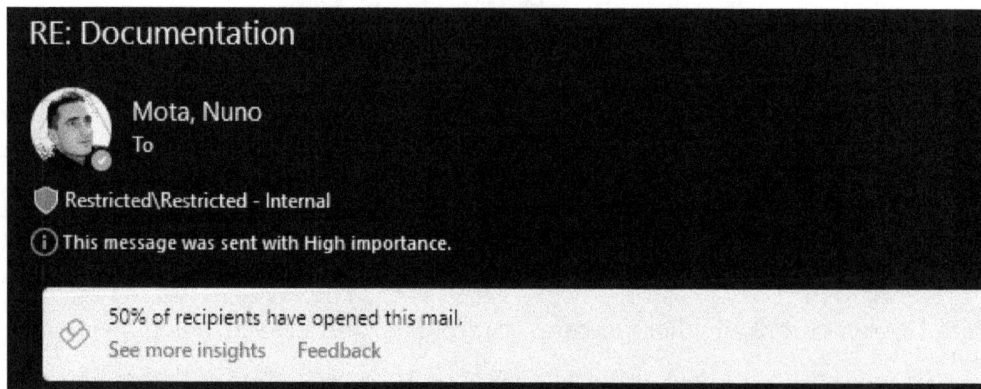

Figure 18.20: Email read rates information

Click on **See more insights** to see more insights regarding the email:

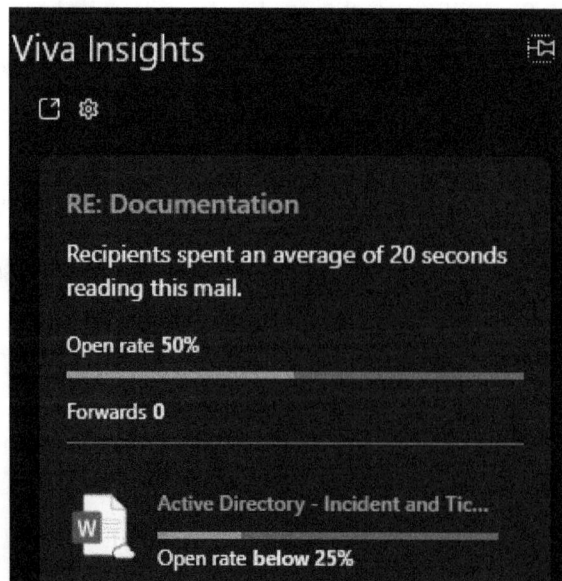

Figure 18.21: Email read rates details

Insights will show the average time recipients spend reading the email, the email's open rate, and also the open rate for linked or attached documents that are stored in OneDrive for Business or in SharePoint.

Catch up on documents

The **Catch up on documents** feature displays a list of shared documents from OneDrive and SharePoint that you have yet to open. This list includes documents shared with you via email from the last 14 days. It helps you stay on top of important files and ensures you do not miss any critical information that may have been shared during this period.

To access this feature, navigate to the Viva Insights add-in pane and select **Catch up on documents**:

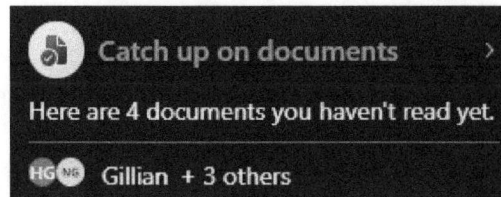

Figure 18.22: Catch up on documents card

From here, you can easily open the relevant email or meeting where the unread documents were shared, or book time on your calendar specifically dedicated to reviewing these documents:

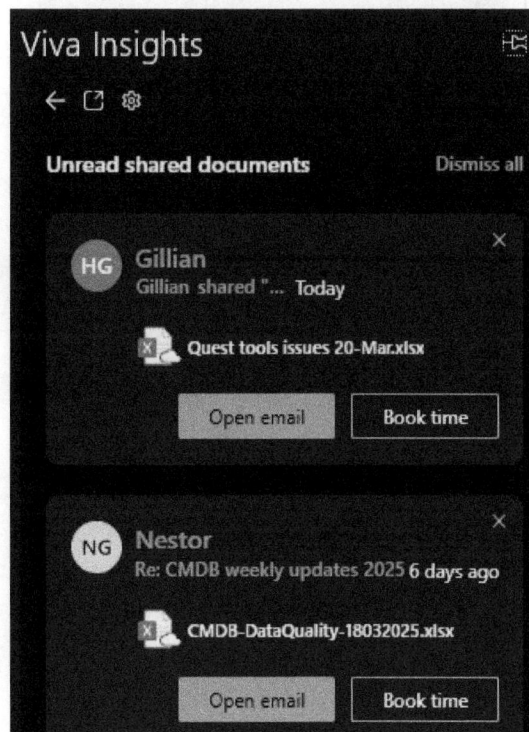

Figure 18.23: Catch up on documents card details

Inline suggestions

Inline suggestions are brief, data and AI-driven notifications that appear in Outlook while you are reading or composing an email or a meeting invitation. These suggestions are designed to optimize your communication and scheduling, providing timely advice to enhance your efficiency. Whether it is recommending a more productive meeting time or suggesting a follow-up action, these notifications help you stay organized and proactive.

One example of an inline suggestion is the **Schedule send suggestions**, which provide recommendations for the most effective times to send emails or schedule meetings based on data insights. This feature is designed to ensure that communications are received at optimal times, thereby enhancing engagement and response rates while minimizing disruptions to colleagues outside of their working hours or during periods of absence, as you can see in the following figure:

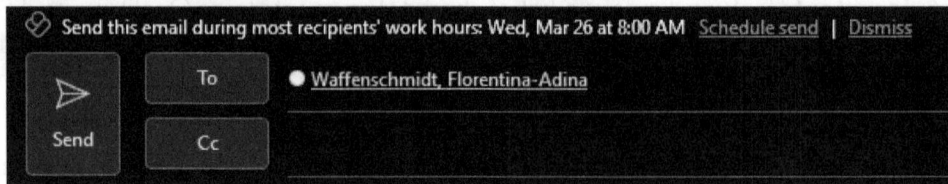

Figure 18.24: Schedule send suggestion

After selecting **Schedule send**, an insight opens to the right of your message confirming that date and time:

- To keep the suggested date and time, press **Send** within the email.
- To change when the recipient receives your email, use the date and time boxes in the insight to make changes as shown in *Figure18.25*. After adjusting these settings, press **Send** within the email.

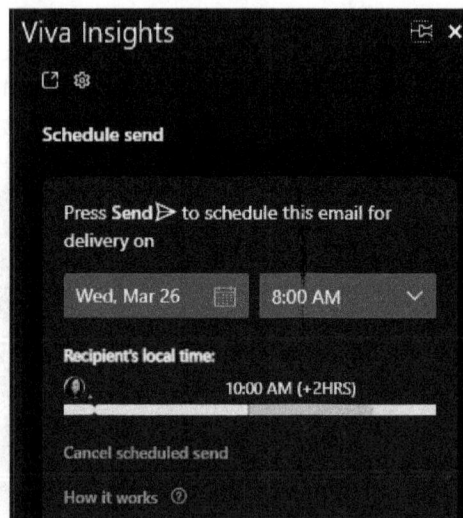

Figure 18.25: Scheduling an email to be sent later

After sending a scheduled message, it is saved in one of two places:

- In the **Drafts** folder when using Outlook on the web.
- In the **Sent items** folder when using Outlook for Windows.

The email is automatically delivered to all recipients in the To, Cc, and Bcc fields at the scheduled delivery time.

Conclusion

Microsoft Personal Insights is a powerful tool designed to help users gain a deeper understanding of their work habits and improve their overall productivity and well-being. Through this chapter, readers have learned how to access and utilize various features of Microsoft Personal Insights to help understand their work habits and improve productivity and well-being through document management, optimized email and meeting schedules, and proactive suggestions.

In the next chapter, we will explore *Planner*, a task management tool that helps teams create plans, organize and assign tasks, and collaborate more efficiently to streamline projects and track progress.

CHAPTER 19

Microsoft Planner

Introduction

Microsoft Planner is a powerful tool within the Microsoft 365 suite designed to help teams plan, organize, and collaborate on tasks and projects. In this chapter, we will delve into the functionalities, benefits, and practical steps to use Planner effectively.

Structure

The chapter covers the following topics:

- Understanding Microsoft Planner
- Accessing Planner
- Plans
- Buckets
- Tasks
- Planner in Outlook Calendar
- Advanced features

Objectives

This chapter will provide readers with an understanding of Microsoft Planner. By the end of this chapter, readers will learn what Planner is and its core features, the licensing options available, who can benefit from using Planner, and how to get started with Planner, including step-by-step instructions.

Understanding Microsoft Planner

Planner is a versatile task management application that is part of the Microsoft 365 suite. It allows users to create and organize plans, assign tasks, and collaborate with team members. The tool is designed to enhance project management by offering visual dashboards that provide an overview of progress and help identify any bottlenecks. With its user-friendly interface, it is accessible even to those with limited technical skills.

Planner integrates seamlessly with other Microsoft 365 applications such as Teams, Outlook, and SharePoint, enabling real-time collaboration and streamlining workflows. Users can link their Planner tasks to their calendar or communicate about tasks within Teams, enhancing productivity and coordination. Linking Planner tasks to Outlook Calendars helps in keeping track of deadlines, while integrating with Teams facilitates communication about tasks without leaving the chat platform. This seamless interaction between applications creates a cohesive environment where progress tracking and task management are streamlined.

The customizable task boards and labels in Microsoft Planner allow users to create different boards for various projects or teams, assign tasks, set due dates, and categorize tasks using labels, making it a flexible tool that can be tailored to the needs of any project or team. Here is an example of a Planner board:

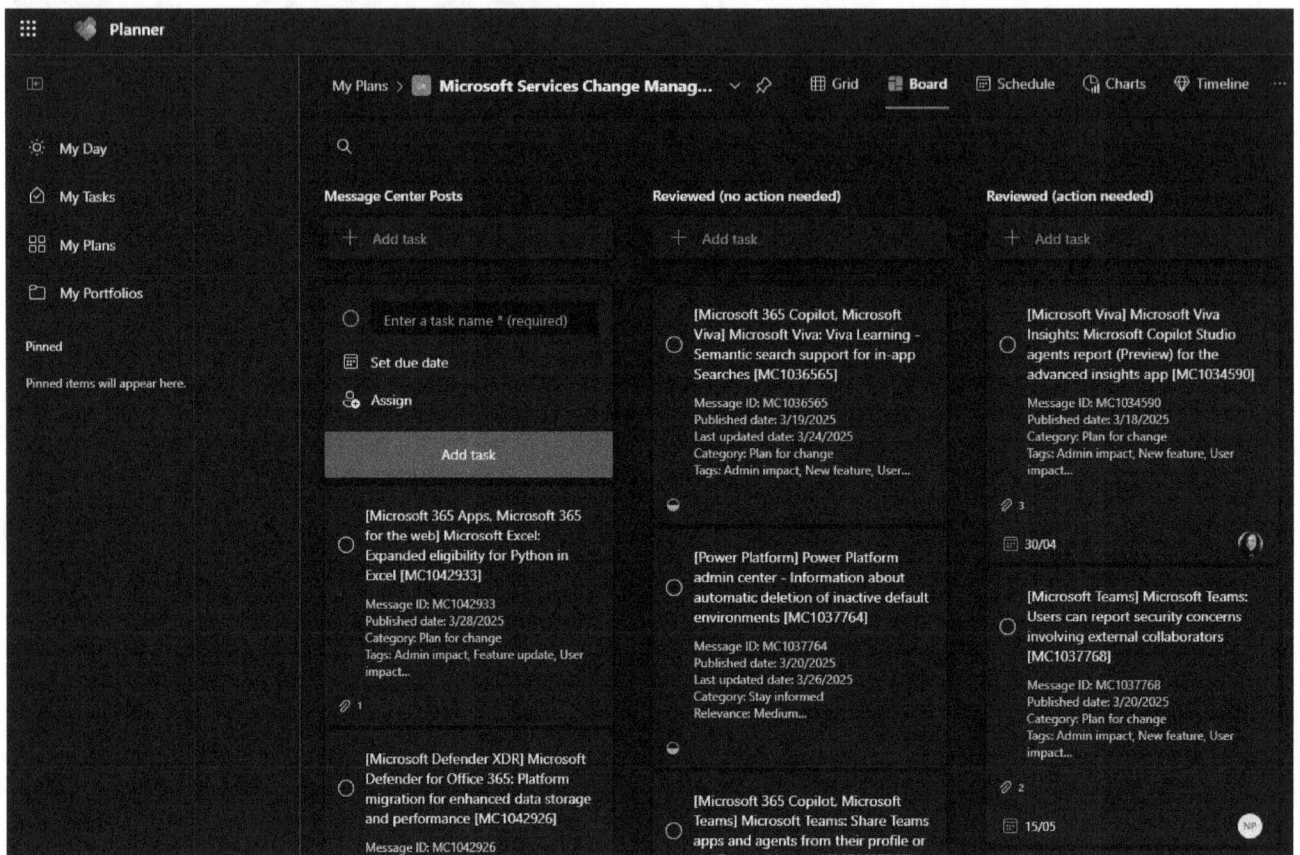

Figure 19.1: Example of a Planner board

Here are a few examples of what Planner can be used for:

- **Project management**: Planner can help organize, assign, and track various tasks within a project, ensuring that deadlines are met, and responsibilities are clear.

- **Event planning**: From corporate conferences to social gatherings, Planner can manage timelines, delegate tasks, and keep track of essential details to ensure the event runs smoothly.

- **Marketing campaigns**: Coordinate efforts across different teams, schedule promotional activities, and monitor the progress and effectiveness of marketing strategies.

- **Product development**: Facilitate collaboration among development, design, and marketing teams, laying out each phase of the product lifecycle and ensuring seamless transitions between stages.

- **Educational projects**: Teachers and students can use Planner to organize assignments, track progress on group projects, and manage classroom activities.

Despite all these benefits, Microsoft Planner has some limitations. Its reporting capabilities are somewhat limited, which may be a drawback for teams needing detailed project analysis and metrics. Additionally, Planner may not be ideal for managing complex projects that require extensive planning and tracking. Another limitation is that it does not offer offline access, which means users must be online to access their plans and tasks.

Licensing

Microsoft Planner is included with various Office 365 and Microsoft 365 plans, such as:

- Microsoft 365 Business Basic, Standard, and Premium
- Office 365 E1, E3, and E5
- Microsoft 365 E3 and E5

Additionally, Planner is also available in a **Premium** capacity as an annual subscription plan called *Planner Plan 1*, *Planner and Project Plan 3*, or *Planner and Project Plan 5*. Here is a description of what each plan offers.

Planner in Microsoft 365 includes:

- Real-time collaboration, commenting, and sharing using the Planner app in Microsoft Teams or the Planner web app
- Creation and management of content-rich tasks with features including files, checklists, and labels
- Tasks are organized by *My Day*, *My Tasks*, and *Assigned to me*
- Basic plan templates
- Ability to view reports and dashboards
- Grid, Board, Schedule, and Charts views
- Ability to view task dependencies
- Security, compliance, data privacy, accessibility, and Microsoft 365 customer support

Planner Plan 1 includes:

- Creation and management of content-rich tasks with features including files, checklists, and labels
- Project goals
- Backlogs and sprints
- Premium plan templates
- Ability to build reports and dashboards
- Grid, Board, Timeline (Gantt), and Charts views
- Task dependencies
- Customization and integration
- Security, compliance, data privacy, accessibility, and Microsoft 365 customer support

Planner and Project Plan 3 include everything in *Planner Plan 1*, plus:

- Microsoft 365 Copilot in Planner (preview)
- Task history
- Roadmaps
- Baselines and critical path
- Resource request capabilities

- Program management
- Portfolios in Planner
- Project financials, budgeting, and costing
- Advanced dependencies with lead and lag
- Project Online desktop client
- Project Online

Planner and Project Plan 5 include everything in *Planner and Project Plan 3*, plus:

- Advanced portfolio management
- Enterprise resource management and allocation

As a summary, some of the features only available in premium plans that are not in the basic plans are:

- Viewing tasks in Timeline (Gantt chart)
- People view: see where people may be over- or under-allocated
- Adding dependencies between tasks
- Adding milestones, task custom fields, and conditional coloring
- Seeing the critical path in the plan
- Colored buckets
- Agile project management with backlogs and sprints
- Goals
- Custom calendars
- Task history

Ideal users of Planner

Microsoft Planner is designed for anyone seeking to enhance their task and project management capabilities. It is particularly beneficial for teams and individuals aiming to improve organization, streamline workflows, and promote collaboration. The application caters to diverse needs, offering a flexible platform that adapts to various working styles and project requirements.

Whether you are managing daily tasks, coordinating complex projects, or ensuring the timely completion of assignments, Planner provides a user-friendly interface to keep track of progress and ensure that team members are aware of each other's progress. This intuitive interface allows users to create, assign, and monitor tasks effortlessly, making it an ideal choice for those who value simplicity and efficiency in their work processes. The tool empowers users to visualize their work through customizable task boards and labels, aiding in better organization and prioritization of activities.

Planner's versatility ensures it can accommodate various project scopes, from small-scale initiatives to more comprehensive undertakings, providing a robust solution for task management across different contexts.

Accessing Planner

To access Planner, first log in to your Microsoft 365 portal at **https://www.microsoft365.com** and open the Planner application from the app launcher, located in the top left corner of Office 365. Alternatively, navigate directly to Planner at **https://planner.cloud.microsoft**.

You can also access Planner in Microsoft Teams through a dedicated Teams app, which brings together tasks from both services, giving you a unified place to view personal (To Do) and team (Planner) tasks.

Plans

A **plan** is a structured framework designed to organize tasks and projects efficiently. It functions as a central hub where teams can manage their workflow, assign tasks, set deadlines, and collaborate seamlessly. Each plan includes task boards, buckets, and labels that aid in categorizing and prioritizing tasks, ensuring that everything remains organized and on track.

To create a new plan, click on **New Plan** at the bottom left corner, then select the **Basic** or **Premium** option to start a plan from scratch, or choose one of the available templates to help you get started:

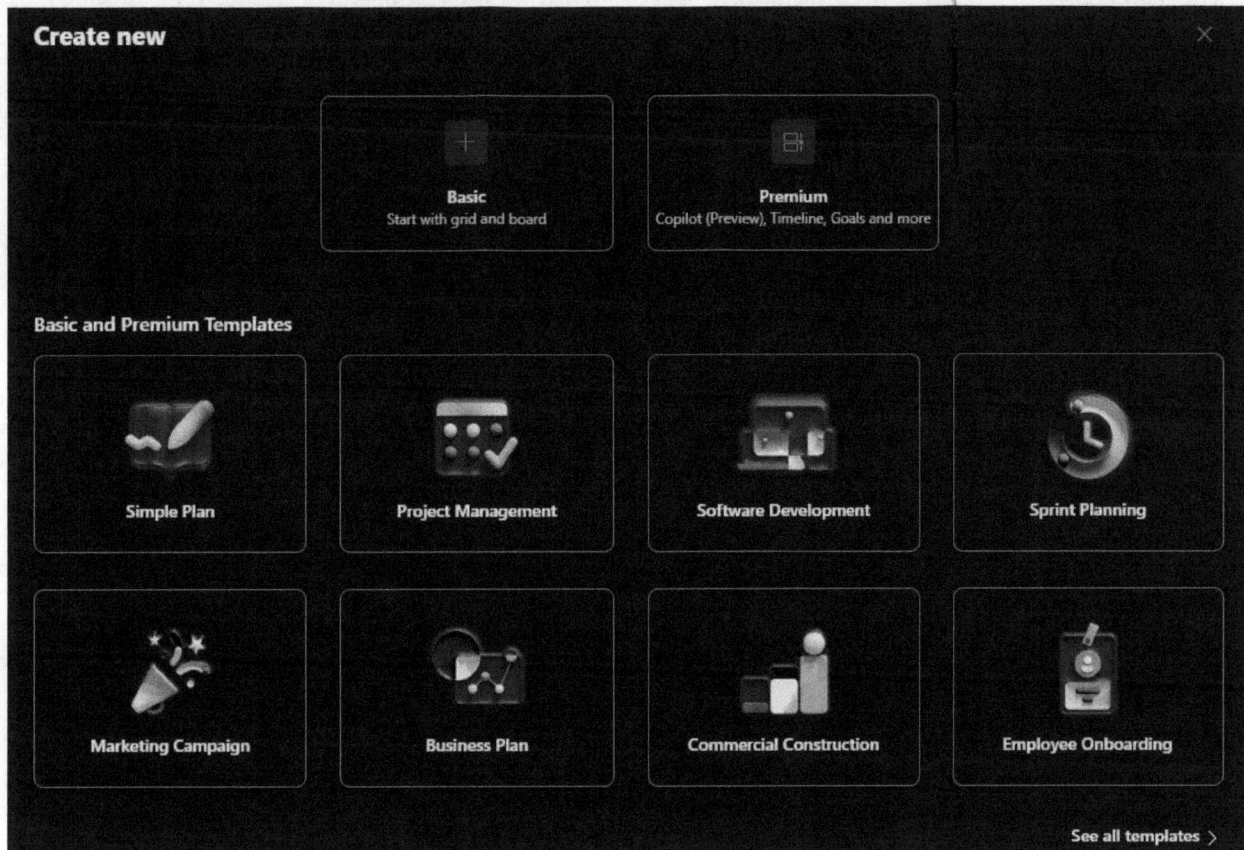

Figure 19.2: *Creating a new Plan*

Next, give your new plan a name, decide if you want to pin it to your plans, and if you want to add it to an existing Microsoft 365 group:

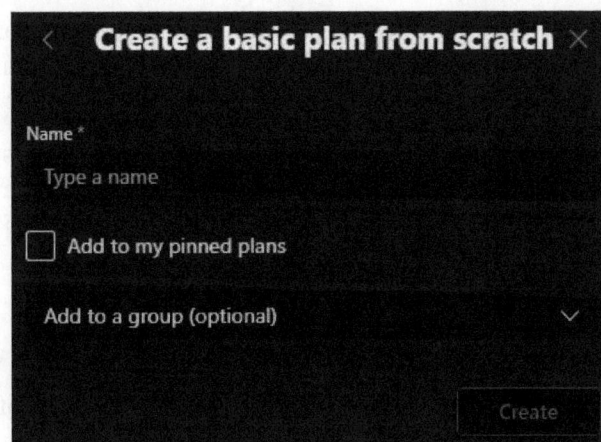

Figure 19.3: *Creating a new plan*

Once your plan is created, you will notice it is made of a single bucket called *To do* with no tasks yet created:

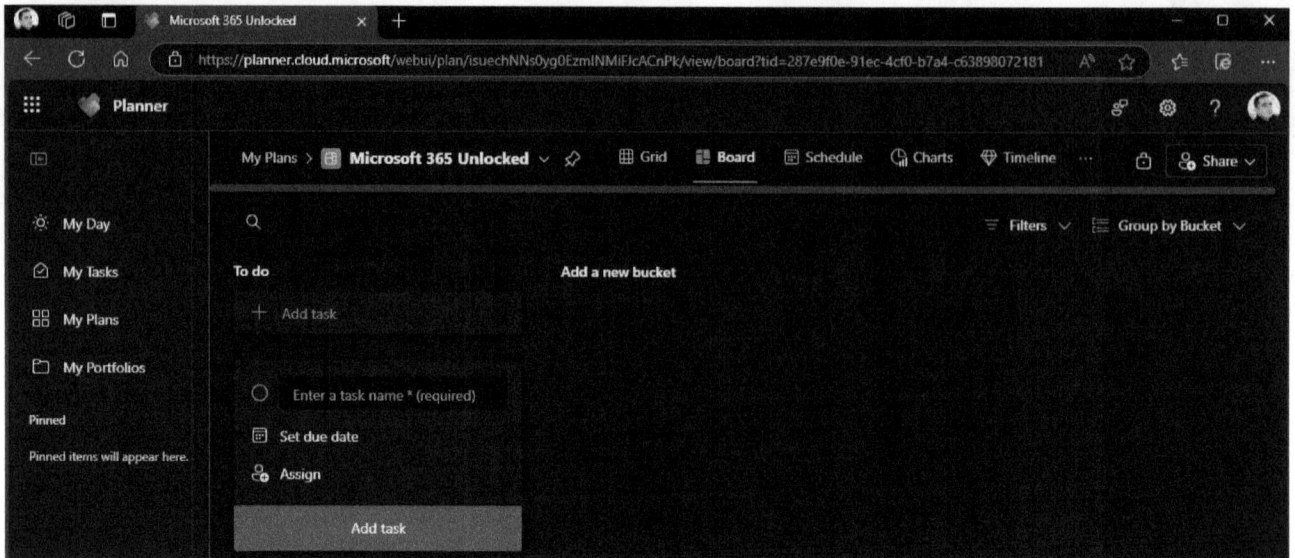

Figure 19.4: A brand new plan

A Plan can easily be added to a tab in Teams, allowing any of its team members to view, assign, and track tasks within the same platform, facilitating better communication and coordination without needing to switch between multiple applications.

To integrate a plan with Teams, follow these steps:

1. Go to the Teams channel where you want to make your plan visible and click on + to add a new tab.

2. Choose **Planner**.

3. Decide whether to **Create a new plan** or **Add an existing plan** from this team, and select the desired plan.

4. Click **Save**.

Buckets

A **bucket** is a container used to organize tasks within a plan. Buckets help in categorizing and structuring tasks, making it easier to manage and track progress. You can create different buckets to represent various stages of a project, types of work, departments, or any other categorization that makes sense for your plan. For example, you might have buckets named *To Do, In Progress*, and *Completed* to reflect the status of tasks.

Buckets are particularly useful for breaking down tasks into manageable sections, allowing you to focus on specific areas of work. You can drag and drop tasks into different buckets to maintain order and structure in your plan. Additionally, buckets can be renamed to better suit the needs of your project.

Using buckets in Planner enhances collaboration by providing a clear visual representation of task organization. This helps team members understand their responsibilities and track their progress more effectively. Buckets also allow for better prioritization and categorization of tasks, making it easier to identify important tasks and organize them based on priority or category.

To create a new bucket in Microsoft Planner, follow these steps:

1. Navigate to the plan where you want to add the bucket.

2. Click on the **Add new bucket** option, typically found on the right side of your existing buckets.

3. Enter a name for the new bucket that reflects the categorization or stage of tasks it will contain, as shown here:

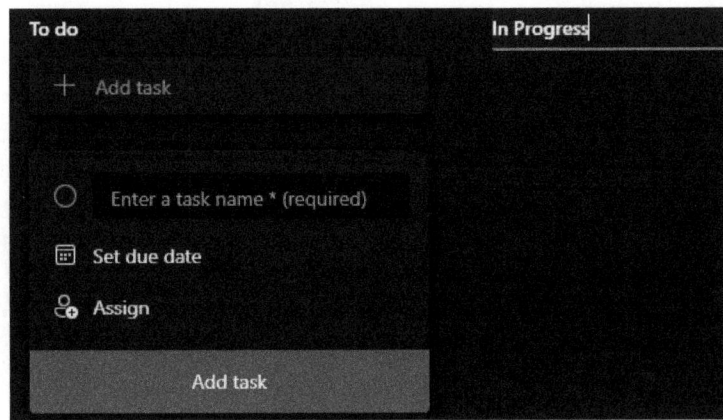

Figure 19.5: Creating a new bucket

4. Press *Enter* to confirm the creation of the new bucket.

Once you have created your buckets, you can manage them to ensure that tasks are organized and structured effectively: you can rename them, delete them, or reorder them.

Once you have your buckets ready, it is time to start creating and assigning tasks.

Tasks

Tasks are units of work that can be assigned to team members within Planner. Each task can include a variety of details to help ensure clarity and accountability. Key components of a task include:

-   **Task name**: A brief description of the work to be done.
-   **Due date**: The deadline by which the task needs to be completed.
-   **Assigned members**: The individuals responsible for completing the task.
-   **Notes**: Additional information that provides context and specifics about the task.
-   **Checklist items**: Sub-tasks or steps to be completed as part of the main task.
-   **Attachments**: Files related to the task that can be uploaded for easy access.
-   **Progress**: Details if the task is in *Not started*, *In progress* or *Completed* status.
-   **Labels**: Customizable color codes that help categorize and prioritize tasks.

To create a task in Microsoft Planner:

1. Within your plan, click on the **+ Add Task** option under the bucket you want to create the task in:

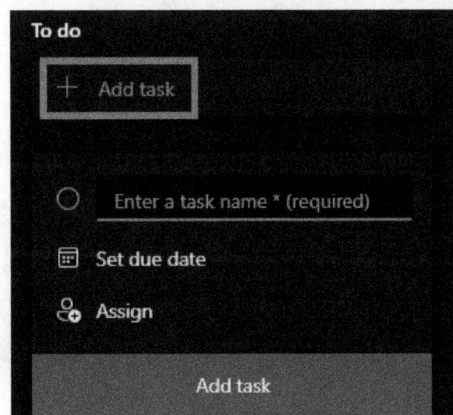

Figure 19.6: Creating a new task

2. Enter the task name to describe the work.

3. Set a due date to specify the deadline.

4. Assign the task to one or more team members responsible for its completion.

5. Click on **Add task**. The new task will now appear in the bucket with the details that you entered:

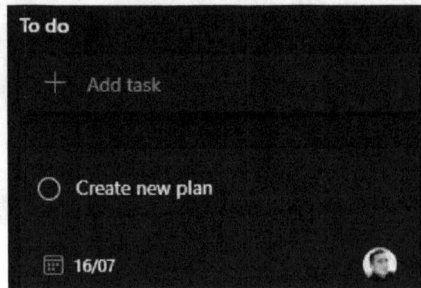

Figure 19.7: *New task created*

These are just the most basic details needed to create a task. However, as mentioned above, there are many more details that can be added to a task. All you have to do is click on a task and a new window will appear where you can enter more information:

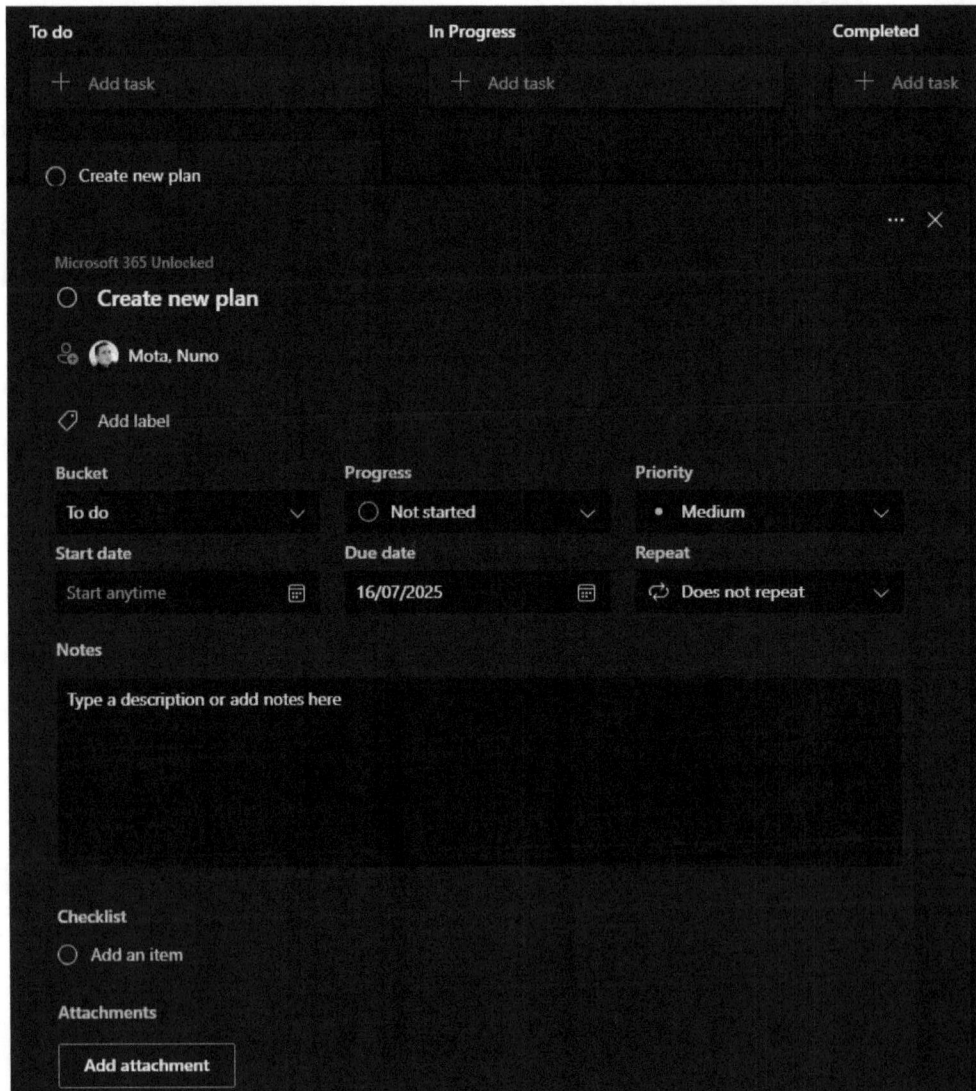

Figure 19.8: *Task details pane*

Entering detailed information in a task allows for better organization, tracking, and collaboration. Detailed information helps team members understand the scope and requirements of the task, ensures that everyone is on the same page regarding expectations, and provides a clear timeline for completion. By including specifics like descriptions, attachments, labels, and comments, team members can more efficiently manage their work and communicate effectively. For example:

- *Files* related to tasks can be uploaded directly to Planner, ensuring all relevant documents are easily accessible.

- *Comments* allow team members to communicate and provide updates on task progress.

- *Labels*, which are customizable color codes, help in highlighting important tasks and organizing them based on priority, category, or other criteria.

- The *Checklist* helps break down tasks into smaller steps. Each checklist item can be checked off upon completion, giving a visual progress update. This is particularly useful for complex tasks involving multiple actions or stages. Checklist items are flexible and can be added, edited, or removed as needed. This ensures all necessary steps are covered, reducing the risk of oversight and enhancing task clarity. Additionally, checklists serve as guides to help team members prioritize efforts and track progress incrementally.

To move a task to a new bucket, you can simply drag and drop it between buckets. Alternatively, you can click on the "**...**" option on the top right side of a task and select **Move task**. On the window that opens, you can move the task to a different plan or to a different bucket within the same plan:

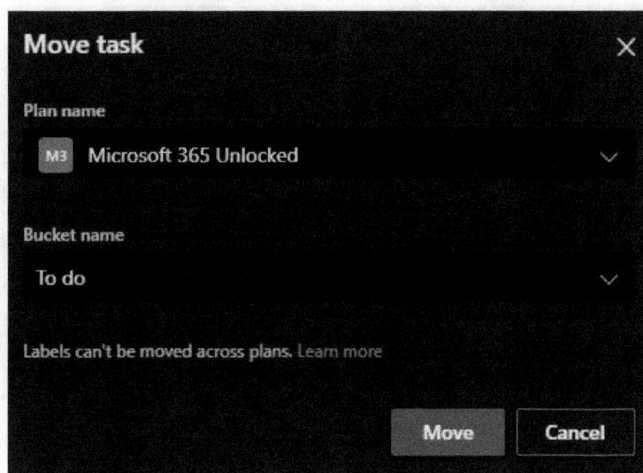

Figure 19.9: Moving a task

Tasks can also be created and/or viewed in Microsoft Loop components (Loop was covered in *Chapter 4, Microsoft Loop*). When you add a Planner component in the Loop app, your team can collaborate in real time within a shared space that supports lists, tables, notes, and more. Any changes made, whether in Planner or directly in the Loop component, automatically stay in sync, so everyone always sees the latest updates, no matter where they are working.

Filter and group tasks

Filtering tasks allows users to narrow down their view to specific tasks based on various criteria. To filter tasks, users can select the **Filter** option and enter a keyword or choose from categories such as **Due date**, **Priority**, **Progress**, **Labels**, **Bucket**, or the user the task is assigned to, as you can see from the following figure:

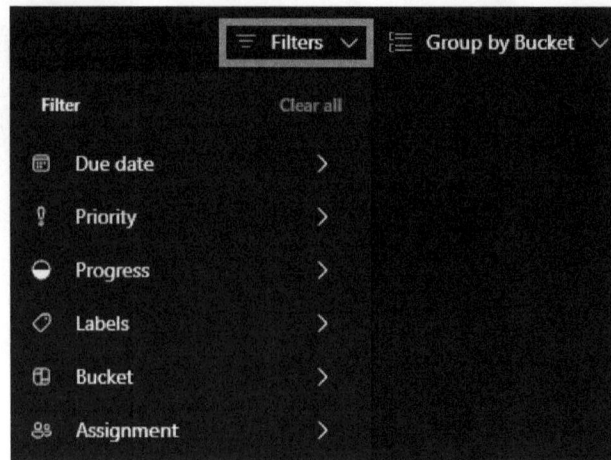

Figure 19.10: Filtering tasks

This is particularly useful for locating tasks quickly and managing those that fall within certain parameters or need immediate attention. Clearing a filter is straightforward: users can simply select **Clear all** to remove the applied filter(s) and return to the default view of all tasks.

Another way of viewing the tasks assigned to yourself, besides using the **Assignment** filter option, is to select **My tasks** in the left pane. This will show all the tasks assigned to you across all plans, as you can see here:

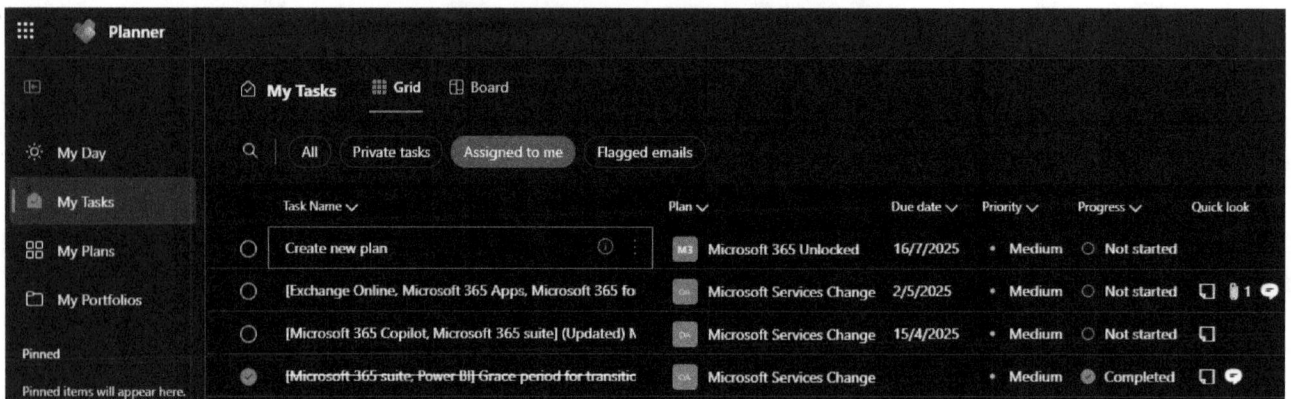

Figure 19.11: My tasks

Grouping tasks is another powerful feature that enhances task management by organizing tasks based on different attributes. Users can select **Group by** and choose options such as **Bucket**, **Assigned to**, **Progress**, **Due date**, **Labels**, or **Priority**:

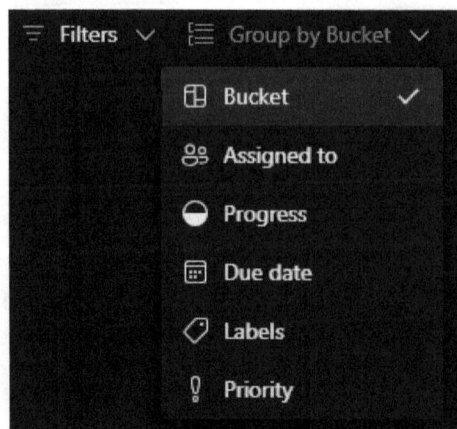

Figure 19.12: Group tasks

This functionality provides a visual representation of tasks, making it easier to understand task distribution, monitor progress, and allocate resources efficiently. In the following screenshot, we changed the default grouping from *Bucket* to *Assigned to* in order to easily view the tasks assigned to each user:

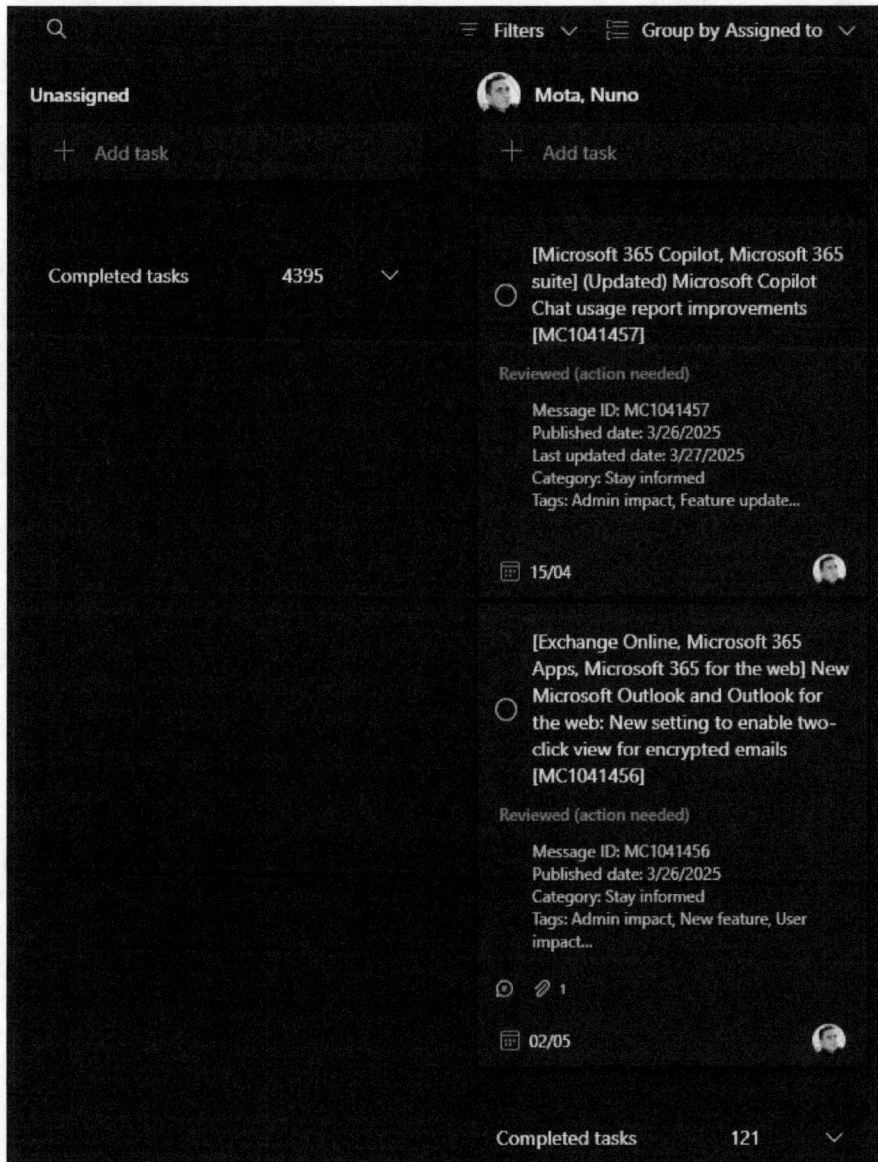

Figure 19.13: *Tasks grouped by assignment*

Charts

Charts in Planner offer a graphical representation of task status, enhancing the ability to monitor and evaluate the progress of various assignments. Users can utilize Charts to gain a visual summary of their team's tasks, helping identify bottlenecks or areas requiring additional attention to ensure efficient workflow management. The Charts feature is particularly useful for project managers and team leaders who need to keep track of task completion rates, member availability, and the overall progress within different buckets.

Here, we can see an example of a visualization of tasks using Charts:

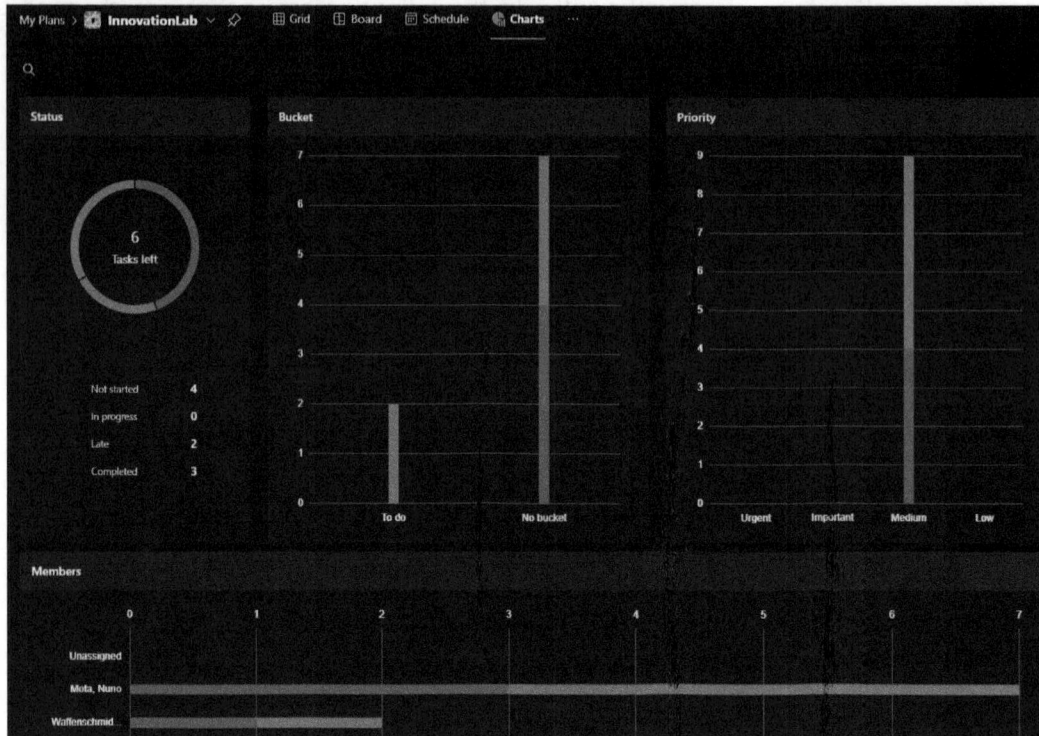

Figure 19.14: Visualizing tasks using Charts

Schedule

The **Schedule** option allows users to organize and view their tasks on a calendar. By selecting **Schedule**, users can see where their tasks are placed over time, facilitating better planning and time management. The Schedule view provides two formats: *Week* and *Month*, offering flexibility in how tasks are visualized. Users can point to a date and easily add new tasks, making it a dynamic tool for managing deadlines and ensuring that no task is overlooked. Additionally, the Schedule feature helps in managing unscheduled tasks by listing them under *Unscheduled tasks*, as you can see in *Figure 19.15*; allowing users to al locate specific dates for these tasks as needed, simply by dragging an unscheduled task to the calendar to schedule it.

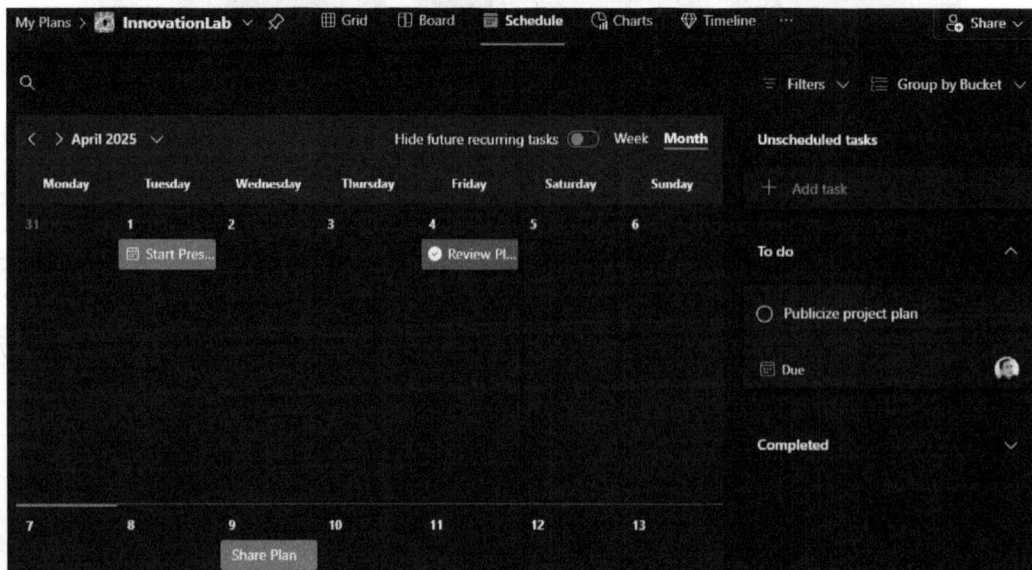

Figure 19.15: Visualizing tasks using Schedule

Grid

The **Grid** option offers a structured and detailed view of tasks within a plan. Unlike visual representations such as charts or schedules, the **Grid** option presents tasks in a tabular format, similar to a spreadsheet. This layout allows users to see all tasks at a glance, with columns for various attributes including task name, due date, assigned user, status, and more:

Figure 19.16: Visualizing tasks using Grid

The Grid option is equipped with several key features that make it very useful, such as:

- **Comprehensive task details**: Each task is displayed with its essential details, enabling users to quickly assess the status and specifics of each assignment.

- **Filtering and sorting**: The Grid view allows users to filter tasks based on various criteria, such as due date or assigned user, and sort them to prioritize actions.

- **Bulk actions**: Users can perform bulk actions on multiple tasks, such as changing the status or assigning them to different team members, streamlining task management.

Planner in Outlook Calendar

Another convenient feature is the ability to integrate your Planner tasks with your Microsoft Outlook Calendar. This functionality enables you to synchronize your task schedules and view them directly within your Outlook Calendar, thus providing a cohesive and unified approach to time management.

To add a plan to your Outlook Calendar, simply open the plan in Microsoft Planner and select the option to add it to your Outlook Calendar from the plan menu:

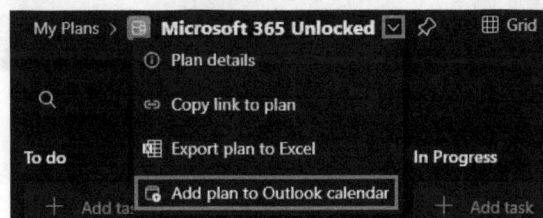

Figure 19.17: Publishing a plan to the Outlook Calendar

If you are the plan owner, you will need to publish the plan to an iCalendar feed first. This integration is available for basic plans and **Assigned to me** tasks, as shown in the following figure:

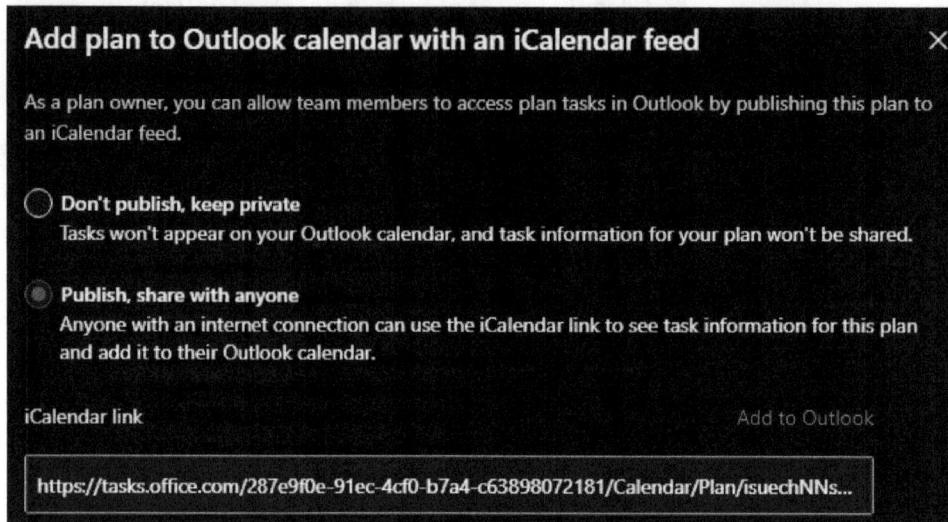

Figure 19.18: Creating an iCalendar feed

Select the **Publish, share with anyone** option to publish the plan to an iCalendar feed, but be careful not to share the iCalendar link where unauthorized users may access it, as anyone with internet access will be able to use the iCalendar link to view task details from the plan. Next, click **Add to Outlook** to automatically open Outlook and begin the setup to add the plan to your calendar.

On the **Subscribe from web** window, change the calendar name if you would like, configure other aspects like the color the calendar items will have, icons, etc., and select **Import**:

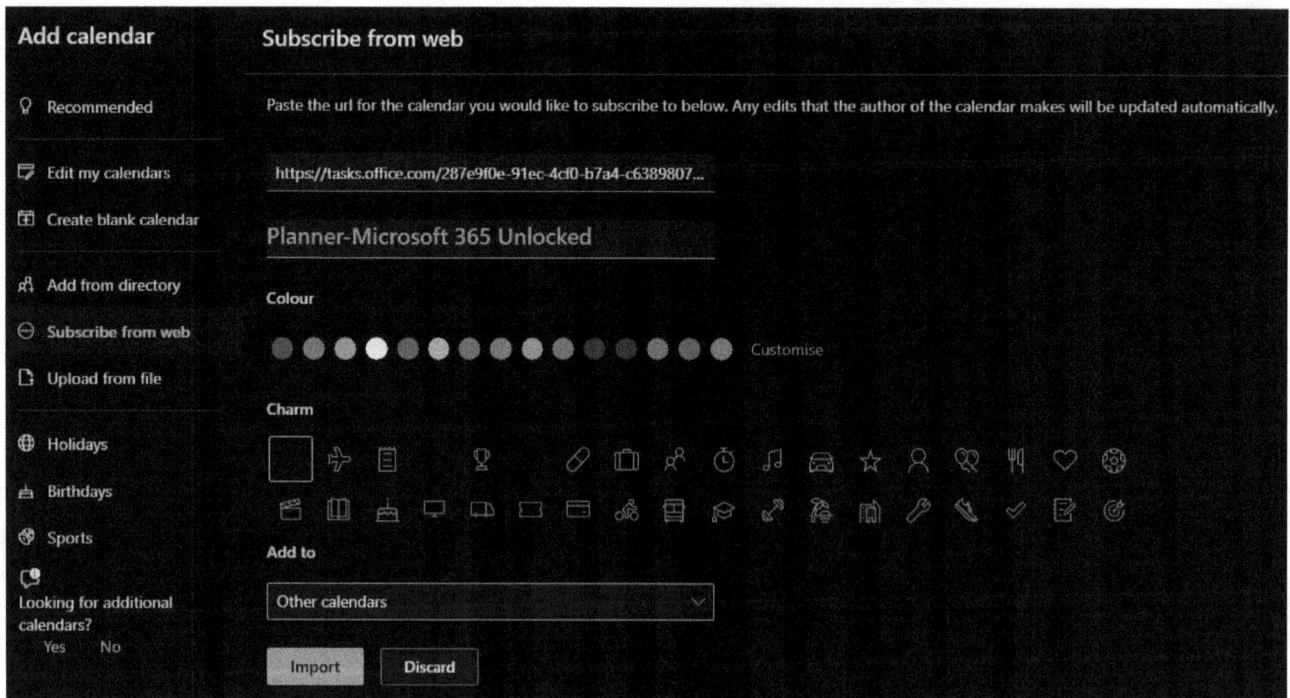

Figure 19.19: Importing Planner into Outlook Calendar

Once the import is complete, all the tasks associated with the plan will appear in your calendar with basic details for each task:

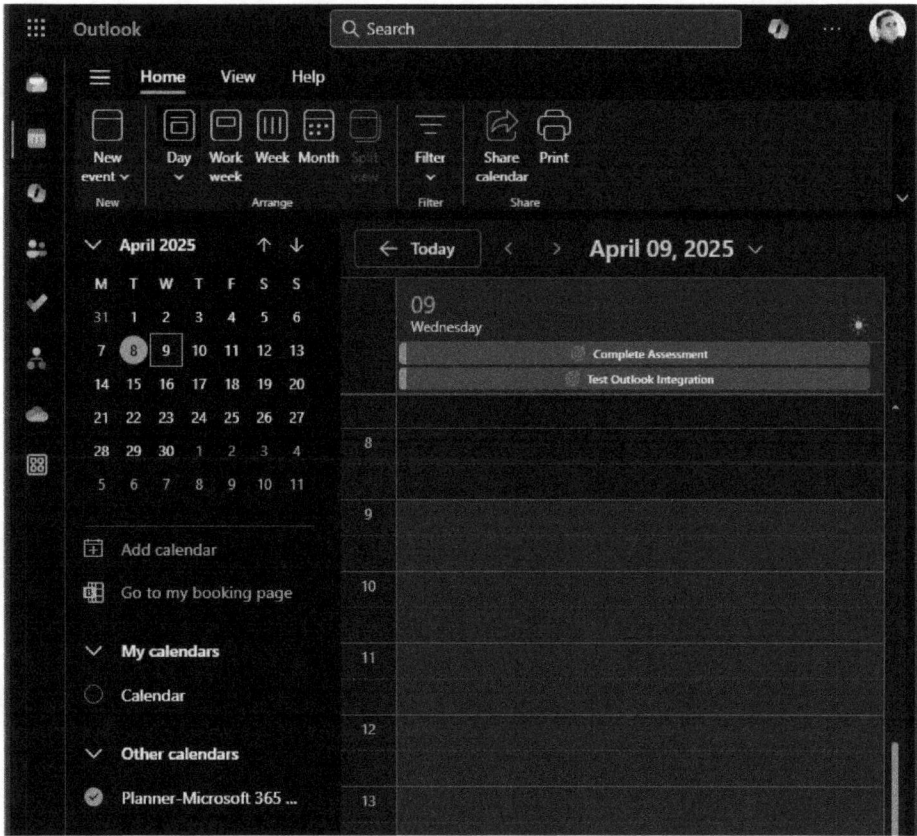

Figure 19.20: Planner tasks in Outlook Calendar

Note: **Synchronization feature is only available for basic plans, and your Assigned to me tasks in My Tasks. It is not available for premium plans, To Do lists, or other tasks in My Tasks.**

Alternatively, if you do not want to synchronize all the plan's tasks, but only your ones, the process is also very straightforward and mostly identical. Simply open **My Tasks** and select **Assigned to me** to view the tasks assigned to you. Next, select the three-dot menu (**...**) at the top of the view, and select **Add Assigned to me tasks to Outlook Calendar**:

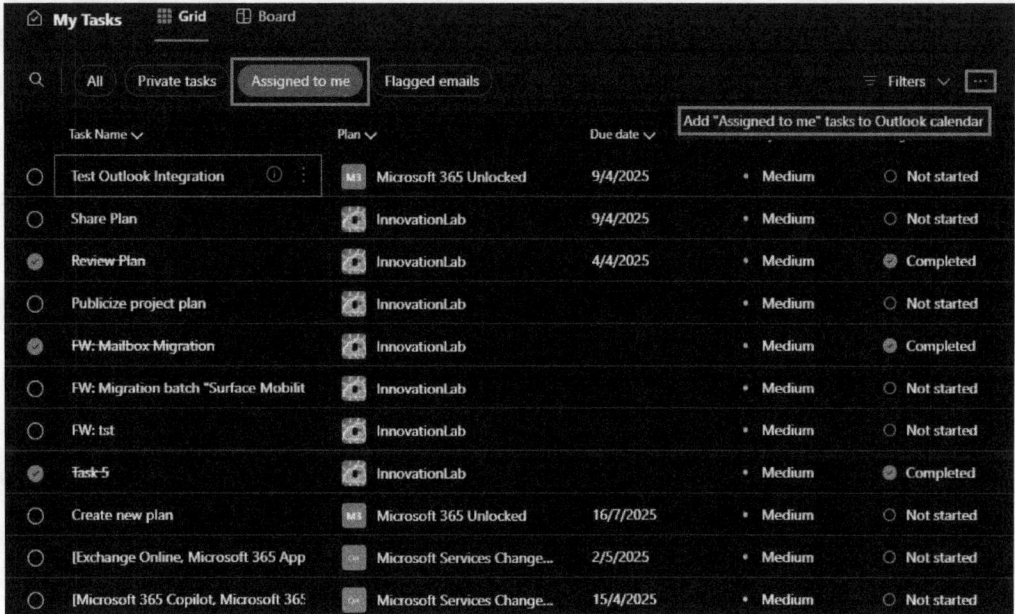

Figure 19.21: Adding Assigned to me tasks to the Outlook Calendar

If you decide that you no longer want your Planner task information to be accessible via your Outlook Calendar, you can easily disable the iCalendar feed. To do this, follow the steps mentioned above to access the iCalendar feed settings for your plan or **Assigned to me** tasks. Once there, select the option **Don't publish, keep private** to turn off the iCalendar feed.

Disabling the iCalendar feed ensures that your task details remain private and inaccessible to unauthorized users. It is a good practice to review and manage the sharing settings of your calendar regularly to maintain the security and privacy of your information.

Advanced features

So far, we have only covered the features available by default in Planner with a Microsoft 365 license. In this section, we will cover a few advanced features available with a Premium license, which can significantly enhance your project management capabilities and streamline your workflow.

Goals

Setting goals in Planner aligns your team and stakeholders by clearly prioritizing tasks. The Goals feature lets you set and track objectives, linking them to specific tasks to ensure alignment and progress.

Goals can be defined using SMART criteria: specific, measurable, achievable, relevant, and time-bound objectives. Breaking goals into smaller tasks assigned to team members ensures clarity and accountability.

The feature includes tracking and reporting options to monitor progress, identify issues, and provide real-time visibility for informed decision-making and stakeholder updates.

Here is an example of the goals feature in use:

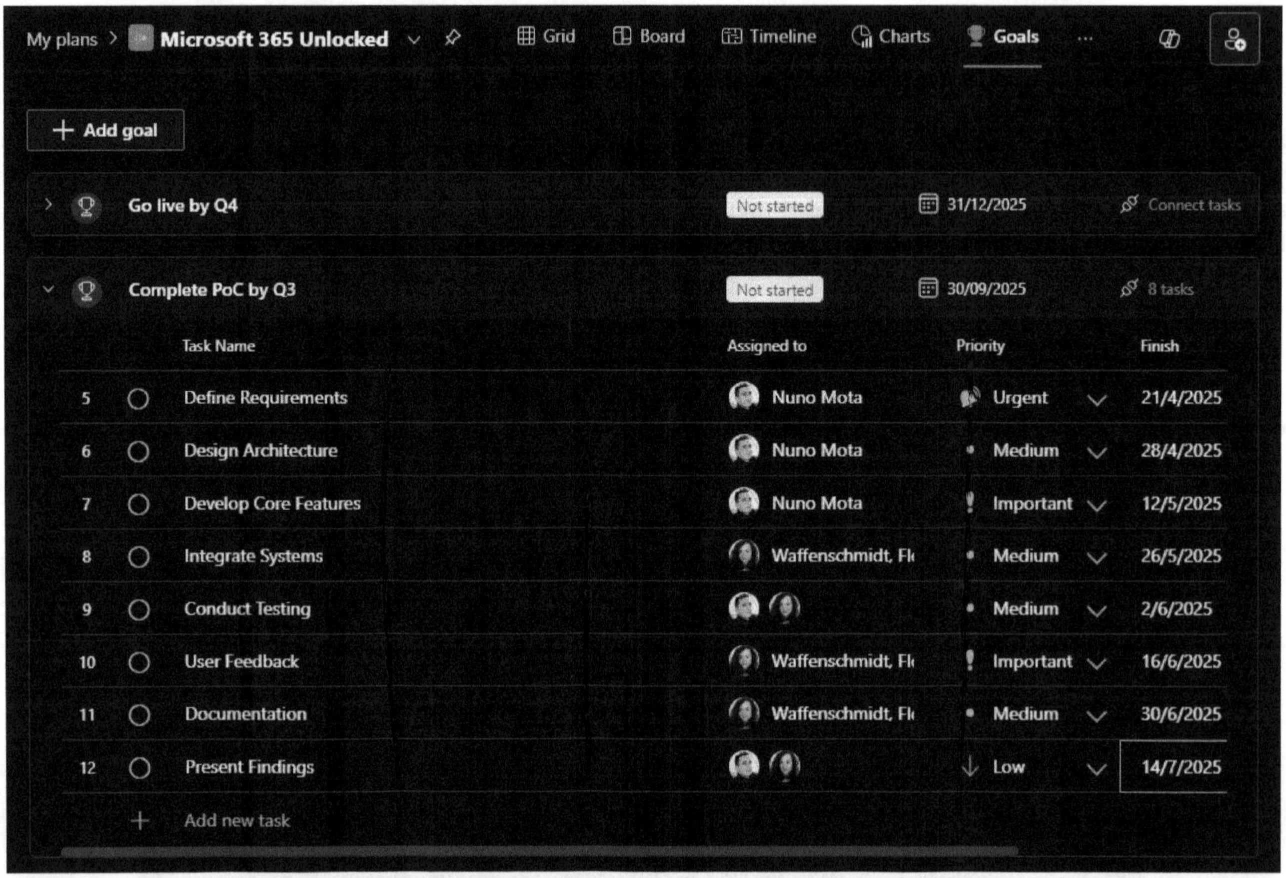

Figure 19.22: Goals in Planner

People view

The People view feature in Planner helps project managers understand the distribution of tasks among team members. It provides a visual representation of each team member's workload, identifying who is over- or under-allocated. This allows managers to make informed decisions about reassigning tasks for better workload balance. Key functionalities include:

- Viewing task allocation among team members to spot imbalances.
- Identifying reassignment opportunities to boost efficiency.
- Monitoring task progress to ensure timely completion.
- Understanding team collaboration for improved communication.

People view is particularly useful for managing large teams or complex projects, making it easier to maintain balanced workloads and achieve project goals effectively.

In the following figure, we can see a fairly balanced task allocation:

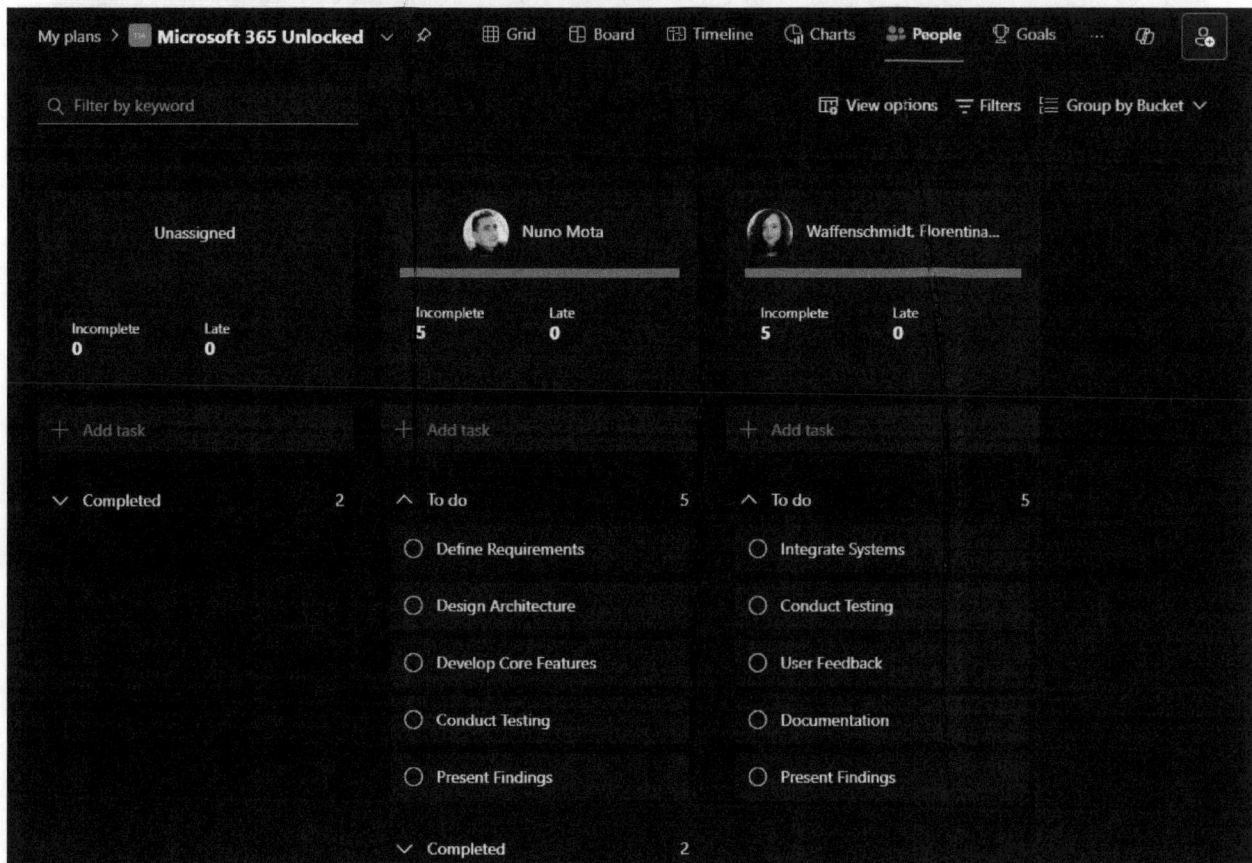

Figure 19.23: People view in Planner

Sprints

Sprints are an essential feature for agile project management. They allow you to plan and structure your projects in defined time periods, known as sprints. By creating and prioritizing a backlog of tasks, you can organize work into manageable segments, ensuring that high-priority items are addressed first. During each sprint, teams can collaborate on planning, tracking, and completing tasks, facilitating a focused and cohesive workflow. This iterative approach enables continuous improvement and adaptation, vital for dynamic and complex projects. The sprint feature in Planner not only enhances productivity but also encourages regular assessment and adjustment, leading to optimal project outcomes.

Task conversations

Task conversations in Planner facilitate efficient communication about individual tasks within your team. This feature integrates seamlessly with Microsoft Teams, enabling team members to discuss updates, coordinate schedules, and seek clarifications directly within the task. By utilizing all the functionalities of Teams messages, such as @ mentions, emojis, GIFs, and more, task conversations ensure that discussion remains lively and engaging, fostering a collaborative environment. This helps in addressing issues promptly and keeping everyone on the same page, ultimately contributing to the project's success.

The following figure shows the detail window of a particular task, with the **Task conversation** button at the bottom:

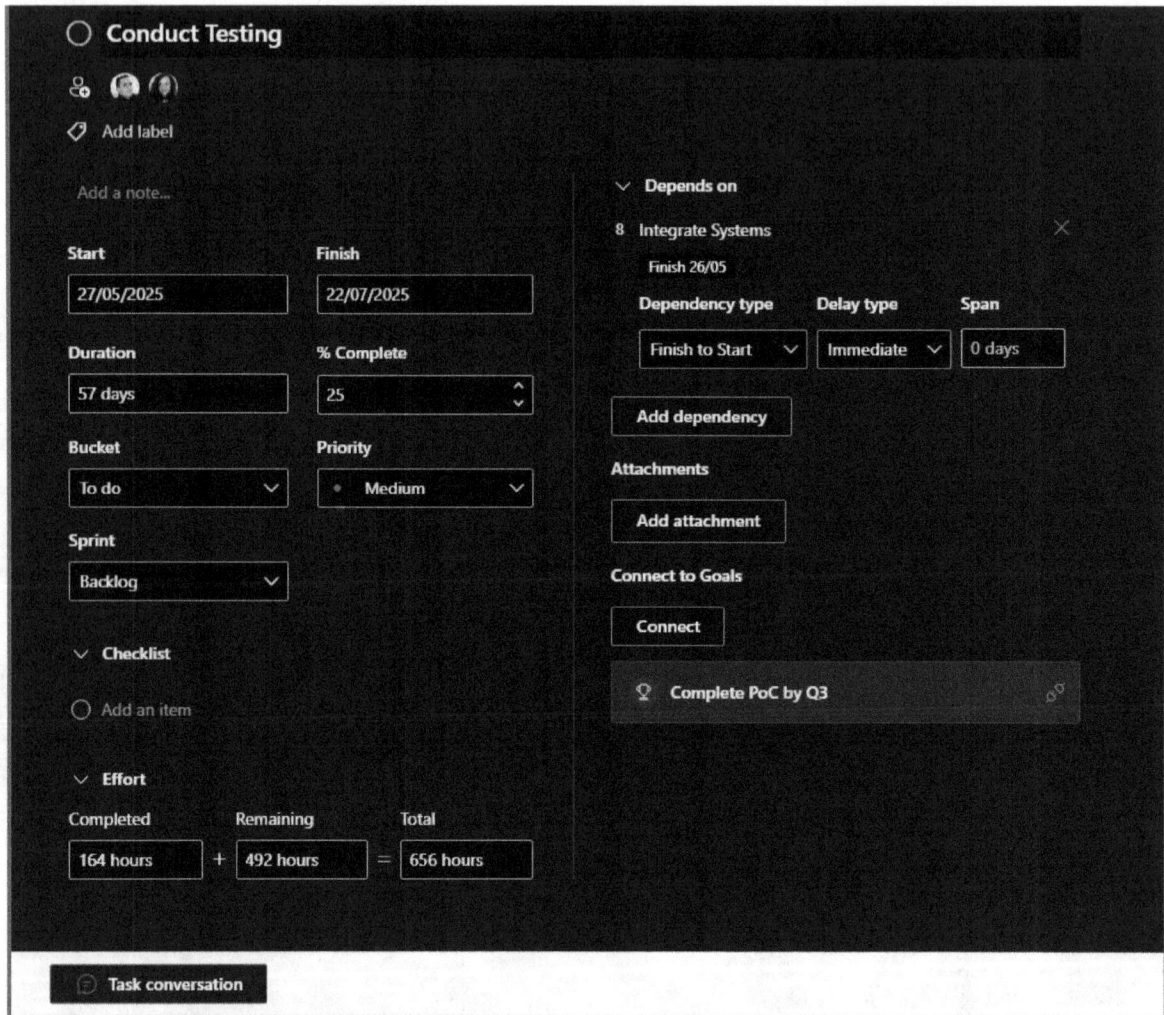

Figure 19.24: Task conversations in Planner

Task history

The task history feature is designed to help task owners stay on top of their assignments by providing a detailed record of all changes and updates. This feature allows users to quickly identify recent progress, modifications, or any alterations that have impacted the schedule. Edits to tasks, such as adding or removing labels, changing durations, or updates to other tasks that affect the overall schedule, are all recorded in the **Changes** pane within **Task Details**, as you can see in *Figure 19.25*. This comprehensive view ensures that users can track the evolution of their tasks and make informed decisions based on the latest information:

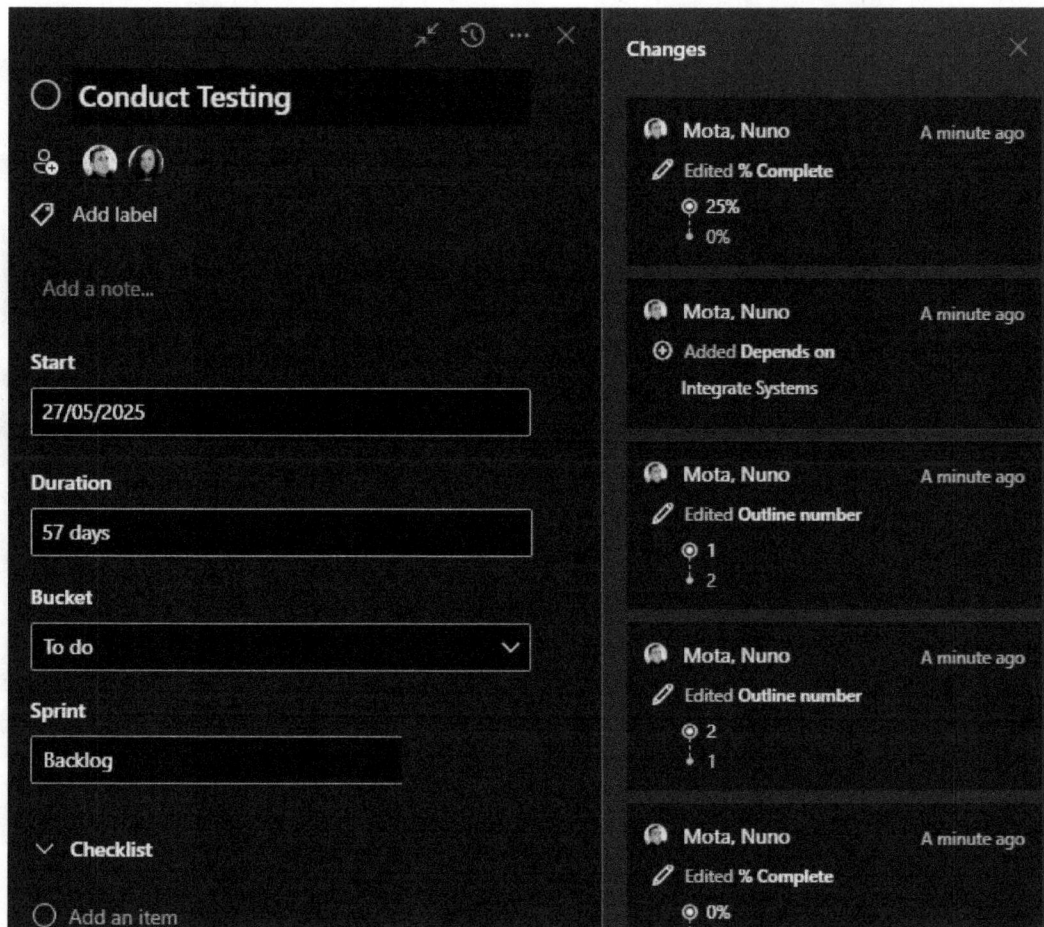

Figure 19.25: Task history in Planner

Advanced dependencies and Timeline view

Advanced dependencies provide a sophisticated method for linking tasks within your projects. By utilizing **finish to start (FS)**, **start to start (SS)**, **start to finish (SF)**, **or finish to finish (FF)** dependencies, you can establish clear relationships between tasks, ensuring that the progression of one task is contingent on the status of another. For example, a finish to start dependency means that a task cannot commence until the preceding task has been completed. These advanced dependencies enable precise project planning and execution, ensuring that tasks are aligned with the overall project timeline and objectives. The Planner scheduling engine automatically adjusts execution dates based on these dependencies, maintaining a coherent flow and preventing scheduling conflicts.

The **Timeline view** offers a visual representation of your tasks in a Gantt chart format, allowing you to oversee the entire project schedule at a glance. This feature illustrates all tasks and their dependencies, providing a comprehensive overview of how each task fits within the project's timeline. The Gantt chart format is particularly useful for tracking progress, identifying potential bottlenecks, and ensuring that deadlines are met. With the Timeline view, project managers can visualize the sequence of tasks, monitor their completion, and make adjustments as needed to keep the project on track.

The following figure shows a Gantt chart with a list of tasks and their interdependencies:

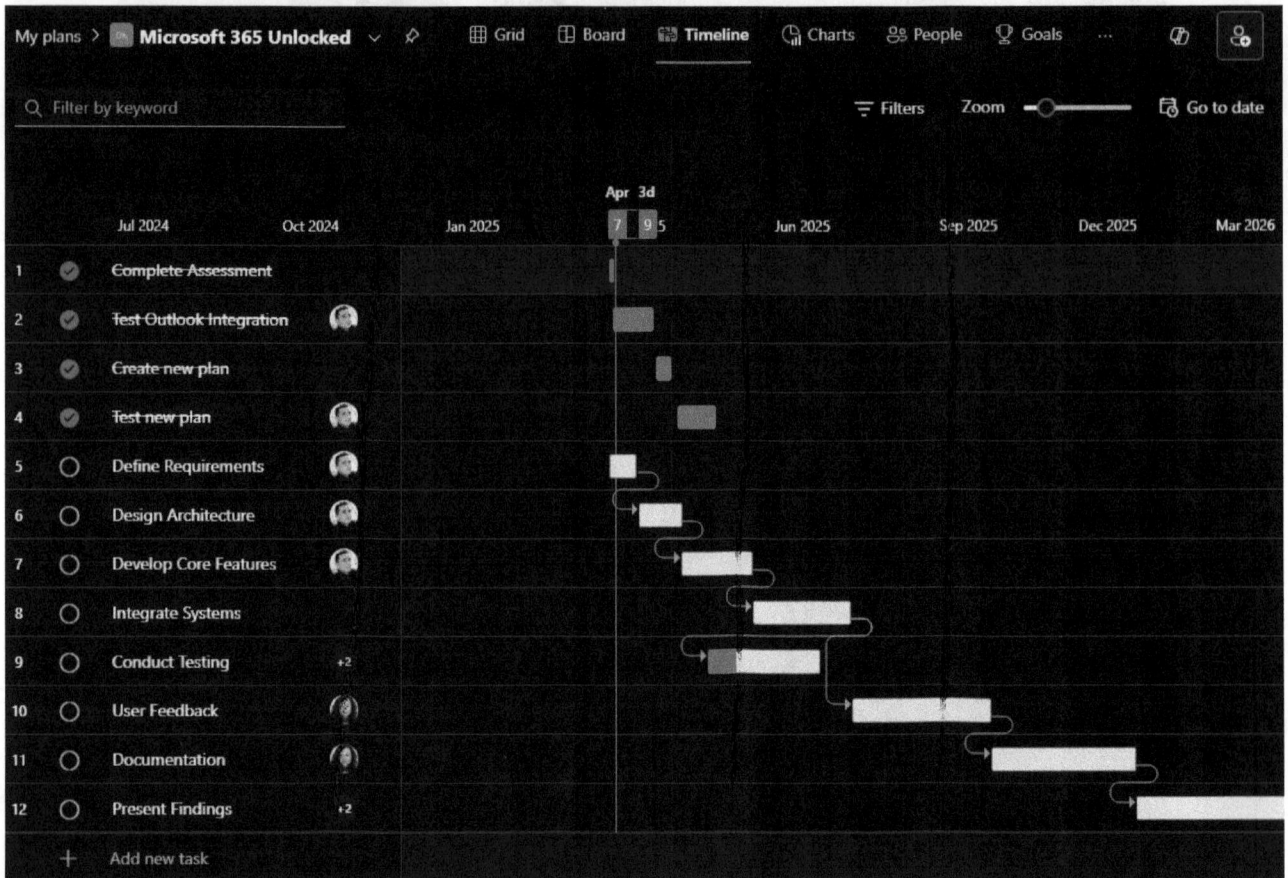

Figure 19.26: *Advanced dependencies and Timeline view in Planner*

Conclusion

In this chapter, readers have learnt how to use Microsoft Planner to plan, organize, and collaborate on tasks and projects. The chapter covers creating plans, assigning tasks, and integrating Planner with other Microsoft 365 applications like Teams and Outlook. It also discusses customizable task boards and examples of Planner's applications in various contexts. Additionally, readers have learnt about licensing options and step-by-step instructions for getting started with Planner.

In the next chapter, we will look at Microsoft Bookings, an appointment scheduling tool that allows businesses and teams to manage and streamline their booking processes efficiently.

Join our Discord space

Join our Discord workspace for latest updates, offers, tech happenings around the world, new releases, and sessions with the authors:

https://discord.bpbonline.com

CHAPTER 20
Microsoft Bookings

Introduction

In this chapter, we will explore the various aspects of Microsoft Bookings, a versatile tool designed to simplify appointment scheduling and enhance customer engagement.

The tool provides a range of features that address both individual and team scheduling needs. Whether you are managing personal appointments or coordinating bookings for a team, Microsoft Bookings provides a seamless and efficient solution.

Structure

This chapter covers the following topics:

- Understanding Microsoft Bookings
- Getting started with Microsoft Bookings
- Personal bookings
- Shared bookings

Objectives

By the end of this chapter, readers will have a comprehensive understanding of the key features and functionalities of Microsoft Bookings, navigate its interface, and understand its applicability, including when to use Microsoft Bookings for personal and shared booking pages. Readers will also understand how to create and manage different types of meetings, as well as setting up and customizing booking pages.

Understanding Microsoft Bookings

Microsoft Bookings is a dynamic scheduling tool that simplifies managing appointments and bookings for businesses and individuals. Part of the Microsoft 365 suite, it helps organize meetings, consultations, and services through a customized booking page.

Bookings integrate seamlessly with Microsoft Outlook to keep your calendar up-to-date and prevent double-booking. It also supports automated reminders and notifications to reduce missed appointments and enhance efficiency.

Microsoft Bookings is available in various Microsoft 365 subscriptions, including Office 365 (A3, A5, E1, E3, E5, F1, F3, G1, G3, and G5) and Microsoft 365 (A3, A5, E1, E3, E5, F1, F3, Business Basic, Business Standard, Business Premium, Teams Essentials, and Teams Premium).

Getting started with Microsoft Bookings

Accessing Microsoft Bookings is straightforward and can be done through the Microsoft 365 portal by navigating to **https://m365.cloud.microsoft**, signing in with your Microsoft 365 credentials and selecting **Bookings** from the list of apps in the app launcher.

Alternatively, you can conveniently access Microsoft Bookings by navigating directly to the following URL: **https://outlook.office.com/bookings**.

Microsoft Bookings home page showcases its two primary components:

- **Personal booking page**: Designed for personal use. A suitable feature for individual users, enabling them to manage their appointments independently.

- **Shared booking pages**: Designed for teams, groups, and organizations. It facilitates seamless coordination and booking among multiple team members.

Personal bookings

Personal bookings is a feature within Microsoft Bookings that caters to individuals who need to manage their own appointments and meetings. It allows users to configure and share a personalized booking page, making it easy for clients and colleagues to schedule one-on-one meetings directly with them.

With Personal bookings, users can customize their availability, set up different types of appointments, and automate reminders, ensuring an efficient scheduling experience.

Exploring meeting types

A meeting type in Microsoft Bookings refers to a specific category or format of an appointment that you can schedule. Each meeting type is designed to address different scheduling needs and can have unique settings such as duration, location, and availability.

When you access your Personal booking page, you will find default appointment types ready for use, such as *30-minute meeting* or *15-minute meeting* options. These appointments are fully customizable, allowing you to modify the settings as needed, but you can also create a new meeting type that suits your needs.

Creating a new meeting type

Let us explore how to create a new meeting type in Microsoft Bookings:

1. On the home page, under the **Personal booking page** section, select **Create meeting type**, as shown in *Figure 20.1*:

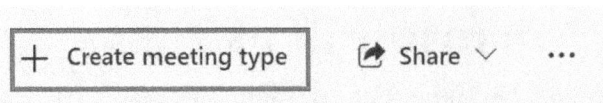

Figure 20.1: Create meeting type

2. Customize your meeting type by choosing a name, assigning a color category, adding a description, selecting the meeting location, setting the duration, and selecting the visibility level (public or private), as shown in *Figure 20.2*.

Note: **Only public meeting types will be visible on your Personal booking page when people access the page link you share. Private meeting types must be shared individually to enable others to book these types of appointments with you.**

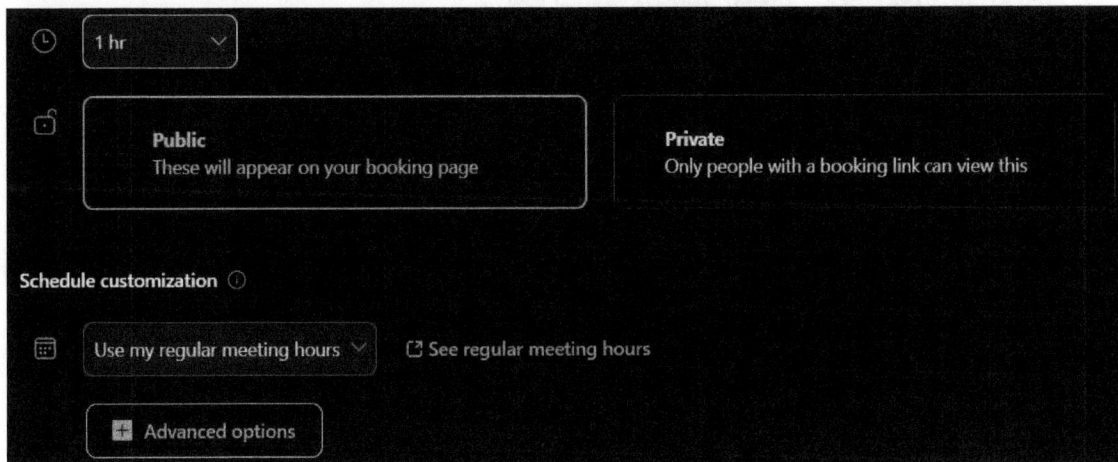

Figure 20.2: New meeting type options

By expanding **Advanced options**, you will be able to configure additional settings, like:

a. **Buffer time**: Add extra time before and after meetings for preparation and wrap-up.

b. **Limit start time to**: Set the time intervals for the meetings. For instance, if you choose *20-min intervals* option, meetings can only be booked at 20-minute intervals using the respective meeting type (example of available times shown: 15:20, 15.40, 16:00, 16:20, etc.). The available times will also be displayed as per the meeting duration, buffer time and the availability you have configured.

c. **Lead time**: Define the minimum and maximum periods for when an appointment can be booked with you.

d. **Email reminders**: Automated email reminders can be configured to be sent before the meeting, reducing the likelihood of no-shows and ensuring everyone is prepared.

e. **Email follow-up**: Set up automated follow-up emails to collect feedback and enhance client experience.

3. Once you have configured all the settings, click **Save** to finalize your new meeting type.

Meeting types

Let us discuss a practical scenario related to meeting types to gain a clearer understanding of how they work.

A Microsoft 365 expert, Page offers training sessions to help individuals and businesses maximize their Microsoft 365 subscriptions. These sessions cover productivity tips, advanced features, and best practices for tools like Teams, SharePoint, and OneDrive.

The details are as follows:

- **Public meeting type use case**: Page creates a public meeting type called *Microsoft 365 Basics Webinar* to offer free, open-to-all webinars on Microsoft 365 basics.

  o **Name**: Microsoft 365 Basics Webinar

o **Description**: A free, one-hour webinar covering the fundamentals of Microsoft 365, including key applications and productivity tips.

o **Duration**: 1 hour

o **Location**: Online (via Microsoft Teams)

o **Visibility**: Public

o **Availability**: Weekly on Wednesdays at 3 PM

Page shares the meeting type link on social media, email newsletters, and community forums.

- **Private meeting type use case**: Page also offers personalized training sessions for businesses needing tailored guidance on Microsoft 365. These sessions are private and customized to the client's specific needs.

o **Name**: Custom Microsoft 365 Training

o **Description**: A personalized training session tailored to your business needs, covering advanced features and best practices for Microsoft 365.

o **Duration**: 2 hours

o **Location**: Online (via Microsoft Teams) or In-person (at the client's office)

o **Visibility**: Private

o **Availability**: Flexible, based on mutual agreement

Page sends the meeting type link directly to clients via email.

These two meeting types allow Page to effectively manage both public and private learning sessions, providing valuable training to a diverse audience while maintaining control over scheduling and accessibility.

Customize and share your personal booking page

To customize your Personal booking page, you can edit the banner image, ensuring it is both visually appealing and user-friendly as follows:

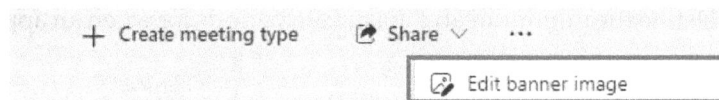

Figure 20.3: Edit banner image

Once you are satisfied with the changes and the meeting types you have created, you can easily share your Personal booking page. Simply copy the link and share it directly with your clients or colleagues. You can also send the link via email or include it in your email signature for easy access as follows:

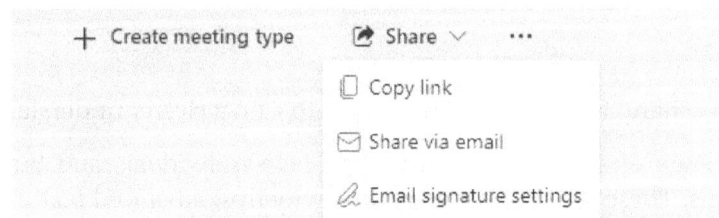

Figure 20.4: Share your Personal booking page

This ensures that your booking page is available to anyone who needs to schedule a meeting with you.

After accessing your booking page, clients or colleagues can easily select an available meeting type and schedule a meeting with you, as shown in *Figure 20.5*:

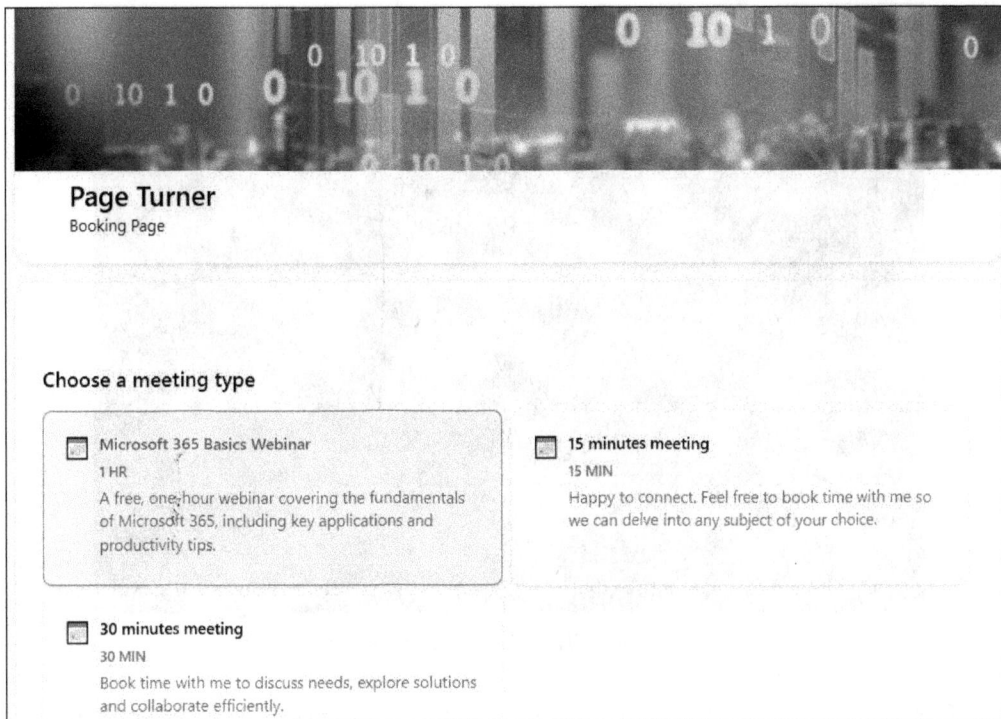

Figure 20.5: *Personal booking page*

You can unpublish your Personal booking page whenever you decide to take it offline. Simply turn off the page from the Microsoft Bookings home page, as shown in *Figure 20.6*.

The page can be republished at any time to make it available again for users to book meetings with you.

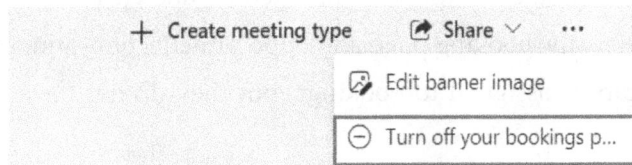

Figure 20.6: *Turn off your bookings page*

Shared bookings

Shared bookings are a powerful feature designed to streamline scheduling for teams and organizations. It allows multiple team members to manage appointments and bookings collaboratively, ensuring that clients can easily book services with the right person at the right time. This feature is particularly useful for businesses with multiple service providers, where clients need to choose from a variety of available professionals. It is also beneficial when multiple users are leading an appointment, as it allows the person booking the meeting to do so without needing to see the specific individuals who will be delivering the session. By using Shared bookings, you can enhance your team's efficiency, reduce scheduling conflicts, and provide a seamless booking experience for your clients.

Create a shared booking page

Let us discuss the steps for creating a shared booking page:

1. On your Bookings homepage, click **Create booking page** under **Shared booking pages**.

2. Give your booking page a name, add a logo (optional), choose a business type (optional), and change your business hours if needed:

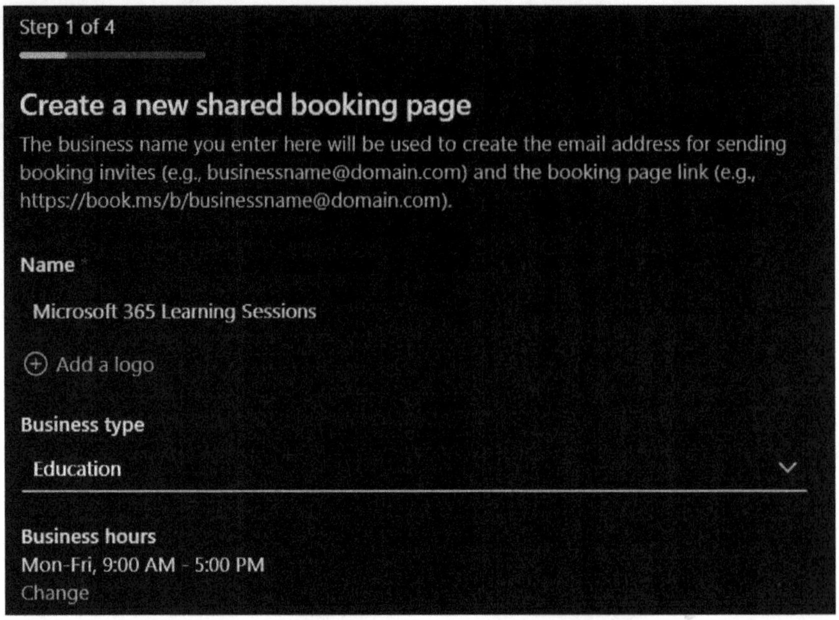

Figure 20.7: Shared booking page creation

3. Invite staff members you want to be part of the shared booking page. Assign appropriate roles to each team member. The roles available for assignment are:

a. **Administrators**: Can manage all settings, staff, and bookings.

b. **Team members**: Can manage bookings assigned to them and their availability in the booking mailbox.

c. **Schedulers**: Can manage bookings on the calendar and customer details.

d. **Viewers**: Can view the booking page and appointments but cannot make any changes.

e. **Guests**: They can be assigned to bookings, but they do not have access to open the booking mailbox.

The following figure shows the **Invite staff** step as part of the share booking page creation:

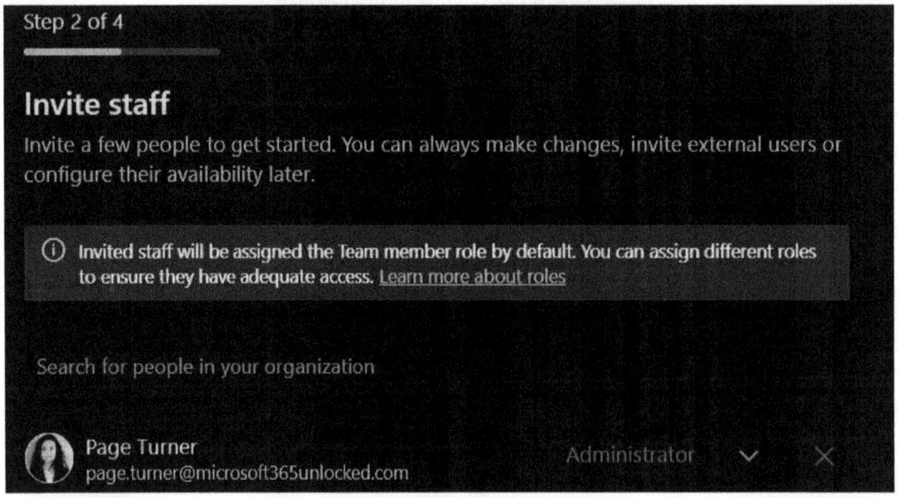

Figure 20.8: Invite staff

1. Set up a service (optional). A service is basically an appointment type. An initial service is created by default, as shown in the following figure. Additional services can be added later, after the page creation.

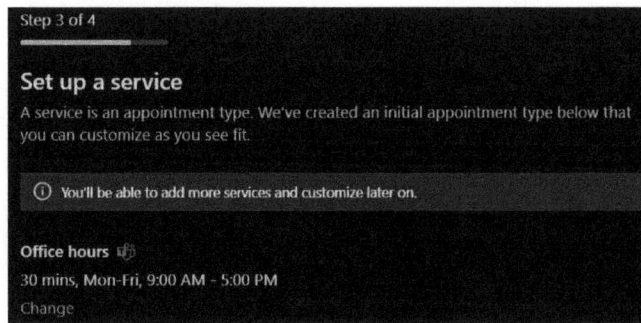

Figure 20.9: Set up a service

2. Choose who can book appointments using this booking page, as shown in *Figure 20.10*. You can select between the following options:

    a. **No self-service**: Appointments can be scheduled only from the Bookings app.

    b. **People in my organization**: An internal-only self-service page will be available for people within the organization.

    c. **Anyone**: A public self-service page will be available.

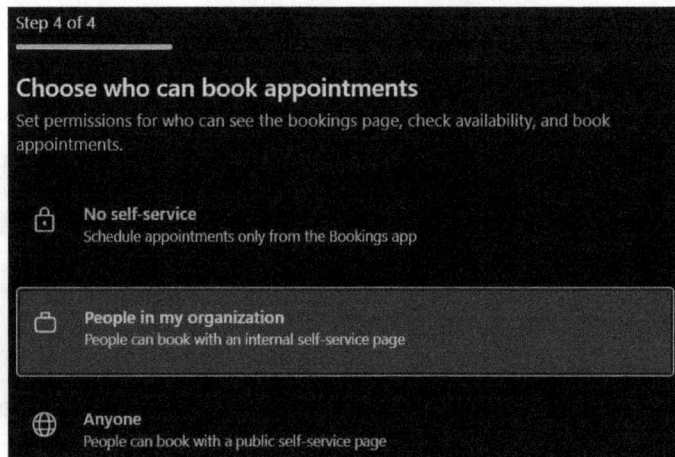

Figure 20.10: Choose who can book appointments

3. Once the booking page has been created, you have the option to share the page or click on **Get started** to further configure and customize your shared booking page:

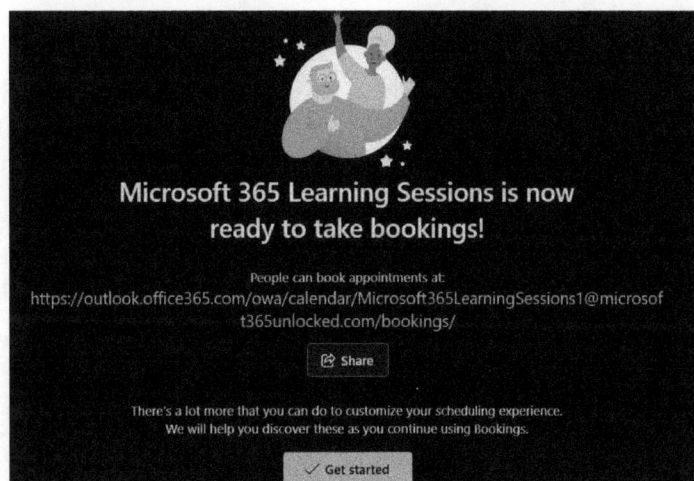

Figure 20.11: Shared booking page created

Set up your shared booking page

After creating your shared booking page, you can configure it to better suit your business needs. Setting up your shared booking page involves configuring various options to ensure a seamless booking experience for your customers.

Configure and manage a shared booking page

We can configure each section under the **Booking Page** tab.

Let us understand how to configure your booking page.

This section allows you to set up your booking page's basic functionality and appearance. The following are the options you can configure:

- **Privacy**: Choose who can access your booking page. Options include:
  - Available to people in your organization
  - No self-service
  - Available to anyone

- **Copy the link to the booking page**: Easily copy the URL of your booking page to share with customers.

- **Email or embed**: You can choose to email the booking page link to customers or embed it on your website for easy access as follows:

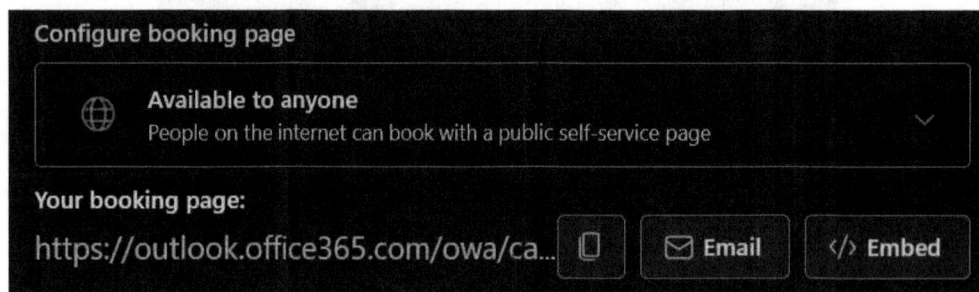

Figure 20.12: Configure booking page

Let us understand how to manage our booking page.

This section provides more advanced settings to manage how your booking page operates. The following are the options you can configure:

- **Business page access control**: Add additional control for your booking page. You can:
  - **Disable direct search engine indexing of the booking page (disabled by default)**: This option prevents search engines from indexing your booking page, making it less likely to appear in search results. This can help maintain privacy and control over who can find and access your booking page.
  - **Require a one-time password to create bookings (disabled by default)**: This option adds an extra layer of security by requiring users to enter a one-time password to create bookings.

- **Customer data usage consent**: Ensure compliance with data protection regulations by setting up consent options for customers to agree to how their data will be used.

- **Default scheduling policy**: Define the default policy for scheduling, including how far in advance customers can book appointments, minimum lead time for bookings and cancellations, time increments, as well as staff control and availability.

- **Customize your page**: Personalize the appearance of your booking page by choosing a color theme and the page template you want to use (new or classic). You can also choose if you want to display the business logo on the booking page.

- **Region and time zone settings**: Set the region and time zone for your booking page to ensure all appointments are scheduled correctly according to your local time. The following figure displays the configurable options under the **Manage your booking page** section:

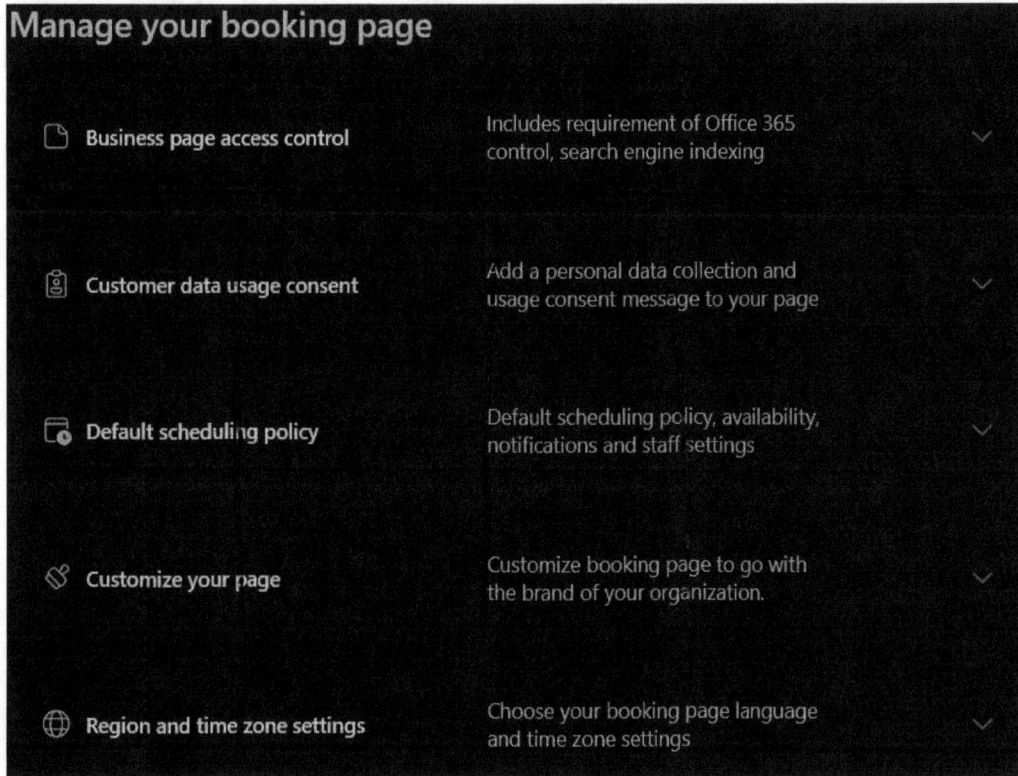

Figure 20.13: Options for managing your booking page

Customers

The **Customers** tab enables you to efficiently add and manage customer information, including their name, email, and chat details. Once a customer is added, you can easily use their profile to book appointments directly with them. The following figure shows the **Customers** section. One customer has been added in this example:

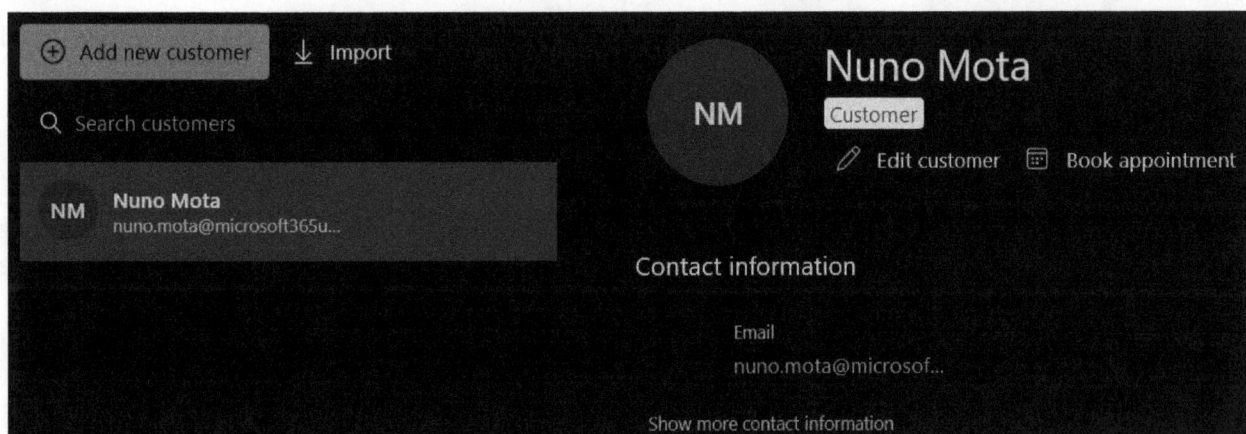

Figure 20.14: Customers

Staff

The **Staff** tab allows you to manage existing staff and their availability as well as adding new staff. From here you can:

- Add additional staff members and manage existing staff information, including their names, contact information, and roles. Staff members who are outside of the organization can only be added as guests.

- Enable or disable for each staff member the email notifications related to booking creation or change.

- Define the working hours and days for each staff member. You can either use the business hours or set specific time slots when they are available for bookings.

The following figure shows some of the options available for configuration when editing a staff member:

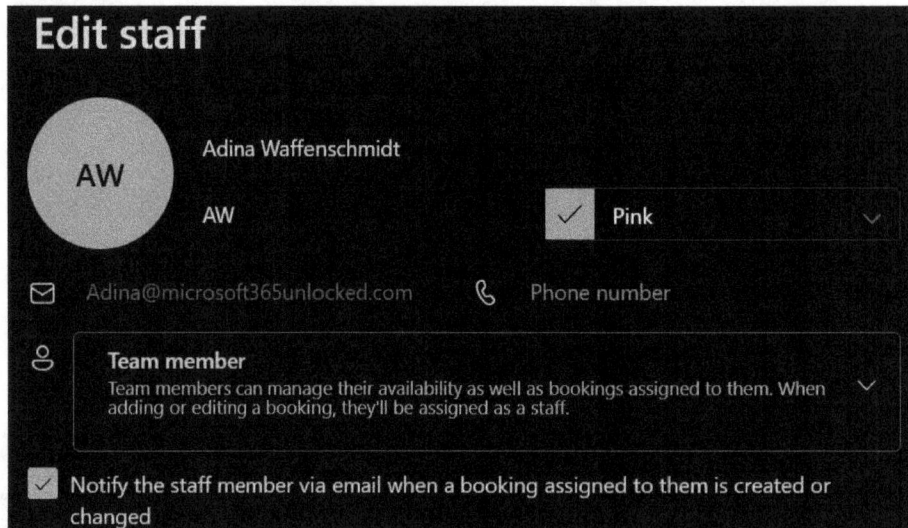

Figure 20.15: Edit staff

Services

The **Services** tab allows you to add a new service and to edit existing services. When adding a new **service** in Microsoft Bookings, you have several options to configure it effectively.

The following are the available options:

- **Basic details**: Start by defining the essential information for the service, like:
  - **Name**: Choose a clear and descriptive name for the service.
  - **Description**: Provide a detailed description to inform customers about what the service entails.
  - **Location**: Choose the location for the service (online or in person).
  - **Duration**: Set the service duration and configure buffer time, if needed.
  - **Price**: Set the cost of the service.
  - **Maximum number of attendees**: Define the maximum number of customers who can book the service at the same time. You can also choose if you want to let customers manage their appointment when it is booked by the staff on their behalf.

- **Availability options**: Determine when the service is available for booking:
  - **Scheduling policy**: Set the scheduling rules to manage bookings effectively:
    - **Time increments**: Define the intervals at which appointments can be scheduled (e.g., every 15 minutes, 30 minutes, etc.).

- **Minimum lead time**: Set the minimum amount of time (in hours) required before a customer can book or cancel an appointment.

- **Maximum lead time**: Specify the maximum amount of time (in days) in advance that customers can book an appointment.

  o **Availability**: Specify the days and times when the service can be booked. This can be aligned with the working hours of the staff members providing the service.

- **Assign staff**: Use this option to assign the right staff members to provide the service. You can set up the appointment to be scheduled with a single staff or with multiple assigned members.

  You can also allow customers to see the names of the staff (for appointments scheduled with multiple assigned members) or allow them to choose a particular staff for booking (for appointments that can be scheduled with a single member).

- **Custom fields**: Collect specific information from customers during the booking process:

  o **Customer information**: Gather details such as customer email, phone number, address, and notes. These fields can be set as required if needed.

  o **Custom fields**: Add any additional fields to collect specific information relevant to the service.

- **Notifications**: Keep both customers and staff informed about bookings:

  o **Email confirmation**: Enable automated email notifications for the customer and the assigned staff to receive a confirmation when an appointment is scheduled, changed, or canceled.

  o **Email reminders**: Ensure that the staff members and the customer receive reminder emails before the appointment.

  o **Email follow-up**: Add a follow-up email that will be sent automatically to the customers after the appointment.

By carefully configuring these options, you can ensure that your services are clearly defined and easily accessible to your customers, leading to a better overall booking experience.

The following figure shows some of the details that can be configured as part of a service:

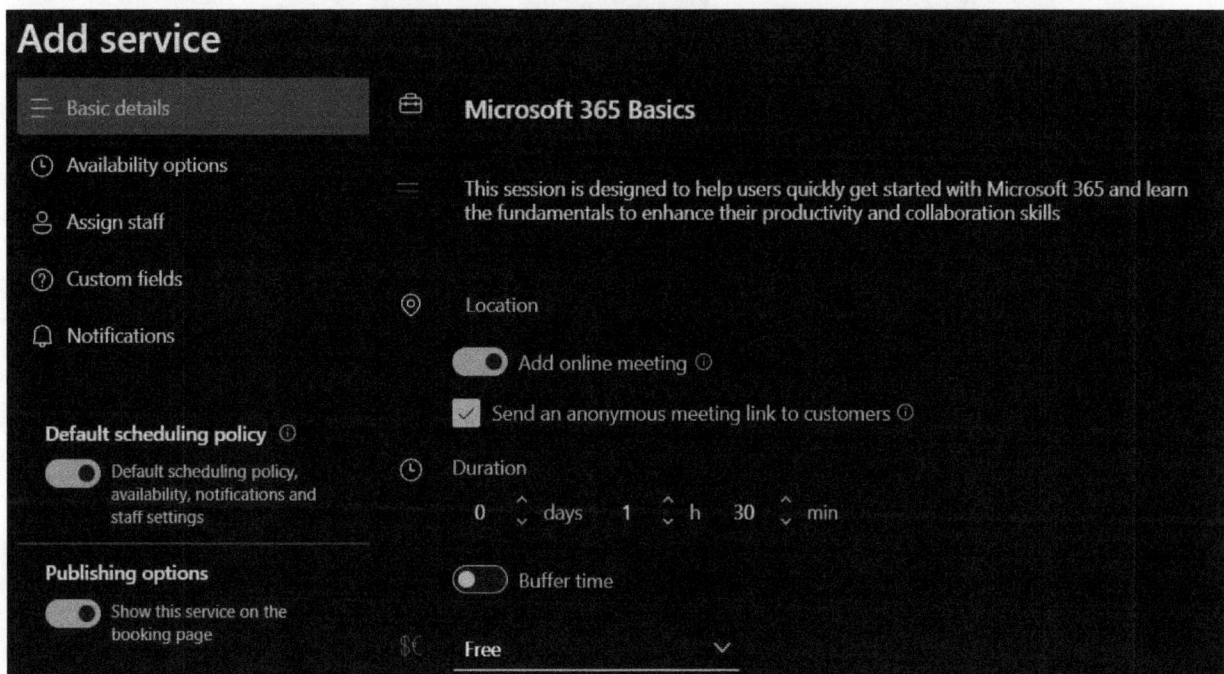

Figure 20.16: Configure services

Queue

The **Queue** tab in Microsoft Bookings allows you to see the scheduled appointments as part of the respective Shared booking page, as seen in the following image:

Figure 20.17: Bookings Queue

From this page, you can add a new booking, modify the date to view appointments on a different day and join an appointment. You can also send an email reminder or SMS reminder for an appointment by clicking on the ellipsis next to each appointment. Email reminders can be sent to assigned staff or to attendees while SMS reminders are only for the attendees.

The **Status** of each appointment can be updated accordingly, as shown in the following figure:

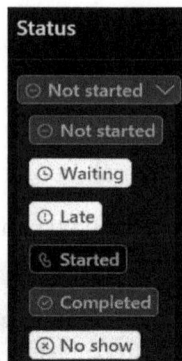

Figure 20.18: Booking Status

Additionally, automatic status updates are triggered when an attendee or staff member joins or concludes a call.

> Note: **Bookings Queue is a premium feature and is available only to users with Teams Premium license.**

Business information

Configuring the business information section in Microsoft Bookings helps provide essential details about your business to your customers.

We can set up each option as follows:

- **Basic details**: Start by providing the fundamental information about your business, such as business name, phone number, address, website URL and business type.

- **Privacy policy and Terms and conditions**: Ensure transparency and compliance by adding your business policies:

o **Privacy policy**: Provide a link to your privacy policy to inform customers about how their data will be used and protected.

o **Terms and conditions**: Include a link to your terms and conditions to outline the rules and guidelines for using your services.

- **Business logo**: Upload an image of your business logo to be displayed on your booking page. This helps create a professional and recognizable appearance.

- **Business hours**: Specify the days and times when your business is open. This information will be displayed on your booking page to help customers know when they can book appointments.

By configuring these options, you can ensure that your business information is clearly presented and easily accessible to your customers, leading to a more professional and trustworthy booking experience.

The following figure illustrates the options that can be configured as part of the **Business information** section:

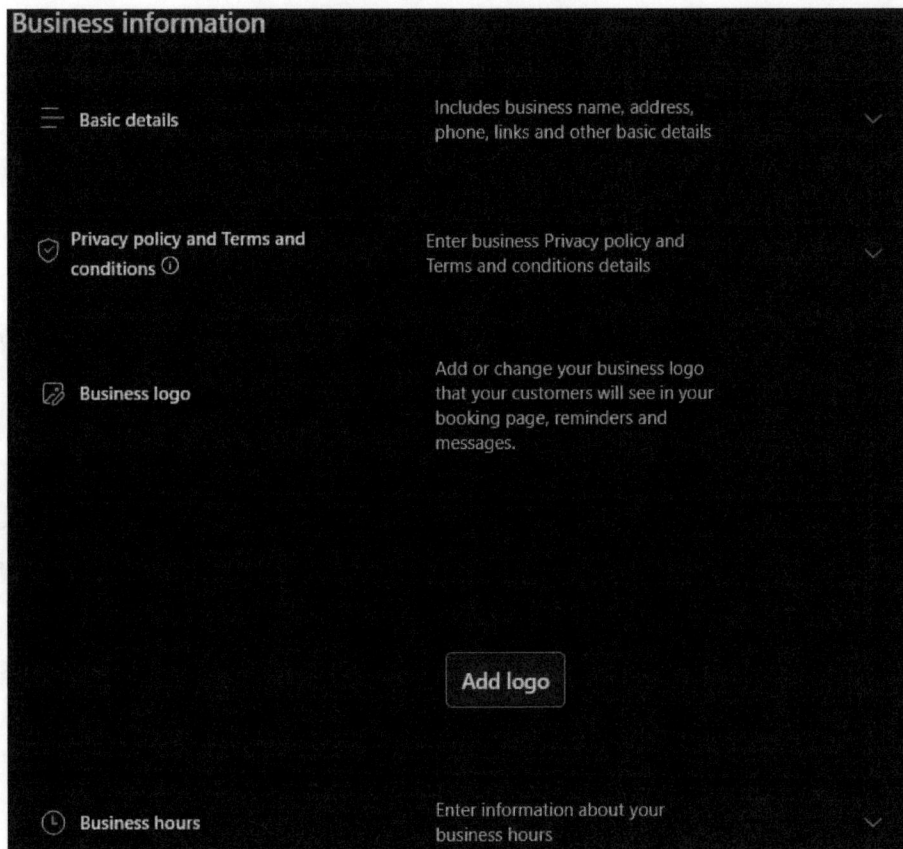

Business information

☰ Basic details	Includes business name, address, phone, links and other basic details ⌄
🛡 Privacy policy and Terms and conditions ⓘ	Enter business Privacy policy and Terms and conditions details ⌄
🖼 Business logo	Add or change your business logo that your customers will see in your booking page, reminders and messages.
	Add logo
🕐 Business hours	Enter information about your business hours ⌄

Figure 20.19: Business information options

Share your booking page

Once you have created and customized your shared booking page, you can share it with clients and colleagues.

The following are the options available:

- **Copy link**: You can copy the link to your shared booking page and share it via email, social media, or any other communication platform. This is the simplest way to distribute your booking page.

- **Embed**: If you have a website, you can get the embed code and embed your shared booking page directly onto it. This allows clients to book appointments without leaving your site.

- **Email**: Send an email with the link to your shared booking page.

After accessing your booking page, clients or colleagues can easily select an available service offering and schedule a meeting with you or your team, as shown in *Figure 20.20*:

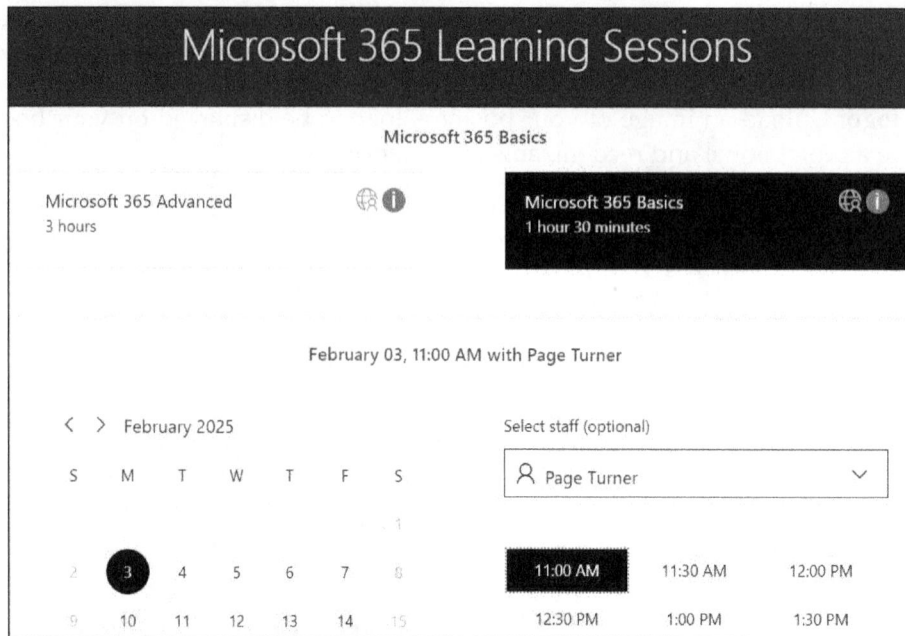

Figure 20.20: *Accessed shared booking page*

Note: An end-user cannot delete a shared booking page. Only Microsoft 365 Admins can delete a shared booking page.

Conclusion

By the end of this chapter, we understood how Microsoft Bookings can simplify the process of scheduling appointments and managing bookings. Whether using Personal bookings to manage individual appointments or Shared bookings to coordinate with a team, this tool offers a range of features to enhance efficiency and improve customer engagement. By understanding and utilizing the various roles, settings, and customization options available, you can create a seamless booking experience that meets your specific needs and enhances overall productivity, taking your bookings to the next level.

In the next chapter, we will explore Microsoft To Do, a versatile tool that offers a centralized task management and productivity enhancement platform.

Join our Discord space

Join our Discord workspace for latest updates, offers, tech happenings around the world, new releases, and sessions with the authors:

https://discord.bpbonline.com

CHAPTER 21

Microsoft To Do

Introduction

In this chapter, we will cover Microsoft To Do, a cloud-based task management application, and look at how it can be used to help users organize their tasks, set reminders, and manage day-to-day activities efficiently.

Structure

The chapter covers the following topics:

- Understanding Microsoft To Do
- Accessing To Do
- Creating and managing tasks
- Lists
- To Do and Outlook
- To Do vs. Planner

Objectives

This chapter describes how to use Microsoft To Do for organizing tasks, setting reminders, and managing daily activities. Readers will understand the application's integration with other Microsoft services, such as Outlook, and explore its features like creating custom lists, syncing tasks across devices, collaboration via shared lists, goal setting and tracking, and customization options for an enhanced user experience.

Understanding Microsoft To Do

To Do is a powerful task management application designed to help users organize, track, and complete tasks efficiently. It integrates seamlessly with other Microsoft services such as Outlook, providing a cohesive experience for managing daily activities. To Do offers an intuitive interface that makes it easy for users to create, manage, and prioritize tasks. Users can create custom lists for different categories such as work, personal projects, or daily errands. Each task can be detailed with due dates, reminders, notes, and steps to ensure thorough tracking and completion.

Like other Microsoft 365 apps, To Do syncs seamlessly across various devices. This cloud-based functionality ensures that users can access their task lists from their computer, smartphone, or tablet, making it convenient to stay organized regardless of the device being used. The integration with Outlook allows users to turn emails into tasks and synchronize their calendar events with their to-do lists, enhancing productivity and ensuring that nothing falls through the cracks.

Microsoft To Do can be used for various purposes, including:

- **Personal task management**: Users can create lists for personal tasks such as grocery shopping, household chores, and fitness routines.

- **Professional task management**: It is ideal for work-related tasks such as meeting preparation, project deadlines, and follow-up actions.

- **Collaboration**: Users can share task lists with colleagues, family, and friends to collaborate on projects or shared responsibilities.

- **Goal setting**: Helps users set and track goals, whether short-term or long-term, by breaking them down into manageable tasks.

Licensing

Microsoft To Do is available at no cost when using a personal Microsoft Account. Consequently, all Microsoft 365 Family or Personal subscribers have access to this service.

You may also utilize a work or school Microsoft Account. The following Microsoft 365 suites contain the required licenses to enable the use of Microsoft To Do:

- **Business plans**: Microsoft 365 Business Basic, Standard, Premium

- **Enterprise plans**: Office 365 E1 - E5, and Microsoft 365 E3 - E5

- **Education plans**: Office 365 A1 - A5, and Microsoft 365 A3 - A5

- **Frontline plans**: Office 365 F2 - F3, Microsoft 365 F3

Accessing To Do

To Do is accessible through multiple platforms, ensuring users can manage their tasks regardless of the device they are using. Here is a look at the various ways and applications available to use To Do.

Web application

Users can access To Do through its web application by visiting **https://to-do.office.com**. Alternatively, log in to your Microsoft 365 portal at **https://www.microsoft365.com** and open To Do from the app launcher, located in the top left corner of the Office 365.

This option is perfect for those who prefer not to download any software but still wish to manage their tasks online. The web application provides full functionality, allowing users to create, edit, and organize their tasks with ease. It also syncs seamlessly with other devices. The following is an example of what To Do looks like on the web client:

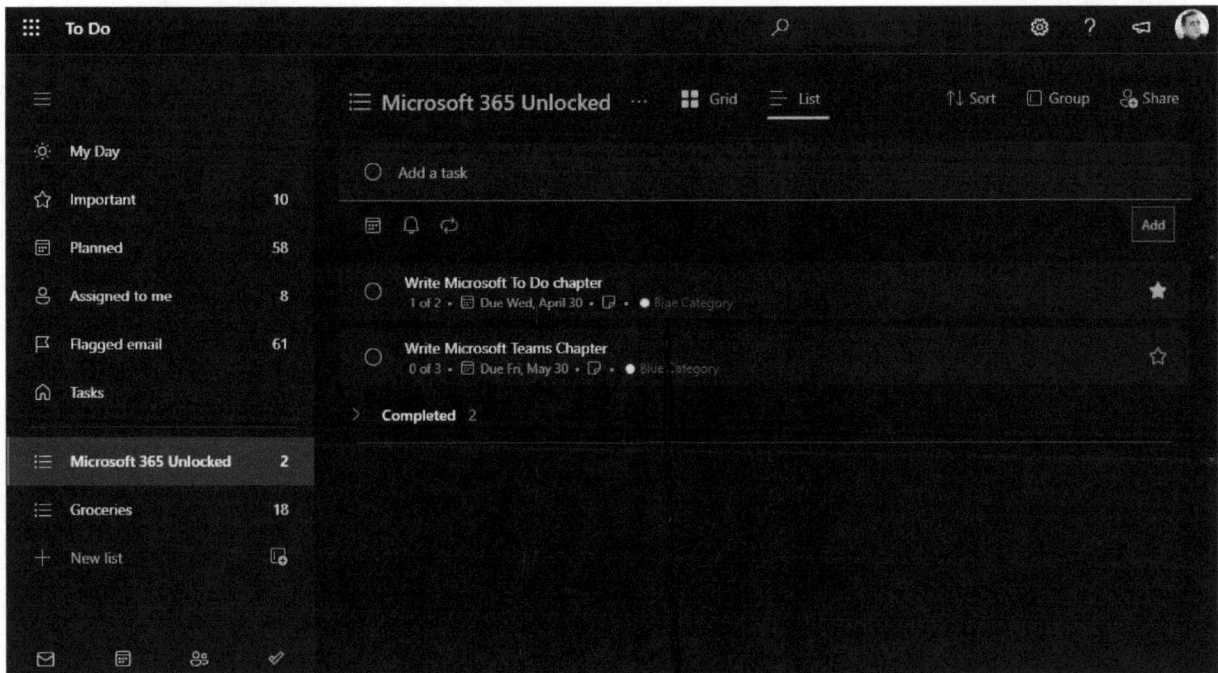

Figure 21.1: *To Do web client*

Windows application

To Do is available for Windows users and can be downloaded from the Microsoft Store. The Windows application offers a comprehensive and robust interface that integrates well with the Windows operating system. Using this app, users can enjoy features such as task notifications and desktop widgets. The following figure shows the Windows app:

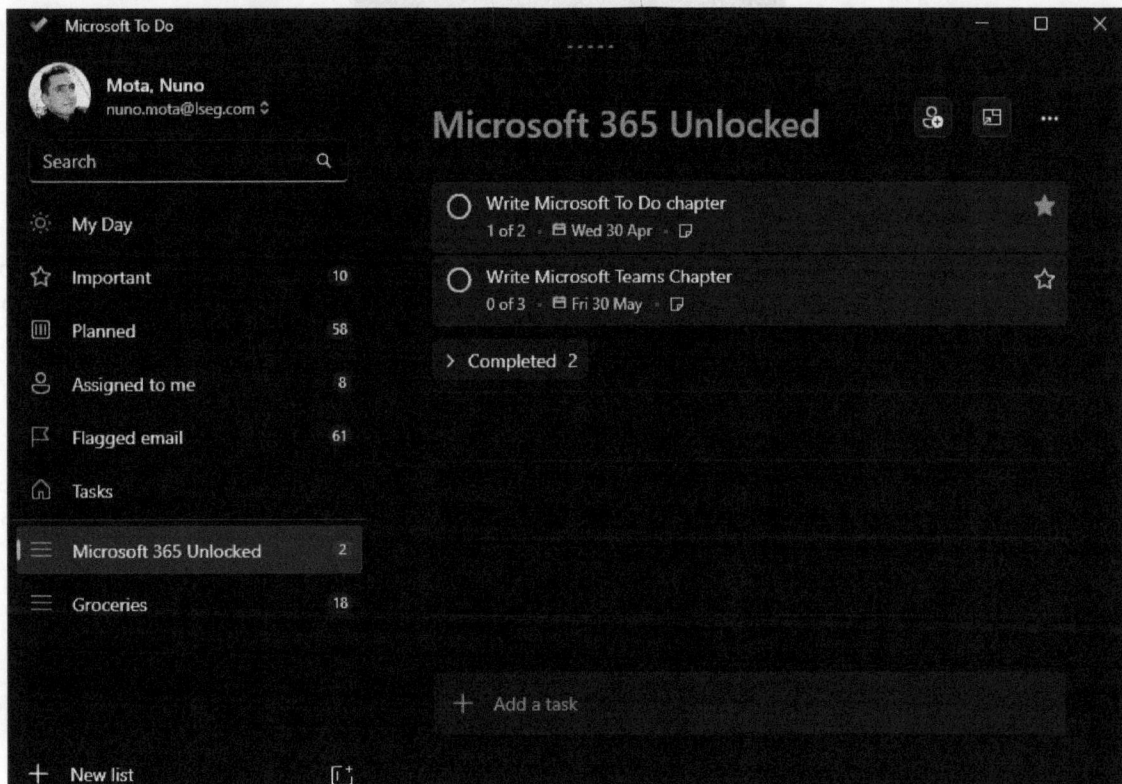

Figure 21.2: *To Do Windows app*

Mobile applications

For those who prefer managing tasks on the go, To Do offers mobile applications for both iOS and Android devices. These apps can be downloaded from the Apple App Store and Google Play Store, respectively. The mobile applications provide a user-friendly interface that is optimized for touch screens, allowing users to effortlessly create and manage tasks from their smartphones or tablets. The apps also support features like task reminders and notifications to ensure users stay on top of their to-do lists. The following figure shows the To Do app on an iPhone:

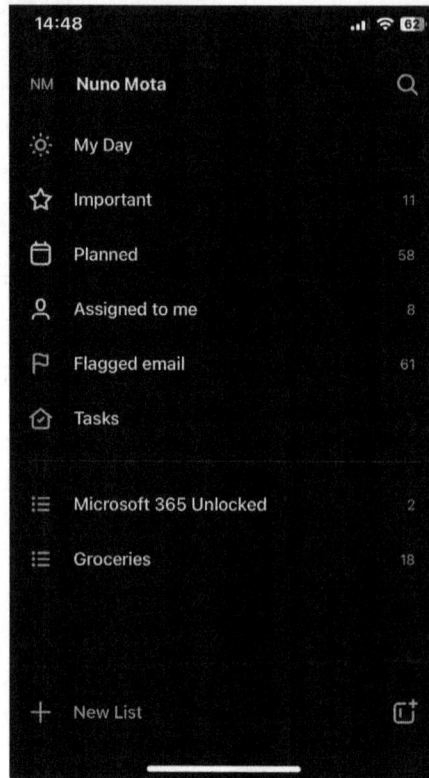

Figure 21.3: To Do mobile app

Mac application

To Do is also available for Mac users. The Mac application can be downloaded from the Mac App Store, providing Apple users with the same level of functionality and integration as the Windows application. This ensures that users can manage their tasks efficiently across different operating systems.

Creating and managing tasks

To Do offers a user-friendly interface for creating and managing tasks, ensuring that you stay organized and on top of your to-do lists. The application is designed to be intuitive and accessible, making it easy for users of all levels to navigate and utilize its features effectively.

To create a task in the web app, follow these steps:

1. Open the Microsoft To Do application.

2. Select the list where you want to create a new task or create a new list if needed, using the **+ New list** button shown as follows:

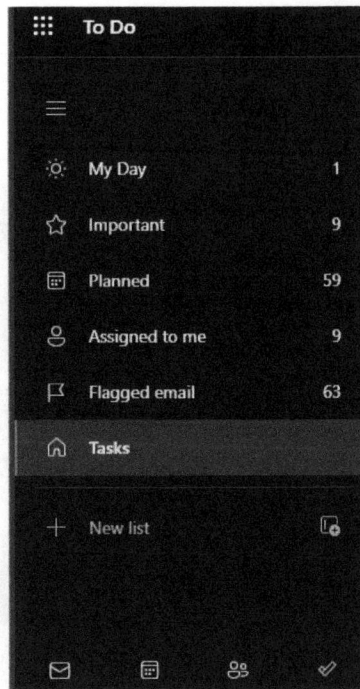

Figure 21.4: Creating a new list

3. Click on the + **Add a Task** button.

4. Enter the task name and press *Enter* to add it to your list. At the same time, you can also set a due date, add a reminder, or set the task to repeat as shown in the following figure:

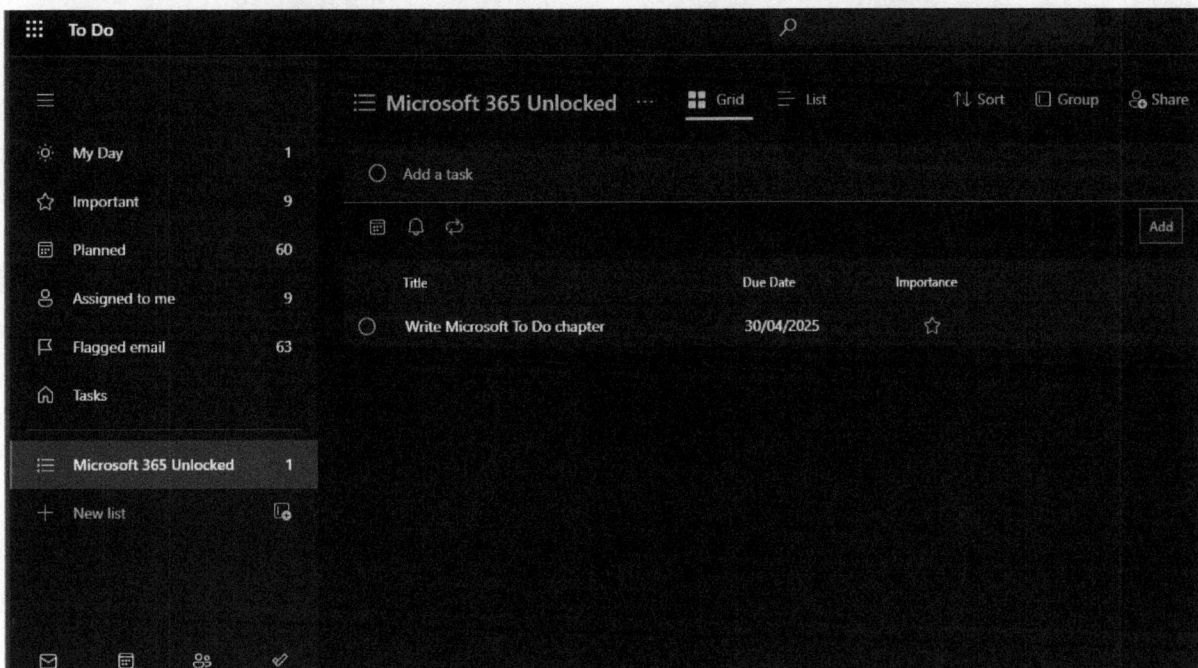

Figure 21.5: Creating a new task

Once you have created your tasks, you can click on a task to edit it, which allows you to update it or add additional information to the task. For instance, you can add notes to provide more context or details about the task. You can also assign different priority levels to your tasks, helping you to focus on what is most important. Additionally, To Do allows you to attach files to tasks, ensuring all relevant documents are readily accessible.

To stay on top of your deadlines, you can set reminders and due dates for your tasks. You also have the option to create recurring tasks for activities that need to be done regularly. The app ensures you receive notifications for upcoming deadlines, helping you to manage your time efficiently.

The following figure shows these options and more:

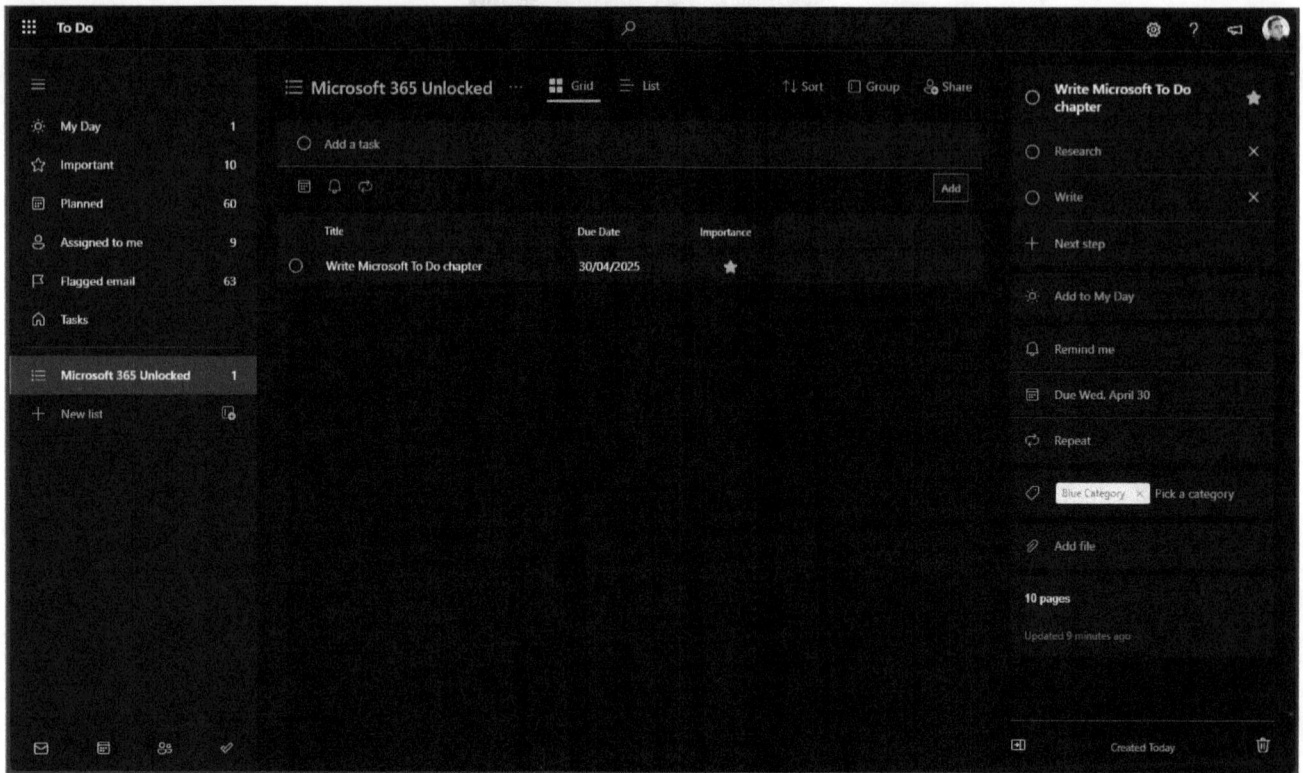

Figure 21.6: Editing a task

Managing your tasks effectively is crucial for staying organized and productive. To Do provides a variety of features to help you accomplish just that, which are listed as follows:

- Drag and drop tasks to reorder them within a list.

- Add hashtags to task names or in the **Notes** section to categorize tasks and make them easier to find. This feature allows you to group similar tasks together, making it simple to manage and locate tasks based on specific projects or themes.

- Group tasks into different lists for better organization. For example, you can have separate lists for work, personal tasks, and special projects, ensuring you keep all aspects of your life well-organized.

- Color-code tasks for visual prioritization. Assign different colors to tasks based on their urgency or category, making it quick and easy to identify high-priority items at a glance.

- Attach files to your tasks to keep all the necessary information and resources associated with a task in one place. Whether it is a project report, a visual reference, or data collection, attaching files ensures that you have quick access to everything needed to complete the task efficiently.

- Use the *Important* flag to highlight critical tasks. By marking certain tasks as important, you can ensure they stand out and receive the attention they need.

- Break down tasks into smaller, manageable steps. By outlining the specific steps needed to complete a task, you can make even the most daunting projects feel achievable. This method allows you to tackle each step one at a time, ensuring steady progress and a clear path to completion.

In the following figure, we can see steps and hashtags being used:

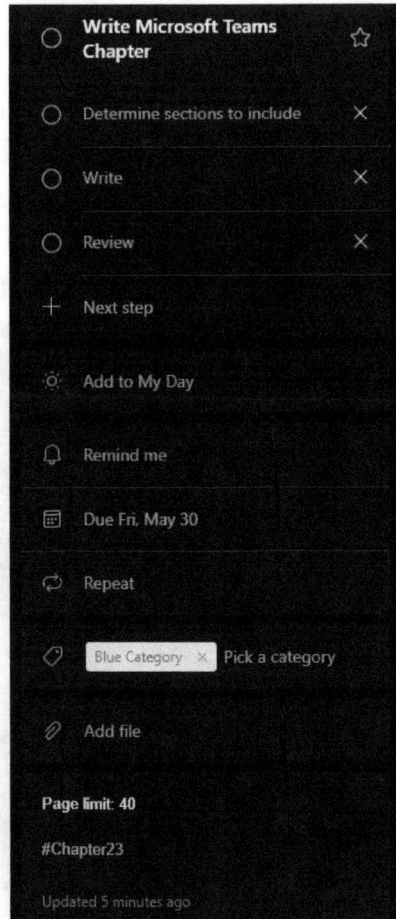

Figure 21.7: Steps and hashtags in tasks

Once a task is complete, simply click the checkbox next to its name to mark it as complete. Completed tasks will move to the **Completed** section at the bottom of the list.

Lists

In To Do, lists serve as an essential organizational tool designed to help users manage tasks and projects efficiently. A list is essentially a collection of related tasks, grouped together for ease of planning, prioritization, and tracking. Lists allow users to categorize their tasks based on different projects, areas of life, or specific goals, ensuring that all tasks are systematically arranged and easily accessible. There are several possible uses for lists:

- **Task organization**: Lists enable users to group tasks by projects or categories, making it easy to see what needs to be done for specific objectives.

- **Prioritization**: By creating separate lists for different priorities, users can focus on the most critical tasks first.

- **Tracking progress**: Lists help in monitoring progress by allowing users to see completed tasks and outstanding tasks within each list.

- **Goal setting**: Break larger goals into smaller, manageable tasks and organize them within lists to keep track of progress.

- **Collaboration**: Share lists with family, friends, or colleagues to manage joint projects, household chores, or event planning.

Creating a new list in To Do is extremely simple, as we have seen *in Figure 21.4:*

1. Click on the **+ New List** button.
2. Name the list based on the category or project it represents.
3. Customize the list with themes and colors for better visual distinction.

Once a list has been created, it can be shared with others. Shared lists are perfect for managing joint projects, household chores, or planning events. Collaborators can add, edit, and complete tasks within shared lists and use comments to communicate and discuss tasks.

To share a list, click on the sharing icon located at the top right corner of any list you have created:

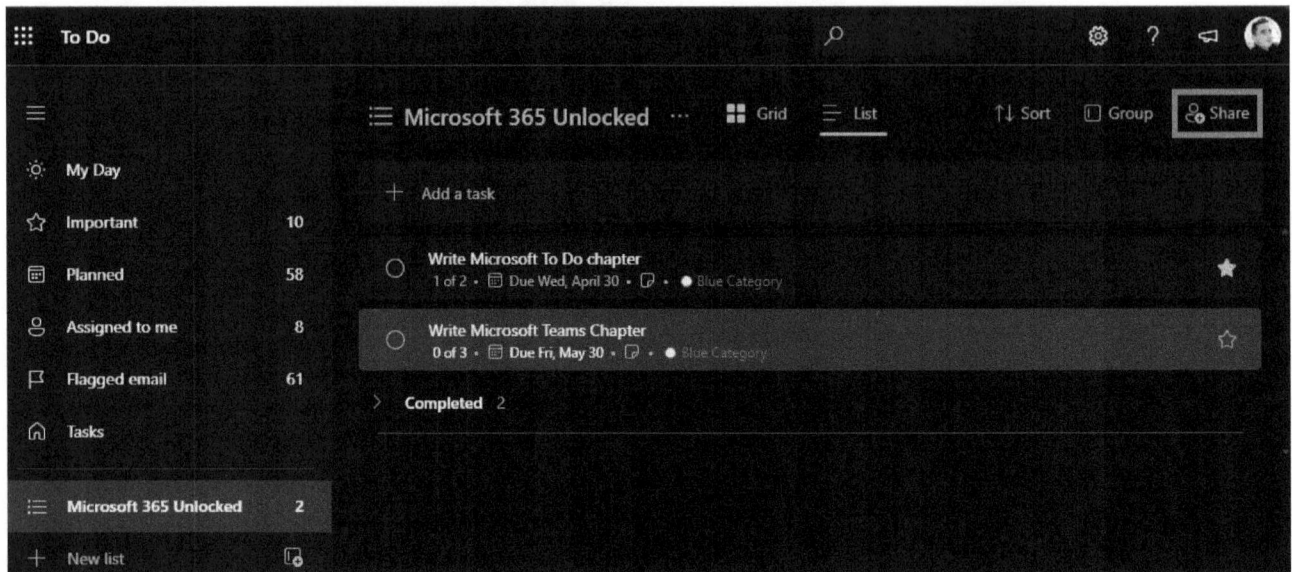

Figure 21.8: List sharing icon

Once the sharing menu opens, you can create an invitation link to share with collaborators by selecting **Create invitation link**, shown as follows, and then **Copy link**:

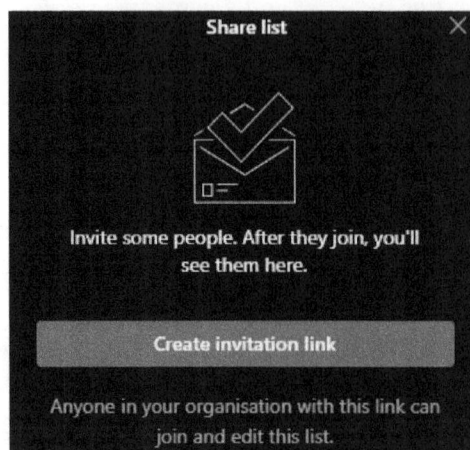

Figure 21.9: Sharing a list

This link can be pasted into an email or messaging app to send to your collaborators, allowing them to join the list and participate in managing tasks.

To disable the sharing link or restrict sharing to the current members of the list, click on the sharing icon to open the sharing menu. Then, select **Manage access** and choose **Limit access to current members**. This will prevent any additional members from joining the list.

You may also click on **Stop Sharing** to disable the sharing link. After stopping sharing, current list members will lose access, and your list will revert to private status.

To Do supports list sharing between personal Microsoft accounts and between accounts within the same place of work or education.

To Do and Outlook

To Do integrates with Outlook Tasks, allowing users to manage their tasks across both platforms efficiently. By signing in to both To Do and Outlook with the same Microsoft account, users can ensure all their tasks are synchronized. Consequently, tasks will be visible both in To Do and in Outlook Tasks, streamlining the process of task management, as can be seen in the following figure:

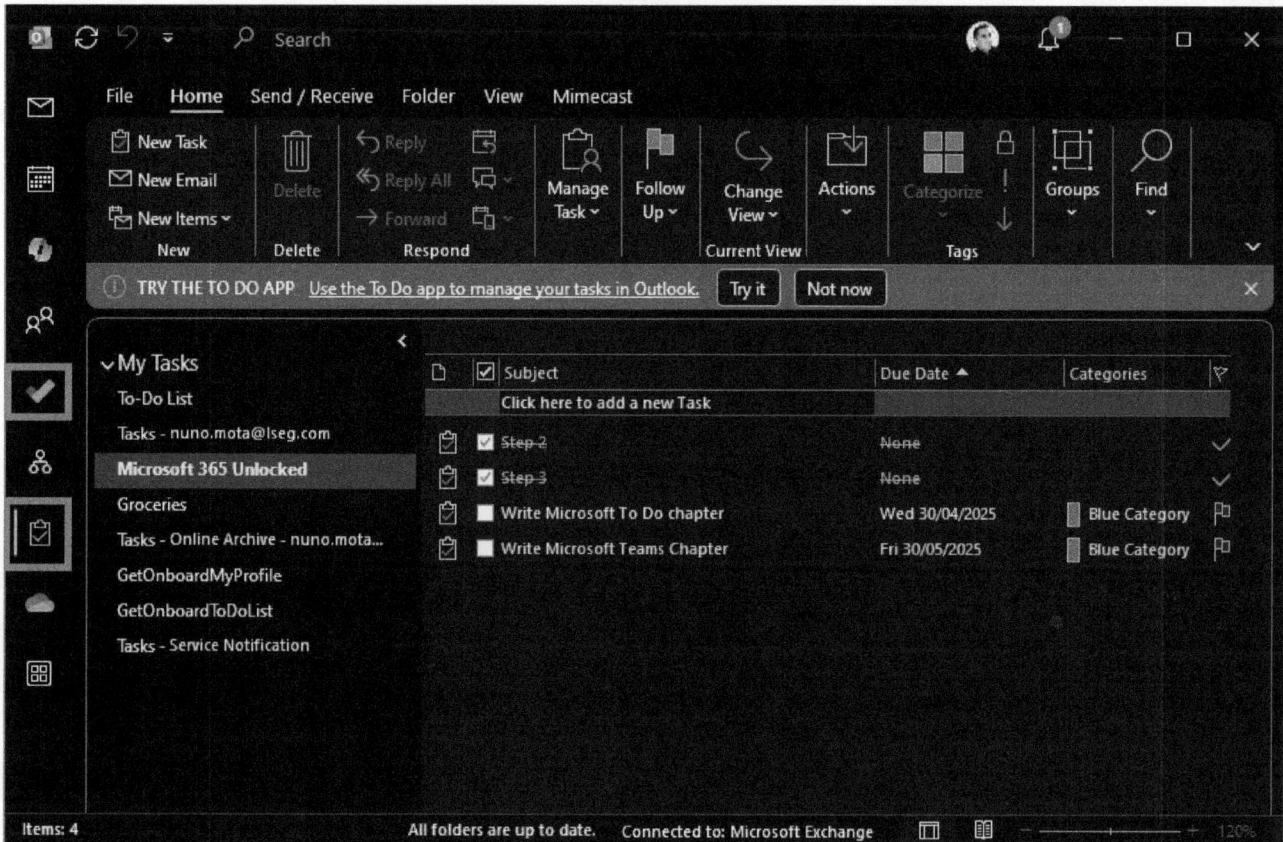

Figure 21.10: To Do tasks in Outlook Calendar

You will also notice the To Do icon present in the left bar of the Outlook desktop client, giving access to the To Do app within Outlook itself.

Additionally, tasks can be viewed directly within the Outlook Calendar, providing users with a comprehensive overview of their schedule and responsibilities. This integration enhances productivity by consolidating tasks and calendar events in one place, making it easier to track and prioritize daily activities, all without any configuration required.

It is important to note, however, that To Do does not yet support all the features available in Outlook Tasks. Although data entered in additional details in Outlook Tasks will be securely stored in Exchange Online, it will not be displayed in To Do. Also, start and end dates, task status, task completion percentage, multiple priority levels, task work hours, task colors, or categories are available in Outlook Tasks but not yet supported in To Do. The opposite is also true where some To Do features are not supported in Outlook. For example, if you create a task with multiple steps, these will not be visible in Outlook.

Flagged email

To Do's **Flagged email** section helps manage tasks directly from your inbox by converting flagged emails in Outlook into actionable tasks. This integration ensures that flagged emails are accessible and manageable within To Do. Flagged emails in Outlook automatically appear in the To Do's *flagged email* section, where users can view, edit, and complete these tasks. Users can manage flagged emails like other tasks, including setting due dates, reminders, and categorizing tasks. Changes in To Do are reflected in Outlook.

To Do vs. Planner

To Do is ideal for managing individual tasks and personal to-do lists. If you need to keep track of your daily activities, set reminders, prioritize tasks, and share lists with friends or family, To Do offers a streamlined and user-friendly interface that integrates well with Outlook and Office 365. Use To Do for personal task management and simple collaboration.

On the other hand, **Planner** is designed for team collaboration and project management. It allows organizations with a Microsoft 365 subscription to visually manage and schedule teamwork. With Planner, you can create plans, assign tasks, set deadlines, and track progress using charts. It integrates with Teams, Outlook, and other Office applications, making it a powerful tool for coordinating group efforts and managing complex projects.

The following table provides an overview of when to use each app:

To Do	Planner
Manage individual tasks across To Do, Outlook, and Planner	Your organization has a Microsoft 365 subscription
Make daily to-do lists	Manage and schedule teamwork visually
Share specific lists with teammates and friends	Use charts to track progress
	Collaborate across Planner, Teams, and Outlook using Microsoft Groups

Table 21.1: To Do vs. Planner

The best part is that you can use To Do and Planner together to complement each other. In fact, when navigating through To Do, users can select the option labeled **Assigned to me** to view tasks specifically assigned to them.

By leveraging the strengths of both applications, users can optimize their productivity and ensure that no task falls through the cracks.

Conclusion

Microsoft To Do is a versatile and intuitive tool that can significantly boost productivity by streamlining task management. Whether for personal use or professional collaboration, its features are designed to accommodate diverse needs and ensure that tasks are completed efficiently. By mastering To-Do, users can enhance their organizational skills and achieve their goals more effectively.

In the next and final chapter, we will go through some security and privacy settings that Microsoft 365 users should be aware of.

CHAPTER 22

Security and Privacy

Introduction

In today's connected world, keeping your Microsoft 365 account secure is crucial. This chapter looks at key steps to prevent unauthorized access and protect your private information. Protecting your account not only ensures the safety of your information but also fosters confidence in the platform. Whether you are collaborating with teammates, managing work files, or securing documents, having confidence in the safety of your information allows you to use Microsoft 365 with ease and peace of mind.

Structure

This chapter covers the following topics:

- My Account portal
- Changing and resetting your password
- Multi-factor authentication
- Managing your devices
- Monitoring sign-in activity

Objectives

By the end of this chapter, readers will understand how to safeguard their Microsoft 365 work or school accounts effectively. They will learn how to navigate the *My Account* portal to configure essential security and privacy features, thus ensuring their data remains protected. Additionally, readers will gain practical knowledge on how to change or reset their passwords, a critical step in maintaining account security, and learn about the importance and how to implement **multi-factor authentication (MFA)** to add an extra layer of protection. Furthermore, it addresses how to manage devices connected to your account and monitor sign-in activity to detect potential unauthorized access.

My Account portal

Your Microsoft 365 account comes with several security and privacy features that you can configure via the *My Account* portal. This portal can be accessed by navigating directly to **https://myaccount.microsoft.com** and signing in with your Microsoft 365 work or school account. Alternatively, you can access the *My Account* portal from your Microsoft 365 homepage (**https://m365.cloud.microsoft**) by clicking on your user account manager icon and then selecting **View account**, as shown in the following figure:

Figure 22.1: Accessing the My Account portal

My Account portal allows you to protect your account from unauthorized access and gives you control over your data. This portal also serves as a central hub for accessing and managing your apps as well as your groups. The following figure shows the **Overview** page of the *My Account* portal for a work or school Microsoft 365 account:

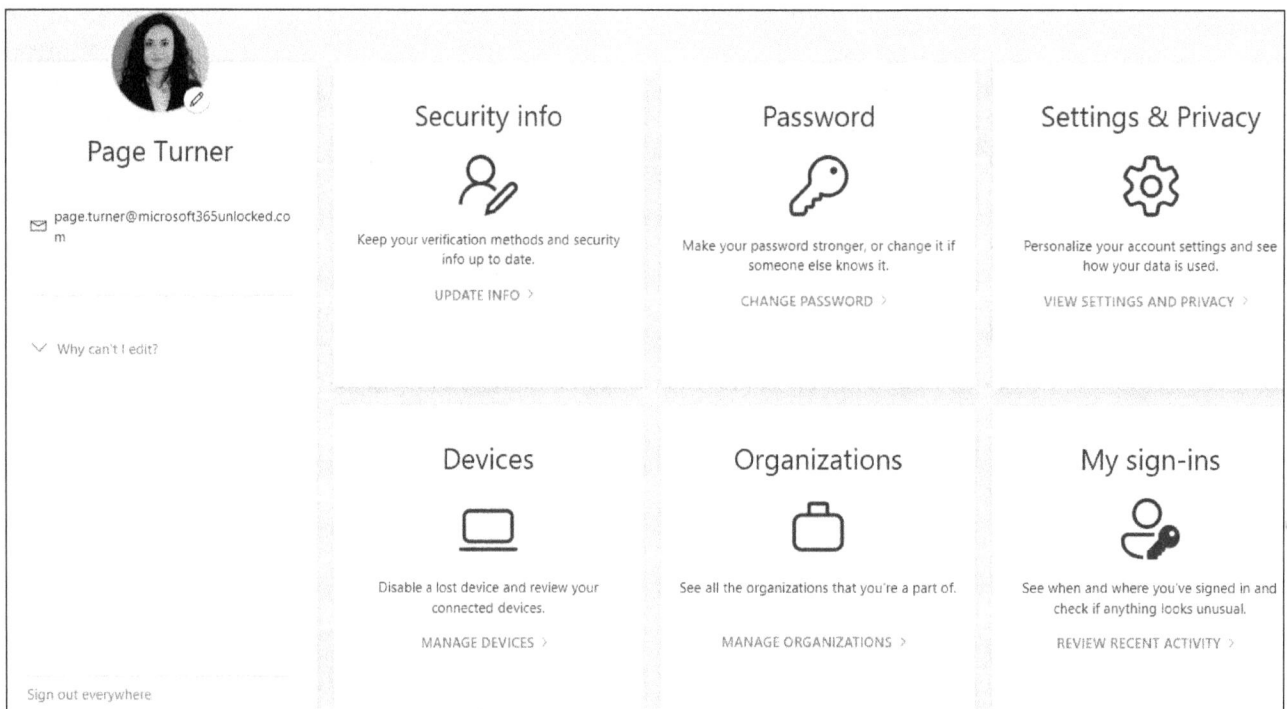

Figure 22.2: Overview page of the My Account portal

Changing and resetting your password

This portal allows you to change your password anytime and offers self-service options to recover your account if you forget your password or if your account is locked. Keeping your password updated and knowing how to reset it are fundamental to account security.

Note: **It is important to keep in mind that some of these features might have been disabled by your organization.**

Changing your password

If you know your current password and simply wish to change it, for example, to comply with a policy or after detecting suspicious activity, you can do so in the *My Account* portal by following these steps:

1. Sign in to the *My Account* portal with your work or school account using your current password.

2. On the left navigation menu, click **Password** (you might also find it under the **Security info** section) or click the **Change Password** link on the portal's overview page.

3. Enter your current password, then choose a new password and confirm it. Make sure the new password meets your organization's requirements (minimum length, complexity, etc.).

4. Save the changes by clicking **Submit**.

The following figure shows the **Change Password** window:

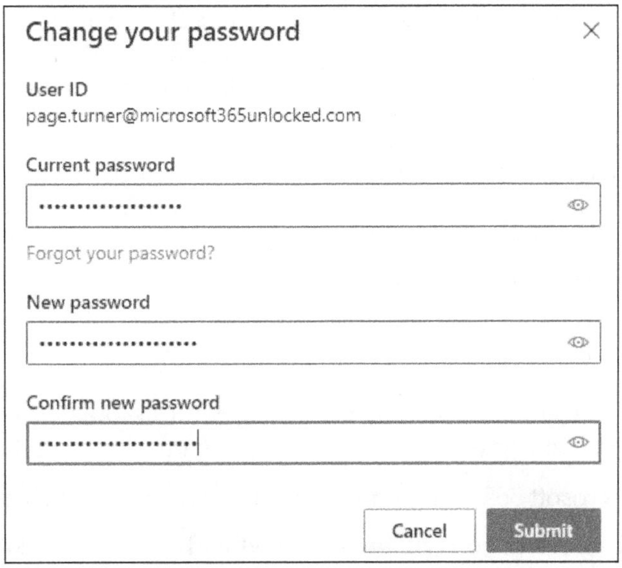

Figure 22.3: Change your password

Your password will be updated immediately. You may be asked to sign in again with the new password as a security measure.

Note: **When changing your password, ensure the new password is strong and has not been used previously. If your organization does not enforce regular password changes, it is still recommended to update your password periodically or whenever you suspect it may have been compromised.**

Resetting your password

If you forgot your password or your account is locked, you could use Microsoft's **self-service password reset** (**SSPR**) feature if your organization enabled it. Follow these steps to reset a forgotten password:

1. On the sign-in page, click **Can't access your account?** link and then select **Work or school account**, which will redirect you to the recovery portal. Alternatively, you can navigate directly to **https://passwordreset.microsoftonline.com**.

2. Verify your identity by entering your account email/username and complete the CAPTCHA to prove you are not a robot, then click **Next**.

3. The system will present you with your configured security verification options, such as your phone number, alternate email, or authenticator app. Choose a verification method (e.g. receive a text message or use the authenticator app) to prove your identity. You may need to perform two verification steps if your organization requires it (for example, approve a notification on the authenticator app and entering a code sent to your phone).

4. Once you have successfully verified your identity through the chosen method(s), you will be allowed to reset your password. Create a new password and submit.

5. After resetting your password, go back to the sign-in page and log in with the new credentials.

Note: **Your organization's administrator must have turned on the self-service password reset feature for your account for you to use these steps. If this feature is not available, the recovery page might direct you to contact your administrator. Additionally, these self-service steps will only work if you have previously set up your security information (like a phone number or the authenticator app) for your account.**

Multi-factor authentication

Passwords alone can sometimes be stolen or guessed, so Microsoft 365 supports MFA, which is an extra layer of security. With MFA enabled, even if someone learns your password, they still cannot access your account without a second verification step that you control (like a code on your phone).

MFA requires you to verify your identity using a second factor beyond just your password, adding a powerful layer of protection to your account. For example, after you enter your password, you might also need to enter a random code from an authenticator app or a text message sent to your phone. This means an attacker would need both your password and your phone unlocked (or access to your second factor) to break in. Enabling MFA greatly reduces the chance of unauthorized access.

Setting up multi-factor authentication

Typically, your organization's IT admin will enable MFA for your account or tenant. Once it is enabled, the setup process usually occurs when you next sign in. Here is what to expect and do:

1. Sign in as usual to Microsoft 365 using your work or school account credentials.

2. Upon entering your password, you will be presented with a prompt to keep your account secure. This indicates that an MFA setup is needed. Click **Next** to begin:

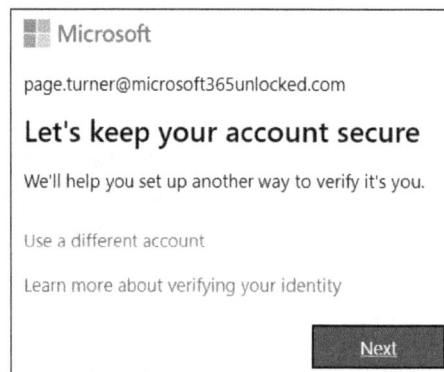

Figure 22.4: Begin MFA setup

3. Choose your MFA method. The default recommendation is to use the **Microsoft Authenticator** app, a free Microsoft mobile app that provides a seamless and secure way to enhance account protection with a second layer of verification. If you have not installed it already, there will be a link to get it. If you prefer not to use this app, you can select **I want to set up a different method** (you might choose to receive text messages or phone calls as your second factor):

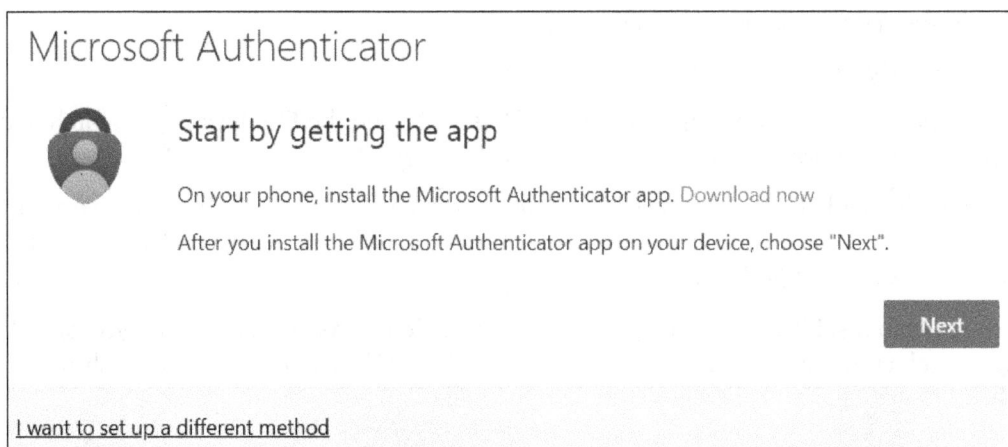

Figure 22.5: Choose MFA method

> Note: **The options available for second-factor authentication depend on the configuration set by your administrator through authentication method policies.**

4. Set up the Authenticator app (if using it):

   a. Download and install the Microsoft Authenticator app on your phone (available for iOS and Android).

   b. In the MFA setup prompt on your computer, click **Next** to continue setting up your account with the Authenticator app and a QR code will appear on screen.

   c. Open the app on your phone, click on + icon and then select **Work or school account** and scan the QR code. This registers your account within the app.

   d. Back on the computer, click **Next** after scanning the QR code, and enter the verification code from the app to confirm it is working.

5. Set up phone verification (if using a different method like text messaging):

   a. Select the country code and enter your mobile number when prompted and select **Receive a code**.

   b. Microsoft 365 will send a 6-digit code via SMS. Enter that code on the prompt to verify your phone number.

6. Complete the setup: Once you have verified at least one secondary method (app or phone), MFA is active on your account. The next time you sign in, after entering your password, you will be asked to approve the sign-in using the method you set up.

In the **Security info** tab within the *My Account* portal, you will be able to view and manage the newly added authentication method as well as add and manage other sign-in options available for you.

By setting up MFA, you considerably improve your account's security. Even if someone guesses or steals your password through phishing, they will be stopped by the second authentication step. It is a small one-time inconvenience for a big long-term benefit in protecting your data.

Managing your devices

Your Microsoft 365 account might be used on multiple devices, such as your laptop, smartphone, tablet, etc. Microsoft provides a way for you to see all the devices that are connected to your work or school account and manage them. For example, if you lose a device or stop using it, you can disable it from accessing your account. This section covers how to view and manage your devices through the *My Account* portal.

To view your connected devices, follow these steps:

1. Sign in to the *My Account* portal.

2. Click on **Devices** in the left navigation menu. This will open the **Devices** page, which lists all devices registered to your work or school account.

3. Review the device list. You will see information for each device, such as device name, operating system, and activity state. Look through and ensure you recognize all of them as devices you currently use or have used in the past.

From this view, you can disable a device that is lost, that you do not recognize, or that you simply do not use anymore. You can select the respective device and then click on **Disable lost device**, as shown the following figure:

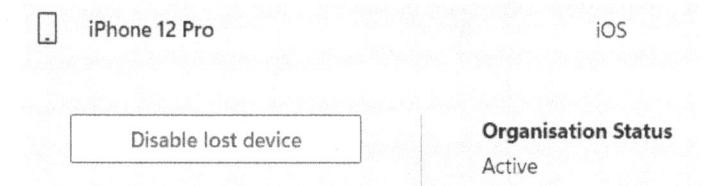

▯ iPhone 12 Pro		iOS

Disable lost device	**Organisation Status**
	Active

Figure 22.6: Disable device

Note: **Keep in mind that once a device is disabled, the action cannot be undone. To re-enable the device, you might need to reach out to your organization's administrator for assistance.**

If one of your Windows devices (like a laptop) is encrypted with **BitLocker** and you are locked out, the **Devices** page can help. You can choose the **View BitLocker Keys** option after selecting the respective device, as shown:

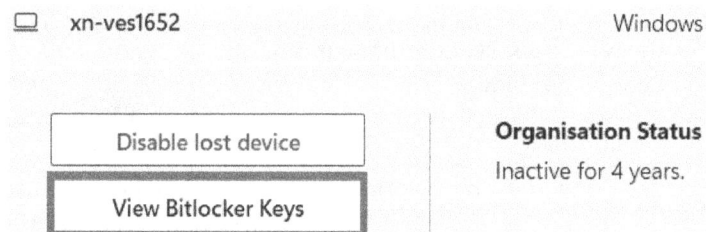

▭ xn-ves1652		Windows

Disable lost device	**Organisation Status**
View Bitlocker Keys	Inactive for 4 years.

Figure 22.7: View BitLocker Keys

This is especially useful if, for example, you forgot the BitLocker PIN on your work laptop. In this case, you can grab the recovery key from another device via this portal.

Regularly reviewing your device list is a good habit. It ensures you know where your account is being used and lets you promptly cut off access from any device that is misplaced or retired.

Monitoring sign-in activity

Another important feature available to users is the ability to monitor their own sign-in activity. This means you can see a log of when and where your account has been accessed. Regularly checking this can help you catch any unusual or unauthorized access early. Microsoft's *My Account* portal includes a **My Sign-ins** page that shows your recent login history.

Microsoft 365's sign-in activity report helps you see if someone might be trying to guess your password, or if an attacker actually managed to sign in, and from what location and device. It essentially gives you a timeline of access to your account. The following figure illustrates an example of sign-in activities:

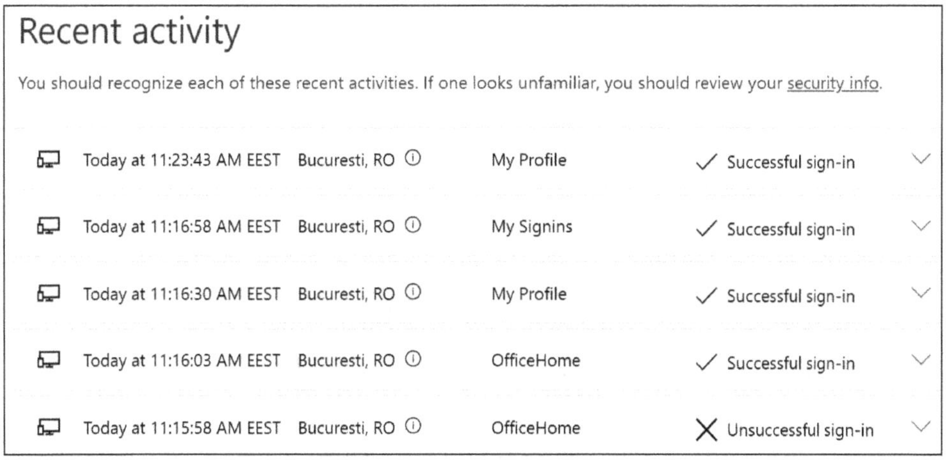

Figure 22.8: *Sign-in activities*

Here is how to view your recent sign-in activity:

1. Sign in to the *My Account* portal.

2. Click on **My sign-ins** in the left navigation menu. This will open a list of your recent sign-in events.

3. Review the list and expand entries: You will see entries each time your account was used to log in. For each sign-in event, it typically shows:

    a. Date and time of the sign-in

    b. App or service used (e.g., Exchange Online, Teams, SharePoint, etc.)

    c. Location (IP address) from where the sign-in occurred, often mapped to a general location (city, country)

    d. Device/Browser information (e.g., Windows 10 & Chrome)

    e. Status (Successful or unsuccessful sign-in)

As you review your sign-in history, look for any anomalies. A successful login from an unknown location or device, such as a sign-in from another country, could signal a breach. Multiple failed attempts might indicate someone trying to guess your password.

If anything seems suspicious, take immediate action. Change your password and enable MFA if not already in place. Additionally, notify your IT admin immediately if it looks like a breach.

Keep in mind that not every unfamiliar detail indicates a security breach. The location can be skewed by network routing. Likewise, an *unsuccessful* sign-in could simply be you mistyping your password once. However, patterns matter, if you see a lot of failures or any obvious anomalies, those are important signals.

Regularly checking your sign-in activity, alongside acting promptly on alerts, helps maintain account security.

Conclusion

This chapter emphasized the critical importance of maintaining vigilance over your account security by regularly reviewing sign-in activity and responding promptly to any anomalies. It also highlighted key practices like changing and resetting passwords, setting up MFA for an additional layer of protection, and monitoring the devices and browsers used for account access. These measures collectively ensure a stronger defense against potential breaches and safeguard your digital presence.

This marks the final chapter of the book. Let it serve as a reminder that safeguarding your accounts and information is an essential part of navigating today's interconnected world. By applying the knowledge gained here, you are better equipped to protect your digital presence and contribute to a safer online environment.

Join our Discord space

Join our Discord workspace for latest updates, offers, tech happenings around the world, new releases, and sessions with the authors:

https://discord.bpbonline.com

Index

O

www.ingramcontent.com/pod-product-compliance
Lightning Source LLC
Chambersburg PA
CBHW061739210326
41599CB00034B/6729

```
* 9 7 8 9 3 6 5 8 9 3 0 5 2 *
```